Applied Econometrics

Second Edition

Dimitrios Asteriou
*Associate Professor at the Department of Business Administration,
Hellenic Open University, Greece*

Stephen G. Hall
Professor of Economics, University of Leicester

First edition 2006
Revised edition 2007
Second edition 2011

Published by
PALGRAVE MACMILLAN

Palgrave Macmillan in the UK is an imprint of Macmillan Publishers Limited, registered in England, company number 785998, of Houndmills, Basingstoke, Hampshire RG21 6XS.

Palgrave Macmillan in the US is a division of St Martin's Press LLC, 175 Fifth Avenue, New York, NY 10010.

Palgrave Macmillan is the global academic imprint of the above companies and has companies and representatives throughout the world.

Palgrave® and Macmillan® are registered trademarks in the United States, the United Kingdom, Europe and other countries.

ISBN: 978–0–230–27182–1

This book is printed on paper suitable for recycling and made from fully managed and sustained forest sources. Logging, pulping and manufacturing processes are expected to conform to the environmental regulations of the country of origin.

A catalogue record for this book is available from the British Library.

A catalog record for this book is available from the Library of Congress.

10 9 8 7 6 5 4 3 2 1
20 19 18 17 16 15 14 13 12 11

Printed and bound in China

To Athina, for all her love – D.A.

To Jacquie, for all her help and understanding – S.G.H.

Brief Contents

Contents

List of Figures

List of Tables

Preface

What is econometrics?

The study of econometrics has become an essential part of every undergraduate course in economics, and it is not an exaggeration to say that it is also an essential part of every economist's training. This is because the importance of applied economics is constantly increasing, and the ability to quantify and evaluate economic theories and hypotheses constitutes now, more than ever, a bare necessity. Theoretical economics may suggest that there is a relationship between two or more variables, but applied economics demands both evidence that this relationship is a real one, observed in everyday life, and quantification of the relationship between the variables. The study of the methods that enable us to quantify economic relationships using actual data is known as econometrics.

Literally, econometrics means 'measurement [the meaning of the Greek word *metrics*] in economics'. However, econometrics includes all those statistical and mathematical techniques that are utilized in the analysis of economic data. The main aim of using these tools is to prove or disprove particular economic propositions and models.

The stages of applied econometric work

Applied econometric work always takes (or, at least, should take) as its starting point a model or an economic theory. From this theory, the first task of the applied econometrician is to formulate an econometric model that can be tested empirically. The next tasks are to collect data that can be used to perform the test and, after that, to proceed with the estimation of the model.

After this estimation of the model, the applied econometrician performs specification tests to ensure that the model used was appropriate and to check the performance and accuracy of the estimation procedure. If these tests suggest that the model is adequate, hypothesis testing is applied to check the validity of the theoretical predictions, and then the model can be used to make predictions and policy recommendations. If the specification tests and diagnostics suggest that the model used was not appropriate, the econometrician must go back to the formulation stage and revise the econometric model, repeating the whole procedure from the beginning.

The purpose of this textbook

This book provides students with the basic mathematical and analytical tools they require to carry out applied econometric work of this kind.

For the first task, formulating an econometric theory, the book adopts a very analytical and simplified approach. For the subsequent tasks, it explains all the basic commands for obtaining the required results from economic data sets using econometric software.

The use and level of mathematics

The use of mathematics in econometrics is unavoidable, but the book tries to satisfy both those students who do not have a solid mathematical background and those who prefer the use of mathematics for a more thorough understanding. To achieve this aim, the book provides, when required, both a general and a mathematical treatment of the subject, in separate sections. Thus students who do not want to get involved with proofs and mathematical manipulations can concentrate on the general (verbal) approach, skipping the more mathematical material, without any loss of continuity. On the other hand, readers who want to go through the mathematics involved in every topic can study these mathematical sections in each chapter. To accommodate this choice, the text uses matrix algebra to prove some important concepts mathematically, while the main points of the analysis are also presented in a simplified manner to make the concept accessible to those who have not taken a course in matrix algebra.

Another important feature of the text is that it presents all the calculations required to get the student from one equation to another, as well as providing explanations of the mathematical techniques used to derive these equations. Students with a limited background in mathematics will find some of the mathematical proofs quite accessible, and should therefore not be disheartened when progressing through them.

The use of econometric software and real data examples

From the practical or applied econometrics point of view, this book is innovative in two ways: (1) it presents all the statistical tests analytically (step by step), and (2) it explains how each test can be carried out using econometric software such as EViews, Stata and Microfit. We think this approach is one of the strongest features of the book, and hope that students will find it useful when they apply these techniques to real data. It was chosen because, from our teaching experience, we realized that students find econometrics a relatively hard course simply because they cannot see the 'beauty' of it, which emerges only when they are able to obtain results from actual data and know how to interpret those results to draw conclusions. Applied econometric analysis is the essence of econometrics, and we hope that using EViews, Stata and Microfit will make the study of econometrics fascinating and its practice more satisfying and enjoyable. Readers who need a basic introduction to EViews, Stata and Microfit should first read the final chapter (Chapter 23), which discusses the practicalities of using these three econometric packages.

Finally

Although this is an introductory text intended primarily for undergraduates, it can also be used by students on a postgraduate course that requires applied work (perhaps for an MSc project). All the empirical results from the examples in the book are reproducible. All the files required to plot the figures, re-estimate the regressions and replicate relevant tests can be downloaded from the companion website. The files are available in four formats: xls (for Excel), wf1 (for EViews), dta (for Stata) and fit (for Microfit). If you find any errors or typos, please let Dimitrios know by e-mailing him at D.A.Asteriou@eap.gr.

DIMITRIOS ASTERIOU
STEPHEN G. HALL

Acknowledgements

I would like to thank my friends and colleagues Keith Pilbeam (City University) and Costas Siriopoulos (University of Patras) for their constant encouragement and support. I would also like to thank Sofia Dimakou for her help with, and discussions about, the Stata software adaptation. Melody Nishino from Quantitative Micro Software provided me with a complimentary copy of EViews 7.0, helping massively with the EViews adaptation process, and her help is greatly appreciated. Finally, I have benefited from discussions about earlier versions of the textbook with the following people, whom I would like to thank one more time: Dionysios Glycopantis, John Thomson, Alistair McGuire, George Agiomirgianakis, Kerry Patterson and Vassilis Monastiriotis.

D.A.

Any remaining mistakes or omissions are, of course, our responsibility.

D.A. and S.G.H.

Part

I

Statistical Background and Basic Data Handling

1 Fundamental Concepts

CHAPTER CONTENTS

Introduction

This chapter outlines some of the fundamental concepts that lie behind much of the rest of this book, including the ideas of a population distribution and a sampling distribution, the importance of random sampling, the law of large numbers and the central limit theorem. It then goes on to show how these ideas underpin the conventional approach to testing hypotheses and constructing confidence intervals.

Econometrics has a number of roles in terms of forecasting and analysing real data and problems. At the core of these roles, however, is the desire to pin down the magnitudes of effects and test their significance. Economic theory often points to the direction of a causal relationship (if income rises we may expect consumption to rise), but theory rarely suggests an exact magnitude. Yet, in a policy or business context, having a clear idea of the magnitude of an effect may be extremely important, and this is the realm of econometrics.

The aim of this chapter is to clarify some basic definitions and ideas in order to give the student an intuitive understanding of these underlying concepts. The account given here will therefore deliberately be less formal than much of the material later in the book.

A simple example

Consider a very simple example to illustrate the idea we are putting forward here. Table 1.1 shows the average age at death for both men and women in the 15 European countries that made up the European Union (EU) before its enlargement.

Simply looking at these figures makes it fairly obvious that women can expect to live longer than men in each of these countries, and if we take the average across

Table 1.1   Average age at death for the EU15 countries (2002)

	Women	Men
Austria	81.2	75.4
Belgium	81.4	75.1
Denmark	79.2	74.5
Finland	81.5	74.6
France	83.0	75.5
Germany	80.8	74.8
Greece	80.7	75.4
Ireland	78.5	73.0
Italy	82.9	76.7
Luxembourg	81.3	74.9
Netherlands	80.6	75.5
Portugal	79.4	72.4
Spain	82.9	75.6
Sweden	82.1	77.5
UK	79.7	75.0
Mean	81.0	75.1
Standard deviation	1.3886616	1.2391241

all countries we can clearly see that again, on a Europe-wide basis, women tend to live longer than men. However, there is quite considerable variation between the countries, and it might be reasonable to ask whether in general, in the world population, we would expect women to live longer than men.

A natural way to approach this would be to look at the difference in the mean life expectancy for the whole of Europe and to ask whether this is significantly different from zero. This involves a number of fundamental steps: first the difference in average life expectancy has to be estimated, then a measure of its uncertainty must be constructed, and finally the hypothesis that the difference is zero needs to be tested.

Table 1.1 gives the average (or mean) life expectancy for men and women for the EU as a whole, simply defined as:

$$\bar{Y}_w = \frac{1}{15} \sum_{i=1}^{15} Y_{wi} \qquad \bar{Y}_m = \frac{1}{15} \sum_{i=1}^{15} Y_{mi} \tag{1.1}$$

where $\bar{Y}_w$ is the EU average life expectancy for women and $\bar{Y}_m$ is the EU average life expectancy for men. A natural estimate of the difference between the two means is $(\bar{Y}_w - \bar{Y}_m)$. Table 1.1 also gives the average dispersion for each of these means, defined as the standard deviation, which is given by:

$$S.D._j = \sqrt{\sum_{i=1}^{15} (Y_{ji} - \bar{Y}_j)^2} \quad j = w, m \tag{1.2}$$

As we have an estimate of the difference and an estimate of the uncertainty of our measures, we can now construct a formal hypothesis test. The test for the difference between two means is:

$$t = \frac{\bar{Y}_w - \bar{Y}_m}{\sqrt{\frac{s_w^2}{15} + \frac{s_m^2}{15}}} = \frac{81 - 75.1}{\sqrt{\frac{1.389^2}{15} + \frac{1.24^2}{15}}} = 12.27 \tag{1.3}$$

The t-statistic of $12.27 > 1.96$, which means that there is less than a 5% chance of finding a t-statistic of 12.27 purely by chance when the true difference is zero. Hence we can conclude that there is a significant difference between the life expectancies of men and women.

Although this appears very intuitive and simple, there are some underlying subtleties, and these are the subject of this chapter. The questions to be explored are: what theoretical framework justifies all this? Why is the difference in means a good estimate of extra length of life for women? Is this a good estimate for the world as a whole? What is the measure of uncertainty captured by the standard deviation, and what does it really mean? In essence, what is the underlying theoretical framework that justifies what happened?

A statistical framework

The statistical framework that underlies the approach above rests on a number of key concepts, the first of which is the population. We assume that there is a population of events or entities that we are interested in. This population is assumed to be infinitely large and comprises all the outcomes that concern us. The data in Table 1.1 are for the EU15 countries for the year 2002. If we were interested only in this one year for this one set of countries, then there would be no statistical question to be asked. According to the data, women lived longer than men in that year in that area. That is simply a fact. But the population is much larger; it comprises all men and women in all periods, and to make an inference about this population we need some statistical framework. It might, for example, just be chance that women lived longer than men in that one year. How can we determine this?

The next important concepts are random variables and the population distribution. A random variable is simply a measurement of any event that occurs in an uncertain way. So, for example, the age at which a person dies is uncertain, and therefore the age of an individual at death is a random variable. Once a person dies, the age at death ceases to be a random variable and simply becomes an observation or a number. The population distribution defines the probability of a certain event happening; for example, it is the population distribution that would define the probability of a man dying before he is 60 ($\Pr(Y_m < 60)$). The population distribution has various moments that define its shape. The first two moments are the mean (sometimes called the expected value, $E(Y_m) = \mu_{Y_m}$, or the average) and the variance ($E(Y_m - \mu_{Y_m})^2$, which is the square of the standard deviation and is often defined as $\sigma^2_{Y_m}$).

The moments described above are sometimes referred to as the unconditional moments; that is to say, they apply to the whole population distribution. But we can also condition the distribution and the moments on a particular piece of information. To make this clear, consider the life expectancy of a man living in the UK. Table 1.1 tells us that this is 75 years. What, then, is the life expectancy of a man living in the UK who is already 80? Clearly not 75! An unconditional moment is the moment for the complete distribution under consideration; a conditional moment is the moment for those members of the population who fulfil some condition, in this case being 80. We can consider a conditional mean $E(Y_m|Y_{im} = 80)$, in this case the mean of men aged 80, or conditional higher moments such as the conditional variance, which will be the subject of a later chapter. This is another way of thinking of subgroups of the population; we could think of the population as consisting of all people, or we could think of the distribution of the population of men and women separately. What we would like to know about is the distribution of the population we are interested in, that is, the mean of the life expectancy of all men and all women. If we could measure this, again there would be no statistical issue to address; we would simply know whether, on average, women live longer than men. Unfortunately, typically we can only ever have direct measures on a sample drawn from the population. And we have to use this sample to draw some inference about the population.

If the sample obeys some basic properties we can proceed to construct a method of deriving inference. The first key idea is that of random sampling: the individuals who make up our sample should be drawn at random from the population. The life expectancy of a man is a random variable; that is to say, the age at death of any individual is uncertain. Once we have observed the age at death and the observation becomes part of our sample it ceases to be a random variable. The data set then comprises a set of individual observations, each of which has been drawn at random from the population. So our sample of ages at death for men becomes $Y_m = (Y_{1m}, Y_{2m}, \ldots, Y_{nm})$. The idea of random sampling has some strong implications: because any two individuals are drawn at random from the population they should be **independent** of each other; that is to say, knowing the age at death of one man tells us nothing about the age at death of the other man. Also, as both individuals have been drawn from the same population, they should have an **identical distribution**. So, based on the assumption of random sampling, we can assert that each of the observations in our sample should have an independent and identical distribution; this is often expressed as IID.

We are now in a position to begin to construct a statistical framework. We want to make some inference about a population distribution from which only a sample has been observed. How can we know whether the method we choose to analyse the sample is a good one or not? The answer to this question lies in another concept, called the sampling distribution. If we draw a sample from our population, let's suppose we have a method for analysing that sample. It could be anything; for example, take the odd-numbered observations and sum them and divide by 20. This will give us an estimate. If we had another sample this would give us another estimate, and if we kept drawing samples this would give us a whole sequence of estimates based on this technique. We could then look at the distribution of all these estimates, and this would be the sampling distribution of this particular technique. Suppose the estimation procedure produces an estimate of the population mean which we call $\tilde{Y}_m$, then the sampling distribution will have a mean and a variance $E(\tilde{Y}_m)$ and $E(\tilde{Y}_m - E(\tilde{Y}_m))^2$; in essence, the sampling distribution of a particular technique tells us most of what we need to know about the technique. A good estimator will generally have the property of **unbiasedness**, which implies that its mean value is equal to the population feature we want to estimate. That is, $E(\tilde{Y}_m) = \eta$, where η is the feature of the population we wish to measure. In the case of unbiasedness, even in a small sample we expect the estimator to get the right answer on average. A slightly weaker requirement is **consistency**; here we only expect the estimator to get the answer correct if we have an infinitely large sample, $\lim_{n \to \infty} E(\tilde{Y}_m) = \eta$. A good estimator will be either unbiased or consistent, but there may be more than one possible procedure which has this property. In this case we can choose between a number of estimators on the basis of **efficiency**; this is simply given by the variance of the sampling distribution. Suppose we have another estimation technique, which gives rise to $\overset{\leftrightarrow}{Y}$, which is also unbiased; then we would prefer $\tilde{Y}$ to this procedure if $\text{var}(\tilde{Y}) < \text{var}(\overset{\leftrightarrow}{Y})$. This simply means that, on average, both techniques get the answer right, but the errors made by the first technique are, on average, smaller.

Properties of the sampling distribution of the mean

In the example above, based on Table 1.1, we calculated the mean life expectancy of men and women. Why is this a good idea? The answer lies in the sampling distribution of the mean as an estimate of the population mean. The mean of the sampling distribution of the mean is given by:

$$E\left(\frac{1}{n}\sum_{i=1}^{n}Y_i\right) = \frac{1}{n}\sum_{i=1}^{n}E(Y_i) = \frac{1}{n}\sum_{i=1}^{n}\mu_Y = \mu_Y \tag{1.4}$$

So the expected value of the mean of a sample is equal to the population mean, and hence the mean of a sample is an unbiased estimate of the mean of the population distribution. The mean thus fulfils our first criterion for being a good estimator. But what about the variance of the mean?

$$\mathrm{var}(\bar{Y}) = E(\bar{Y} - \mu_Y)^2 = E\left(\frac{1}{n^2}\sum_{i=1}^{n}\sum_{j=1}^{n}(Y_i - \mu_Y)(Y_j - \mu_Y)\right)$$

$$= \frac{1}{n^2}\left(\sum_{i=1}^{n}\mathrm{var}(Y_i) + \sum_{i=1}^{n}\sum_{j=1, j\neq i}^{n}\mathrm{cov}(Y_i, Y_j)\right) = \frac{\sigma_Y^2}{n} \tag{1.5}$$

So the variance of the mean around the true population mean is related to the sample size that is used to construct the mean and the variance of the population distribution. As the sample size increases, the variance in the population shrinks, which is quite intuitive, as a large sample gives rise to a better estimate of the population mean. If the true population distribution has a smaller mean the sampling distribution will also have a smaller mean. Again, this is very intuitive; if everyone died at exactly the same age the population variance would be zero, and any sample we drew from the population would have a mean exactly the same as the true population mean.

Hypothesis testing and the central limit theorem

It would seem that the mean fulfils our two criteria for being a good estimate of the population as a whole: it is unbiased and its efficiency increases with the sample size. However, before we can begin to test a hypothesis about this mean, we need some idea of the shape of the whole sampling distribution. Unfortunately, while we have derived a simple expression for the mean and the variance, it is not in general possible to derive the shape of the complete sampling distribution. A hypothesis test proceeds by making an assumption about the truth; we call this the null hypothesis, often referred to as H_0. We then set up a specific alternative hypothesis, typically called H_1. The test consists of calculating the probability that the observed value of the statistic could have arisen purely by chance, assuming that the null hypothesis is true. Suppose that our null hypothesis is that the true population mean for age at death for men is 70, H_0: $E(\bar{Y}_m) = 70$. Having observed a mean of 75.1, we might then test the alternative that it is greater than 70. We would do this by calculating the probability that 75.1 could arise purely by chance when the true value of the population mean is 70. With a continuous distribution the probability of any exact point coming up is zero, so strictly what we are calculating is the probability of drawing any value for the mean that is greater than 75.1. We can then compare this probability with a predetermined value, which we call the **significance level** of the test. If the probability is less than the significance level, we reject the null hypothesis in favour of the alternative. In traditional statistics the significance level is usually set at 1%, 5% or 10%. If we were using a 5% significance level and we found that the probability of observing a mean greater than 75.1 was 0.01, as $0.01 < 0.05$ we would reject the hypothesis that the true value of the population mean is 70 against the alternative that it is greater than 70.

The alternative hypothesis can typically be specified in two ways, which give rise to either a one-sided test or a two-sided test. The example above is a one-sided test, as the alternative was that the age at death was greater than 70, but we could equally have tested the possibility that the true mean was either greater or less than 70, in which case we would have been conducting a two-sided test. In the case of a two-sided test we would be calculating the probability that a value either greater than 75.1 or less than $70 - (75.1 - 70) = 64.9$ could occur by chance. Clearly this probability would be higher than in the one-sided test.

Figure 1.1 shows the basic idea of hypothesis testing. It illustrates a possible sampling distribution for the mean life expectancy of men under the null hypothesis that the population mean is 70. It is an unlikely shape, being effectively a triangle, but we will discuss this later; for the moment, simply assume that this is the shape of the distribution. By definition, the complete area under the triangle sums to 1. This simply means that with probability 1 (certainty) the mean will lie between 62 and 78 and that it is centred on 70. We actually observe a mean of 75.1, and if we wish to test the hypothesis that the true mean is 70 against the alternative that it is greater than 70 (a one-sided test) we calculate the probability of observing a value of 75.1 or greater. This is given by area C in the figure. If we wished to conduct the two-sided test, that the alternative is either greater than 75.1 or less than 64.9, we would calculate the sum of

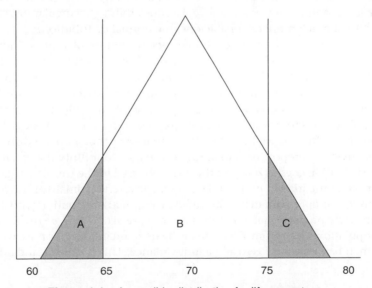

Figure 1.1 A possible distribution for life expectancy

areas A and C, which is clearly greater than C. If we adopted a 5% critical value and if $C < 0.05$, we would reject the null on a one-sided test. If $C + A < 0.05$, we would reject the null at a 5% level on the two-sided test.

As noted above, while we have calculated the mean and the variance of the sampling distribution in the case of the mean, it is not generally possible to calculate the shape of the complete distribution. However, there is a remarkable theorem which does generally allow us to do this as the sample size grows large. This is the central limit theorem.

Central limit theorem

If a set of data is IID with n observations, $(Y_1, Y_2, \ldots Y_n)$, and with a finite variance then as n goes to infinity the distribution of $\bar{Y}$ becomes normal. So as long as n is reasonably large we can think of the distribution of the mean as being approximately normal.

This is a remarkable result; what it says is that, regardless of the form of the population distribution, the sampling distribution will be normal as long as it is based on a large enough sample. To take an extreme example, suppose we think of a lottery which pays out one winning ticket for every 100 tickets sold. If the prize for a winning ticket is $100 and the cost of each ticket is $1, then, on average, we would expect to earn $1 per ticket bought. But the population distribution would look very strange; 99 out of every 100 tickets would have a return of zero and one ticket would have a return of $100. If we tried to graph the distribution of returns it would have a huge spike at zero and a small spike at $100 and no observations anywhere else. But, as long as we draw a reasonably large sample, when we calculate the mean return over the sample it will be centred on $1 with a normal distribution around 1.

The importance of the central limit theorem is that it allows us to know what the sampling distribution of the mean should look like as long as the mean is based on a reasonably large sample. So we can now replace the arbitrary triangular distribution in Figure 1.1 with a much more reasonable one, the normal distribution.

A final small piece of our statistical framework is the **law of large numbers**. This simply states that if a sample $(Y_1, Y_2, \ldots Y_n)$ is IID with a finite variance then $\bar{Y}$ is a consistent estimator of μ, the true population mean. This can be formally stated as $\Pr(|\bar{Y} - \mu| < \varepsilon) \to 1$ as $n \to \infty$, meaning that the probability that the absolute difference between the mean estimate and the true population mean will be less than a small positive number tends to one as the sample size tends to infinity. This can be proved straightforwardly, since, as we have seen, the variance of the sampling distribution of the mean is inversely proportional to n; hence as n goes to infinity the variance of the sampling distribution goes to zero and the mean is forced to the true population mean.

We can now summarize: $\bar{Y}$ is an unbiased and consistent estimate of the true population mean μ; it is approximately distributed as a normal distribution with a variance which is inversely proportional to n; this may be expressed as $N(\mu, \sigma^2/n)$. So if we subtract the population mean from $\bar{Y}$ and divide by its standard deviation we will create a variable which has a mean of zero and a unit variance. This is called standardizing the variable.

$$\frac{\bar{Y} - \mu}{\sqrt{\sigma^2/n}} \sim N(0, 1) \tag{1.6}$$

One small problem with this formula, however, is that it involves σ^2. This is the population variance, which is unknown, and we need to derive an estimate of it. We may estimate the population variance by:

$$S^2 = \frac{1}{n-1} \sum_{i=1}^{n} (Y_i - \bar{Y})^2 \tag{1.7}$$

Here we divide by $n-1$ because we effectively lose one observation when we estimate the mean. Consider what happens when we have a sample of one. The estimate of the mean would be identical to the one observation, and if we divided by $n = 1$ we would estimate a variance of zero. By dividing by $n - 1$ the variance is undefined for a sample of one. Why is S^2 a good estimate of the population variance? The answer is that it is essentially simply another average; hence the law of large numbers applies and it will be a consistent estimate of the true population variance.

Now we are finally in a position to construct a formal hypothesis test. The basic test is known as the student 't' test and is given by:

$$t = \frac{\bar{Y} - \mu}{\sqrt{S^2/n}} \tag{1.8}$$

When the sample is small this will follow a student t-distribution, which can be looked up in any standard set of statistical tables. In practice, however, once the sample is larger than 30 or 40, the t-distribution is almost identical to the standard normal distribution, and in econometrics it is common practice simply to use the normal distribution. The value of the normal distribution that implies 0.025 in each tail of the distribution is 1.96. This is the critical value that goes with a two-tailed test at a 5% significance level. So if we want to test the hypothesis that our estimate of the life expectancy of men of 75.1 actually is a random draw from a population with a mean of 70, then the test would be:

$$t = \frac{75.1 - 70}{\sqrt{S^2/3.87}} = \frac{5.1}{.355} = 14.2$$

This is greater than the 5% significance level of 1.96, and so we would reject the null hypothesis that the true population mean is 70. Equivalently, we could evaluate the proportion of the distribution that is associated with an absolute t-value greater than 4.1, which would then be the probability value discussed above. Formally the probability or p-value is given by:

$$p\text{-value} = \Pr{}_{H_0}(|Y - \mu| > |\bar{Y}^{act} - \mu|) = \Pr{}_{H_0}(|t| > |t^{act}|)$$

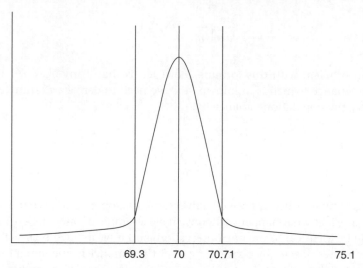

69.3   70   70.71   75.1

Figure 1.2   A normal distribution for life expectancy around the null

So if the *t*-value is exactly 1.96 the *p*-value will be 0.05, and when the *t*-value is greater than 1.96 the *p*-value will be less than 0.05. They contain exactly the same information, simply expressed in a different way. The *p*-value is useful in other circumstances, however, as it can be calculated for a range of different distributions and can avoid the need to consult statistical tables, as its interpretation is always straightforward.

Figure 1.2 illustrates this procedure. It shows an approximately normal distribution centred on the null hypothesis with the two tails of the distribution defined by 69.3 and 70.71. Ninety-five per cent of the area under the distribution lies between these two points. The estimated value of 75.1 lies well outside this central region, and so we can reject the null hypothesis that the true value is 70 and we observed 75.1 purely by chance. The *p*-value is twice the area under the curve which lies beyond 75.1, and clearly this is very small indeed.

One final way to think about the confidence we have in our estimate is to construct a confidence interval around the estimated parameter. We have an estimated mean value of 75.1, but we know there is some uncertainty as to what the true value is. The law of large numbers tells us that this is a consistent estimate of the true value, so with just this one observation our best guess is that the true value is 75.1. The central limit theorem tells us that the distribution around this value is approximately normal, and we know the variance of this distribution. So we can construct an interval around 75.1 that will contain any required amount of the distribution. The convention again is to use a 95% confidence interval, and this may be constructed as follows:

$$CI_{95\%} = \left\{ \bar{Y} + 1.96\frac{S}{\sqrt{n}}, \ \bar{Y} - 1.96\frac{S}{\sqrt{n}} \right\} = \bar{Y} + 0.71, \ \bar{Y} - 0.71$$

So with 95% confidence we can say that the true mean lies between 75.81 and 74.39. This is shown in Figure 1.3; all that has happened here is that the picture has been moved so that it now centres on the estimated value of 75.1 and 95% of the figure lies inside the confidence interval. Clearly the null value of 70 lies way outside this

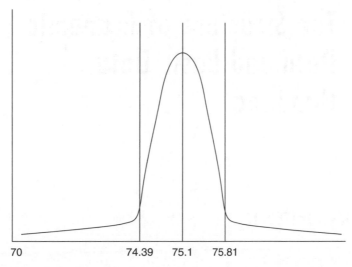

70   74.39   75.1   75.81

Figure 1.3 A 95% confidence interval around the estimated mean

region, and so we can again conclude that the true value of the mean is highly unlikely to be 70.

The same conclusion arises from calculating the formal t-test or the p-value or considering the confidence interval, because they are all simply different ways of expressing the same underlying distribution.

Conclusion

In this chapter we have outlined the basic steps in constructing a theory of estimation and hypothesis testing. We began from the simple idea of random sampling, which gave rise to the proposition that the elements of a sample will have an IID distribution. From this we were able to define a population distribution and to make some inference about this distribution by constructing the mean and then defining the sampling distribution of the mean. By using the law of large numbers and the central limit theorem, we were able to define the shape of the sampling distribution, and finally, given this, we were able to outline the basic testing procedure used in classical econometrics.

While at first sight this may appear to relate specifically to a simple estimation procedure, the mean, the same steps may be applied to almost any estimation procedure, as we will see in later chapters of this book. So when we estimate a parameter in a model from a data set we are essentially following the same steps. Any estimation procedure is essentially just taking a sample of data and averaging it together in some way. We have a sampling distribution for the parameter and we can investigate the unbiasedness and consistency of the estimation procedure. We can go on to apply the central limit theorem, which will establish that this sampling distribution will tend to a normal distribution as the sample size grows. Finally, we can use this result to construct hypothesis tests about the parameters that have been estimated and to calculate p-values and confidence intervals.

2 The Structure of Economic Data and Basic Data Handling

CHAPTER CONTENTS

LEARNING OBJECTIVES

After studying this chapter you should be able to:

1. Understand the various forms of economic data.
2. Differentiate among cross-sectional, time series and panel data.
3. Work with real data and generate graphs of data using econometric software.
4. Obtain summary statistics for your data using econometric software.
5. Perform data transformations when necessary using econometric software.

14

The structure of economic data

Economic data sets come in various forms. While some econometric methods can be applied straightforwardly to different types of data set, it is essential to examine the special features of some sets. In the following sections we describe the most important data structures encountered in applied econometrics.

Cross-sectional data

A cross-sectional data set consists of a sample of individuals, households, firms, cities, countries, regions or any other type of unit at a specific point in time. In some cases, the data across all units do not correspond to exactly the same time period. Consider a survey that collects data from questionnaire surveys of different families on different days within a month. In this case, we can ignore the minor time differences in collection and the data collected will still be viewed as a cross-sectional data set.

In econometrics, cross-sectional variables are usually denoted by the subscript i, with i taking values of $1, 2, 3, \ldots, N$, for N number of cross-sections. So if, for example, Y denotes the income data we have collected for N individuals, this variable, in a cross-sectional framework, will be denoted by:

$$Y_i \quad \text{for } i = 1, 2, 3, \ldots, N \tag{2.1}$$

Cross-sectional data are widely used in economics and other social sciences. In economics, the analysis of cross-sectional data is associated mainly with applied microeconomics. Labour economics, state and local public finance, business economics, demographic economics and health economics are some of the prominent fields in microeconomics. Data collected at a given point in time are used in these cases to test microeconomic hypotheses and evaluate economic policies.

Time series data

A time series data set consists of observations of one or more variables over time. Time series data are arranged in chronological order and can have different time frequencies, such as biannual, annual, quarterly, monthly, weekly, daily and hourly. Examples of time series data include stock prices, gross domestic product (GDP), money supply and ice cream sales figures, among many others.

Time series data are denoted by the subscript t. So, for example, if Y denotes the GDP of a country between 1990 and 2002 we denote that as:

$$Y_t \quad \text{for } t = 1, 2, 3, \ldots, T \tag{2.2}$$

where $t = 1$ for 1990 and $t = T = 13$ for 2002.

Because past events can influence those in the future, and lags in behaviour are prevalent in the social sciences, time is a very important dimension in time series data sets. A variable that is lagged one period will be denoted as Y_{t-1}, and when it is lagged s periods will be denoted as Y_{t-s}. Similarly, if it is leading k periods it will be denoted as Y_{t+k}.

A key feature of time series data, which makes them more difficult to analyse than cross-sectional data, is that economic observations are commonly dependent across time; that is, most economic time series are closely related to their recent histories. So, while most econometric procedures can be applied to both cross-sectional and time series data sets, in the case of time series more things need to be done to specify the appropriate econometric model. Additionally, the fact that economic time series display clear trends over time has led to new econometric techniques that attempt to address these features.

Another important feature is that time series data that follow certain frequencies might exhibit a strong seasonal pattern. This feature is encountered mainly with weekly, monthly and quarterly time series. Finally, it is important to note that time series data are mainly associated with macroeconomic applications.

Panel data

A panel data set consists of a time series for each cross-sectional member in the data set; as an example we could consider the sales and the number of employees for 50 firms over a five-year period. Panel data can also be collected on a geographical basis; for example, we might have GDP and money supply data for a set of 20 countries and for a 20-year period.

Panel data are denoted by the use of both i and t subscripts, which we have used before for cross-sectional and time series data, respectively. This is simply because panel data have both cross-sectional and time series dimensions. So, we might denote GDP for a set of countries and for a specific time period as:

$$Y_{it} \quad \text{for } t = 1, 2, 3, \ldots, T \quad \text{and} \quad i = 1, 2, 3, \ldots, N \tag{2.3}$$

To better understand the structure of panel data, consider a cross-sectional and a time series variable as $N \times 1$ and $T \times 1$ matrices, respectively:

$$Y_t^{ARGENTINA} = \begin{pmatrix} Y_{1990} \\ Y_{1991} \\ Y_{1992} \\ \vdots \\ Y_{2012} \end{pmatrix} ; \quad Y_i^{1990} = \begin{pmatrix} Y_{ARGENTINA} \\ Y_{BRAZIL} \\ Y_{URUGUAY} \\ \vdots \\ Y_{VENEZUELA} \end{pmatrix} \tag{2.4}$$

Here $Y_t^{ARGENTINA}$ is the GDP for Argentina from 1990 to 2012 and Y_i^{1990} is the GDP for 20 different Latin American countries.

The panel data Y_{it} variable will then be a $T \times N$ matrix of the following form:

$$Y_{it} = \begin{pmatrix} Y_{ARG,1990} & Y_{BRA,1990} & \cdots & Y_{VEN,1990} \\ Y_{ARG,1991} & Y_{BRA,1991} & \cdots & Y_{VEN,1991} \\ \vdots & \vdots & & \vdots \\ Y_{ARG,2012} & Y_{BRA,2012} & \cdots & Y_{VEN,2012} \end{pmatrix} \qquad (2.5)$$

where the t dimension is depicted vertically and the i dimension horizontally.

Most undergraduate econometrics textbooks do not contain a discussion of panel data. However, the advantages of panel data, combined with the fact that many issues in economics are difficult, if not impossible, to analyse satisfactorily without panel data, make their use more than necessary. Part VI of this book is for this reason devoted to panel data techniques and methods of estimation.

Basic data handling

Before getting into the statistical and econometric tools, a preliminary analysis is extremely important to get a basic 'feel' for your data. This section briefly describes ways of viewing and analysing data by examining various types of graphs and summary statistics. This process provides the necessary background for the sound application of regression analysis and interpretation of results. In addition, we shall see how to apply several types of transformation to the raw data to isolate or remove one or more components of a time series and/or to obtain the format most suitable for the ultimate regression analysis. While the focus is on time series data, some of the points and procedures also apply to cross-sectional data.

Looking at raw data

The point of departure is simply to look at the numbers in a spreadsheet, taking note of the number of series, start and end dates, range of values and so on. If we look more closely at the figures, we may notice outliers or certain discontinuities/structural breaks (for example a large jump in the values at a point in time). These are very important as they can have a substantial impact on regression results, and must therefore be kept in mind when formulating the model and interpreting the output.

Graphical analysis

Looking at the raw data (that is the actual numbers) may tell us certain things, but graphs facilitate the inspection process considerably. Graphs are essential tools for seeing the 'big picture', and they reveal a large amount of information about the series in one view. They also make checking for outliers or structural breaks much easier than poring over a spreadsheet! The main graphical tools are:

1 Histograms: give an indication of the distribution of a variable;

2 Scatter plots: give combinations of values from two series for the purpose of determining their relationship (if any);

3 Line graphs: facilitate comparisons of series;

4 Bar graphs; and

5 Pie charts.

Graphs in MFit

Creating graphs   To create a line graph of a variable against time, we type in the Microfit Command Editor window:

```
plot x
```

This command produces a plot of variable x against time over the entire sample period. If we need a certain sample period then we type:

```
sample t0 t1; plot x
```

where t0 and t1 stand for the start and end of our sub-sample period, respectively. For example,

```
sample 1990q1 1994q4; plot x
```

We can plot up to a maximum of 50 variables against another variable. When issuing this command, namely xplot, we must specify at least two variable names. For example:

```
xplot x y
```

or

```
sample 1990q1 1994q4; xplot x y z
```

These commands produce a plot of the variables x and z against the variable y for the sub-sample period 1990q1 to 1994q4 (note that all graphs are produced from the Process menu). The default graph display may be edited using the graph control facility. Click the **graph** button to access it. Graph control contains many options for adjusting the various features of the graph; each option has its own property page. Click the appropriate page tab to view it. To apply a change we have made without closing graph control, click the **apply now** button. To exit graph control without implementing the changes click **cancel**. The most commonly used page tabs are: **2D Gallery, Titles, Trends** and **Background**.

Saving graphs   When we plot a graph, the Graph Editor window opens. A displayed graph can be saved as a bitmap (BMP) (click on the second button) or as a Windows metafile (WMF) (click on the third button). If we are using MS Word then we can copy and paste the graph by clicking on the fourth button first, and then opening MS Word and pasting the graph. The first button sends the graph to the nearest printer.

Graphs in EViews

In EViews we can plot/graph the data in a wide variety of ways. One way is to double-click on the variable of interest (the one from which we want to obtain a graph); a new window will appear that looks like a spreadsheet with the values of the variable we double-clicked. Then we go to **View/Line Graph** in order to generate a plot of the series against time (if it is a time series) or against observations (for **undated or irregular** cross-sectional data). Another option is to click on **View/Bar Graph**, which gives a similar figure to the line option but with bars for every observation instead of a line plot. Obviously, the line graph option is preferable in describing time series, and the bar graph for cross-sectional data.

If we need to plot more than one series together, we may first open/create a **group** of series in EViews. To open a group we select the series we want to be in the group by clicking on them with the mouse one by one, with the control button held down, or by typing on the EViews command line the word:

```
group
```

and then pressing enter. This will open a new EViews window in which to specify the series to include in the group. In this window, we type the names of the series we want to plot together, and then click **OK**. Again, a spreadsheet opens with the values for the variables selected to appear in the group. When we click on **View** two graph options are shown: **Graph** will create graphs of all series in the group together, while **Multiple Graphs** will create graphs for each individual series in the group. In both **Graph** and **Multiple Graphs** options for different types of graphs are available. One type that can be very useful in econometric analysis is the scatter plot. To obtain a scatter plot of two series in EViews we open a group (following the procedure described above) with the two series we want to plot and then go to **View/Graph/Scatter**. There are four different options for scatter plots: (a) simple scatter; (b) scatter with a fitted regression line; (c) scatter with a line that fits as closely as possible to the data; and (d) scatter with a kernel density function.

Another simple and convenient way of generating a scatter plot in EViews is to use the command:

```
scat X Y
```

where X and Y should be replaced by the names of the series to be plotted on the x and y axes, respectively. Similarly, a very easy way of producing a time plot of a time series is to use the command:

```
plot X
```

where, again, X is the name of the series we want to plot. The plot command can be used to generate time plots of more than one series in the same graph by specifying more than one variable, separated by spaces, such as:

```
plot X Y Z
```

A final option to generate graphs in EViews is to click on **Quick/Graph** and then specify the names of the series to plot (one or more). A new window opens which offers different options for graph types and scales. After making a choice, we press **OK** to obtain the graph.

We can easily copy and paste graphs from EViews into a document in a word processor. To do this we first need to make sure that the active object is the window that contains the graph (the title bar of the window should be bright; if it is not, click anywhere on the graph and it will be activated). We then either press **CTRL+C** or click on **Edit/Copy**. The **Copy Graph as Metafile** window appears with various options: either to copy the file to the clipboard in order to paste it into another program (the word processor, for example), or to copy the file to disk. We can also choose whether the graph will be in colour or have bold lines. If we copy the graph to the clipboard, we can paste it into a different program very easily either by pressing **CTRL+V** or by clicking on **Edit/Paste**. Conventional Windows programs allow the graph to be edited, changing its size or position in the document.

Graphs in Stata

In Stata it is easy to produce graphs of various kinds. All graphs are accessed through the Graphics menu. This menu has a special option for time series graphs, which includes various types of graphs in addition to the simple line plot (which is the first option in the time series graphs menu). The Graphics menu also includes bar charts, pie charts and histograms, as well as twoway graphs, which produce scatter plots. In each case Stata requires the user to define the variables to be plotted on the graph together with other parameters (for example, number of bins and bin range for histograms) if necessary. The Graphics menu in Stata works like in any other Windows-based program, and is, on the whole, very user-friendly. We shall see examples of various graphs produced in Stata later in the text.

Summary statistics

To gain a more precise idea of the distribution of a variable x_t we can estimate various simple measures such as the mean (or average), often denoted as $\bar{x}$, the variance, often denoted as σ_x^2, and its square root, the standard deviation, stated as σ_x. Thus:

$$\bar{x} = \frac{1}{T} \sum_{i=1}^{T} x_i \qquad (2.6)$$

$$\sigma_x^2 = \frac{1}{T-1} \sum_{i=1}^{T} (x_i - \bar{x})^2 \tag{2.7}$$

$$\sigma_x = \sqrt{\sigma_x^2} \tag{2.8}$$

To analyse two or more variables we might also consider their covariance and correlations (defined later). However, these summary statistics contain far less information than a graph, and the starting point for any good piece of empirical analysis should be a graphical check of all the data.

Summary statistics in MFit

To obtain summary statistics in Microfit we type the command:

```
cor X
```

where X is the name of the variable from which to obtain summary statistics. As well as summary statistics (minimum, maximum, mean, standard deviation, skewness, kurtosis and coefficient of variation), Microfit will give the autocorrelation function of this variable. To generate a histogram of a variable, the command is:

```
hist X
```

The histogram may be printed, copied and saved like any other graph from Microfit.

Summary statistics in EViews

To obtain summary descriptive statistics in EViews, we need again either to double-click and open the series window or to create a group with more than one series, as described in the graphs section above. After that, we click on **View/Descriptive Statistics/Histogram and Stats** for the one variable window case. This will provide summary statistics such as the mean, median, minimum, maximum, standard deviation, skewness and kurtosis, and the Jarque–Bera Statistic for testing for normality of the series, together with its probability limit. If we have opened a group, clicking **View/Descriptive Statistics** provides two choices: one using a common sample for all series, and another using the greatest possible number of observations by ignoring differences in sample sizes among variables.

Summary statistics in Stata

To obtain summary statistics for a series of variables, we go to the Statistics menu and choose the path **Statistics/Summaries, Tables and Tests/Summary and Descriptive Statistics/Summary Statistics**. In the new window we either specify the variables for which we want summary statistics or leave it blank and allow Stata to calculate summary statistics automatically for all the variables in the file. Alternatively, a much quicker and easier way is to type:

```
summarize
```

in the command window, followed by the names of the variables for which we want summary statistics (again, if we leave this blank, summary statistics will be provided for all variables), and simply press enter.

This command provides the number of observations, mean values, standard deviations and minimum and maximum values for the data. Other specific statistics (the median or the coefficient of skewness, for example) can be obtained either by going to the menu **Statistics/Summaries, Tables and Tests/Tables/Table of Summary Statistics** and then defining which statistics to generate, for which variables, or with the command:

```
tabstat variable_name, statistics(median skewness)
columns(variables)
```

For `variable_name` we type the name of the variable exactly as it appears in the 'Variables' list in Stata, and in parentheses after `Statistics` we list the statistics we want.

Components of a time series

An economic or financial time series consists of up to four components:

1 Trend (smooth, long-term/consistent upward or downward movement);
2 Cycle (rise and fall over periods longer than a year, for example resulting from a business cycle);
3 Seasonal (within-year pattern seen in weekly, monthly or quarterly data); and
4 Irregular (random component; can be subdivided into episodic [unpredictable but identifiable] and residual [unpredictable and unidentifiable]).

Note that not all time series have all four components, though the irregular component is present in every series. As we shall see later, various techniques are available for removing one or more components from a time series.

Indices and base dates

An index is a number that expresses the relative change in value (for example price or quantity) from one period to another. The change is measured relative to the value at a base date (which may be revised from time to time). Familiar examples of indices are the consumer price index (CPI) and the FTSE-100 share price index. In many cases, such as these two examples, indices are used as a convenient way of summarizing many prices in one series (the index comprises many individual companies' share prices). Note that two indices may be compared directly only if they have the same base date, which may lead to the need to change the base date of an index.

Splicing two indices and changing the base date of an index   Suppose we have the following data:

Year	Price index (1985 base year)	Price index (1990 base year)	Standardized price index (1990 base year)
1985	100		45.9
1986	132		60.6
1987	196		89.9
1988	213		97.7
1989	258		118.3
1990	218	100	100
1991		85	85
1992		62	62

In this (hypothetical) example, the price index for the years 1985 to 1990 (column 2) uses 1985 as its base year (that is the index takes a value of 100 in 1985), while from 1991 onwards (column 3) the base year is 1990. To make the two periods compatible, we need to convert the data in one of the columns so that a single base year is used. This procedure is known as splicing two indices.

- If we want 1990 as our base year, we need to divide all the previous values (that is those in column 2) by a factor of 2.18 (so that the first series now takes a value of 100 in 1990). The standardized series is shown in the last column in the table.

- Similarly, to obtain a single series in 1985 prices, we would need to multiply the values for the years 1991 to 1992 by a factor of 2.18.

Even if we have a complete series with a single base date, we may for some reason want to change that base date. The procedure is similar: simply multiply or divide – depending on whether the new base date is earlier or later than the old one – the entire series by the appropriate factor to get a value of 100 for the chosen base year.

Data transformations

Changing the frequency of time series data   EViews allows us to convert the frequency of a time series (for example reducing the frequency from monthly to quarterly figures). The choice of method for calculating a series with reduced frequency depends partly on whether we have a stock variable or a flow variable. In general, for stock variables (and indices such as the CPI) we would choose specific dates (for example beginning, middle or end of period) or averaging, while for flow variables we would sum the values (for example annual GDP in 1998 is the sum of quarterly GDP in each of the four quarters of 1998). Increasing the frequency of a time series (for example from quarterly to monthly) involves extrapolation and should be done with great caution. The resultant 'manufactured' series will appear quite smooth and would normally be used for ease of comparison with a series of similar frequency.

Nominal versus real data   A rather tricky issue in econometrics is the choice between nominal and real terms for data. The problem with nominal series is that they incorporate a price component that can obscure the fundamental features we are interested in. This is particularly problematic when two nominal variables are being compared, since the dominant price component in each will produce close matches between the series, resulting in a spuriously high correlation coefficient. To circumvent this problem, we can convert nominal series to real terms using an appropriate price deflator (for example the CPI for consumption expenditure or the producer price index, PPI, for manufacturing production). However, sometimes no appropriate deflator is available, which renders the conversion process somewhat arbitrary.

The bottom line is: think carefully about the variables you are using and the relationships you are investigating, choose the most appropriate format for the data – and be consistent.

Logs   Logarithmic transformations are very popular in econometrics, for several reasons. First, many economic time series exhibit a strong trend (that is a consistent upward or downward movement in the value). When this is caused by some underlying growth process, a plot of the series will reveal an exponential curve. In such cases, the exponential/growth component dominates other features of the series (for example cyclical and irregular components of time series) and may thus obscure a more interesting relationship between this variable and another growing variable. Taking the natural logarithm of such a series effectively linearizes the exponential trend (since the log function is the inverse of an exponential function). For example, we may want to work with the (natural) log of GDP, which will appear on a graph as a roughly straight line, rather than the exponential curve exhibited by the raw GDP series.

Second, logs may also be used to linearize a model that is non-linear in its parameters. An example is the Cobb–Douglas production function:

$$Y = AL^\alpha K^\beta e^u \tag{2.9}$$

(where u is a disturbance term and e is the base of the natural log). Taking logs of both sides, we obtain:

$$\ln(Y) = \ln(A) + \alpha \ln(L) + \beta \ln(K) + u \tag{2.10}$$

Each variable (and the constant term) can be redefined as follows: $y = \ln(Y)$; $k = \ln(K)$; $l = \ln(L)$; $a = \ln(A)$, so that the transformed model becomes:

$$y = a + \alpha l + \beta k + u \tag{2.11}$$

which is linear in the parameters and hence can easily be estimated using ordinary least squares (OLS) regression.

A third advantage of using logarithmic transformations is that they allow the regression coefficients to be interpreted as elasticities, since, for small changes in any variable x, (change in $\ln x$) $\simeq$ (relative change in x itself). (This follows from elementary differentiation: $d(\ln x)/dx = 1/x$ and thus $d(\ln x) = dx/x$.)

In the log-linear production function above, a measures the change in $\ln(Y)$ associated with a small change in $\ln(K)$; that is, it represents the elasticity of output with respect to capital.

Differencing   In the previous section it was noted that a log transformation linearizes an exponential trend. If we want to remove the trend component from a (time) series entirely – that is to render it stationary – we need to apply differencing; that is, we compute absolute changes from one period to the next. Symbolically,

$$\Delta Y_t = Y_t - Y_{t-1} \tag{2.12}$$

which is known as first-order differencing. If a differenced series still exhibits a trend, it needs to be differenced again (one or more times) to render it stationary. Thus we have second-order differencing:

$$\Delta^2 y_t = \Delta(Y_t - Y_{t-1}) = \Delta Y_t - \Delta Y_{t-1}$$

$$= (Y_t - Y_{t-1}) - (Y_{t-1} - Y_{t-2}) = Y_t - 2Y_{t-1} + Y_{t-2} \tag{2.13}$$

and so on.

Growth rates   In many instances, it makes economic sense to analyse data and model relationships in growth-rate terms. A prime example is GDP, which is far more commonly discussed in growth-rate terms than in terms of levels. Using growth rates allows us to investigate the way that changes (over time) in one variable are related to changes (over the same time period) in another variable. Because of the differencing involved, the calculation of growth rates in effect removes the trend component from a series.

There are two types of growth rates: discretely compounded and continuously compounded. Discretely compounded growth rates are computed as follows:

$$\text{growth rate of } Y_t = (Y_t - Y_{t-1})/Y_{t-1}$$

where t refers to the time period.

It is more usual in econometrics to calculate continuously compounded growth rates, which combine the logarithmic and differencing transformations. Dealing with annual data is simple: the continuously compounded growth rate is the natural log of the ratio of the value of the variable in one period to the value in the previous period (or, alternatively, the difference between the log of the value in one year and the log of the value in the previous year):

$$\text{growth rate of } Y_t = \ln(Y_t/Y_{t-1}) = \ln(Y_t) - \ln(Y_{t-1})$$

For monthly data, there is a choice between calculating the (annualized) month-on-previous-month growth rate and calculating the year-on-year growth rate. The advantage of the former is that it provides the most up-to-date rate and is therefore less biased than a year-on-year rate. Month-on-month growth rates are usually annualized, that is multiplied by a factor of 12 to give the amount the series would grow in a whole year if that monthly rate applied throughout the year. The relevant formulae are as follows:

annualized month-on-month growth rate

$= 12 * \ln(Y_t/Y_{t-1})$ (continuous)

OR $[(Y_t/Y_{t-1})^{12} - 1]$ (discrete)

annualized quarter-on-quarter growth rate

$= 4 * \ln(Y_t/Y_{t-1})$ (continuous)

OR $[(Y_t/Y_{t-1})^4 - 1]$ (discrete)

(Multiply these growth rates by 100 to obtain percentage growth rates.)

However, month-on-previous-month growth rates (whether annualized or not) are often highly volatile, in large part because time series are frequently subject to seasonal factors (the Christmas boom being the best-known). It is in order to avoid this seasonal effect that growth rates usually compare one period with the corresponding period a year earlier (for example January 2000 with January 1999). This is how the headline inflation rate is calculated, for instance. Similar arguments apply to quarterly and other data. (Another advantage of using these rates in regression analysis is that it allows one year for the impact of one variable to take effect on another variable.) This type of growth-rate computation involves seasonal differencing:

$$\Delta^s Y_t = Y_t - Y_{t-s}$$

The formula for calculating the year-on-year growth rate using monthly data is:

$$\text{growth rate of } Y_t = \ln(Y_t/Y_{t-12}) = \ln(Y_t) - \ln(Y_{t-12})$$

In sum, calculating year-on-year growth rates simultaneously removes trend and seasonal components from time series, and thus facilitates the examination (say, in correlation or regression analysis) of other characteristics of the data (such as cycles or irregular components).

Part

II

The Classical Linear Regression Model

3 Simple Regression

CHAPTER CONTENTS

LEARNING OBJECTIVES

After studying this chapter you should be able to:

1. Understand the concepts of correlation and regression.
2. Derive mathematically the regression coefficients of a simple regression model.
3. Understand estimation of simple regression models with the ordinary least squares method.
4. Understand the concept of goodness of fit measured by the R^2 in simple regression models.
5. Conduct hypothesis testing and construct confidence intervals for the estimated coefficients of a simple regression model.
6. Perform a simple regression estimation using econometric software.
7. Interpret and discuss the results of a simple regression estimation output.

29

Introduction to regression: the classical linear regression model (CLRM)

Why do we do regressions?

Econometric methods such as regression can help to overcome the problem of complete uncertainty and guide planning and decision-making. Of course, building a model is not an easy task. Models should meet certain criteria (for example, a model should not suffer from serial correlation) in order to be valid and a lot of work is usually needed before we achieve a good model. Furthermore, much decision-making is required regarding which variables to include in the model. Too many may cause problems (unneeded variables misspecification), while too few may cause other problems (omitted variables misspecification or incorrect functional form).

The classical linear regression model

The classical linear regression model is a way of examining the nature and form of the relationships among two or more variables. In this chapter we consider the case of only two variables. One important issue in the regression analysis is the direction of causation between the two variables; in other words, we want to know which variable is affecting the other. Alternatively, this can be stated as which variable depends on the other. Therefore, we refer to the two variables as the dependent variable (usually denoted by Y) and the independent or explanatory variable (usually denoted by X). We want to explain/predict the value of Y for different values of the explanatory variable X. Let us assume that X and Y are linked by a simple linear relationship:

$$E(Y_t) = a + \beta X_t \tag{3.1}$$

where $E(Y_t)$ denotes the average value of Y_t for given X_t and unknown population parameters a and β (the subscript t indicates that we have time series data). Equation (3.1) is called the population regression equation. The actual value of Y_t will not always equal its expected value $E(Y_t)$. There are various factors that can 'disturb' its actual behaviour and therefore we can write actual Y_t as:

$$Y_t = E(Y_t) + u_t$$

or

$$Y_t = a + \beta X_t + u_t \tag{3.2}$$

where u_t is a disturbance. There are several reasons why a disturbance exists:

1 Omission of explanatory variables. There might be other factors (other than X_t) affecting Y_t that have been left out of Equation (3.2). This may be because we do not

know these factors, or even if we know them we might be unable to measure them in order to use them in a regression analysis.

2 Aggregation of variables. In some cases it is desirable to avoid having too many variables and therefore we attempt to summarize in aggregate a number of relationships in only one variable. Therefore, eventually we have only a good approximation of Y_t, with discrepancies that are captured by the disturbance term.

3 Model misspecification. We might have a misspecified model in terms of its structure. For example, it might be that Y_t is not affected by X_t, but it is affected by the value of X in the previous period (that is X_{t-1}). In this case, if X_t and X_{t-1} are closely related, the estimation of Equation (3.2) will lead to discrepancies that are again captured by the error term.

4 Functional misspecification. The relationship between X and Y might be non-linear. We shall deal with non-linearities in other chapters of this text.

5 Measurement errors. If the measurement of one or more variables is not correct then errors appear in the relationship and these contribute to the disturbance term.

Now the question is whether it is possible to estimate the population regression function based on sample information. The answer is that we may not be able to estimate it 'accurately' because of sampling fluctuations. However, while the population regression equation is unknown – and will remain unknown – to any investigator, it is possible to estimate it after gathering data from a sample. The first step for the researcher is to do a scatter plot of the sample data and try to fix a straight line to the scatter of points, as shown in Figure 3.1.

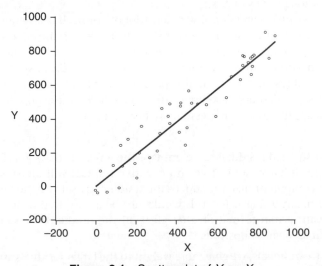

Figure 3.1   Scatter plot of Y on X

There are many ways of fixing a line, including:

1 Drawing it by eye.
2 Connecting the first with the last observation.
3 Taking the average of the first two observations and the average of the last two observations and connecting those two points.
4 Applying the method of ordinary least squares (OLS).

The first three methods are naïve ones, while the last is the most appropriate method for this type of situation. The OLS method is the topic of the next section.

The ordinary least squares (OLS) method of estimation

Consider again the population regression equation:

$$Y_t = a + \beta X_t + u_t \qquad (3.3)$$

This equation is not directly observable. However, we can gather data and obtain estimates of a and β from a sample of the population. This gives us the following relationship, which is a fitted straight line with intercept $\hat{a}$ and slope $\hat{\beta}$:

$$\hat{Y}_t = \hat{a} + \hat{\beta} X_t \qquad (3.4)$$

Equation (3.4) can be referred to as the sample regression equation. Here, $\hat{a}$ and $\hat{\beta}$ are sample estimates of the population parameters a and β, and $\hat{Y}_t$ denotes the predicted value of Y. (Once we have the estimated sample regression equation we can easily predict Y for various values of X.)

When we fit a sample regression line to a scatter of points, it is obviously desirable to select the line in such a manner that it is as close as possible to the actual Y, or, in other words, that it provides the smallest possible number of residuals. To do this we adopt the following criterion: choose the sample regression function in such a way that the sum of the squared residuals is as small as possible (that is minimized). This method of estimation has some desirable properties that make it the most popular technique in uncomplicated applications of regression analysis, namely:

1 By using the squared residuals we eliminate the effect of the sign of the residuals, so it is not possible that a positive and negative residual will offset each other. For example, we could minimize the sum of the residuals by setting the forecast for $Y(\hat{Y})$ equal to the mean of $Y(\bar{Y})$. But this would not be a very well-fitting line at all. So clearly we want a transformation that gives all the residuals the same sign before making them as small as possible.

2 By squaring the residuals, we give more weight to the larger residuals and so, in effect, we work harder to reduce the very large errors.

3 The OLS method chooses $\hat{a}$ and $\hat{\beta}$ estimators that have certain numerical and statistical properties (such as unbiasedness and efficiency) that we shall discuss later.

We can now see how to derive the OLS estimators. Denoting by *RSS* the sum of the squared residuals, we have:

$$RSS = \hat{u}_1^2 + \hat{u}_2^2 + \cdots + \hat{u}_n^2 = \sum_{t=1}^{n} \hat{u}_t^2 \tag{3.5}$$

However, we know that:

$$\hat{u}_t = (Y_t - \hat{Y}_t) = (Y_t - \hat{a} - \hat{\beta}X_t) \tag{3.6}$$

and therefore:

$$RSS = \sum_{t=1}^{n} \hat{u}_t^2 = \sum_{t=1}^{n}(Y_t - \hat{Y}_t)^2 = \sum_{t=1}^{n}(Y_t - \hat{a} - \hat{\beta}X_t)^2 \tag{3.7}$$

To minimize Equation (3.7), the first-order condition is to take the partial derivatives of *RSS* with respect to $\hat{a}$ and $\hat{\beta}$ and set them to zero. Thus, we have:

$$\frac{\partial RSS}{\partial \hat{a}} = -2 \sum_{t=1}^{n}(Y_t - \hat{a} - \hat{\beta}X_t) = 0 \tag{3.8}$$

and

$$\frac{\partial RSS}{\partial \hat{\beta}} = -2 \sum_{t=1}^{n} X_t(Y_t - \hat{a} - \hat{\beta}X_t) = 0 \tag{3.9}$$

The second-order partial derivatives are:

$$\frac{\partial^2 RSS}{\partial \hat{a}^2} = 2n \tag{3.10}$$

$$\frac{\partial^2 RSS}{\partial \hat{\beta}^2} = 2 \sum_{t=1}^{n} X_t^2 \tag{3.11}$$

$$\frac{\partial^2 RSS}{\partial \hat{a}\partial \hat{\beta}} = 2 \sum_{t=1}^{n} X_t \tag{3.12}$$

Therefore, it is easy to verify that the second-order conditions for a minimum are met.

Since $\sum \hat{a} = n\hat{a}$ (for simplicity of notation we omit the upper and lower limits of the summation symbol), we can (by using that and rearranging) rewrite Equations (3.8) and (3.9) as follows:

$$\sum Y_t = n\hat{a} - \hat{\beta} \sum X_t \tag{3.13}$$

and

$$\sum X_t Y_t = \hat{a} \sum X_t + \hat{\beta} \sum X_t^2 \qquad (3.14)$$

The only unknowns in these two equations are $\hat{a}$ and $\hat{\beta}$. Therefore we can solve this system of two equations with two unknowns to obtain $\hat{a}$ and $\hat{\beta}$. First, we divide both sides of Equation (3.13) by n to get:

$$\frac{\sum Y_t}{n} = \frac{n\hat{a}}{n} - \frac{\hat{\beta} \sum X_t}{n} \qquad (3.15)$$

Denoting $\sum Y_t/n$ by $\bar{Y}$ and $\sum X_t/n$ by $\bar{X}$, and rearranging, we obtain:

$$\hat{a} = \bar{Y} - \hat{\beta}\bar{X} \qquad (3.16)$$

Substituting Equation (3.16) into Equation (3.14), we get:

$$\sum X_t Y_t = \bar{Y} \sum X_t - \hat{\beta}\bar{X} \sum X_t + \hat{\beta} \sum X_t^2 \qquad (3.17)$$

or

$$\sum X_t Y_t = \frac{1}{n} \sum Y_t \sum X_t - \hat{\beta}\frac{1}{n} \sum X_t \sum X_t + \hat{\beta} \sum X_t^2 \qquad (3.18)$$

and finally, factorizing the $\hat{\beta}$ terms, we have:

$$\sum X_t Y_t = \frac{\sum Y_t \sum X_t}{n} + \hat{\beta}\left[\sum X_t^2 - \frac{(\sum X_t)^2}{n}\right] \qquad (3.19)$$

Thus, we can obtain $\hat{\beta}$ as:

$$\hat{\beta} = \frac{\sum X_t Y_t - 1/n \sum Y_t \sum X_t}{\sum X_t^2 - 1/n \left(\sum X_t\right)^2} \qquad (3.20)$$

And given $\hat{\beta}$ we can use Equation (3.16) to obtain $\hat{a}$.

Alternative expressions for $\hat{\beta}$

We can express the numerator and denominator of Equation (3.20) as follows:

$$\sum (X_t - \bar{X})(Y_t - \bar{Y}) = \sum X_t Y_t - \frac{1}{n} \sum Y_t \sum X_t \qquad (3.21)$$

$$\sum (X_t - \bar{X})^2 = \sum X_t^2 - \frac{1}{n} \left(\sum X_t\right)^2 \qquad (3.22)$$

So then we have:

$$\hat{\beta} = \frac{\sum (X_t - \bar{X})(Y_t - \bar{Y})}{\sum (X_t - \bar{X})^2} \tag{3.23}$$

or even

$$\hat{\beta} = \frac{\sum x_t y_t}{\sum x_t^2} \tag{3.24}$$

where obviously $x_t = (X_t - \bar{X})$ and $y_t = (Y_t - \bar{Y})$, which are deviations from their respective means.

We can use the definitions of $Cov(X, Y)$ and $Var(X)$ to obtain an alternative expression for $\hat{\beta}$ as:

$$\hat{\beta} = \frac{\sum X_t Y_t - 1/n \sum Y_t \sum X_t}{\sum X_t^2 - 1/n \left(\sum X_t\right)^2} = \frac{\sum X_t Y_t - \bar{Y}\bar{X}}{\sum X_t^2 - \left(\bar{X}\right)^2} \tag{3.25}$$

or

$$\hat{\beta} = \frac{\sum (X_t - \bar{X})(Y_t - \bar{Y})}{\sum (X_t - \bar{X})^2} \tag{3.26}$$

If we further divide both nominator and denominator by $1/n$ we have:

$$\hat{\beta} = \frac{1/n \sum (X_t - \bar{X})(Y_t - \bar{Y})}{1/n \sum (X_t - \bar{X})^2} \tag{3.27}$$

and finally we can express $\hat{\beta}$ as:

$$\hat{\beta} = \frac{Cov(X_t, Y_t)}{Var(X_t)} \tag{3.28}$$

where $Cov(X_t, Y_t)$ and $Var(X_t)$ are sample covariances and variances.

The assumptions of the CLRM

General

In the previous section we described the desirable properties of estimators. However, we need to make clear that there is no guarantee that the OLS estimators will possess any of these properties unless a number of assumptions – which this section presents – hold.

In general, when we calculate estimators of population parameters from sample data we are bound to make some initial assumptions about the population distribution.

Usually, they amount to a set of statements about the distribution of the variables we are investigating, without which our model and estimates cannot be justified. Therefore, it is important not only to present the assumptions but also to move beyond them, to the extent that we will at least study what happens when they go wrong, and how we may test whether they have gone wrong. This will be examined in the third part of this book.

The assumptions

The CLRM consists of eight basic assumptions about the ways in which the observations are generated:

1 *Linearity*. The first assumption is that the dependent variable can be calculated as a linear function of a specific set of independent variables, plus a disturbance term. This can be expressed mathematically as follows: the regression model is linear in the unknown coefficients α and β so that $Y_t = \alpha + \beta X_t + u_t$, for $t = 1, 2, 3, \ldots, n$.

2 *X_t has some variation*. By this assumption we mean that not all observations of X_t are the same; at least one has to be different so that the sample $Var(X)$ is not 0. It is important to distinguish between the sample variance, which simply shows how much X varies over the particular sample, and the stochastic nature of X. In many places in this book we shall make the assumption that X is non-stochastic (see point 3 below). This means that the variance of X at any point in time is zero, so $Var(X_t) = 0$, and if we could somehow repeat the world over again X would always take exactly the same values. But, of course, over any sample there will (indeed must) be some variation in X.

3 *X_t is non-stochastic and fixed in repeated samples*. By this assumption we mean first that X_t is a variable whose values are not determined by some chance mechanism – they are determined by an experimenter or investigator; and second that it is possible to repeat the sample with the same independent variable values. This implies that $Cov(X_s, u_t) = 0$ for all s, and $t = 1, 2, \ldots, n$; that is, X_t and u_t are uncorrelated.

4 *The expected value of the disturbance term is zero*. This means that the disturbance is a genuine disturbance, so that if we took a large number of samples the mean disturbance would be zero. This can be denoted as $E(u_t) = 0$. We need this assumption in order to interpret the deterministic part of a regression model, $\alpha + \beta X_t$, as a 'statistical average' relation.

5 *Homoskedasticity*. This requires that all disturbance terms have the same variance, so that $Var(u_t) = \sigma^2 = $ constant for all t.

6 *Serial independence*. This requires that all disturbance terms are independently distributed, or, more easily, are not correlated with one another, so that $Cov(u_t, u_s) = E(u_t - Eu_t)(u_s - Eu_s) = E(u_t u_s) = 0$ for all $t \neq s$. This assumption has a special significance in economics; to grasp what it means in practice, recall that we nearly always obtain our data from time series in which each t is one year, or one quarter, or one

week ahead of the last. The condition means, therefore, that the disturbance in one period should not be related to a disturbance in the next or previous periods. This condition is frequently violated since, if there is a disturbing effect at one time, it is likely to persist. In this discussion we shall be studying violations of this assumption quite carefully.

7 *Normality of residuals.* The disturbances $u_1, u_2, \ldots, u_n$ are assumed to be independently and identically normally distributed, with mean zero and common variance σ^2.

8 *$n > 2$ and multicollinearity.* This assumption says that the number of observations must be greater than two, or in general must be greater than the number of independent variables, and that there are no exact linear relationships among the variables.

Violations of the assumptions

The first three assumptions basically state that X_t is a 'well-behaved' variable that was not chosen by chance, and that we can in some sense 'control' for it by choosing it repeatedly. These are needed because X_t is used to explain what is happening (the explanatory variable).

Violation of assumption 1 creates problems that are in general called misspecification errors, such as wrong regressors, non-linearities and hanging parameters. We discuss these problems analytically in Chapter 8. Violation of assumptions 2 and 3 results in errors in variables and problems which are also discussed in Chapter 8. Violation of assumption 4 leads to a biased intercept, while violations of assumptions 5 and 6 lead to problems of heteroskedasticity and serial correlation, respectively. These problems are discussed in Chapters 6 and 7, respectively. Finally, assumption 7 has important implications in hypothesis testing, and violation of assumption 8 leads to problems of perfect multicollinearity, which are discussed in Chapter 5 (see Table 3.1).

Table 3.1 The assumptions of the CLRM

Assumption	Mathematical expression	Violation may imply	Chapter
(1) Linearity of the model	$Y_t = \alpha + \beta X_t + u_t$	Wrong regressors Non-linearity Changing parameters	8 8 8
(2) X is variable	$Var(X)$ is not 0	Errors in variables	8
(3) X is non-stochastic and fixed in repeated samples	$Cov(X_s, u_t) = 0$ for all s and $t = 1, 2, \ldots, n$	Autoregression	10
(4) Expected value of disturbance is zero	$E(u_t) = 0$	Biased intercept	—
(5) Homoskedasticity	$Var(u_t) = \sigma^2 = $ constant	Heteroskedasticity	6
(6) Serial independence	$Cov(u_t, u_s) = 0$ for all $t \neq s$	Autocorrelation	7
(7) Normality of disturbance	$u_t \sim N(\mu, \sigma^2)$	Outliers	8
(8) No linear relationships	$\sum_{t=1}^{T}(\delta_i X_{it} + \delta_j X_{jt}) \neq 0 \quad i \neq j$	Multicollinearity	5

Properties of the OLS estimators

We now return to the properties that we would like our estimators to have. Based on the assumptions of the CLRM we can prove that the OLS estimators are best linear unbiased estimators (BLUE). To do so, we first have to decompose the regression coefficients estimated under OLS into their random and non-random components.

As a starting point, note that Y_t has a non-random component $(a + \beta X_t)$, as well as a random component, captured by the residuals u_t. Therefore, $Cov(X, Y)$ – which depends on values of Y_t – will have a random and a non-random component:

$$Cov(X, Y) = Cov(X_t, [a + \beta X + u])$$
$$= Cov(X, a) + Cov(X, \beta X) + Cov(X, u) \qquad (3.29)$$

However, because a and β are constants we have that $Cov(X, a) = 0$ and that $Cov(X, \beta X) = \beta Cov(X, X) = \beta Var(X)$. Thus:

$$Cov(X, Y) = \beta Var(X) + Cov(X, u) \qquad (3.30)$$

and substituting that in Equation (3.28) yields:

$$\hat{\beta} = \frac{Cov(X, Y)}{Var(X)} = \beta + \frac{Cov(X, u)}{Var(X)} \qquad (3.31)$$

which says that the OLS coefficient $\hat{\beta}$ estimated from any sample has a non-random component, β, and a random component which depends on $Cov(X_t, u_t)$.

Linearity

Based on assumption 3, we have that X is non-stochastic and fixed in repeated samples. Therefore, the X values can be treated as constants and we need merely to concentrate on the Y values. If the OLS estimators are linear functions of the Y values then they are linear estimators. From Equation (3.24) we have that:

$$\hat{\beta} = \frac{\sum x_t y_t}{\sum x_t^2} \qquad (3.32)$$

Since the X_t are regarded as constants, then the x_t are regarded as constants as well. We have that:

$$\hat{\beta} = \frac{\sum x_t y_t}{\sum x_t^2} = \frac{\sum x_t (Y_t - \bar{Y})}{\sum x_t^2} = \frac{\sum x_t Y_t - \bar{Y} \sum x_t}{\sum x_t^2} \qquad (3.33)$$

but because $\bar{Y} \sum x_t = 0$, we have that:

$$\hat{\beta} = \frac{\sum x_t Y_t}{\sum x_t^2} = \sum z_t Y_t \qquad (3.34)$$

where $z_t = x_t / \sum x_t^2$ can also be regarded as constant and therefore $\hat{\beta}$ is indeed a linear estimator of the Y_t.

Unbiasedness

Unbiasedness of $\hat{\beta}$

To prove that $\hat{\beta}$ is an unbiased estimator of β we need to show that $E(\hat{\beta}) = \beta$. We have:

$$E(\hat{\beta}) = E\left[\beta + \frac{Cov(X, u)}{Var(X)}\right] \qquad (3.35)$$

However, β is a constant, and using assumption 3 – that X_t is non-random – we can take $Var(X)$ as a fixed constant to take them out of the expectation expression and have:

$$E(\hat{\beta}) = E(\beta) + \frac{1}{Var(X)} E[Cov(X, u)] \qquad (3.36)$$

Therefore, it is enough to show that $E[Cov(X, u)] = 0$. We know that:

$$E[Cov(X, u)] = E\left[\frac{1}{n}\sum_{t=1}^{n}(X_t - \bar{X})(u_t - \bar{u})\right] \qquad (3.37)$$

where $1/n$ is constant, so we can take it out of the expectation expression, and we can also break the sum down into the sum of its expectations to give:

$$E[Cov(X_t, u_t)] = \frac{1}{n}\left[E(X_1 - \bar{X})(u_1 - \bar{u}) + \cdots + E(X_n - \bar{X})(u_n - \bar{u})\right]$$

$$= \frac{1}{n}\sum_{t=1}^{n} E\left[(X_t - \bar{X})(u_t - \bar{u})\right] \qquad (3.38)$$

Furthermore, because X_t is non-random (again from assumption 3) we can take it out of the expectation term to give:

$$E[Cov(X, u)] = \frac{1}{n}\sum_{t=1}^{n}(X_t - \bar{X})E(u_t - \bar{u}) \qquad (3.39)$$

Finally, using assumption 4, we have that $E(u_t) = 0$ and therefore $E(\bar{u}) = 0$. So $E[Cov(X, u)] = 0$ and this proves that:

$$E(\hat{\beta}) = \beta$$

or, to put it in words, that $\hat{\beta}$ is an unbiased estimator of the true population parameter β.

Unbiasedness of $\hat{a}$

We know that $\hat{a} = \bar{Y} - \hat{\beta}\bar{X}$, so:

$$E(\hat{a}) = E(\bar{Y}) - E(\hat{\beta})\bar{X} \tag{3.40}$$

But we also have that:

$$E(Y_t) = a + \beta X_t + E(u_t) = a + \beta X_t \tag{3.41}$$

where we eliminated the $E(u_t)$ term because, according to assumption 4, $E(u_t) = 0$. So:

$$E(\bar{Y}) = a + \beta\bar{X} \tag{3.42}$$

Substituting Equation (3.42) into Equation (3.40) gives:

$$E(\hat{a}) = a + \beta\bar{X} - E(\hat{\beta})\bar{X} \tag{3.43}$$

We have proved before that $E(\hat{\beta}) = \beta$; therefore:

$$E(\hat{a}) = a + \beta\bar{X} - \beta\bar{X} = a \tag{3.44}$$

which proves that $\hat{a}$ is an unbiased estimator of a.

Efficiency and BLUEness

Under assumptions 5 and 6, we can prove that the OLS estimators are the most efficient among all unbiased linear estimators. Thus we can conclude that the OLS procedure yields BLU estimators.

The proof that the OLS estimators are BLU estimators is relatively complicated. It entails a procedure which goes the opposite way from that followed so far. We start the estimation from the beginning, trying to derive a BLU estimator of β based on the properties of linearity, unbiasedness and minimum variance one by one, and then we check whether the BLU estimator derived by this procedure is the same as the OLS estimator.

Thus, we want to derive the BLU estimator of β, say $\breve{\beta}$, concentrating first on the property of linearity. For $\breve{\beta}$ to be linear we need to have:

$$\breve{\beta} = \delta_1 Y_1 + \delta_2 Y_2 + \cdots + \delta_n Y_n = \sum \delta_t Y_t \tag{3.45}$$

where the δ_t terms are constants, the values of which are to be determined.

Proceeding with the property of unbiasedness, for $\breve{\beta}$ to be unbiased we must have $E(\breve{\beta}) = \beta$. We know that:

$$E(\breve{\beta}) = E\left(\sum \delta_t Y_t\right) = \sum \delta_t E(Y_t) \tag{3.46}$$

Substituting $E(Y_t) = a + \beta X_t$ (because $Y_t = a + \beta X_t + u_t$, and also because X_t is non-stochastic and $E(u_t) = 0$, given by the basic assumptions of the model), we get:

$$E(\breve{\beta}) = \sum \delta_t (a + \beta X_t) = a \sum \delta_t + \beta \sum \delta_t X_t \qquad (3.47)$$

and therefore, in order to have unbiased $\breve{\beta}$, we need:

$$\sum \delta_t = 0 \quad \text{and} \quad \sum \delta_t X_t = 1 \qquad (3.48)$$

Next, we proceed by deriving an expression for the variance (which we need to minimize) of $\breve{\beta}$:

$$
\begin{aligned}
Var(\breve{\beta}) &= E\left[\breve{\beta} - E(\breve{\beta})\right]^2 \\
&= E\left[\sum \delta_t Y_t - E\left(\sum \delta_t Y_t\right)\right]^2 \\
&= E\left[\sum \delta_t Y_t - \sum \delta_t E(Y_t)\right]^2 \\
&= E\left[\sum \delta_t (Y_t - E(Y_t))\right]^2 \qquad (3.49)
\end{aligned}
$$

In this expression we can use $Y_t = a + \beta X_t + u_t$ and $E(Y_t) = a + \beta X_t$ to give:

$$
\begin{aligned}
Var(\breve{\beta}) &= E\left[\sum \delta_t (a + \beta X_t + u_t - (a + \beta X_t))\right]^2 \\
&= E\left(\sum \delta_t u_t\right)^2 \\
&= E(\delta_1^2 u_1^2 + \delta_2^2 u_2^2 + \delta_3^2 u_3^2 + \cdots + \delta_n^2 u_n^2 \\
&\quad + 2\delta_1\delta_2 u_1 u_2 + 2\delta_1\delta_3 u_1 u_3 + \cdots) \\
&= \delta_1^2 E(u_1^2) + \delta_2^2 E(u_2^2) + \delta_3^2 E(u_3^2) + \cdots + \delta_n^2 E(u_n^2) \\
&\quad + 2\delta_1\delta_2 E(u_1 u_2) + 2\delta_1\delta_3 E(u_1 u_3) + \cdots) \qquad (3.50)
\end{aligned}
$$

Using assumptions 5 ($Var(u_t) = \sigma^2$) and 6 ($Cov(u_t, u_s) = E(u_t u_s) = 0$ for all $t \neq s$) we obtain that:

$$Var(\breve{\beta}) = \sum \delta_t^2 \sigma^2 \qquad (3.51)$$

We now need to choose δ_t in the linear estimator (Equation (3.46)) to be such as to minimize the variance (Equation (3.51)) subject to the constraints (Equation (3.48)) which ensure unbiasedness (with this then having a linear, unbiased minimum variance estimator). We formulate the Lagrangian function:

$$L = \sigma^2 \sum \delta_t^2 - \lambda_1 \left(\sum \delta_t\right) - \lambda_2 \left(\sum \delta_t X_t - 1\right) \qquad (3.52)$$

where λ_1 and λ_2 are Lagrangian multipliers.

Following the regular procedure, which is to take the first-order conditions (that is the partial derivatives of L with respect to δ_t, λ_1 and λ_2) and set them equal to zero, and after rearrangement and mathematical manipulations (we omit the mathematical details of the derivation because it is very lengthy and tedious, and because it does not use any of the assumptions of the model in any case), we obtain the optimal δ_t as:

$$\delta_t = \frac{x_t}{\sum x_t^2} \tag{3.53}$$

Therefore we have that $\delta_t = z_t$ of the OLS expression given by Equation (3.34). So, substituting this into our linear estimator $\breve{\beta}$ we have:

$$\begin{aligned}
\breve{\beta} &= \sum \delta_t Y_t = \sum z_t Y_t \\
&= \sum z_t (Y_t - \bar{Y} + \bar{Y})^* \\
&= \sum z_t (Y_t - \bar{Y}) + \bar{Y} \sum z_t \\
&= \sum z_t y_t = \frac{\sum x_t y_t}{\sum x_t^2} \\
&= \hat{\beta} \tag{3.54}
\end{aligned}$$

Thus, the $\hat{\beta}$ of the OLS is BLU.

The advantage of the BLUEness condition is that it provides us with an expression for the variance by substituting the optimal δ_t given in Equation (3.53) into Equation (3.51) to give:

$$\begin{aligned}
Var(\breve{\beta}) = Var(\hat{\beta}) &= \sum \left(\frac{x_t}{\sum x_t^2} \right)^2 \sigma^2 \\
&= \frac{\sum x_t^2 \sigma^2}{\left(\sum x_t^2 \right)^2} = \sigma^2 \frac{1}{\sum x_t^2} \tag{3.55}
\end{aligned}$$

Consistency

Consistency is the idea that, as the sample becomes infinitely large, the parameter estimate given by a procedure such as OLS converges on the true parameter value. This is obviously true when the estimator is unbiased, as shown above, as consistency is really just a weaker form of unbiasedness. However, the proof above rests on our assumption 3, that the X variables are fixed. If we relax this assumption it is no longer possible to prove the unbiasedness of OLS but we can still establish that it is a consistent estimator. That is, when we relax assumption 3, OLS is no longer a BLU estimator but it is still consistent.

---

* We add and subtract $\bar{Y}$.

We showed in Equation (3.31) that $\hat{\beta} = \beta + Cov(X, u)/Var(X)$. Dividing the top and the bottom of the last term by n gives

$$\hat{\beta} = \beta + \frac{Cov(X, u)/n}{Var(X)/n} \tag{3.56}$$

Using the law of large numbers, we know that $Cov(X, u)/n$ converges to its expectation, which is $Cov(X_t, u_t)$. Similarly, $Var(X)/n$ converges to $Var(X_t)$. So, as $n \to \infty$, $\hat{\beta} \to \beta + Cov(X_t, u_t)/Var(X_t)$, which is equal to the true population parameter β if $Cov(X_t, u_t) = 0$ (that is if X_t and u_t are uncorrelated). Thus $\hat{\beta}$ is a consistent estimator of the true population parameter β.

The overall goodness of fit

We showed earlier that the regression equation obtained from the OLS method fits a scatter diagram quite closely. However, we need to know how close it is to the scattered observed values to be able to judge whether one particular line describes the relationship between Y_t and X_t better than an alternative line. In other words, it is desirable to know a measure that describes the closeness of fit. This measure will also inform us how well the equation we have obtained accounts for the behaviour of the dependent variable.

To obtain such a measure, we first have to decompose the actual value of Y_t into a predicted value, which comes from the regression equation, $\hat{Y}_t$, plus the equation's residuals:

$$Y_t = \hat{Y}_t + \hat{u}_t \tag{3.57}$$

Subtracting $\bar{Y}$ from both sides we have:

$$Y_t - \bar{Y} = \hat{Y}_t - \bar{Y} + \hat{u}_t \tag{3.58}$$

We need to obtain a measure of the total variation in Y_t from its mean $\bar{Y}$. Therefore, we take the sum of Equation (3.58):

$$\sum(Y_t - \bar{Y}) = \sum(\hat{Y}_t - \bar{Y} + \hat{u}_t) \tag{3.59}$$

then square both terms to get:

$$\sum(Y_t - \bar{Y})^2 = \sum(\hat{Y}_t - \bar{Y} + \hat{u}_t)^2 \tag{3.60}$$

Note that, if we divided the measure on the left-hand side of the above equation by n, we would simply get the sample variance of Y_t. So $\sum(Y_t - \bar{Y})^2$ is an appropriate measure of the total variation in Y_t, often called the total sum of squares (TSS).

Continuing:

$$\sum (Y_t - \bar{Y})^2 = \sum (\hat{Y}_t - \bar{Y})^2 + \sum \hat{u}_t^2 + 2 \sum (\hat{Y}_t - \bar{Y})\hat{u}_t \qquad (3.61)$$

where $\sum (\hat{Y}_t - \bar{Y})^2$ is the explained sum of squares from the OLS – usually called the ESS – and $\sum \hat{u}_t^2$ is the unexplained part of the total variation in Y_t, or the remaining or residual sum of squares (RSS). It is easy to show that the cross-product term drops out of the equation using the properties of the OLS residuals (from the first-order conditions we had that $-2 \sum (Y_t - \hat{a} - \hat{\beta} X_t) = 0$ and $-2 \sum X_t(Y_t - \hat{a} - \hat{\beta} X_t) = 0$, which says that $-2 \sum \hat{u}_t = 0$ and $-2 \sum X_t \hat{u}_t = 0$):

$$\sum (Y_t - \bar{Y})\hat{u}_t = \sum (\hat{a} + \hat{\beta} X_t - \bar{Y})\hat{u}_t$$

$$= \hat{a} \sum \hat{u}_t + \hat{\beta} \sum X_t \hat{u}_t - \bar{Y} \sum \hat{u}_t = 0 \qquad (3.62)$$

Thus Equation (3.61) reduces to:

$$TSS = ESS + RSS \qquad (3.63)$$

where both TSS and ESS are expressed in units of Y squared. By relating ESS to TSS we can derive a pure number called the coefficient of determination (and denoted by R^2):

$$R^2 = \frac{ESS}{TSS} \qquad (3.64)$$

which measures the proportion of the total variation in Y_t (TSS) that is explained by the sample regression equation (ESS). By dividing each of the terms in Equation (3.63) by TSS we obtain an alternative equation that gives us the range of the values of R^2:

$$1 = R^2 + \frac{RSS}{TSS} \qquad (3.65)$$

When the sample regression function fails to account for any of the variation in Y_t then ESS = 0 and all the variation in Y_t is left unexplained: RSS = TSS. In this case, $R^2 = 0$ and this is its lower bound. At the opposite extreme, when the sample regression equation predicts perfectly every value of Y_t, no equation error occurs; thus RSS = 0 and ESS = TSS, which gives us an R^2 equal to its upper bound value of 1.

Therefore the value of R^2 lies between 0 and 1, and shows how closely the equation fits the data. An R^2 of 0.4 is better than a value of 0.2, but not twice as good. The value of 0.4 indicates that 40% of the variation in Y_t is explained by the sample regression equation (or by the regressors).

Problems associated with R^2

There are a number of serious problems associated with the use of R^2 to judge the performance of a single equation or as a basis of comparison of different equations:

1 *Spurious regression problem (this problem will be discussed fully in Chapters 16 and 17).* In the case where two or more variables are actually unrelated, but exhibit strong trend-like behaviour, the R^2 can reach very high values (sometimes even greater than 0.9). This may mislead the researcher into believing there is actually a strong relationship between the variables.

2 *High correlation of X_t with another variable Z_t.* It might be that there is a variable Z_t that determines the behaviour of Y_t and is highly correlated with X_t. Then, even though a large value of R^2 shows the importance of X_t in determining Y_t, the omitted variable Z_t may be responsible for this.

3 *Correlation does not necessarily imply causality.* No matter how high the value of R^2, this cannot suggest causality between Y_t and X_t, because R^2 is a measure of correlation between the observed value Y_t and the predicted value $\hat{Y}_t$. To whatever extent possible, we should refer to economic theory, previous empirical work and intuition to determine a causally related variable to include in a sample regression.

4 *Time series equations versus cross-section equations.* Time series equations almost always generate higher R^2 values than cross-section equations. This is because cross-sectional data contain a great deal of random variation (usually called 'noise'), which makes ESS small relative to TSS. On the other hand, even badly specified time series equations can give R^2s of 0.999 for the spurious regression reasons presented in point 1 above. Therefore, comparisons of time series and cross-sectional equations using R^2 are not possible.

5 *Low R^2 does not mean the wrong choice of X_t.* Low values of R^2 are not necessarily the result of using a wrong explanatory variable. The functional form used might be an inappropriate one (that is linear instead of quadratic), or – in the case of time series – the choice of time period might be incorrect and lagged terms might need to be included instead.

6 *R^2s from equations with different forms of Y_t are not comparable.* Assume we estimate the following population regression equations:

$$Y_t = a_0 + b_0 X_t + e_t \tag{3.66}$$

$$\ln Y_t = a_1 + b_1 \ln X_t + u_t \tag{3.67}$$

comparing their R^2 values is not appropriate. This is because of the definition of R^2. The R^2 in the first equation shows the proportion of variation in Y_t explained by X_t, while in the second equation it shows the proportion of the variation in the natural logarithm of Y_t explained by the natural logarithm of X_t. In general, whenever the dependent variable is changed in any way, R^2 values should not be used to compare the models.

Hypothesis testing and confidence intervals

Under the assumptions of the CLRM, we know that the estimators $\hat{a}$ and $\hat{\beta}$ obtained by OLS follow a normal distribution with means a and β and variances $\sigma_{\hat{a}}^2$ and $\sigma_{\hat{\beta}}^2$, respectively. It follows that the variables:

$$\frac{\hat{a} - a}{\sigma_{\hat{a}}} \quad \text{and} \quad \frac{\hat{\beta} - \beta}{\sigma_{\hat{\beta}}} \tag{3.68}$$

have a standard normal distribution (that is a normal distribution with mean 0 and variance 1). If we replace the unknown $\sigma_{\hat{a}}$ and $\sigma_{\hat{\beta}}$ by their estimates $s_{\hat{a}}$ and $s_{\hat{\beta}}$ this is no longer true. However, it is relatively easy (based on Chapter 1) to show that the following random variables (after the replacement):

$$\frac{\hat{a} - a}{s_{\hat{a}}} \quad \text{and} \quad \frac{\hat{\beta} - \beta}{s_{\hat{\beta}}} \tag{3.69}$$

follow the student's t-distribution with $n - 2$ degrees of freedom. The student's t-distribution is close to the standard normal distribution except that it has fatter tails, particularly when the number of degrees of freedom is small.

Testing the significance of the OLS coefficients

Knowing the distribution of our estimated coefficients, we are able to conduct hypothesis testing to assess their statistical significance. In general, the following steps should be followed:

Step 1: Set the null and alternative hypotheses. They can be either $H_0: \beta = 0$; $H_a: \beta \neq 0$ (two-tailed test) or, if there is prior knowledge about the sign of the estimated coefficient (let's assume it is positive), $H_0: \beta = 0$; $H_a: \beta > 0$ (one-tailed test).

Step 2: Calculate the t-statistic as $t = (\hat{\beta} - \beta)/s_{\hat{\beta}}$, where, because β under the null hypothesis is equal to zero, it becomes $\hat{\beta}/s_{\hat{\beta}}$ (note that this is the t-statistic that is automatically provided by EViews and Microfit in their standard regression outputs).

Step 3: Find from the t-tables the t-critical value for $n - 2$ degrees of freedom.

Step 4: If $|t_{stat}| > |t_{crit}|$ reject the null hypothesis.

Note that if we want to test a different hypothesis (that is that $\beta = 1$), then we need to change our null and alternative hypotheses in step 1 and calculate the t-statistic manually using the $t = (\hat{\beta} - \beta)/s_{\hat{\beta}}$ formula. In this case it is not appropriate to use the t-statistic provided by EViews and Microfit.

A rule of thumb of significance tests

The procedure for hypothesis testing outlined above presupposes that the researcher selects a significance level and then compares the value of the t-statistic with the critical value for this level. Several rules of thumb based on this approach have been developed, and these are useful in the sense that we do not need to consult statistical tables in cases of large samples (degrees of freedom >30).

Note that the critical value for a 5% level of significance and for a very large sample ($n \to \infty$) reaches ± 1.96. For the same level and for 30 degrees of freedom it is ± 2.045, while for 60 degrees of freedom it is exactly ± 2.00. Therefore, for large samples it is quite safe to use as a rule of thumb a critical value of $|t| > 2$. For a one-tailed test the rule of thumb changes, with the t-value being $|t| > 1.65$. The rules stated above are nothing more than convenient approximations to these values. For 'small' samples we must use the specific values given in the t-table, as the above rules are not appropriate.

The p-value approach

EViews and Microfit, as well as reporting t-statistics for the estimated coefficients, also report p-values, which can be used as an alternative approach in assessing the significance of regression coefficients. The p-value shows the lowest level at which we would be able to accept the null hypothesis for a test. It is very useful because the significance levels chosen for a test are always arbitrary: why, for example, 5% and not 1% or 10%? The p-value approach is also more informative than the 'choose significance levels and find critical values' approach, because one can obtain exactly the level of significance of the estimated coefficient. For example, a p-value of 0.339 says that if the true $\beta = 0$ there is a probability of 0.339 of observing an estimated value of $\hat{\beta}$ which is greater than or equal to the OLS estimate purely by chance. So the estimated value could have arisen by chance with a fairly high probability even if the true value is zero. Similarly, if the p-value is 0.01, this says that there is a very small probability of a value for $\hat{\beta}$ equal to or greater than the OLS estimate arising purely by chance when the true value of β is zero. Furthermore, if we adopt a conventional significance level (let's say 5% or 0.05) we conclude that the coefficient is significantly different from zero at the 5% level if the p-value is less than or equal to 0.05. If it is greater than 0.05 we cannot reject the null hypothesis that the coefficient is actually zero at our 5% significance level.

Confidence intervals

For the null hypothesis that $H_0: \beta = \beta_1$ and for an r% significance level we can accept the null when our t-test lies in the following region:

$$-t_{r,n-2} \le \frac{\hat{\beta} - \beta_1}{s_{\hat{\beta}}} \le t_{r,n-2} \tag{3.70}$$

where $t_{r,n-2}$ is the critical value from the student's t-tables for an r% significance level and $n - 2$ degrees of freedom (as we assume there are only two parameters being estimated). So we can construct a confidence interval for the range of values of β_1 for which we would accept the null hypothesis:

$$\hat{\beta} - t_{r,n-2}s_{\hat{\beta}} \le \beta_1 \le \hat{\beta} + t_{r,n-2}s_{\hat{\beta}} \tag{3.71}$$

Alternatively:

$$\hat{\beta} \pm t_{r,n-2} s_{\hat{\beta}} \tag{3.72}$$

Of course, the same holds for α, being $\hat{\alpha} \pm t_{r,n-2} s_{\hat{\alpha}}$.

How to estimate a simple regression in Microfit, EViews and Stata

Simple regression in Microfit

Step 1: Open Microfit.

Step 2: Click on **File/New** in order to create a new file.

Step 3: Choose the required frequency for time series or 'undated' for cross-sectional data and specify the number of variables as well as the start and end dates for time series data or the number of observations for cross-sectional data.

Step 4: When asked to provide names and descriptions for variables, give the names Y and X, and descriptions you think will enable you to remember the definitions of your variables (giving descriptions is optional but is recommended as it is sometimes really helpful). Press **GO**.

Step 5: Either type the data into Microfit or copy/paste the data from Excel. Be very careful in pasting the data to provide the appropriate information required by Microfit. Press **GO** at the end.

Step 6: Once you have put the data into Microfit, you have to create a constant. Either go to the **process** editor (by pressing the **process** button) and type C = 1 (and then press **GO**), or click on **Edit/Constant (intercept) term** and provide a name for your intercept by typing it in the corresponding window (let us assume that you name your constant term C).

Step 7: Go to the single editor (by clicking the **single** button) and type into the single editor:

    Y C X

and then click **START**. The regression output is presented in a new window which provides estimates for alpha (the coefficient of the constant term), beta (the coefficient of X) and some additional statistics that will be discussed in later chapters of this book.

Simple regression in EViews

Step 1: Open EViews.

Step 2: Click on **File/New/Workfile** in order to create a new file.

Step 3: Choose the frequency of the data in the case of time series data or **Undated or Irregular** in the case of cross-sectional data, and specify the start and end of your data set. EViews will open a new window which automatically contains a constant (**c**) and a residual (**resid**) series.

Step 4: On the command line type:

```
genr x=0 (press enter)
genr y=0 (press enter)
```

which creates two new series named x and y that contain zeros for every observation. Open x and y as a group by selecting them and double-clicking with your mouse.

Step 5: Then either type the data into EViews or copy/paste the data from Excel. To be able to type (edit) the data of your series or to paste anything into the EViews cells, the **edit +/−** button must be pressed. After editing the series press the **edit +/−** button again to lock or secure the data.

Step 6: Once the data have been entered into EViews, the regression line (to obtain alpha and beta) may be estimated either by typing:

```
ls y c x (press enter)
```

on the command line, or by clicking on **Quick/Estimate equation** and then writing your equation (that is y c x) in the new window. Note that the option for OLS (LS – Least Squares (NLS and ARMA)) is chosen automatically by EViews and the sample is automatically selected to be the maximum possible.

Either way, the regression result is shown in a new window which provides estimates for alpha (the coefficient of the constant term), beta (the coefficient of X) and some additional statistics that will be discussed in later chapters of this book.

Simple regression in Stata

Step 1: Open Stata.

Step 2: Click on the **Data Editor** button to open the Data Editor Window, which looks like a spreadsheet. Start entering data manually or copy/paste data from Excel or any other spreadsheet. After you have finished entering the data, double-click on the variable label (the default names are var1, var2 and so on). A new window opens where you can specify the name of the variable and can (optionally) give a description of the variable in the Label area. Let's assume that we entered data for two variables only (variable Y and variable X).

Step 3: In the Command Window type the command:

```
regress y x (press enter)
```

and you get the regression results. Note that there is no need to include a constant here as Stata includes the constant automatically in the results (in the output it is labelled as _cons).

Reading the Microfit simple regression results output

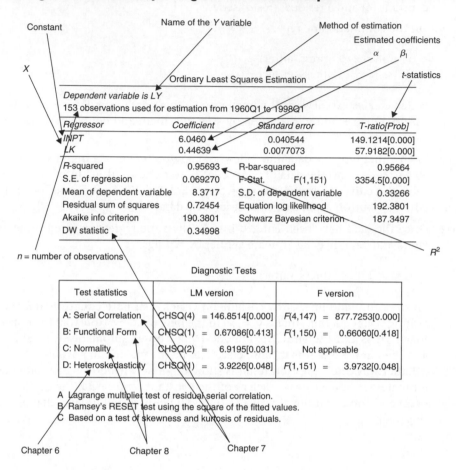

Reading the Stata simple regression results output

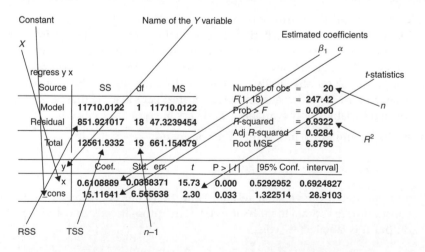

Reading the EViews simple regression results output

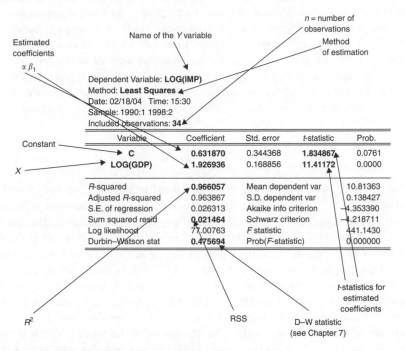

Presentation of regression results

The results of a regression analysis can be presented in a range of different ways. However, the most common way is to write the estimated equation with standard errors of the coefficients in brackets below the estimated coefficients and to include further statistics below the equation. For the consumption function that will be presented in Computer Example 2, the results are summarized as shown below:

$$\hat{C}_t = 15.116 + 0.160 Y_t^d$$

$$(6.565) \quad (0.038) \tag{3.73}$$

$$R^2 = 0.932 \quad n = 20 \quad \hat{\sigma} = 6.879 \tag{3.74}$$

From this summary we can (a) read estimated effects of changes in the explanatory variables on the dependent variable; (b) predict values of the dependent variable for given values of the explanatory variable; (c) perform hypothesis testing for the estimated coefficients; and (d) construct confidence intervals for the estimated coefficients.

Applications

Application 1: the demand function

From economic theory we know that the demand for a commodity depends basically on the price of that commodity (the law of demand). Other possible determinants can include prices of competing goods (close substitutes) or goods that complement that commodity (close complements), and, of course, the level of income of the consumer. To include all these determinants we need to employ a multiple regression analysis. However, for pedagogical purposes we restrict ourselves here to one explanatory variable. Therefore, we assume a partial demand function where the quantity demanded is affected only by the price of the product. (Another way of doing this is to use a *ceteris paribus* (other things remaining the same) demand function, in which we simply assume that the other variables entering the relationship remain constant, and thus do not affect the quantity demanded.) The population regression function will have the form:

$$q_t = a_0 + a_1 p_t + u_t \tag{3.75}$$

where the standard notation is used, with q_t denoting quantity demanded and p_t the price of the product. From economic theory we expect a_1 to be negative, reflecting the law of demand (the higher the price, the less the quantity demanded). We can collect time series data for sales of a product and the price level of this product and estimate the above specification. The interpretation of the results will be as follows. For a_1: if the price of the product is increased by one unit (that is, if measured in £ sterling, an increase of £1.00), the consumption of this product will decrease (because a_1 will be negative) by $\hat{a}_1$ units. For a_0: if the price of the product is zero, consumers will consume $\hat{a}_0$ quantity of this product. R^2 is expected to be rather low (let's say 0.6), suggesting that there are additional variables affecting the quantity demanded which we did not include in our equation. It is also possible to obtain the price elasticity of this product for a given year (let's say 1999) from the equation:

$$\frac{p_{99}}{\hat{q}_{99}} \frac{\Delta q}{\Delta p} = \frac{p_{99}}{\hat{q}_{99}} \hat{a}_1 \tag{3.76}$$

Application 2: the production function

One of the most basic relationships in economic theory is the production function, which generally relates output (denoted by Y) to the possible factor inputs affecting production, such as labour (L) and capital (K). The general form of this relationship can be expressed as:

$$Y_t = f(K_t, L_t) \tag{3.77}$$

A frequently used form of this function – because of properties that we shall see later – is the well-known Cobb–Douglas production function:

$$Y_t = A K_t^a L_t^\beta \tag{3.78}$$

where a and β are constant terms that express the responsiveness of output to capital and labour, respectively. A can be regarded as an exogenous efficiency/technology parameter. Obviously, the greater is A, the higher is maximum output, keeping labour and capital constant. In the short run we can assume that the stock of capital is fixed (the short run can be viewed here as a period during which, once the decision about capital has been made, the producer cannot change the decision until the next period). Then, in the short run, maximum output depends only on the labour input, and the production function becomes:

$$Y_t = g(L_t) \tag{3.79}$$

Using the Cobb–Douglas form of the function (and for K_t constant and equal to K_0) we have:

$$Y_t = (AK_0^a)L_t^\beta = A^*L_t^\beta \tag{3.80}$$

where $A^* = (AK_0^a)$. This short-run production function is now a bivariate model, and after applying a logarithmic transformation can be estimated with the OLS method. Taking the natural logarithm of both sides and adding an error term we have:

$$\ln Y_t = \ln(A^*) + \beta \ln(L_t) + u_t$$
$$= c + \beta \ln(L_t) + u_t \tag{3.81}$$

where $c = \ln(A^*)$, and β is the elasticity of output with respect to labour (one of the properties of the Cobb–Douglas production function). This elasticity denotes the percentage change in output that results from a 1% change in the labour input.

We can use time series data on production and employment for the manufacturing sector of a country (or aggregate GDP and employment data) to obtain estimates of c and β for the above model.

Application 3: Okun's law

Okun (1962) derived an empirical relationship, using quarterly data from 1947q2 to 1960q4, between changes in the state of the economy (captured by changes in gross national product – GNP) and changes in the unemployment rate. This relationship is known as Okun's law. His results provide an important insight into the sensitivity of the unemployment rate to economic growth. The basic relationship is that connecting the growth rate of unemployment (*UNEMP*) (which constitutes the dependent variable) to a constant and the growth rate of GNP (the independent variable), as follows:

$$\Delta UNEMP_t = a + b\Delta GNP_t + u_t \tag{3.82}$$

Applying OLS, the sample regression equation that Okun obtained was:

$$\widehat{\Delta UNEMP}_t = 0.3 - 0.3\Delta GNP_t$$
$$R^2 = 0.63 \tag{3.83}$$

The constant in this equation shows the mean change in the unemployment rate when the growth rate of the economy is equal to zero, so from the obtained results we conclude that when the economy does not grow, the unemployment rate rises by 0.3%. The negative b coefficient suggests that when the state of the economy improves, the unemployment rate falls. The relationship, though, is less than one to one. A 1% increase in GNP is associated with only a 0.3% decrease in the unemployment rate. It is easy to collect data on GNP and unemployment, calculate their respective growth rates and check whether Okun's law is valid for different countries and different time periods.

Application 4: the Keynesian consumption function

Another basic relationship in economic theory is the Keynesian consumption function, which simply states that consumption (C_t) is a positive linear function of disposable (after tax) income (Y_t^d). The relationship is as follows:

$$C_t = a + \delta Y_t^d \tag{3.84}$$

where a is autonomous consumption (consumption even when disposable income is zero) and δ is the marginal propensity to consume. In this function we expect $a > 0$ and $0 < \delta < 1$. A $\hat{\delta} = 0.7$ means that the marginal propensity to consume is 0.7. A Keynesian consumption function is estimated below as a worked-through computer exercise example.

Computer example: the Keynesian consumption function

Table 3.2 provides data for consumption and disposable income for 20 randomly selected people.

(a) Put the data in Excel and calculate α and β, assuming a linear relationship between X and Y, using both expressions for β given by Equations (3.20) and (3.28).

(b) Calculate α and β using the 'Data Analysis' menu provided in Excel and check whether the results are the same as the ones obtained in (a).

(c) Create a scatter plot of X and Y.

(d) Use Microfit to calculate α and β and scatter plots of X and Y.

(e) Use Eviews to calculate α and β and scatter plots of X and Y.

(f) Use Stata to calculate α and β and scatter plots of X and Y.

Solution

(a) First, we must obtain the products $X * Y$ and X^2 as well as the summations of X, Y, $X * Y$ and X^2. These are given in Table 3.3.

The command for cell C2 is '=B2*A2'; C3 is '=B3*A3' and so on; D2 is '=B2*B2' or '=B2^2'. For the summations in A22 the command is '=SUM(A2:A21)', and similarly for B22 the command is '=SUM(B2:B21)' and so on.

Table 3.2 Data for simple regression example

Consumption Y	Disposable income X
72.30	100
91.65	120
135.20	200
94.60	130
163.50	240
100.00	114
86.50	126
142.36	213
120.00	156
112.56	167
132.30	189
149.80	214
115.30	188
132.20	197
149.50	206
100.25	142
79.60	112
90.20	134
116.50	169
126.00	170

Table 3.3 Excel calculations

	A	B	C	D
	Y	X	X*Y	X-squared
1				
2	72.30	100.00	7230.00	10000.00
3	91.65	120.00	10998.00	14400.00
4	135.20	200.00	27040.00	40000.00
5	94.60	130.00	12298.00	16900.00
6	163.50	240.00	39240.00	57600.00
7	100.00	114.00	11400.00	12996.00
8	86.50	126.00	10899.00	15876.00
9	142.36	213.00	30322.68	45369.00
10	120.00	156.00	18720.00	24336.00
11	112.56	167.00	18797.52	27889.00
12	132.30	189.00	25004.70	35721.00
13	149.80	214.00	32057.20	45796.00
14	115.30	188.00	21676.40	35344.00
15	132.20	197.00	26043.40	38809.00
16	149.50	206.00	30797.00	42436.00
17	100.25	142.00	14235.50	20164.00
18	79.60	112.00	8915.20	12544.00
19	90.20	134.00	12086.80	17956.00
20	116.50	169.00	19688.50	28561.00
21	126.00	170.00	21420.00	28900.00
22	2310.32	3287.00	398869.90	571597.00

We can then calculate β using Equation (3.20) as follows: for β we need to type in a cell (let's do that in cell G2) the following '=(C22−(A22*B22)/20)/(D22−((B22^2)/20))'. Then in order to obtain a value for α we need to type in a different cell (let's say G3) the following '= AVERAGE(A2:A21)−G2*AVERAGE(B2:B21)'.

If we do this correctly we should find that $\beta = 0.610888903$ and $\alpha = 15.11640873$.

Table 3.4   Excel calculations (continued)

	A	...	F	G	H
1	Y	...			
2	72.30	...	beta	0.610888903	
3	91.65	...	alpha	15.11640873	
4	135.20	...			
5	94.60	...		Y	X
6	163.50	...	Y	628.096654	
7	100.00	...	X	958.4404	1568.9275

Table 3.5   Regression output from Excel

Regression statistics					
Multiple *R*	0.9654959				
R-squared	0.93218233				
Adjusted *R*-squared	0.92841469				
Standard error	6.87960343				
Observations	20				
ANOVA					
	df	*SS*	*MS*	*F*	*Significance F*
Regression	1	11710.0121	11710.0121	247.41757	5.80822E-12
Residual	18	851.9209813	47.3289434		
Total	19	12561.93308			
	Coefficients	*Standard error*	*t stat*	*p-value*	*Lower 95%*
Intercept	15.1164087	6.565638115	2.302351799	0.0334684	1.322504225
X	0.6108889	0.038837116	15.72951266	5.808E–12	0.529295088

Alternatively, using Equation (3.28), we may go to the menu **Tools/Data Analysis** and from the data analysis menu choose the command **Covariance**. We are then asked to specify the **Input Range**, the columns that contain the data for Y and X (enter '\$A\$1:\$B\$21' or simply select this area using the mouse). Note that if we include the labels (Y, X) in our selection we have to tick the **Labels in the First Row** box. We are asked to specify our **Output Range** as well, which can be either a different sheet (not recommended) or any empty cell in the current sheet (for example we might specify cell F5). By clicking **OK** we obtain the display shown in Table 3.4.

In order to calculate β we have to write in cell G2 '=G7/H7'. The command for α remains the same as in the previous case.

(b) Go to **Tools/Data Analysis** and from the data analysis menu choose the command **Regression**. We are then asked to specify our **Input Y Range**, which is the column that contains the data for the dependent (Y) variable (write '\$A\$1:\$A\$21'), and **Input X Range**, which is the column that contains the data for the independent (X) variable (write '\$B\$1:\$B\$21'). Again, we can select these two areas using the mouse, and if we include the labels (Y, X) in our selection we have to tick the **Labels in the First Row** box. We will also be asked to specify the **Output Range**, as above. Clicking **OK** generates the display shown in Table 3.5.

In addition to estimates for α (which is the coefficient of the intercept) and β (the coefficient of X), Table 3.5 shows more statistics that will be discussed later in this book.

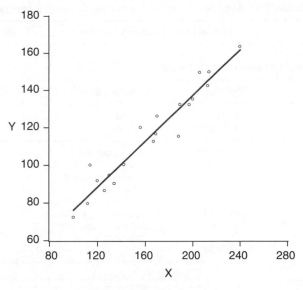

Figure 3.2 Scatter plot

(c) To obtain a scatter plot of Y and X, first click on the **chart wizard** button and then specify **XY scatter** and click **next**. Go to **series** and enter the values for X and Y using the mouse; click **next** again. Enter titles for the diagram and the X and Y variables and then click **finish** to obtain the graph. Clicking on the dots of the scatter plot and using the right button of the mouse brings up the **Add Trendline** command for the graph. The graph will look like Figure 3.2.

(d) To obtain the regression results in Microfit we take the following steps:

1 Open Microfit.

2 Choose **File/New** in order to create a new file.

3 Choose **Undated** and specify the number of variables (in this case 2) as well as the number of observations (in this case 20).

4 When asked to provide names and descriptions for the variables, give the names Y and X, and the descriptions 'Consumption' and 'Disposable Income', respectively (giving descriptions is optional but it is recommended). Press **GO**.

5 Either type the data into Microfit or copy/paste the data from Excel. Press **GO** at the end.

6 Having entered the data in Microfit, we need to create a constant. Either go to the **process** editor (by pressing the **process** button) and write:

    C=1 (and then press **GO**)

or go to **Edit/Constant (intercept) term** and provide a name for the intercept by typing it in the corresponding window (let's assume that we name the constant term C).

Table 3.6 Microfit results from a simple regression model

Ordinary Least Squares Estimation

Dependent variable is Y
20 observations used for estimation from 1 to 20

Regressor	Coefficient	Standard error	t-ratio [Prob].
INPT	15.1164	6.5656	2.3024 [0.033]
X	0.61089	0.038837	15.7295 [0.000]

R-squared	0.93218	*R*-bar-squared	0.92841
S.E. of regression	6.8796	*F*-stat. $F(1, 18)$	247.4176 [0.000]
Mean of dependent variable	115.5160	S.D. of dependent variable	25.7129
Residual sum of squares	851.9210	Equation log likelihood	−65.8964
Akaike info criterion	−67.8964	Schwarz Bayesian criterion	−68.8921
DW statistic	2.2838		

Diagnostic Tests

Test statistics	LM version	F version
A: Serial correlation	CHSQ(1) = 0.72444 [0.395]	$F(1, 17) = 0.63891$ [0.435]
B: Functional form	CHSQ(1) = 0.19091 [0.662]	$F(1, 17) = 0.16384$ [0.691]
C: Normality	CHSQ(2) = 0.35743 [0.836]	Not applicable
D: Heteroscedasticity	CHSQ(1) = 0.40046 [0.527]	$F(1, 18) = 0.36778$ [0.552]

A   Lagrange multiplier test of residual serial correlation.
B   Ramsey's RESET test using the square of the fitted values.
C   Based on a test of skewness and kurtosis of residuals.

7 Go to the single editor (by clicking the **single** button); write:

```
Y C X
```

and click **START**. The output in Table 3.6 is shown in a new window and provides estimates for alpha (the coefficient of the constant term), beta (the coefficient of *X*) and some additional statistics that will be discussed in later chapters.

(e) To obtain regression results in EViews, the following steps are required:

1 Open EViews.

2 Choose **File/New/Workfile** in order to create a new file.

3 Choose **Undated or Irregular** and specify the number of observations (in this case 20). A new window appears which automatically contains a constant (**c**) and a residual (**resid**) series.

4 In the command line type:

```
genr x=0 (press enter)
genr y=0 (press enter)
```

Table 3.7 EViews results from a simple regression model

Dependent variable: Y
Method: least squares
Date: 01/09/04 Time: 16:13
Sample: 1–20
Included observations: 20

Variable	Coefficient	Std. error	t-statistic	Prob.
C	15.11641	6.565638	2.302352	0.0335
X	0.610889	0.038837	15.72951	0.0000

R-squared	0.932182	Mean dependent var		115.5160
Adjusted R-squared	0.928415	S.D. dependent var		25.71292
S.E. of regression	6.879603	Akaike info criterion		6.789639
Sum squared resid	851.9210	Schwarz criterion		6.889212
Log likelihood	−65.89639	F-statistic		247.4176
Durbin–Watson stat	2.283770	Prob(F-statistic)		0.000000

which creates two new series named **x** and **y** that contain zeros for every observation. Open **x** and **y** as a group by selecting them and double-clicking with the mouse.

5 Either type the data into EViews or copy/paste the data from Excel. To edit the series press the **edit +/−** button. After you have finished editing the series press the **edit +/−** button again to lock or secure the data.

6 After entering the data into EViews, the regression line (to obtain alpha and beta) can be estimated either by writing:

```
ls y c x (press enter)
```

on the EViews command line, or by clicking on **Quick/Estimate equation** and then writing the equation (that is y c x) in the new window. Note that the option for **OLS (LS – Least Squares (NLS and ARMA))** is chosen automatically by EViews and the sample is automatically selected to be from 1 to 20.

Either way, the output in Table 3.7 is shown in a new window which provides estimates for alpha (the coefficient of the constant term) and beta (the coefficient of X).

(f) To obtain regression results in Stata, the following steps are required:

1 Open Stata.

2 Click on the **Data Editor** button and enter the data manually or copy/paste them from Excel. Label the variables as Y and X respectively.

3 The command for the scatter plot is:

```
scatter y x (press enter)
```

The graph in Figure 3.3 will be obtained.

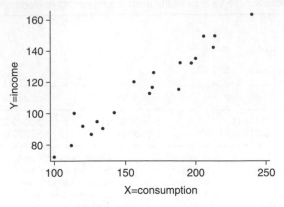

Figure 3.3   Scatter plot

Table 3.8   Stata results from a simple regression model

Regress y x

Source	SS	df	MS		Number of obs	=	20
					F(1, 18)	=	247.42
Model	11710.0122	1	11710.0122		Prob > F	=	0.0000
Residual	851.921017	18	47.3289754		R-squared	=	0.9322
					Adj R-squared	=	0.9284
Total	12561.9332	19	661.154379		Root MSE	=	6.8796

y	Coef.	Std. Err.	t	P > |t|	[95% Conf. Interval]	
x	0.6108889	0.0388371	15.73	0.000	0.5292952	0.6924827
_cons	15.11641	6.565638	2.30	0.033	1.322514	28.9103

4 To generate the regression results for α and β the command is:

    regress y x (press **enter**)

The output is shown in Table 3.8.

Questions and exercises

Questions

1 An outlier is an observation that is very far from the sample regression function. Suppose the equation is initially estimated using all observations and then re-estimated omitting outliers. How will the estimated slope coefficient change? How will R^2 change? Explain.

2 Regression equations are sometimes estimated using an explanatory variable that is a deviation from some value of interest. An example is a capacity utilization rate–unemployment rate equation, such as:

$$u_t = a_0 + a_1(CAP_t - CAP_t^f) + e_t$$

where CAP_t^f is a single value representing the capacity utilization rate corresponding to full employment (the value of 87.5% is sometimes used for this purpose).

(a) Will the estimated intercept for this equation differ from that for the equation with only CAP_t as an explanatory variable? Explain.

(b) Will the estimated slope coefficient for this equation differ from that for the equation with only CAP_t as an explanatory variable? Explain.

3 Prove that the OLS coefficient for the slope parameter in the simple linear regression model is unbiased.

4 Prove that the OLS coefficient for the slope parameter in the simple linear regression model is a BLU estimator.

5 State the assumptions of the simple linear regression model and explain why they are necessary.

Exercise 3.1

The following data refer to the quantity sold of good Y (measured in kg), and the price of that good X (measured in pence per kg), for 10 different market locations:

Y:	198	181	170	179	163	145	167	203	251	147
X:	23	24.5	24	27.2	27	24.4	24.7	22.1	21	25

(a) Assuming a linear relationship between the two variables, obtain the OLS estimators of a and β.

(b) On a scatter diagram of the data, draw your OLS sample regression line.

(c) Estimate the elasticity of demand for this good at the point of the sample means (that is when $Y = \bar{Y}$ and $X = \bar{X}$).

Exercise 3.2

The table below shows the average growth rates of GDP and employment for 25 OECD countries for the period 1988–97.

Countries	Empl.	GDP	Countries	Empl.	GDP
Australia	1.68	3.04	Korea	2.57	7.73
Austria	0.65	2.55	Luxembourg	3.02	5.64
Belgium	0.34	2.16	Netherlands	1.88	2.86
Canada	1.17	2.03	New Zealand	0.91	2.01
Denmark	0.02	2.02	Norway	0.36	2.98
Finland	−1.06	1.78	Portugal	0.33	2.79
France	0.28	2.08	Spain	0.89	2.60
Germany	0.08	2.71	Sweden	−0.94	1.17
Greece	0.87	2.08	Switzerland	0.79	1.15
Iceland	−0.13	1.54	Turkey	2.02	4.18
Ireland	2.16	6.40	United Kingdom	0.66	1.97
Italy	−0.30	1.68	United States	1.53	2.46
Japan	1.06	2.81			

(a) Assuming a linear relationship, obtain the OLS estimators.

(b) Provide an interpretation of the coefficients.

Exercise 3.3

In the Keynesian consumption function:

$$C_t = a + \delta Y_t^d$$

the estimated marginal propensity to consume is $\hat{\delta}$, and the average propensity to consume is $C/Y^d = \hat{a}/Y^d + \hat{\delta}$. Using data on annual income and consumption (both of which were measured in £ sterling) from 200 UK households we found the following regression equation:

$$C_t = 138.52 + 0.725 Y_t^d \quad R^2 = 0.862$$

(a) Provide an interpretation of the constant in this equation and discuss its sign and magnitude.

(b) Calculate the predicted consumption of a hypothetical household with an annual income of £40,000.

(c) With Y_t^d on the x-axis, draw a graph of the estimated Marginal Propensity to Consumption (MPC) and Autonomous Consumption Path (ACP).

Exercise 3.4

Obtain annual data for the inflation rate and the unemployment rate of a country.

(a) Estimate the following regression, which is known as the Phillips curve:

$$\pi_t = a_0 + a_1 UNEMP_t + u_t$$

where π_t is inflation and $UNEMP_t$ is unemployment. Present the results in the usual way.

(b) Estimate the alternative model:

$$\pi_t - \pi_{t-1} = a_0 + a_1 UNEMP_{t-1} + u_t$$

and calculate the Non-Accelerating Inflation Rate of Unemployment (NAIRU) (that is when $\pi_t - \pi_{t-1} = 0$).

(c) Re-estimate the above equations splitting your sample into different decades. What factors account for differences in the results? Which period has the 'best-fitting' equation? State the criteria you have used.

Exercise 3.5

The following equation has been estimated by OLS:

$$\hat{R}_t = 0.567 + 1.045 R_{mt} \quad n = 250$$

$$(0.33) \quad (0.066)$$

where R_t and R_{mt} denote the excess return of a stock and the excess return of the market index for the London Stock Exchange.

(a) Derive a 95% confidence interval for each coefficient.

(b) Are these coefficients statistically significant? Explain the meaning of your findings with regard to the Capital Asset Pricing Model (CAPM) theory.

(c) Test the hypotheses $H_0: \beta = 1$ and $H_a: \beta < 1$ at the 1% level of significance. If you reject H_0 what does this indicate about this stock?

Exercise 3.6

Obtain time series data on real business fixed investment (I) and an appropriate rate of interest (r). Consider the following population regression function:

$$I_t = \alpha_0 + \alpha_1 r_t + e_t$$

(a) What are the expected signs of the coefficients in this equation?

(b) Explain your reasoning in each case.

(c) How can you use this equation to estimate the interest elasticity of investment?

(d) Estimate the population regression function.

(e) Which coefficients are statistically significant? Are the signs those expected?

(f) Construct a 99% confidence interval for the coefficient of r_t.

(g) Estimate the log-linear version of the population regression function:

$$\ln I_t = a_0 + a_1 \ln r_t + u_t$$

(h) Is the estimated interest rate elasticity of investment significant?

(i) Do you expect this elasticity to be elastic or inelastic, and why?

(j) Perform a hypothesis test of whether investment is interest-elastic.

Exercise 3.7

The file salaries_01.wf1 contains data for senior officers from a number of UK firms. The variable *salary* is the salary that each officer gets, measured in thousands of pounds. The variable *years_senior* measures the number of years they have been senior officers, and the variable *years_comp* measures the number of years they had worked for the company at the time of the research.

(a) Calculate summary statistics for these three variables and discuss them.

(b) Estimate a simple regression that explains whether and how salary level is affected by the number of years they have been senior officers. Estimate another regression that explains whether and how salary level is affected by the number of years they have worked for the same company. Report your results and comment on them. Which relationship seems to be more robust, and why?

4 Multiple Regression

CHAPTER CONTENTS

LEARNING OBJECTIVES

After studying this chapter you should be able to:

1. Derive mathematically the regression coefficients of a multiple regression model.
2. Understand the difference between the R^2 and the adjusted R^2 for a multiple regression model.
3. Appreciate the importance of the various selection criteria for the best regression model.
4. Conduct hypothesis testing and test linear restrictions, omitted and redundant variables, as well as the overall significance of the explanatory variables.
5. Obtain the output of a multiple regression estimation using econometric software.
6. Interpret and discuss the results of a multiple regression estimation output.

Introduction

So far, we have restricted ourselves to the single case of a two-variable relationship in a regression equation. However, in economics it is quite rare to have such relationships. Usually the dependent variable, Y, depends on a larger set of explanatory variables or regressors, and so we have to extend our analysis to more than one regressor. The multiple regression model generally has the following form:

$$Y_t = \beta_1 X_{1t} + \beta_2 X_{2t} + \beta_3 X_{3t} + \cdots + \beta_k X_{kt} + u_t \tag{4.1}$$

where X_{1t} is a vector equal to unity (to allow for the constant term) and can be omitted from Equation (4.1), and X_{jt} ($j = 2, 3, \ldots, k$) is the set of explanatory variables or regressors. From this it follows that Equation (4.1) contains k parameters to be estimated, which gives the degrees of freedom as well.

Derivation of multiple regression coefficients

The three-variable model

The three-variable model relates Y to a constant and two explanatory variables X_2 and X_3. Thus we have:

$$Y_t = \beta_1 + \beta_2 X_{2t} + \beta_3 X_{3t} + u_t \tag{4.2}$$

As before, we need to minimize the sum of the squared residuals (RSS):

$$RSS = \sum_{t=1}^{n} \hat{u}_t^2 \tag{4.3}$$

where $\hat{u}_t$ is the difference between the actual Y_t and the fitted $\hat{Y}_t$, predicted by the regression equation. Therefore:

$$\hat{u}_t = Y_t - \hat{Y}_t = Y_t - \hat{\beta}_1 - \hat{\beta}_2 X_{2t} - \hat{\beta}_3 X_{3t} \tag{4.4}$$

Substituting Equation (4.4) into Equation (4.3) we get:

$$RSS = \sum_{t=1}^{n} \hat{u}_t^2 = \sum_{t=1}^{n} \left(Y_t - \hat{\beta}_1 - \hat{\beta}_2 X_{2t} - \hat{\beta}_3 X_{3t} \right)^2 \tag{4.5}$$

The next step is to take the First Order Conditions (FOCs) for a minimum:

$$\frac{\partial RSS}{\partial \hat{\beta}_1} = -2 \sum_{t=1}^{n} \left(Y_t - \hat{\beta}_1 - \hat{\beta}_2 X_{2t} - \hat{\beta}_3 X_{3t} \right) = 0 \tag{4.6}$$

$$\frac{\partial RSS}{\partial \hat{\beta}_2} = -2 \sum_{t=1}^{n} X_{2t} \left(Y_t - \hat{\beta}_1 - \hat{\beta}_2 X_{2t} - \hat{\beta}_3 X_{3t} \right) = 0 \qquad (4.7)$$

$$\frac{\partial RSS}{\partial \hat{\beta}_3} = -2 \sum_{t=1}^{n} X_{3t} \left(Y_t - \hat{\beta}_1 - \hat{\beta}_2 X_{2t} - \hat{\beta}_3 X_{3t} \right) = 0 \qquad (4.8)$$

Again we arrive at a system of three equations with three unknowns $\hat{\beta}_1$, $\hat{\beta}_2$ and $\hat{\beta}_3$, which can easily be solved to give estimates of the unknowns. Equation (4.6) can easily be transformed, for example, to give:

$$\sum_{t=1}^{n} Y_t = \sum_{t=1}^{n} \hat{\beta}_1 + \sum_{t=1}^{n} \hat{\beta}_2 X_{2t} + \sum_{t=1}^{n} \hat{\beta}_3 X_{3t} \qquad (4.9)$$

$$\sum_{t=1}^{n} Y_t = n\hat{\beta}_1 + \hat{\beta}_2 \sum_{t=1}^{n} X_{2t} + \hat{\beta}_3 \sum_{t=1}^{n} X_{3t} \qquad (4.10)$$

Dividing throughout by n and defining $\bar{X}_i = \sum_{t=1}^{n} X_{it} n$:

$$\bar{Y} = \hat{\beta}_1 + \hat{\beta}_2 \bar{X}_2 + \hat{\beta}_3 \bar{X}_3 \qquad (4.11)$$

and we derive a solution for $\hat{\beta}_1$:

$$\hat{\beta}_1 = \bar{Y} - \hat{\beta}_2 \bar{X} - \hat{\beta}_3 \bar{X} \qquad (4.12)$$

Using Equation (4.12) and the second and third of the FOCs after manipulation, we obtain a solution for $\hat{\beta}_2$:

$$\hat{\beta}_2 = \frac{Cov(X_2, Y)Var(X_3) - Cov(X_3, Y)Cov(X_2, X_3)}{Var(X_2)Var(X_3) - [Cov(X_2, X_3)]^2} \qquad (4.13)$$

and $\hat{\beta}_3$ will be similar to Equation (4.13) by rearranging X_{2t} and X_{3t}:

$$\hat{\beta}_3 = \frac{Cov(X_3, Y)Var(X_2) - Cov(X_2, Y)Cov(X_3, X_2)}{Var(X_3)Var(X_2) - [Cov(X_3, X_2)]^2} \qquad (4.14)$$

The *k*-variables case

With k explanatory variables the model is as presented initially in Equation (4.1), so we have:

$$Y_t = \beta_1 X_{1t} + \beta_2 X_{2t} + \beta_3 X_{3t} + \cdots + \beta_k X_{kt} + u_t \qquad (4.15)$$

while again we derive fitted values as:

$$\hat{Y}_t = \hat{\beta}_1 X_{1t} + \hat{\beta}_2 X_{2t} + \hat{\beta}_3 X_{3t} + \cdots + \hat{\beta}_k X_{kt} \qquad (4.16)$$

and

$$\hat{u}_t = Y_t - \hat{Y}_t = Y_t - \hat{\beta}_1 X_{1t} - \hat{\beta}_2 X_{2t} - \hat{\beta}_3 X_{3t} - \cdots - \hat{\beta}_k X_{kt} \tag{4.17}$$

We again want to minimize RSS, so:

$$RSS = \sum_{t=1}^{n} \hat{u}_t^2 = \sum_{t=1}^{n} \left(Y_t - \hat{\beta}_1 X_{1t} - \hat{\beta}_2 X_{2t} - \hat{\beta}_3 X_{3t} - \cdots - \hat{\beta}_k X_{kt} \right)^2 \tag{4.18}$$

Taking the FOCs for a minimum this time we obtain k equations for k unknown regression coefficients, as:

$$\sum_{t=1}^{n} Y_t = n\hat{\beta}_1 + \hat{\beta}_2 \sum_{t=1}^{n} X_{2t} + \cdots + \hat{\beta}_k \sum_{t=1}^{n} X_{kt} \tag{4.19}$$

$$\sum_{t=1}^{n} Y_t X_{2t} = \hat{\beta}_1 \sum_{t=1}^{n} X_{2t} + \hat{\beta}_2 \sum_{t=1}^{n} X_{2t}^2 + \cdots + \hat{\beta}_k \sum_{t=1}^{n} X_{kt} X_{2t} \tag{4.20}$$

$$\cdots \tag{4.21}$$

$$\sum_{t=1}^{n} Y_t X_{k-1,t} = \hat{\beta}_1 \sum_{t=1}^{n} X_{k-1t} + \hat{\beta}_2 \sum_{t=1}^{n} X_{2t} X_{k-1t} + \cdots + \hat{\beta}_k \sum_{t=1}^{n} X_{kt} X_{k-1,t} \tag{4.22}$$

$$\sum_{t=1}^{n} Y_t X_{k,t} = \hat{\beta}_1 \sum_{t=1}^{n} X_{kt} + \hat{\beta}_2 \sum_{t=1}^{n} X_{2t} X_{k,t} + \cdots + \hat{\beta}_k \sum_{t=1}^{n} X_{kt}^2 \tag{4.23}$$

The above k equations can be solved uniquely for the βs, and it is easy to show that:

$$\hat{\beta}_1 = \bar{Y} - \hat{\beta}_2 \bar{X}_2 - \cdots - \hat{\beta}_k \bar{X}_k \tag{4.24}$$

However, the expressions for $\hat{\beta}_2, \hat{\beta}_3, \ldots, \hat{\beta}_k$ are very complicated and the mathematics will not be presented here. The analysis requires matrix algebra, which is the subject of the next section. Standard computer programs can carry out all the calculations and provide estimates immediately.

Derivation of the coefficients with matrix algebra

Equation (4.1) can easily be written in matrix notation as:

$$\mathbf{Y} = \mathbf{X}\boldsymbol{\beta} + \mathbf{u} \tag{4.25}$$

where

$$\mathbf{Y} = \begin{pmatrix} Y_1 \\ Y_2 \\ \vdots \\ Y_T \end{pmatrix}, \quad \mathbf{X} = \begin{pmatrix} 1 & X_{21} & X_{31} & \ldots & X_{k1} \\ 1 & X_{22} & X_{32} & \ldots & X_{k3} \\ \vdots & \vdots & \vdots & & \vdots \\ 1 & X_{2T} & X_{3T} & \ldots & X_{kT} \end{pmatrix},$$

$$\beta = \begin{pmatrix} \beta_1 \\ \beta_2 \\ \vdots \\ \beta_k \end{pmatrix}, \quad \mathbf{u} = \begin{pmatrix} u_1 \\ u_2 \\ \vdots \\ u_n \end{pmatrix}$$

Thus, $\mathbf{Y}$ is a $T \times 1$ vector, $\mathbf{X}$ is a $T \times k$ matrix, β is a $k \times 1$ vector and $\mathbf{u}$ is a $T \times 1$ vector. Our aim is to minimize RSS. Note that in matrix notation RSS $= \hat{\mathbf{u}}'\hat{\mathbf{u}}$. Thus, we have:

$$\hat{\mathbf{u}}'\hat{\mathbf{u}} = (\mathbf{Y} - \mathbf{X}\hat{\beta})'(\mathbf{Y} - \mathbf{X}\hat{\beta}) \tag{4.26}$$

$$= (\mathbf{Y}' - \hat{\beta}'\mathbf{X}')(\mathbf{Y} - \mathbf{X}\hat{\beta}) \tag{4.27}$$

$$= \mathbf{Y}'\mathbf{Y} - \mathbf{Y}'\mathbf{X}\hat{\beta} - \hat{\beta}'\mathbf{X}'\mathbf{Y} + \hat{\beta}'\mathbf{X}'\mathbf{X}\hat{\beta} \tag{4.28}$$

$$= \mathbf{Y}'\mathbf{Y} - 2\mathbf{Y}\mathbf{X}'\hat{\beta}' + \hat{\beta}'\mathbf{X}'\mathbf{X}\hat{\beta} \tag{4.29}$$

We now need to differentiate the above expression with respect to $\hat{\beta}$ and set this result equal to zero:

$$\frac{\partial RSS}{\partial \hat{\beta}} = -2\mathbf{X}'\mathbf{Y} + 2\mathbf{X}'\mathbf{X}\hat{\beta} = 0 \tag{4.30}$$

which is a set of k equations and k unknowns. Rewriting Equation (4.30) we have:

$$\mathbf{X}'\mathbf{X}\hat{\beta} = \mathbf{X}'\mathbf{Y} \tag{4.31}$$

and multiplying both sides by the inverse matrix $(\mathbf{X}'\mathbf{X})^{-1}$ we get:

$$\hat{\beta} = (\mathbf{X}'\mathbf{X})^{-1}\mathbf{X}'\mathbf{Y} \tag{4.32}$$

which is the solution for the OLS estimators in the case of multiple regression analysis.

The structure of the X'X and X'Y matrices

For a better understanding of the above solution, it is useful to examine the structure of the $(\mathbf{X}'\mathbf{X})$ and $(\mathbf{X}'\mathbf{Y})$ matrices that give us the solution for $\hat{\beta}$. Recall that $\tilde{x}_t = (X_t - \bar{X})$ denotes deviations of variables from their means, so we have:

$$(\tilde{\mathbf{x}}'\tilde{\mathbf{x}}) = \begin{pmatrix} \sum \tilde{x}_{2t}^2 & \sum \tilde{x}_{2t}\tilde{x}_{3t} & \sum \tilde{x}_{2t}\tilde{x}_{4t} & \cdots & \sum \tilde{x}_{2t}\tilde{x}_{kt} \\ \sum \tilde{x}_{3t}\tilde{x}_{2t} & \sum \tilde{x}_{3t}^2 & \sum \tilde{x}_{3t}\tilde{x}_{4t} & \cdots & \sum \tilde{x}_{3t}\tilde{x}_{kt} \\ \sum \tilde{x}_{4t}\tilde{x}_{2t} & \sum \tilde{x}_{4t}\tilde{x}_{3t} & \sum \tilde{x}_{4t}^2 & \cdots & \sum \tilde{x}_{4t}\tilde{x}_{kt} \\ \cdots & & \cdots & & \\ \sum \tilde{x}_{kt}\tilde{x}_{2t} & \sum \tilde{x}_{kt}\tilde{x}_{3t} & \sum \tilde{x}_{kt}\tilde{x}_{4t} & \cdots & \sum \tilde{x}_{kt}^2 \end{pmatrix} \tag{4.33}$$

and

$$(\tilde{\mathbf{x}}'\mathbf{y}) = \begin{pmatrix} \sum \tilde{x}_{2t}\tilde{y}_t \\ \sum \tilde{x}_{3t}\tilde{y}_t \\ \sum \tilde{x}_{4t}\tilde{y}_t \\ \cdots \\ \sum \tilde{x}_{kt}\tilde{y}_t \end{pmatrix} \tag{4.34}$$

It is clear that the matrix $(\tilde{\mathbf{x}}'\tilde{\mathbf{x}})$ in the case of a four explanatory variables regression model $(k = 4)$ will reduce to its 3×3 equivalent; for $k = 3$ to its 2×2 equivalent, and so on. When we have the simple linear regression model with two explanatory variables ($k = 2$, the constant and the slope coefficient), we shall have $(\tilde{\mathbf{x}}'\tilde{\mathbf{x}}) = \sum \tilde{x}_{2t}^2$ and $(\tilde{\mathbf{x}}'\tilde{\mathbf{y}}) = \sum \tilde{x}_{2t}\tilde{y}_t 8$. The OLS formula will be:

$$\hat{\beta}_2 = (\tilde{\mathbf{x}}'\tilde{\mathbf{x}})^{-1}(\tilde{\mathbf{x}}'\tilde{\mathbf{y}})$$

$$= \left(\sum \tilde{x}_2^2\right)^{-1}\left(\sum \tilde{x}_2\tilde{y}\right) \tag{4.35}$$

$$= \frac{\sum \tilde{x}_2\tilde{y}}{\sum \tilde{x}_2^2} = \hat{\beta}^* \tag{4.36}$$

which is the same as with Equation (4.24) that we derived analytically without matrix algebra.

The assumptions of the multiple regression model

We can briefly restate the assumptions of the model, which are not very different from the simple two-variable case:

1 The dependent variable is a linear function of the explanatory variables.

2 All explanatory variables are non-random.

3 All explanatory variables have values that are fixed in repeated samples, and as $n \to \infty$ the variance of their sample values $1/n \sum(X_{jt} - \bar{X}_j)^2 \to Q_j$ $(j = 2, 3, \ldots, k)$, where the Q_j are fixed constants.

4 $E(u_t) = 0$ for all t.

5 $Var(u_t) = E(u_t^2) = \sigma^2 = $ constant for all t.

6 $Cov(u_t, u_j) = E(u_t, u_j) = 0$ for all $j \neq t$.

7 Each u_t is normally distributed.

8 There are no exact linear relationships among the sample values of any two or more of the explanatory variables.

The variance–covariance matrix of the errors

Recall from the matrix representation of the model that we have an $n \times 1$ vector $\mathbf{u}$ of error terms. If we form an $n \times n$ matrix $\mathbf{u}'\mathbf{u}$ and take the expected value of this matrix we get:

$$E(\mathbf{uu}') = \begin{pmatrix} E(u_1^2) & E(u_1u_2) & E(u_1u_3) & \cdots & E(u_1u_n) \\ E(u_2u_1) & E(u_2^2) & E(u_2u_3) & \cdots & E(u_2u_n) \\ E(u_3u_1) & E(u_3u_2) & E(u_3^2) & \cdots & E(u_3u_n) \\ \cdots & \cdots & \cdots & & \cdots \\ E(u_nu_1) & E(u_nu_2) & E(u_nu_3) & \cdots & E(u_n^2) \end{pmatrix} \tag{4.37}$$

Since each error term, u_t, has a zero mean, the diagonal elements of this matrix will represent the variance of the disturbances, and the non-diagonal terms will be the covariances among the different disturbances. Hence this matrix is called the variance–covariance matrix of the errors, and using assumptions 5 ($Var(u_t) = E(u_t^2) = \sigma^2$) and 6 ($Cov(u_t, u_j) = E(u_t, u_j) = 0$) will be in the form:

$$E(\mathbf{uu}') = \begin{pmatrix} \sigma^2 & 0 & 0 & \cdots & 0 \\ 0 & \sigma^2 & 0 & 0 & 0 \\ 0 & 0 & \sigma^2 & \cdots & 0 \\ \cdots & \cdots & \cdots & & \cdots \\ 0 & 0 & 0 & \cdots & \sigma^2 \end{pmatrix} = \sigma^2\mathbf{I_n} \tag{4.38}$$

where $\mathbf{I_n}$ is an $n \times n$ identity matrix.

Properties of multiple regression model OLS estimators

As in the simple two-variable regression model, based on the assumptions of the CLRM, we can prove that the OLS estimators are best linear unbiased (BLU) estimators. We concentrate on the slope coefficients ($\beta_2, \beta_3, \beta_4, \ldots, \beta_k$) rather than the constant (β_1) because these parameters are of greater interest.

Linearity

For OLS estimators to be linear, assumptions 2 and 3 are needed. Since the values of the explanatory variables are fixed constants, it can easily be shown that the OLS estimators are linear functions of the Y-values. Recall the solution for $\hat{\beta}$:

$$\hat{\beta} = (\mathbf{X}'\mathbf{X})^{-1}\mathbf{X}'\mathbf{Y} \tag{4.39}$$

where, since $\mathbf{X}$ is a matrix of fixed constants, $\mathbf{W} = (\mathbf{X}'\mathbf{X})^{-1}\mathbf{X}'$ is also a $n \times k$ matrix of fixed constants. Since $\mathbf{W}$ is a matrix of fixed constants, $\hat{\beta}$ is a linear function of Y, so by definition it is a linear estimator.

Unbiasedness

We know that:

$$\hat{\beta} = (X'X)^{-1}X'Y \tag{4.40}$$

and we also have that:

$$Y = X\beta + u \tag{4.41}$$

Substituting Equation (4.41) into Equation (4.40) we get:

$$\hat{\beta} = (X'X)^{-1}X'(X\beta + u)$$

$$= (X'X)^{-1}X'X\beta + (X'X)^{-1}X'u$$

$$= \beta + (X'X)^{-1}X'u \quad [\text{since } (X'X)^{-1}X'X = I] \tag{4.42}$$

Taking the expectations of Equation (4.42) yields:

$$E(\hat{\beta}) = E(\beta) + (X'X)^{-1}X'E(u) \tag{4.43}$$

$$= \beta \quad [\text{since } E(\beta) = \beta \text{ and } E(u) = 0] \tag{4.44}$$

Therefore $\hat{\beta}$ is an unbiased estimator of β.

Consistency

Unbiasedness means simply that, whatever the sample size, we expect that on average the estimated $\hat{\beta}$ will equal the true β; however, the above proof of this rests on the assumption that X is fixed, and this is a strong and often unrealistic assumption. If we relax this assumption, however, we can still establish that $\hat{\beta}$ is consistent; this means that as the estimation sample size approaches infinity $\hat{\beta}$ will converge in probability to its true value. Thus $p\lim(\hat{\beta}) = \beta$. The proof of consistency will not be presented here as it is tedious and beyond the scope of this book. However, the key assumption to this proof is that the X-variable, while not being fixed, must be uncorrelated with the error term.

BLUEness

Before we proceed with the proof that the OLS estimators for the multiple regression model are BLU estimators, it is good to first find expressions for the variances and convariances of the OLS estimators.

Consider the symmetric $k \times k$ matrix of the form:

$$E(\hat{\boldsymbol{\beta}} - \boldsymbol{\beta})(\hat{\boldsymbol{\beta}} - \boldsymbol{\beta})'$$

$$= \begin{pmatrix} E(\hat{\beta}_1 - \beta_1)^2 & E(\hat{\beta}_1 - \beta_1)(\hat{\beta}_2 - \beta_2) & \cdots & E(\hat{\beta}_1 - \beta_1)(\hat{\beta}_k - \beta_k) \\ E(\hat{\beta}_2 - \beta_2)(\hat{\beta}_1 - \beta_1) & E(\hat{\beta}_2 - \beta_2)^2 & \cdots & E(\hat{\beta}_2 - \beta_2)(\hat{\beta}_k - \beta_k) \\ \cdots & \cdots & & \cdots \\ E(\hat{\beta}_k - \beta_k)(\hat{\beta}_1 - \beta_1) & E(\hat{\beta}_k - \beta_k)(\hat{\beta}_2 - \beta_2) & \cdots & E(\hat{\beta}_k - \beta_k)^2 \end{pmatrix} \tag{4.45}$$

Because of the unbiasedness of $\hat{\boldsymbol{\beta}}$ we have that $E(\hat{\boldsymbol{\beta}}) = \boldsymbol{\beta}$. Therefore:

$$E(\hat{\boldsymbol{\beta}} - \boldsymbol{\beta})(\hat{\boldsymbol{\beta}} - \boldsymbol{\beta})' = \begin{pmatrix} Var(\hat{\beta}_1)^2 & Cov(\hat{\beta}_1, \hat{\beta}_2) & \cdots & Cov(\hat{\beta}_1, \hat{\beta}_k) \\ Cov(\hat{\beta}_2, \hat{\beta}_1) & Var(\hat{\beta}_2) & \cdots & Cov(\hat{\beta}_2, \hat{\beta}_k) \\ \cdots & \cdots & & \cdots \\ Cov(\hat{\beta}_k, \hat{\beta}_1) & Cov(\hat{\beta}_k, \hat{\beta}_2) & \cdots & Var(\hat{\beta}_k) \end{pmatrix} \tag{4.46}$$

which is called the variance–covariance matrix of $\hat{\boldsymbol{\beta}}$. We need to find an expression for this. Consider that from Equation (4.32) we have:

$$\hat{\boldsymbol{\beta}} = (\mathbf{X}'\mathbf{X})^{-1}\mathbf{X}'\mathbf{Y} \tag{4.47}$$

Substituting $\mathbf{Y} = \mathbf{X}\boldsymbol{\beta} + \mathbf{u}$, we get:

$$\begin{aligned} \hat{\boldsymbol{\beta}} &= (\mathbf{X}'\mathbf{X})^{-1}\mathbf{X}'(\mathbf{X}\boldsymbol{\beta} + \mathbf{u}) \\ &= (\mathbf{X}'\mathbf{X})^{-1}\mathbf{X}'\mathbf{X}\boldsymbol{\beta} + (\mathbf{X}'\mathbf{X})^{-1}\mathbf{X}'\mathbf{u} \\ &= \boldsymbol{\beta} + (\mathbf{X}'\mathbf{X})^{-1}\mathbf{X}'\mathbf{u} \end{aligned} \tag{4.48}$$

or

$$\hat{\boldsymbol{\beta}} - \boldsymbol{\beta} = (\mathbf{X}'\mathbf{X})^{-1}\mathbf{X}'\mathbf{u} \tag{4.49}$$

By the definition of variance–covariance we have that:

$$\begin{aligned} Var(\hat{\boldsymbol{\beta}}) &= \mathbf{E}[(\hat{\boldsymbol{\beta}} - \boldsymbol{\beta})(\hat{\boldsymbol{\beta}} - \boldsymbol{\beta})'] \\ &= E\{[(\mathbf{X}'\mathbf{X})^{-1}\mathbf{X}'\mathbf{u}][(\mathbf{X}'\mathbf{X})^{-1}\mathbf{X}'\mathbf{u}]'\} \\ &= E\{(\mathbf{X}'\mathbf{X})^{-1}\mathbf{X}'\mathbf{u}\mathbf{u}'\mathbf{X}(\mathbf{X}'\mathbf{X})^{-1}\}^* \\ &= (\mathbf{X}'\mathbf{X})^{-1}\mathbf{X}'E(\mathbf{u}\mathbf{u}')\mathbf{X}(\mathbf{X}'\mathbf{X})^{-1}{}^{**} \\ &= (\mathbf{X}'\mathbf{X})^{-1}\mathbf{X}'\sigma^2\mathbf{I}\mathbf{X}(\mathbf{X}'\mathbf{X})^{-1} \\ &= \sigma^2(\mathbf{X}'\mathbf{X})^{-1} \end{aligned} \tag{4.50}$$

---

* This is because $(BA)' = A'B'$.
** This is because, by assumption 2, the Xs are non-random.

Now for the BLUEness of $\hat{\beta}$, let us assume that there is $\hat{\beta}^*$, which is any other linear estimator of β. This can be expressed as:

$$\hat{\beta}^* = [(X'X)^{-1}X' + Z](Y) \tag{4.51}$$

where Z is a matrix of constants. Substituting for $Y = X\beta + u$, we get:

$$\hat{\beta}^* = [(X'X)^{-1}X' + Z](X\beta + u)$$
$$= \beta + ZX\beta + (X'X)^{-1}X'u + Zu \tag{4.52}$$

and for $\hat{\beta}^*$ to be unbiased we require that:

$$ZX = 0 \tag{4.53}$$

Using Equation (4.53), we can rewrite Equation (4.52) as:

$$\hat{\beta}^* - \beta = (X'X)^{-1}X'u + Zu \tag{4.54}$$

Going back to the definition of variance–covariance:

$$E[(\hat{\beta} - \beta)(\hat{\beta} - \beta)'] = \{(X'X)^{-1}X'u + Zu\}\{(X'X)^{-1}X'u + Zu\}' \tag{4.55}$$
$$= \sigma^2(X'X)^{-1} + \sigma^2 ZZ' \tag{4.56}$$

which says that the variance–covariance matrix of the alternative estimator $\hat{\beta}^*$ is equal to the variance–covariance matrix of the OLS estimator $\hat{\beta}$ plus σ^2 times ZZ', and therefore greater than the variance–covariance of $\hat{\beta}$. Hence $\hat{\beta}$ is a BLU estimator.

R^2 and adjusted R^2

The regular coefficient of determination, R^2, is again a measure of the closeness of fit in the multiple regression model as in the simple two-variable model. However, R^2 cannot be used as a means of comparing two different equations containing different numbers of explanatory variables. This is because, when additional explanatory variables are included, the proportion of variation in Y explained by the Xs, R^2, will always be increased. We shall always obtain a higher R^2 regardless of the importance or not of the additional regressor. For this reason we require a different measure that will take into account the number of explanatory variables included in each model. This measure is called the adjusted R^2 (and is denoted by $\bar{R}^2$) because it is adjusted for the number of regressors (or adjusted for the degrees of freedom).

Since $R^2 = ESS/TSS = 1 - RSS/TSS$, the adjusted R^2 is just:

$$\bar{R}^2 = 1 - \frac{RSS/(n-k)}{TSS/(n-1)} = 1 - \frac{RSS(n-1)}{TSS(n-k)} \tag{4.57}$$

Thus an increase in the number of Xs included in the regression function increases k and this will reduce RSS (which, if we do not make adjustments, will increase R^2). Dividing RSS by $n-k$, the increase in k tends to offset the fall in RSS, which is why $\bar{R}^2$ is a 'fairer' measure when comparing different equations. The criterion for selecting a model is to include an extra variable only if it increases $\bar{R}^2$. Note that because $(n-1)/(n-k)$ is never less than 1, $\bar{R}^2$ will never be higher than R^2. However, while R^2 has values only between 0 and 1, and can never be negative, $\bar{R}^2$ can have a negative value in some cases. A negative $\bar{R}^2$ indicates that the model does not adequately describe the data-generating process.

General criteria for model selection

We noted earlier that increasing the number of explanatory variables in a multiple regression model will decrease the RSS, and R^2 will therefore increase. However, the cost of that is a loss in terms of degrees of freedom. A different method – apart from $\bar{R}^2$ – of allowing for the number of Xs to change when assessing goodness of fit is to use different criteria for model comparison, such as the Akaike Information Criterion (AIC) developed by Akaike (1974) and given by:

$$AIC = \left(\frac{RSS}{n}\right) e^{2k/n} \tag{4.58}$$

the Finite Prediction Error (FPE), again developed by Akaike (1970):

$$FPE = \left(\frac{RSS}{n}\right) \frac{n+k}{n-k} \tag{4.59}$$

the Schwarz Bayesian Criterion (SBC) developed by Schwarz (1978):

$$SBC = \left(\frac{RSS}{n}\right) e^{k/n} \tag{4.60}$$

or the Hannan and Quin (1979) Criterion (HQC):

$$HQC = \left(\frac{RSS}{n}\right) (\ln n)^{2k/n} \tag{4.61}$$

among many others. (Other criteria include those by Shibata (1981), Rice (1984), and a Generalized Gross Validation (GGV) method developed by Craven and Wahba (1979). Note that some programs, including EViews, report the logarithm of the AIC – Equations (4.58) and (4.61).

Ideally, we select the model that minimizes all those statistics. In general, however, it is quite common to have contradictory results arising from different criteria. For example, the SBC penalizes model complexity more heavily than any other measure, and might therefore give a different conclusion. A model that outperforms another in several of these criteria might generally be preferred. However, in general, the AIC is one of the most commonly used methods in time series analysis. Both AIC and SBC are provided by EViews in the standard regression results output, while Microfit provides only SBC.

Multiple regression estimation in Microfit, EViews and Stata

Multiple regression in Microfit

Step 1   Open Microfit.

Step 2   Click on **File/New** in order to create a new file, or **File/Open** to open an existing file.

Step 3   If it is a new file, follow steps 3–6 described in the simple regression case.

Step 4   Go to the single editor (by clicking the **single** button) and type into this:

        Y C X2 X3 X4 ... XK

where X2 , . . . , XK are the names of the variables to add to the explanatory variables list. Of course, Y is the dependent variable and C is the constant created in Microfit. After determining the equation, click **START**. The regression result is output in a new window which provides estimates for β_1 (the coefficient of the constant term C), and $\beta_2, \ldots, \beta_k$ (the coefficients of Xs) and some additional statistics that will be discussed in later chapters of this book.

Multiple regression in EViews

Step 1   Open EViews.

Step 2   Click **File/New/Workfile** in order to create a new file, or **File/Open** to open an existing file.

Step 3   If it is a new file, follow steps 3–5 described in the simple regression case.

Step 4   Once the data have been entered in EViews, the regression line can be estimated, to obtain β_1 (the coefficient of the constant term C) and $\beta_2, \ldots, \beta_k$ (the coefficients of Xs), in two different ways. One is by typing in the EViews command line:

        ls y c x2 x3 ... xk   (press **enter**)

where y is to be substituted with the name of the dependent variable as it appears in the EViews file, and, similarly, x2 , . . . xk will be the names of the explanatory variables.

The second way is to click on **Quick/Estimate equation** and then write the equation (that is y c x2 . . . xk) in the new window. Note that the option for OLS (LS – Least Squares (NLS and ARMA)) is chosen automatically by EViews and the sample selected to be the maximum possible.

Below we show an example of a regression result output from EViews (the case of Microfit is similar).

Multiple regression in Stata

Step 1   Open Stata

Step 2   Click on the **Data Editor** button to open the Data Editor Window, which looks like a spreadsheet. Start entering the data manually or copy/paste the data from Excel or any other spreadsheet. After you have finished entering the data, double-click on the variable label (the default name is var1, var2 and so on) and a new window opens up where you can specify the name of the variable and can (optionally) enter a description of it in the Label area. We will assume that for this example we entered data for the following variables given in Step 2 (variable y is the dependent variable and variables x2, x3, x4 and x5 are four explanatory variables).

Step 2   In the Command Window, type the command:

```
regress y x2 x3 x4 x5  (press enter)
```

and you will obtain the regression results. Note that there is no requirement to provide a constant here as Stata includes it automatically in the results (in the output it is labelled as _cons). The $\beta1$ coefficient is the one next to _cons in the Stata regression output and $\beta2$, $\beta3$, $\beta4$ and $\beta5$ are the coefficients derived in Stata, and you will see them next to the x2, x3, x4 and x5 variables in the results. For a better explanation of the Stata output, refer to Chapter 3.

Reading the EViews multiple regression results output

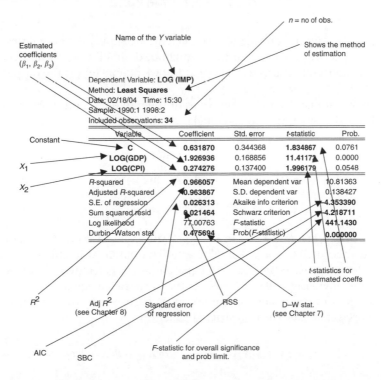

Hypothesis testing

Testing individual coefficients

As in simple regression analysis, in multiple regression a single test of hypothesis on a regression coefficient is carried out as a normal t-test. We can again have one-tail tests (if there is some prior belief/theory for the sign of the coefficient) or two-tail tests, carried out in the usual way ($(\hat{\beta} - \beta)/s_{\hat{\beta}}$ follows t_{n-k}), and we can immediately make a decision about the significance or not of the $\hat{\beta}$s using the criterion $|t\text{-}stat| > |t\text{-}crit|$, having the t-statistic provided immediately by either Microfit or EViews (note that, especially for large samples, we can use the 'rule of thumb' $|t\text{-}stat| > 2$).

Testing linear restrictions

Sometimes in economics we need to test whether there are particular relationships between the estimated coefficients. Take, for example, a production function of the standard Cobb–Douglas type:

$$Q = AL^a K^\beta \tag{4.62}$$

where Q is output, L denotes labour units, K is capital and A is an exogenous technology parameter. If we take logarithms and add an error term we have:

$$\ln Q = c + a \ln L + \beta \ln K + u \tag{4.63}$$

where $c = \ln A$, a constant, and a and β coefficients are simply the elasticities of labour and capital, respectively. In this example it might be desirable to test whether $a + \beta = 1$, which implies constant returns to scale (that is if we double inputs the output will also be doubled).

We now have estimates $\hat{a}$ and $\hat{\beta}$ and we want them to obey a linear restriction. If we impose this restriction on the Cobb–Douglas production function we have:

$$\ln Q = c + (1 - \beta) \ln L + \beta \ln K + u$$
$$\ln Q - \ln L = c + \beta(\ln K - \ln L) + u \tag{4.64}$$
$$Q^* = c + \beta K^* + u$$

where $Q^* = \ln Q - \ln L$ and $K^* = \ln K - \ln L$. Thus we can estimate Equation (4.64) to get $\hat{\beta}$ and then derive $\hat{a} = 1 - \hat{\beta}$. The estimates obtained in this way are known as restricted least squares estimates, and Equation (4.64) is referred to as the restricted equation while obviously Equation (4.63) is the unrestricted equation.

Sometimes it is even possible to impose more than one restriction at a time. For example, suppose we have the unrestricted equation:

$$Y_t = \beta_1 + \beta_2 X_{2t} + \beta_3 X_{3t} + \beta_4 X_{4t} + \beta_5 X_{5t} + e_t \tag{4.65}$$

and we need to impose the following restrictions:

$$\beta_3 + \beta_4 = 1 \quad \text{and} \quad \beta_2 = \beta_5$$

Substituting the restrictions into the unrestricted equation we have:

$$
\begin{aligned}
Y_t &= \beta_1 + \beta_5 X_{2t} + (1 - \beta_4) X_{3t} + \beta_4 X_{4t} + \beta_5 X_{5t} + e_t \\
Y_t &= \beta_1 + \beta_5 X_{2t} + X_{3t} - \beta_4 X_{3t} + \beta_4 X_{4t} + \beta_5 X_{5t} + e_t \\
Y_t - X_{3t} &= \beta_1 + \beta_5 (X_{2t} + X_{5t}) + \beta_4 (X_{4t} - X_{3t}) + e_t \\
Y_t^* &= \beta_1 + \beta_5 (X_{1t}^*) + \beta_4 (X_{2t}^*) + e_t
\end{aligned}
\tag{4.66}
$$

where $Y_t^* = Y_t - X_{3t}$, $X_{1t}^* = X_{2t} + X_{5t}$ and $X_{2t}^* = X_{4t} - X_{3t}$.

In this case we can estimate the restricted Equation (4.66) and get $\hat{\beta}_1, \hat{\beta}_5$ and $\hat{\beta}_4$, then calculate $\hat{\beta}_3$ and $\hat{\beta}_2$ from the restrictions imposed above.

So far, things have been simple. However, the problem is that we are usually not able merely to accept the restrictions as given without testing for their validity. There are three basic ways of constructing a test: the Likelihood Ratio procedure; the Wald procedure; and the Lagrange Multiplier (or LM) procedure. The exact derivation of these procedures is beyond the scope of this book but we shall attempt to give an intuitive account of these three. The aim of most tests is to assess the difference between an unrestricted model and a restricted version of the same model. If the restriction does not affect the fit of the model very much then we can accept the restriction as being valid. If, on the other hand, the model is a much worse fit, then we reject it.

Of course, this means we have to have some firm measure of how much worse the fit can get and still be insignificant. In general, this comes from a measure of how good a model is, called the likelihood function. At an intuitive level this shows us how likely the model is to be correct. We use this to form a test based on the fact that if we take twice the difference between the likelihood function of the unrestricted and restricted models this value will have a χ^2 distribution, with the number of degrees of freedom equal to the number of restrictions imposed on the model. This gives rise to the basic Likelihood Ratio test, which simply involves estimating the model both with the restriction and without it and constructing a test based on these two estimates. The χ^2 distribution is asymptotic, which means that it is only correct for an infinitely large sample; however, in some cases we can calculate a version of the Likelihood Ratio test that is correct in small samples and then it may have an F-distribution, for example. Any test that involves estimating the model both with and without the restriction is a form of Likelihood Ratio test. There are, however, two approximations to the Likelihood Ratio test that only require us to estimate one model. If we only estimate the unrestricted model and then use a formula to approximate the full Likelihood Ratio test, this is called a Wald test. The t-test associated with OLS coefficients, for example, a particular form of Wald test. We estimate the unrestricted model and then we can test the hypothesis that the true coefficient is zero, but we do not estimate the complete model subject to this restriction. The final method (the LM procedure) only estimates a restricted model and then tests for a relaxation of the restrictions by again applying a formula but not actually re-estimating the model. This final procedure has proved very useful in recent years as it allows us to test a model for many possible forms of mis-specification without having to estimate many different models. All three forms may have asymptotic χ^2 distributions or they may have distributions which correct for the small sample, such as an F- or t-distribution.

The F-form of the Likelihood Ratio test

The most common method is to estimate both the unrestricted and restricted equations and to take the RSS of both models denoted as RSS_U and RSS_R respectively (the subscript U stands for unrestricted, R for restricted).

It should be obvious that $RSS_R > RSS_U$. However, if the restrictions are valid, then this difference should be minimal. It is beyond the scope of this text to prove that there is a statistic given by the following expression:

$$\frac{(RSS_R - RSS_U)/(k_U - k_R)}{SSR_U/(n - k_U)} \tag{4.67}$$

This follows an F-type distribution with $(k_U - k_R, n - k_U)$ degrees of freedom, which is the appropriate statistic to help us determine whether the restrictions are valid or not. In summary, the F-test (which is a special form of the Likelihood Ratio procedure) for testing linear restrictions can be conducted as follows:

Step 1   The null hypothesis is that the restrictions are valid.

Step 2   Estimate both the restricted and unrestricted models and derive RSS_R and RSS_U.

Step 3   Calculate F-statistical by Equation (4.67) above, where k_U and k_R are the number of regressors in each model.

Step 4   Find F-critical for $(k_U - k_R, n - k_U)$ degrees of freedom from the F-tables.

Step 5   If F-statistical > F-critical reject the null hypothesis.

Testing the joint significance of the Xs

This is simply the F-type test for the overall goodness of fit, but it can be understood more easily as a special case of an LR-type test. Consider the following two (unrestricted and super-restricted) models:

$$Y_t = \beta_1 + \beta_2 X_{2t} + \beta_3 X_{3t} + \beta_4 X_{4t} + \beta_5 X_{5t} + e_t \tag{4.68}$$

$$Y_t = \beta_1 + \epsilon_t \tag{4.69}$$

The second model is described as super-restricted because we impose a number of restrictions equal to the number of explanatory variables excluding the constant (that is $k - 1$ restrictions).

The null hypothesis in this case is $\beta_2 = \beta_3 = \beta_4 = \beta_5 = 0$, or to put it in words, 'none of the coefficients in the model apart from the intercept is statistically significant'. If we fail to reject this hypothesis, this means that we have a very poor model and must reformulate it.

In this special case we can show that we do not have to estimate both models in order to calculate the F-statistic. First, we can get RSS_U by estimating the full model. Then we can get RSS_{SR} by minimizing $\sum \epsilon_t^2 = \sum (Y_t - \beta_1)^2$ with respect to β_1. However, we know that $\beta_1 = \bar{Y}_t$ and therefore $RSS_{SR} = \sum (Y_t - \bar{Y}_t)^2$, which is the same as TSS_U.

The F-statistic is now:

$$\frac{(TSS_U - RSS_U)/(k-1)}{RSS_U/(n-k)} = \frac{ESS_U/(k-1)}{RSS_U/(n-k)} = \frac{R^2/(k-1)}{(1-R^2)/(n-k)} \tag{4.70}$$

which can easily be calculated by the R^2 of the unrestricted model.

F-test for overall significance in Microfit and EViews

Both Microfit and EViews provide the F-statistic for the overall significance of the Xs as a part of the summary statistics for a regression model. We just have to make sure that F-statistical > F-critical $(k-1, n-k)$ in order to reject the null hypothesis. If we cannot reject the null, then we have to reformulate our model.

Adding or deleting explanatory variables

Frequently we might face the problem of deciding whether to add or delete one or more explanatory variables from an estimated model. When only one variable is involved, a safe criterion is to check its t-ratio, but when a set of variables is involved we might need to assess their combined influence in the model. Consider the following model:

$$Y_t = \beta_1 + \beta_2 X_{2t} + \cdots + \beta_k X_{kt} + e_t \tag{4.71}$$

$$Y_t = \beta_1 + \beta_2 X_{2t} + \cdots + \beta_k X_{kt} + \beta_{k+1} X_{k+1t} + \cdots + \beta_m X_{mt} + \epsilon_t \tag{4.72}$$

In this case we again have a restricted and unrestricted model with $m - k$ more variables in which we are interested in assessing their combined effect. The null hypothesis here is $\beta_{k+1} = \beta_{k+2} = \cdots = \beta_m = 0$, which says that the joint significance of these omitted variables is zero. Alternatively, we can have the model in Equation (4.72) as the initial model and might want to test that variables $X_{k+1} = X_{k+2} = \cdots = X_{mt}$ are redundant to this model. This can be tested by either a regular F-test or a Likelihood Ratio (LR) test. The F-type test, as we explained above, is based on the difference of the RSS of the restricted and unrestricted regressions.

The LR-statistic is computed as:

$$LR = -2(l_R - l_U)$$

where l_R and l_U are the maximized values of the log likelihood function of the unrestricted and restricted equations, respectively. The LR-statistic follows a χ^2 distribution with degrees of freedom equal to the number of restrictions (that is the number of omitted or added variables).

Omitted and redundant variables test in EViews

Suppose that we have estimated the unrestricted model:

$$ls \quad Y \quad C \quad X1 \quad X2 \quad X3$$

and want to test whether $X4$ and $X5$ are omitted from the model. From the regression window select **View/Coefficient Diagnostics/Omitted Variables-Likelihood Ratio**. A new window with a dialog box opens, where we specify the names of the variables we want to test (that is write $X4$ $X5$) and click **OK**. EViews reports the two statistics concerning the hypothesis testing (namely, the F and LR-statistics with their probability limits). If F-statistical > F-critical or if LR-statistical > χ^2-critical then we reject the null that the two series do not belong to the equation. Similar steps have to be carried out for a variable deletion test, where we choose **View/Coefficient Diagnostics/Redundant Variables-Likelihood Ratio** and specify the names of the variables that were included in the initial model and whose significance we want to test.

Omitted and redundant variables test in Microfit

Similarly, in Microfit, after estimating a regression and closing the results window, a new window pops up with 10 different choices numbered consecutively from 0 to 9. Choice 2 is about hypothesis testing, which we discussed in the second part of this chapter. Choosing 2: **Move to hypothesis testing menu**, click **OK** and a new window opens with 10 different choices. From those choices, choice 5 concerns the variable deletion test and choice 6 the variable addition test. In each case we need to specify the names/labels of variables to add or delete. Microfit reports results of LR, F and Lagrange Multiplier (LM) test statistics. In each case, if the statistical value is greater than the critical value we reject the null hypothesis that the restrictions are valid.

How to perform the Wald test in EViews and Microfit

As noted above, a particular set of restrictions or hypotheses may be tested in three different ways, the Likelihood Ratio procedure gives rise to the F-test detailed above, which involves estimating the model twice and this may be cumbersome to do. The Wald procedure, however, allows us to test any restriction on a model once we have estimated it without estimating any further models. It is therefore often quite convenient to use a series of Wald tests after we have estimated our model.

The Wald test in EViews

We can test various linear restrictions in EViews and Microfit using the Wald test. For EViews we first estimate the unrestricted equation, then from the regression output window we choose **View/Coefficient Diagnostics/Wald-Coefficient Restrictions** .... We must then enter the restrictions in the new dialog box (in the case of more than one restriction we have to separate them by commas). The restrictions should be entered as equations involving the estimated coefficients and constants. The coefficients should be referred to as **C(1)** for the constant, **C(2)** for the coefficient of the first explanatory variable and so on. After entering the restrictions, click **OK**. EViews reports the F statistic of the Wald test and a Chi-square statistic. If the statistical value is greater than the critical we reject the null hypothesis.

The Wald test in Microfit

Similarly, in Microfit, after estimating a regression and closing the results window a new window pops up with 10 different choices numbered consecutively from 0 to 9. Choosing 2: **Move to hypothesis testing menu**, click **OK** and a new window opens, again with 10 different choices. From those choices, choice 7 concerns the Wald test for linear restrictions. We need to specify the restrictions as equations, where this time the coefficients should be referred to as **A1** for the constant, **A2** for the coefficient of the first explanatory variable and so on. Microfit reports the Wald statistics as a Chi-square distributed statistic. If the statistical value is greater than the critical value we reject the null hypothesis.

The *t* test (a special case of the Wald procedure)

A third method is to test the restriction without actually estimating the restricted equation, but simply using a t-test on the actual restriction. Think of the Cobb–Douglas production function:

$$\ln Q = c + a \ln L + \beta \ln K + u \tag{4.73}$$

and the restriction $a + \beta = 1$. We can obtain $\hat{a}$ and $\hat{\beta}$ by OLS and test whether $\hat{a} + \hat{\beta} = 1$. We know that $\hat{a}$ and $\hat{\beta}$ are normally distributed:

$$\hat{a} \sim N\left(a, \sigma_{\hat{a}}^2\right) \quad \text{and} \quad \hat{\beta} \sim N\left(\beta, \sigma_{\hat{\beta}}^2\right)$$

where σ^2 refers to the respective variances. Furthermore, we know that any linear combination of two normal variables will also be normal. So, we have:

$$\hat{a} + \hat{\beta} \sim N(a + \beta, Var(\hat{a} + \hat{\beta}))$$

where

$$Var(\hat{a} + \hat{\beta}) = Var(\hat{a}) + Var(\hat{\beta}) + 2Cov(\hat{a}, \hat{\beta})$$

Converting the above into standard normal distribution we obtain:

$$\frac{\hat{a} + \hat{\beta} - (a + \beta)}{Var(\hat{a}) + Var(\hat{\beta}) + 2Cov(\hat{a}, \hat{\beta})} \sim N(0, 1)$$

or

$$\frac{\hat{a} + \hat{\beta} - 1}{Var(\hat{a}) + Var(\hat{\beta}) + 2Cov(\hat{a}, \hat{\beta})} \sim N(0, 1)$$

because under the null hypothesis $a + \beta = 1$. We do not know the variances and covariances exactly, but these can be estimated. If we substitute an estimated value for the denominator in the above equation (u) that can be taken from the residuals variance–covariance matrix, then its statistical distribution changes to the student's t-distribution with $n - k$ degrees of freedom. Thus, we can apply a t-test calculating the following:

$$t_{stat} = \frac{\hat{a} + \hat{\beta} - 1}{Var(\hat{a}) + Var(\hat{\beta}) + 2Cov(\hat{a}, \hat{\beta})} \tag{4.74}$$

and as always if $|t_{stat}| > |t\text{-}crit|$ then we reject the null. Because this test requires several auxiliary calculations, one of the previously presented methods is generally recommended.

The LM test

The final way to test a set of restrictions on a model rests on estimating only the restricted model, the Lagrange Multiplier (LM) test. This is particularly useful, as we shall see later, as it allows us to test for more general models that might often be much more difficult to estimate. Assuming again have the unrestricted model:

$$Y_t = \beta_1 + \beta_2 X_{2t} + \beta_3 X_{3t} + \beta_4 X_{4t} + \beta_5 X_{5t} + u_t \tag{4.75}$$

and imposing:

$$\beta_3 + \beta_4 = 1 \quad \text{and} \quad \beta_2 = \beta_5$$

we have:

$$Y_t^* = \beta_1 + \beta_5(X_{1t}^*) + \beta_4(X_{2t}^*) + u_t \tag{4.76}$$

as was shown above.

The LM test involves the following steps:

Step 1 The null hypothesis is that the restrictions are valid.

Step 2 Estimate the restricted model in Equation (4.76) and save the residuals $\hat{u}_R$.

Step 3 Regress $\hat{u}_R$ on the four explanatory variables of the unrestricted model in Equation (4.75):

$$\hat{u}_R = \hat{\delta}_1 + \hat{\delta}_2 X_{2t} + \hat{\delta}_3 X_{3t} + \hat{\delta}_4 X_{4t} + \hat{\delta}_5 X_{5t} + \varepsilon_t$$

Step 4 Calculate the χ^2-statistic $= nR^2$, which is distributed with h degrees of freedom, where h is the number of restrictions (in this case 2).

Step 5 Find χ^2-critical for h degrees of freedom.

Step 6 If χ^2-statistical $> \chi^2$-critical reject the null hypothesis.

The LM test in Microfit and EViews

There is no routine used to calculate the LM procedure to test simple linear restrictions in Microfit and EViews as it is almost always more convenient to use a Wald or Likelihood Ratio test, so to calculate the LM test for the above restrictions we would have to follow the steps above manually. However, when we come to test more complex departures from our model such as serial correlation or ARCH effects, the LM procedure becomes very useful and both programs have a number of routines that make use of this procedure, as we shall see later.

Computer example: Wald, omitted and redundant variables tests

The file wage.xls contains data regarding wage rates (*wage*), years of education (*educ*), years of working experience (*exper*) and years spent with the same company (*tenure*) for 900 UK financial analysts. We want to estimate an equation that includes, as determinants of the logarithm of the wage rate, the variables *educ*, *exper* and *tenure*.

First we have to construct/generate the dependent variable. To do that we must type the following command in the EViews command line:

```
genr lnwage = log(wage)
```

Then, to estimate the multiple regression model, we select from the EViews toolbar **Quick/Estimate Equation** and type into the **Equation Specification** box the required model as:

```
lnwage c educ exper tenure
```

The results from this equation are shown in Table 4.1.

Table 4.1 Results from the wage equation

Dependent Variable: LNWAGE
Method: Least Squares
Date: 02/02/04 Time: 11:10
Sample: 1 900
Included observations: 900

Variable	Coefficient	Std. error	t-statistic	Prob.
C	5.528329	0.112795	49.01237	0.0000
EDUC	0.073117	0.006636	11.01871	0.0000
EXPER	0.015358	0.003425	4.483631	0.0000
TENURE	0.012964	0.002631	4.927939	0.0000

R-squared	0.148647	Mean dependent var	6.786164
Adjusted R-squared	0.145797	S.D. dependent var	0.420312
S.E. of regression	0.388465	Akaike info criterion	0.951208
Sum squared resid	135.2110	Schwarz criterion	0.972552
Log likelihood	−424.0434	F-statistic	52.14758
Durbin–Watson stat	1.750376	Prob(F-statistic)	0.000000

We can also save the equation (named **unrestrict01**) and save the regression results (by clicking on the **'freeze'** button) to an output table (named **Table01** in the file). As may be seen from the equation, all three variables have positive coefficients. These are all above the 'rule of thumb' critical *t*-value of 2, hence all are significant. It may be said that wages will increase as education, experience and tenure increase. Despite the significance of these three variables, the adjusted R^2 is quite low (0.145) as there are probably other variables that affect wages.

A Wald test of coefficient restrictions

Let's now assume that we want to test whether the effect of the *tenure* variable is the same as that of experience (*exper* variable). Referring to the estimation equation, we can see that the coefficient of *exper* is $C(3)$ and the coefficient of *tenure* is $C(4)$.

To test the hypothesis that the two effects are equal we need to conduct a Wald test in EViews. This is done by clicking on **View/Coefficient Diagnostics/Wald-Coefficient Restrictions** in the regression results output and then typing the restriction as:

$$C(3) = C(4) \qquad\qquad (4.77)$$

in the **Wald Test** window (then click **OK**). EViews then generates the *F* statistic (we saved this output as **Table02WALD**). The results of the Wald test are reported in Table 4.2.

The *F*-statistic is equal to 0.248, lower than the *F* critical value of 3.84. As *F*-statistical is less than *F*-critical, we cannot reject the null hypothesis. The null hypothesis is that the two coefficients are the same, and hence we accept this conclusion.

A redundant variable test

Suppose we want to conduct a redundant variable test for the explanatory variable *tenure* – that is years with current employer – to determine whether this variable is significant in determining the logarithm of the wage rate. To do that we click on **View/Coefficient Diagnostics/Redundant variables-Likelihood ratio** and type the name of the variable (*tenure*) we want to check. The results of this test are shown in Table 4.3.

Table 4.2 Wald test results

Equation: Untitled			
Null Hypothesis:	$C(3) = C(4)$		
F-statistic	0.248656	Probability	0.618145
Chi-square	0.248656	Probability	0.618023

Table 4.3 Redundant variable test results

Redundant variable: TENURE

F-statistic	24.28459	Probability	0.000001
Log likelihood ratio	24.06829	Probability	0.000001

Test Equation:
Dependent variable: LNWAGE
Method: Least Squares
Date: 01/30/04 Time: 16:47
Sample: 1 900
Included observations: 900

Variable	Coefficient	Std. error	t-statistic	Prob.
C	5.537798	0.114233	48.47827	0.0000
EDUC	0.075865	0.006697	11.32741	0.0000
EXPER	0.019470	0.003365	5.786278	0.0000

R-squared	0.125573	Mean dependent var	6.786164
Adjusted R-squared	0.123623	S.D. dependent var	0.420312
S.E. of regression	0.393475	Akaike info criterion	0.975728
Sum squared resid	138.8757	Schwarz criterion	0.991736
Log likelihood	−436.0776	F-statistic	64.40718
Durbin–Watson stat	1.770020	Prob(F-statistic)	0.000000

We can now save this output as **Table03REDUNDANT**. The results give us an F-statistic of 24.285, in comparison with the F-critical value of 3.84. As F-statistical is greater than F-critical, we can reject the null hypothesis. Thus, we can conclude that the coefficient of the variable *tenure* is not zero, and therefore *tenure* is not redundant – that is, it has a significant effect in determining the wage rate.

An omitted variable test

Suppose now that we want to conduct an omitted variable test for the explanatory variable *educ*. To do this, we first have to estimate a model that does not include *educ* as an explanatory variable and then check whether the omission of *educ* was of importance in the model or not. We estimate the following equation by typing in the EViews command line:

```
ls lnwage c exper tenure
```

The results of this regression model are shown in Table 4.4.

To conduct the omitted variable test we now need to click on **View/Coefficient Diagnostics/Omitted variables-Likelihood ratio** and type in the name of the variable (*educ*) we want to check. The results of this test are shown in Table 4.5.

We see from these results that the F-statistic is equal to 121.41, which is much greater than the critical value (see also the very small value of the probability limit), suggesting that the variable *educ* was an omitted variable that plays a very important role in the determination of the log of the wage rate.

Table 4.4   Wage equation test results

Dependent variable: LNWAGE
Method: Least Squares
Date: 02/02/04 Time: 11:57
Sample: 1 900
Included observations: 900

Variable	Coefficient	Std. error	t-statistic	Prob.
C	6.697589	0.040722	164.4699	0.0000
EXPER	−0.002011	0.003239	−0.621069	0.5347
TENURE	0.015400	0.002792	5.516228	0.0000
R-squared	0.033285		Mean dependent var	6.786164
Adjusted R-squared	0.031130		S.D. dependent var	0.420312
S.E. of regression	0.413718		Akaike info criterion	1.076062
Sum squared resid	153.5327		Schwarz criterion	1.092070
Log likelihood	−481.2280		F-statistic	15.44241
Durbin–Watson stat	1.662338		Prob(F-statistic)	0.000000

Table 4.5   Omitted variable test results

Omitted variable: EDUC

F-statistic	121.4120	Probability	0.000000
Log likelihood ratio	114.3693	Probability	0.000000

Test equation:
Dependent variable: LNWAGE
Method: Least Squares
Date: 02/02/04 Time: 12:02
Sample: 1 900
Included observations: 900

Variable	Coefficient	Std. error	t-statistic	Prob.
C	5.528329	0.112795	49.01237	0.0000
EXPER	0.015358	0.003425	4.483631	0.0000
TENURE	0.012964	0.002631	4.927939	0.0000
EDUC	0.073117	0.006636	11.01871	0.0000
R-squared	0.148647		Mean dependent var	6.786164
Adjusted R-squared	0.145797		S.D. dependent var	0.420312
S.E. of regression	0.388465		Akaike info criterion	0.951208
Sum squared resid	135.2110		Schwarz criterion	0.972552
Log likelihood	−424.0434		F-statistic	52.14758
Durbin–Watson stat	1.750376		Prob(F-statistic)	0.000000

Computer example: commands for Stata

In Stata, to perform a Wald test for coefficient restrictions we use the command:

```
test [restriction]
```

immediately after we run and derive the regression results, where in [restriction] we write the restriction we want to test. The example shown previously in EViews can be performed in Stata as follows (the file with the data is wage.dta).

First we use the command:

```
g lwage = log(wage)
```

to calculate the logarithm of the wage variable. Note that a new variable will be created in Stata called *lwage*.

Then, to obtain the regression results, we use the command:

```
regress lwage educ exper tenure
```

The results are reported below, and are the same as those obtained using EViews:

regress y x Source	SS	df	MS			Number of obs =	900
						F(3, 896) =	52.15
Model	23.3080086	3	7.86933619			Prob > F =	0.0000
Residual	135.21098	892	.150905112			R-squared =	0.1486
						Adj R-squared =	0.1458
Total	158.818989	899	.176661834			Root MSE =	0.38847

lwage	Coef.	Std. err.	t	P > |t|	[95% Conf. interval]	
educ	.0731166	.0066357	11.02	0.000	.0600933	.0861399
exper	.0153578	.0034253	4.48	0.033	.0086353	.0220804
tenure	.129641	.0026307	4.93	0.000	.007807	.0181272
_cons	5.528329	.1127946	49.01	0.000	5.306957	5.749702

To test for the coefficient restrictions $c(3) = c(4)$ in Stata, the restriction is written using the names of the relevant variables. Since we want to test whether the coefficient of *exper* is the same as that of *tenure*, we type the following command:

```
test  exper = tenure
```

The results are given below:

```
. test exper = tenure (1) exper - tenure = 0
       f(1,  896) =  0.25
          Prob > F =  0.6181
```

We see that the results are identical to the those obtained previously using EViews. Similarly, for the redundant variable test, if we want to test whether *educ* is redundant the restriction is:

```
test educ = 0
```

and we get the following results:

```
. test educ = 0
(1)  educ - 0
       F(1,  896) =  121.41
          Prob > F =    0.0000
```

The omitted variable test cannot be conducted in Stata.

Questions and exercises

Questions

1 Derive the OLS solutions for $\hat{\beta}$ for the k explanatory variables case using matrix algebra.

2 Prove that the OLS estimates for the k explanatory variables case are BLU estimators.

3 Show how one can test for constant returns to scale for the following Cobb–Douglas type production function:

$$Q = AL^a K^\beta$$

where Q is output, L denotes labour units, K is capital and A is an exogenous technology parameter.

4 Describe the steps involved in performing the Wald test for linear restrictions.

5 Write down a regression equation and show how you can test whether one of the explanatory variables is redundant.

Exercise 4.1

The file health.xls contains data for the following variables: *birth_weight* = the weight of infants after birth; when low this can put an infant at risk of illness; *cig* = number of cigarettes the mother was smoking during pregnancy; and *fam_inc* = the income of the family; the higher the family income the better the access to prenatal care for the family in general. We would expect that the latter two variables should affect *birth_weight*.

(a) Run a regression that includes both variables and explain the signs of the coefficients.

(b) Estimate a regression that includes only *fam_inc*, and comment on your results.

(c) Estimate a regression that includes only *cig* and comment on your results.

(d) Present all three regressions summarized in a table and comment on your results, especially by comparing the changes in the estimated effects and the R^2 of the three different models. What does the F statistic suggest about the joint significance of the explanatory variables in the multiple regression case?

(e) Test the hypothesis that the effect of *cig* is two times greater than the respective effect of *fam_inc*, using the Wald test.

Exercise 4.2

Use the data from the file wage.wf1 and estimate an equation that includes as determinants of the logarithm of the wage rate the variables, *educ*, *exper* and *tenure*.

(a) Comment on your results.

(b) Conduct a test of whether another year of general workforce experience (captured by *exper*) has the same effect on log (wage) as another year of education (captured by *educ*). State clearly your null and alternative hypotheses and your restricted and unrestricted models. Use the Wald test to check for that hypothesis.

(c) Conduct a redundant variable test for the explanatory variable *exper*. Comment on your results.

(d) Estimate a model with *exper* and *educ* only and then conduct an omitted variable test for *tenure* in the model. Comment on your results.

Exercise 4.3

Use the data in the file money_uk.wf1 to estimate the parameters α, β and γ in the equation below:

$$\ln(M/P)_t = a + \beta \ln Y_t + \gamma \ln R_t + u_t$$

(a) Briefly outline the theory behind the aggregate demand for money. Relate your discussion to the specification of the equation given above. In particular, explain first the meaning of the dependent variable and then the interpretation of β and γ.

(b) Perform appropriate tests of significance on the estimated parameters to investigate each of the following propositions: (i) that the demand for money increases with the level of real income; (ii) the demand for money is income-elastic; and (iii) the demand for money is inversely related to the rate of interest.

Exercise 4.4

The file Cobb_Douglas_us.wf1 contains data for output (Y), labour (L) and stock of capital (K) for the United States. Estimate a Cobb–Douglas type regression equation and check for constant returns to scale using the Wald test.

Part

III Violating the Assumptions of the CLRM

5 Multicollinearity

CHAPTER CONTENTS

LEARNING OBJECTIVES

After studying this chapter you should be able to:

1. Recognize the problem of multicollinearity in the CLRM.
2. Distinguish between perfect and imperfect multicollinearity.
3. Understand and appreciate the consequences of perfect and imperfect multicol-linearity for OLS estimates.
4. Detect problematic multicollinearity using econometric software.
5. Find ways of resolving problematic multicollinearity.

Introduction

Assumption 8 of the CLRM (see page 37) requires that there are no exact linear relationships among the sample values of the explanatory variables. This requirement can also be stated as the absence of perfect multicollinearity. This chapter explains how the existence of perfect multicollinearity means that the OLS method cannot provide estimates for population parameters. It also examines the more common and realistic case of imperfect multicollinearity and its effects on OLS estimators. Finally, possible ways of detecting problematic multicollinearity are discussed and ways of resolving these problems are suggested.

Perfect multicollinearity

To understand multicollinearity, consider the following model:

$$Y = \beta_1 + \beta_2 X_2 + \beta_3 X_3 + u \tag{5.1}$$

where hypothetical sample values for X_2 and X_3 are given below:

$$
\begin{array}{lcccccc}
X_2': & 1 & 2 & 3 & 4 & 5 & 6 \\
X_3': & 2 & 4 & 6 & 8 & 10 & 12
\end{array}
$$

From this we can easily observe that $X_3 = 2X_2$. Therefore, while Equation (5.1) seems to contain two distinct explanatory variables (X_2 and X_3), in fact the information provided by X_3 is not distinct from that of X_2. This is because, as we have seen, X_3 is an exact linear function of X_2. When this situation occurs, X_2 and X_3 are said to be linearly dependent, which implies that X_2 and X_3 are perfectly collinear. More formally, two variables X_2 and X_3 are linearly dependent if one variable can be expressed as a linear function of the other. When this occurs the equation:

$$\delta_1 X_2 + \delta_2 X_3 = 0 \tag{5.2}$$

can be satisfied for non-zero values of both δ_1 and δ_2. In our example we have: $X_3 = 2X_2$, therefore $(-2)X_2 + (1)X_3 = 0$, so $\delta_1 = -2$ and $\delta_2 = 1$. Obviously, if the only solution in Equation (5.2) is $\delta_1 = \delta_2 = 0$ (usually called the trivial solution) then X_2 and X_3 are linearly independent. The absence of perfect multicollinearity requires that does not hold.

Equation (5.2) where there are more than two explanatory variables (let's take five), linear dependence means that one variable can be expressed as an exact linear function of one or more, or even all, of the other variables. So this time the expression:

$$\delta_1 X_1 + \delta_2 X_2 + \delta_3 X_3 + \delta_4 X_4 + \delta_5 X_5 = 0 \tag{5.3}$$

can be satisfied with at least two non-zero coefficients.

This concept can be understood better by using the dummy variable trap. Take, for example, X_1 to be the intercept (so $X_1 = 1$), and X_2, X_3, X_4 and X_5 to be seasonal dummies for quarterly time series data (that is, X_2 takes the value of 1 for the first quarter, 0 otherwise; X_3 takes the value of 1 for the second quarter, 0 otherwise and so on). Then in this case $X_2 + X_3 + X_4 + X_5 = 1$; and because $X_1 = 1$ then $X_1 = X_2 + X_3 + X_4 + X_5$. So, the solution is $\delta_1 = 1$, $\delta_2 = -1$, $\delta_3 = -1$, $\delta_4 = -1$, and $\delta_5 = -1$, and this set of variables is linearly dependent.

Consequences of perfect multicollinearity

It is fairly easy to show that under conditions of perfect multicollinearity, the OLS estimators are not unique. Consider, for example, the model:

$$Y = \beta_1 + \beta_2 X_2 + \beta_3 X_3 + u_t \tag{5.4}$$

where $X_3 = \delta_1 + \delta_2 X_2$; and δ_1 and δ_2 are known constants. Substituting this into Equation (5.4) gives:

$$\begin{aligned} Y &= \beta_1 + \beta_2 X_2 + \beta_3 (\delta_1 + \delta_2 X_2) + u \\ &= (\beta_1 + \beta_3 \delta_1) + (\beta_2 + \beta_3 \delta_2) X_2 + u \\ &= \vartheta_1 + \vartheta_2 X_2 + \varepsilon \end{aligned} \tag{5.5}$$

where, of course, $\vartheta_1 = (\beta_1 + \beta_3 \delta_1)$ and $\vartheta_2 = (\beta_2 + \beta_3 \delta_2)$.

What we can therefore estimate from our sample data are the coefficients ϑ_1 and ϑ_2. However, no matter how good the estimates of ϑ_1 and ϑ_2 are, we shall never be able to obtain unique estimates of β_1, β_2 and β_3. To obtain these we would have to solve the following equations:

$$\hat{\vartheta}_1 = \hat{\beta}_1 + \hat{\beta}_3 \delta_1$$

$$\hat{\vartheta}_2 = \hat{\beta}_2 + \hat{\beta}_3 \delta_2$$

However, this is a system of two equations and three unknowns: $\hat{\beta}_1$, $\hat{\beta}_2$ and $\hat{\beta}_3$. Unfortunately, as in any system that has more variables than equations, this has an infinite number of solutions. For example, select an arbitrary value for $\hat{\beta}_3$, let's say k. Then for $\hat{\beta}_3 = k$ we can find $\hat{\beta}_1$ and $\hat{\beta}_2$ as:

$$\hat{\beta}_1 = \hat{\vartheta}_1 - \delta_1 k$$

$$\hat{\beta}_2 = \hat{\vartheta}_2 - \delta_2 k$$

Since there are infinite values that can be used for k, there are an infinite number of solutions for $\hat{\beta}_1$, $\hat{\beta}_2$ and $\hat{\beta}_3$. So, under perfect multicollinearity, no method can provide us with unique estimates for population parameters. In terms of matrix notation, and for the more general case if one of the columns of matrix $\mathbf{X}$ is an exact linear function of one or more of the other columns, the matrix $\mathbf{X'X}$ is singular, which implies that its determinant is zero ($|\mathbf{X'X}| = 0$). Since the OLS estimators are given by:

$$\hat{\beta} = (\mathbf{X'X})^{-1} \mathbf{X'Y}$$

we need the inverse matrix of $X'X$, which is calculated by the expression:

$$(X'X)^{-1} = \frac{1}{|X'X|}[\mathbf{adj}(X'X)]$$

and because $|X'X| = 0$ then it cannot be inverted.

Another way of showing this is by trying to evaluate the expression for the least squares estimator. From Equation (4.13):

$$\hat{\beta}_2 = \frac{Cov(X_2, Y)Var(X_3) - Cov(X_3, Y)Cov(X_2, X_3)}{Var(X_2)Var(X_3) - [Cov(X_2, X_3)]^2}$$

substituting $X_3 = \delta_1 + \delta_2 X_2$:

$$\hat{\beta}_2 = \frac{Cov(X_2, Y)Var(\delta_1 + \delta_2 X_2) - Cov(\delta_1 + \delta_2 X_2, Y)Cov(X_2, \delta_1 + \delta_2 X_2)}{Var(X_2)Var(\delta_1 + \delta_2 X_2) - [Cov(X_2, \delta_1 + \delta_2 X_2)]^2}$$

dropping the additive δ_1 term:

$$\hat{\beta}_2 = \frac{Cov(X_2, Y)Var(\delta_2 X_2) - Cov(\delta_2 X_2, Y)Cov(X_2, \delta_2 X_2)}{Var(X_2)Var(\delta_2 X_2) - [Cov(X_2, \delta_2 X_2)]^2}$$

taking out of the *Var* and *Cov* the term δ_2:

$$\hat{\beta}_2 = \frac{Cov(X_2, Y)\delta_2^2 Var(X_2) - \delta_2 Cov(X_2, Y)\delta_2 Cov(X_2, X_2)}{Var(X_2)\delta_2^2 Var(X_2) - [\delta_2 Cov(X_2, X_2)]^2}$$

and using the fact that $Cov(X_2, X_2) = Var(X_2)$:

$$\hat{\beta}_2 = \frac{\delta_2^2 Cov(X_2, Y)Var(X_2) - \delta_2^2 Cov(X_2, Y)Var(X_2)}{\delta_2^2 Var(X_2)^2 - \delta_2^2 Var(X_2)^2} = \frac{0}{0}$$

which means that the regression coefficient is indeterminate. So we have seen that the consequences of perfect multicollinearity are extremely serious. However, perfect multicollinearity seldom arises with actual data. The occurrence of perfect multicollinearity often results from correctable mistakes, such as the dummy variable trap presented above, or including variables as $\ln X$ and $\ln X^2$ in the same equation. The more relevant question and the real problem is how to deal with the more common case of imperfect multicollinearity, examined in the next section.

Imperfect multicollinearity

Imperfect multicollinearity exists when the explanatory variables in an equation are correlated, but this correlation is less than perfect. Imperfect multicollinearity can be expressed as follows: when the relationship between the two explanatory variables in Equation (5.4), for example, is $X_3 = X_2 + v$ (where v is a random variable that can be viewed as the 'error' in the exact linear relationship among the two variables), then if v has non-zero values we can obtain OLS estimates. On a practical note, in reality every multiple regression equation will contain some degree of correlation among its explanatory variables. For example, time series data frequently contain a common upward time trend that causes variables of this kind to be highly correlated. The problem is to identify whether the degree of multicollinearity observed in one relationship is high enough to create problems. Before discussing that we need to examine the effects of imperfect multicollinearity in the OLS estimators.

Consequences of imperfect multicollinearity

In general, when imperfect multicollinearity exists among two or more explanatory variables, not only are we able to obtain OLS estimates but these will also be the best (BLUE). However, the BLUEness of these should be examined in a more detailed way. Implicit in the BLUE property is the efficiency of the OLS coefficients. As we shall show later, while OLS estimators are those with the smallest possible variance of all linear unbiased estimators, imperfect multicollinearity affects the attainable values of these variances and therefore also estimation precision. Using the matrix solution again, imperfect multicollinearity implies that one column of the $\mathbf{X}$ matrix is now an approximate linear function of one or more of the others. Therefore, matrix $|\mathbf{X}'\mathbf{X}|$ will be close to singularity, which again implies that its determinant will be close to zero. As stated earlier, when forming the inverse $(\mathbf{X}'\mathbf{X})^{-1}$ we multiply by the reciprocal of $|\mathbf{X}'\mathbf{X}|$, which means that the elements (and particularly the diagonal elements) of $(\mathbf{X}'\mathbf{X})^{-1}$ will be large. Because the variance of $\hat{\beta}$ is given by:

$$var(\hat{\beta}) = \sigma^2 (\mathbf{X}'\mathbf{X})^{-1} \qquad (5.6)$$

the variances, and consequently the standard errors, of the OLS estimators will tend to be large when there is a relatively high degree of multicollinearity. In other words, while OLS provides linear unbiased estimators with the minimum variance property, these variances are often substantially larger than those obtained in the absence of multicollinearity.

To explain this in more detail, consider the expression that gives the variance of the partial slope of variable X_j which is given by (in the case of two explanatory variables):

$$var(\hat{\beta}_2) = \frac{\sigma^2}{\sum (X_2 - \bar{X}_2)^2 (1 - r^2)} \qquad (5.7)$$

$$var(\hat{\beta}_3) = \frac{\sigma^2}{\sum (X_3 - \bar{X}_3)^2 (1 - r^2)} \qquad (5.8)$$

where r^2 is the square of the sample correlation coefficient between X_2 and X_3. Other things being equal, a rise in r (which means a higher degree of multicollinearity) will lead to an increase in the variances and therefore also to an increase in the standard errors of the OLS estimators.

Extending this to more than two explanatory variables, the variance of β_j will be given by:

$$var(\hat{\beta}_j) = \frac{\sigma^2}{\sum (X_j - \bar{X}_j)^2 (1 - R_j^2)} \qquad (5.9)$$

where R_j^2 is the coefficient of determination from the auxiliary regression of X_j on all other explanatory variables in the original equation. The expression can be rewritten as:

$$var(\hat{\beta}_j) = \frac{\sigma^2}{\sum(X_j - \bar{X}_j)^2} \frac{1}{(1 - R_j^2)} \qquad (5.10)$$

The second term in this expression is called the variance inflation factor (VIF) for X_j:

$$VIF_j = \frac{1}{(1 - R_j^2)}$$

It is called the variance inflation factor because high degrees of intercorrelation among the Xs will result in a high value of R_j^2, which will inflate the variance of $\hat{\beta}_j$. If $R_j^2 = 0$ then $VIF = 1$ (which is its lowest value). As R_j^2 rises, VIF_j rises at an increasing rate, approaching infinity in the case of perfect multicollinearity ($R_j^2 = 1$). The table below presents various values for R_j^2 and the corresponding VIF_j.

R_j^2	VIF_j
0	1
0.5	2
0.8	5
0.9	10
0.95	20
0.975	40
0.99	100
0.995	200
0.999	1000

VIF values exceeding 10 are generally viewed as evidence of the existence of problematic multicollinearity, which will be discussed below. From the table we can see that this occurs when $R^2 > 0.9$. In conclusion, imperfect multicollinearity can substantially diminish the precision with which the OLS estimators are obtained. This obviously has more negative effects on the estimated coefficients. One important consequence is that large standard errors will lead to confidence intervals for the $\hat{\beta}_j$ parameters calculated by:

$$\hat{\beta}_j \pm t_{a,n-k} s_{\hat{\beta}_j}$$

being very wide, thereby increasing uncertainty about the true parameter values.

Another consequence is related to the statistical inference of the OLS estimates. Since the t-ratio is given by $t = \hat{\beta}_j/s_{\hat{\beta}_j}$, the inflated variance associated with multicollinearity raises the denominator of this statistic and causes its value to fall. Therefore we might have t-statistics that suggest the insignificance of the coefficients but this is only a result of multicollinearity. Note here that the existence of multicollinearity does not necessarily mean small t-stats. This can be because the variance is also affected by the variance of X_j (presented by writing $\sum(X_j - \bar{X}_j)^2$) and the residual's variance (σ^2). Multicollinearity affects not only the variances of the OLS estimators, but also the covariances. Thus, the possibility of sign reversal arises. Also, when there is severe multicollinearity, the addition or deletion of just a few sample observations can change the estimated coefficient substantially, causing 'unstable' OLS estimators. The consequences of imperfect multicollinearity can be summarized as follows:

1 Estimates of the OLS coefficients may be imprecise in the sense that large standard errors lead to wide confidence intervals.

2 Affected coefficients may fail to attain statistical significance because of low t-statistics, which may lead us mistakenly to drop an influential variable from a regression model.

3 The signs of the estimated coefficients can be the opposite of those expected.

4 The addition or deletion of a few observations may result in substantial changes in the estimated coefficients.

Detecting problematic multicollinearity

Simple correlation coefficient

Multicollinearity is caused by intercorrelations between the explanatory variables. Therefore, the most logical way to detect multicollinearity problems would appear to be through the correlation coefficient for these two variables. When an equation contains only two explanatory variables, the simple correlation coefficient is an adequate measure for detecting multicollinearity. If the value of the correlation coefficient is large then problems from multicollinearity might emerge. The problem here is to define what value can be considered as large, and most researchers consider the value of 0.9 as the threshold beyond which problems are likely to occur. This can be understood from the VIF for a value of $r = 0.9$ as well.

R^2 from auxiliary regressions

In the case where we have more than two variables, the use of the simple correlation coefficient to detect bivariate correlations, and therefore problematic multicollinearity, is highly unreliable, because an exact linear dependency can occur among three or more variables simultaneously. In these cases, we use auxiliary regressions. Candidates for dependent variables in auxiliary regressions are those displaying the symptoms of problematic multicollinearity discussed above. If a near-linear dependency exists, the auxiliary regression will display a small equation standard error, a large R^2 and a statistically significant t-value for the overall significance of the regressors.

Computer examples

Example 1: induced multicollinearity

The file multicol.wf1 contains data for three different variables, namely Y, $X2$ and $X3$, where $X2$ and $X3$ are constructed to be highly collinear. The correlation matrix of the three variables can be obtained from EViews by opening all three variables together in a group, by clicking on **Quick/Group Statistics/Correlations**. EViews requires us to define the series list that we want to include in the group and we type:

```
Y X2 X3
```

and then click **OK**. The results will be as shown in Table 5.1.

Table 5.1   Correlation matrix

	Y	$X2$	$X3$
Y	1	0.8573686	0.857437
$X2$	0.8573686	1	0.999995
$X3$	0.8574376	0.999995	1

The results are, of course, symmetrical, while the diagonal elements are equal to 1 because they are correlation coefficients of the same series. We can see that Y is highly positively correlated with both $X2$ and $X3$, and that $X2$ and $X3$ are nearly the same (the correlation coefficient is equal to 0.999995; that is very close to 1). From this we obviously suspect that there is a strong possibility of the negative effects of multicollinearity.

Estimate a regression with both explanatory variables by typing in the EViews command line:

```
ls y c x2 x3
```

We get the results shown in Table 5.2. Here we see that the effect of $X2$ on Y is negative and the effect of $X3$ is positive, while both variables appear to be insignificant. This latter result is strange, considering that both variables are highly correlated with Y, as we saw above. However, estimating the model by including only $X2$, either by typing on the EViews command line:

```
ls y c x2
```

or by clicking on the **Estimate** button of the **Equation Results** window and respecifying the equation by excluding/deleting the $X3$ variable, we get the results shown in Table 5.3. This time, we see that $X2$ is positive and statistically significant (with a t-statistic of 7.98).

Re-estimating the model, this time including only $X3$, we get the results shown in Table 5.4. This time, we see that $X3$ is highly significant and positive.

Table 5.2 Regression results (full model)

Dependent variable: Y
Method: least squares
Date: 02/17/04 Time: 01:53
Sample: 1 25
Included observations: 25

Variable	Coefficient	Std. error	t-statistic	Prob.
C	35.86766	19.38717	1.850073	0.0778
X2	−6.326498	33.75096	−0.187446	0.8530
X3	1.789761	8.438325	0.212099	0.8340
R-squared	0.735622	Mean dependent var		169.3680
Adjusted R-squared	0.711587	S.D. dependent var		79.05857
S.E. of regression	42.45768	Akaike info criterion		10.44706
Sum squared resid	39658.40	Schwarz criterion		10.59332
Log likelihood	−127.5882	F-statistic		30.60702
Durbin–Watson stat	2.875574	Prob(F-statistic)		0.000000

Table 5.3 Regression results (omitting X3)

Dependent variable: Y
Method: least squares
Date: 02/17/04 Time: 01:56
Sample: 1 25
Included observations: 25

Variable	Coefficient	Std. error	t-statistic	Prob.
C	36.71861	18.56953	1.977358	0.0601
X2	0.832012	0.104149	7.988678	0.0000
R-squared	0.735081	Mean dependent var		169.3680
Adjusted R-squared	0.723563	S.D. dependent var		79.05857
S.E. of regression	41.56686	Akaike info criterion		10.36910
Sum squared resid	39739.49	Schwarz criterion		10.46661
Log likelihood	−127.6138	F-statistic		63.81897
Durbin–Watson stat	2.921548	Prob(F-statistic)		0.000000

Table 5.4 Regression results (omitting X2)

Dependent variable: Y
Method: least squares
Date: 02/17/04 Time: 01:58
Sample: 1 25
Included observations: 25

Variable	Coefficient	Std. error	t-statistic	Prob.
C	36.60968	18.57637	1.970766	0.0609
X3	0.208034	0.026033	7.991106	0.0000
R-squared	0.735199	Mean dependent var		169.3680
Adjusted R-squared	0.723686	S.D. dependent var		79.05857
S.E. of regression	41.55758	Akaike info criterion		10.36866
Sum squared resid	39721.74	Schwarz criterion		10.46617
Log likelihood	−127.6082	F-statistic		63.85778
Durbin–Watson stat	2.916396	Prob(F-statistic)		0.000000

Table 5.5   Auxiliary regression results (regressing $X2$ to $X3$)

Dependent variable: $X2$
Method: least squares
Date: 02/17/04   Time: 02:03
Sample: 1 25
Included observations: 25

Variable	Coefficient	Std. error	t-statistic	Prob.
C	−0.117288	0.117251	−1.000310	0.3276
X3	0.250016	0.000164	**1521.542**	0.0000
R-squared	**0.999990**	Mean dependent var		159.4320
Adjusted R-squared	0.999990	S.D. dependent var		81.46795
S.E. of regression	0.262305	Akaike info criterion		0.237999
Sum squared resid	1.582488	Schwarz criterion		0.335509
Log likelihood	− 0.974992	F-statistic		2315090.
Durbin–Watson stat	2.082420	Prob(F-statistic)		0.000000

Finally, running an auxiliary regression of $X2$ on a constant and $X3$ yields the results shown in Table 5.5. Note that the value of the t-statistic is extremely high (1521.542!) while R^2 is nearly 1.

The conclusions from this analysis can be summarized as follows:

1 The correlation among the explanatory variables is very high, suggesting that multicollinearity is present and that it might be serious. However, as mentioned above, looking at the correlation coefficients of the explanatory variables alone is not enough to detect multicollinearity.

2 Standard errors or t-ratios of the estimated coefficients changed from estimation to estimation, suggesting that the problem of multicollinearity in this case was serious.

3 The stability of the estimated coefficients was also problematic, with negative and positive coefficients being estimated for the same variable in two alternative specifications.

4 R^2 from auxiliary regressions is substantially high, suggesting that multicollinearity exists and that it has been an unavoidable effect on our estimations.

Example 2: with the use of real economic data

Let us examine the problem of multicollinearity again, but this time using real economic data. The file imports_uk.wf1 contains quarterly data for four different variables for the UK economy: namely, imports (*IMP*); gross domestic product (*GDP*), the consumer price index (*CPI*); and the producer price index (*PPI*).

The correlation matrix of the three variables can be obtained from EViews by opening all the variables together, by clicking on **Quick/Group Statistics/Correlations**. EViews asks us to define the series list we want to include in the group and we type in:

```
imp gdp cpi ppi
```

Table 5.6   Correlation matrix

	IMP	GDP	CPI	PPI
IMP	1.000000	0.979713	0.916331	0.883530
GDP	0.979713	1.000000	0.910961	0.899851
CPI	0.916331	0.910961	1.000000	**0.981983**
PPI	0.883530	0.899851	0.981983	1.000000

Table 5.7   First model regression results (including only *CPI*)

Dependent variable: LOG(IMP)
Method: least squares
Date: 02/17/04 Time: 02:16
Sample: 1990:1 1998:2
Included observations: 34

Variable	Coefficient	Std. error	t-statistic	Prob.
C	0.631870	0.344368	1.834867	0.0761
LOG(GDP)	1.926936	0.168856	11.41172	0.0000
LOG(CPI)	0.274276	0.137400	1.996179	0.0548

R-squared	0.966057	Mean dependent var	10.81363
Adjusted R-squared	0.963867	S.D. dependent var	0.138427
S.E. of regression	0.026313	Akaike info criterion	−4.353390
Sum squared resid	0.021464	Schwarz criterion	−4.218711
Log likelihood	77.00763	F-statistic	441.1430
Durbin–Watson stat	0.475694	Prob(F-statistic)	0.000000

and then click **OK**. The results are shown in Table 5.6. From the correlation matrix we can see that, in general, the correlations among the variables are very high, but the highest correlations are between *CPI* and *PPI*, (0.98), as expected.

Estimating a regression with the logarithm of imports as the dependent variable and the logarithms of *GDP* and *CPI* only as explanatory variables by typing in the EViews command line:

```
ls log(imp) c log(gdp) log(cpi)
```

we get the results shown in Table 5.7. The R^2 of this regression is very high, and both variables appear to be positive, with the log(*GDP*) also being highly significant. The log(*CPI*) is only marginally significant.

However, estimating the model also including the logarithm of *PPI*, either by typing on the EViews command line:

```
ls log(imp) c log(gdp) log(cpi) log(ppi)
```

or by clicking on the **Estimate** button of the **Equation Results** window and respecifying the equation by adding the log(*PPI*) variable to the list of variables, we get the results shown in Table 5.8. Now log(*CPI*) is highly significant, while log(*PPI*) (which is highly correlated with log(*CPI*) and therefore should have more or less the same effect on log(*IMP*)) is negative and highly significant. This, of course, is because of the inclusion of both price indices in the same equation specification, as a result of the problem of multicollinearity.

Table 5.8 Second model regression results (including both *CPI* and *PPI*)

Dependent variable: LOG(IMP)
Method: least squares
Date: 02/17/04 Time: 02:19
Sample: 1990:1 1998:2
Included observations: 34

Variable	Coefficient	Std. error	t-statistic	Prob.
C	0.213906	0.358425	0.596795	0.5551
LOG(GDP)	1.969713	0.156800	12.56198	0.0000
LOG(CPI)	1.025473	0.323427	3.170645	0.0035
LOG(PPI)	−0.770644	0.305218	−2.524894	0.0171

R-squared	0.972006	Mean dependent var	10.81363
Adjusted R-squared	0.969206	S.D. dependent var	0.138427
S.E. of regression	0.024291	Akaike info criterion	−4.487253
Sum squared resid	0.017702	Schwarz criterion	−4.307682
Log likelihood	80.28331	F-statistic	347.2135
Durbin–Watson stat	0.608648	Prob(F-statistic)	0.000000

Table 5.9 Third model regression results (including only *PPI*)

Dependent variable: LOG(IMP)
Method: least squares
Date: 02/17/04 Time: 02:22
Sample: 1990:1 1998:2
Included observations: 34

Variable	Coefficient	Std. error	t-statistic	Prob.
C	0.685704	0.370644	1.850031	0.0739
LOG(GDP)	2.093849	0.172585	12.13228	0.0000
LOG(PPI)	0.119566	0.136062	0.878764	0.3863

R-squared	0.962625	Mean dependent var	10.81363
Adjusted R-squared	0.960213	S.D. dependent var	0.138427
S.E. of regression	0.027612	Akaike info criterion	−4.257071
Sum squared resid	0.023634	Schwarz criterion	−4.122392
Log likelihood	75.37021	F-statistic	399.2113
Durbin–Watson stat	0.448237	Prob(F-statistic)	0.000000

Estimating the equation this time without log(*CPI*) but with log(*PPI*) we get the results in Table 5.9, which show that log(*PPI*) is positive and insignificant. It is clear that the significance of log(*PPI*) in the specification above was a result of the linear relationship that connects the two price variables.

The conclusions from this analysis are similar to the case of the collinear data set in Example 1 above, and can be summarized as follows:

1 The correlation among the explanatory variables was very high.

2 Standard errors or *t*-ratios of the estimated coefficients changed from estimation to estimation.

3 The stability of the estimated coefficients was also quite problematic, with negative and positive coefficients being estimated for the same variable in alternative specifications.

In this case it is clear that multicollinearity is present, and that it is also serious, because we included two price variables that are quite strongly correlated. We leave it as an exercise for the reader to check the presence and the seriousness of multicollinearity with only the inclusion of log(*GDP*) and log(*CPI*) as explanatory variables (see Exercise 5.1 below).

Questions and exercises

Questions

1 Define multicollinearity and explain its consequences in simple OLS estimates.
2 In the following model:

$$Y = \beta_1 + \beta_2 X_2 + \beta_3 X_3 + \beta_4 X_4 + u_t$$

assume that X_4 is a perfect linear combination of X_2. Show that in this case it is impossible to obtain OLS estimates.

3 From Chapter 4 we know that $\hat{\beta} = (X'X)^{-1}(X'Y)$. What happens to $\hat{\beta}$ when there is perfect collinearity among the Xs? How would you know if perfect collinearity exists?

4 Explain what the VIF is and its use.

5 Show how to detect possible multicollinearity in a regression model.

Exercise 5.1

The file imports_uk.wf1 contains quarterly data for imports (*imp*), gross domestic product (*gdp*) and the consumer price index (*cpi*) for the USA. Use these data to estimate the following model:

$$\ln imp_t = \beta_1 + \beta_2 \ln gdp_t + \beta_3 \ln cpi_t + u_t$$

Check whether there is multicollinearity in the data. Calculate the correlation matrix of the variables and comment regarding the possibility of multicollinearity. Also, run the following additional regressions:

$$\ln imp_t = \beta_1 + \beta_2 \ln gdp_t + u_t$$
$$\ln imp_t = \beta_1 + \beta_2 \ln cpi_t + u_t$$
$$\ln gdp_t = \beta_1 + \beta_2 \ln cpi_t + u_t$$

What can you conclude about the nature of multicollinearity from these results?

Exercise 5.2

The file imports_uk_y.wf1 contains yearly observations of the variables mentioned in Exercise 5.1. Repeat Exercise 5.1 using the yearly data. Do your results change?

Exercise 5.3

Use the data in the file money_uk02.wf1 to estimate the parameters α, β and γ, in the equation below:

$$\ln(M/P)_t = a + \beta \ln Y_t + \gamma \ln R_{1t} + u_t$$

where R_{1t} is the 3-month treasury bill rate. For the rest of the variables the usual notation applies.

(a) Use as an additional variable in the above equation R_{2t}, which is the dollar interest rate.

(b) Do you expect to find multicollinearity? Why?

(c) Calculate the correlation matrix of all the variables. Which correlation coefficient is the largest?

(d) Calculate auxiliary regressions and conclude whether the degree of multicollinearity in (a) is serious or not.

6 Heteroskedasticity

CHAPTER CONTENTS

LEARNING OBJECTIVES

After studying this chapter you should be able to:

1. Understand the meaning of heteroskedasticity and homoskedasticity through examples.
2. Understand the consequences of heteroskedasticity for OLS estimates.
3. Detect heteroskedasticity through graph inspection.
4. Detect heteroskedasticity using formal econometric tests.
5. Distinguish among the wide range of available tests for detecting heteroskedasticity.
6. Perform heteroskedasticity tests using econometric software.
7. Resolve heteroskedasticity using econometric software.

Introduction: what is heteroskedasticity?

A good start might be made by first defining the words homoskedasticity and heteroskedasticity. Some authors spell the former homoscedasticity, but McCulloch (1985) appears to have settled this controversy in favour of homoskedasticity, based on the fact that the word has a Greek origin.

Both words can be split into two parts, having as a first part the Greek words *homo* (meaning same or equal) or *hetero* (meaning different or unequal), and as the second part the Greek word *skedasmos* (meaning spread or scatter). So, homoskedasticity means equal spread, and heteroskedasticity means unequal spread. In econometrics the measure we usually use for spread is the variance, and therefore heteroskedasticity deals with unequal variances.

Recalling the assumptions of the classical linear regression model presented in Chapters 4 and 5, assumption 5 was that the disturbances should have a constant (equal) variance independent of i, given in mathematical form by the following equation:*

$$var(u_i) = \sigma^2 \tag{6.1}$$

Therefore, having an equal variance means that the disturbances are homoskedastic.

However, it is quite common in regression analysis for this assumption to be violated. (In general heteroskedasticity is more likely to occur within a cross-sectional framework, although this does not mean that heteroskedasticity in time series models is impossible.) In such cases we say that the homoskedasticity assumption is violated, and that the variance of the error terms depends on which observation is being discussed, that is:

$$var(u_i) = \sigma_i^2 \tag{6.2}$$

Note that the only difference between Equations (6.1) and (6.2) is the subscript i attached to the σ^2, which means that the variance can change for every different observation in the sample $i = 1, 2, 3, \ldots, n$.

In order to make this clearer, it is useful to go back to the simple two-variable regression model of the form:

$$Y_i = a + \beta X_i + u_i \tag{6.3}$$

Consider a scatter plot with a population regression line of the form given in Figure 6.1 and compare it with Figure 6.2. Points X_1, X_2 and X_3 in Figure 6.1, although referring to different values of X ($X_1 < X_2 < X_3$), are concentrated closely around

---

*Because heteroskedasticity is often analysed in a pure cross-section setting, in most of this chapter we will index our variables by i rather than t.

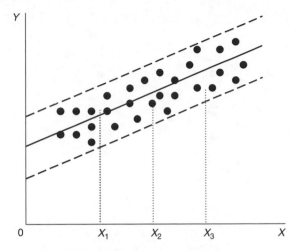

Figure 6.1   Data with a constant variance

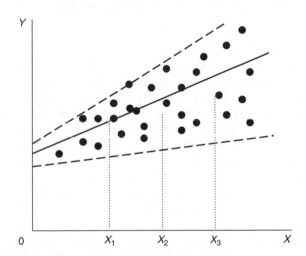

Figure 6.2   An example of heteroskedasticity with increasing variance

the regression line with an equal spread above and below (that is equal spread, or homoskedastic).

On the other hand, points X_1, X_2 and X_3 in Figure 6.2 again refer to different values of X, but this time, it is clear that the higher the value of X, the higher is the spread around the line. In this case the spread is unequal for each X_i (shown by the dashed lines above and below the regression line), and therefore we have heteroskedasticity. It is now clear that in Figure 6.3 we have the opposite case (for lower X_i the variance is higher).

An example of the first case of heteroskedasticity (shown in Figure 6.2) can be derived from looking at income and consumption patterns. People with low levels of income do not have much flexibility in spending their money. A large proportion of their income will be spent on buying food, clothing and transportation; so, at low levels of income,

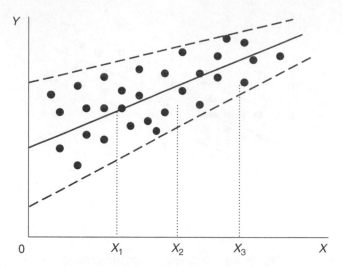

Figure 6.3 An example of heteroskedasticity with falling variance

consumption patterns will not differ much and the spread will be relatively low. On the other hand, rich people have much more choice and flexibility. Some might consume a lot, some might be large savers or investors in the stock market, implying that the average consumption (given by the regression line) can be quite different from the actual consumption. So the spread for high incomes will definitely be higher than that for lower incomes.

The opposite case (such as the one shown in Figure 6.3) can be illustrated by examples such as improvements in data collection techniques (think here of large banks that have sophisticated data processing facilities and therefore are able to calculate customer estimates with fewer errors than smaller banks with no such facilities), or to error-learning models where experience decreases the chances of making large errors (for example, where the Y-variable is score performance on a test and the X-variable the times that individuals have taken the test in the past, or hours of preparation for the test; the larger the X, the smaller the variability in terms of Y will be).

The aims of this chapter are to examine the consequences of heteroskedasticity for OLS estimators, to present tests for detecting heteroskedasticity in econometric models, and to show ways of resolving heteroskedasticity.

Consequences of heteroskedasticity for OLS estimators

A general approach

Consider the classical linear regression model:

$$Y_i = \beta_1 + \beta_2 X_{2i} + \beta_3 X_{3i} + \cdots + \beta_k X_{ki} + u_i \tag{6.4}$$

If the error term u_i in this equation is heteroskedastic, the consequences for the OLS estimators $\hat{\beta}$s (or $\hat{\boldsymbol{\beta}}$) can be summarized as follows:

1 The OLS estimators for the $\hat{\beta}$s are still unbiased and consistent. This is because none of the explanatory variables is correlated with the error term. So, a correctly specified equation that suffers only from the presence of heteroskedasticity will give us values of $\hat{\beta}$ that are relatively good.

2 Heteroskedasticity affects the distribution of the $\hat{\beta}$s increasing the variances of the distributions and therefore making the estimators of the OLS method inefficient (because it violates the minimum variance property). To understand this consider Figure 6.4, which shows the distribution of an estimator $\hat{\beta}$ with and without heteroskedasticity. It is obvious that heteroskedasticity does not cause bias because $\hat{\beta}$ is centred around β (so $E(\hat{\beta}) = \beta$), but widening the distribution makes it no longer efficient.

3 Heteroskedasticity also affects the variances (and therefore the standard errors as well) of the estimated $\hat{\beta}$s. In fact the presence of heteroskedasticity causes the OLS method to underestimate the variances (and standard errors), leading to higher than expected values of t-statistics and F-statistics. Therefore, heteroskedasticity has a wide impact on hypothesis testing: both the t-statistics and the F-statistics are no longer reliable for hypothesis testing because they lead us to reject the null hypothesis too often.

A mathematical approach

In order to observe the effect of heteroskedasticity on the OLS estimators, first the simple regression model will be examined, then the effect of heteroskedasticity in the form of the variance–covariance matrix of the error terms of the multiple regression model

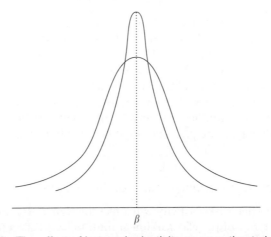

Figure 6.4 The effect of heteroskedasticity on an estimated parameter

will be presented, and finally, using matrix algebra, the effect of heteroskedasticity in a multiple regression framework will be shown.

Effect on the OLS estimators of the simple regression model

For the simple linear regression model – with only one explanatory variable and a constant regressed on Y, like the one analysed in Chapter 3 – it is easy to show that the variance of the slope estimator will be affected by the presence of heteroskedasticity. Equation (3.56) for the variance of the OLS coefficient $\hat{\beta}$ showed that:

$$Var(\hat{\beta}) = \sum \left(\frac{x_i}{\sum x_i^2} \right)^2 \sigma^2$$

$$= \frac{\sum x_i^2 \sigma^2}{\left(\sum x_i^2 \right)^2} = \sigma^2 \frac{1}{\sum x_i^2} \tag{6.5}$$

This applies only when the error terms are homoskedastic, so that the variance of the residuals is constant σ^2. The only difference between Equation (3.56) and the equation presented here is that the subscript i is used instead of t, because this chapter is dealing mainly with models of cross-sectional data. In the case of heteroskedasticity, the variance changes with every individual observation i, and therefore the variance of $\hat{\beta}$ will now be given by:

$$Var(\hat{\beta}) = \sum \left(\frac{x_i}{\sum x_i^2} \right)^2 \sigma_i^2 = \frac{\sum x_i^2 \sigma_i^2}{\left(\sum x_i^2 \right)^2} \tag{6.6}$$

which is clearly different from Equation (6.5). The bias that occurs in the presence of heteroskedasticity can now be explained. If heteroskedasticity is present and the variance of $\hat{\beta}$ is given by the standard OLS formula, Equation (6.5), instead of the correct one, Equation (6.6), then we will be bound to underestimate the true variance and standard error of $\hat{\beta}$. The t-ratios will therefore be falsely high, leading to the erroneous conclusion that an explanatory variable X is statistically significant, whereas its impact on Y is in fact zero. The confidence intervals for β will also be narrower than their correct values, implying a more precise estimate than is in fact statistically justifiable.

Effect on the variance–covariance matrix of the error terms

It is useful to see how heteroskedasticity will affect the form of the variance–covariance matrix of the error terms of the classical linear multiple regression model.

Chapter 4 showed that the variance–covariance matrix of the errors, because of assumptions 5 and 6, looks like:

$$E(\mathbf{uu'}) = \begin{pmatrix} \sigma^2 & 0 & 0 & \ldots & 0 \\ 0 & \sigma^2 & 0 & 0 & 0 \\ 0 & 0 & \sigma^2 & \ldots & 0 \\ \ldots & \ldots & \ldots & & \ldots \\ 0 & 0 & 0 & \ldots & \sigma^2 \end{pmatrix} = \sigma^2 \mathbf{I_n} \tag{6.7}$$

where $\mathbf{I_n}$ is an $n \times n$ identity matrix.

Assumption 5 is no longer valid in the presence of heteroskedasticity, so the variance–covariance matrix of the residuals will be as follows:

$$E(\mathbf{uu'}) = \begin{pmatrix} \sigma_1^2 & 0 & 0 & \ldots & 0 \\ 0 & \sigma_2^2 & 0 & 0 & 0 \\ 0 & 0 & \sigma_3^2 & \ldots & 0 \\ \ldots & \ldots & \ldots & & \ldots \\ 0 & 0 & 0 & \ldots & \sigma_n^2 \end{pmatrix} = \Omega \tag{6.8}$$

Effect on the OLS estimators of the multiple regression model

The variance–covariance matrix of the OLS estimators $\hat{\boldsymbol{\beta}}$ is given by:

$$Cov(\hat{\boldsymbol{\beta}}) = \mathbf{E}[(\hat{\beta} - \beta)(\hat{\beta} - \beta)']$$

$$= E\{[(\mathbf{X'X})^{-1}\mathbf{X'u}][(\mathbf{X'X})^{-1}\mathbf{X'u}]'\}$$

$$= E\{(\mathbf{X'X})^{-1}\mathbf{X'uu'X}(\mathbf{X'X})^{-1}\}^*$$

$$= (\mathbf{X'X})^{-1}\mathbf{X'}E(\mathbf{uu'})\mathbf{X}(\mathbf{X'X})^{-1\dagger}$$

$$= (\mathbf{X'X})^{-1}\mathbf{X'}\Omega\mathbf{X}(\mathbf{X'X})^{-1} \tag{6.9}$$

which is totally different from the classical expression $\sigma^2(\mathbf{X'X})^{-1}$. This is because assumption 5 no longer holds, and Ω denotes the new variance–covariance matrix presented above, whatever form it may happen to take. Therefore, using the classical expression to calculate the variances, standard errors and t-statistics of the estimated $\hat{\beta}$s will lead to the wrong conclusions. The formulae in Equation (6.9) form the basis for what is often called 'robust' inference, that is the derivation of standard errors and t-statistics that are correct even when some of the OLS assumptions are violated; a

---

* This is because $(AB)' = B'A'$.

† This is because, according to assumption 2, the Xs are non-random.

particular form is assumed for the Ω matrix and Equation (6.9) is used to calculate a corrected covariance matrix.

Detecting heteroskedasticity

In general there are two ways of detecting heteroskedasticity. The first, known as the informal way, is by inspection of different graphs, while the second is by applying appropriate tests.

The informal way

In the informal way, and in the two-variable case that we have seen before, heteroskedasticity can easily be detected by simple inspection of the scatter plot. However, this cannot be done in the multiple regression case. In this case useful information about the possible presence of heteroskedasticity can be given by plotting the squared residuals against the dependent variable and/or the explanatory variables.

Gujarati (1978) presents cases in which useful information about heteroskedasticity can be deduced from this kind of graph pattern. The possible patterns are presented in Figures 6.5 to 6.9. In Figure 6.5 there is no systematic pattern between the two variables, which suggests that it is a 'healthy' model, or at least one that does not suffer from heteroskedasticity. In Figure 6.6 there is a clear pattern that suggests heteroskedasticity, in Figure 6.7 there is a clear linear relationship between Y_i (or X_i) and u_i^2, while Figures 6.8 and 6.9 exhibit a quadratic relationship. Knowing the relationship between the two variables can be very useful because it enables the data to be transformed in such a way as to eliminate the heteroskedasticity.

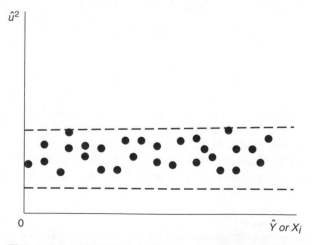

Figure 6.5   A 'healthy' distribution of squared residuals

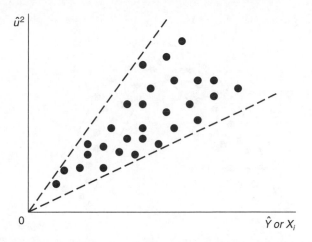

Figure 6.6   An indication of the presence of heteroskedasticity

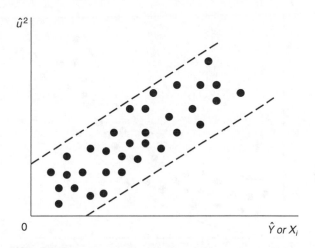

Figure 6.7   Another indication of heteroskedasticity

The Breusch–Pagan LM test

Breusch and Pagan (1979) developed a Lagrange Multiplier (LM) test for heteroskedasticity. In the following model:

$$Y_i = \beta_1 + \beta_2 X_{2i} + \beta_3 X_{3i} + \cdots + \beta_k X_{ki} + u_i \tag{6.10}$$

$var(u_i) = \sigma_i^2$. The Breusch–Pagan test involves the following steps:

Step 1   Run a regression of Equation (6.10) and obtain the residuals $\hat{u}_i$ of this regression equation.

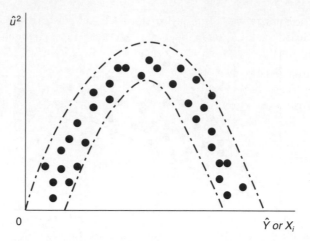

Figure 6.8 A non-linear relationship leading to heteroskedasticity

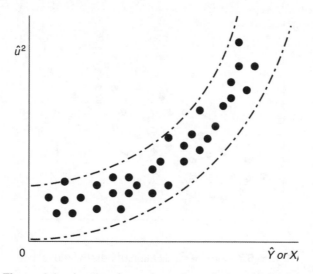

Figure 6.9 Another form of non-linear heteroskedasticity

Step 2 Run the following auxiliary regression:

$$\hat{u}_i^2 = a_1 + a_2 Z_{2i} + a_3 Z_{3i} + \cdots + a_p Z_{pi} + v_i \tag{6.11}$$

where Z_{ki} is a set of variables thought to determine the variance of the error term. (Usually for Z_{ki} the explanatory variables of the original regression equation are used, that is the Xs.)

Step 3 Formulate the null and the alternative hypotheses. The null hypothesis of homoskedasticity is:

$$H_0: \quad a_1 = a_2 = \cdots = a_p = 0 \tag{6.12}$$

while the alternative is that at least one of the as is different from zero and that at least one of the Zs affects the variance of the residuals, which will be different for different t.

Step 4 Compute the $LM = nR^2$ statistic, where n is the number of observations used in order to estimate the auxiliary regression in step 2, and R^2 is the coefficient of determination of this regression. The LM statistic follows the χ^2 distribution with $p - 1$ degrees of freedom.

Step 5 Reject the null and conclude that there is significant evidence of heteroskedasticity when LM-statistical is bigger than the critical value (LM-*stat* $>$ $\chi^2_{p-1,\alpha}$). Alternatively, compute the p-value and reject the null if the p-value is less than the level of significance α (usually $\alpha = 0.05$).

In this – as in all other LM tests that we will examine later – the auxiliary equation makes an explicit assumption about the form of heteroskedasticity that can be expected in the data. There are three more LM tests, which introduce different forms of auxiliary regressions, suggesting different functional forms about the relationship of the squared residuals ($\hat{u}_i^2$, which is a proxy for σ^2 since it is not known) and the explanatory variables.

The Breusch–Pagan test in EViews

The Breusch–Pagan test can be performed in EViews as follows. The regression equation model must first be estimated with OLS using the command:

```
ls y c x1 x2 x3 ... xk
```

where y is the dependent variable and x1 to xk the explanatory variables. Next the *generate* (genr) command is used to obtain the residuals:

```
genr ut=resid
```

Note that it is important to type and execute this command immediately after obtaining the equation results so that the resid vector has the residual of the equation estimated previously. Here *ut* is used for the error terms of this model.

The squared residuals are then calculated as follows:

```
genr utsq=ut^2
```

and the estimate of the auxiliary regression is obtained from the command:

```
ls utsq c z1 z2 z3 ... zp
```

In order to compute the LM-statistic, the calculation $LM = n * R^2$ is performed, where n is the number of observations and R^2 is the coefficient of determination of the auxiliary regression.

Finally, conclusions are drawn from the comparison of LM-critical and LM-statistical.

The Breusch–Pagan LM test in Stata

To perform the Breusch–Pagan test in Stata, the first regression equation model is estimated with OLS, using the command:

```
regress y x1 x2 x3 x4 ... xk
```

where y is the dependent variable and x1 to xk the explanatory variables. The residuals are obtained by using the *predict* command as follows:

```
predict ut , residual
```

where *ut* represents the residuals. The squared residuals are then calculated as follows:

```
g utsq = ut^ 2
```

and the estimate for the auxiliary regression obtained from the command:

```
regress utsq z1 z2 z3 ... zp
```

To compute the LM-statistic, the calculation $LM = n * R^2$ is performed, where n is the number of observations and R^2 is the coefficient of determination of the auxiliary regression.

Finally, conclusions are drawn from the comparison of LM-critical and LM-statistical.

The Glesjer LM test

Glesjer's (1969) test is described below – note that the steps are the same as the Breusch–Pagan test above with the exception of Step 2, which involves a different auxiliary regression equation.

Step 1 Run a regression of Equation (6.10) and obtain the residuals $\hat{u}_i$ of this regression equation.

Step 2 Run the following auxiliary regression:

$$|\hat{u}_i| = a_1 + a_2 Z_{2i} + a_3 Z_{3i} + \cdots + a_p Z_{pi} + v_i \tag{6.13}$$

Step 3 Formulate the null and the alternative hypotheses. The null hypothesis of homoskedasticity is:

$$H_0: \quad a_1 = a_2 = \cdots = a_p = 0 \tag{6.14}$$

while the alternative is that at least one of the *as* is different from zero.

Step 4 Compute the $LM = nR^2$ statistic, where n is the number of observations used in order to estimate the auxiliary regression in step 2, and R^2 is the coefficient of determination of this regression. The *LM*-statistic follows the χ^2 distribution with $p - 1$ degrees of freedom.

Step 5 Reject the null and conclude that there is significant evidence of heteroskedasticity when *LM*-statistical is bigger than the critical value ($LM\text{-}stat > \chi^2_{p-1,\alpha}$). Alternatively, compute the *p*-value and reject the null if the *p*-value is less than the level of significance α (usually $\alpha = 0.05$).

The Glesjer test in EViews

The Glesjer test can be performed in EViews as follows. First the regression equation model is estimated with OLS, using the command:

```
ls y c x1 x2 x3 ... xk
```

where y is the dependent variable and x1 to xk the explanatory variables. The *generate* (genr) command is used to obtain the residuals:

```
genr ut=resid
```

Note that it is important to type and execute this command immediately after obtaining the equation results so that the resid vector has the residual of the equation estimated previously. *ut* is used for the error terms of this model. The absolute value of the residuals is then calculated as follows:

```
genr absut=abs(ut)
```

and the estimate of the auxiliary regression obtained from the command:

```
ls absut c z1 z2 z3 ... zp
```

To compute the *LM*-statistic the calculation $LM = n * R^2$ is performed, where n is the number of observations and R^2 is the coefficient of determination of the auxiliary regression.

Finally, conclusions are drawn from the comparison of *LM*-critical and *LM*-statistical.

The Glesjer LM test in Stata

The Glesjer test can be performed in Stata as follows. First, the regression equation model is estimated with OLS, using the command:

```
regress y x1 x2 x3 x4 ... xk
```

where y is the dependent variable and x1 to xk the explanatory variables. The residuals are obtained using the *predict* command:

```
predict ut , residual
```

where ut represents the residuals. The absolute value of the residuals is then calculated as follows:

```
g absut = abs(ut)
```

and the estimate for the auxiliary regression obtained from the command:

```
regress absut z1 z2 z3 ... zp
```

In order to compute the LM-statistic, the calculation $LM=n*R^2$ is performed, where n is the number of observations and R^2 is the coefficient of determination of the auxiliary regression.

Finally, the conclusions are drawn from the comparison of LM-critical and LM-statistical.

The Harvey–Godfrey LM test

Harvey (1976) and Godfrey (1978) developed the following test:

Step 1 Run a regression of Equation (6.10) and obtain the residuals $\hat{u}_i$ of this regression equation.

Step 2 Run the following auxiliary regression:

$$\ln(\hat{u}_i^2) = a_1 + a_2 Z_{2i} + a_3 Z_{3i} + \cdots + a_p Z_{pi} + v_i \qquad (6.15)$$

Step 3 Formulate the null and the alternative hypotheses. The null hypothesis of homoskedasticity is:

$$H_0: \quad a_1 = a_2 = \cdots = a_p = 0 \qquad (6.16)$$

while the alternative is that at least one of the as is different from zero.

Step 4 Compute the $LM = nR^2$ statistic, where n is the number of observations used in order to estimate the auxiliary regression in step 2, and R^2 is the coefficient of determination of this regression. The LM statistic follows the χ^2 distribution with $p - 1$ degrees of freedom.

Step 5 Reject the null and conclude that there is significant evidence of heteroskedasticity when LM-statistical is bigger than the critical value (LM-stat $>$ $\chi^2_{p-1,\alpha}$). Alternatively, compute the p-value and reject the null if the p-value is less than the level of significance α (usually $\alpha = 0.05$).

The Harvey–Godfrey test in EViews

The Harvey–Godfrey test can be performed in EViews as follows. First the regression equation model is estimated with OLS using the command:

```
ls y c x1 x2 x3 ... xk
```

where y is the dependent variable and x1 to xk the explanatory variables. The residuals are obtained using the *generate* (genr) command:

```
genr ut=resid
```

Note that it is important to type and execute this command immediately after obtaining the equation results so that the resid vector has the residual of the equation estimated previously. Here *ut* represents the error terms of the model.

The squared residuals are calculated as follows:

```
genr utsq=ut^2
```

and the estimate of the auxiliary regression obtained from the command:

```
ls log(utsq) c z1 z2 z3 ... zp
```

The *LM*-statistic is calculated as $LM = n * R^2$, where n is the number of observations and R^2 is the coefficient of determination of the auxiliary regression.

Finally, conclusions are drawn from the comparison of *LM*-critical and *LM*-statistical.

The Harvey–Godfrey test in Stata

After the squared residuals have been obtained as described in the previous tests, the log of the squared residuals must also be obtained. This is performed in Stata using the following command:

```
g lutsq = log(utsq)
```

where *lutsq* represents the log of squared residuals variable. The auxiliary regression for the Harvey–Godfrey test in Stata is:

```
regress lutsq z1 z2 z3 ... zp
```

The *LM*-statistic is computed using the calculation $LM = n * R^2$, where n is the number of observations and R^2 is the coefficient of determination of the auxiliary regression.

Finally, conclusions are drawn from the comparison of *LM*-critical and *LM*-statistical.

The Park LM test

Park (1966) developed an alternative LM test, involving the following steps:

Step 1 Run a regression of Equation (6.10) and obtain the residuals $\hat{u}_i$ of this regression equation.

Step 2 Run the following auxiliary regression:

$$\ln(\hat{u}_i^2) = a_1 + a_2 \ln Z_{2i} + a_3 \ln Z_{3i} + \cdots + a_p \ln Z_{pi} + v_i \tag{6.17}$$

Step 3 Formulate the null and the alternative hypotheses. The null hypothesis of homoskedasticity is:

$$H_0: \quad a_1 = a_2 = \cdots = a_p = 0 \tag{6.18}$$

while the alternative is that at least one of the as is different from zero, in which case at least one of the Zs affects the variance of the residuals, which will be different for different t.

Step 4 Compute the $LM = nR^2$ statistic, where n is the number of observations used in order to estimate the auxiliary regression in step 2, and R^2 is the coefficient of determination of this regression. The LM-statistic follows the χ^2 distribution with $p - 1$ degrees of freedom.

Step 5 Reject the null and conclude that there is significant evidence of heteroskedasticity when LM-statistical is bigger than the critical value ($LM\text{-}stat > \chi^2_{p-1,\alpha}$). Alternatively, compute the p-value and reject the null if the p-value is less than the level of significance α (usually $\alpha = 0.05$).

The Park test in EViews

The Park test can be performed in EViews as follows. First, the regression equation model is estimated with OLS, using the command:

```
ls y c x1 x2 x3 ... xk
```

where y is the dependent variable and x1 to xk the explanatory variables. The residuals are then obtained the *generate* (genr) command:

```
genr ut=resid
```

Note that it is important to type and execute this command immediately after deriving the equation results so that the resid vector has the residual of the equation estimated previously. Here *ut* represents the error terms of the model. The squared residuals are then calculated as follows:

```
genr utsq=ut^2
```

and the auxiliary regression estimated using this command:

```
ls log(utsq) c log(z1) log(z2) log(z3) ... log(zp)
```

The LM-statistic is calculated using $LM = n*R^2$, where n is the number of observations and R^2 is the coefficient of determination of the auxiliary regression.

Finally, conclusions are drawn by comparing LM-critical and LM-statistical.

The Park test in Stata

The Park test can be performed in Stata in a similar way to the other Stata tests already described, using the following auxiliary regression:

```
regress lutsq lz1 lz2 lz3 ... lzp
```

which simply requires that we first obtained the logs of the $z1, \ldots, zp$ variables with the *generate* (g) command in Stata.

Criticism of the LM tests

An obvious criticism of all the LM tests described above is that they require prior knowledge of what might be causing the heteroskedasticity captured in the form of the auxiliary equation. Alternative models have been proposed and they are presented below.

The Goldfeld–Quandt test

Goldfeld and Quandt (1965) proposed an alternative test based on the idea that if the variances of the residuals are the same across all observations (that is homoskedastic), then the variance for one part of the sample should be the same as the variance for another. To apply the test it is necessary to identify a variable to which the variance of the residuals is mostly related (this can be done with plots of the residuals against the explanatory variables). The steps of the Goldfeld–Quandt test are as follows:

Step 1 Identify one variable that is closely related to the variance of the disturbance term, and order (or rank) the observations of this variable in descending order (from the highest to the lowest value).

Step 2 Split the ordered sample into two equal-sized sub-samples by omitting c central observations, so that the two sub-samples will contain $\frac{1}{2}(n - c)$ observations. The first will contain the highest values and the second the lowest ones.

Step 3 Run an OLS regression of Y on the X-variable used in Step 1 for each sub-sample and obtain the RSS for each equation.

Step 4 Calculate the F-statistic as follows:

$$F = \frac{RSS_1}{RSS_2} \tag{6.19}$$

where the *RSS* with the largest value is in the numerator. The F-statistic is distributed with $F_{(1/2(n-c)-k, 1/2(n-c)-k)}$ degrees of freedom.

Step 5 Reject the null hypothesis of homoskedasticity if F-statistical $>$ F-critical.

If the error terms are homoskedastic then the variance of the residuals will be the same for each sample, so that the ratio is unity. If the ratio is significantly larger, the null of equal variances will be rejected. The value of c is arbitrarily chosen and it should usually be between 1/6 and 1/3 of the observations.

The problems with the Goldfeld–Quandt test are that it does not take into account cases where heteroskedasticity is caused by more than one variable and it is not always suitable for time series data. However, it is a very popular model for the simple regression case (with only one explanatory variable).

The Goldfeld–Quandt test in EViews

To perform the Goldfeld–Quandt test in EViews, the data first needs to be sorted in descending order according to the variable thought to be causing the heteroskedasticity X. To do this click on **Procs/Sort Series**, enter the name of the variable (in this case X) in the sort key dialog box and tick 'descending' for the sort order. The sample is then divided into two different sub-samples and OLS of Y on X run for both sub-samples in order to obtain the RSSs. The following commands are used for the first sample:

```
smpl start end
ls y c x
scalar rss1=@ssr
```

and

```
smpl start end
ls y c x
scalar rss2=@ssr
```

with the start and end points defined appropriately in each case, depending on the frequency of the data set and the number of middle-point observations that should be excluded.

The F-statistic is then calculated, given by RRS1/RSS2 or the following command:

```
genr F_GQ=RSS1/RSS2
```

and compared with the F-critical value given by:

```
scalar f_crit=@qfdist(.95,n1-k,n2-k)
```

Alternatively the p-value can be obtained and conclusions drawn by:

```
scalar p_value=1-@fdist(.05,n1-k,n2-k)
```

The Goldfeld–Quandt test in Stata

In order to perform the Goldfeld–Quandt test in Stata the data must first be sorted in descending order according to the variable thought to be causing the heteroskedasticity (variable X in this example), using the command:

```
sort x
```

The sample is then broken into two different sub-samples and OLS of Y on X run for both sub-samples in order to obtain the RSSs. The following commands (assuming here a sample of 100 observations in total, with the sample split into the first 40 (1–40) and the last 40 (61–100), leaving 20 middle observations (41–60) out of the estimation window):

```
regress y x in 1/40
scalar rss1 = e(rmse)^2
scalar df_rss1 = e(df_r)
```

for the first sample and for the second:

```
regress y x in 61/100
scalar rss2 = e(rmse)^2
scalar df_rss2 = e(df_r)
```

The Goldfeld–Quandt F-statistic is then calculated from:

```
scalar FGQ = rss2/rss1
```

and compared with the *F*-critical value given by the following command:

```
scalar Fcrit = invFtail(df_rss2,df_rss1,.05)
```

Alternatively the *p*-value:

```
scalar pvalue = Ftail(df_rss2,df_rss1,FGQ)
```

The results are viewed by entering in the command editor the following:

```
scalar list FGQ pvalue Fcrit
```

White's test

White (1980) developed a more general test for heteroskedasticity that eliminates the problems that appeared in the previous tests. White's test is also an LM test, but it has the advantages that (a) it does not assume any prior determination of heteroskedasticity, (b) unlike the Breusch–Pagan test, it does not depend on normality assumption, and (c) it proposes a particular choice for the Zs in the auxiliary regression.

The steps involved in White's test assuming a model with two explanatory variables like the one presented here:

$$Y_i = \beta_1 + \beta_2 X_{2i} + \beta_3 X_{3i} + u_i \tag{6.20}$$

are the following:

Step 1 Run a regression of Equation (6.20) and obtain the residuals $\hat{u}_i$ of this regression equation.

Step 2 Run the following auxiliary regression:

$$\hat{u}_i^2 = a_1 + a_2 X_{2i} + a_3 X_{3i} + a_4 X_{2i}^2 + a_5 X_{3i}^2 + a_6 X_{2i} X_{3i} + v_i \tag{6.21}$$

That is, regress the squared residuals on a constant, all the explanatory variables, the squared explanatory variables, and their respective cross products.

Step 3 Formulate the null and the alternative hypotheses. The null hypothesis of homoskedasticity is:

$$H_0: \quad a_1 = a_2 = \cdots = a_p = 0 \tag{6.22}$$

while the alternative is that at least one of the as is different from zero.

Step 4 Compute the $LM = nR^2$ statistic, where n is the number of observations used in order to estimate the auxiliary regression in step 2, and R^2 is the coefficient of determination of this regression. The LM-statistic follows the χ^2 distribution with $6 - 1$ degrees of freedom.

Step 5 Reject the null and conclude that there is significant evidence of heteroskedasticity when LM-statistical is bigger than the critical value (LM-*stat* $>$ $\chi^2_{6-1,\alpha}$). Alternatively, compute the p-value and reject the null if the p-value is less than the level of significance α (usually $\alpha = 0.05$).

White's test in EViews

EViews already includes a routine for executing White's test for heteroskedasticity. After obtaining the OLS results, click on **View/Residual Diagnostics/Heteroskedasticity Tests**. A new window opens that includes various tests, from which **White** test should be chosen. Note that EViews provides the option of including or excluding cross terms by clicking or not clicking next to the **Include White cross terms** button. In either case EViews provides the results of the auxiliary regression equation that is estimated, as well as the LM test and its respective p-value.

White's test in Stata

White's test can be performed in Stata as follows. First, the regression equation model needs to be estimated with OLS, assuming for simplicity that there are only two explanatory variables (x2 and x3), using the command:

```
regress y x2 x3
```

The residuals are obtained using the *predict* command as follows:

```
predict ut , residual
```

where *ut* represents residuals. The squared residuals are calculated as follows:

```
g utsq = ut^ 2
```

and the estimate for the auxiliary regression obtained from the command:

```
regress utsq x2 x3 x2^ 2 x3^ 2 x2*x3
```

The *LM*-statistic is calculated using $LM = n*R^2$, where n is the number of observations and R^2 is the coefficient of determination of the auxiliary regression.

Finally, conclusions are drawn by comparing *LM*-critical and *LM*-statistical.

Computer example: heteroskedasticity tests

The file houseprice.wf1 contains house price data from of a sample of 88 London houses together with some of their characteristics. The variables are:

Price = the price of the houses measured in pounds

Rooms = the number of bedrooms in each house

Sqfeet = the size of the house measured in square feet

We want to see whether the number of bedrooms and the size of the house play an important role in determining the price of each house.

A simple scatter plot inspection of the two explanatory variables against the dependent variable (Figures 6.10 and 6.11) shows clear evidence of heteroskedasticity in the relationship as regards the *Rooms* variable, but also some evidence of the same problem for the size proxy (*Sqfeet*) variable with larger variations in prices for larger houses.

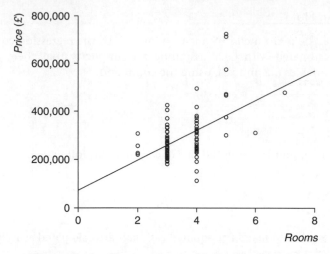

Figure 6.10   Clear evidence of heteroskedasticity

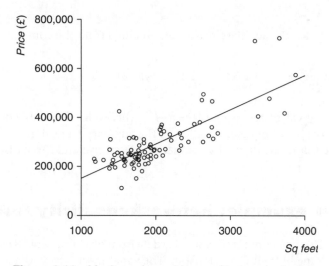

Figure 6.11   Much weaker evidence of heteroskedasticity

The Breusch–Pagan test

To test for heteroskedasticity in a more formal way, the Breusch–Pagan test can first be applied:

Step 1   The regression equation is estimated:

$$price = b_1 + b_2 rooms + b_3 sqfeet + u$$

the results of which are presented in Table 6.1.

Table 6.1 Basic regression model results

Dependent bariable: PRICE
Method: least squares
Date: 02/03/04 Time: 01:52
Sample: 1 88
Included observations: 88

Variable	Coefficient	Std. error	t-statistic	Prob.
C	−19315.00	31046.62	−0.622129	0.5355
Rooms	15198.19	9483.517	1.602590	0.1127
Sqfeet	128.4362	13.82446	9.290506	0.0000

R-squared	0.631918	Mean dependent var.	293546.0
Adjusted R-squared	0.623258	S.D. dependent var.	102713.4
S.E. of regression	63044.84	Akaike info criterion	24.97458
Sum squared resid.	3.38E+11	Schwarz criterion	25.05903
Log likelihood	−1095.881	F-statistic	72.96353
Durbin–Watson stat.	1.858074	Prob(F-statistic)	0.000000

Step 2 The residuals of this regression model (represented here by ut) are obtained by typing the following command in the command line:

```
genr ut=resid
```

and the squared residuals by typing the command:

```
genr utsq=ut^sq
```

The auxiliary regression is then estimated using as Zs the explanatory variables from the original equation model:

$$utsq = a_1 + a_2 rooms + a_3 sqfeet + v$$

The results of this equation are presented in Table 6.2.

The LM-statistic is distributed under a chi-square distribution with degrees of freedom equal to the number of slope coefficients included in the auxiliary regression (or $k - 1$), which in our case is 2. The chi-square critical can be given by:

```
genr chi=@qchisq(.95,2)
```

and is equal to 5.991465.

Step 3 Because the LM-stat > chi-square critical value we can conclude that the null can be rejected, and therefore there is evidence of heteroskedasticity.

Table 6.2   The Breusch–Pagan test auxiliary regression

Dependent variable: UTSQ
Method: least squares
Date: 02/03/04 Time: 02:09
Sample: 1 88
Included observations: 88

Variable	Coefficient	Std. error	t-statistic	Prob.
C	−8.22E + 09	3.91E + 09	−2.103344	0.0384
Rooms	1.19E + 09	1.19E + 09	0.995771	0.3222
Sqfeet	3881720.	1739736.	2.231213	0.0283

R-squared	0.120185	Mean dependent var.	3.84E + 09
Adjusted R-squared	0.099484	S.D. dependent var.	8.36E + 09
S.E. of regression	7.93E + 09	Akaike info criterion	48.46019
Sum squared resid.	5.35E + 21	Schwarz criterion	48.54464
Log likelihood	−2129.248	F-statistic	5.805633
Durbin–Watson stat.	2.091083	Prob(F-statistic)	0.004331

The Glesjer test

For the Glesjer test the steps are similar but the dependent variable in the auxiliary regression is now the absolute value of the error terms. This variable should be constructed as follows:

```
genr absut=abs(ut)
```

and the auxiliary equation estimated as:

$$absut = a_1 + a_2 rooms + a_3 sqfeet + v$$

The results of this model are given in Table 6.3. Again the *LM*-statistic must be calculated:

$$LM = \text{obs} * R^2 = 88 * 0.149244 = 13.133472$$

which is again bigger than the chi-square critical value, and therefore again it can be concluded that there is sufficient evidence of heteroskedasticity.

The Harvey–Godfrey test

For the Harvey–Godfrey test the auxiliary regression takes the form:

$$log(utsq) = a_1 + a_2 rooms + a_3 sqfeet + v$$

The results of this auxiliary regression model are given in Table 6.4. In this case the *LM*-statistic is:

$$LM = \text{obs} * R^2 = 88 * 0.098290 = 8.64952$$

Table 6.3   The Glesjer test auxiliary regression

Dependent variable: ABSUT
Method: least squares
Date: 02/03/04 Time: 02:42
Sample: 1 88
Included observations: 88

Variable	Coefficient	Std. error	t-statistic	Prob.
C	−23493.96	19197.00	−1.223835	0.2244
Rooms	8718.698	5863.926	1.486836	0.1408
Sqfeet	19.04985	8.548052	2.228560	0.0285
R-squared	0.149244		Mean dependent var.	45976.49
Adjusted R-squared	0.129226		S.D. dependent var.	41774.94
S.E. of regression	38982.40		Akaike info criterion	24.01310
Sum squared resid.	1.29E+11		Schwarz criterion	24.09756
Log likelihood	−1053.577		F-statistic	7.455547
Durbin–Watson stat.	2.351422		Prob(F-statistic)	0.001039

Table 6.4   The Harvey–Godfrey test auxiliary regression

Dependent variable: LOG(UTSQ)
Method: least squares
Date: 02/03/04 Time: 02:46
Sample: 1 88
Included observations: 88

Variable	Coefficient	Std. error	t-statistic	Prob.
C	17.77296	0.980629	18.12405	0.0000
Rooms	0.453464	0.299543	1.513852	0.1338
Sqfeet	0.000625	0.000437	1.432339	0.1557
R-squared	0.098290		Mean dependent var.	20.65045
Adjusted R-squared	0.077073		S.D. dependent var.	2.072794
S.E. of regression	1.991314		Akaike info criterion	4.248963
Sum squared resid.	337.0532		Schwarz criterion	4.333418
Log likelihood	−183.9544		F-statistic	4.632651
Durbin–Watson stat.	2.375378		Prob(F-statistic)	0.012313

which is again bigger than the chi-square critical value, and therefore it can be again concluded that there is sufficient evidence of heteroskedasticity.

The Park test

Finally, for the Park test the auxiliary regression takes the form:

$$log(utsq) = a_1 + a_2 log(rooms) + a_3 log(sqfeet) + v \tag{6.23}$$

the results of which are given in Table 6.5. In this case the LM-statistic is:

$$LM = \text{obs} * R^2 = 88 * 0.084176 = 7.407488$$

Table 6.5 The Park test auxiliary regression

Dependent variable: LOG(UTSQ)
Method: least squares
Date: 02/03/04 Time: 02:50
Sample: 1 88
Included observations: 88

Variable	Coefficient	Std. error	t-statistic	Prob.
C	9.257004	6.741695	1.373097	0.1733
Log(Rooms)	1.631570	1.102917	1.479322	0.1428
Log(Sqfeet)	1.236057	0.969302	1.275204	0.2057
R-squared	0.084176	Mean dependent var.		20.65045
Adjusted R-squared	0.062627	S.D. dependent var.		2.072794
S.E. of regression	2.006838	Akaike info criterion		4.264494
Sum squared resid.	342.3290	Schwarz criterion		4.348949
Log likelihood	−184.6377	F-statistic		3.906274
Durbin–Watson stat.	2.381246	Prob(F-statistic)		0.023824

which is again bigger than the chi-square critical value, and therefore again it can be concluded that there is sufficient evidence of heteroskedasticity.

The Goldfeld–Quandt test

The Goldfeld–Quandt test requires first that the observations are ordered according to the variable thought principally to be causing the heteroskedasticity. Taking this to be the *rooms* variable, this test is performed in the sequence described below:

Step 1   Click on **Procs/Sort Current page**, enter the name of the variable (in this case *rooms*) in the sort key dialog box and click on the box to tick **descending** for the sort order.

Step 2   Break the sample into two different sub-samples, subtracting c number of intermediate observations. Choosing c close to 1/6 of the total observations gives $c = 14$. Therefore each sub-sample will contain $(88 − 14)/2 = 37$ observations. The first sample will have observations 1 to 37 and the second will have observations 51 to 88.

Step 3   Now run an OLS of *price* on rooms for both sub-samples in order to obtain the RSSs, using the following commands:

```
smpl  1 37            [sets the sample to
                         sub-sample 1]
ls price c rooms      [estimates the regression
                         equation]
scalar rss1=@ssr      [creates a scalar that will
                         be the value of the RSS
                         of the regression equation
                         estimated by the previous
                         command]
```

Table 6.6 The Goldfeld–Quandt test (first sub-sample results)

Dependent variable: PRICE
Method: least squares
Date: 02/03/04 Time: 03:05
Sample: 1 37
Included observations: 37

Variable	Coefficient	Std. error	t-statistic	Prob.
C	−150240.0	124584.0	−1.205933	0.2359
Rooms	110020.7	28480.42	3.863028	0.0005

R-squared	0.298920	Mean dependent var.		325525.0
Adjusted R-squared	0.278889	S.D. dependent var.		134607.0
S.E. of regression	114305.9	Akaike info criterion		26.18368
Sum squared resid.	**4.57E + 11**	Schwarz criterion		26.27076
Log likelihood	−482.3981	F-statistic		14.92298
Durbin–Watson stat.	1.718938	Prob(F-statistic)		0.000463

Table 6.7 The Goldfeld–Quandt test (second sub-sample results)

Dependent variable: PRICE
Method: least squares
Date: 02/03/04 Time: 03:05
Sample: 51 88
Included observations: 38

Variable	Coefficient	Std. error	t-statistic	Prob.
C	227419.1	85213.84	2.668805	0.0113
Rooms	11915.44	29273.46	0.407039	0.6864

R-squared	0.004581	Mean dependent var.		261911.2
Adjusted R-squared	−0.023069	S.D. dependent var.		54751.89
S.E. of regression	55379.83	Akaike info criterion		24.73301
Sum squared resid.	**1.10E + 11**	Schwarz criterion		24.81920
Log likelihood	−467.9273	F-statistic		0.165681
Durbin–Watson stat.	1.983220	Prob(F-statistic)		0.686389

Similarly for the second sub-sample, type the following commands:

```
smpl 51 88
ls price c rooms
scalar rss2=@ssr
```

The results for both sub-samples are presented in Tables 6.6 and 6.7. Since *RSS*1 is bigger than *RSS*2, the *F*-statistic can be calculated as follows:

```
genr F_GQ=RSS1/RSS2
```

and *F*-critical will be given by:

```
genr F_crit=@qfdist(.95,37,37)
```

The *F*-statistic 4.1419 is bigger than *F*-critical 1.7295, and therefore there is evidence of heteroskedasticity.

Table 6.8 White's test (no cross products)

White heteroskedasticity test:

F-statistic	4.683121	Probability	0.001857
Obs*R-squared	**16.20386**	**Probability**	**0.002757**

Test equation:
Dependent variable: RESID^2
Method: least squares
Date: 02/03/04 Time: 03:15
Sample: 1 88
Included observations: 88

Variable	Coefficient	Std. error	t-statistic	Prob.
C	7.16E+09	1.27E+10	0.562940	0.5750
Rooms	7.21E+09	5.67E+09	1.272138	0.2069
Rooms^2	−7.67E+08	6.96E+08	−1.102270	0.2735
Sqfeet	−20305674	9675923.	−2.098577	0.0389
Sqfeet^2	5049.013	1987.370	2.540550	0.0129

R-squared	0.184135	Mean dependent var.	3.84E+09
Adjusted R-squared	0.144816	S.D. dependent var.	8.36E+09
S.E. of regression	7.73E+09	Akaike info criterion	48.43018
Sum squared resid.	4.96E+21	Schwarz criterion	48.57094
Log likelihood	−2125.928	F-statistic	4.683121
Durbin–Watson stat.	1.640895	Prob(F-statistic)	0.001857

White's test

For White's test, the equation model (presented in the first table with results of this example) should be estimated and the results shown in Table 6.8 viewed then by clicking on **View/Residual Tests/White (no cross products)**. Note that the auxiliary regression does not include the cross products of the explanatory variables in this case. The *LM-stat* 16.20386 is bigger than the critical value and the *p*-value also next to the *LM*-test provided by EViews is 0.02757, both suggesting evidence of heteroskedasticity.

If the version of White's test with the cross products is chosen by clicking on **View/Residual Tests/White (cross products)**, the results shown in Table 6.9 are obtained. In this case, as well as in all cases above, the *LM*-stat (17.22519) is bigger than the critical and therefore there is evidence of heteroskedasticity.

Commands for the computer example in Stata

First open the file houseprice.dat in Stata. Then perform commands as follows.
   For the Breusch–Pagan LM test:

```
regress price rooms sqfeet
predict ut, residual
g utsq = ut^ 2
regress utsq rooms sqfeet
```

The results should be identical to those in Table 6.2.

Table 6.9 White's test (cross products)

White heteroskedasticity test:

F-statistic	3.991436	Probability	0.002728
Obs*R-squared**	**17.22519**	**Probability**	**0.004092**

Test equation:
Dependent variable: RESID^2
Method: least squares
Date: 02/03/04 Time: 03:18
Sample: 1 88
Included observations: 88

Variable	Coefficient	Std. error	t-statistic	Prob.
C	1.08E + 10	1.31E + 10	0.822323	0.4133
Rooms	7.00E + 09	5.67E + 09	1.234867	0.2204
Rooms^2	−1.28E + 09	8.39E + 08	−1.523220	0.1316
Rooms*Sqfeet	1979155.	1819402.	1.087805	0.2799
Sqfeet	−23404693	10076371	−2.322730	0.0227
Sqfeet^2	4020.876	2198.691	1.828759	0.0711

R-squared	0.195741	Mean dependent var.	3.84E + 09
Adjusted *R*-squared	0.146701	S.D. dependent var.	8.36E + 09
S.E. of regression	7.72E + 09	Akaike info criterion	48.43858
Sum squared resid.	4.89E + 21	Schwarz criterion	48.60749
Log likelihood	−2125.297	*F*-statistic	3.991436
Durbin–Watson stat.	1.681398	Prob(*F*-statistic)	0.002728

For the Glesjer LM test:

```
g absut = abs(ut)
regress absut rooms sqfeet
```

The results should be identical to those in Table 6.3.

For the Harvey–Godfrey test:

```
g lutsq = log(utsq)
regress lutsq rooms sqfeet
```

The results should be identical to those in Table 6.4.

For the Park LM test:

```
g lrooms = log(rooms)
g lsqfeet = log(sqfeet)
regress lutsq lrooms lsqfeet
```

The results should be identical to those in Table 6.5.

For the Goldfeld–Quandt test:

```
sort rooms
regress price rooms in 1/37
scalar rss1 = e(rmse)^ 2
```

```
scalar df_rss1 = e(df_r)
regress price rooms in 51/88
scalar rss2 = e(rmse)^ 2
scalar df_rss2 = e(df_r)
scalar FGQ = rss2/rss1
scalar Fcrit = invFtail(df_rss2,df_rss1,.05)
scalar pvalue = Ftail(df_rss2,df_rss1,FGQ)
scalar list FGQ pvalue Fcrit
```

Finally for White's test (no cross products):

```
regress utsq rooms rooms^ 2 sqfeet sqfeet^ 2
```

and for White's test (with cross products):

```
regress utsq rooms rooms^ 2 sqfeet sqfeet^ 2 rooms*sqfeet
```

Engle's ARCH test*

So far we have looked for the presence of autocorrelation in the error terms of a regression model. Engle (1982) introduced a new concept allowing for autocorrelation to occur in the variance of the error terms, rather than in the error terms themselves. To capture this autocorrelation Engle developed the Autoregressive Conditional Heteroskedasticity (ARCH) model, the key idea behind which is that the variance of u_t depends on the size of the squared error term lagged one period (that is u_{t-1}^2).

More analytically, consider the regression model:

$$Y_t = \beta_1 + \beta_2 X_{2t} + \beta_3 X_{3t} + \cdots + \beta_k X_{kt} + u_t \tag{6.24}$$

and assume that the variance of the error term follows an ARCH(1) process:

$$Var(u_t) = \sigma_t^2 = \gamma_0 + \gamma_1 u_{t-1}^2 \tag{6.25}$$

If there is no autocorrelation in $Var(u_t)$, then γ_1 should be zero and therefore $\sigma_t^2 = \gamma_0$. So there is a constant (homoskedastic) variance.

The model can easily be extended for higher-order ARCH(p) effects:

$$Var(u_t) = \sigma_t^2 = \gamma_0 + \gamma_1 u_{t-1}^2 + \gamma_2 u_{t-2}^2 + \cdots + \gamma_p u_{t-p}^2 \tag{6.26}$$

---

* This test only applies to a time series context and so in this section the variables are indexed by t.

Here the null hypothesis is:

$$H_0: \quad \gamma_1 = \gamma_2 = \cdots = \gamma_p = 0 \tag{6.27}$$

that is, no ARCH effects are present. The steps involved in the ARCH test are:

Step 1 Estimate equation (6.24) by OLS and obtain the residuals, $\hat{u}_t$.

Step 2 Regress the squared residuals (u_t^2) against a constant, u_{t-1}^2, u_{t-2}^2, ..., u_{t-p}^2 (the value of p will be determined by the order of ARCH(p) being tested for).

Step 3 Compute the *LM* statistic $= (n - p)R^2$, from the regression in step 2. If $LM > \chi_p^2$ for a given level of significance, reject the null of no ARCH effects and conclude that ARCH effects are indeed present.

The ARCH-LM test in EViews, Microfit and Stata

After estimating a regression equation in EViews, click on **View/Residual Diagnostics/Heteroskedasticity Tests**. A new window appears, which includes various possible tests (note here that this window offers the opportunity to do the tests examined above in a different manner). From the various possibilities, choose the **ARCH** test by highlighting with the mouse, specify the number of lags we want to use and click **OK** to obtain the test results. These are interpreted in the usual way.

In Microfit, after estimating the regression model, close the results window by clicking on **close** to obtain the **Post Regression** menu. From that menu choose option 2, move to the **Hypothesis Testing** menu and click **OK**. From the hypothesis testing menu choose option 2, **Autoregressive Conditional Heteroskedasticity tests (OLS & NLS)**, and again click **OK**. Specify the number of lags in the Input, an integer window, and click **OK** to obtain the results of the test.

Finally, in Stata, after estimating a regression model, the ARCH-LM test can be performed using the **Statistics** menu, and choosing **Statistics/Linear models and related/Regression Diagnostics/Specification tests**, etc. Select from the list 'Test for ARCH effects in the residuals (archlm test – time series only)', and specify the number of lags to be tested. The results appear immediately in the **Results window**. A simpler and much faster way is through the use of the following command:

```
estat archlm , lag(number)
```

where (number) should be replaced by the number of lags to be tested for ARCH effects. Therefore, to test for four lagged squared residual terms, type:

```
estat archlm , lags(4)
```

Similarly, for other lag orders, change the number in brackets.

Table 6.10   The ARCH-LM test results

ARCH test:

F-statistic	12.47713	Probability	0.001178
Obs*R-squared	**9.723707**	Probability	**0.001819**

Test equation:
Dependent variable: RESID^2
Method: least squares
Date: 02/12/04 Time: 23:21
Sample(adjusted): 1985:2 1994:2
Included observations: 37 after adjusting endpoints

Variable	Coefficient	Std. error	*t*-statistic	Prob.
C	0.000911	0.000448	2.030735	0.0499
RESID^2(−1)	0.512658	0.145135	**3.532298**	0.0012

R-squared	0.262803	Mean dependent var.	0.001869
Adjusted *R*-squared	0.241740	S.D. dependent var.	0.002495
S.E. of regression	0.002173	Akaike info. criterion	−9.373304
Sum squared resid.	0.000165	Schwarz criterion	−9.286227
Log likelihood	175.4061	*F*-statistic	12.47713
Durbin–Watson stat.	1.454936	Prob(*F*-statistic)	0.001178

Computer example of the ARCH-LM test

To apply the ARCH-LM test, estimate the equation, click on **View/Residual Tests/ARCH LM Test** and specify the lag order. Applying the ARCH-LM test to the initial model (for ARCH(1) effects enter 1, in lag order):

$$C_t = b_1 + b_2 D_t + b_3 P_t + u_t \tag{6.28}$$

we obtain the results shown in Table 6.10, where it is obvious from both the *LM*-statistic (and the probability limit) as well as from the *t*-statistic of the lagged squared residual term that it is highly significant that this equation has ARCH(1) effects.

Resolving heteroskedasticity

If heteroskedasticity is found, there are two ways of proceeding. First, the model can be re-estimated in a way that fully recognizes the presence of the problem, and that would involve applying the generalized (or weighted) least squares method. This would then produce a new set of parameter estimates that would be more efficient than the OLS ones and a correct set of covariances and *t*-statistics. Alternatively, we can recognize that while OLS is no longer best it is still consistent and the real problem is that the covariances and *t*-statistics are simply wrong. We can then correct the covariances and *t*-statistics by basing them on a set of formulae such as Equation (6.9). Of course this will not change the actual parameter estimates, which will remain less than fully efficient.

Generalized (or weighted) least squares

Generalized least squares

Consider the following model:

$$Y_i = \beta_1 + \beta_2 X_{2i} + \beta_3 X_{3i} + \cdots + \beta_k X_{ki} + u_i \tag{6.29}$$

where the variance of the error term, instead of being constant, is heteroskedastic, that is $Var(u_i) = \sigma_i^2$.

If each term in Equation (6.29) is divided by the standard deviation of the error term, σ_i, one of these modified models is obtained:

$$\frac{Y_i}{\sigma_i} = \beta_1 \frac{1}{\sigma_i} + \beta_2 \frac{X_{2i}}{\sigma_i} + \beta_3 \frac{X_{3i}}{\sigma_i} + \cdots + \beta_k \frac{X_{ki}}{\sigma_i} + \frac{u_i}{\sigma_i} \tag{6.30}$$

or:

$$Y_i^* = \beta_1 X_{1i}^* + \beta_2 X_{2i}^* + \beta_3 X_{3i}^* + \cdots + \beta_k X_{ki}^* + u_i^* \tag{6.31}$$

For the modified model:

$$Var(u_i^*) = Var\left(\frac{u_i}{\sigma_i}\right) = \frac{Var(u_i)}{\sigma_i^2} = 1 \tag{6.32}$$

Therefore, estimates obtained by OLS of regressing Y_i^* to X_{1i}^*, X_{2i}^*, X_{3i}^*, ..., X_{ki}^* are now BLUE. This procedure is called generalized least squares (GLS).

Weighted least squares

The GLS procedure is also the same as the weighted least squares (WLS), where we have weights, ω_i, adjusting our variables. The similarity can be identified by defining $\omega_i = \frac{1}{\sigma_i}$, and rewriting the original model as:

$$\omega_i Y_i = \beta_1 \omega_i + \beta_2 (X_{2i}\omega_i) + \beta_3 (X_{3i}\omega_i) + \cdots + \beta_k (X_{ki}\omega_i) + (u_i\omega_i) \tag{6.33}$$

which, if defined as $\omega_i Y_i = Y_i^*$, and $(X_{ki}\omega_i) = X_{ki}^*$, gives same equation as (6.31):

$$Y_i^* = \beta_1 X_{1i}^* + \beta_2 X_{2i}^* + \beta_3 X_{3i}^* + \cdots + \beta_k X_{ki}^* + u_i^* \tag{6.34}$$

Assumptions about the structure of σ^2

A major practical problem with the otherwise straightforward GLS and WLS is that σ_i^2 is unknown and therefore Equation (6.31) and/or Equation (6.33) cannot be estimated without making explicit assumptions about the structure of σ_i^2.

However, if there is a prior belief about the structure of σ_i^2, then GLS and WLS work in practice. Consider the case where in Equation (6.29):

$$Var(u_i) = \sigma_i^2 = \sigma^2 Z_i^2 \tag{6.35}$$

where Z_i is a variable whose values are known for all i. Dividing each term in Equation (6.29) by Z_i gives:

$$\frac{Y_i}{Z_i} = \beta_1 \frac{1}{Z_i} + \beta_2 \frac{X_{2i}}{Z_i} + \beta_3 \frac{X_{3i}}{Z_i} + \cdots + \beta_k \frac{X_{ki}}{Z_i} + \frac{u_i}{Z_i} \tag{6.36}$$

or:

$$Y_i^* = \beta_1 X_{1i}^* + \beta_2 X_{2i}^* + \beta_3 X_{3i}^* + \cdots + \beta_k X_{ki}^* + u_i^* \tag{6.37}$$

where starred terms denote variables divided by Z_i. In this case:

$$Var(u_i^*) = Var\left(\frac{u_i}{Z_i}\right) = \sigma^2 \tag{6.38}$$

The heteroskedasticity problem has been resolved from the original model. Note, however, that this equation has no constant term; the constant in the original regression (β_1 in Equation (6.24)) becomes the coefficient on X_i^* in Equation (6.37). Care should be taken in interpreting the coefficients, especially when Z_i is an explanatory variable in the original model – Equation (6.29). If, for example, $Z_i = X_{3i}$, then:

$$\frac{Y_i}{Z_i} = \beta_1 \frac{1}{Z_i} + \beta_2 \frac{X_{2i}}{Z_i} + \beta_3 \frac{X_{3i}}{Z_i} + \cdots + \beta_k \frac{X_{ki}}{Z_i} + \frac{u_i}{Z_i} \tag{6.39}$$

or:

$$\frac{Y_i}{Z_i} = \beta_1 \frac{1}{Z_i} + \beta_2 \frac{X_{2i}}{Z_i} + \beta_3 + \cdots + \beta_k \frac{X_{ki}}{Z_i} + \frac{u_i}{Z_i} \tag{6.40}$$

If this form of WLS is used, then the coefficients obtained should be interpreted very carefully. Note that β_3 is now the constant term of Equation (6.37), whereas it was a slope coefficient in Equation (6.29), and β_1 is now a slope coefficient in Equation (6.37), while it was the intercept in the original model, Equation (6.29). The effect of X_{3i} in Equation (6.29) can therefore be researched by examining the intercept in Equation (6.37); the other case can be approached similarly.

Heteroskedasticity-consistent estimation methods

White (1980) proposed a method of obtaining consistent estimators of the variances and covariances of the OLS estimators. The mathematical details of this method are beyond the scope of this book. However, several computer packages, including EViews, are now able to compute White's heteroskedasticity-corrected variances and standard errors. An example of White's method of estimation in EViews is given in the computer example below.

Computer example: resolving heteroskedasticity

If, as in the example heteroskedasticity tests given above, all tests show evidence of heteroskedasticity, alternative methods of estimation are required instead of OLS. Estimating the equation by OLS gives the results shown in Table 6.11.

However, we know that because of heteroskedasticity, the standard errors of the OLS coefficient estimates are incorrect. To obtain White's corrected standard error estimates, click on **Quick/Estimate Equation** and then on the **Options** button that is located at the lower right of the **Equation Specification** window. In the **Estimation Options** window that opens, click on the **Heteroskedasticity-Consistent Covariance** box, then on the box next to **White** and finally on **OK**. Returning to the Equation Specification window, enter the required regression equation by typing:

```
price c rooms sqfeet
```

and then click **OK**. The results obtained will be as shown in Table 6.11 where now the White's standard errors are not the same as those from the simple OLS case, although the coefficients are, of course, identical.

Calculating the confidence interval for the coefficient of *sqfeet* for the simple OLS case (the incorrect case) gives (the *t*-stat for 0.05 and 86 degrees of freedom is 1.662765):

$$128.4362 - 1.662765 * 13.82446 < b_3 < 128.4362 + 1.662765 * 13.82446$$

$$105.44 < b_3 < 151.42$$

while for the White corrected case it will be:

$$128.4362 - 1.662765 * 19.59089 < b_3 < 128.4362 + 1.662765 * 19.59089$$

$$112.44 < b_3 < 144.38$$

Table 6.11   Regression results with heteroskedasticity

Dependent variable: PRICE
Method: least squares
Date: 02/03/04 Time: 01:52
Sample: 1 88
Included observations: 88

Variable	Coefficient	Std. error	t-statistic	Prob.
C	−19315.00	31046.62	−0.622129	0.5355
Rooms	15198.19	9483.517	1.602590	0.1127
Sqfeet	128.4362	13.82446	9.290506	0.0000

R-squared	0.631918	Mean dependent var.	293546.0
Adjusted R-squared	0.623258	S.D. dependent var.	102713.4
S.E. of regression	63044.84	Akaike info criterion	24.97458
Sum squared resid.	3.38E+11	Schwarz criterion	25.05903
Log likelihood	−1095.881	F-statistic	72.96353
Durbin–Watson stat.	1.858074	Prob(F-statistic)	0.000000

Table 6.12   Heteroskedasticity-corrected regression results (White's method)

Dependent variable: PRICE
Method: least squares
Date: 02/05/04 Time: 20:30
Sample: 1 88
Included observations: 88
White Heteroskedasticity-consistent standard errors & covariance

Variable	Coefficient	Std. error	t-statistic	Prob.
C	−19315.00	**41520.50**	−0.465192	0.6430
Rooms	15198.19	**8943.735**	1.699311	0.0929
Sqfeet	128.4362	**19.59089**	6.555914	0.0000
R-squared	0.631918		Mean dependent var.	293546.0
Adjusted R-squared	0.623258		S.D. dependent var.	102713.4
S.E. of regression	63044.84		Akaike info criterion	24.97458
Sum squared resid.	3.38E + 11		Schwarz criterion	25.05903
Log likelihood	−1095.881		F-statistic	72.96353
Durbin–Watson stat.	1.757956		Prob(F-statistic)	0.000000

The White's corrected standard errors thus provide a better (more accurate) estimate.

Alternatively, EViews allows us to use the weighted or generalized least squares method as well. Assuming that the variable causing the heteroskedasticity is the *sqfeet* variable (or in mathematical notation assuming that):

$$Var(u_i) = \sigma_i^2 = \sigma^2 sqfeet \tag{6.41}$$

then the weight variable will be $1/\sqrt{sqfeet}$. To do this, click on **Quick/Estimate Equation** and then on **Options**, this time ticking the **Weighted LS/TSLS** box and entering the weighting variable $1/\sqrt{sqfeet}$ in the box by typing:

```
sqfeet^(-.5)
```

The results from this method are given in Table 6.13 and are clearly different from simple OLS estimation. The reader can use it as an exercise to calculate and compare standard errors and confidence intervals for this case.

Similarly, in Stata, in order to obtain heteroskedasticity-corrected results through the weighted or generalized least squares, go to **Statistics/Linear models and related/Linear regression** to obtain the **regress – linear regression** dialogue window. Complete the dependent and explanatory variables in the **Model** tab, while in the **Weights** tab tick the **Analytic weights** button and specify the desired weight (in this case it is *1/sqfeet*) in the box. Click **OK** to obtain the heteroskedasticity-corrected results, which are identical to those reported in Table 6.13. Alternatively, this can be done more simply using the command:

```
regress price rooms sqfeet [aweight = 1/sqfeet]
```

Table 6.13 Heteroskedasticity-corrected regression results (weighted LS method)

Date: 02/05/04 Time: 20:54
Sample: 1 88
Included observations: 88
Weighting series: SQFEET^(−.5)
White heteroskedasticity-consistent standard errors & covariance

Variable	Coefficient	Std. error	t-statistic	Prob.
C	8008.412	36830.04	0.217442	0.8284
Rooms	11578.30	9036.235	1.281319	0.2036
Sqfeet	121.2817	18.36504	6.603944	0.0000

Weighted statistics

R-squared	0.243745	Mean dependent var.	284445.3
Adjusted R-squared	0.225950	S.D. dependent var.	67372.90
S.E. of regression	59274.73	Akaike info criterion	24.85125
Sum squared resid.	2.99E+11	Schwarz criterion	24.93570
Log likelihood	−1090.455	F-statistic	53.20881
Durbin–Watson stat.	1.791178	Prob(F-statistic)	0.000000

Unweighted statistics

R-squared	0.628156	Mean dependent var.	293546.0
Adjusted R-squared	0.619406	S.D. dependent var.	102713.4
S.E. of regression	63366.27	Sum squared resid.	3.41E+11
Durbin–Watson stat.	1.719838		

Questions and exercises

Questions

1 Briefly state the consequences of heteroskedasticity in simple OLS.

2 Describe the Goldfeld–Quandt test for detection of heteroskedasticity.

3 Show how the weighted least squares can be applied in order to resolve heteroskedasticity.

4 When applying WLS and where the weight is an explanatory variable of the original model, discuss and show mathematically the problem of interpreting the estimated coefficients.

5 Consider the following model:

$$Y_i = \beta_1 + \beta_2 X_{2i} + \beta_3 X_{3i} + u_i$$

where $Var(u_i) = \sigma^2 X_{2i}$. Find the generalized least squares estimates.

6 Define heteroskedasticity and provide examples of econometric models where heteroskedasticity is likely to exist.

Exercise 6.1

Use the data in the file houseprice.wf1 to estimate a model of:

$$price_i = \beta_1 + \beta_2 sqfeet_i + u_i$$

Check for heteroskedasticity using the White and the Goldfeld–Quandt tests. Obtain GLS estimates for the following assumptions: (a) $Var(u_i) = \sigma^2 sqfeet_i$ and (b) $Var(u_i) = \sigma^2 sqfeet_i^2$. Comment on the sensitivity of the estimates and their standard errors to the heteroskedastic specification. For each of the two cases, use both the White and the Goldfeld–Quandt tests to see whether heteroskedasticity has been eliminated.

Exercise 6.2

Use the data in Greek_SME.wf1 to estimate the effect of size (proxied by number of employees) on the profit/sales ratio. Check whether the residuals in this equation are heteroskedastic by applying all the tests for detection of heteroskedasticity (both formal and informal) described in this chapter. If there is heteroskedasticity, obtain the White's corrected standard error estimates and construct confidence intervals to find the differences between the simple OLS and the White's estimates.

Exercise 6.3

Use the data in police.wf1 to estimate the equation that relates the actual value of the current budget (Y) with the expected value of the budget (X). Check for heteroskedasticity in this regression equation with all the known tests described in this chapter.

Exercise 6.4

The file sleep.xls contains data for 706 individuals concerning sleeping habits and possible determinants of sleeping time. Estimate the following regression equation:

$$sleep = b_0 + b_1 totwrk + b_2 educ + b_3 age + b_4 yngkid + b_5 male + u \qquad (6.42)$$

(a) Check whether there is evidence of heteroskedasticity.

(b) Is the estimated variance of u higher for men than women?

(c) Re-estimate the model, correcting for heteroskedasticity. Compare the results obtained with those in part from the simple OLS estimation.

Exercise 6.5

Use the data in the file houseprice.xls to estimate the following equation:

$$price = b_0 + b_1 lotsize + b_2 sqrft + b_3 bdrms + u \tag{6.43}$$

(a) Check whether there is evidence of heteroskedasticity.

(b) Re-estimate the equation but this time instead of *price* use log(*price*) as the dependent variable. Check for heteroskedasticity again. Is there any change in your conclusion in (a)?

(c) What does this example suggest about heteroskedasticity and the transformation used for the dependent variable?

7 Autocorrelation

CHAPTER CONTENTS

LEARNING OBJECTIVES

After studying this chapter you should be able to:

1. Understand the meaning of autocorrelation in the CLRM.
2. Find out what causes autocorrelation.
3. Distinguish among first and higher orders of autocorrelation.
4. Understand the consequences of autocorrelation on OLS estimates.
5. Detect autocorrelation through graph inspection.
6. Detect autocorrelation using formal econometric tests.
7. Distinguish among the wide range of available tests for detecting autocorrelation.
8. Perform autocorrelation tests using econometric software.
9. Resolve autocorrelation using econometric software.

Introduction: what is autocorrelation?

We know that the use of OLS to estimate a regression model leads us to BLUE estimates of the parameters only when all the assumptions of the CLRM are satisfied. In the previous chapter we examined the case where assumption 5 does not hold. This chapter examines the effects on the OLS estimators when assumption 6 of the CLRM is violated.

Assumption 6 of the CLRM states that the covariances and correlations between different disturbances are all zero:

$$Cov(u_t, u_s) = 0 \quad \text{for all } t \neq s \tag{7.1}$$

This assumption states that the error terms u_t and u_s are independently distributed, termed serial independence. If this assumption is no longer true, then the disturbances are not pairwise independent, but are pairwise autocorrelated (or serially correlated). In this situation:

$$Cov(u_t, u_s) \neq 0 \quad \text{for some } t \neq s \tag{7.2}$$

which means that an error occurring at period t may be correlated with one at period s.

Autocorrelation is most likely to occur in a time series framework. When data are arranged in chronological order, the error in one period may affect the error in the next (or other) time period(s). It is highly likely that there will be intercorrelations among successive observations, especially when the interval is short, such as daily, weekly or monthly frequencies, compared to a cross-sectional data set. For example, an unexpected increase in consumer confidence can cause a consumption function equation to underestimate consumption for two or more periods. In cross-sectional data, the problem of autocorrelation is less likely to exist because we can easily change the arrangement of the data without meaningfully altering the results. (This is not true in the case of spatial autocorrelation, but this is beyond the scope of this text.)

What causes autocorrelation?

One factor that can cause autocorrelation is *omitted variables*. Suppose that Y_t is related to X_{2t} and X_{3t} but we, in error, do not include X_{3t} in our model. The effect of X_{3t} will be captured by the disturbances u_t. If X_{3t}, as in many economic time series, depends on $X_{3,t-1}, X_{3,t-2}$ and so on, this will lead to unavoidable correlation among u_t and u_{t-1}, u_{t-2} and so on, thus omitted variables can be a cause of autocorrelation.

Autocorrelation can also occur because of *misspecification* of the model. Suppose that Y_t is connected to X_{2t} with a quadratic relationship $Y_t = \beta_1 + \beta_2 X_{2t}^2 + u_t$, but we, wrongly, assume and estimate a straight-line $Y_t = \beta_1 + \beta_2 X_{2t} + u_t$. Then, the error term obtained from the straight-line specification will depend on X_{2t}^2. If X_{2t} is increasing or decreasing over time, u_t will be doing the same, indicating autocorrelation.

A third factor is *systematic errors in measurement*. Suppose a company updates its inventory at a given period in time; if a systematic error occurs in its measurement, then the cumulative inventory stock will exhibit accumulated measurement errors. These errors will show up as an autocorrelated procedure.

First- and higher-order autocorrelation

The simplest and most commonly observed case of autocorrelation is first-order serial correlation. (The terms serial correlation and autocorrelation are identical and will be used in this text interchangeably.) Consider the multiple regression model:

$$Y_t = \beta_1 + \beta_2 X_{2t} + \beta_3 X_{3t} + \cdots + \beta_k X_{kt} + u_t \tag{7.3}$$

in which the current observation of the error term (u_t) is a function of the previous (lagged) observation of the error term (u_{t-1}); that is:

$$u_t = \rho u_{t-1} + \varepsilon_t \tag{7.4}$$

where ρ is the parameter depicting the functional relationship among observations of the error term (u_t), and ε_t is a new error term that is identically independently distributed (iid). The coefficient ρ is called the first-order autocorrelation coefficient and takes values from -1 to 1 (or $|\rho| < 1$) in order to avoid explosive behaviour (this will be explained this analytically in Chapter 12, where we describe the ARIMA models).

It is obvious that the size of ρ will determine the strength of serial correlation, and we can differentiate three cases:

(a) If ρ is zero, then we have no serial correlation, because $u_t = \varepsilon_t$ and therefore an iid error term.

(b) If ρ approaches $+1$, the value of the previous observation of the error (u_{t-1}) becomes more important in determining the value of the current error term (u_t) and therefore greater positive serial correlation exists. In this case the current observation of the error term tends to have the same sign as the previous observation of the error term (that is negative will lead to negative, and positive to positive). This is called positive serial correlation. Figure 7.1 shows how the residuals of a case of positive serial correlation appear.

(c) If ρ approaches -1, obviously the strength of serial correlation will be very high. This time, however, we have negative serial correlation. Negative serial correlation implies that there is some saw-tooth-like behaviour in the time plot of the error

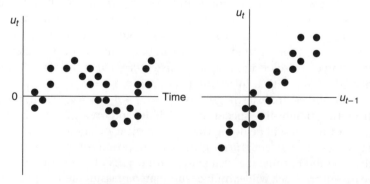

Figure 7.1   Positive serial correlation

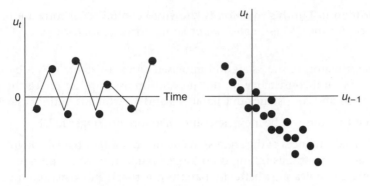

Figure 7.2 Negative serial correlation

terms. The signs of the error terms have a tendency to switch from negative to positive and vice versa in consecutive observations. Figure 7.2 depicts the case of negative serial correlation.

In general, in economics, negative serial correlation is much less likely to happen than positive serial correlation.

Serial correlation can take many forms and we can have disturbances that follow higher orders of serial correlation. Consider the following model:

$$Y_t = \beta_1 + \beta_2 X_{2t} + \beta_3 X_{3t} + \cdots + \beta_k X_{kt} + u_t \tag{7.5}$$

where:

$$u_t = \rho_1 u_{t-1} + \rho_2 u_{t-2} + \cdots + \rho_p u_{t-p} + \varepsilon_t \tag{7.6}$$

In this case, we say that we have pth-order serial correlation. If we have quarterly data and omit seasonal effects, for example, we might expect to find that fourth-order serial correlation is present; while, similarly, monthly data might exhibit 12th-order serial correlation. In general, however, cases of higher-order serial correlation are not as likely to happen as the first-order type we examined analytically above.

Consequences of autocorrelation for the OLS estimators

A general approach

Consider the classical linear regression model:

$$Y_t = \beta_1 + \beta_2 X_{2t} + \beta_3 X_{3t} + \cdots + \beta_k X_{kt} + u_t \tag{7.7}$$

If the error term (u_t) in this equation is known to exhibit serial correlation, then the consequences for the OLS estimates can be summarized as follows:

1 The OLS estimators of the $\hat{\beta}$s are still unbiased and consistent. This is because both unbiasedness and consistency do not depend on assumption 6 (see the proofs of unbiasedness and consistency in Chapters 3 and 4), which is in this case violated.

2 The OLS estimators will be inefficient and therefore no longer BLUE.

3 The estimated variances of the regression coefficients will be biased and inconsistent, and therefore hypothesis testing is no longer valid. In most of the cases, R^2 will be overestimated (indicating a better fit than the one that truly exists) and the t-statistics will tend to be higher (indicating a higher significance of our estimates than for the correct one).

A more mathematical approach

We now examine how serial correlation affects the form of the variance–covariance matrix of the residuals, and then use this to show why the variance of the $\hat{\beta}$s in a multiple regression model will no longer be correct.

Effect on the variance–covariance matrix of the error terms

Recall from Chapter 4 (pp. 71ff.) that the variance–covariance matrix of the residuals, because of assumptions 5 and 6, looks like:

$$E(\mathbf{uu'}) = \begin{pmatrix} \sigma^2 & 0 & 0 & \dots & 0 \\ 0 & \sigma^2 & 0 & 0 & 0 \\ 0 & 0 & \sigma^2 & \dots & 0 \\ \dots & \dots & \dots & & \dots \\ 0 & 0 & 0 & \dots & \sigma^2 \end{pmatrix} = \sigma^2 \mathbf{I_n} \tag{7.8}$$

where $\mathbf{I_n}$ is an $n \times n$ identity matrix.

The presence of serial correlation shows clearly that assumption 6 has been violated. Therefore, the non-diagonal terms of the variance–covariance matrix of the residuals will no longer be zero. Let's assume that the error terms are serially correlated of order one. We therefore have:

$$u_t = \rho u_{t-1} + \varepsilon_t \tag{7.9}$$

Using the lag operator, $LX_t = X_{t-1}$, Equation (7.9) can be rewritten:

$$(1 - \rho L)u_t = \varepsilon_t \tag{7.10}$$

or:

$$u_t = \frac{1}{(1 - \rho L)}\varepsilon_t$$

$$= (1 + \rho L + \rho^2 L^2 + \cdots)\varepsilon_t$$

$$= \varepsilon_t + \rho \varepsilon_{t-1} + \rho^2 \varepsilon_{t-2} + \rho^3 \varepsilon_{t-3} + \cdots \tag{7.11}$$

Squaring both sides of (7.11) and taking expectations yields:

$$E(u_t^2) = Var(u_t) = \frac{\sigma_\varepsilon^2}{1 - \rho^2} \tag{7.12}$$

Note that the solution for $Var(u_t)$ does not involve t, therefore the u_t series has a constant variance given by:

$$\sigma_u^2 = \frac{\sigma_\varepsilon^2}{1 - \rho^2} \tag{7.13}$$

Using Equation (7.11) it is simple to show that the covariances $E(u_t, u_{t-1})$ will be given by:

$$E(u_t, u_{t-1}) = \rho \sigma_u^2 \tag{7.14}$$

$$E(u_t, u_{t-2}) = \rho^2 \sigma_u^2 \tag{7.15}$$

$$\cdots \tag{7.16}$$

$$E(u_t, u_{t-s}) = \rho^s \sigma_u^2 \tag{7.17}$$

Thus the variance–covariance matrix of the disturbances (for the first-order serial correlation case) will be given by:

$$E(\mathbf{uu}') = \sigma^2 \begin{pmatrix} 1 & \rho & \rho^2 & \cdots & \rho^{n-1} \\ \rho & 1 & \rho & \cdots & \rho^{n-2} \\ \cdots & \cdots & \cdots & & \cdots \\ \rho^{n-1} & \rho^{n-2} & \rho^{n-3} & \cdots & 1 \end{pmatrix} = \mathbf{\Omega}_2 \text{ *} \tag{7.18}$$

Effect on the OLS estimators of the multiple regression model

Recall that the variance–covariance matrix of the OLS estimators $\hat{\boldsymbol{\beta}}$ is given by:

$$\begin{aligned} Cov(\hat{\boldsymbol{\beta}}) &= \mathbf{E}[(\hat{\boldsymbol{\beta}} - \boldsymbol{\beta})(\hat{\boldsymbol{\beta}} - \boldsymbol{\beta})'] \\ &= E\{[(\mathbf{X}'\mathbf{X})^{-1}\mathbf{X}'\mathbf{u}][(\mathbf{X}'\mathbf{X})^{-1}\mathbf{X}'\mathbf{u}]'\} \\ &= E\{(\mathbf{X}'\mathbf{X})^{-1}\mathbf{X}'\mathbf{uu}'\mathbf{X}(\mathbf{X}'\mathbf{X})^{-1}\}^\dagger \\ &= (\mathbf{X}'\mathbf{X})^{-1}\mathbf{X}'E(\mathbf{uu}')\mathbf{X}(\mathbf{X}'\mathbf{X})^{-1\ddagger} \\ &= (\mathbf{X}'\mathbf{X})^{-1}\mathbf{X}'\mathbf{\Omega}_2\mathbf{X}(\mathbf{X}'\mathbf{X})^{-1} \end{aligned} \tag{7.19}$$

which is totally different from the classical expression $\sigma^2(\mathbf{X}'\mathbf{X})^{-1}$. This is because assumption 6 is no longer valid, and of course $\mathbf{\Omega}_2$ denotes the new variance–covariance matrix presented above, whatever form it may happen to take. Therefore, using the classical expression to calculate the variances, standard errors and t-statistics of

---

*We denote this matrix of $\mathbf{\Omega}_2$ in order to differentiate from the $\mathbf{\Omega}$ matrix in the heteroskedasticity case in Chapter 9.

† This is because $(AB)' = B'A'$.

‡ This is because, according to assumption 2, the Xs are non-random.

the estimated $\hat{\beta}$s will lead us to incorrect conclusions. Equation (7.19) (which is similar to Equation (7.9)) forms the basis for what is often called 'robust' inference; that is, the derivation of standard errors and t-statistics that are correct even when some of the OLS assumptions are violated. What happens is that we assume a particular form for the Ω matrix and then use Equation (7.19) to calculate a corrected covariance matrix.

Detecting autocorrelation

The graphical method

One simple way to detect autocorrelation is to examine whether the residual plots against time and the scatter plot of $\hat{u}_t$ against $\hat{u}_{t-1}$ exhibit patterns similar to those presented in Figures 7.1 and 7.2 above. In such cases we say that we have evidence of positive serial correlation if the pattern is similar to that of Figure 7.1, and negative serial correlation if it is similar to that of Figure 7.2. An example with real data is given below.

Example: detecting autocorrelation using the graphical method

The file ser_corr.wf1 contains the following quarterly data from 1985q1 to 1994q2:
   lcons = consumers' expenditure on food in £millions at constant
         1992 prices.
   ldisp = disposable income in £millions at constant 1992 prices.
   lprice = the relative price index of food (1992 = 100).
Denoting *lcons*, *ldisp* and *lprice* by C_t, D_t and P_t, respectively, we estimate in EViews the following regression equation:

$$C_t = b_1 + b_2 D_t + b_3 P_t + u_t$$

by typing in the EViews command line:

```
ls lcons c ldisp lprice
```

Results from this regression are shown in Table 7.1.

   After estimating the regression, we store the residuals of the regression in a vector by typing the command:

```
genr res01=resid
```

A plot of the residuals obtained by the command:

```
plot res01
```

is presented in Figure 7.3, while a scatter plot of the residuals against the residuals at $t - 1$ obtained by using the command:

```
scat res01(-1) res01
```

is given in Figure 7.4.

Table 7.1 Regression results from the computer example

Dependent variable: LCONS
Method: least squares
Date: 02/12/04 Time: 14:25
Sample: 1985:1 1994:2
Included observations: 38

Variable	Coefficient	Std. error	t-statistic	Prob.
C	2.485434	0.788349	3.152708	0.0033
LDISP	0.529285	0.292327	1.810589	0.0788
LPRICE	−0.064029	0.146506	−0.437040	0.6648

R-squared	0.234408	Mean dependent var	4.609274
Adjusted R-squared	0.190660	S.D. dependent var	0.051415
S.E. of regression	0.046255	Akaike info criterion	−3.233656
Sum squared resid	0.074882	Schwarz criterion	−3.104373
Log likelihood	64.43946	F-statistic	5.358118
Durbin–Watson stat	0.370186	Prob(F-statistic)	0.009332

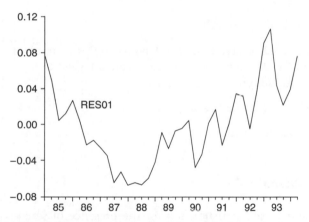

Figure 7.3 Residuals plot from computer example

From Figures 7.3 and 7.4, it is clear that the residuals are serially correlated and particularly positively serially correlated.

A similar analysis can be conducted in Stata with the use of the ser_cor.dat file. The commands used to obtain the regression results, construct the residual series and obtain Figures 7.3 and 7.4 are as follows (explanations are given in parentheses):

```
regress lcons ldisp lprice
```

(this command is for the regression results)

```
predict res01, residual
```

(this command is in order to save the residuals)

```
twoway (tsline res01)
```

(this command is for the time plot of the residuals)

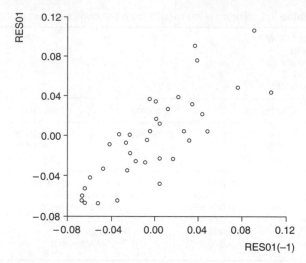

Figure 7.4   Residuals scatter plot from computer example

```
g res01_1=L1.res01
```

(this command is used to create the $t - 1$ lagged series of residuals. Here L1. is for the lag operator of first order; if we want to create a lagged two-period series we use L2.nameofseries, and so on)

```
twoway (scatter res01_1 res01)
```

(this command is for the scatter plot).

The Durbin–Watson test

The most frequently used statistical test for the presence of serial correlation is the Durbin–Watson (DW) test (see Durbin and Watson, 1950), which is valid when the following assumptions are met:

(a) the regression model includes a constant;

(b) serial correlation is assumed to be of first-order only; and

(c) the equation does not include a lagged dependent variable as an explanatory variable.

Consider the model:

$$Y_t = \beta_1 + \beta_2 X_{2t} + \beta_3 X_{3t} + \cdots + \beta_k X_{kt} + u_t \tag{7.20}$$

where:

$$u_t = \rho u_{t-1} + \varepsilon_t \quad |\rho| < 1 \tag{7.21}$$

Table 7.2 The DW test

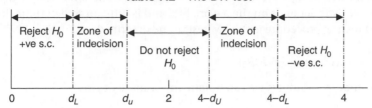

Then under the null hypothesis H_0: $\rho = 0$ the DW test involves the following steps:

Step 1   Estimate the model by using OLS and obtain the residuals $\hat{u}_t$.

Step 2   Calculate the DW test statistic given by:

$$d = \frac{\sum_{t=2}^{n}(\hat{u}_t - \hat{u}_{t-1})^2}{\sum_{t=1}^{n}\hat{u}_t^2} \qquad (7.22)$$

Step 3   Construct Table 7.2, substituting with your calculated d_U, d_L, $4-d_U$ and $4-d_L$ that you will obtain from the DW critical values table given in the Appendix to this chapter. Note that the table of critical values is according to k', which is the number of explanatory variables excluding the constant.

Step 4a   To test for positive serial correlation, the hypotheses are:

$$H_0: \quad \rho = 0 \text{ no autocorrelation.}$$

$$H_a: \quad \rho > 0 \text{ positive autocorrelation.}$$

1 If $d \leq d_L$ we reject H_0 and conclude in favour of positive serial correlation.

2 If $d \geq d_U$ we cannot reject H_0 and therefore there is no positive serial correlation.

3 In the special case where $d_L < d < d_U$ the test is inconclusive.

Step 4b   To test for negative serial correlation the hypotheses are:

$$H_0: \quad \rho = 0 \text{ no autocorrelation.}$$

$$H_a: \quad \rho < 0 \text{ negative autocorrelation.}$$

1 If $d \geq 4 - d_L$ we reject H_0 and conclude in favour of negative serial correlation.

2 If $d \leq 4 - d_U$ we cannot reject H_0 and therefore there is no negative serial correlation.

3 In the special case where $4 - d_U < d < 4 - d_L$ the test is inconclusive.

The reason for the inconclusiveness of the DW test is that the small sample distribution for the DW statistic depends on the X-variables and is difficult to determine in general. A preferred testing procedure is the LM test, to be described later.

A rule of thumb for the DW test

From the estimated residuals we can obtain an estimate of ρ as:

$$\hat{\rho} = \frac{\sum_{t=2}^{n} \hat{u}_t \hat{u}_{t-1}}{\sum_{t=1}^{n} \hat{u}_t^2} \tag{7.23}$$

It is shown in the Appendix that the DW statistic is approximately equal to $d = 2(1 - \hat{\rho})$. Because ρ by definition ranges from -1 to 1, the range for d will be from 0 to 4. Therefore, we can have three different cases:

(a) $\rho = 0$; $d = 2$: therefore, a value of d close to 2 indicates that there is no evidence of serial correlation.

(b) $\rho \simeq 1$; $d \simeq 0$: a strong positive autocorrelation means that ρ will be close to $+1$, and thus d will have very low values (close to zero) for positive autocorrelation.

(c) $\rho \simeq -1$; $d \simeq 4$: similarly, when ρ is close to -1 then d will be close to 4, indicating a strong negative serial correlation.

From this analysis we can see that, as a rule of thumb, when the DW test statistic is very close to 2 we do not have serial correlation.

The DW test in EViews, Microfit and Stata

Both EViews and Microfit report the DW test statistic directly in the diagnostics of every regression output, in the final line in the left-hand corner. Stata regression results do not contain the DW statistic automatically, but this can be obtained very easily by using the following command (the command should be typed and executed immediately after obtaining the regression results you want to test for autocorrelation):

```
estat dwatson
```

The result is reported in the results window of Stata. Therefore, for all three software packages, the only work that remains for the researcher to do is to construct the table with the critical values and check whether serial correlation exists, and of what kind it is. An example is given below.

Computer example of the DW test

From the regression results output of the previous example (graphical detection of autocorrelation) we observe that the DW statistic is equal to 0.37. Finding the 1% significance level critical values d_L and d_U for $n = 38$ and $k' = 2$ from Appendix A on page 387 and putting them into the DW table, we have the results shown in

Table 7.3 An example of the DW test

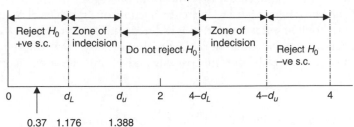

Table 7.3. Since $d = 0.37$ is less than $d_L = 1.176$, there is strong evidence of positive serial correlation.

The Breusch–Godfrey LM test for serial correlation

The DW test has several drawbacks that make its use inappropriate in various cases. For example (a) it may give inconclusive results; (b) it is not applicable when a lagged dependent variable is used; and (c) it can't take into account higher orders of serial correlation.

For these reasons, Breusch (1978) and Godfrey (1978) developed an *LM* test that can accommodate all the above cases. Consider the model:

$$Y_t = \beta_1 + \beta_2 X_{2t} + \beta_3 X_{3t} + \cdots + \beta_k X_{kt} + u_t \tag{7.24}$$

where:

$$u_t = \rho_1 u_{t-1} + \rho_2 u_{t-2} + \cdots + \rho_p u_{t-p} + \varepsilon_t \tag{7.25}$$

The Breusch–Godfrey *LM* test combines these two equations:

$$Y_t = \beta_1 + \beta_2 X_{2t} + \beta_3 X_{3t} + \cdots + \beta_k X_{kt} + \rho_1 u_{t-1} + \rho_2 u_{t-2} + \cdots$$
$$+ \rho_p u_{t-p} + \varepsilon_t \tag{7.26}$$

and therefore the null and the alternative hypotheses are:

H_0: $\rho_1 = \rho_2 = \cdots = \rho_p = 0$ no autocorrelation.

H_a: at least one of the ρs is not zero, thus serial correlation.

The steps for carrying out the test are as follows:

Step 1   Estimate Equation (7.24) by OLS and obtain $\hat{u}_t$.

Step 2   Run the following regression model with the number of lags used (p) being determined according to the order of serial correlation to be tested.

$$\hat{u}_t = \alpha_0 + \alpha_1 X_{2t} \ldots \alpha_R X_{Rt} + \alpha_{R+1} \hat{u}_{t-1} \ldots \alpha_{R+P} \hat{u}_{t-p}$$

Step 3 Compute the *LM* statistic $= (n - p)R^2$ from the regression run in step 2. If this *LM*-statistic is bigger than the χ_p^2 critical value for a given level of significance, then the null of serial correlation is rejected and we conclude that serial correlation is present. Note that the choice of p is arbitrary. However, the periodicity of the data (quarterly, monthly, weekly and so on) will often suggest the size of p.

The Breusch–Godfrey test in EViews, Microfit and Stata

After estimating a regression equation in EViews, in order to perform the Breusch–Godfrey LM test we move from the estimation results window to **View/Residual Tests/Serial Correlation LM test**. EViews asks for the number of lags to be included in the test, and after specifying that and clicking **OK** the results of the test are obtained. The interpretation is as usual.

Microfit reports the LM test for first-order serial correlation directly in the diagnostic tests section of the regression results output. The Breusch–Godfrey *LM*-test is for Microfit test A. If we need to test for higher-order serial correlation we close the results window by clicking on **close** to obtain the **Post Regression** menu. From that menu choose option 2. Move to the **Hypothesis Testing** menu and click **OK**. From the hypothesis testing menu choose option 1, **LM tests for Serial Correlation (OLS, IV, NLS and IV-NLS)**, and click **OK**. You will then be asked to determine the number of lags in the **Input an integer** window and after clicking **OK** the results of the test will be obtained. An example with the use of EViews is given below.

In Stata the command used to obtain the Breusch–Godfrey test results is:

```
estat bgodfrey , lags(number)
```

where (number) should be substituted by the number of lags we want to test for autocorrelation. Therefore, if we want to test for the fourth order of autocorrelation, the command is:

```
estat bgodfrey , lags(4)
```

Similarly for other orders we simply change the number in the parentheses.

Computer example of the Breusch–Godfrey test

Continuing with the consumption, disposable income and price relationship, we proceed by testing for the fourth-order serial correlation because we have quarterly data. To test for this serial correlation we use the Breusch–Godfrey LM test. From the estimated regression results window go to **View/Residual Tests/Serial Correlation LM Test** and specify 4 as the number of lags. The results of this test are shown in Table 7.4.

We can see from the first columns that the values of both the *LM*-statistic and the *F*-statistic are quite high, suggesting the rejection of the null of no serial correlation. It is also clear that this is because the p-values are very small (less than 0.05 for a 95% confidence interval). Therefore, serial correlation is definitely present. However, if we observe the regression results, we see that only the first lagged residual term is statistically significant, indicating most probably that the serial correlation is of the

Table 7.4   Results of the Breusch–Godfrey test (fourth-order s.c.)

Breusch-Godfrey Serial Correlation LM Test:

F-statistic	17.25931	Probability	0.000000
Obs*R-squared	**26.22439**	Probability	**0.000029**

Test equation:
Dependent variable: RESID
Method: least squares
Date: 02/12/04 Time: 22:51

Variable	Coefficient	Std. error	t-statistic	Prob.
C	−0.483704	0.489336	−0.988491	0.3306
LDISP	0.178048	0.185788	0.958341	0.3453
LPRICE	−0.071428	0.093945	−0.760322	0.4528
RESID(−1)	0.840743	0.176658	**4.759155**	0.0000
RESID(−2)	−0.340727	0.233486	−1.459306	0.1545
RESID(−3)	0.256762	0.231219	1.110471	0.2753
RESID(−4)	0.196959	0.186608	1.055465	0.2994

R-squared	0.690115	Mean dependent var	1.28E−15
Adjusted R-squared	0.630138	S.D. dependent var	0.044987
S.E. of regression	0.027359	Akaike info criterion	−4.194685
Sum squared resid	0.023205	Schwarz criterion	−3.893024
Log likelihood	86.69901	F-statistic	11.50621
Durbin–Watson stat	1.554119	Prob(F-statistic)	0.000001

Table 7.5   Results of the Breusch–Godfrey test (first-order s.c.)

Breusch–Godfrey Serial Correlation LM Test:

F-statistic	53.47468	Probability	0.000000
Obs*R-squared	**23.23001**	Probability	**0.000001**

Test equation:
Dependent variable: RESID
Method: least squares
Date: 02/12/04 Time: 22:55

Variable	Coefficient	Std. error	t-statistic	Prob.
C	−0.585980	0.505065	−1.160208	0.2540
LDISP	0.245740	0.187940	1.307546	0.1998
LPRICE	−0.116819	0.094039	−1.242247	0.2226
RESID(−1)	0.828094	0.113241	**7.312638**	0.0000

R-squared	0.611316	Mean dependent var	1.28E − 15
Adjusted R-squared	0.577020	S.D. dependent var	0.044987
S.E. of regression	0.029258	Akaike info criterion	−4.126013
Sum squared resid	0.029105	Schwarz criterion	−3.953636
Log likelihood	82.39425	F-statistic	17.82489
Durbin–Watson stat	1.549850	Prob(F-statistic)	0.000000

first order. Rerunning the test for a first-order serial correlation, the results are as shown in Table 7.5.

This time the *LM*-statistic is much higher, as well as the *t*-statistic of the lagged residual term. So, the autocorrelation is definitely of the first order.

Durbin's *h* test in the presence of lagged dependent variables

We mentioned earlier, in the assumptions of this test, that this test is not applicable when the regression model includes lagged dependent variables as explanatory variables. Therefore, if the model under examination has the form:

$$Y_t = \beta_1 + \beta_2 X_{2t} + \beta_3 X_{3t} + \cdots + \beta_k X_{kt} + \gamma Y_{t-1} + u_t \qquad (7.27)$$

the DW test is not valid.

Durbin (1970) devised a test statistic that can be used for such models, and this *h*-statistic has the form:

$$h = \left(1 - \frac{d}{2}\right) \sqrt{\frac{n}{1 - n\sigma_{\hat{\gamma}}^2}} \qquad (7.28)$$

where n is the number of observations, d is the regular DW statistic defined in Equation (7.22) and $\sigma_{\hat{\gamma}}^2$ is the estimated variance of the coefficient of the lagged dependent variable. For large samples, this statistic follows a normal distribution. The steps involved in the *h*-test are as follows:

Step 1 Estimate Equation (7.27) by OLS to obtain the residuals and calculate the DW statistic given by Equation (7.22). (As we noted earlier, in practical terms this step using EViews involves only the estimation of the equation by OLS. EViews provides the DW statistic in its reported regression diagnostics. Using Microfit this step alone will also give the *h*-statistic, so step 2 will not be needed.)

Step 2 Calculate the *h*-statistic given by Equation (7.28).

Step 3 The hypotheses are:

$$H_0: \quad \rho = 0 \text{ no autocorrelation.}$$

$$H_a: \quad \rho \neq 0 \text{ autocorrelation is present.}$$

Step 4 Compare the *h*-statistic with the critical value (for large samples and for $\alpha = 0.05$, $z = \pm 1.96$). If the *h*-statistic exceeds the critical value, then H_0 is rejected and we conclude that there is serial correlation (see also Figure 7.5).

The *h*-test in EViews, Microfit and Stata

EViews reports only the DW test, regardless of whether a lagged dependent variable is used as a regressor or not. Therefore step 2 is needed in order to calculate the *h*-statistic. In Microfit, though, the inclusion of a lagged dependent variable gives by default the *h*-statistic in the diagnostics of the regression results output window. This is located next to the DW statistic and is the last line of the right-hand side. Microfit also reports the probability limit for this statistic, so if it is greater than 0.05 it is very clear that serial correlation is not present. An example of the *h*-test using EViews is given below.

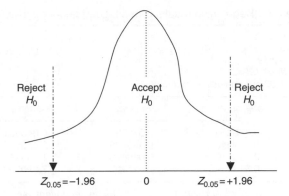

Figure 7.5 Durbin's *h*-test, displayed graphically

In Stata, after estimating the regression with the lagged dependent variable, we need to use the DW test command:

```
estat dwatson
```

followed by the calculation of the *h*-statistic as described in step 2. A computer example using EViews is given below. It is very easy to produce the same results with Stata.

Computer example of Durbin's *h* test

If we want to estimate the following regression model:

$$C_t = b_1 + b_2 D_t + b_3 P_t + b_4 C_{t-1} + u_t$$

which includes a lagged dependent variable, we know that the DW test is no longer valid. Thus, in this case, we need to use either Durbin's *h*-test or the LM test. Running the regression model by typing:

```
ls lcons c ldisp lprice lcons(-1)
```

we get the results shown in Table 7.6.

The DW statistic is equal to 1.727455, and from this we can get the *h*-statistic from the formula:

$$h = \left(1 - \frac{d}{2}\right)\sqrt{\frac{n}{1 - n\sigma_{\hat{\gamma}}^2}}$$

where $\sigma_{\hat{\gamma}}^2$ is the variance of the coefficient of LCONS(−1) = $(0.103707)^2 = 0.0107551$. Typing the following command in Eviews, we get the value of the *h*-statistic:

```
scalar h= (1-1.727455/2)(37/(1-37*0.103707^2))^(.5)
```

and by double-clicking on the scalar *h* we can see the value at the lower left-hand corner as:

```
scalar h=1.0682889
```

Table 7.6   Regression results with a lagged dependent variable

Dependent variable: LCONS
Method: least squares
Date: 02/12/04 Time: 22:59
Sample(adjusted): 1985:2 1994:2
Included observations: 37 after adjusting endpoints

Variable	Coefficient	Std. error	t-statistic	Prob.
C	−0.488356	0.575327	−0.848831	0.4021
LDISP	0.411340	0.169728	2.423524	0.0210
LPRICE	−0.120416	0.086416	−1.393442	0.1728
LCONS(−1)	0.818289	**0.103707**	7.890392	0.0000

R-squared	0.758453	Mean dependent var	4.608665
Adjusted R-squared	0.736494	S.D. dependent var	0.051985
S.E. of regression	0.026685	Akaike info criterion	−4.307599
Sum squared resid	0.023500	Schwarz criterion	−4.133446
Log likelihood	83.69058	F-statistic	34.53976
Durbin–Watson stat	**1.727455**	Prob(F-statistic)	0.000000

Table 7.7   The Breusch–Godfrey LM test (again)

Breusch–Godfrey Serial Correlation LM Test:

F-statistic	0.680879	Probability	0.415393
Obs*R-squared	**0.770865**	Probability	**0.379950**

Test equation:
Dependent variable: RESID
Method: least squares
Date: 02/12/04 Time: 23:10

Variable	Coefficient	Std. error	t-statistic	Prob.
C	0.153347	0.607265	0.252521	0.8023
LDISP	0.018085	0.171957	0.105171	0.9169
LPRICE	0.003521	0.086942	0.040502	0.9679
LCONS(−1)	−0.054709	0.123515	−0.442932	0.6608
RESID(−1)	0.174392	0.211345	0.825154	0.4154

R-squared	0.020834	Mean dependent var	9.98E-16
Adjusted R-squared	−0.101562	S.D. dependent var	0.025549
S.E. of regression	0.026815	Akaike info criterion	−4.274599
Sum squared resid	0.023010	Schwarz criterion	−4.056908
Log likelihood	84.08009	F-statistic	0.170220
Durbin–Watson stat	1.855257	Prob(F-statistic)	0.952013

and therefore because $h < z -$ critical $= 1.96$ we fail to reject the H_0 hypothesis and conclude that this model does not suffer from serial correlation.

Applying the LM test for this regression equation by clicking on **View/Residual Tests/Serial Correlation LM Test** and specifying the lag order to be equal to 1 (by typing 1 in the relevant box) we get the results shown in Table 7.7. From these results it is again clear that there is no serial correlation in this model.

Resolving autocorrelation

Since the presence of autocorrelation provides us with inefficient OLS estimators, it is important to have ways of correcting our estimates. Two different cases are presented in the next two sections.

When ρ is known

Consider the model:

$$Y_t = \beta_1 + \beta_2 X_{2t} + \beta_3 X_{3t} + \cdots + \beta_k X_{kt} + u_t \tag{7.29}$$

where we know that u_t is autocorrelated and we speculate that it follows a first-order serial correlation, so that:

$$u_t = \rho u_{t-1} + \varepsilon_t \tag{7.30}$$

If Equation (7.29) holds for period t, it will also hold for period $t - 1$, so:

$$Y_{t-1} = \beta_1 + \beta_2 X_{2t-1} + \beta_3 X_{3t-1} + \cdots + \beta_k X_{kt-1} + u_{t-1} \tag{7.31}$$

Multiplying both sides of Equation (7.31) by ρ, yields:

$$\rho Y_{t-1} = \beta_1 \rho + \beta_2 \rho X_{2t-1} + \beta_3 \rho X_{3t-1} + \cdots + \beta_k \rho X_{kt-1} + \rho u_{t-1} \tag{7.32}$$

and subtracting Equation (7.32) from Equation (7.29) we obtain:

$$Y_t - \rho Y_{t-1} = \beta_1(1 - \rho) + \beta_2(X_{2t} - \rho X_{2t-1}) + \beta_3(X_{3t} - \rho X_{3t-1}) + \cdots$$
$$+ \beta_k(X_{kt} - \rho X_{kt-1}) + (u_t - \rho u_{t-1}) \tag{7.33}$$

or:

$$Y_t^* = \beta_1^* + \beta_2 X_{2t}^* + \beta_3 X_{3t}^* + \cdots + \beta_k X_{kt}^* + \varepsilon_t \tag{7.34}$$

where $Y_t^* = Y_t - \rho Y_{t-1}$, $\beta_1^* = \beta_1(1 - \rho)$, and $X_{it}^* = (X_{it} - \rho X_{it-1})$.

Note that with this differencing procedure we lose one observation. To avoid this loss, it is suggested that Y_1 and X_{i1} should be transformed for the first observation, as follows:

$$Y_1^* = Y_1\sqrt{1 - \rho^2} \quad \text{and} \quad X_{i1}^* = X_{i1}\sqrt{1 - \rho^2} \tag{7.35}$$

The transformation that generated Y_t^*, β_1^* and X_{it}^* is known as quasi-differencing or generalized differencing. Note that the error term in Equation (7.34) satisfies all the CLRM assumptions. So, if ρ is known we can apply OLS to Equation (7.34) and obtain estimates that are BLUE. An example of the use of generalized differencing is provided below.

Table 7.8   Regression results for determining the value of ρ

Dependent variable: RES01
Method: least squares
Date: 02/12/04 Time: 23:26
Sample(adjusted): 1985:2 1994:2
Included observations: 37 after adjusting endpoints

Variable	Coefficient	Std. error	t-statistic	Prob.
RES01(−1)	**0.799544**	0.100105	7.987073	0.0000

R-squared	0.638443	Mean dependent var		−0.002048
Adjusted R-squared	0.638443	S.D. dependent var		0.043775
S.E. of regression	0.026322	Akaike info criterion		−4.410184
Sum squared resid	0.024942	Schwarz criterion		−4.366646
Log likelihood	82.58841	Durbin–Watson stat		1.629360

Table 7.9   The generalized differencing regression results

Dependent variable: LCONS_STAR
Method: least squares
Date: 02/12/04 Time: 23:49
Sample: 1985:1 1994:2
Included observations: 38

Variable	Coefficient	Std. error	t-statistic	Prob.
BETA1_STAR	4.089403	1.055839	3.873131	0.0004
LDISP_STAR	0.349452	0.231708	1.508155	0.1405
LPRICE_STAR	−0.235900	0.074854	−3.151460	0.0033

R-squared	0.993284	Mean dependent var		0.974724
Adjusted R-squared	0.992900	S.D. dependent var		0.302420
S.E. of regression	0.025482	Akaike info criterion		−4.426070
Sum squared resid	0.022726	Schwarz criterion		−4.296787
Log likelihood	87.09532	Durbin–Watson stat		1.686825

Computer example of the generalized differencing approach

To apply the generalized differencing estimators we first need to find an estimate of the ρ coefficient. Remember that, from the first computer example, we obtained the residual terms and named them *res*01. Running a regression of *res*01 to *res*01(−1) we get the results shown in Table 7.8, from which the ρ coefficient is equal to 0.799.

In order to transform the variables for the first observation we need to enter the following commands in the EViews command window:

```
scalar rho=c(1)              [saves the estimate of the r coefficient]
smpl 1985:1 1985:1           [sets the sample to be only the first observation]
genr lcons_star=((1-rho^2)^(0.5))*lcons
genr ldisp_star=((1-rho^2)^(0.5))*ldisp
genr lprice_star=((1-rho^2)^(0.5))*lprice
genr beta1_star=((1-rho^2)^(0.5))
```

where the three commands generate the starred variables and the final command creates the new constant.

To transform the variables for observations 2 to 38 we need to type the following commands in the EViews command window:

```
smpl 1985:2 1994:2
genr lcons_star=lcons-rho*lcons(-1)
genr ldisp_star=ldisp-rho*disp(-1)
genr lprice_star=lprice-rho*lprice(-1)
genr beta1_star=1-rho
```

And to estimate the generalized differenced equation we need first to change the sample to all observations by typing:

```
smpl 1985:1 1994:2
```

and then to execute the following command:

```
ls lcons_star beta1_star ldisp_star lprice_star
```

the results of which are shown in Table 7.9.

When ρ is unknown

Although the method of generalized differencing seems to be very easy to apply, in practice the value of ρ is not known. Therefore, alternative procedures need to be developed to provide us with estimates of ρ and then of the regression model in Equation (7.34). Several procedures have been developed, with two being the most popular and important: (a) the Cochrane–Orcutt iterative procedure; and (b) the Hildreth–Lu search procedure. These two procedures are presented below.

The Cochrane–Orcutt iterative procedure

Cochrane and Orcutt (1949) developed an iterative procedure that can be presented through the following steps:

Step 1 Estimate the regression model from Equation (7.29) and obtain the residuals $\hat{u}_t$.

Step 2 Estimate the first-order serial correlation coefficient ρ by OLS from $\hat{u}_t = \rho\hat{u}_{t-1} + \varepsilon_t$.

Step 3 Transform the original variables as $Y_t^* = Y_t - \hat{\rho}Y_{t-1}$, $\beta_1^* = \beta_1(1 - \hat{\rho})$, and $X_{it}^* = (X_{it} - \hat{\rho}X_{it-1})$ for $t = 2, \ldots, n$ and as $Y_1^* = Y_1\sqrt{1 - \hat{\rho}^2}$ and $X_{i1}^* = X_{i1}\sqrt{1 - \hat{\rho}^2}$ for $t = 1$.

Step 4 Run the regression using the transformed variables and find the residuals of this regression. Since we do not know that the $\hat{\rho}$ obtained from step 2 is the 'best' estimate of ρ, go back to step 2 and repeat steps 2 to 4 for several rounds until the following stopping rule holds.

Stopping rule The iterative procedure can be stopped when the estimates of ρ from two successive iterations differ by no more than some preselected (very small) value, such as 0.001. The final $\hat{\rho}$ is used to get the estimates of Equation (7.34). In general, the iterative procedure converges quickly and does not require more than 3 to 6 iterations.

EViews utilizes an iterative non-linear method for estimating generalized differencing results with AR(1) errors (autoregressive errors of order 1) in the presence of serial correlation. Since the procedure is iterative, it requires a number of repetitions to achieve convergence, which is reported in the EViews results below the **included observations** information. The estimates from this iterative method can be obtained by simply adding the AR(1) error terms to the end of the equation specification list. So, if we have a model with variables Y and X, the simple linear regression command is:

```
ls y c x
```

If we know that the estimates suffer from serial correlation of order 1, results can be obtained through the iterative process by using the command:

```
ls y c x ar(1)
```

EViews provides results in the usual way regarding the constant and coefficient of the X-variable, together with an estimate for ρ, which will be the coefficient of the AR(1) term. An example is provided at the end of this section.

The Hildreth–Lu search procedure

Hildreth and Lu (1960) developed an alternative method to the Cochrane–Orcutt iterative procedure. Their method consists of the following steps:

Step 1 Choose a value for ρ (say ρ_1), and for this value transform the model as in Equation (7.34) and estimate it by OLS.

Step 2 From the estimation in step 1 obtain the residuals $\hat{\varepsilon}_t$ and the residual sum of squares (RSS(ρ_1)). Next choose a different value of ρ (say ρ_2) and repeat steps 1 and 2.

Step 3 By varying ρ from -1 to $+1$ in some predetermined systematic way (let's say at steps of length 0.05), we can get a series of values for RSS(ρ_i). We choose the ρ for which RSS is minimized and Equation (7.34), which was estimated using the chosen ρ as the optimal solution.

This procedure is very complex and involves many calculations. EViews provides results very quickly with the Cochrane–Orcutt iterative method (as we have shown above), and is usually preferred in cases of autocorrelation.

Computer example of the iterative procedure

To obtain results with the EViews iterative method, and assuming a serial correlation of order one, we type the following command in EViews:

```
ls lcons c ldisp lprice ar(1)
```

the results from which are shown in Table 7.10.

Table 7.10 Results with the iterative procedure

Dependent variable: LCONS
Method: least squares
Date: 02/12/04 Time: 23:51
Sample(adjusted): 1985:2 1994:2
Included observations: 37 after adjusting endpoints
Convergence achieved after 13 iterations

Variable	Coefficient	Std. error	t-statistic	Prob.
C	9.762759	1.067582	9.144742	0.0000
LDISP	−0.180461	0.222169	-0.812269	0.4225
LPRICE	−0.850378	0.057714	-14.73431	0.0000
AR(1)	**0.974505**	0.013289	**73.33297**	0.0000

R-squared	0.962878	Mean dependent var.	4.608665
Adjusted R-squared	0.959503	S.D. dependent var.	0.051985
S.E. of regression	0.010461	Akaike info. criterion	−6.180445
Sum squared resid	0.003612	Schwarz criterion	−6.006291
Log likelihood	118.3382	F-statistic	285.3174
Durbin–Watson stat	2.254662	Prob(F-statistic)	0.000000

Inverted AR roots	0.97

It needed 13 iterations to obtain convergent results. Also, the AR(1) coefficient (which is in fact the ρ) is equal to 0.974, which is much bigger than that obtained in the previous computer example. However, this is not always the case; other examples lead to smaller discrepancies. The case here might be affected by the quarterly frequency of the data. If we add an AR(4) term using the command:

```
ls lcons c ldisp lprice ar(1) ar(4)
```

we get a ρ coefficient (see Table 7.11) that is very close to that in the previous example.

Resolving autocorrelation in Stata

To resolve autocorrelation in Stata, we can re-estimate the model with the Cochrane–Orcutt iterative procedure by using this command:

```
prais lcons ldisp lprice , corc
```

Stata does all the necessary iterations and provides corrected results for a first-order autoregressive process. The results obtained from this command will be identical to those in Table 7.10.

Table 7.11   Results with the iterative procedure and AR(4) term

Dependent variable: LCONS
Method: least squares
Date: 02/12/04 Time: 23:57
Sample(adjusted): 1986:1 1994:2
Included observations: 34 after adjusting endpoints
Convergence achieved after 11 iterations

Variable	Coefficient	Std. error	t-statistic	Prob.
C	10.21009	0.984930	10.36632	0.0000
LDISP	−0.308133	0.200046	−1.540312	0.1343
LPRICE	−0.820114	0.065876	−12.44932	0.0000
AR(1)	**0.797678**	0.123851	**6.440611**	0.0000
AR(4)	0.160974	0.115526	1.393404	0.1741

R-squared	0.967582	Mean dependent var	4.610894
Adjusted R-squared	0.963111	S.D. dependent var	0.053370
S.E. of regression	0.010251	Akaike info criterion	−6.187920
Sum squared resid	0.003047	Schwarz criterion	−5.963455
Log likelihood	110.1946	F-statistic	216.3924
Durbin–Watson stat	2.045794	Prob(F-statistic)	0.000000

Inverted AR roots	0.97	0.16+0.55i	0.16−0.55i	−0.50

Questions and exercises

Questions

1 What is autocorrelation? Which assumption of the CLRM is violated, and why?

2 Explain the consequences of autocorrelation and how they can be resolved when ρ is known.

3 Explain how autocorrelation can be resolved when ρ is unknown.

4 Describe the steps of the DW test for autocorrelation. What are its disadvantages and which alternative tests can you suggest?

Exercise 7.1

The file investment.wf1 contains data for the following variables, I = investment, Y = income and R = interest rate. Estimate a regression equation that has investment as the dependent variable, and income and the interest rate as explanatory variables. Check for autocorrelation using both the informal and all the formal ways (tests) that we have covered in Chapter 7. If autocorrelation exists, use the Cochrane–Orcutt iterative procedure to resolve this.

Exercise 7.2

The file product.wf1 contains data for the following variables, q = quantity of a good produced during various years, p = price of the good, f = amount of fertilizer used in the production of this good and r = amount of rainfall during each production year. Estimate a regression equation that explains the quantity produced of this product. Check for autocorrelation using both the informal and all the formal ways (tests) that we have covered in Chapter 7. If autocorrelation exists, use the Cochrane–Orcutt iterative procedure to resolve this.

Appendix

The DW test statistic given in Equation (7.22) can be expanded to give:

$$d = \frac{\sum_{t=2}^{n} \hat{u}_t^2 + \sum_{t=2}^{n} \hat{u}_{t-1}^2 - 2 \sum_{t=2}^{n} \hat{u}_t \hat{u}_{t-1}}{\sum_{t=1}^{n} \hat{u}_t^2} \tag{7.36}$$

Because $\hat{u}_t$ are generally small, the summations from 2 to n or from 2 to $n-1$ will both be approximately equal to the summation from 1 to n. Thus:

$$\sum_{t=2}^{n} \hat{u}_t^2 \simeq \sum_{t=2}^{n} \hat{u}_{t-1}^2 \simeq \sum_{t=1}^{n} \hat{u}_t^2 \tag{7.37}$$

So, we have that Equation (7.36) is now:

$$d \simeq 1 + 1 - \frac{2 \sum_{t=2}^{n} \hat{u}_t \hat{u}_{t-1}}{\sum_{t=1}^{n} \hat{u}_t^2} \tag{7.38}$$

but from Equation (7.23) we have that $\hat{\rho} = 2 \sum_{t=2}^{n} \hat{u}_t \hat{u}_{t-1} / \sum_{t=1}^{n} \hat{u}_t^2$, and therefore:

$$d \simeq 2 - 2\rho \simeq 2(1 - \rho) \tag{7.39}$$

Finally, because ρ takes values from $+1$ to -1, then d will take values from 0 to 4.

8 Misspecification: Wrong Regressors, Measurement Errors and Wrong Functional Forms

CHAPTER CONTENTS

LEARNING OBJECTIVES

After studying this chapter you should be able to:

1. Understand the various forms of possible misspecification in the CLRM.
2. Appreciate the importance and learn the consequences of omitting influential variables in the CLRM.
3. Distinguish among the wide range of functional forms and understand the meaning and interpretation of their coefficients.
4. Understand the importance of measurement errors in the data.
5. Perform misspecification tests using econometric software.
6. Understand the meaning of nested and non-nested models.
7. Be familiar with the concept of data mining and choose an appropriate econometric model.

Introduction

One of the most important problems in econometrics is that we are never certain about the form or specification of the equation we want to estimate. For example, one of the most common specification errors is to estimate an equation that omits one or more influential explanatory variables, or an equation that contains explanatory variables that do not belong to the 'true' specification. This chapter will show how these problems affect the OLS estimates, and then provide ways of resolving them.

Other misspecification problems related to the functional form can result from an incorrect assumption that the relation between the Ys and Xs is linear. Therefore, this chapter presents a variety of models that allow us to formulate and estimate various non-linear relationships.

In addition, it examines the problems emerging from measurement errors regarding our variables, as well as formal tests for misspecification. Alternative approaches to selecting the best model are presented in the final section.

Omitting influential or including non-influential explanatory variables

Consequences of omitting influential variables

Omitting explanatory variables that play an important role in the determination of the dependent variable causes these variables to become a part of the error term in the population function. Therefore, one or more of the CLRM assumptions will be violated. To explain this in detail, consider the population regression function:

$$Y = \beta_1 + \beta_2 X_2 + \beta_3 X_3 + u \tag{8.1}$$

where $\beta_2 \neq 0$ and $\beta_3 \neq 0$, and assume that this is the 'correct' form of this relationship.

However, let us also suppose that we make an error in our specification and we estimate:

$$Y = \beta_1 + \beta_2 X_2 + u^* \tag{8.2}$$

where X_3 is wrongly omitted. In this equation we are forcing u to include the omitted variable X_3 as well as any other purely random factors. In fact, in Equation (8.2) the error term is:

$$u^* = \beta_3 X_3 + u \tag{8.3}$$

Based on the assumptions of the CLRM, now the assumption that the mean error is zero is violated:

$$E(u^*) = E(\beta_3 X_3 + u) = E(\beta_3 X_3) + E(u) = E(\beta_3 X_3) \neq 0 \tag{8.4}$$

and, if the excluded variable X_3 happens to be correlated with X_2, then the error term in Equation (8.2) is no longer independent of X_2. The result of both these complications leads to estimators of β_1 and β_2 that are biased and inconsistent. This is often called omitted variable bias. It is easy to show that the situation is the same when we omit more than one variable from the 'true' population equation.

Including a non-influential variable

We have seen that omitting influential explanatory variables causes particular complications for the OLS estimators. However, if an estimated equation includes variables that are not influential the problem is less serious. In this case, assume that the correct equation is:

$$Y = \beta_1 + \beta_2 X_2 + u \tag{8.5}$$

and this time estimate:

$$Y = \beta_1 + \beta_2 X_2 + \beta_3 X_3 + u \tag{8.6}$$

where X_3 is wrongly included in the model specification.

Here, since X_3 does not belong to Equation (8.6), its population coefficient should be equal to zero ($\beta_3 = 0$). If $\beta_3 = 0$ then none of the CLRM assumptions is violated when we estimate Equation (8.6) and therefore OLS estimators will yield both unbiased and consistent estimators. However, while the inclusion of an irrelevant variable does not lead to bias, the OLS estimators of β_1 and β_2 are unlikely to be fully efficient. In the case that X_3 is correlated with X_2, an unnecessary element of multicollinearity will be introduced into the estimation, which will lead unavoidably to a higher standard error in the coefficient of X_2. This might also lead to the wrong conclusion of having non-significant t-values for explanatory variables that are influential.

Therefore, because of the inclusion of irrelevant variables, it does not necessarily follow that a coefficient with an insignificant t-statistic is also irrelevant. So, dropping insignificant variables from a regression model has to be done very cautiously. In general, in non-influential conditions we should expect that:

1 The value of $\bar{R}^2$ will fall, since degrees of freedom increase, while the residual sums of squares (RSS) should remain more or less unchanged.

2 Sign reversal will not occur for the coefficients of the remaining regressors, nor should their magnitudes change appreciably.

3 t-statistics of the remaining variables with not be affected appreciably.

However, the selection of a non-influential variable that is highly correlated with one or more of the remaining variables can affect their t-statistics. Thus these guidelines are valid only under ideal circumstances, as noted earlier. Intuition, economic theory and previous empirical findings should be used to determine whether to delete variables from an equation.

Omission and inclusion of relevant and irrelevant variables at the same time

In this case, suppose the correct equation is:

$$Y = \beta_1 + \beta_2 X_2 + \beta_3 X_3 + u \tag{8.7}$$

and we estimate:

$$Y = \beta_1 + \beta_2 X_2 + \beta_4 X_4 + u^* \tag{8.8}$$

Here we not only omit the relevant variable X_3, but also include the non-influential variable X_4 at the same time. As was analysed above, the consequences of the first case are to have biased and inconsistent estimates, and the second gives inefficient estimates. In general, the consequences of omitting an influential variable are serious and we therefore need to have ways of detecting such problems. One way of doing this is by observing the residuals of the estimated equation. We have already seen in Chapter 7 that visual observation of the residuals can give us an indication of problems of autocorrelation. Here we will also describe formal tests to detect autocorrelation and to resolve it.

The plug-in solution in the omitted variable bias

Sometimes omitted variable bias occurs because a key variable that affects Y is not available. For example, consider a model where the monthly salary of an individual is associated with whether the person is male or female (*sex*), and the years each individual has spent in education (*education*). Both these factors can be quantified easily and included in the model. However, if we also assume that the salary level can be affected by the socio-economic environment in which each person was raised, then it is difficult to find a variable that captures that aspect:

$$(salary\_level) = \beta_1 + \beta_2(sex) + \beta_3(education) + \beta_4(background) \tag{8.9}$$

Not including the *background* variable in this model may lead to biased and inconsistent estimates of β_2 and β_3. Our major interest, however, is to obtain appropriate estimates for those two slope coefficients. We do not care that much about β_1, and we can never hope for a consistent estimator of β_3, since *background* is unobserved. Therefore, a way to resolve this problem and obtain appropriate slope coefficients is to include a proxy variable for the omitted variable, such as, in this example, the family income (*fm_inc*) of each individual. In this case, of course, *fm_inc* does not have to be the same as *background*, but we need *fm_inc* to be correlated with the unobserved variable *background*.

To illustrate this in more detail, consider the following model:

$$Y = \beta_1 + \beta_2 X_2 + \beta_3 X_3 + \beta_4 X_4^* + u \tag{8.10}$$

where X_2 and X_3 are variables that are observed (such as *sex* and *education*), while X_4^* is unobserved (such as *background*), but we have a variable X_4 that is a 'good' proxy variable for X_4^* (such as *fm_inc*).

For X_4 we require at least some relationship to X_4^*; for example, a simple linear form such as:

$$X_4^* = \gamma_1 + \gamma_2 X_4 + e \tag{8.11}$$

where an error e should be included because X_4^* and X_4 are not exactly related. Obviously, if then the variable X_4^* is not an appropriate proxy for X_4, while in general we include proxies that have a positive correlation, so, $\gamma_2 > 0$. The coefficient γ_1 is included in order to allow X_4^* and X_4 to be measured on different scales, and obviously they can be related either positively or negatively.

Therefore, to resolve the omitted variable bias, we can assume that X_4 and X_4^* are the same and run the regression:

$$\begin{aligned} Y &= \beta_1 + \beta_2 X_2 + \beta_3 X_3 + \beta_4(\gamma_1 + \gamma_2 X_4 + e) + u \\ &= (\beta_1 + \beta_4\gamma_1) + \beta_2 X_2 + \beta_3 X_3 + \beta_4\gamma_2 X_4 + (u + \beta_4 e) \\ &= a_1 + \beta_2 X_2 + \beta_3 X_3 + a_4 X_4 + \varkappa \end{aligned} \tag{8.12}$$

where $\varkappa = u + \beta_4 e$ is a composite error that depends on the model of interest in Equation (8.10) and the error from the proxy variable equation (Equation (8.11)). Obviously, $a_1 = (\beta_1 + \beta_4\gamma_1)$ is the new intercept and $a_4 = \beta_4\gamma_2$ is the slope parameter of the proxy variable. As noted earlier, by estimating Equation (8.12) we do not get unbiased estimators of β_1 and β_4, but we do obtain unbiased estimators of a_1, β_2, β_3 and a_4. The important thing is that we get 'appropriate' estimates for the parameters β_2 and β_3, which are of most interest in our analysis.

On the other hand, it is easy to show that using a proxy variable can still lead to bias. Suppose that the unobserved variable X_4^* is related to all (or some) of the observed variables. Then Equation (8.11) becomes:

$$X_4^* = \gamma_1 + \gamma_2 X_2 + \gamma_3 X_3 + \gamma_4 X_4 + w \tag{8.13}$$

Equation (8.11) simply assumes that $\gamma_2 = \gamma_3 = 0$, and by substituting Equation (8.13) into Equation (8.10) we have:

$$\begin{aligned} Y &= (\beta_1 + \beta_4\gamma_1) + (\beta_2 + \beta_4\gamma_2)X_2 + (\beta_3 + \beta_4\gamma_3)X_3 \\ &\quad + \beta_4\gamma_4 X_4 + (u + \beta_4 w) \end{aligned} \tag{8.14}$$

from which we get $plim(\hat{\beta}_2) = \beta_2 + \beta_4\gamma_2$ and $plim(\hat{\beta}_3) = \beta_3 + \beta_4\gamma_3$. Connecting this to the previous example, if *education* has a positive partial correlation with *fm_inc*, there will be a positive bias (inconsistency) in the estimate of the *education* coefficient. However, we can reasonably hope that the bias faced in this case will be smaller than where the variable is omitted entirely.

Various functional forms

Introduction

A different situation where specification errors may be found is when an incorrect functional form is used. The most obvious case relates to the basic assumption of having an equation that can be represented by a linear relationship. If this is not true, then a linear estimating equation might be adopted while the real population relationship is non-linear.

For example, if the true regression equation is:

$$Y = AX_2^{\beta}X_3^{\gamma}e^u \tag{8.15}$$

and we estimate the linear form given by:

$$Y = a + \beta X_2 + \gamma X_3 + u \tag{8.16}$$

then the parameters β and γ in the non-linear model represent elasticities, while β (and γ) in the linear model show an estimate of the change in Y after a one-unit change in X_2 (and X_3). Therefore, β and γ are clearly incorrect estimators of the true population parameters.

One way to detect incorrect functional forms is visually to inspect the pattern of the residuals. If a systematic pattern is observed in the residuals we may suspect the possibility of misspecification. However, it is also useful to know the various possible non-linear functional forms that might have to be estimated, together with the properties regarding marginal effects and elasticities. Table 8.1 presents a summary of the forms and features of the various alternative models.

Linear-log functional form

In a linear-log model, the dependent variable remains the same but the independent variable appears in logs. Thus the model is:

$$Y = \beta_1 + \beta_2 \ln X + u \tag{8.17}$$

Table 8.1 Features of different functional forms

Name	Functional form	Marginal effect (dY/dX)	Elasticity $(X/Y)(dY/dX)$
Linear	$Y = \beta_1 + \beta_2 X$	β_2	$\beta_2 X/Y$
Linear-log	$Y = \beta_1 + \beta_2 \ln X$	β_2/X	β_2/Y
Reciprocal	$Y = \beta_1 + \beta_2(1/X)$	$-\beta_2/X^2$	$-\beta_2/(XY)$
Quadratic	$Y = \beta_1 + \beta_2 X + \beta_3 X^2$	$\beta_2 + 2\beta_3 X$	$(\beta_2 + 2\beta_3 X)X/Y$
Interaction	$Y = \beta_1 + \beta_2 X + \beta_3 XZ$	$\beta_2 + \beta_3 Z$	$(\beta_2 + \beta_3 Z)X/Y$
Log-linear	$\ln Y = \beta_1 + \beta_2 X$	$\beta_2 Y$	$\beta_2 X$
Log-reciprocal	$\ln Y = \beta_1 + \beta_2(1/X)$	$-\beta_2 Y/X^2$	$-\beta_2 X$
Log-quadratic	$\ln Y = \beta_1 + \beta_2 X + \beta_3 X^2$	$Y(\beta_2 + 2\beta_3 X)$	$X(\beta_2 + 2\beta_3 X)$
Double-log	$\ln Y = \beta_1 + \beta_2 \ln X$	$\beta_2 Y/X$	β_2
Logistic	$\ln[Y/(1-Y)] = \beta_1 + \beta_2 X$	$\beta_2 Y(1-Y)$	$\beta_2(1-Y)X$

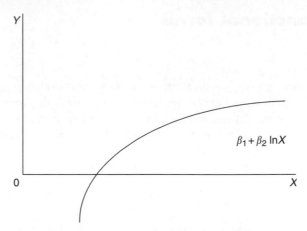

Figure 8.1   A linear-log functional form

This relation gives a marginal effect (dY/dX) equal to $dY/dX = \beta_2/X$. Solving this for dY:

$$dY = \beta_2 \frac{dX}{X} = \frac{\beta_2}{100}\left[100\frac{dX}{X}\right] = \frac{\beta_2}{100} \quad (\% \text{ change in } X) \tag{8.18}$$

So, a 1 per cent change in X will lead to a $\beta_2/100$ units change on Y (note that this is not a percentage but a unit change).

A plot of this function for positive β_1 and β_2 is given in Figure 8.1, and an example from economic theory is the production of the total output of an agricultural product (Y) with respect to hectares of land used for its cultivation (X).

Reciprocal functional form

A different model is:

$$Y = \beta_1 + \beta_2(1/X) + u \tag{8.19}$$

a plot of which is shown in Figure 8.2.

This form is frequently used with demand curve applications. Note that because demand curves are typically downward-sloping, we expect β_2 to be positive and, while X becomes sufficiently large, Y asymptotically approaches β_1.

Polynomial functional form

This model includes terms of the explanatory variable X increased in different powers according to the degree of the polynomial (k). We have:

$$Y = \beta_1 + \beta_2 X + \beta_3 X^2 + \cdots + \beta_k X^k + u \tag{8.20}$$

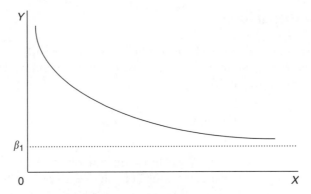

Figure 8.2 A reciprocal functional form

To estimate this model we simply generate new variables X^2, X^3 and so on, and then regress these variables to Y. Obviously if $k = 3$ then the polynomial is cubic, while for $k = 2$ it is quadratic. Quadratic formulations are frequently used to fit U-shaped curves (as, for example, cost functions). In general, polynomials of orders higher than 2 should be avoided, first because of the reduction of the degrees of freedom, and second because there is a possibility of a high correlation between X and X^2, and the estimated coefficients are unreliable.

Functional form including interaction terms

Sometimes the marginal effect of a variable depends on another variable. For example, Klein and Morgan (1951) suggested that the marginal propensity to consume is affected by the asset holdings of individuals, meaning that a wealthier person is likely to have a higher marginal propensity to consume from his income. Thus, in the Keynesian consumption function:

$$C = a + \beta Y + u \tag{8.21}$$

where C denotes consumption and y income, β is the marginal propensity to consume, we have $\beta = \beta_1 + \beta_2 A$, where A denotes assets. Substituting this into Equation (8.21) we get:

$$C = a + (\beta_1 + \beta_2 A)Y + u$$
$$= a + \beta_1 Y + \beta_2 AY + u \tag{8.22}$$

The term AY is known as the interaction term. Note that in this case the marginal effect will be given by $dC/dY = \beta_2 + \beta_2 A$, so we need to know the value of A in order to calculate it.

Log-linear functional form

So far we have examined models where non-linearity emerges only from the explanatory variables. Now we examine a model in which the dependent variable appears transformed. Consider the model:

$$\ln Y = \beta_1 + \beta_2 X + u \tag{8.23}$$

β_2 is now the marginal effect of X on $\ln Y$ and not on Y. This is known as the instantaneous rate of growth. Differentiating both sides with respect to X, we obtain:

$$\beta_2 = \frac{d \ln Y}{dX} = \frac{1}{Y}\frac{dY}{dX} = \frac{dY}{Y}\frac{1}{dX} \tag{8.24}$$

The term dY/Y is the change in Y divided by Y. Therefore, when multiplied by 100, β_2 gives the percentage change in Y per unit change in X.

The log-linear model is widely applied in economics (and, recently, especially in the human capital literature). This theory suggests, for example, that the more educated a person, the higher his/her salary should be. Therefore, let us say that there is a return on an extra year of education, labelled θ. Then, for the first period, the monthly salary will be equal to $s_1 = (1 + \theta)s_0$, for a two-year return it will be $s_2 = (1 + \theta)^2 s_0$, and so on. For k years it will be $s_k = (1 + \theta)^k s_0$. Taking logarithms of both sides we have:

$$\ln s_k = k \ln(1 + \theta) + \ln(s_0) = \beta_1 + \beta_2 k \tag{8.25}$$

where, of course, k is years in education for each individual. Thus we have obtained a log-linear relationship between salary and years of education, where the OLS coefficient β_2 indicates that one more year of education will give $100\beta_2\%$ more in monthly salary.

The double-log functional form

The double-log model is very popular in cases where we expect variables to have constant ratios. A common specification is the Cobb–Douglas type of production function of the form:

$$Y_t = AK_t^a L_t^\beta \tag{8.26}$$

where standard notation is used. Taking logarithms of both sides and adding an error term we get:

$$\ln Y_t = \gamma + a \ln K_t + \beta \ln L_t + u_t \tag{8.27}$$

and it can be shown here that a and β are the elasticities of K_t and L_t, respectively. To demonstrate that, consider changes in K while keeping L constant. We have:

$$a = \frac{d \ln Y}{d \ln K} = \frac{(1/Y)dY}{(1/K)dK} = \frac{K}{Y}\frac{dY}{dK} \quad (8.28)$$

Another way to show this is by taking the derivative of Y with respect to K; from the initial function in Equation (8.26):

$$\frac{dY}{dK} = aAK_t^{a-1}L_t^{\beta} = a\frac{AK_t^a L_t^{\beta}}{K} = a\frac{Y}{K} \quad (8.29)$$

and therefore:

$$a = \frac{dY}{dK}\frac{K}{Y} \quad (8.30)$$

It can be shown that the same holds for β. We leave this as an exercise for the reader. Table 8.2 provides interpretations of the marginal effects in the various logarithmic models.

The Box–Cox transformation

As was demonstrated above, the choice of functional form plays a very important role in the interpretation of the estimated coefficients, and therefore a formal test is needed to direct the choice of functional form where there is uncertainty about the population relationship.

For example, consider a model with two explanatory variables (X_2 and X_3). We must be able to determine whether to use the linear, log-linear, linear-log or double-log specification. The choice between the linear and linear-log model, or the log-linear and double-log specification, is simple because we have the same dependent variable in each of the two models. So, we can estimate both models and choose the functional

Table 8.2 Interpretation of marginal effects in logarithmic models

Name	Functional form	Marginal effect	Interpretation
Linear	$Y = \beta_1 + \beta_2 X$	$\Delta Y = \beta_2 \Delta X$	1-*unit* change in X will induce a β_2 *unit* change in Y
Linear-log	$Y = \beta_1 + \beta_2 \ln X$	$\Delta Y = \beta_2/100[100\Delta X/X]$	1% change in X will induce a $\beta_2/100$ *unit* change in Y
Log-linear	$\ln Y = \beta_1 + \beta_2 X$	$100\Delta Y/Y = 100\beta_2 \Delta X$	1-*unit* change in X will induce a $100\beta_2$% change in Y
Double-log	$\ln Y = \beta_1 + \beta_2 \ln X$	$100\Delta Y/Y = \beta_2[100\Delta X/X]$	1% change in X will induce a β_2% change in Y

form that yields the higher R^2. However, in cases where the dependent variable is not the same, as for example in the linear form:

$$Y = \beta_1 + \beta_2 X \tag{8.31}$$

and the double-log form:

$$\ln Y = \beta_1 + \beta_2 \ln X \tag{8.32}$$

it is not possible to compare the two by using R^2.

In such examples, the Y-variable must be scaled in such a way that the two models can be compared. The procedure is based on the work of Box and Cox (1964), and is usually known as the Box–Cox transformation. The procedure follows these steps:

Step 1   Obtain the geometric mean of the sample Y-values. This is:

$$\tilde{Y} = (Y_1 Y_2 Y_3 \cdots Y_n)^{1/n} = \exp\left(1/n \sum \ln Y_i\right) \tag{8.33}$$

Step 2   Transform the sample Y-values by dividing each of them by $\tilde{Y}$ obtained above to get:

$$Y_i^* = Y_i/\tilde{Y} \tag{8.34}$$

Step 3   Estimate Equations (8.31) and (8.32), substituting Y_i^* as the dependent variable in both. The RSSs of the two equations are now directly comparable, and the equation with the lower RSS is preferred.

Step 4   If we need to know whether one of the equations is significantly better than the other, we have to calculate the following statistic:

$$\left(\frac{1}{2}n\right) \ln\left(\frac{RSS_2}{RSS_1}\right) \tag{8.35}$$

where RSS_2 is the higher RSS, and RSS_1 is the lower. The above statistic follows a χ^2 distribution with 1 degree of freedom. If χ^2-statistical exceeds the χ^2-critical value we can say with confidence that the model with the lower RSS is superior at the level of significance for which the χ^2-critical is obtained.

Measurement errors

Up to this point our discussion has dealt with situations where explanatory variables are either omitted or included contrary to the correct model specification. However, another possibility exists that can create problems in the OLS coefficients. Sometimes in econometrics it is not possible to collect data on the variable that truly affects economic behaviour, or we might even collect data for which one or more variables are measured incorrectly. In such cases, variables used in the econometric analysis are different from the correct values and can therefore potentially create serious estimation problems.

Measurement error in the dependent variable

We begin by examining the case where there is a measurement error only in the dependent variable and we assume that the true population equation is:

$$Y = \beta_1 + \beta_2 X_2 + \cdots + \beta_k X_k + u \tag{8.36}$$

which we further assume satisfies the assumptions of the CLRM, but we are unable to observe the actual values of Y. Not having information about the correct values of Y leads us to use available data on Y containing measurement errors.

The observed values of Y^* will differ from the actual relationship as follows:

$$Y^* = Y + w \tag{8.37}$$

where w denotes the measurement error in Y.

To obtain a model that can be estimated econometrically, we have that $Y = Y^* - w$ and we insert this into Equation (8.36) to obtain:

$$Y^* = \beta_1 + \beta_2 X_2 + \cdots + \beta_k X_k + (u + w) \tag{8.38}$$

Therefore, we now have an error term $(u+w)$. Since $Y^*, X_2, \ldots, X_k$ are now observed, we can ignore the fact that Y^* is not a perfect measure of Y and estimate the model. The obtained OLS coefficients will be unaffected only if certain conditions about w occur. First, we know from the CLRM assumptions that u has a zero mean and is uncorrelated with all Xs. If the measurement error w also has a zero mean, then we get an unbiased estimator for the constant β_1 in the equation; if not, then the OLS estimator for β_1 is biased, but this is rarely important in econometrics. Second, we need to have a condition for the relationship of w with the explanatory variables.

If the measurement error in Y is uncorrelated with the Xs then the OLS estimators for the slope coefficients are unbiased and consistent, and vice versa. As a final note, in a case where u and w are uncorrelated then $var(u+w) = \sigma_u^2 + \sigma_w^2 > \sigma_u^2$.

Therefore, the measurement error leads to a larger residual variance, which, of course, leads to larger variances in the OLS estimated coefficients. However, this is expected and nothing can be done to avoid it.

Measurement error in the explanatory variable

In this case we have as the true population equation:

$$Y = \beta_1 + \beta_2 X_2 + u \tag{8.39}$$

which satisfies the assumption of the CLRM and therefore OLS will provide unbiased and consistent estimators of both β_1 and β_2. Now with X_2 non-observed, we have only a measure of X_2, let's say X_2^*. The relationship between X_2 and X_2^* is:

$$X_2 = X_2^* - v \tag{8.40}$$

and inserting this into the population model gives:

$$Y = \beta_1 + \beta_2(X_2^* - v) + u \tag{8.41}$$

$$= \beta_1 + \beta_2 X_2^* + (u - \beta_2 v) \tag{8.42}$$

If ε and v were uncorrelated with X_2^* and both had a zero mean, then the OLS estimators would be consistent estimators for both β_1 and β_2. However, as shown below, this is not generally the case. Also, again since ε and v are uncorrelated, the residual variance is $var(\varepsilon - \beta_2 v) = \sigma_\varepsilon^2 + \beta_2^2 \sigma_v^2$. Thus, only when $\beta_2 = 0$ does the measurement error not increase the variance, and the variances of β_1 and β_2 will again be higher.

Recall that the OLS slope estimator is given by:

$$\hat{\beta}_2 = \frac{\sum (X_2^* - \bar{X}_2^*)(Y - \bar{Y})}{\sum (X_2^* - \bar{X}_2^*)^2}$$

$$= \frac{\sum (X_2^* - \bar{X}_2^*)(\beta_1 + \beta_2 X_2^* + u - \beta_2 v) - \beta_1 - \beta_2 \bar{X}_2^* - \bar{u} + \beta_2 \bar{v}}{\sum (X_2^* - \bar{X}_2^*)^2}$$

$$= \frac{\sum (X_2^* - \bar{X}_2^*)(\beta_2 (X_2^* - \bar{X}_2^*) + (u - \bar{u}) - \beta_2 (v - \bar{v}))}{\sum (X_2^* - \bar{X}_2^*)^2} \tag{8.43}$$

For unbiasedness we want $E(\hat{\beta}_2) = \beta_2$. Taking the expected value of Equation (8.43) we have:

$$E(\hat{\beta}_2) = \beta_2 + E\left(\frac{\sum (X_2^* - \bar{X}_2^*)(u - \bar{u})}{\sum (X_2^* - \bar{X}_2^*)^2} - \beta_2 \frac{\sum (X_2^* - \bar{X}_2^*)(v - \bar{v})}{\sum (X_2^* - \bar{X}_2^*)^2}\right)$$

$$= \beta_2 + E\left(\frac{Cov(X_2^*, u)}{Var(X_2^*)} - \beta_2 \frac{Cov(X_2^*, v)}{Var(X_2^*)}\right) \tag{8.44}$$

Therefore we need to check whether these covariances are equal to zero. We have that:

$$Cov(X_2^*, u) = E(X_2^* u) - E(X_2^*) E(u) \tag{8.45}$$

But because $E(\varepsilon) = 0$ this reduces to:

$$Cov(X_2^*, u) = E(X_2^* u) = E[(X_2 + v)u] = E(X_2 u) + E(vu) \tag{8.46}$$

Since the actual X is uncorrelated with u, the first expectation in Equation (8.46) equals zero. Also, assuming that the two errors (v and u) are independent, the second expectation is also zero.

For the covariance of X_2^* with v we have:

$$Cov\left(X_2^*, v\right) = E\left(X_2^* v\right) - E\left(X_2^*\right) E(v) \tag{8.47}$$

$$= E\left[(X_2 + v)v\right] \tag{8.48}$$

$$= E(X_2 v) + E(v^2) = 0 + \sigma_v^2 \tag{8.49}$$

The term $E(X_2 v)$ is zero because the actual X_2 is independent of the measurement error. However, because $Cov(X_2^*, v) = \sigma_v^2$ is non-zero, the observed X_2 (that is X_2^*) is correlated with its measurement error. Thus the slope coefficient is biased (because $E(\hat{\beta}_2) = \beta_2 + \sigma_v^2$). Finally, since its magnitude of bias is not affected by its sample size, the OLS estimator under measurement error in one of the explanatory variables is not only biased but also inconsistent.

Tests for misspecification

Normality of residuals

It was mentioned earlier that one way of detecting misspecification problems is by observing the regression residuals. One of the assumptions of the CLRM is that the residuals are normally distributed with a zero mean and a constant variance. Violation of this assumption leads to the inferential statistics of a regression model (that is t-stats, F-stats, etc.) not being valid. Therefore, it is essential to test for the normality of residuals.

To test for this we first calculate the second, third and fourth moments of the residuals and then compute the Jarque–Berra (1990) (JB) statistic. The test can be done by following these four steps:

Step 1 Calculate the second, third and fourth moments of the residuals ($\hat{u}$) (note that μ_3 is the skewness and μ_4 is the kurtosis of these) in the regression equation as:

$$\mu_2 = \frac{\sum \hat{u}^2}{n}; \quad \mu_3 = \frac{\sum \hat{u}^3}{n}; \quad \mu_4 = \frac{\sum \hat{u}^4}{n} \tag{8.50}$$

Step 2 Calculate the Jarque–Berra statistic by

$$JB = n\left[\frac{\mu_3^2}{6} + \frac{(\mu_4 - 3)^2}{24}\right] \tag{8.51}$$

which has a χ^2 distribution with 2 degrees of freedom.

Step 3 Find the $\chi^2(2)$ critical value from the tables of χ^2 distribution.

Step 4 If $JB > \chi^2$-critical we reject the null hypothesis of normality of residuals. Alternatively, if the p-value is less than 0.05 (for a 95% significance level), then we again reject the null hypothesis of normality.

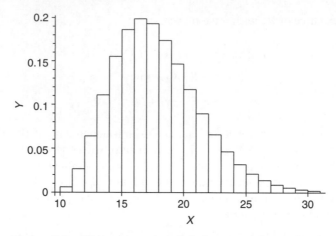

Figure 8.3   Histogram and statistic for regression residuals

The JB normality test for residuals in EViews

To check for normality of residuals in a regression model we need to examine the histogram and the JB statistic. To do this we first need to estimate the desired equation, either by typing the command for the equation estimation in the EViews command line, or by choosing **Quick/Estimate Equation**, then specifying the equation and clicking **OK**. After the estimation the series RESID, which is in every EViews workfile, will contain the residuals of this regression (Note: the series RESID contains the residuals of the most recent estimated equation in EViews, so if another equation is estimated later the series RESID will change). To check for normality, double-click on the RESID series and from the series object toolbar click on **View/Descriptive Statistics/Histogram and Stats**. This procedure will provide the graph and summary statistics shown in Figure 8.3.

From the histogram it can be seen that the residuals do not seem to be normally distributed. Also, at the lower right-hand corner of the figure we can see the value of the JB statistic and its respective probability limit. The residuals come from a simple regression model that includes only one explanatory variable and 38 observations. So we can obtain the χ^2 critical value for 2 degrees of freedom, $a = 0.05$ and $n = 38$, by typing the following command into EViews:

```
scalar chi_crit=@qchisq(.95,2)
```

This will create a scalar named chi_crit in our workfile, and the result of the scalar can be displayed in the status line at the bottom of the EViews main window, after double-clicking on the scalar. The value of the chi_crit is equal to 3.841, and since it is higher than the JB statistic we cannot reject the null hypothesis that the residuals are normally distributed. Also, since the *p*-value is equal to 0.415 and greater than the chosen level of significance (0.05), we again conclude that we cannot reject the null hypothesis of normality.

The JB normality test for residuals in Stata

In Stata we can obtain a histogram of the residuals (let's assume they are labelled resid01) using the following command:

```
histogram resid01
```

Since we want to see whether the residuals follow the normal distribution closely, a graph that includes the normal line can be obtained by re-entering the above command as follows:

```
histogram resid01 , normal
```

Finally, for the formal χ^2 test and the JB statistic we need to enter the command:

```
sktest res01
```

The results of this command for a hypothetical data set are shown below. The statistical value is given under the heading 'adj chi2(2)'; in this example it is equal to 1.51, and next to it is the probability limit. Since the probability limit is 0.47, we cannot reject the null of normality.

```
. sktest res01
                Skewness/Kurtosis tests for Normality
                                                        — joint —
    Variable| Obs Pr(Skewness) Pr(Kurtosis) adj chi2(2) Prob>chi2
       res01|  38     0.239        0.852        1.51       0.4701
```

The Ramsey RESET test for general misspecification

One of the most commonly used tests for general misspecification is Ramsey's (1969) Regressions Specification Error Test (RESET). As with many tests, this has both an F form and an LM form. Suppose the 'true' population model is:

$$Y = \beta_1 + \beta_2 X_2 + \beta_3 X_2^2 + u \tag{8.52}$$

and we wrongly estimate:

$$Y = \beta_1 + \beta_2 X_2 + \hat{u}^* \tag{8.53}$$

where we omit X_2^2 because we do not know the real nature of Y.

The RESET test for such misspecification is based on the fitted values of Y obtained from the regression in Equation (8.53) as:

$$\hat{Y} = \hat{\beta}_1 + \hat{\beta}_2 X_2 \tag{8.54}$$

The RESET test involves including various powers of $\hat{Y}$ as proxies for X_2^2 that can capture possible non-linear relationships. Before implementing the test we need to decide how many terms are to be included in the expanded regression. There is no formal answer to this question, but in general the squared and cubed terms have proved to be useful in most applications; so the expanded equation will be:

$$Y = \beta_1 + \beta_2 X_2 + \delta_1 \hat{Y}^2 + \delta_2 \hat{Y}^3 + \epsilon \qquad (8.55)$$

Then the situation boils down to a regular F-type test for the additional explanatory variables $\hat{Y}^2$ and $\hat{Y}^3$. If one or more of the coefficients is significant this is evidence of general misspecification. A big drawback of the RESET test is that if we reject the null hypothesis of a correct specification, this merely indicates that the equation is misspecified in one way or another, without providing us with alternative models that are correct.

So, summing up, the RESET test can be performed step by step as follows:

Step 1   Estimate the model that is thought to be correct in describing the population equation, and obtain the fitted values of the dependent variable $\hat{Y}$.

Step 2   Estimate the model in step 1 again, this time including $\hat{Y}^2$ and $\hat{Y}^3$ as additional explanatory variables.

Step 3   The model in step 1 is the restricted model and that in step 2 is the unrestricted model. Calculate the F-statistic for these two models.

Step 4   Find the F-critical value from the F-tables for 2, $n - k - 3$ degrees of freedom.

Step 5   If F-statistic $>$ F-critical we reject the null hypothesis of correct specification and conclude that our model is somehow misspecified in some way. Alternatively, we can use the p-value approach. If the p-value for the F-statistic is smaller than the required level of significance (usually 0.05), we again reject the null hypothesis of correct specification.

The RESET test can also be calculated using the LM procedure described in Chapter 4. To perform this, take the residuals from the restricted model in Equation (8.53) and regress them on $\hat{Y}^2$ and $\hat{Y}^3$. TR^2 from this regression would give an LM test with a χ^2 distribution with 2 degrees of freedom.

Ramsey's RESET test in EViews

Assume that we estimated the following regression model from the file cons.wf1, by typing into the EViews command line:

```
ls lcons c ldisp
```

which regresses the logarithm of a consumer's expenditure on food (`lcons`) on the logarithm of disposable income (`ldisp`). The results obtained from this regression are shown in Table 8.3.

To test for general misspecification with Ramsey's RESET test we click on **View/Stability Diagnostics/Ramsey RESET Test** ..., after which a new window opens (**RESET Specification**) that asks us to specify the number of fitted terms we want to

Table 8.3 Ramsey RESET test example

Dependent variable: LCONS
Method: least squares
Date: 02/16/04 Time: 15:03
Sample: 1985:1 1994:2
Included observations: 38

Variable	Coefficient	Std. error	t-statistic	Prob.
C	2.717238	0.576652	4.712091	0.0000
LDISP	0.414366	0.126279	3.281340	0.0023

R-squared	0.230230	Mean dependent var	4.609274
Adjusted R-squared	0.208847	S.D. dependent var	0.051415
S.E. of regression	0.045732	Akaike info criterion	−3.280845
Sum squared resid	0.075291	Schwarz criterion	−3.194656
Log likelihood	64.33606	F-statistic	10.76719
Durbin–Watson stat	0.412845	Prob(F-statistic)	0.002301

use. If we choose 1 it will include only $\hat{Y}^2$, if we choose 2 it will include both $\hat{Y}^2$ and $\hat{Y}^3$, and so on. Assume that we choose only 1 and click **OK**. The results are shown in Table 8.4.

From the results we can see that *F*-stat is quite high. Even though we do not have *F*-critical, from the *p*-value we can see that because the *p*-value for *F*-stat is smaller than the required level of significance (0.05), we can safely reject the null hypothesis of correct specification and conclude that our model is misspecified. Notice also that the coefficient of the squared fitted term is statistically significant (*t*-stat = 4.66).

Ramsey's RESET test in Microfit

Microfit reports Ramsey's test in the regression results output under diagnostic tests, as test B, and it includes one fitted squared term. It reports statistical values and *p*-values for both the LM test and the *F*-type test described above. The interpretation is as usual, with the use of the *p*-value approach as presented in the example above.

Ramsey's RESET test in Stata

To perform Ramsey's RESET test in Stata, after running a regression the following command should be used:

```
estat ovtest
```

Stata gives the F-statistic and the probability limit directly. The test in Stata is slightly different from the one in EViews. The Stata test takes as its restricted model one that does not contain any explanatory variables (which is why the F-statistic reported has different degrees of freedom from the one in EViews) and therefore there will be differences in the results obtained from the two programs. However, in most – if not all – cases, the conclusion will be the same.

Table 8.4   Ramsey RESET test example (continued)

Ramsey RESET test
Equation: UNTITLED
Specification: LCONS C LDISP
Omitted Variables: Squares of fitted values

	Value	df	Probability
t-statistic	4.663918	35	0.0000
F-statistic	*21.75213*	*(1, 35)*	*0.0000*
Likelihood ratio	18.36711	1	0.0000

F-test summary:

	Sum of sq.	df	Mean squares
Test SSR	0.028858	1	0.028858
Restricted SSR	0.075291	36	0.002091
Unrestricted SSR	0.046433	35	0.001327
Unrestricted SSR	0.046433	35	0.001327

LR test summary:

	Value	df
Restricted LogL	64.33606	36
Unrestricted LogL	73.51961	35

Unrestricted test equation:
Dependent variable: LCONS
Method: least squares
Date: 04/19/10 Time: 23:06
Sample: 1985Q1 1994Q2
Included observations: 38

Variable	Coefficient	Std. error	*t*-statistic	Prob.
C	−204.0133	44.32788	−4.602369	0.0001
LDISP	−204.4012	43.91502	−4.654470	0.0000
FITTED^2	53.74842	11.52431	*4.663918*	0.0000

R-squared	0.525270	Mean dependent var	4.609274
Adjusted R-squared	0.498142	S.D. dependent var	0.051415
S.E. of regression	0.036423	Akaike info criterion	−3.711559
Sum squared resid	0.046433	Schwarz criterion	−3.582275
Log likelihood	73.51961	Hannan-Quinn criter.	−3.665561
F-statistic	19.36302	Durbin-Watson stat	0.795597
Prob(F-statistic)	0.000002		

Tests for non-nested models

To test models that are non-nested the F-type test cannot be used. By non-nested models we mean models in which neither equation is a special case of the other; in other words, we do not have a restricted and an unrestricted model.

Suppose, for example, that we have the following two models:

$$Y = \beta_1 + \beta_2 X_2 + \beta_3 X_3 + u \tag{8.56}$$

$$Y = \beta_1 + \beta_2 \ln X_2 + \beta_3 \ln X_3 + \varepsilon \tag{8.57}$$

and that we want to test the first against the second, and vice versa. There are two different approaches.

The first is an approach proposed by Mizon and Richard (1986), who simply suggest the estimation of a comprehensive model of the form:

$$Y = \delta_1 + \delta_2 X_2 + \delta_3 X_3 + \delta_4 \ln X_2 + \delta_5 \ln X_3 + \epsilon \tag{8.58}$$

then applying an F-test for significance of δ_2 and δ_3, having as the restricted model Equation (8.57), or test for δ_4 and δ_5, having as the unrestricted model Equation (8.56).

The second approach is proposed by Davidson and MacKinnon (1993), who suggest that if the model in Equation (8.56) is true, then the fitted values of Equation (8.57) should be insignificant in Equation (8.56) and vice versa. Therefore, in order to test Equation (8.56) we need first to estimate Equation (8.57) and take the fitted values of this model, which may be called $\widetilde{Y}$. The test is then based on the t-statistic of $\widetilde{Y}$ in the following equation:

$$Y = \beta_1 + \beta_2 X_2 + \beta_3 X_3 + \zeta \widetilde{Y} + \nu \tag{8.59}$$

where a significant ζ coefficient will suggest, of course, the rejection of Equation (8.56). A drawback of this test is that the comprehensive Equation (8.58) may not make sense from an economic theory point of view.

The case is exactly the opposite if we want to test Equation (8.57) against Equation (8.56). There are some drawbacks with these testing techniques, however:

1 It is not necessary to have results that clearly suggest which model is better. Both models may be rejected or neither model may be rejected. If neither is rejected, choose the one with the higher $\bar{R}^2$.

2 Rejecting Equation (8.56) does not necessarily mean that Equation (8.57) is the correct alternative.

3 The situation is even more difficult if the two competing models also have different dependent variables. Tests have been proposed to deal with this problem but they are beyond the scope of this text and will not be presented here.

Example: the Box–Cox transformation in EViews

This example looks at the relationship between income and consumption, proposing two functional forms and using the Box–Cox transformation to decide which of the two is preferable. A Ramsey RESET test is also performed.

We use data for income, consumption and the consumer price index, in quarterly frequency from 1985q1 to 1994q2. The file name is box_cox.wf1 and the variable names are *inc*, *cons* and *cpi*, respectively.

The consumption function can be specified in two ways:

$$C_t = \beta_{11} + \beta_{12} Y_t + u_{1t} \tag{8.60}$$

or:

$$\ln C_t = \beta_{21} + \beta_{22} \ln Y_t + u_{2t} \tag{8.61}$$

where C_t is real consumption (adjusted for inflation); β_{11}, β_{12}, β_{21} and β_{22} are coefficients to be estimated; Y_t is real income (adjusted for inflation); and u_{1t} and u_{2t} are the disturbance terms for the two alternative specifications.

We therefore need to restate the nominal data in real terms for both equations, and to create the log of the variables in order to estimate Equation (8.61). We can use *cpi* to remove the effects of price inflation, as follows:

$$X_{real} = X_{nominal} * \left(\frac{CPI_{base}}{CPI_t} \right) \tag{8.62}$$

In EViews, the following commands are used:

```
scalar cpibase=102.7
genr consreal=cons*(cpibase/cpi)
gern increal=inc*(cpibase/cpi)
```

and the logarithm of the variables *consreal* and *increal* can be transformed in EViews using the commands:

```
gern lincr=log(increal)
genr lconsr=log(consreal)
```

All the data sets are now in place for the Box–Cox transformation. First, we need to obtain the geometric mean, which can be calculated as:

$$\tilde{Y} = (Y_1 Y_2 Y_3 \cdots Y_n)^{1/n} = \exp\left(1/n \sum \ln Y_i\right) \tag{8.63}$$

In EViews, the first step is to prepare the sum of the logs of the dependent variable. To do this, type the following command into the EViews command line:

```
scalar scons = @sum(lconsr)
```

To view a scalar value in EViews, we need to double-click on the scalar and its value will appear at the lower right-hand corner. We observe that the sum of the logs is calculated as 174.704. The command to find the geometric mean of the dependent variable, with $n = 38$ observations, is:

```
scalar constilda=exp((1/38)*scons)
```

and we need to transform the sample Y-values, that is *lconsr*, by dividing each by *constilda* to generate a new series *constar*. In EViews the command is:

```
genr constar=lconsr/constilda
```

The new series *constar* can now be substituted as the dependent variable in Equations (8.60) and (8.61) above to provide the following new equations:

$$C_t^* = \beta_{11} + \beta_{12} Y_t + u_{1t} \tag{8.64}$$

and:

$$C_t^* = \beta_{21} + \beta_{22} \ln Y_t + u_{2t} \tag{8.65}$$

To run these two regression in EViews, the commands are:

```
ls constar c increal
ls constar c lincr
```

The results are presented in Tables 8.5 and 8.6, respectively. Summarized results are presented in Table 8.7. From the summarized results we see that the constant and

Table 8.5 Regression model for the Box–Cox test

Dependent variable: CONSTAR
Method: least squares
Date: 02/25/04 Time: 16:56
Sample: 1985:1 1994:2
Included observations: 38

Variable	Coefficient	Std. error	t-statislic	Prob.
C	−0.025836	0.008455	−3.055740	0.0042
LINCR	0.015727	0.001842	8.536165	0.0000
R-squared	0.669319	Mean dependent var		0.046330
Adjusted *R*-squared	0.660133	S.D. dependent var		0.001096
S.E. of regression	0.000639	Akaike info criterion		−11.82230
Sum squared resid	1.47E−05	Schwarz criterion		−11.73611
Log likelihood	226.6238	*F*-statistic		72.86612
Durbin–Watson stat	0.116813	Prob(*F*-statistic)		0.000000

Table 8.6 Regression model for the Box–Cox test (continued)

Dependent variable: CONSTAR
Method: least squares
Date: 02/25/04 Time: 16:56
Sample: 1985:1 1994:2
Included observations: 38

Variable	Coefficient	Std. error	t-statistic	Prob.
C	0.030438	0.001928	15.78874	0.0000
INCREAL	0.000161	1.95E−05	8.255687	0.0000
R-squared	0.654366	Mean dependent var		0.046330
Adjusted *R*-squared	0.644765	S.D. dependent var		0.001096
S.E. of regression	0.000653	Akaike info criterion		−11.77808
Sum squared resid	1.54E−05	Schwarz criterion		−11.69189
Log likelihood	225.7835	*F*-statistic		68.15636
Durbin–Watson stat	0.117352	Prob(*F*-statistic)		0.000000

Table 8.7 Summary of OLS results for the Box–Cox test

Variables	Linear model	Log-Log model
Constant	0.0304	−0.025836
	(15.789)	(−3.056)
Income	0.000161	0.015727
	(8.256)	(8.536)
R^2	0.654366	0.669319
Sample size (n)	38	38

income terms in both functional forms are significant; and the R^2 values are similar at 65–67%.

The residual sums of squares (RSS) of the regressions are 1.54E−05 and 1.47E−05 for the linear (8.64) and the double-log model in Equation (8.65), respectively. Thus Equation (8.65) has the lower RSS, and would be the preferred option. To test this result, we can calculate the Box–Cox test statistic, which is given by the following equation:

$$\left(\frac{1}{2}n\right) \ln\left(\frac{RSS_2}{RSS_1}\right) \tag{8.66}$$

$$= (0.5 * 38) * ln(1.54 * 10^{-5}/1.47 * 10^{-5}) \tag{8.67}$$

$$= 19 * ln(1.0476) = 0.8839 \tag{8.68}$$

where RSS_2 is the higher RSS value, obtained from the linear function in Equation (8.64).

The critical value, taken from the chi-square distribution with one degree of freedom (one independent variable) and an 0.05 level of significance, is 3.841. The test statistic is less than the critical value so we cannot conclude that the log function is superior to the linear function at a 5% level of significance.

Approaches in choosing an appropriate model

The traditional view: average economic regression

In the past, the traditional approach to econometric modelling was to start by formulating the simplest possible model to obey the underlying economic theory, and after estimating that model, to perform various tests in order to determine whether it was satisfactory.

A satisfactory model in that sense would be: (a) one having significant coefficients (that is high t-ratios), and coefficients whose signs correspond with the theoretical predictions; (b) one with a good fit (that is high R^2); and (c) one having residuals that do not suffer from autocorrelation or heteroskedasticity.

If one or more of these points is violated, researchers try to find better methods of estimation (that is the Cochrane–Orcutt iterative method of estimation for the case of serial correlation), or to check other possible causes of bias such as whether important variables have been omitted from the model or whether redundant variables have been included, or to consider alternative functional forms, and so on.

This approach, which essentially starts with a simple model and then 'builds up' the models as the situation demands, is called the 'simple to general approach' or the 'average economic regression (AER)', a term coined by Gilbert (1986), because this was the method that most traditional econometric research was following in practice.

The AER approach has been subject to major criticisms:

1 One obvious criticism is that the procedure followed in the AER approach suffers from data mining. Since generally only the final model is presented by the researcher, no information is available regarding the number of variables used in the model before obtaining the 'final' model results.

2 Another criticism is that the alterations to the original model are carried out in an arbitrary manner, based mainly on the beliefs of the researcher. It is therefore quite possible for two different researchers examining the same case to arrive at totally different conclusions.

3 By definition, the initial starting model is incorrect as it has omitted variables. This means that all the diagnostic tests on this model are incorrect, so we may consider important variables to be insignificant and exclude them.

The Hendry 'general to specific approach'

Following from these three major criticisms of the AER, an alternative approach has been developed called the 'general to specific approach' or the Hendry approach, because it was developed mainly by Professor Hendry of the London School of Economics (see Hendry and Richard, 1983). The approach is to start with a general model that contains – nested within it as special cases – other, simpler, models. Let's use an example to understand this better. Assume that we have a variable Y that can be affected by two explanatory variables X and Z. The general to specific approach proposes as a starting point the estimation of the following regression equation:

$$
\begin{aligned}
Y_t = a &+ \beta_0 X_t + \beta_1 X_{t-1} + \beta_2 X_{t-2} + \cdots + \beta_m X_{t-m} \\
&+ \gamma_0 Z_t + \gamma_1 Z_{t-1} + \gamma_2 Z_{t-2} + \cdots + \gamma_m Z_{t-m} \\
&+ \delta_1 Y_{t-1} + \delta_2 Y_{t-2} + \cdots + \delta_m Y_{t-m} + u_t
\end{aligned} \tag{8.69}
$$

that is, to regress Y_t on contemporaneous and lagged terms X_t and Z_t as well as lagged values of Y_t. This model is called an autoregressive (because lagged values of the dependent variable appear as regressors as well) distributed lag (because the effect of X and Z on Y is spread over a period of time from $t - m$ to t) model (ARDL). Models such as that shown in Equation (8.69) are known as dynamic models because they examine the behaviour of a variable over time.

The procedure then is, after estimating the model, to apply appropriate tests and to narrow down the model to the simpler ones that are nested with the previously estimated model.

Consider the above example for $m = 2$ to see how to proceed in practice with this approach. We have the original model:

$$Y_t = a + \beta_0 X_t + \beta_1 X_{t-1} + \beta_2 X_{t-2}$$
$$+ \gamma_0 Z_t + \gamma_1 Z_{t-1} + \gamma_2 Z_{t-2} + \delta_1 Y_{t-1} + \delta_2 Y_{t-2} + u_t \qquad (8.70)$$

where one restriction may be that all the Xs are non-important in the determination of Y. For this we have the hypothesis $H_0 : \beta_0 = \beta_1 = \beta_2 = 0$; and if we accept that, we have a simpler model such as:

$$Y_t = a\gamma_0 Z_t + \gamma_1 Z_{t-1} + \gamma_2 Z_{t-2} + \delta_1 Y_{t-1} + \delta_2 Y_{t-2} + u_t \qquad (8.71)$$

Another possible restriction may be that the second lagged term of each variable is insignificant; that is hypothesis $H_0 : \beta_2 = \gamma_2 = \delta_2 = 0$. Accepting this restriction will give the following model:

$$Y_t = a + \beta_0 X_t + \beta_1 X_{t-1} + \gamma_0 Z_t + \gamma_1 Z_{t-1} + \delta_1 Y_{t-1} + u_t \qquad (8.72)$$

It should be clear by now that the models in Equations (8.71) and (8.72) are both nested versions of the initial model in Equation (8.70); but Equation (8.72) is not a nested model of Equation (8.71) and therefore we cannot proceed to Equation (8.72) after estimating Equation (8.71).

An important question when we are moving from the general to the more specific model is how to know what the final simplified model should be like. To answer this question, Hendry and Richard (1983) suggested that the simplified model should:

1 be data admissible;

2 be consistent with the theory;

3 use regressors that are not correlated with u_t;

4 exhibit parameter constancy;

5 exhibit data coherency, that is have residuals that are purely random (white noise); and

6 be encompassing, meaning it includes all possible rival models in the sense that it allows us to interpret their results.

Exercises

Exercise 8.1

The file wages_01.wf1 contains data for monthly wage rates (measured in UK pounds) and IQ scores of a large number of City University graduates, after five years of employment:

(a) Find summary statistics for the above-mentioned variables and discuss them.

(b) Estimate a functional form that will show how a one-point increase in the IQ score will change the respective wage rate by a constant amount measured in UK pounds. What is the change in the wage rate for a ten-point increase in the IQ score?

(c) Estimate a functional form that will show how a one-point increase in the IQ score will have a percentage change effect on the wage rate. What is the percentage change in the wage rate for a ten-point increase in the IQ score?

(d) Use the Box–Cox transformation to decide which of the two models is more appropriate.

Questions

1 Show how the plug in solution can resolve the omitted variable bias. Provide an example from the economic theory.

2 What is the use of the Box–Cox transformation? Explain through an example.

3 Describe the Hendry Approach in choosing an appropriate econometric model. Discuss its advantages.

Part

IV Topics in Econometrics

9

Dummy Variables

CHAPTER CONTENTS

LEARNING OBJECTIVES

After studying this chapter you should be able to:

1. Understand the importance of qualitative information in economics.
2. Understand the use of dummy variables in order to quantify qualitative information.
3. Distinguish among a range of cases with dummy variables and learn their uses in econometric analysis.
4. Know how to create and use dummy variables in econometric software.
5. Test for structural stability and for seasonal effects with the use of dummy variables.

Introduction: the nature of qualitative information

So far, we have examined the equation specifications employed in econometric analysis, as well as techniques used to obtain estimates of the parameters in an equation and procedures for assessing the significance, accuracy and precision of those estimates. An assumption made implicitly up to this point has been that we can always obtain a set of numerical values for all the variables we want to use in our models. However, there are variables that can play a very important role in the explanation of an econometric model but are not numerical or easy to quantify. Examples of these are:

(a) gender may be very important in determining salary levels;

(b) different ethnic groups may follow diverse patterns regarding consumption and savings;

(c) educational levels can affect earnings from employment; and/or

(d) being a member of a labour union may imply different treatment/attitudes than not belonging to the union.

All these are cases for cross-sectional analysis.

Not easily quantifiable (or in general qualitative) information could also arise within a time series econometric framework. Consider the following examples:

(a) changes in a political regime may affect production processes or employment conditions;

(b) a war can have an impact on all aspects of economic activity;

(c) certain days in a week or certain months in a year can have different effects on stock prices; and

(d) seasonal effects are frequently observed in the demand for particular products; for example, ice cream in the summer, furs during the winter.

The aim of this chapter is to show the methods used to include information from qualitative variables in econometric models. This is done by using 'dummy' or 'dichotomous' variables. The next section presents the possible effects of qualitative variables in regression equations and how to use them. We then present special cases of dummy variables and the Chow test for structural stability.

The use of dummy variables

Intercept dummy variables

Consider the following cross-sectional regression equation:

$$Y_i = \beta_1 + \beta_2 X_{2i} + u_i \tag{9.1}$$

The constant term (β_1) in this equation measures the mean value of Y_i when X_{2i} is equal to zero. The important thing here is that this regression equation assumes that the value of β_0 will be the same for all the observations in the data set. However, the coefficient might be different, depending on different aspects of the data set. For example, regional differences might exist in the values of Y_i; or Y_i might represent the growth of GDP for European Union (EU) countries. Differences in growth rates are quite possible between core and peripheral countries. The question is, how can we quantify this information in order to enter it in the regression equation and check for the validity of this possible difference? The answer is: with the use of a special type of variable – a dummy (or fake) that captures qualitative effects by coding the different possible outcomes with numerical values.

This can usually be done quite simply by dichotomizing the possible outcomes and arbitrarily assigning the values of 0 and 1 to the two possibilities. So, for the EU countries example, we can have a new variable, D, which can take the following values:

$$D = \begin{cases} 1 & \text{for core country} \\ 0 & \text{for peripheral country} \end{cases} \tag{9.2}$$

Note that the choice of which of the alternative outcomes is to be assigned the value of 1 does not alter the results in an important way, as we shall show later.

Thus, entering this dummy variable in the regression model in Equation (9.1) we get:

$$Y_i = \beta_1 + \beta_2 X_{2i} + \beta_3 D_i + u_i \tag{9.3}$$

and in order to obtain the interpretation of D_i, consider the two possible values of D and how these will affect the specification of Equation (9.3). For $D = 0$ we have:

$$Y_i = \beta_1 + \beta_2 X_{2i} + \beta_3 (0)_i + u_i \tag{9.4}$$

$$= \beta_1 + \beta_2 X_{2i} + u_i \tag{9.5}$$

which is the same as for the initial model, and for $D = 1$ we have:

$$Y_i = \beta_1 + \beta_2 X_{2i} + \beta_3 (1)_i + u_i \tag{9.6}$$

$$= (\beta_1 + \beta_3) + \beta_2 X_{2i} + u_i \tag{9.7}$$

where the constant is now different from β_1 and equal to ($\beta_1 + \beta_3$). We can see that, by including the dummy variable, the value of the intercept has changed, shifting the function (and therefore the regression line) up or down, depending on whether the observation in question corresponds to a core or a peripheral country.

This is depicted graphically in Figures 9.1 and 9.2, which show two possibilities for β_3: (a) the first being positive and shifting the regression line up, suggesting that (if X_{2i} is investment rates) the mean GDP growth for core countries is greater than for peripheral countries for any given level of investment; and (b) the second being negative, suggesting the opposite conclusion.

Once regression Equation (9.3) has been estimated, the coefficient β_3 will be tested in the usual way with the t-statistic. Only if β_3 is significantly different from zero can we conclude that we have a relationship such as that depicted in Figures 9.1 and 9.2.

For other examples we could consider Y as the salary level and X the years of experience of various individuals, with a dummy variable being the gender of each individual (male $= 1$; female $= 0$); or, in the time series framework, we might have dummy variables for certain periods (for example, war dummies that take the value of 1 for

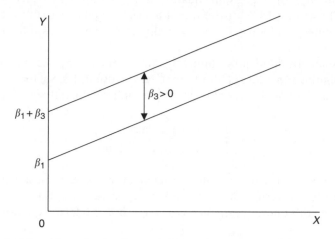

Figure 9.1   The effect of a dummy variable on the constant of the regression line

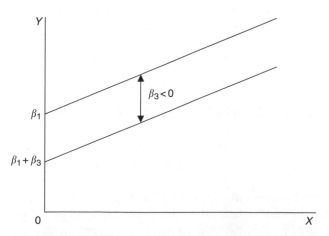

Figure 9.2   The effect of a dummy variable on the constant of the regression line

the period during the war and zero otherwise); or for certain events (such as dummy variables for oil price shock).

Slope dummy variables

In the previous section, we examined how qualitative information can affect the regression model, and saw that only the constant in the relationship is allowed to change. The implicit assumption underlying this is that the relationship between Y and the Xs is not affected by the inclusion of the qualitative dummy variable.

The relationship between Y and the Xs is represented by the derivative (or slope) of the function in the simple linear regression model, and by the partial derivatives in the multiple regression model. Sometimes, however, the slope coefficients might be affected by differences in dummy variables.

Consider, for example, the Keynesian consumption function model, relating consumer expenditure (Y_t) to disposable income (X_{2t}). This simple regression model has the following form:

$$Y_t = \beta_1 + \beta_2 X_{2t} + u_t \tag{9.8}$$

The slope coefficient (β_2) of this regression is the marginal propensity to consume given by:

$$\frac{dY_t}{dX_{2t}} = \beta_2 \tag{9.9}$$

and shows the percentage of the disposable income that will be consumed. Assume that we have time series observations for total consumer expenditure and disposable income from 1970 to 1999 for the UK economy. Assume, further, that we think a change in the marginal propensity to consume occurred in 1982 as a result of the oil price shock that had a general effect on the economic environment. To test this, we need to construct a dummy variable (D_t) that will take the following values:

$$D = \begin{cases} 0 & \text{for years from 1970–81} \\ 1 & \text{for years from 1982–99} \end{cases} \tag{9.10}$$

This dummy variable, because we assume that it will affect the slope parameter, must be included in the model in the following multiplicative way:

$$Y_t = \beta_1 + \beta_2 X_{2t} + \beta_3 D_t X_{2t} + u_t \tag{9.11}$$

The effect of the dummy variable can be dichotomized again according to two different outcomes. For $D_t = 0$ we have:

$$Y_t = \beta_1 + \beta_2 X_{2t} + \beta_3 (0) X_{2t} + u_t \tag{9.12}$$

$$= \beta_1 + \beta_2 X_{2t} + u_t \tag{9.13}$$

which is the same as with the initial model; and for $D = 1$:

$$Y_t = \beta_1 + \beta_2 X_{2t} + \beta_3(1)X_{2t} + u_t \tag{9.14}$$

$$= \beta_1 + (\beta_2 + \beta_3)X_{2i} + u_t \tag{9.15}$$

So, before 1982 the marginal propensity to consume is given by β_2, and after 1982 it is $\beta_2 + \beta_3$ (higher if β_3 is higher, and lower if β_3 is lower). To illustrate the effect better, see Figures 9.3 and 9.4 for the cases where $\beta_3 > 0$ and $\beta_3 < 0$, respectively.

The combined effect of intercept and slope dummies

It is now easy to understand what the outcome will be when using a dummy variable that is allowed to affect both the intercept and the slope coefficients. Consider the model:

$$Y_t = \beta_1 + \beta_2 X_{2t} + \beta_3 X_{3t} + u_t \tag{9.16}$$

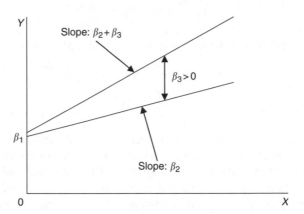

Figure 9.3   The effect of a dummy variable on the slope of the regression line (positive coefficient)

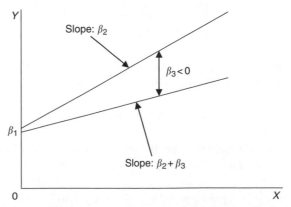

Figure 9.4   The effect of a dummy variable on the slope of the regression line (negative coefficient)

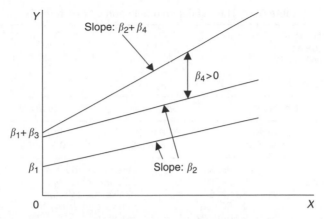

Figure 9.5 The combined effect of a dummy variable on the constant and the slope of the regression line

and let us assume that we have a dummy variable defined as follows:

$$D = \begin{cases} 0 & \text{for } t = 1, \ldots, s \\ 1 & \text{for } t = s+1, \ldots, T \end{cases} \tag{9.17}$$

Then, using the dummy variable to examine its effects on both the constant and the slope coefficients, we have:

$$Y_t = \beta_1 + \beta_2 X_{2t} + \beta_3 D_t + \beta_4 D_t X_{2t} + u_t \tag{9.18}$$

and the different outcomes will be, for $D_t = 0$:

$$Y_t = \beta_1 + \beta_2 X_{2t} + u_t \tag{9.19}$$

which is the same as for the initial model; and for $D = 1$:

$$Y_t = (\beta_1 + \beta_3) + (\beta_2 + \beta_4)X_{2t} + u_t \tag{9.20}$$

The effects are shown graphically in Figure 9.5.

Computer example of the use of dummy variables

The file dummies.wf1 contains data on wages (*wage*) and IQ levels (*iq*) of 935 individuals. It also includes various dummy variables for specific characteristics of the 935 individuals. One is the dummy variable *male*, which takes the value of 1 when the individual is male and the value of 0 if the individual is female.

We want to see the possible effects of the *male* dummy on the wage rates (that is to examine whether males get different wages from females). First, regress only wages on the IQ levels and a constant, to examine whether IQ plays a part in wage determination.

Table 9.1   The relationship between wages and IQ

Dependent Variable: WAGE
Method: Least Squares
Date: 03/30/04 Time: 14:20
Sample: 1 935
Included observations: 935

Variable	Coefficient	Std. Error	t-Statistic	Prob.
C	116.9916	85.64153	1.366061	0.1722
IQ	8.303064	0.836395	9.927203	0.0000

R-squared	0.095535	Mean dependent var	957.9455
Adjusted R-squared	0.094566	S.D. dependent var	404.3608
S.E. of regression	384.7667	Akaike info criterion	14.74529
Sum squared resid	1.38E+08	Schwarz criterion	14.75564
Log likelihood	−6891.422	F-statistic	98.54936
Durbin–Watson stat	0.188070	Prob(F-statistic)	0.000000

The results are obtained by using the following command in EViews:

```
ls wage c iq
```

and are presented in Table 9.1.

From these results we understand that IQ is indeed an important determinant (its *t*-statistic is highly significant), and because our model is linear there is also a one-unit increase in the IQ level, which corresponds to an 8.3-unit increase in the wage rate of the individual. Independent of the IQ level, the wage rate is 116.9 units.

Using a constant dummy

Including the male dummy as a dummy affecting only the constant, we find the regression results (shown in Table 9.2). The command in EViews for this estimation is:

```
ls wage c iq male
```

From these results we can see that, independent of the IQ, if the individual is a female she will have a wage of 224.8 units, while if the individual is a male he will have a wage of 722.8 units (224.8 + 498.0). This interpretation is, of course, based on the fact that the coefficient of the dummy variable is highly statistically significant, reflecting that, indeed, males receive higher wages than females.

Using a slope dummy

We want now to check whether the marginal effect is also affected by an individual's gender. In other words, we want to see whether, on average, an increase in the IQ level of men will mean higher wage increases than for women. To do this we estimate

Table 9.2 Wages and IQ and the role of gender (using a constant dummy)

Dependent variable: WAGE
Method: least squares
Date: 03/30/04 Time: 14:21
Sample: 1 935
Included observations: 935

Variable	Coefficient	Std. error	t-statistic	Prob.
C	224.8438	66.64243	3.373884	0.0008
IQ	5.076630	0.662354	7.664527	0.0000
MALE	498.0493	20.07684	24.80715	0.0000

R-squared	0.455239	Mean dependent var	957.9455
Adjusted R-squared	0.454070	S.D. dependent var	404.3608
S.E. of regression	298.7705	Akaike info criterion	14.24043
Sum squared resid	83193885	Schwarz criterion	14.25596
Log likelihood	−6654.402	F-statistic	389.4203
Durbin–Watson stat	0.445380	Prob(F-statistic)	0.000000

Table 9.3 Wages and IQ and the role of gender (using a slope dummy)

Dependent variable: WAGE
Method: least squares
Date: 03/30/04 Time: 14:21
Sample: 1 935
Included observations: 935

Variable	Coefficient	Std. error	t-statistic	Prob.
C	412.8602	67.36367	6.128825	0.0000
IQ	3.184180	0.679283	4.687559	0.0000
MALE ∗ IQ	4.840134	0.193746	24.98181	0.0000

R-squared	0.458283	Mean dependent var	957.9455
Adjusted R-squared	0.457120	S.D. dependent var	404.3608
S.E. of regression	297.9346	Akaike info criterion	14.23483
Sum squared resid	82728978	Schwarz criterion	14.25036
Log likelihood	−6651.782	F-statistic	394.2274
Durbin–Watson stat	0.455835	Prob(F-statistic)	0.000000

a regression in EViews that includes a multiplicative slope dummy (*male* ∗ *iq*), using the command:

```
ls wage c iq male*iq
```

The results of this are presented in Table 9.3. We observe that the slope dummy is statistically significant indicating that there is a difference in the slope coefficient for different sexes. Particularly, we have that the marginal effect for women is 3.18 while that for men is equal to $3.18 + 4.84 = 8.02$.

Using both dummies together

Finally, we examine the above relationship further by using both dummies at the same time, to see the difference in the results. The results of this model are presented in

Table 9.4   Wages and IQ and the role of gender (using both constant and slope dummies)

Dependent variable: WAGE
Method: least squares
Date: 03/30/04 Time: 14:23
Sample: 1 935
Included observations: 935

Variable	Coefficient	Std. error	t-statistic	Prob.
C	357.8567	84.78941	4.220535	0.0000
IQ	3.728518	0.849174	4.390756	0.0000
MALE	149.1039	139.6018	1.068066	0.2858
MALE $*$ IQ	3.412121	1.350971	2.525680	0.0117

R-squared	0.458946	Mean dependent var		957.9455
Adjusted R-squared	0.457202	S.D. dependent var		404.3608
S.E. of regression	297.9121	Akaike info criterion		14.23574
Sum squared resid	82627733	Schwarz criterion		14.25645
Log likelihood	−6651.210	F-statistic		263.2382
Durbin–Watson stat	0.450852	Prob(F-statistic)		0.000000

Table 9.4 and suggest that only the effect on the slope is now significant, and the effect on the constant is equal to zero.

Special cases of the use of dummy variables

Using dummy variables with multiple categories

A dummy variable might have more than two categories. Consider, for example, a model of wage determination where Y_i is the wage rate of a number of individuals and X_{2i} is the years of experience of each individual in the sample. It is logical to assume that the educational attainment level will also affect the wage rate of each individual. Therefore, in this case, we can have several dummies defined for the highest level of educational attainment of each individual, given by:

$$D_1 = \begin{cases} 1 & \text{if primary only} \\ 0 & \text{otherwise} \end{cases} \tag{9.21}$$

$$D_2 = \begin{cases} 1 & \text{if secondary only} \\ 0 & \text{otherwise} \end{cases} \tag{9.22}$$

$$D_3 = \begin{cases} 1 & \text{if BSc only} \\ 0 & \text{otherwise} \end{cases} \tag{9.23}$$

$$D_4 = \begin{cases} 1 & \text{if MSc only} \\ 0 & \text{otherwise} \end{cases} \tag{9.24}$$

We then have a wage equation of the form:

$$Y_i = \beta_1 + \beta_2 X_{2i} + a_2 D_{2i} + a_3 D_{3i} + a_4 D_{4i} + u_i \tag{9.25}$$

Note that we did not use all four dummy variables. This is because if we use all four there will be exact multicollinearity, since $D_1 + D_2 + D_3 + D_4$ will always be equal to 1, and therefore they will form an exact linear relationship with the constant β_1. This known as the *dummy variable trap*. To avoid this, the rule is that the number of dummy variables we use will always be one less than the total number of possible categories. The dummy variables omitted will define a reference group, as will become clear in the interpretation of the dummies in the model.

The wage equation can be separated according to the use of the dummies, as follows. If $D_2 = 1$; $D_3 = D_4 = 0$:

$$Y_i = \beta_1 + \beta_2 X_{2i} + a_2 D_{2i} + u_i \tag{9.26}$$

$$= (\beta_1 + a_2) + \beta_2 X_{2i} + u_i \tag{9.27}$$

so the constant for the case of secondary education is $(\beta_1 + a_2)$.
   If $D_3 = 1$; $D_2 = D_4 = 0$:

$$Y_i = \beta_1 + \beta_2 X_{2i} + a_3 D_{3i} + u_i \tag{9.28}$$

$$= (\beta_1 + a_3) + \beta_2 X_{2i} + u_i \tag{9.29}$$

so the constant in the case of BSc degree holders is $(\beta_1 + a_3)$.
   If $D_4 = 1$; $D_2 = D_3 = 0$:

$$Y_i = \beta_1 + \beta_2 X_{2i} + a_3 D_{4i} + u_i \tag{9.30}$$

$$= (\beta_1 + a_4) + \beta_2 X_{2i} + u_i \tag{9.31}$$

so the constant in the case of MSc degree holders is $(\beta_1 + a_4)$.
   While if $D_2 = D_3 = D_4 = 0$:

$$Y_i = \beta_1 + \beta_2 X_{2i} \tag{9.32}$$

and for this case the constant for the primary education is equal to the constant of the original model, β_1.

Therefore we do not need all four variables to depict the four outcomes. Taking as a reference variable primary education, coefficients a_2, a_3 and a_4 measure the expected wage differential that workers with secondary education, BSc and MSc degrees will have compared to those with primary education alone.

It is important to note that, mathematically, it does not matter which dummy variable is omitted. We leave this as an exercise for the reader to understand why this is the case. However, the choice of the D_1 dummy to be used as the reference dummy variable is a convenient one, because it is the lowest level of education and therefore the lowest wage rates are expected to correspond to this category.

In terms of graphical depiction, the effect of the multiple dummy variable 'educational level' is shown in Figure 9.6.

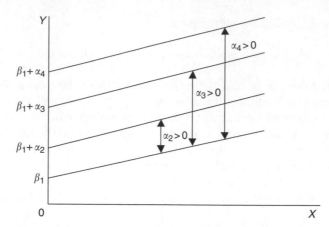

Figure 9.6 The effect of a dummy variable on the constant of the regression line

The dummy variable trap is a serious mistake and should be avoided at all costs. Fortunately, computer software will signal to the researcher that OLS estimation is not possible, which suggests that there is a possibility of the mistake of committing exact multicollinearity as a result of the dummy variable trap (for more about exact multicollinearity; see Chapter 6).

Using more than one dummy variable

Dummy variable analysis can easily be extended to cases of more than one dummy variable, some of which may have more than one category. In such cases, the interpretation of the dummy variables, while following the regular form, might appear more complicated and the researcher should take care when using them.

To illustrate this, consider the previous model, hypothesizing that apart from the educational level there are other qualitative aspects determining the wage rate, such as age, gender and category of occupation. In this case we have the following model:

$$
\begin{aligned}
Yi = \beta_1 + \beta_2 X_{2i} &+ \beta_3 EDUC_{2i} + \beta_4 EDUC_{3i} + \beta_5 EDUC_{4i} \\
&+ \beta_6 SEXM_i + \beta_7 AGE_{2i} + \beta_8 AGE_{3i} \\
&+ \beta_9 OCUP_{2i} + \beta_{10} OCUP_{3i} + \beta_{11} OCUP_{4i} + u_i
\end{aligned}
\tag{9.33}
$$

where we have the following dummies:

$$
EDUC_1 = \begin{cases} 1 & \text{if primary only} \\ 0 & \text{otherwise} \end{cases}
\tag{9.34}
$$

$$
EDUC_2 = \begin{cases} 1 & \text{if secondary only} \\ 0 & \text{otherwise} \end{cases}
\tag{9.35}
$$

$$EDUC_3 = \begin{cases} 1 & \text{if BSc only} \\ 0 & \text{otherwise} \end{cases} \tag{9.36}$$

$$EDUC_4 = \begin{cases} 1 & \text{if MSc only} \\ 0 & \text{otherwise} \end{cases} \tag{9.37}$$

and $EDUC_1$ defines the reference group.

$$SEXM = \begin{cases} 1 & \text{if male} \\ 0 & \text{if female} \end{cases} \tag{9.38}$$

$$SEXF = \begin{cases} 1 & \text{if female} \\ 0 & \text{if male} \end{cases} \tag{9.39}$$

and $SEXF$ defines the reference group.

$$AGE_1 = \begin{cases} 1 & \text{for less than 30} \\ 0 & \text{otherwise} \end{cases} \tag{9.40}$$

$$AGE_2 = \begin{cases} 1 & \text{for 30 to 40} \\ 0 & \text{otherwise} \end{cases} \tag{9.41}$$

$$AGE_3 = \begin{cases} 1 & \text{for more than 40} \\ 0 & \text{otherwise} \end{cases} \tag{9.42}$$

and AGE_1 is the reference group. And finally:

$$OCUP_1 = \begin{cases} 1 & \text{if unskilled} \\ 0 & \text{otherwise} \end{cases} \tag{9.43}$$

$$OCUP_2 = \begin{cases} 1 & \text{if skilled} \\ 0 & \text{otherwise} \end{cases} \tag{9.44}$$

$$OCUP_3 = \begin{cases} 1 & \text{if clerical} \\ 0 & \text{otherwise} \end{cases} \tag{9.45}$$

$$OCUP_4 = \begin{cases} 1 & \text{if self-employed} \\ 0 & \text{otherwise} \end{cases} \tag{9.46}$$

with $OCUP_1$ being the reference group in this case.

Using seasonal dummy variables

In the analysis of time series data, seasonal effects might play a very important role, and the seasonal variations can easily be examined with the use of dummy variables.

So, for example, for quarterly time series data we can introduce four dummy variables as follows:

$$D_1 = \begin{cases} 1 & \text{for the first quarter} \\ 0 & \text{otherwise} \end{cases} \qquad (9.47)$$

$$D_2 = \begin{cases} 1 & \text{for the second quarter} \\ 0 & \text{otherwise} \end{cases} \qquad (9.48)$$

$$D_3 = \begin{cases} 1 & \text{for the third quarter} \\ 0 & \text{otherwise} \end{cases} \qquad (9.49)$$

$$D_4 = \begin{cases} 1 & \text{for the fourth quarter} \\ 0 & \text{otherwise} \end{cases} \qquad (9.50)$$

and in a regression model we can use them as:

$$Y_t = \beta_1 + \beta_2 X_{2t} + a_2 D_{2t} + a_3 D_{3t} + a_4 D_{4t} + u_t \qquad (9.51)$$

and can analyse (using the procedure described above) the effects on the average level of Y of each of these dummies. Note that we have used only three of the four dummies, to avoid the dummy variable trap described above. Similarly, for monthly data sets there will be twelve dummy variables. If the constant is included we need to use only eleven, keeping one as a reference group. An illustrative example is given below using the January effect hypothesis for monthly stock returns.

Computer example of dummy variables with multiple categories

Again using the data in the file dummies.wf1, we examine the case of dummy variables with multiple categories. To see the effect we can use, for example, the educational level variable with its four different classifications as defined in the previous section. The command to examine the effect of educational levels, in EViews, is:

```
ls wage c educ2 educ3 educ4
```

Note that we do not use all four dummies, because we have the constant and therefore we should not include them all, to avoid the dummy variable trap. The results are given in Table 9.5.

The results provide statistically significant estimates for all coefficients, so we can proceed with the interpretation. The effect on wages if an individual has finished only primary education is given by the constant and is equal to 774.2. An individual who has completed secondary education will have a wage 88.4 units higher than those with primary education alone; an individual with a BSc degree will have 221.4 units more than that of primary; and an individual with an MSc degree will have 369.1 more

Table 9.5 Dummy variables with multiple categories

Dependent variable: WAGE
Method: least squares
Date: 03/30/04 Time: 14:48
Sample: 1 935
Included observations: 935

Variable	Coefficient	Std. error	t-statistic	Prob.
C	774.2500	40.95109	18.90670	0.0000
EDUC2	88.42176	45.30454	1.951719	0.0513
EDUC3	221.4167	48.88677	4.529174	0.0000
EDUC4	369.1184	47.69133	7.739739	0.0000

R-squared	0.100340	Mean dependent var		957.9455
Adjusted R-squared	0.097441	S.D. dependent var		404.3608
S.E. of regression	384.1553	Akaike info criterion		14.74424
Sum squared resid	1.37E+08	Schwarz criterion		14.76495
Log likelihood	−6888.932	F-statistic		34.61189
Durbin–Watson stat	0.166327	Prob(F-statistic)		0.000000

Table 9.6 Changing the reference dummy variable

Dependent variable: WAGE
Method: least squares
Date: 03/30/04 Time: 14:58
Sample: 1 935
Included observations: 935

Variable	Coefficient	Std. error	t-statistic	Prob.
C	1143.368	24.44322	46.77651	0.0000
EDUC1	−369.1184	47.69133	−7.739739	0.0000
EDUC2	−280.6967	31.19263	−8.998812	0.0000
EDUC3	−147.7018	36.19938	−4.080229	0.0000

R-squared	0.100340	Mean dependent var		957.9455
Adjusted R-squared	0.097441	S.D. dependent var		404.3608
S.E. of regression	384.1553	Akaike info criterion		14.74424
Sum squared resid	1.37E+08	Schwarz criterion		14.76495
Log likelihood	−6888.932	F-statistic		34.61189
Durbin–Watson stat	0.166327	Prob(F-statistic)		0.000000

units of wage than someone with primary education alone. So the final effects can be summarized as follows:

Primary	774.2
Secondary	862.6
BSc	995.6
MSc	1,143.3

It is easy to show that if we change the reference variable the results will remain unchanged. Consider the following regression equation model, which uses as a reference category the *educ*4 dummy (the command in EViews is: ls wage c educ1 educ2 educ3), the results of this are presented in Table 9.6. We leave it to the reader to do the simple calculations and see that the final effects are identical to those of the previous case. Thus changing the reference dummy does not affect the results at all.

Table 9.7 Using more than one dummy together

Dependent variable: WAGE
Method: least squares
Date: 03/30/04 Time: 15:03
Sample: 1 935
Included observations: 935

Variable	Coefficient	Std. error	t-statistic	Prob.
C	641.3229	41.16019	15.58115	0.0000
EDUC2	19.73155	35.27278	0.559399	0.5760
EDUC3	112.4091	38.39894	2.927402	0.0035
EDUC4	197.5036	37.74860	5.232077	0.0000
AGE2	−17.94827	29.59479	−0.606467	0.5444
AGE3	71.25035	30.88441	2.307001	0.0213
MALE	488.0926	20.22037	24.13865	0.0000

R-squared	0.462438	Mean dependent var		957.9455
Adjusted R-squared	0.458963	S.D. dependent var		404.3608
S.E. of regression	297.4286	Akaike info criterion		14.23568
Sum squared resid	82094357	Schwarz criterion		14.27192
Log likelihood	−6648.182	F-statistic		133.0523
Durbin–Watson stat	0.451689	Prob(F-statistic)		0.000000

The reader can check that changing the reference category to *educ2* or *educ3* yields identical results.

Finally, we may have an example using three different dummies (*educ*, *age* and *male*) together in the same equation (we will use *educ1*, *age1* and *female* as reference dummies to avoid the dummy variable trap). We leave this as an exercise for the reader to interpret the results of this model. The results are presented in Table 9.7.

Application: the January effect in emerging stock markets

Asteriou and Kavetsos (2003) examined the efficient market hypothesis – in terms of the presence (or not) of the 'January effect' for eight transition economies, namely the Czech Republic, Hungary, Lithuania, Poland, Romania, Russia, Slovakia and Slovenia. (For more details on the January effect, see Gultekin and Gultekin, 1983, and Jaffe and Westerfield, 1989.) In their analysis Asteriou and Kavestsos used a monthly data set from 1991 to the early months of 2003 using monthly time series data, for the stock markets of each of the countries listed above. The test for January effects is based strongly on the use of seasonal dummy variables. In practice, what is required is to create twelve dummies (one for each month) that take the following values:

$$D_{it} = \begin{cases} 1 & \text{if the return at time } t \text{ corresponds to month } i \\ 0 & \text{otherwise} \end{cases} \qquad (9.52)$$

Table 9.8 Tests for seasonal effects

Variables	Czech Rep.		Hungary		Lithuania		Poland	
	coef	t-stat	coef	t-stat	coef	t-stat	coef	t-stat
D1	0.016	0.631	**0.072**	**2.471**	−0.008	−0.248	**0.072**	**1.784**
D2	0.004	0.146	−0.008	−0.280	0.018	0.543	0.033	0.826
D3	−0.001	−0.031	0.017	0.626	0.041	1.220	−0.026	−0.650
D4	0.001	0.023	0.022	0.800	−0.014	−0.421	0.041	1.024
D5	−0.013	−0.514	−0.005	−0.180	−0.036	−1.137	0.049	1.261
D6	−0.041	−1.605	0.004	0.126	**−0.071**	**−2.106**	−0.051	−1.265
D7	0.036	1.413	0.017	0.583	−0.013	−0.381	0.033	0.814
D8	−0.022	−0.849	0.007	0.245	−0.009	−0.264	0.014	0.341
D9	−0.029	−1.127	−0.027	−0.926	**−0.086**	**−2.547**	−0.034	−0.842
D10	−0.014	−0.532	0.011	0.387	−0.014	−0.420	0.025	0.611
D11	−0.039	−1.519	−0.002	−0.058	0.048	1.427	0.012	0.287
D12	0.033	1.294	**0.060**	**2.083**	−0.011	−0.325	0.061	1.528
R^2(OLS)	0.105		0.070		0.196		0.070	
B-G test	12.934 (0.374)		12.409 (0.413)		34.718 (0.001)		34.591 (0.001)	
LM(1) test	0.351 (0.553)		0.039 (0.843)		4.705 (0.030)		2.883 (0.090)	

	Romania		Russia		Slovakia		Slovenia	
	coef	t-stat	coef	t-stat	coef	t-stat	coef	t-stat
D1	0.088	1.873	0.034	0.581	0.044	1.223	**0.061**	**2.479**
D2	0.007	0.154	0.065	1.125	**0.081**	**2.274**	−0.012	−0.482
D3	−0.064	−1.367	0.089	1.536	−0.012	−0.327	−0.023	−0.934
D4	0.036	0.846	0.078	1.347	−0.048	−1.329	−0.013	−0.537
D5	0.009	0.218	0.027	0.471	−0.034	−0.939	0.011	0.455
D6	0.034	0.727	0.067	1.100	−0.012	−0.313	−0.028	−1.089
D7	−0.032	−0.689	−0.025	−0.404	0.002	0.044	**0.048**	**1.854**
D8	−0.023	−0.499	−0.041	−0.669	0.032	0.846	**0.045**	**1.855**
D9	−0.041	−0.877	−0.056	−0.919	−0.024	−0.631	0.006	0.232
D10	0.007	0.147	0.047	0.810	−0.012	−0.340	0.033	1.336
D11	0.002	0.033	0.035	0.599	−0.018	−0.501	0.006	0.243
D12	−0.005	−0.103	0.086	1.487	0.037	1.028	0.007	0.305
R^2(OLS)	0.141		0.075		0.103		0.155	
B-G test	16.476 (0.170)		17.014 (0.149)		24.517 (0.017)		27.700 (0.006)	
LM(1) test	1.355 (0.244)		0.904 (0.342)		13.754 (0.000)		0.612 (0.434)	

From the methodology point of view, to test for seasonal effects in general corresponds to estimating the following equation:

$$R_{it} = a_1 D_{1t} + a_2 D_{2t} + a_3 D_{3t} + \cdots + a_{12} D_{12t} + u_t \tag{9.53}$$

where R_t indicates the stock market return at time t, a_i is the average return of month i, D_{it} are the seasonal dummy variables as defined above, and u_t is an iid (identically independently distributed) error term. The null hypothesis to be tested is that the coefficients a_i are equal. If they are equal there are no seasonal effects, and seasonal effects apply if they are unequal.

Then, to test explicitly for January effects, the regression model is modified as follows:

$$R_{it} = c + a_2 D_{2t} + a_3 D_{3t} + \cdots + a_{12} D_{12t} + u_t \tag{9.54}$$

Table 9.9 Tests for the January effect

Variables	Czech Rep.		Hungary		Lithuania		Poland	
	coef	t-stat	coef	t-stat	coef	t-stat	coef	t-stat
C	0.016	0.631	**0.072**	**2.471**	−0.008	−0.248	**0.072**	**1.784**
D2	−0.012	−0.327	−0.079	−1.976	0.027	0.559	−0.039	−0.677
D3	−0.017	−0.455	−0.054	−1.348	0.050	1.038	−0.098	−1.721
D4	−0.015	−0.416	−0.049	−1.227	−0.006	−0.123	−0.031	−0.537
D5	−0.029	−0.809	−0.077	−1.906	−0.027	−0.591	−0.023	−0.413
D6	−0.057	−1.581	−0.068	−1.658	−0.063	−1.314	−0.123	−2.156
D7	0.020	0.553	−0.055	−1.335	−0.005	−0.094	−0.039	−0.686
D8	−0.038	−1.046	−0.064	−1.574	−0.001	−0.012	−0.058	−1.020
D9	−0.045	−1.243	**−0.098**	**−2.402**	−0.078	−1.626	**−0.106**	**−1.856**
D10	−0.030	−0.822	−0.060	−1.474	−0.006	−0.122	−0.047	−0.829
D11	−0.055	−1.520	**−0.073**	**−1.788**	0.057	1.184	−0.060	−1.058
D12	0.017	0.469	−0.011	−0.274	−0.003	−0.055	−0.010	−0.181
R^2(OLS)	0.105		0.070		0.196		0.070	
B-G test	12.934 (0.374)		12.409 (0.413)		34.718 (0.001)		34.591 (0.001)	
LM(1) test	0.351 (0.553)		0.039 (0.843)		4.705 (0.030)		2.883 (0.090)	

	Romania		Russia		Slovakia		Slovenia	
	coef	t-stat	coef	t-stat	coef	t-stat	coef	t-stat
C	**0.088**	**1.873**	0.034	0.581	0.044	1.223	**0.061**	**2.479**
D2	−0.081	−1.215	0.031	0.385	0.038	0.743	**−0.072**	**−2.094**
D3	**−0.152**	**−2.290**	0.055	0.676	−0.055	−1.096	**−0.084**	**−2.413**
D4	−0.052	−0.813	0.044	0.542	**−0.091**	**−1.805**	**−0.074**	**−2.133**
D5	−0.078	−1.236	−0.006	−0.077	−0.077	−1.529	−0.050	−1.431
D6	−0.054	−0.810	0.034	0.402	−0.056	−1.069	**−0.089**	**−2.489**
D7	−0.120	−1.811	−0.058	−0.693	−0.042	−0.810	−0.012	−0.339
D8	−0.111	−1.677	−0.074	−0.885	−0.012	−0.228	−0.015	−0.441
D9	**−0.129**	**−1.944**	−0.090	−1.067	−0.068	−1.300	−0.055	−1.589
D10	−0.081	−1.220	0.013	0.162	−0.056	−1.105	−0.028	−0.808
D11	−0.086	−1.301	0.001	0.013	−0.062	−1.219	−0.055	−1.581
D12	−0.093	−1.397	0.052	0.641	−0.007	−0.138	−0.053	−1.537
R^2(OLS)	0.141		0.075		0.103		0.155	
B-G test	16.476 (0.170)		17.014 (0.149)		24.517 (0.017)		27.700 (0.006)	
LM(1) test	1.355 (0.244)		0.904 (0.342)		13.754 (0.000)		0.612 (0.434)	

where R_t again indicates stock market returns, the intercept c represents the mean return for January, and in this case the coefficients a_i, represent the difference between the return for January and month i.

The null hypothesis to be tested in this case is that all dummy variable coefficients are equal to zero. A negative value of a dummy coefficient would be proof of the January effect. The estimation of the coefficients in Equation (9.54) will specify which months have lower average returns than those obtained in January.

The summarized results obtained from Asteriou and Kavetsos (2003) for Equation (9.54) are presented in Table 9.8, while those for the January effect are given in Table 9.9. From these results we see, first, that there are significant seasonal effects for five out of the eight countries in the sample (note that data in bold type indicates that the coefficients are significant in Table 9.8), while they also found evidence in favour of the January effect (data in bold type indicates coefficients in Table 9.9) for Hungary,

Poland, Romania, Slovakia and Slovenia. For more details regarding the interpretation of these results, see Asteriou and Kavetsos (2003).

Tests for structural stability

The dummy variable approach

The use of dummy variables can be considered as a test for stability of the estimated parameters in a regression equation. When an equation includes both a dummy variable for the intercept and a multiplicative dummy variable for each of the explanatory variables, the intercept and each partial slope is allowed to vary, implying different underlying structures for the two conditions (0 and 1) associated with the dummy variable.

Therefore, using dummy variables is like conducting a test for structural stability. In essence, two different equations are being estimated from the coefficients of a single-equation model. Individual t-statistics are used to test the significance of each term, including a dummy variable, while the statistical significance of the entire equation can be established by a Wald test as described in Chapter 5.

The advantages of using the dummy variable approach when testing for structural stability are:

(a) a single equation is used to provide a set of estimated coefficients for two or more structures;

(b) only one degree of freedom is lost for every dummy variable used in the equation;

(c) a larger sample is used for the estimation of the model (than the Chow test case described below), improving the precision of the estimated coefficients; and

(d) it provides information about the exact nature of the parameter instability (that is whether or not it affects the intercept and one or more of the partial slope coefficients).

The Chow test for structural stability

An alternative way to test for structural stability is provided by the Chow test (Chow, 1960). The test consists of breaking the sample into two (or more, according to the case) structures, estimating the equation for each, and then comparing the SSR from the separate equations with that of the whole sample.

To illustrate this, consider the case of the Keynesian consumption function for the UK data set, examined with the use of dummy variables. To apply the Chow test the following steps are followed:

Step 1   Estimate the basic regression equation:

$$Y_t = \beta_1 + \beta_2 X_{2t} + u_t \tag{9.55}$$

for three different data sets:

(a) the whole sample (n);

(b) the period before the oil shock (n_1); and

(c) the period after the oil shock (n_2).

Step 2   Obtain the SSR for each of the three subsets and label them as SSR_n, SSR_{n_1} and SSR_{n_2}, respectively.

Step 3   Calculate the following F-statistic:

$$F = \frac{(SSR_n - (SSR_{n_1} + SSR_{n_2}))/k}{(SSR_{n_1} + SSR_{n_2})/(n_1 + n_2 + 2k)} \tag{9.56}$$

where k is the number of parameters estimated in the equation in step 1 (for this case $k = 2$).

Step 4   Compare the F-statistic obtained above with the critical $F_{(k, n_1 + n_2 + 2k)}$ for the required significance level. If F-statistical $> F$-critical we reject the hypothesis H_0 that the parameters are stable for the entire data set, and conclude that there is evidence of structural instability.

Note that while the Chow test might suggest there is parameter instability, it does not give us any information about which parameters are affected. For this reason dummy variables provide a better and more direct way of examining structural stability.

Questions

Questions

1 Explain how we can use dummy variables to quantify qualitative information in a regression model. Use appropriate examples from economic theory.

2 Show (both graphically and mathematically) the combined effect of the use of a dichotomous dummy variable on the constant and the slope coefficient of the simple regression model.

3 Provide an example from economic theory where the use of seasonal dummy variables is required. Explain why, when there is a constant included in the model, we cannot use all the dummies together but must exclude one dummy, which will act as the reference dummy. What is the meaning of a reference dummy variable?

4 Describe the steps involved in conducting the Chow test for structural stability. Is the Chow test preferable to the dummy variables approach? Explain why or why not.

10 Dynamic Econometric Models

CHAPTER CONTENTS

LEARNING OBJECTIVES

After studying this chapter you should be able to:

1. Understand the meaning of and differentiate between distributed lag models and autoregressive models.
2. Understand and use the Koyck and Almon transformations.
3. Understand and use the partial adjustment and the adaptive expectations models.
4. Understand the meaning and use of panels in applied econometrics data.

Introduction

Despite many econometric models being formulated in static terms, it is possible in time series models to have relationships in which the concept of time plays a more central role. So, for example, we might find ourselves with a model that has the following form:

$$Y_t = a + \beta_0 X_t + \beta_1 X_{t-1} + \beta_2 X_{t-2} + \cdots + \beta_p X_{t-p} + u_t \tag{10.1}$$

In this model we see that Y_t is not dependent on the current value of X_t alone, but also on past (lagged) values of X_t. There are various reasons why lags might need to be introduced in a model. Consider, for example, an exogenous shock stimulating the purchase of capital goods. It is unavoidable that some time will elapse between the moment the shock occurred and the firm's awareness of the situation. This can be for instance because (a) it takes some time to gather the relevant statistical information; or (b) it takes time for the firm's managers to draw up plans for the new capital project; or (c) the firm might want to obtain different prices from competing suppliers of capital equipment. Therefore, lagged effects will occur, and dynamic models that can capture the effects of the time paths of exogenous variables and/or disturbances on the time path of the endogenous variables are needed.

In general there are two types of dynamic models:

(1) **distributed lag** models that include lagged terms of the independent (or explanatory variables); and

(2) **autoregressive** models that include lagged terms of the dependent variable.

Both types of model are described in this chapter.

Distributed lag models

Consider the model:

$$Y_t = \alpha + \beta_0 X_t + \beta_1 X_{t-1} + \beta_2 X_{t-2} + \cdots + \beta_p X_{t-p} + u_t$$

$$= \alpha + \sum_{i=0}^{p} \beta_i X_{t-i} + u_t \tag{10.2}$$

in which the βs are coefficients of the lagged X terms. With this model, the reaction to Y_t after a change in X_t is distributed over a number of time periods. In the model we have p lagged terms and the current X_t term, so, it takes $p+1$ periods for the full effect of a change in X_t to influence Y_t.

It is interesting to examine the effect of the βs:

(a) The coefficient β_0 is the weight attached to the current X (X_t) given by $\Delta Y_t / \Delta X_t$. It therefore shows how much the average change in Y_t will be when X_t changes by one unit. For this reason, β_0 is called the impact multiplier.

(b) β_i is similarly given by $\Delta Y_t / \Delta X_{t-i}$ and shows the average change in Y_t for a unit increase in X_{t-i}; that is, for a unit increase in X made i periods prior to t. For this reason the β_is are called the interim multipliers of order i.

(c) The total effect is given by the sum of the effects on all periods:

$$\sum_{i=0}^{p} \beta_i = \beta_0 + \beta_1 + \beta_2 + \cdots + \beta_p \tag{10.3}$$

This is also called the long-run equilibrium effect when the economy is at the steady state (equilibrium) level. In the long run:

$$X^* = X_t = X_{t-1} = \cdots = X_{t-p} \tag{10.4}$$

and therefore:

$$Y_t^* = \alpha + \beta_0 X^* + \beta_1 X^* + \beta_2 X^* + \cdots + \beta_p X^* + u_t$$

$$= \alpha + X^* \sum_{i=0}^{p} \beta_i + u_t \tag{10.5}$$

Under the assumption that the Xs are weakly exogenous, distributed lag models can be estimated by simple OLS and the estimators of the βs are BLUE. The question here is, how many lags are required in order to have a correctly specified equation? Or, in other words, what is the optimal lag length?

One way to resolve this is to use a relatively large value for p, estimate the model for $p, p-1, p-2, \ldots$ lags and choose the model with the lowest value of AIC (Akaike Information Criterion), SBC (Schwarz Bayesian Criterion) or any other criterion. However, this approach generates two considerable problems:

(a) it can suffer from severe multicollinearity problems, because of close relationships between $X_t, X_{t-1}, X_{t-2}, \ldots, X_{t-p}$; and

(b) a large number of p means a considerable loss of degrees of freedom because we can use only the $p+1$ to n observations.

Therefore, an alternative approach is needed to provide methods that can resolve these difficulties. The typical approach is to impose restrictions regarding the structure of the βs and then reduce from $p+1$ to only a few of the number of parameters to be estimated. Two of the most popular methods of doing this are the Koyck (geometrical lag) and the Almon (polynomial lag) transformations, both of which are presented below.

The Koyck transformation

Koyck (1954) proposed a geometrically declining scheme for the βs. To understand this, consider again the distributed lag model:

$$Y_t = \alpha + \beta_0 X_t + \beta_1 X_{t-1} + \beta_2 X_{t-2} + \cdots + \beta_p X_{t-p} + u_t \tag{10.6}$$

Koyck made two assumptions:

(a) all the βs have the same sign; and

(b) the βs decline geometrically, as in the following equation:

$$\beta_i = \beta_0 \lambda^i \tag{10.7}$$

where λ takes values between 0 and 1 and $i = 0, 1, 2, \ldots$

It is easy to see that it is declining. Since λ is positive and less than one and all the β_i have the same sign, then $\beta_0 \lambda^1 > \beta_0 \lambda^2 > \beta_0 \lambda^3$ and so on; and therefore $\beta_1 > \beta_2 > \beta_3$ and so on (for a graphical depiction of this, see Figure 10.1).

Let us consider an infinite distributed lag model:

$$Y_t = \alpha + \beta_0 X_t + \beta_1 X_{t-1} + \beta_2 X_{t-2} + \cdots + u_t \tag{10.8}$$

Substituting $\beta_i = \beta_0 \lambda^i$ we have:

$$Y_t = \alpha + \beta_0 \lambda^0 X_t + \beta_0 \lambda^1 X_{t-1} + \beta_0 \lambda^2 X_{t-2} + \cdots + u_t \tag{10.9}$$

For this infinite lag model the immediate impact is given by β_0 (because $\lambda^0 = 1$), while the long-run effect will be the sum of an infinite geometric series. Koyck transforms this model in to a much simpler one, as follows:

Step 1   Lag both sides of Equation (10.9) one period to get:

$$Y_{t-1} = \alpha + \beta_0 \lambda^0 X_{t-1} + \beta_0 \lambda^1 X_{t-2} + \beta_0 \lambda^2 X_{t-3} + \cdots + u_{t-1} \tag{10.10}$$

Step 2   Multiply both sides of Equation (10.10) by λ to get:

$$\lambda Y_{t-1} = \lambda \alpha + \beta_0 \lambda^1 X_{t-1} + \beta_0 \lambda^2 X_{t-2} + \beta_0 \lambda^3 X_{t-3} + \cdots + \lambda u_{t-1} \tag{10.11}$$

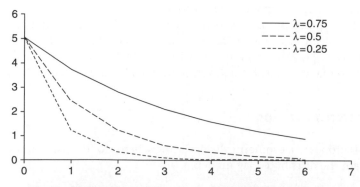

Figure 10.1   Koyck distributed lag for different values of λ

Step 3   Subtract Equation (10.11) from Equation (10.9) to obtain:

$$Y_t - \lambda Y_{t-1} = \alpha(1 - \lambda) + \beta_0 X_t + u_t - \lambda u_{t-1} \tag{10.12}$$

or:

$$Y_t = \alpha(1 - \lambda) + \beta_0 X_t + \lambda Y_{t-1} + v_t \tag{10.13}$$

where $v_t = u_t - \lambda u_{t-1}$. In this case the immediate effect is β_0 and the long-run effect is $\beta_0/(1 - \lambda)$ (consider again that in the long run we have $Y^* = Y_t = Y_{t-1} = \ldots$). So Equation (10.13) now gives both the immediate and long-run coefficients.

The Almon transformation

An alternative procedure is provided by Almon (1965). Almon assumes that the coefficients β_i can be approximated by polynomials in i, such as:

$$\beta_i = f(i) = a_0 i^0 + a_1 i^1 + a_2 i^2 + a_3 i^3 + \cdots + a_r i^r \tag{10.14}$$

The Almon procedure requires prior selection of the degree of the polynomial (r) as well as of the largest lag to be used in the model (p). Therefore, unlike the Koyck transformation, where the distributed lag is infinite, the Almon procedure must be finite.

Suppose we choose $r = 3$ and $p = 4$; then we have:

$$\beta_0 = f(0) = a_0$$
$$\beta_1 = f(1) = a_0 + a_1 + a_2 + a_3$$
$$\beta_2 = f(2) = a_0 + 2a_1 + 4a_2 + 8a_3$$
$$\beta_3 = f(3) = a_0 + 3a_1 + 9a_2 + 27a_3$$
$$\beta_4 = f(4) = a_0 + 4a_1 + 16a_2 + 64a_3$$

Substituting these into the distributed lag model of order $p = 4$ we have:

$$
\begin{aligned}
Y_t = \alpha &+ (a_0)X_t + (a_0 + a_1 + a_2 + a_3)X_{t-1} \\
&+ (a_0 + 2a_1 + 4a_2 + 8a_3)X_{t-2} \\
&+ (a_0 + 3a_1 + 9a_2 + 27a_3)X_{t-3} \\
&+ (a_0 + 4a_1 + 16a_2 + 64a_3)X_{t-4} + u_t
\end{aligned} \tag{10.15}
$$

and factorizing the a_is we get:

$$
\begin{aligned}
Y_t = \alpha &+ a_0(X_t + X_{t-1} + X_{t-2} + X_{t-3} + X_{t-4}) \\
&+ a_1(X_{t-1} + 2X_{t-2} + 3X_{t-3} + 4X_{t-4})
\end{aligned}
$$

$$+ a_2(X_{t-1} + 4X_{t-2} + 9X_{t-3} + 16X_{t-4})$$
$$+ a_3(X_{t-1} + 8X_{t-2} + 27X_{t-3} + 64X_{t-4}) + u_t \qquad (10.16)$$

Therefore what is required is to apply appropriate transformations of the Xs such as the ones given in parentheses. If α_3 is not statistically significant, a second-degree polynomial might be preferable. If we want to include additional terms we can easily do that. The best model will be either the one that maximizes R^2 (for different model combinations regarding r and p), or the one that minimizes AIC, SBC or any other criteria.

Other models of lag structures

There are several other models for reducing the number of parameters in a distributed lag model. Some of the most important ones are the Pascal lag, the gamma lag, the LaGuerre lag and the Shiller lag. For a full explanation of these models, see Kmenta (1986).

Autoregressive models

Autoregressive models are models that simply include lagged dependent (or endogenous) variables as regressors. In the Koyck transformation discussed above, we saw that Y_{t-1} appears as a regressor, so it can be considered as a case of a distributed lag model that has been transformed into an autoregressive model. There are two more specifications involving lag-dependent variables:

(a) the partial adjustment model; and

(b) the adaptive expectations model.

These two models will be examined in detail below.

The partial adjustment model

Suppose that the adjustment of the actual value of a variable Y_t to its optimal (or desired) level (denoted by Y_t^*) needs to be modelled. One way to do this is by using the partial adjustment model, which assumes that the change in actual Y_t ($Y_t - Y_{t-1}$) will be equal to a proportion of the optimal change ($Y_t^* - Y_{t-1}$) or:

$$Y_t - Y_{t-1} = \lambda(Y_t^* - Y_{t-1}) \qquad (10.17)$$

where λ is the adjustment coefficient, which takes values from 0 to 1, and $1/\lambda$ denotes the speed of adjustment.

Consider the two extreme cases: (a) if $\lambda = 1$ then $Y_t = Y_t^*$ and therefore the adjustment to the optimal level is instantaneous; while (b) if $\lambda = 0$ then $Y_t = Y_{t-1}$, which means that there is no adjustment of Y_t. Therefore, the closer λ is to unity, the faster the adjustment will be. To understand this better, we can use a model from economic theory. Suppose Y_t^* is the desired level of inventories for a firm i, and that this depends on the level of the sales of the firm X_t:

$$Y_t^* = \beta_1 + \beta_2 X_t \tag{10.18}$$

Because there are 'frictions' in the market, there is bound to be a gap between the actual level of inventories and the desired one. Suppose also that only a part of the gap can be closed during each period. Then the equation that will determine the actual level of inventories will be given by:

$$Y_t = Y_{t-1} + \lambda(Y_t^* - Y_{t-1}) + u_t \tag{10.19}$$

That is, the actual level of inventories is equal to that at time $t - 1$ plus an adjustment factor and a random component.

Combining Equations (10.18) and (10.19):

$$\begin{aligned} Y_t &= Y_{t-1} + \lambda(\beta_1 + \beta_2 X_t - Y_{t-1}) + u_t \\ &= \beta_1\lambda + (1 - \lambda)Y_{t-1} + \beta_2\lambda X_t + u_t \end{aligned} \tag{10.20}$$

From this model we have the following:

(a) the short-run reaction of Y to a unit change in X is $\beta_2\lambda$;

(b) the long-run reaction is given by β_1; and

(c) an estimate of β_1 can be obtained by dividing the estimate of $\beta_2\lambda$ by 1 minus the estimate of $(1 - \lambda)$, that is $\beta_1 = \beta_2\lambda/[1 - (1 - \lambda)]$.

Here it is useful to note that the error correction model is also an adjustment model. However, we provide a full examination of these kinds of models in Chapter 17.

A computer example of the partial adjustment model

Consider the money-demand function:

$$M_t^* = aY_t^{b_1} R_t^{b_2} e_t^{u_t} \tag{10.21}$$

where the usual notation applies. Taking logarithms of this equation, we get:

$$\ln M_t^* = \ln a + b_1 \ln Y_t + b_2 \ln R_t + u_t \tag{10.22}$$

The partial adjustment hypothesis can be written as:

$$\frac{M_t}{M_{t-1}} = \left(\frac{M_t^*}{M_{t-1}}\right)^\lambda \tag{10.23}$$

where, if we take logarithms, we get:

$$\ln M_t - \ln M_{t-1} = \lambda \left(\ln M_t^* - \ln M_{t-1} \right) \tag{10.24}$$

Substituting Equation (10.22) into Equation (10.24) we get:

$$\ln M_t - \ln M_{t-1} = \lambda \left(\ln a + b_1 \ln Y_t + b_2 \ln R_t + u_t - \ln M_{t-1} \right) \tag{10.25}$$

$$\ln M_t = \lambda \ln a + \lambda b_1 \ln Y_t + \lambda b_2 \ln R_t + (1 - \lambda) \ln M_{t-1} + \lambda u_t \tag{10.26}$$

or:

$$\ln M_t = \gamma_1 + \gamma_2 \ln Y_t + \gamma_3 \ln R_t + \gamma_4 \ln M_{t-1} + v_t \tag{10.27}$$

We shall use EViews to obtain OLS results for this model using data for the Italian economy (gross domestic product (*GDP*), the consumer price index (*cpi*) the M2 monetary aggregate (*M2*), plus the official discount interest rate (*R*)). The data are quarterly observations from 1975q1 to 1997q4. First we need to divide both *GDP* and *M2* by the consumer price index in order to obtain real *GDP* and real money balances. We do this by creating the following variables:

```
genr lm2_p=log(m2/cpi)
genr lgdp_p=log(gdp/cpi)
```

Then we need to calculate the logarithm of the interest rate (*R*). We can do that with the following command:

```
genr lr=log(r)
```

Now we are able to estimate the model given in Equation (10.27) by OLS by typing the following command on the command line:

```
ls lm2_p c lgdp_p lr lm2_p(-1)
```

the results of which are given in Table 10.1.

The coefficients have their expected (according to economic theory) signs and all are significantly different from zero. The R^2 is very high (0.93) but this is mainly because one of the explanatory variables is the lagged dependent variable. We leave it as an exercise for the reader to test for possible serial correlation for this model (see Chapter 8 and note the inclusion of the lagged dependent variable).

From the results we can obtain an estimate for the adjustment coefficient (λ) by using the fact that $\gamma_4 = 1 - \lambda$. So, we have that $1 - 0.959 = 0.041$. This tells us that 4.1% of the difference between the desired and actual demand for money is eliminated in each quarter, or that 16.4% of the difference is eliminated each year.

The estimated coefficients in Table 10.1 are of the short-run demand for money and they are the short-run elasticities with respect to *GDP* and *R*, respectively. The short-run income elasticity is 0.026 and the short-run interest rate elasticity is −0.017.

The long-run demand for money is given by Equation (10.22). Estimates of these long-run parameters can be obtained by dividing each of the short-run coefficients by

Table 10.1 Results for the Italian money supply example

Dependent variable: LM2_P
Method: least squares
Date: 03/02/04 Time: 17:17
Sample (adjusted): 1975:2 1997:4
Included observations: 91 after adjusting endpoints

Variable	Coefficient	Std. error	t-statistic	Prob.
C	0.184265	0.049705	3.707204	0.0004
LGDP_P	0.026614	0.010571	2.517746	0.0136
LR	−0.017358	0.005859	−2.962483	0.0039
LM2_P(−1)	0.959451	0.030822	31.12873	0.0000

R-squared	0.933470	Mean dependent var		1.859009
Adjusted R-squared	0.931176	S.D. dependent var		0.059485
S.E. of regression	0.015605	Akaike info criterion		−5.439433
Sum squared resid	0.021187	Schwarz criterion		−5.329065
Log likelihood	251.4942	F-statistic		406.8954
Durbin–Watson stat	1.544176	Prob (F-statistic)		0.000000

the estimate of the adjustment coefficient ($\lambda = 0.041$). So the long-run function is:

$$\ln M_t^* = 4.487 + 0.634 \ln Y_t - 0.414 \ln R_t + u_t \tag{10.28}$$

Note that these are the quarterly elasticities. To obtain the yearly elasticities, multiply the respective coefficients by 4.

The adaptive expectations model

The second of the autoregressive models is the adaptive expectations model, which is based on the adaptive expectations hypothesis formulated by Cagan (1956). Before exploring the model it is crucial to have a clear picture of the adaptive expectations hypothesis. Consider an agent who forms expectations of a variable X_t. If we denote by the superscript e expectations, then X_{t-1}^e is the expectation formed at time $t-1$ for X in t.

The adaptive expectations hypothesis assumes that agents make errors in their expectations (given by $X_t - X_{t-1}^e$) and that they revise their expectations by a constant proportion of the most recent error. Thus:

$$X_t^e - X_{t-1}^e = \theta(X_t - X_{t-1}^e) \quad 0 < \theta \leq 1 \tag{10.29}$$

where θ is the adjustment parameter.
If we consider again the two extreme cases we have:

(a) if $\theta = 0$ then $X_t^e = X_{t-1}^e$ and no revision in the expectations is made; while

(b) if $\theta = 1$ then $X_t^e = X_t$ and we have an instantaneous adjustment in the expectations.

The adaptive expectations hypothesis can now be incorporated into an econometric model. Suppose that we have the following model:

$$Y_t = \beta_1 + \beta_2 X_t^e + u_t \tag{10.30}$$

where, for example, we can think of Y_t as consumption and of X_t^e as expected income. Assume, then, that for the specific model the expected income follows the adaptive expectations hypothesis, so that:

$$X_t^e - X_{t-1}^e = \theta(X_t - X_{t-1}^e) \tag{10.31}$$

If actual X in period $t-1$ exceeds expectations, we would expect agents to revise their expectations upwards. Equation (10.31) then becomes:

$$X_t^e = \theta X_t + (1 - \theta) X_{t-1}^e \tag{10.32}$$

Substituting Equation (10.32) into Equation (10.30) we obtain:

$$
\begin{aligned}
Y_t &= \beta_1 + \beta_2(\theta X_t + (1 - \theta) X_{t-1}^e) + u_t \\
&= \beta_1 + \beta_2 \theta X_t + \beta_2(1 - \theta) X_{t-1}^e + u_t
\end{aligned} \tag{10.33}
$$

To estimate the X_{t-1}^e variable from Equation (10.33) to obtain an estimable econometric model, we need to follow the following procedure:
Lagging Equation (10.30) one period we get:

$$Y_{t-1} = \beta_1 + \beta_2 X_{t-1}^e + u_{t-1} \tag{10.34}$$

Multiplying both sides of Equation (10.34) by $(1 - \theta)$ we get:

$$(1 - \theta)Y_{t-1} = (1 - \theta)\beta_1 + (1 - \theta)\beta_2 X_{t-1}^e + (1 - \theta)u_{t-1} \tag{10.35}$$

Subtracting Equation (10.35) from Equation (10.33) we get:

$$Y_t - (1 - \theta)Y_{t-1} = \beta_1 - (1 - \theta)\beta_1 + \beta_2 \theta X_t + u_t - (1 - \theta)u_{t-1} \tag{10.36}$$

or:

$$Y_t = \beta_1 \theta + \beta_2 \theta X_t + (1 - \theta)Y_{t-1} + u_t - (1 - \theta)u_{t-1} \tag{10.37}$$

and finally:

$$Y_t = \beta_1^* + \beta_2^* X_t + \beta_3^* Y_{t-1} + v_t \tag{10.38}$$

where $\beta_1^* = \beta_1 \theta$, $\beta_2^* = \beta_2 \theta$, $\beta_3^* = (1 - \theta)$ and $v_t = u_t - (1 - \theta)u_{t-1}$. Once estimates of the β^*s have been obtained, β_1, β_2 and θ can be estimated as follows:

$$\hat{\theta} = 1 - \beta_3^*, \quad \hat{\beta}_1 = \frac{\beta_1^*}{\theta} \quad \text{and} \quad \hat{\beta}_2 = \frac{\beta_2^*}{\theta} \tag{10.39}$$

By using this procedure we are able to obtain an estimate of the marginal propensity to consume out of expected income, though we do not have data for expected income.

Tests of autocorrelation in autoregressive models

It is of great importance to test for autocorrelation in models with lagged dependent variables. In Chapter 7 we mentioned that in such cases the DW test statistic is not appropriate and Durbin's h-test should be used instead, or the LM test for autocorrelation. Both tests were presented analytically in Chapter 7.

Exercises

Exercise 10.1

Show how we might obtain an estimate of the marginal propensity to consume out of expected income, despite not having the data for expected income, using the adaptive expectations autoregressive model.

Exercise 10.2

Derive the Almon polynomial transformation for $p = 5$ and $r = 4$. Explain how to proceed with the estimation of this model.

Exercise 10.3

Explain how we can test for serial correlation in autoregressive models.

Exercise 10.4

Show how the Koyck transformation transforms an infinite distributed lag model into an autoregressive model. Explain the advantages of this transformation.

Exercise 10.5

Assume we have the following distributed lag model:

$$Y_t = 0.847 + 0.236X_t + 0.366X_{t-1} + 0.581X_{t-2}$$
$$+ 0.324X_{t-3} + 0.145X_{t-4} \tag{10.40}$$

Find (a) the impact effect, and (b) the long-run effect of a unit change in X on Y.

Table 10.2   Results for an adaptive expectations model

Dependent variable: CE
Method: least squares
Date: 03/02/04 Time: 18:00
Sample (adjusted): 1976:1 1997:4
Included observations: 88 after adjusting endpoints

Variable	Coefficient	Std. error	t-statistic	Prob.
C	−7.692041	3.124125	−2.462146	0.0310
YD	0.521338	0.234703	2.221233	0.0290
CE(−1)	0.442484	0.045323	9.762089	0.0000

R-squared	0.958482	Mean dependent var	1.863129
Adjusted *R*-squared	0.588722	S.D. dependent var	0.055804
S.E. of regression	0.032454	Akaike info criterion	−3.650434
Sum squared resid	0.148036	Schwarz criterion	−3.565979
Log likelihood	161.6191	*F*-statistic	49.58733
Durbin–Watson stat	0.869852	Prob (*F*-statistic)	0.000000

Exercise 10.6

The model:

$$CE_t = \beta_1 + \beta_2 YD_t + \beta_3 CE_{t-1} + v_t \tag{10.41}$$

(where CE = aggregate consumer expenditure and YD = personal disposable income) was estimated by simple OLS using data for the UK economy. The results are given in Table 10.2. Is this model a satisfactory one? Explain (using the adaptive expectations hypothesis) the meaning of each of the estimated coefficients.

Exercise 10.7

The file cons_us.wf1 contains data on consumption expenditure (CE) and personal disposable income (PDI) (measured in constant prices) for the US economy.

(a) Estimate the partial adjustment model for CE by OLS.

(b) Provide an interpretation of the estimated coefficients.

(c) Calculate the implied adjustment coefficient.

(d) Test for serial correlation using Durbin's h method and the LM test.

11 Simultaneous Equation Models

CHAPTER CONTENTS

LEARNING OBJECTIVES

After studying this chapter you should be able to:

1. Understand the problem of simultaneity and its consequences.
2. Understand the identification problem through macroeconomic examples.
3. Understand and use the two-stage least squares method of estimation.

Introduction: basic definitions

All econometric models covered so far have dealt with a single dependent variable and estimations of single equations. However, in modern world economics, interdependence is very commonly encountered. Several dependent variables are determined simultaneously, therefore appearing both as dependent and explanatory variables in a set of different equations. For example, in the single-equation case that we have explored so far, we have had equations such as demand functions of the form:

$$Q_t^d = \beta_1 + \beta_2 P_t + \beta_3 Y_t + u_t \tag{11.1}$$

where Q_t^d is quantity demanded, P_t is the relative price of the commodity, and Y_t is income. However, economic analysis suggests that price and quantity typically are determined simultaneously by the market processes, and therefore a full market model is not captured by a single equation but consists of a set of three different equations: the demand function, the supply function and the condition for equilibrium in the market of the product. So we have:

$$Q_t^d = \beta_1 + \beta_2 P_t + \beta_3 Y_t + u_{1t} \tag{11.2}$$

$$Q_t^s = \gamma_1 + \gamma_2 P_t + u_{2t} \tag{11.3}$$

$$Q_t^d = Q_t^s \tag{11.4}$$

where, of course, Q_t^s denotes the quantity supplied.

Equations (11.2), (11.3) and (11.4) are called structural equations of the simultaneous equations model, and the coefficients β and γ are called structural parameters.

Because price and quantity are jointly determined, they are both endogenous variables, and because income is not determined by the specified model, income is characterized as an exogenous variable. Note, here, that in the single-equation models, we used the terms exogenous variable and explanatory variable interchangeably, but this is no longer possible in simultaneous equation models. So we have price as an explanatory variable but not as an exogenous variable as well.

Equating Equations (11.3) to (11.2) and solving for P_t we get:

$$P_t = \frac{\beta_1 - \gamma_1}{\beta_2 - \gamma_2} + \frac{\beta_3}{\beta_2 - \gamma_2} Y_t + \frac{u_{1t} - u_{2t}}{\beta_2 - \gamma_2} \tag{11.5}$$

which can be rewritten:

$$P_t = \pi_1 + \pi_2 Y_t + v_{1t} \tag{11.6}$$

substituting Equation (11.6) into Equation (11.3) we get:

$$\begin{aligned}
Q &= \gamma_1 + \gamma_2(\pi_1 + \pi_2 Y_t + v_{1t}) + u_{1t} \\
&= \gamma_1 + \gamma_2 \pi_1 + \gamma_2 \pi_2 Y_t + \gamma_2 v_{1t} + u_{2t} \\
&= \pi_3 + \pi_4 Y_t + v_{2t}
\end{aligned} \tag{11.7}$$

Now Equations (11.3) and (11.7) specify each of the endogenous variables in terms only of the exogenous variables, the parameters of the model and the stochastic error terms. These two equations are known as reduced form equations and the πs are known as reduced form parameters. In general, reduced form equations can be obtained by solving for each of the endogenous variables in terms of the exogenous variables, the unknown parameters and the error terms.

Consequences of ignoring simultaneity

One of the assumptions of the CLRM states that the error term of an equation should be uncorrelated with each of the explanatory variables in the equation. If such a correlation exists, then the OLS regression equation is biased. It should be evident from the reduced form equations that, in cases of simultaneous equation models, such a bias exists. Recall that the new error terms v_{1t} and v_{2t} depend on u_{1t} and u_{2t}. However, to show this more clearly, consider the following general form of a simultaneous equation model:

$$Y_{1t} = a_1 + a_2 Y_{2t} + a_3 X_{1t} + a_4 X_{3t} + e_{1t} \tag{11.8}$$

$$Y_{2t} = \beta_1 + \beta_2 Y_{1t} + \beta_3 X_{3t} + \beta_4 X_{2t} + e_{2t} \tag{11.9}$$

In this model we have two structural equations, with two endogenous variables (Y_{1t} and Y_{2t}) and three exogenous variables (X_{1t}, X_{2t} and X_{3t}). Let us see what happens if one of the error terms increases, assuming everything else in the equations remains constant:

(a) if e_{1t} increases, this causes Y_{1t} to increase because of Equation (11.8); then

(b) if Y_{1t} increases (assuming that β_2 is positive) Y_{2t} will also increase because of the relationship in Equation (11.9); but

(c) if Y_{2t} increases in Equation (11.9) it also increases in Equation (11.8) where it is an explanatory variable.

Therefore an increase in the error term of an equation causes an increase in an explanatory variable in the same equation. So the assumption of no correlation among the error term and the explanatory variables is violated, leading to biased estimates.

The identification problem

Basic definitions

We saw earlier that reduced form equations express the endogenous variables only as functions of the exogenous variables. Therefore it is possible to apply OLS to these equations to obtain consistent and efficient estimations of the reduced form parameters (the πs).

The question here is whether we can obtain consistent estimates (the βs and the γs) by going back and solving for those parameters. The answer is that there are three possible situations:

(1) it is not possible to go back from the reduced form to the structural form;

(2) it is possible to go back in a unique way; or

(3) there is more than one way to go back.

This problem of being (or not being) able to go back and determine estimates of the structural parameters from estimators of the reduced form coefficients is called the identification problem.

The first situation (not possible to go back) is called under-identification, the second situation (the unique case) is called exact identification and the third situation (where there is more than one way) is called over-identification.

Conditions for identification

There are two conditions required for an equation to be identified: the order condition and the rank condition. First the two conditions are described, and then examples are given to illustrate their use.

The order condition

Let us define as G the number of endogenous variables in the system, and as M the number of variables missing from the equation under consideration (these can be endogenous, exogenous or lagged endogenous variables). Then the order condition states that:

(a) if $M < G - 1$, the equation is under-identified;

(b) if $M = G - 1$, the equation is exactly identified; and

(c) if $M > G - 1$, the equation is over-identified.

The order condition is necessary but not sufficient. By this we mean that if this condition does not hold, then the equation is not identified, but if it does hold we cannot be certain that it is identified, thus we still need to use the rank condition to conclude.

The rank condition

For the rank condition we first need to construct a table with a column for each variable and a row for each equation. For each equation put a $\sqrt{}$ in the column if the variable that corresponds to this column is included in the equation, otherwise put a 0. This gives an array of $\sqrt{}$s and 0s for each equation. Then, for a particular equation:

(a) delete the row of the equation that is under examination;

(b) write out the remaining elements of each column for which there is a zero in the equation under examination; and

(c) consider the resulting array: if there are at least $G - 1$ rows and columns that are not all zeros, then the equation is identified; otherwise it is not identified.

The rank condition is necessary and sufficient, but the order condition is needed to indicate whether the equation is exactly identified or over-identified.

Example of the identification procedure

Consider the demand and supply model described in Equations (11.2), (11.3) and (11.4). First produce a table with a column for each variable and a row for each of the three equations:

	Q^d	Q^s	P	Y
Equation 1	✓	0	✓	✓
Equation 2	0	✓	✓	0
Equation 3	✓	✓	0	0

Here we have three endogenous variables (Q^d, Q^s and P), so $G = 3$ and $G - 1 = 2$.

Now consider the order condition. For the demand function the number of excluded variables is 1, so $M = 1$, and because $M < G - 1$ the demand function is not identified. For the supply function, $M = 1$ and because $M = G - 1$ the supply function is exactly identified.

Proceeding with the rank condition we need to check only for the supply function (because we saw that the demand is not identified). The resulting array (after deleting the Q^s and P columns and the Equation 2 line) will be given by:

	Q^d	Q^s	P	Y
Equation 1	✓	0	✓	✓
Equation 2	0	✓	✓	0
Equation 3	✓	✓	0	0

	Q^d	Y
Equation 1	✓	✓
Equation 3	✓	0

The question is, are there at least $G - 1 = 2$ rows and columns that are not all zeros? The answer is 'yes', and therefore the rank condition is satisfied and the supply function is indeed exactly identified.

A second example: the macroeconomic model of a closed economy

Consider the simple macroeconomic model for a closed economy described by the equations below:

$$C_t = \beta_1 + \beta_2 Y_t \tag{11.10}$$

$$I_t = \gamma_1 + \gamma_2 Y_t + \gamma_3 R_t \tag{11.11}$$

$$Y_t = C_t + I_t + G_t \tag{11.12}$$

where C_t denotes consumption, Y_t is GDP, I_t is investments, R_t denotes the interest rate and G_t is government expenditure. Here, C_t, I_t and Y_t are endogenous variables, while R_t and G_t are exogenous. First, produce a table with five columns (one for each variable) and three rows (one for each equation):

	C	Y	I	R	G
Equation 1	✓	✓	0	0	0
Equation 2	0	✓	✓	✓	0
Equation 3	✓	✓	✓	0	✓

From the table we see that for Equation 1, $M = 3$ (I, R and G are excluded) while $G = 3$ and therefore, $M > G - 1$, so the consumption function appears to be over-identified. Similarly, for Equation 2 $M = G - 1$ and it therefore appears to be exactly identified.

Employing the rank condition for the consumption function, we have (after excluding the C and Y columns and the Equation 1 row) the following table:

	I	R	G
Equation 2	✓	✓	0
Equation 3	✓	0	✓

So, there are $G - 1 = 2$ rows and columns with no all-zero elements and therefore it is over-identified. For the investment function (after excluding the I, Y and R columns and the Equation 2 row) we have:

	C	G
Equation 1	✓	0
Equation 3	✓	✓

Again there are $G - 1 = 2$ rows and columns with no all-zero elements so the rank condition is satisfied once more and we conclude that the investment function is indeed identified.

Estimation of simultaneous equation models

The question of identification is closely related to the problem of estimating the structural parameters in a simultaneous equation model. Thus when an equation is not identified, such an estimation is not possible. In cases, however, of exact identification or overidentification there are procedures that allow us to obtain estimates of the structural parameters. These procedures are different from simple OLS in order to avoid the simultaneity bias presented earlier.

In general, in cases of exact identification, the appropriate method is the so-called method of indirect least squares (ILS), while in cases of over-identified equations the two-stage least squares (TSLS) method is the one used most commonly. The next two sections briefly present these procedures.

Estimation of an exactly identified equation: the ILS method

This method can be used only when the equations in the simultaneous equation model are found to be exactly identified. The ILS procedure involves these three steps:

Step 1 Find the reduced form equations;

Step 2 Estimate the reduced form parameters by applying simple OLS to the reduced form equations; and

Step 3 Obtain unique estimates of the structural parameters from the estimates of the parameters of the reduced form equation in step 2.

The OLS estimates of the reduced form parameters are unbiased, but when transformed the structural parameter estimates they provide are consistent. In the rare case where all the structural form equations are exactly identified, ILS provides estimates that are consistent, asymptotic-efficient and asymptotically normal.

However, the ILS method is not commonly used, for two reasons:

(1) Most simultaneous equation models tend to be over-identified; and

(2) If the system has several equations, solving for the reduced form and then for the structural form can be very tedious. An alternative is the TSLS method.

Estimation of an over-identified equation: the TSLS method

The basic idea behind the TSLS method is to replace the stochastic endogenous regressor (which is correlated with the error term and causes the bias) with one that is non-stochastic and consequently independent of the error term. This involves the following two stages (hence *two-stage* least squares):

Stage 1 Regress each endogenous variable that is also a regressor, on all the endogenous and lagged endogenous variables in the entire system by using simple OLS (this is equivalent to estimating the reduced form equations) and obtain the fitted values of the endogenous variables of these regressions ($\hat{Y}$).

Stage 2 Use the fitted values from stage 1 as proxies or instruments for the endogenous regressors in the original (structural form) equations.

One requirement is that the R^2s of the estimate equations in stage 1 should be relatively high. This is to ensure that $\hat{Y}$ and Y are highly correlated and therefore $\hat{Y}$ is a good instrument for Y. One advantage of the TSLS method is that, for equations that are exactly identified, it will yield estimates identical to those obtained from the ILS, while TSLS is also appropriate even for over-identified equations.

Example: the IS–LM model

Consider the following IS–LM model:

$$R_t = \beta_{11} + \beta_{12}M_t + \beta_{13}Y_t + \beta_{14}M_{t-1} + u_{1t} \tag{11.13}$$

$$Y_t = \beta_{21} + \beta_{22}R_t + \beta_{23}I_t + u_{1t} \tag{11.14}$$

where R denotes the interest rate, M the money stock, Y is GDP and I is investment expenditure. In this model, R and Y are the endogenous variables and M and I exogenous variables. We shall leave it as an exercise for the reader to prove that Equation (11.13) is exactly identified and Equation (11.14) is over-identified.

We want to estimate the model and, because the second equation is over-identified, we shall have to use the TSLS method. The data for this example are in the file simult.wf1 and are quarterly time series data from 1972q1 to 1998q3 for the UK economy.

To estimate an equation by using TSLS, either go to **Quick/Estimate Equation** and in the **Equation Specification** window change the method from the default **LS – Least Squares (NLS and ARMA)** to **TSLS – Two-stage Least Squares (TSNLS and ARMA)** and then specify the equation you want to estimate in the first box and the list of instruments in the second; or type the following command into EViews:

```
tsls r c m y m(-1) @ c m i m(-1)
```

where before the @ symbol is the equation to be estimated, and after the @ symbol the variable names are included that are to be used as instruments. The results of this calculation are given in Table 11.1.

The interest rate equation can be viewed as the LM relationship. The coefficient of Y is very small and positive (but insignificant), suggesting that the LM function is very flat, while increases in the money stock reduce the rate of interest. Also, R^2 is very small, suggesting that there are variables missing from the equation.

Table 11.1   TSLS estimation of the R (LM) equation

Dependent variable: R
Method: two-stage least squares
Date: 03/02/04 Time: 23:52
Sample(adjusted): 1972:1 1998:3
Included observations: 107 after adjusting endpoints
Instrument list: C M I M(−1)

Variable	Coefficient	Std. error	t-statistic	Prob.
C	9.069599	5.732089	1.582250	0.1167
M	−0.008878	0.002614	−3.396474	0.0010
Y	4.65E−05	6.44E−05	0.722214	0.4718
M(−1)	0.008598	0.002566	3.350368	0.0011
R-squared	0.182612	Mean dependent var.		9.919252
Adjusted R-squared	0.158805	S.D. dependent var.		3.165781
S.E. of regression	2.903549	Sum squared resid.		868.3518
F-statistic	8.370503	Durbin–Watson stat.		0.362635
Prob(F-statistic)	0.000049			

Table 11.2 TSLS estimation of the *Y* (IS) equation

Dependent variable: *Y*
Method: two-stage least squares
Date: 03/02/04 Time: 23:56
Sample(adjusted): 1972:1 1998:3
Included observations: 107 after adjusting endpoints
Instrument list: *C M I M*(−1)

Variable	Coefficient	Std. error	t-statistic	Prob.
C	72538.68	14250.19	5.090368	0.0000
R	−3029.112	921.8960	−3.285742	0.0014
I	4.258678	0.266492	15.98049	0.0000
R-squared	0.834395	Mean dependent var.		145171.7
Adjusted R-squared	0.831210	S.D. dependent var.		24614.16
S.E. of regression	10112.50	Sum squared resid.		1.06E+10
F-statistic	294.8554	Durbin–Watson stat.		0.217378
Prob(F-statistic)	0.000000			

Table 11.3 The first stage of the TSLS method

Dependent variable: *Y*
Method: least squares
Date: 03/03/04 Time: 00:03
Sample(adjusted): 1969:3 1998:3
Included observations: 117 after adjusting endpoints

Variable	Coefficient	Std. error	t-statistic	Prob.
C	60411.05	1561.051	38.69896	0.0000
M	6.363346	1.912864	3.326607	0.0012
I	1.941795	0.102333	18.97519	0.0000
M(−1)	−3.819978	1.921678	−1.987835	0.0492
R-squared	0.992349	Mean dependent var.		141712.3
Adjusted R-squared	0.992146	S.D. dependent var.		26136.02
S.E. of regression	2316.276	Akaike info criterion		18.36690
Sum squared resid.	6.06E+08	Schwarz criterion		18.46133
Log likelihood	−1070.464	F-statistic		4885.393
Durbin–Watson stat.	0.523453	Prob(F-statistic)		0.000000

To estimate the second equation (which can be viewed as the IS relationship), type the following command:

```
TSLS y c r i @ c m i m(-1)
```

The results of this are presented in Table 11.2.

Interpreting these results, we can see that income and the rate of interest are negatively related, according to the theoretical prediction, and income is quite sensitive to changes in the rate of interest. Also, a change in investments would cause the function to shift to the right, again as theory suggests. The R^2 of this specification is quite high.

To better understand the two-stage least squares method we can carry out the estimation stage by stage. We shall do so for the second equation only. The first

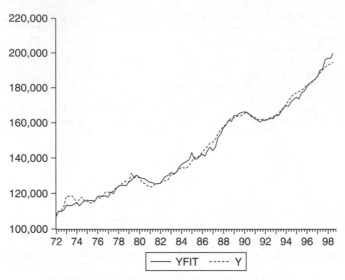

Figure 11.1   Actual and fitted values of Y

Table 11.4   The second stage of the TSLS method

Dependent variable: YFIT
Method: least squares
Date: 03/03/04 Time: 00:14
Sample(adjusted): 1972:1 1998:3
Included observations: 107 after adjusting endpoints

Variable	Coefficient	Std. error	t-statistic	Prob.
C	75890.95	8497.518	8.930955	0.0000
RFIT	−3379.407	549.7351	−6.147337	0.0000
I	4.252729	0.158912	26.76155	0.0000

R-squared	0.942570	Mean dependent var.	144905.9
Adjusted R-squared	0.941466	S.D. dependent var.	24924.47
S.E. of regression	6030.176	Akaike info criterion	20.27458
Sum squared resid.	3.78E + 09	Schwarz criterion	20.34952
Log likelihood	−1081.690	F-statistic	853.4572
Durbin–Watson stat.	0.341516	Prob(F-statistic)	0.000000

stage involves regressing Y on a constant M, I and $M(-1)$, so type the following command:

```
ls y c m i m(-1)
```

The results are presented in Table 11.3. A positive result here is that R^2 is very high, so the fitted Y-variable is a very good proxy for Y.

Next we need to obtain the fitted values of this regression equation. This can be done by subtracting the residuals of the model from the actual Y-variable. The EViews command is:

```
genr yfit=y-resid
```

Plotting these two variables together by the command:

```
plot y yfit
```

we see (Figure 11.1) that they are moving very closely together.

Do the same for *R* to obtain the rfit variable and then, as the second stage, estimate the model with the fitted endogenous variables instead of the actual *Y* and *R*. The command for this is:

```
ls yfit c rfit i
```

The results are reported in Table 11.4.

Estimation of simultaneous equations in Stata

In Stata, to estimate a model of simultaneous equations the command is:

```
reg3 (first equation) (second equation) , 2sls
```

where, in the first parentheses, we put the first of the two equations we need to estimate and, in the second parentheses, the second equation. The 2sls in the command line indicates that the method of estimation should be the two-stage least squares method.

Therefore, in our example of IS–LM the command is:

```
reg3 (r = m y L.m) (y = r i) , 2sls
```

The results of this command (use the file simult.dat for this analysis) are shown in Table 11.5 and are very similar to the EViews example.

Table 11.5 Two-stage least squares regression

Equation	Obs	Parms	RMSE	"R-sq"	F-stat	P
r	106	3	2.82336	0.2115	10.23	0.0000
y	106	2	9657.933	0.8469	317.21	0.0000

	Coef.	Std.	Err.	t	P>|t|	[95% Conf. Interval]	
r							
m	−0.0093748	0.0025448	−3.68	0.000	−0.0143922	−0.0043575	
y	0.0000622	0.0000626	0.99	0.322	−0.0000612	0.0001856	
m							
L1.	0.0090177	0.002498	3.61	0.000	0.0040926	0.0139428	
_cons	8.079159	5.565536	1.45	0.148	−2.89387	19.05219	
y							
r	−3030.804	815.5647	−3.72	0.000	−4640.774	−1424.833	
i	4.188473	0.254951	16.43	0.000	3.685862	4.691084	
_cons	74573.4	13054.1	5.71	0.000	48835.9	100310.9	

Endogenous variables: r y
Exogenous variables: m L.m i

12 Limited Dependent Variable Regression Models

CHAPTER CONTENTS

LEARNING OBJECTIVES

After studying this chapter you should be able to:

1. Understand the problems caused by estimating a model with a dummy dependent variable using the simple linear model.
2. Be familiar with the logit and probit models for dummy dependent variables.
3. Estimate logit and probit models and interpret the results obtained through econometric software.
4. Be familiar with and learn how to estimate the multinomial and ordered logit and probit models.
5. Understand the meaning of censored data and learn the use of the Tobit model.
6. Estimate the Tobit model for censored data.

Introduction

So far, we have examined cases in which dummy variables, carrying qualitative information, were used as explanatory variables in a regression model (see Chapter 10). However, there are frequently cases in which the dependent variable is of a qualitative nature and therefore a dummy is being used in the left-hand side of the regression model. Assume, for example, we want to examine why some people go to university while others do not, or why some people decide to enter the labour force and others do not. Both these variables are dichotomous (they take 0 or 1 values) dummy variables of the types discussed in Chapter 10. However, here we want to use this variable as the dependent variable.

Things can be even further complicated by having a dependent variable that is of a qualitative nature but can take more than two responses (a polychotomous variable). For example, consider the ratings of various goods from consumer surveys – answers to questionnaires on various issues taking the form: strongly disagree, disagree, indifferent, agree, strongly agree and so on.

In these cases, models and estimation techniques are used other than the ones we have examined already. The presentation and analysis of these models is the aim of this chapter. We start with the linear probability model, followed by the logit, probit and Tobit models. Ordered and multinomial logit and probit models are also presented.

The linear probability model

We begin with an examination of the simplest possible model, which has a dichotomous dummy variable as the dependent variable. For simplicity, we assume that the dummy dependent variable is explained by only one regressor. For example, we are interested in examining the labour force participation decision of adult females. The question is: why do some women enter the labour force while others do not? Labour economics suggests that the decision to go out to work or not is a function of the unemployment rate, average wage rate, level of education, family income, age and so on. However, for simplicity, we assume that the decision to go out to work or not is affected by only one explanatory variable (X_{2i}) – the level of family income.

The model is:

$$Y_i = \beta_1 + \beta_2 X_{2i} + u_i \tag{12.1}$$

But since Y_i is a dummy variable, we can rewrite the model as:

$$D_i = \beta_1 + \beta_2 X_{2i} + u_i \tag{12.2}$$

where X_{2i} is the level of family income (a continuous variable); D_i is a dichotomous dummy defined as:

$$D_i = \begin{cases} 1 & \text{if the } i\text{th individual is working} \\ 0 & \text{if the } i\text{th individual is not working} \end{cases} \tag{12.3}$$

and u_i as usual is the disturbance.

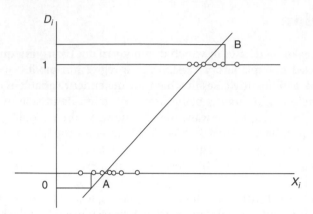

Figure 12.1   The linear probability model

One of the basic assumptions of the CLRM is that $E(u_i) = 0$. Thus, for given X_{2i}:

$$E(D_i) = \beta_1 + \beta_2 X_{2i} \tag{12.4}$$

However, since D_i is of a qualitative nature, here the interpretation is different. Let us define P_i as the probability of $D_i = 1(P_i = \Pr(D_i = 1))$; therefore $1 - P_i$ is the probability of $D_i = 0(1 - P_i = \Pr(D_i = 0))$. To put this mathematically:

$$E(D_i) = 1 \Pr(D_i = 1) + 0 \Pr(D_i = 0)$$
$$= 1P_i + 0(1 - P_i)$$
$$= P_i \tag{12.5}$$

Equation (12.5) simply suggests that the expected value of D_i is equal to the probability that the ith individual is working. For this reason, this model is called the linear probability model. Therefore the values obtained, β_1 and β_2, enable us to estimate the probabilities that a woman with a given level of family income will enter the labour force.

Problems with the linear probability model

$\hat{D}_i$ is not bounded by the (0,1) range

The linear probability model can be estimated by simple OLS. However, an estimation using OLS can cause significant problems. Consider the case depicted in Figure 12.1. Since the dependent dummy variable, D_i, can take only two values, 0 and 1, the scatter diagram will simply be two horizontal rows of points, one at the 0 level (the X axis) and one for the value of 1. The problem emerges from the fact that OLS will fit a straight line to these points for the estimated values of β_1 and β_2 (note that nothing prevents β_1 from being negative). Therefore, for low levels of income (such as in point A in

Figure 12.1) we have negative probability, while also for high levels of income (such as in point B) we shall obtain probability higher than 1. This is obviously a problem, since a negative probability and/or a probability greater than 1 is meaningless. An alternative estimation method that will restrict the values of $\hat{D}_i$ to lying between 0 and 1 is required. The logit and probit methods discussed later resolve this problem.

Non-normality and heteroskedasticity of the disturbances

Another problem with the linear probability model is that the disturbances are not normally distributed, but they follow the binomial distribution. We have that:

$$\text{if } D_i = 1 \Rightarrow u_i = 1 - \beta_1 - \beta_2 X_{2i}$$
$$\text{if } D_i = 0 \Rightarrow u_i = -\beta_1 - \beta_2 X_{2i}$$

which means that u_i takes only the above two values with probabilities P_i and $1 - P_i$, respectively, and is therefore non-normal.

However, the non-normality is not that crucial, because we still get unbiased OLS estimates. The bigger problem is that the disturbances are also heteroskedastic. To see this we need to calculate the variance of the disturbances:

$$\text{Var}(u_i) = E(u_i)^2 = P_i(\text{value of } u_i \text{ when } D_i = 1)^2 + (1 - P_i)(\text{value of } u_i \text{ when } D_i = 0)^2$$
$$(12.6)$$

We know that $E(D_i) = P_i = \beta_1 + \beta_2 X_{2i}$, therefore substituting that into Equation (12.6) we obtain:

$$\text{Var}(u_i) = P_i(1 - P_i)^2 + (1 - P_i)(P_i)^2$$
$$= P_i(1 + P_i^2 - 2P_i) + (1 - P_i)P_i^2$$
$$= P_i + P_i^3 - 2P_i^2 + P_i^2 - P_i^3$$
$$= P_i - P_i^2$$
$$\text{Var}(u_i) = P_i(1 - P_i) \tag{12.7}$$

Thus, since the variance of the disturbances depends on P_i, which differs for every individual according to their level of family income, the disturbance is heteroskedastic.

The coefficient of determination as a measure of overall fit

Another problem associated with the linear probability model is that the value of the coefficient of determination, R^2, obtained from simple OLS does not have any significant value in explaining the model. This can be understood by examining Figure 12.1. Since the values of D_i are either 0 or 1 for any value of X_{2i} all the scatter dots will lie around those two values and will fit well with any regression line obtained. As a result, the R^2 computed from these models is generally much lower than the maximum value of 1, even if the model does exceptionally well in explaining the two distinct choices involved. Therefore, R^2 should not be used in the case of such models.

After discussing the problems concerning the linear probability model, we see that an alternative method is required to examine appropriately cases of models with dummy dependent variables. Such models will be examined in the following sections.

The logit model

A general approach

In the linear probability model, we saw that the dependent variable D_i on the left-hand side, which reflects the probability P_i, can take any real value and is not limited to being in the correct range of probabilities – the $(0,1)$ range.

A simple way to resolve this problem involves the following two steps. First, transform the dependent variable, D_i, as follows, introducing the concept of odds:

$$odds_i = \frac{P_i}{1 - P_i} \tag{12.8}$$

Here, $odds_i$ is defined as the ratio of the probability of success to its complement (the probability of failure). Using the labour force participation example, if the probability for an individual to join the labour force is 0.75 then the odds ratio is $0.75/0.25 = 3/1$, or the odds are three to one that an individual is working. The second step involves taking the natural logarithm of the odds ratio, calculating the logit, L_i, as:

$$L_i = ln\left(\frac{P_i}{1 - P_i}\right) \tag{12.9}$$

Using this in a linear regression we obtain the logit model as:

$$L_i = \beta_1 + \beta_2 X_{2i} + u_i \tag{12.10}$$

It is easy to see that this model (which is linear to both the explanatory variable and the parameters) can be extended to more than one explanatory variable, so as to obtain:

$$L_i = \beta_1 + \beta_2 X_{2i} + \beta_3 X_{3i} + \cdots + \beta_k X_{ki} + u_i \tag{12.11}$$

Notice that the logit model resolves the 0,1 boundary condition problem because:

(a) As the probability P_i approaches 0 the odds approach zero and the logit ($ln(0)$) approaches $-\infty$.

(b) As the probability P_i approaches 1 the odds approach $+\infty$ and the logit ($ln(1)$) approaches $+\infty$.

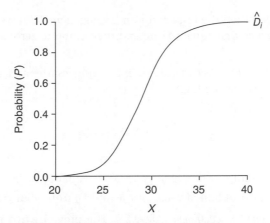

Figure 12.2 The logit function

Therefore, we see that the logit model maps probabilities from the range $(0,1)$ to the entire real line. A graph that depicts the logit model is shown in Figure 12.2, where we can see that $\hat{D}_i$ asymptotically approaches 1 and 0 in the two extreme cases. The S-shape of this curve is known as a sigmoid curve and functions of this type are called sigmoid functions. Estimation of the logit model is done by using the maximum-likelihood method. This method is an iterative estimation technique that is particularly useful for equations that are non-linear in the coefficients.

Interpretation of the estimates in logit models

After estimating a logit model, the regular hypothesis testing analysis can be undertaken using the z-statistics obtained. However, the interpretation of the coefficients is totally different from that of regular OLS. The reason for this is clear if we consider that the dependent variable is a logit equation. Given this, the coefficient β_2 obtained from a logit model estimation shows the change in $L_i = ln(P_i/(1 - P_i))$ for a unit change in X, which has no particular meaning.

What we need to know is the impact of an independent variable on the probability $\hat{P}_i$ and not on $\widehat{ln\left(\frac{P_i}{1-P_i}\right)}$. In general there are three possible ways of interpreting the results obtained.

(a) *Calculate the change in average $\hat{D}_i$:* To do this, first insert the mean values of all the explanatory variables into the estimated logit equation and calculate the average $\hat{D}_i$. Then recalculate, but now increasing the value of the explanatory variable under examination by one unit to obtain the new average $\hat{D}_i$. The difference between the two $\hat{D}_i$s obtained shows the impact of a one-unit increase in that explanatory variable on the probability that $D_i = 1$ (keeping all other explanatory variables constant). This approach should be used cautiously when one or more of the explanatory variables is also a dummy variable (for example how can anyone define the average of gender?). When dummies of this kind (for example gender) exist in the equation, the methodology used is to calculate first the impact for an 'average male' and then the impact for an 'average female' (by setting the dummy explanatory variable first equal to one and then equal to zero) and comparing the two results.

(b) *Take the partial derivative*: As can be seen in the more mathematical approach below, taking the derivative of the logit obtains:

$$\frac{\partial \hat{D}_i}{\partial X_{ji}} = \hat{\beta}_j \hat{D}_i (1 - \hat{D}_i) \tag{12.12}$$

Thus the marginal impact of a change in X_{ji} is equal to $\hat{\beta}_j \hat{D}_i (1 - \hat{D}_i)$. To use this, simply substitute the obtained values for $\hat{\beta}_j$ and $\hat{D}_i$ from your estimation.

(c) *Multiply the obtained β_j coefficients by 0.25*: The previous two methods are quite difficult to use, but are very accurate. A simpler, but not so accurate method is to multiply the coefficients obtained from the probit model by 0.25 and use this for the interpretation of the marginal effect. This comes from the substitution of the value $\hat{D}_i = 0.5$ to Equation (12.12) above:

$$\hat{\beta}_j 0.5 (1 - 0.5) = \hat{\beta}_j 0.25 \tag{12.13}$$

So, where a rough approximation is needed, this method is simple and quick. However, if precision is required the two methods discussed earlier are much more appropriate.

Goodness of fit

As pointed out earlier, the conventional measure of goodness of fit, R^2, is not appropriate for assessing the performance of logit models. Therefore, alternative ways are needed to deal with that. One way is to create a measure based on the percentage of the observations in the sample that the estimated equation explained correctly. This measure is called the *count R^2* and is defined as:

$$count\ R^2 = \frac{number\ of\ correct\ predictions}{number\ of\ observations} \tag{12.14}$$

Here we define as a correct prediction $\hat{D}_i > 0.5$ to predict correctly that $D_i = 1$ and $\hat{D}_i < 0.5$ to predict correctly that $D_i = 0$. Obviously the higher the *count R^2*, the better the fit of the model.

This measure, though easy to calculate and very intuitive, was criticized by Kennedy (2003) because a naïve predictor can do better than any other model if the sample is unbalanced between the 0 and 1 values. Assume, for example, that $D_i = 1$ for 90% of the observations in the sample. A simple rule that the prediction is always 1 is likely to outperform the *count R^2* measure of goodness of fit, though very naïve and clearly wrong. Therefore Kennedy suggests a measure that adds the portion of the correctly predicted $D_i = 1$ values to the correctly predicted $D_i = 0$ values. This new measure of goodness of fit (let's call it R_K^2) is given by:

$$R_k^2 = \frac{number\ of\ correct\ predictions\ of\ D_i = 1}{number\ of\ observations\ of\ D_i = 1} + \frac{number\ of\ correct\ predictions\ of\ D_i = 0}{number\ of\ observations\ of\ D_i = 0}$$

$$(12.15)$$

McFadden (1973) suggests an alternative way to measure the goodness of fit, called McFadden's *pseudo-R²*. To obtain this measure McFadden suggests a likelihood ratio (LR) test as an alternative to the F test for the overall significance of the coefficients that were examined in the CLRM. This involves the estimation of the full model:

$$L_i = \beta_1 + \beta_2 X_{2i} + \beta_3 X_{3i} + \cdots + \beta_k X_{ki} + u_i \qquad (12.16)$$

and after imposing the restriction:

$$\beta_1 = \beta_2 = \beta_3 = \cdots = \beta_k \qquad (12.17)$$

the estimation of the restricted model:

$$L_i = \beta_1 + u_i \qquad (12.18)$$

Both the unrestricted and restricted models are estimated using the maximum likelihood method, and the maximized likelihoods for each model (l_R and I_u for the restricted and the unrestricted model, respectively) are calculated. The restrictions are then tested using the LR test statistic:

$$LR = -2(l_R - I_u) \qquad (12.19)$$

which follows the χ^2 distribution with $k - 1$ degrees of freedom.

The McFadden *pseudo-R²* can then be defined as:

$$pseudo\text{-}R^2 = 1 - \frac{l_u}{l_R} \qquad (12.20)$$

which (since l_R is always smaller than I_u) will always take values between 0 and 1 like the normal R^2. Note, however, that the McFadden *pseudo-R²* does not have the same interpretation as the normal R^2, and for this reason is not used very much by most researchers. Finally, it should be pointed out that, in general, for the dummy dependent variable models, the goodness of fit is not of primary importance. What are of importance, however, are the expected signs of the regression coefficients, their statistical significance and their interpretation.

A more mathematical approach

Recall that, in explaining the decision to join the labour force or not depending on the level of family income, the linear probability model was:

$$D_i = \beta_1 + \beta_2 X_{2i} + u_i \qquad (12.21)$$

If we use the logistic function in explaining this probability we have:

$$P_i = \frac{1}{1 + e^{[-(\beta_1 + \beta_2 X_{2i} + u_i)]}} \tag{12.22}$$

This equation constrains P_i to take values on the (0,1) range, because as X_{2i} becomes very large (approaches ∞) then $P_i = 1$, and as X_{2i} becomes very small (approaches $-\infty$) then $P_i = 0$.

It is easy to see that the complement of P_i is given by:

$$(1 - P_i) = \frac{e^{-(\beta_1 + \beta_2 X_{2i} + u_i)}}{1 + e^{[-(\beta_1 + \beta_2 X_{2i} + u_i)]}} \tag{12.23}$$

Therefore, we have that:

$$\frac{P_i}{(1 - P_i)} = \frac{\frac{1}{1 + e^{[-(\beta_1 + \beta_2 X_{2i} + u_i)]}}}{\frac{e^{-(\beta_1 + \beta_2 X_{2i} + u_i)}}{1 + e^{[-(\beta_1 + \beta_2 X_{2i} + u_i)]}}} = \frac{1}{e^{-(\beta_1 + \beta_2 X_{2i} + u_i)}} \tag{12.24}$$

and if we take natural logarithms of both sides we obtain:

$$\ln \frac{P_i}{(1 - P_i)} = \beta_1 + \beta_2 X_{2i} + u_i \tag{12.25}$$

where the ratio $P_i/(1 - P_i)$ is called the odds ratio and its logarithm is called the logit. Hence the model is known as the logit model.

Notice that in the logit model P_i is not linearly related to X_{2i}, therefore the interpretation of the β_2 coefficient is not straightforward. What we have here is that β_2 measures the change in $ln(P_i/(1 - P_i))$ for a unit change in X_{2i}. In our example, this is how the natural logarithm of the odds in favour of participating in the labour force is affected as family income (X_{2i}) changes by one unit. This interpretation therefore has no logical meaning.

To obtain an interpretation that is logical, it is useful to differentiate the model with respect to X_{2i}:

$$\frac{\partial P_i}{\partial X_{2i}} \frac{1}{P_i} + \frac{\partial P_i}{\partial X_{2i}} \frac{1}{(1 - P_i)} = \beta_2 \tag{12.26}$$

Therefore:

$$\frac{\partial P_i}{\partial X_{2i}} = \beta_2 P_i (1 - P_i) \tag{12.27}$$

or:

$$\frac{\partial \hat{D}_i}{\partial X_{2i}} = \hat{\beta}_2 \hat{D}_i (1 - \hat{D}_i) \tag{12.28}$$

which says that the change in the expected value of $\hat{D}_i$ caused by a one-unit increase in X_{2i} equals $\hat{\beta}_2 \hat{D}_i (1 - \hat{D}_i)$.

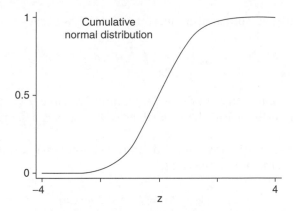

Figure 12.3   Cumulative normal distribution

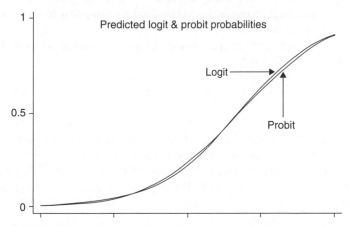

Figure 12.4   Differences between logit and probit probabilities

The probit model

A general approach

The probit model is an alternative method of resolving the problem faced by the linear probability model of having values beyond the acceptable (0,1) range of probabilities. To do this, obtain a sigmoid function similar to that of the logit model by using the cumulative normal distribution, which by definition has an S-shape asymptotical to the (0,1) range (see Figure 12.3).

The logit and probit procedures are so closely related that they rarely produce results that are significantly different. However, the idea behind using the probit model as being more suitable than the logit model is that most economic variables follow the normal distribution and hence it is better to examine them through the cumulative normal distribution. For the high degree of similarity of the two models, compare the two sigmoid functions as shown in Figure 12.4.

Using the cumulative normal distribution to model P_i we have:

$$P_i = \frac{1}{\sqrt{2\pi}} \int_{-\infty}^{Z_i} e^{-\frac{s^2}{2}} ds \tag{12.29}$$

where P_i is the probability that the dependent dummy variable $D_i = 1$, $Z_i = \beta_1 + \beta_2 X_{2i}$ (this can be easily extended to the k-variables case) and s is a standardized normal variable.

The Z_i is modelled as the inverse of the normal cumulative distribution function $(\Phi^{-1}(P_i))$ to give us the probit model, as:

$$Z_i = (\Phi^{-1}(P_i)) = \beta_1 + \beta_2 X_{2i} + u_i \tag{12.30}$$

The probit model is estimated by applying the maximum-likelihood method. Since probit and logit are quite similar, they also have similar properties: interpretation of the coefficients is not straightforward and the R^2 does not provide a valid measure for the overall goodness of fit.

To calculate the marginal effect of a change in X on a change in the probability $P_i = 1$ we need to calculate $\beta_2 f(Z)$ with:

$$f(Z) = \frac{1}{\sqrt{2\pi}} e^{\frac{1}{2} Z^2} \tag{12.31}$$

Generally, logit and probit analysis provide similar results and similar marginal effects, especially for large samples. However, since the shapes of the tails of the logit and probit distributions are different (see Figure 12.4), the two models produce different results in terms of 0 and 1 values in the dependent dummy variable if the sample is unbalanced.

A more mathematical approach

Suppose we want to model:

$$D_i = \beta_1 + \beta_2 X_{2i} + \beta_3 X_{3i} + \cdots + \beta_k X_{ki} + u_i \tag{12.32}$$

where D_i is a dichotomous dummy variable as in the problem of labour force participation discussed earlier. To motivate the probit model, assume that the decision to join the work force or not depends on an unobserved variable (also known as a latent variable) Z_i that is determined by other observable variables (say, level of family income as in our previous example), such as:

$$Z_i = \beta_1 + \beta_2 X_{2i} + \beta_3 X_{3i} + \cdots + \beta_k X_{ki} \tag{12.33}$$

and

$$P_i = F(Z_i) \tag{12.34}$$

If we assume normal distribution, then the $F(Z_i)$ comes from the normal cumulative density function given by:

$$F(Z_i) = \frac{1}{\sqrt{2\pi}} \int_{-\infty}^{Z_i} e^{-\frac{z^2}{2}} dZ \tag{12.35}$$

Expressing Z as the inverse of the normal cumulative density function we have:

$$Z_i = F^{-1}(P_i) = \beta_1 + \beta_2 X_{2i} + \beta_3 X_{3i} + \cdots + \beta_k X_{ki} \tag{12.36}$$

which is the expression for the probit model.

The model is estimated by applying the maximum-likelihood method to Equation (12.36), but the results obtained from the use of any statistical software are given in the form of Equation (12.37).

The interpretation of the marginal effect is obtained by differentiation in order to calculate $\partial P / \partial X_i$ which in this case is:

$$\frac{\partial P}{\partial X_i} = \frac{\partial P}{\partial Z} \frac{\partial Z}{\partial X_i} = F'(Z)\beta_i \tag{12.37}$$

Since $F(Z_i)$ is the standard normal cumulative distribution, $F'(Z_i)$ is just the standard normal distribution itself given by:

$$F'(Z_i) = \frac{1}{\sqrt{2\pi}} e^{-\frac{z^2}{2}} \tag{12.38}$$

In order to obtain a statistic for the marginal effect, first calculate Z for the mean values of the explanatory variables, then calculate $F'(Z_i)$ from Equation (12.37) and then multiply this result by β_i to get the final result, as in Equation (12.38).

The overall goodness of fit is examined as for the logit model.

Multinomial and ordered logit and probit models

In many cases we have variables of qualitative information that are not simply dichotomous (the 0,1 case) but have more than two categories (polychotomous variables). An example is answers in questionnaires of the form: strongly agree, agree, indifferent, disagree, strongly disagree. Another example from financial economics involves one firm intending to take over another using three different methods: (a) by cash; (b) by shares; or (c) by a mixture of the two.

Notice the difference between the two examples. In the first case, the five different options follow a natural ordering of the alternatives, starting with the strongest and going to the weakest. Strongly agree is clearly better than simply agree, and this in turn is better than indifferent and so on. In cases like this, ordered probit and logit models should be used to obtain appropriate estimates. In the second case there is no natural ordering of the three alternatives, meaning that it is not better to carry out the takeover by using cash or by using shares or by a mixture of the two. Therefore, in this case multinomial logit and probit models should be used. We examine these two cases below.

Multinomial logit and probit models

Multinomial logit and probit models are multi-equation models. A dummy dependent variable with k categories will create $k - 1$ equations (and cases to examine). This is easy to see if we consider that for the dichotomous dummy $D = (1, 0)$ we have only one logit/probit equation to capture the probability that the one or the other will be chosen. Therefore, if we have a trichotomous (with three different choices) variable we shall need two equations, and for a k categories variable, $k - 1$ equations.

Consider the example given before. We have a firm that is planning to make a takeover bid by means of (a) cash, (b) shares, or (c) a mixture. Therefore, we have a response variable with three levels. We can define these variable levels as follows:

$$D_S = \begin{cases} 1 & \text{if the takeover is by shares} \\ 0 & \text{if otherwise} \end{cases}$$

$$D_C = \begin{cases} 1 & \text{if the takeover is by cash} \\ 0 & \text{if otherwise} \end{cases}$$

$$D_M = \begin{cases} 1 & \text{if the takeover is by a mixture} \\ 0 & \text{if otherwise} \end{cases}$$

Note that we need only two of the three dummies presented here, because one dummy will be reserved as the reference point. Therefore, we have two equations:

$$D_S = \beta_1 + \beta_2 X_{2i} + \beta_3 X_{3i} + \cdots + \beta_k X_{ki} + u_i \tag{12.39}$$

$$D_C = a_1 + a_2 X_{2i} + a_3 X_{3i} + \cdots + a_k X_{ki} + v_i \tag{12.40}$$

which can be estimated by either the logit or the probit method, based on the assumption to be made for the distribution of the disturbances.

The fitted values of the two equations can be interpreted as the probabilities of using the method of takeover described by each equation. Since all three alternatives should add up to one, by subtracting the two obtained probabilities from unity we can derive the probability for the takeover by using a mixed strategy.

Ordered logit and probit models

In cases where the multiple response categories of a dummy variable follow a rank or order, as in the case of strongly agree, agree and so on, the ordered logit and probit models should be used. These models assume that the observed D_i is determined by D_i^* using the rule:

$$D_i = \begin{cases} 1 & \text{if } D_i^* \leq \gamma_1 \\ 2 & \text{if } \gamma_1 \leq D_i^* \leq \gamma_2 \\ 3 & \text{if } \gamma_2 \leq D_i^* \leq \gamma_3 \\ \vdots \\ M & \text{if } \gamma_M \leq D_i^* \end{cases}$$

with the 1 value in this case being for the lower-rank response (strongly disagree), the 2 value for the next higher response (disagree), and so on.

Note that, since the data are ordered, choosing disagree (which takes the value of 2) does not mean that it is twice as preferable or twice as high as strongly disagree. All we can say is that it is higher because the disagree case seems to be of a lesser degree than the strongly disagree case.

The mathematics and computations behind the ordered logit and probit models are quite complicated and beyond the scope of this textbook. However, econometric software, such as EViews and Stata, provide estimates, and the analysis and interpretation are similar to those of the simple logit and probit models.

The Tobit model

The Tobit model (developed and named after Tobin (1958) is an extension of the probit model that allows us to estimate models that use censored variables. Censored variables are variables that contain regular values for some of the cases in the sample and do not have any values at all for some other cases. We shall illustrate this with an example. Take the simple dummy variable of home ownership, which takes the values of:

$$D_i = \begin{cases} 1 & \text{if the } i\text{th individual is home owner} \\ 0 & \text{if the } i\text{th individual is not home owner} \end{cases}$$

This dummy variable is a standard case in that, if we want to use it as dependent variable, we shall have to employ either logit or probit models, as discussed above.

However, if we transform this variable because what we want to examine now is the amount of money spent in order to buy a house, what we have is a variable that takes continuous values for those who own a house (the values are the amount of money spent on buying the house) and a set of zeros for those individuals who do not own a house. Such variables are called censored variables and require the Tobit model in order to be examined in a regression analysis context.

The problem relies on the fact that a simple OLS estimation of models of this kind will 'ignore' the zero values of the censored dependent variable and hence provide results that are biased and inconsistent. The Tobit model resolves the problem by providing appropriate parameter estimates. The mathematics behind the Tobit model is rather complicated and beyond the scope of this textbook. Interested readers can obtain detailed information from Greene (2000).

Computer example: probit and logit models in EViews, Stata and Microfit

Logit and probit models in EViews

The file binary2.wf1 contains data for an example similar to the labour force participation example discussed above. More specifically, there is a dummy variable (*dummy*)

Table 12.1   Results from the linear probability model

Dependent variable: DUMMY
Method: least squares
Date: 05/01/10 Time: 14:42
Sample: 1 507
Included observations: 507

Variable	Coefficient	Std. error	t-statistic	Prob.
C	1.579630	0.050012	31.58525	0.0000
FAM_INCOME	−0.585599	0.022949	−25.51746	0.0000
R-squared	0.563202	Mean dependent var.		0.355030
Adjusted *R*-squared	0.562337	S.D. dependent var.		0.478995
S.E. of regression	0.316884	Akaike info criterion		0.543377
Sum squared resid.	50.70992	Schwarz criterion		0.560058
Log likelihood	−135.7461	Hannan–Quinn criter.		0.549919
F-statistic	651.1409	Durbin–Watson stat.		1.196107
Prob(*F*-statistic)	0.000000			

that takes the value 1 when the individual is working and 0 when he or she is not working. There are also other variables that will be used as explanatory ones, such as:

fam_inc = family income for every individual

age = the years of age of every individual

exper = the years of working experience for every individual.

The data set is for 507 individuals.

First, we estimate the linear probability model for the role of family income on the decision to join the labour force or not. This can easily be done with the command for OLS, as follows:

```
ls dummy c fam_inc
```

The results are reported in Table 12.1. We have discussed the limitations of this model extensively and it is easy to understand that a logit or probit estimation is appropriate in this case. To get logit results, click on the **Estimate** button of the **Equation** window with the regression results and change the method of estimation in the **Estimation settings** from the drop-down menu from LS to BINARY. In the new **Estimation specification** window that comes up, choose **Logit** by selecting the **Logit** button (note that the default is the probit one) and click **OK**. The results of the logit estimation are given in Table 12.2. We leave it as an exercise for the reader to interpret these results according to the theory provided earlier in this chapter.

Similarly, if we want to obtain the results for the probit model, again click **Estimate** and this time choose the probit model by selecting the **Probit** button in EViews. When **OK** is clicked, the results are obtained immediately. The results of the probit model are shown in Table 12.3. Note that the two sets of results (logit and probit) do not differ substantially. We again leave this for the reader as an exercise.

Table 12.2 Results from the logit model

Dependent variable: DUMMY
Method: ML – binary logit (quadratic hill climbing)
Date: 05/01/10 Time: 15:04
Sample: 1 507
Included observations: 507
Convergence achieved after 5 iterations
Covariance matrix computed using second derivatives

Variable	Coefficient	Std. error	z-statistic	Prob.
C	19.82759	2.386267	8.309040	0.0000
FAM_INCOME	−11.15332	1.337354	−8.339835	0.0000

McFadden R-squared	0.706117	Mean dependent var.		0.355030
S.D. dependent var.	0.478995	S.E. of regression		0.256373
Akaike info criterion	0.390235	Sum squared resid.		33.19227
Schwarz criterion	0.406915	Log likelihood		−96.92449
Hannan–Quinn criter.	0.396776	Deviance		193.8490
Restr. deviance	659.6117	Restr. log likelihood		−329.8059
LR statistic	465.7628	Avg. log likelihood		−0.191173
Prob(LR statistic)	0.000000			

Obs with Dep = 0	327	Total obs	507
Obs with Dep = 1	180		

Table 12.3 Results from the probit model

Dependent variable: DUMMY
Method: ML – binary probit (quadratic hill climbing)
Date: 05/01/10 Time: 15:02
Sample: 1 507
Included observations: 507
Convergence achieved after 6 iterations
Covariance matrix computed using second derivatives

Variable	Coefficient	Std. error	z-statistic	Prob.
C	11.72280	1.380677	8.490614	0.0000
FAM_INCOME	−6.585262	0.771075	−8.540365	0.0000

McFadden R-squared	0.710884	Mean dependent var.		0.355030
S.D. dependent var.	0.478995	S.E. of regression		0.255433
Akaike info criterion	0.384033	Sum squared resid.		32.94917
Schwarz criterion	0.400713	Log likelihood		−95.35225
Hannan–Quinn criter.	0.390574	Deviance		190.7045
Restr. deviance	659.6117	Restr. log likelihood		−329.8059
LR statistic	468.9072	Avg. log likelihood		−0.188071
Prob(LR statistic)	0.000000			

Obs with Dep = 0	327	Total obs	507
Obs with Dep = 1	180		

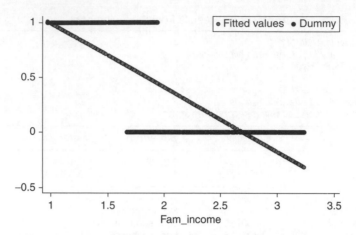

Figure 12.5   Plot of Stata computer example – the linear probability model

EViews has options for estimating ordered logit and probit models as well as the Tobit model (under the ORDERED and TRUNCATED methods of estimation), which are very easy to use and to obtain results from.

Logit and probit models in Stata

In Stata the commands for the logit and probit methods of estimation are easy to use and follow the same syntax as the simple *regress* command for OLS. Using the data in the file binary2.dat (the variables are again *dummy* for labour force participation and *fam_inc* for family income), first obtain the linear probability model estimation results by using the regress function as follows:

```
regress dummy fam_inc
```

The results obtained from this command are similar to those reported in Table 12.1. If we further give the command:

```
predict dumhat
```

which saves the predicted values of the dummy variable (or $\hat{D}_i$) in a series called dumhat, and then the command:

```
graph twoway (scatter dumhat dummy fam_inc)
```

we obtain the graph shown in Figure 12.5, which shows clearly why the linear model is not appropriate (connect this with the discussion of theoretical Figure 12.1).

To estimate the same regression with the logit model, the command is:

```
logit dummy fam_inc
```

and, again, if we give the commands for storing the fitted values of the logit model and plotting them in a graph:

```
predict dumhatlog
graph twoway (scatter dumhatlog dummy fam_inc)
```

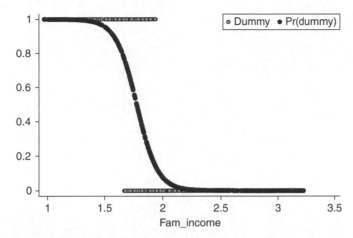

Figure 12.6   Plot of Stata computer example – the logit model

we obtain Figure 12.6, which shows how the logistic function is indeed fitting the data in an appropriate way through its sigmoid form. The results of the logit method of estimation are similar to those reported in Table 12.2.

Similarly, for the probit method of estimation, the command is:

```
probit dummy fam_inc
```

The results of this method are similar to those reported in Table 12.3.

Logit and probit models in Microfit

The file binary2.fit contains data for the labour force participation example discussed above. To estimate the regression of the dummy dependent variable for labour force participation (*dummy*) on the family income (*faminc*) variable, first go to the single equation estimation window by clicking on the button **single**. Then specify the dependent variable followed by the constant and the independent variable by typing in the window:

```
dummy inpt faminc
```

These results are the simple OLS results, or the results of the linear probabilistic model, and are similar to those reported in Table 12.1. To obtain the logit estimation results for this specification, then go to **Univariate/7 Logit and Probit Models/1 Logit** and click on **run**. The results of the logit method are then reported and are similar to those in Table 12.2. Similarly for the probit estimation, go to **Univariate/7 Logit and Probit Models/2 Probit** and click on **run** again. The results of this method of estimation are similar to those in Table 12.3.

Part

V

Time Series Econometrics

13 ARIMA Models and the Box–Jenkins Methodology

CHAPTER CONTENTS

LEARNING OBJECTIVES

After studying this chapter you should be able to:

1. Understand the concept of ARIMA models.
2. Differentiate between univariate and multivariate time series models.
3. Understand the Box–Jenkins approach for model selection in the univariate time series framework.
4. Know how to estimate ARIMA(p, d, q) models using econometric software.

An introduction to time series econometrics

In this section we discuss single equation estimation techniques in a different way from Parts II and III of the text. In those parts we were explaining how to analyse the behaviour and variability of a dependent variable by regressing it using a number of different regressors or explanatory variables. In the time series econometrics framework, the starting point is to exploit the information that can be obtained from a variable that is accessible through the variable itself. An analysis of a single time series is called a univariate time series, and this is the topic of this chapter. In general, the purpose of time series analysis is to capture and examine the dynamics of the data. In time series econometrics we can also have multivariate time series models, which will be discussed in later chapters.

As has been mentioned before, traditional econometricians have emphasized the use of economic theory and the study of contemporaneous relationships in order to explain relationships among dependent and explanatory variables. (From here onwards we use the term *traditional econometrics* to differentiate the econometric analysis examined in Parts II and III from the new ('modern') developments of time series econometrics.) Lagged variables were introduced occasionally, but not in any systematic way, or at least not in a way that attempted to analyse the dynamics or the temporal structure of the data. There are various aspects to time series analysis but one common theme to them all is full use of the dynamic structure of the data; by this we mean that we extract as much information as possible from the past history of the series. The two principal types of time series analysis are time series forecasting and dynamic modelling. Time series forecasting is unlike most other econometrics in that it is not concerned with building structural models, understanding the economy or testing hypotheses. It is only concerned with building efficient forecasting models, usually done by exploiting the dynamic inter-relationship that exists over time for any single variable. Dynamic modelling, on the other hand, is concerned only with understanding the structure of the economy and testing hypotheses; however, it starts from the view that most economic series are slow to adjust to any shock, and so to understand the process we must fully capture the adjustment process, which may be long and complex. Since the early 1980s, the techniques developed in the time series forecasting literature have become increasingly useful in econometrics generally. Hence we begin this chapter with an account of the basic 'work horse' of time series forecasting, the ARIMA model.

ARIMA models

Box and Jenkins (1976) first introduced ARIMA models, the term deriving from:

  AR = autoregressive;
  I = integrated; and
  MA = moving average.

The following sections will present the different versions of ARIMA models and introduce the concept of stationarity, which will be analysed extensively. After defining stationarity, we will begin by examining the simplest model – the autoregressive model of order one then continue with the survey of ARIMA models. Finally, the Box–Jenkins approach for model selection and forecasting will be presented briefly.

Stationarity

A key concept underlying time series processes is that of stationarity. A time series is covariance stationary when it has the following three characteristics:

(a) exhibits mean reversion in that it fluctuates around a constant long-run mean;

(b) has a finite variance that is time-invariant; and

(c) has a theoretical correlogram that diminishes as the lag length increases.

In its simplest terms a time series Y_t is said to be stationary if:

(a) $E(Y_t) = $ constant for all t;

(b) $Var(Y_t) = $ constant for all t; and

(c) $Cov(Y_t, Y_{t+k}) = $ constant for all t and all $k \neq 0$,
  or if its mean, variance and covariances remain constant over time.

Thus these quantities would remain the same whether observations for the time series were, for example, from 1975 to 1985 or from 1985 to 1995. Stationarity is important because, if the series is non-stationary, all the typical results of the classical regression analysis are not valid. Regressions with non-stationary series may have no meaning and are therefore called 'spurious'. (The concepts of spurious regressions will be examined and analysed further in Chapter 16.)

Shocks to a stationary time series are necessarily temporary; over time, the effects of the shocks will dissipate and the series will revert to its long-run mean level. As such, long-term forecasts of a stationary series will converge to the unconditional mean of the series.

Autoregressive time series models

The AR(1) model

The simplest, purely statistical time series model is the autoregressive of order one model, or AR(1) model

$$Y_t = \phi Y_{t-1} + u_t \tag{13.1}$$

where, for simplicity, we do not include a constant and $|\phi| < 1$ and u_t is a Gaussian (white noise) error term. The assumption behind the AR(1) model is that the time series behaviour of Y_t is largely determined by its own value in the preceding period. So what will happen in t is largely dependent on what happened in $t-1$. Alternatively, what will happen in $t+1$ will be determined by the behaviour of the series in the current time t.

Condition for stationarity

Equation (13.1) introduces the constraint $|\phi| < 1$ in order to guarantee stationarity as defined in the previous section. If we have $|\phi| > 1$, then Y_t will tend to get larger in each period, so we would have an explosive series. To illustrate this, consider the following example in EViews.

Example of stationarity in the AR(1) model

Open EViews and create a new workfile by choosing **File/New Workfile**. In the **workfile range** choose **undated or irregular** and define the **start observation** as 1 and the **end observation** as 500. To create a stationary time series process, type the following commands in the EViews command line (the bracketed comments provide a description of each command):

`smpl 1 1`	[sets the sample to be the first observation only]
`genr yt=0`	[generates a new variable yt with the value of 0]
`smpl 2 500`	[sets the sample to range from the second to the five-hundredth observation]
`genr  yt = 0.4*yt(-1) +nrnd`	[creates yt as an AR(1) model with $\phi = 0.4$]
`smpl 1 500`	[sets the sample back to the full sample]
`plot yt`	[provides a plot of the yt series]

The plot of the Y_t series will look like that shown in Figure 13.1. It is clear that this series has a constant mean and a constant variance, which are the first two characteristics of a stationary series.

If we obtain the correlogram of the series we shall see that it indeed diminishes as the lag length increases. To do this in EViews, first double-click on yt to open it in a new window and then go to **View/Correlogram** and click **OK**.

Continuing, to create a time series (say X_t) which has $|\phi| > 1$, type in the following commands:

```
smpl 1 1
genr xt=1
smpl 2 500
genr xt = 1.2*xt(−1) + nrnd
smpl 1 200
plot xt
```

With the final command Figure 13.2 is produced, where it can be seen that the series is exploding. Note that we specified the sample to range from 1 to 200. This is because the explosive behaviour is so great that EViews cannot plot all 500 data values in one graph.

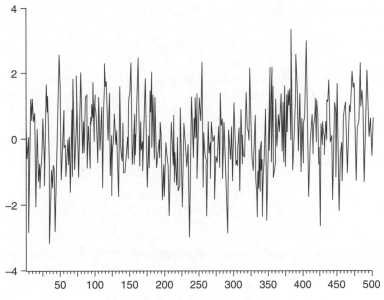

Figure 13.1   Plot of an AR(1) model

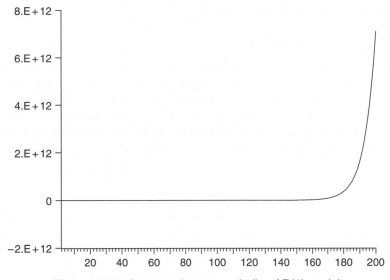

Figure 13.2   A non-stationary, exploding AR(1) model

The AR(p) model

A generalization of the AR(1) model is the AR(p) model; the number in parentheses denotes the order of the autoregressive process and therefore the number of lagged dependent variables the model will have. For example, the AR(2) model will be an autoregressive model of order two, and will have the form:

$$Y_t = \phi_1 Y_{t-1} + \phi_2 Y_{t-2} + u_t \tag{13.2}$$

Similarly, the AR(p) model will be an autoregressive model of order p, and will have p lagged terms, as in the following:

$$Y_t = \phi_1 Y_{t-1} + \phi_2 Y_{t-2} + \cdots + \phi_p Y_{t-p} + u_t \tag{13.3}$$

or, using the summation symbol:

$$Y_t = \sum_{i=1}^{p} \phi_i Y_{t-i} + u_t \tag{13.4}$$

Finally, using the lag operator L (which has the property $L^n Y_t = Y_{t-n}$) we can write the AR(p) model as:

$$Y_t(1 - \phi_1 L - \phi_2 L^2 - \cdots - \phi_p L^p) = u_t \tag{13.5}$$

$$\Phi(L)Y_t = u_t \tag{13.6}$$

where $\Phi(L)Y_t$ is a polynomial function of Y_t.

Stationarity in the AR(p) model

The condition for stationarity of an AR(p) process is guaranteed only if the p roots of the polynomial equation $\Phi(z) = 0$ are greater than 1 in absolute value, where z is a real variable. (Alternatively, this can be expressed with the following terminology: the solutions of the polynomial equation $\Phi(z) = 0$ should lie outside the unit circle.) To see this, consider the AR(1) process. The condition for the AR(1) process according to the polynomial notation reduces to:

$$(1 - \phi z) = 0 \tag{13.7}$$

with its roots being greater than 1 in absolute value. If this is so, and if the first root is equal to λ, then the condition is:

$$|\lambda| = \left| \frac{1}{\phi} \right| > 1 \tag{13.8}$$

$$|\phi| < 1 \tag{13.9}$$

A necessary but not sufficient requirement for the AR(p) model to be stationary is that the summation of the p autoregressive coefficients should be less than 1:

$$\sum_{i=1}^{p} \phi_i < 1 \tag{13.10}$$

Properties of the AR models

We start by defining the unconditional mean and the variance of the AR(1) process, which are given by:

$$E(Y_t) = E(Y_{t-1}) = E(Y_{t+1}) = 0$$

where $Y_{t+1} = \phi Y_t + u_{t+1}$. Substituting repeatedly for lagged Y_t we have:

$$Y_{t+1} = \phi^t Y_0 + (\phi^t u_1 + \phi^{t-1} u_2 + \cdots + \phi^0 u_{t+1})$$

since $|\phi| < 1, \phi^t$ will be close to zero for large t. Thus we have that:

$$E(Y_{t+1}) = 0 \tag{13.11}$$

and:

$$Var(Y_t) = Var(\phi Y_{t-1} + u_t) = \phi^2 \sigma_Y^2 + \sigma_u^2 = \frac{\sigma_u^2}{1 - \phi^2 \sigma_Y^2} \tag{13.12}$$

Time series are also characterized by the autocovariance and autocorrelation functions. The covariance between two random variables X_t and Z_t is defined as:

$$Cov(X_t, Z_t) = E\{[X_t - E(X_t)][Z_t - E(Z_t)]\} \tag{13.13}$$

Thus for two elements of the Y_t process, say Y_t and Y_{t-1}, we have:

$$Cov(Y_t, Y_{t-1}) = E\{[Y_t - E(Y_t)][Y_{t-1} - E(Y_{t-1})]\} \tag{13.14}$$

which is called the autocovariance function. For the AR(1) model the autocovariance function will be given by:

$$
\begin{aligned}
Cov(Y_t, Y_{t-1}) &= E\{[Y_t Y_{t-1}] - [Y_t E(Y_{t-1})] - [E(Y_t) Y_{t-1}] \\
&\quad + [E(Y_t)E(Y_{t-1})]\} \\
&= E[Y_t Y_{t-1}]
\end{aligned}
$$

where $E(Y_t) = E(Y_{t-1}) = E(Y_{t+1}) = 0$. This leads to:

$$
\begin{aligned}
Cov(Y_t, Y_{t-1}) &= E[(\phi Y_{t-1} + u_t) Y_{t-1}] \\
&= E(\phi Y_{t-1} Y_{t-1}) + E(u_t Y_{t-1}) \\
&= \phi \sigma_Y^2
\end{aligned} \tag{13.15}
$$

We can easily show that:

$$
\begin{aligned}
Cov(Y_t, Y_{t-2}) &= E(Y_t Y_{t-2}) \\
&= E[(\phi Y_{t-1} + u_t) Y_{t-2}] \\
&= E[(\phi(\phi Y_{t-2} + u_{t-1}) + u_t) Y_{t-2}] \\
&= E(\phi^2 Y_{t-2} Y_{t-2}) \\
&= \phi^2 \sigma_Y^2
\end{aligned}
\tag{13.16}
$$

and in general:

$$
Cov(Y_t, Y_{t-k}) = \phi^k \sigma_Y^2
\tag{13.17}
$$

The autocorrelation function will be given by:

$$
Cor(Y_t, Y_{t-k}) = \frac{Cov(Y_t, Y_{t-k})}{\sqrt{Var(Y_t)Var(Y_{t-k})}} = \frac{\phi^k \sigma_Y^2}{\sigma_Y^2} = \phi^k
\tag{13.18}
$$

So, for an AR(1) series, the autocorrelation function (ACF) (and the graph of it which plots the values of $Cor(Y_t, Y_{t-k})$ against k and is called a correlogram) will decay exponentially as k increases.

Finally, the partial autocorrelation function (PACF) involves plotting the estimated coefficient Y_{t-k} from an OLS estimate of an AR(k) process, against k. If the observations are generated by an AR(p) process then the theoretical partial autocorrelations will be high and significant for up to p lags and zero for lags beyond p.

Moving average models

The MA(1) model

The simplest moving average model is that of order one, or the MA(1) model, which has the form:

$$
Y_t = u_t + \theta u_{t-1}
\tag{13.19}
$$

Thus the implication behind the MA(1) model is that Y_t depends on the value of the immediate past error, which is known at time t.

The MA(q) model

The general form of the MA model is an MA(q) model of the form:

$$
Y_t = u_t + \theta_1 u_{t-1} + \theta_2 u_{t-2} + \cdots + \theta_q u_{t-q}
\tag{13.20}
$$

which can be rewritten as:

$$Y_t = u_t + \sum_{j=1}^{q} \theta_j u_{t-j} \tag{13.21}$$

or, using the lag operator:

$$Y_t = \left(1 + \theta_1 L + \theta_2 L^2 + \cdots + \theta_q L^q\right) u_t \tag{13.22}$$

$$= \Theta(L) u_t \tag{13.23}$$

Because any MA(q) process is, by definition, an average of q stationary white-noise processes it follows that every moving average model is stationary, as long as q is finite.

Invertibility in MA models

A property often discussed in connection with the moving average processes is that of invertibility. A time series Y_t is invertible if it can be represented by a finite-order MA or convergent autoregressive process. Invertibility is important because the use of the ACF and PACF for identification assumes implicitly that the Y_t sequence can be approximated well by an autoregressive model. As an example, consider the simple MA(1) model:

$$Y_t = u_t + \theta u_{t-1} \tag{13.24}$$

Using the lag operator, this can be rewritten as:

$$Y_t = (1 + \theta L) u_t$$

$$u_t = \frac{Y_t}{(1 + \theta L)} \tag{13.25}$$

If $|\theta| < 1$, then the left-hand side of Equation (13.25) can be considered as the sum of an infinite geometric progression:

$$u_t = Y_t(1 - \theta L + \theta^2 L^2 - \theta^3 L^3 + \cdots) \tag{13.26}$$

To understand this, consider the MA(1) process:

$$Y_t = u_t - \theta u_{t-1}$$

Lagging this relationship one period and solving for u_t we have:

$$u_{t-1} = Y_{t-1} - \theta u_{t-2}$$

Substituting this into the original expression we have:

$$Y_t = u_t - \theta(Y_{t-1} - \theta u_{t-2}) = u_t - \theta Y_{t-1} + \theta^2 u_{t-2}$$

Lagging the above expression one period and solving for u_{t-2} and resubstituting we get:

$$Y_t = u_t - \theta Y_{t-1} + \theta^2 Y_{t-2} - \theta^3 u_{t-3}$$

and repeating this an infinite number of times we finally get the expression Equation (13.26). Thus the MA(1) process has been inverted into an infinite order AR process with geometrically declining weights. Note that for the MA(1) process to be invertible it is necessary that $|\theta| < 1$.

In general, MA(q) processes are invertible if the roots of the polynomial:

$$\Theta(z) = 0 \tag{13.27}$$

are greater than 1 in absolute value.

Properties of the MA models

The mean of the MA process will clearly be equal to zero as it is the mean of white-noise error terms. The variance will be (for the MA(1) model) given by:

$$Var(Y_t) = Var(u_t + \theta u_{t-1}) = \sigma_u^2 + \theta^2 \sigma_u^2 = \sigma_u^2(1 + \theta^2) \tag{13.28}$$

The autocovariance will be given by:

$$Cov(Y_t, Y_{t-1}) = E[(u_t + \theta u_{t-1})(u_{t-1} + \theta u_{t-2})] \tag{13.29}$$

$$= E(u_t u_{t-1}) + \theta E(u_{t-1}^2) + \theta^2 E(u_{t-1} u_{t-2}) \tag{13.30}$$

$$= \theta \sigma_u^2 \tag{13.31}$$

And since u_t is serially uncorrelated it is easy to see that:

$$Cov(Y_t, Y_{t-k}) = 0 \quad \text{for } k > 1 \tag{13.32}$$

From this we can understand that for the MA(1) process the autocorrelation function will be:

$$Cor(Y_t, Y_{t-k}) = \frac{Cov(Y_t, Y_{t-k})}{\sqrt{Var(Y_t)Var(Y_{t-k})}} = \begin{cases} \dfrac{\theta \sigma_u^2}{\sigma_u^2(1 + \theta^2)} = \dfrac{\sigma_u^2}{1 + \theta^2} & \text{for } k = 1 \\ 0 & \text{for } k > 1 \end{cases} \tag{13.33}$$

So, with an MA(q) model the correlogram (the graph of the ACF) is expected to have q spikes for $k = q$, and then go down to zero immediately. Also, since any MA process can be represented as an AR process with geometrically declining coefficients, the PACF for an MA process should decay slowly.

ARMA models

After presenting the AR(p) and the MA(q) processes, it should be clear that there can be combinations of the two processes to give a new series of models called ARMA(p, q) models.

The general form of the ARMA model is an ARMA(p, q) model of the form:

$$Y_t = \phi_1 Y_{t-1} + \phi_2 Y_{t-1} + \cdots + \phi_p Y_{t-p} + u_t$$
$$+ \theta_1 u_{t-1} + \theta_2 u_{t-2} + \cdots + \theta_q u_{t-q} \tag{13.34}$$

which can be rewritten, using the summations, as:

$$Y_t = \sum_{i=1}^{p} \phi_i Y_{t-i} + u_t + \sum_{j=1}^{q} \theta_j u_{t-j} \tag{13.35}$$

or, using the lag operator:

$$Y_t(1 - \phi_1 L - \phi_2 L^2 - \cdots - \phi_p L^p) = (1 + \theta_1 L + \theta_2 L^2 + \cdots + \theta_q L^q)u_t \tag{13.36}$$

$$\Phi(L)Y_t = \Theta(L)u_t \tag{13.37}$$

In the ARMA(p, q) models the condition for stationarity deals only with the AR(p) part of the specification. Therefore the p roots of the polynomial equation $\Phi(z) = 0$ should lie outside the unit circle. Similarly, the property of invertibility for the ARMA(p, q) models will relate only with the MA(q) part of the specification and the roots of the $\Theta(z)$ polynomial should also lie outside the unit circle. The next section will deal with integrated processes and explain the 'I' part of ARIMA models. Here it is useful to note that the ARMA(p, q) model can also be denoted as an ARIMA(p,0,q) model. To give an example, consider the ARMA(2,3) model, which is equivalent to the ARIMA(2,0,3) model and is:

$$Y_t = \phi_1 Y_{t-1} + \phi_2 Y_{t-2} + u_t$$
$$+ \theta_1 u_{t-1} + \theta_2 u_{t-2} + \theta_3 u_{t-3} \tag{13.38}$$

Integrated processes and the ARIMA models

An integrated series

ARMA models can only be made with time series Y_t that are stationary. This means that the mean, variance and covariance of the series are all constant over time. However, most economic and financial time series show trends over time, and so the mean of Y_t during one year will be different from its mean in another year. Thus the mean of most economic and financial time series is not constant over time, which indicates that the series are non-stationary. To avoid this problem, and to induce stationarity, we need to de-trend the raw data through a process called differencing. The first differences of a series Y_t are given by the equation:

$$\Delta Y_t = Y_t - Y_{t-1} \tag{13.39}$$

As most economic and financial time series show trends to some degree, we nearly always take the first differences of the input series. If, after first differencing, a series is stationary, then the series is also called integrated to order one, and denoted I(1) – which completes the abbreviation ARIMA. If the series, even after first differencing, is not stationary, second differences need to be taken, using the equation:

$$\Delta\Delta Y_t = \Delta^2 Y_t = \Delta Y_t - \Delta Y_{t-1} \tag{13.40}$$

If the series becomes stationary after second differencing it is integrated of order two and denoted by I(2). In general, if a series d times is differenced in order to induce stationarity, the series is called integrated of order d and denoted by I(d). Thus the general ARIMA model is called an ARIMA(p, d, q), with p being the number of lags of the dependent variable (the AR terms), d being the number of differences required to take in order to make the series stationary, and q being the number of lagged terms of the error term (the MA terms).

Example of an ARIMA model

To give an example of an ARIMA(p, d, q) model, we can say that in general an integrated series of order d must be differenced d times before it can be represented by a stationary and invertible ARMA process. If this ARMA representation is of order (p, q), then the original, undifferenced series is following an ARIMA(p, d, q) representation. Alternatively, if a process Y_t has an ARIMA(p, d, q) representation, then the $\Delta^d Y_t$ has an ARMA(p, q) representation, as presented by this equation:

$$\Delta^d Y_t (1 - \phi_1 L - \phi_2 L^2 - \cdots - \phi_p L^p) = (1 + \theta_1 L + \theta_2 L^2 + \cdots + \theta_q L^q) u_t \tag{13.41}$$

Box–Jenkins model selection

A fundamental principle in the Box–Jenkins approach is parsimony. Parsimony (meaning sparseness or stinginess) should come as second nature to economists and financial analysts. Incorporating additional coefficients will necessarily increase the fit of the regression equation (that is the value of the R^2 will increase), but the cost will be a reduction of the degrees of freedom. Box and Jenkins argue that parsimonious models produce better forecasts than do overparametrized models. In general, Box and Jenkins popularized a three-stage method aimed at selecting an appropriate (parsimonious) ARIMA model for the purposes of estimating and forecasting a univariate time series. The three stages are: (a) identification; (b) estimation; and (c) diagnostic checking. These are presented below.

We have already seen that a low-order MA model is equivalent to a high-order AR model, and similarly a low-order AR model is equivalent to a high-order MA model.

This gives rise to the main difficulty in using ARIMA models, called the identification problem. The essence of this is that any model may be given more than one (and in most cases many) different representations, which are essentially equivalent. How, then, should we choose the best one and how should it be estimated? Defining the 'best' representation is fairly easy, and here we use the principle of parsimony. This simply means that we pick the form of the model with the smallest number of parameters to be estimated. The trick is to find this model. You might think it is possible to start with a high-order ARMA model and simply remove the insignificant coefficients. But this does not work, because within this high-order model will be many equivalent ways of representing the same model and the estimation process is unable to choose between them. We therefore have to know the form of the model before we can estimate it. In this context this is known as the identification problem and it represents the first stage of the Box–Jenkins procedure.

Identification

In the identification stage (this identification should not be confused with the identification procedure explained in the simultaneous equations chapter), the researcher visually examines the time plot of the series ACF and PACF. Plotting each observation of the Y_t sequence against t provides useful information concerning outliers, missing values and structural breaks in the data. It was mentioned earlier that most economic and financial time series are trended and therefore non-stationary. Typically, non-stationary variables have a pronounced trend (increasing or declining) or appear to meander without a constant long-run mean or variance. Missing values and outliers can be corrected at this point. At one time, the standard practice was to first-difference any series deemed to be non-stationary.

A comparison of the sample ACF and PACF to those of various theoretical ARIMA processes may suggest several plausible models. In theory, if the series is non-stationary, the ACF of the series will not die down or show signs of decay at all. If this is the case, the series needs to be transformed to make it stationary. As was noted above, a common stationarity-inducing transformation is to take logarithms and then first differences of the series.

Once stationarity has been achieved, the next step is to identify the p and q orders of the ARIMA model. For a pure MA(q) process, the ACF will tend to show estimates that are significantly different from zero up to lag q and then die down immediately after the qth lag. The PACF for MA(q) will tend to die down quickly, either by an exponential decay or by a damped sine wave.

In contrast to the MA processes, the pure AR(p) process will have an ACF that will tend to die down quickly, either by an exponential decay or by a damped sine wave, while the PACF will tend to show spikes (significant autocorrelations) for lags up to p and then will die down immediately.

If neither the ACF nor the PACF show a definite cut-off, a mixed process is suggested. In this case it is difficult, but not impossible, to identify the AR and MA orders. We should think of the ACF and PACF of pure AR and MA processes as being superimposed

Table 13.1   ACF and PACF patterns for possible ARMA(p, q) models

Model	ACF	PACF
Pure white noise	All autocorrelations are zero	All partial autocorrelations are zero
MA(1)	Single positive spike at lag 1	Damped sine wave or exponential decay
AR(1)	Damped sine wave or exponential decay	Single positive spike at lag 1
ARMA(1,1)	Decay (exp. or sine wave) beginning at lag 1	Decay (exp. or sine wave) beginning at lag 1
ARMA(p, q)	Decay (exp. or sine wave) beginning at lag q	Decay (exp. or sine wave) beginning at lag p

onto one another. For example, if both ACF and PACF show signs of slow exponential decay, an ARMA(1,1) process may be identified. Similarly, if the ACF shows three significant spikes at lags one, two and three and then an exponential decay, and the PACF spikes at the first lag and then shows an exponential decay, an ARMA(3,1) process should be considered. Table 13.1 reports some possible combinations of ACF and PACF forms that allow us the detection of the order of ARMA processes. In general, it is difficult to identify mixed processes, so sometimes more than one ARMA(p, q) model might be estimated, which is why the estimation and diagnostic checking stages are both important and necessary.

Estimation

In the estimation stage, each of the tentative models is estimated and the various coefficients are examined. In this second stage, the estimated models are compared using the Akaike information criterion (AIC) and the Schwarz Bayesian criterion (SBC). We want a parsimonious model, so we choose the model with the smallest AIC and SBC values. Of the two criteria, the SBC is preferable. Also at this stage we have to be aware of the common factor problem. The Box–Jenkins approach necessitates that the series is stationary and the model invertible.

Diagnostic checking

In the diagnostic checking stage we examine the goodness of fit of the model. The standard practice at this stage is to plot the residuals and look for outliers and evidence of periods in which the model does not fit the data well. Care must be taken here to avoid overfitting (the procedure of adding another coefficient in an appropriate model). The special statistics we use here are the Box–Pierce statistic (BP) and the Ljung–Box (LB) Q-statistic (see Ljung and Box, 1979), which serve to test for autocorrelations of the residuals.

The Box–Jenkins approach step by step

The Box–Jenkins approach involves the following steps:

Step 1 Calculate the ACF and PACF of the raw data, and check whether the series is stationary or not. If the series is stationary, go to step 3; if not, go to step 2.

Step 2 Take the logarithm and the first differences of the raw data and calculate the ACF and PACF for the first logarithmic differenced series.

Step 3 Examine the graphs of the ACF and PACF and determine which models would be good starting points.

Step 4 Estimate those models.

Step 5 For each of the estimated models:

(a) check to see if the parameter of the longest lag is significant. If not, there are probably too many parameters and you should decrease the order of p and/or q.

(b) check the ACF and PACF of the errors. If the model has at least enough parameters, then all error ACFs and PACFs will be insignificant.

(c) check the AIC and SBC together with the adj-R^2 of the estimated models to detect which model is the parsimonious one (that is the one that minimizes AIC and SBC and has the highest adj-R^2).

Step 6 If changes in the original model are needed, go back to step 4.

Example: the Box–Jenkins approach

The Box–Jenkins approach in EViews

The file ARIMA.wf1 contains quarterly data observations for the consumer price index (*cpi*) and gross domestic product (*gdp*) of the UK economy. We shall try to identify the underlying ARMA model for the *gdp* variable.

Step 1 As a first step we need to calculate the ACF and PACF of the raw data. To do this we need to double-click on the *cpi* variable to open the variable in a new EViews window. We can then calculate the ACF and PACF and view their respective graphs by clicking on **View/Correlogram** in the window that contains the *gdp* variable. This will give us Figure 13.3.

From Figure 13.3 we can see that the ACF does not die down at all for all lags (see also the plot of *gdp* to notice that it is clearly trended), which suggests that the series is integrated and we need to proceed with taking logarithms and first differences of the series.

Step 2 We take logs and then first differences of the *gdp* series by typing the following commands into the EViews command line:

```
genr lgdp = log(gdp)
genr dlgdp = lgdp - lgdp(-1)
```

Date: 02/26/04   Time: 15:31
Sample: 1980:1 1998:2
Included observations: 74

Autocorrelation	Partial correlation		AC	PAC	Q-stat	Prob
. |*******|	. |*******|	1	0.963	0.963	71.464	0.000
. |*******|	.*| .	2	0.922	−0.079	137.85	0.000
. |*******|	. | .	3	0.878	−0.049	198.98	0.000
. |******		. | .	4	0.833	−0.047	254.74	0.000
. |******		. | .	5	0.787	−0.038	305.16	0.000
. |******		. | .	6	0.740	−0.021	350.47	0.000
. |*****		. | .	7	0.695	−0.002	391.06	0.000
. |*****		. | .	8	0.650	−0.040	427.05	0.000
. |*****		. | .	9	0.604	−0.029	458.63	0.000
. |****		. | .	10	0.559	−0.026	486.05	0.000

Figure 13.3   ACF and PACF of *gdp*

Date: 02/26/04   Time: 15:43
Sample: 1980:1 1998:2
Included observations: 73

Autocorrelation	Partial correlation		AC	PAC	Q-stat	Prob
. |***		. |***	1	0.454	0.454	15.645	0.000
. |**		. |*.	2	0.288	0.104	22.062	0.000
. |**		. |*.	3	0.312	0.187	29.661	0.000
. |**		. | .	4	0.242	0.037	34.303	0.000
. |*.		. | .	5	0.130	−0.049	35.664	0.000
. |**		. |*.	6	0.238	0.174	40.287	0.000
. | .		.*| .	7	0.055	−0.187	40.536	0.000
.*| .		.*| .	8	−0.085	−0.141	41.149	0.000
. | .		. | .	9	−0.010	−0.032	41.158	0.000
. | .		. | .	10	−0.020	−0.026	41.193	0.000

Figure 13.4   ACF and PACF of *dlgdp*

and then double-click on the newly created *dlgdp* (log-differenced series) and click again on **View/Correlogram** to obtain the correlogram of the *dlgdp* series.

Step 3   From step 2 above we obtain the ACF and PACF of the *dlgdp* series, provided in Figure 13.4. From this correlogram we can see that there are 2 to 3 spikes on the ACF, and then all are zero, while there is also one spike in the PACF which then dies down to zero quickly. This suggests that we might have up to MA(3) and AR(1) specifications. So, the possible models are the ARMA(1,3), ARMA(1,2) or ARMA(1,1) models.

Step 4   We then estimate the three possible models. The command for estimating the ARMA(1,3) model is:

```
ls dlgdp c ar(1) ma(1) ma(2) ma(3)
```

similarly, for ARMA(1,2) it is:

```
ls dlgdp c ar(1) ma(1) ma(2)
```

and for ARMA(1,1) it is:

```
ls dlgdp c ar(1) ma(1)
```

The results are presented in Tables 13.2, 13.3 and 13.4, respectively.

Step 5 Finally, the diagnostics of the three alternative models need to be checked, to see which model is the most appropriate. Summarized results of all three specifications are provided in Table 13.5, from which we see that, in terms of the significance of estimated coefficients, the model that is most appropriate is probably ARMA(1,3). ARMA(1,2) has one insignificant term (the coefficient of the MA(2) term, which should be dropped), but when we include both MA(2) and MA(3), the MA(3) term is highly significant and the MA(2) term is significant at the 90% level. In terms of AIC and SBC we have contradictory results. The AIC suggests the ARMA(1,3) model, but the SBC suggests the ARMA(1,1) model. The adj-R^2 is also higher for the ARMA(1,3) model. So evidence here suggests that the ARMA(1.3) model is probably the most appropriate one. Remembering that we need a parsimonious model, there might be a problem of overfitting here. For this we also check the Q-statistics of the correlograms of the residuals for lags 8, 16 and 24. We see that only the ARMA(1,3) model has insignificant lags for all three cases, while the other two

Table 13.2 Regression results of an ARMA(1,3) model

Dependent variable: DLGDP
Method: least squares
Date: 02/26/04 Time: 15:50
Sample(adjusted): 1980:3 1998:2
Included observations: 72 after adjusting endpoints
Convergence achieved after 10 iterations
Backcast: 1979:4 1980:2

Variable	Coefficient	Std. error	t-statistic	Prob.
C	0.006817	0.001541	4.423742	0.0000
AR(1)	0.710190	0.100980	7.032979	0.0000
MA(1)	−0.448048	0.146908	−3.049866	0.0033
MA(2)	−0.220783	0.123783	−1.783625	0.0790
MA(3)	0.323663	0.113301	2.856665	0.0057
R-squared	0.340617	Mean dependent var.		0.005942
Adjusted *R*-squared	0.301251	S.D. dependent var.		0.006687
S.E. of regression	0.005590	Akaike info criterion		−7.468887
Sum squared resid.	0.002093	Schwarz criterion		−7.310785
Log likelihood	273.8799	*F*-statistic		8.652523
Durbin–Watson stat.	1.892645	Prob(*F*-statistic)		0.000011
Inverted AR Roots	0.71			
Inverted MA Roots	0.55+0.44i		0.55−0.44i	−0.65

Table 13.3   Regression results of an ARMA(1,2) model

Dependent variable: DLGDP
Method: least squares
Date: 02/26/04 Time: 16:00
Sample(adjusted): 1980:3 1998:2
Included observations: 72 after adjusting endpoints
Convergence achieved after 32 iterations
Backcast: 1980:1 1980:2

Variable	Coefficient	Std. error	t-statistic	Prob.
C	0.006782	0.001387	4.890638	0.0000
AR(1)	0.722203	0.114627	6.300451	0.0000
MA(1)	−0.342970	0.171047	−2.005128	0.0489
MA(2)	−0.124164	0.130236	−0.953374	0.3438

R-squared	0.286174	Mean dependent var.		0.005942
Adjusted R-squared	0.254681	S.D. dependent var.		0.006687
S.E. of regression	0.005773	Akaike info criterion		−7.417330
Sum squared resid.	0.002266	Schwarz criterion		−7.290849
Log likelihood	271.0239	F-statistic		9.087094
Durbin–Watson stat.	2.023172	Prob(F-statistic)		0.000039

Inverted AR Roots	0.72		
Inverted MA Roots	0.56	−0.22	

Table 13.4   Regression results of an ARMA(1,1) model

Dependent variable: DLGDP
Method: least squares
Date: 02/26/04 Time: 16:03
Sample(adjusted): 1980:3 1998:2
Included observations: 72 after adjusting endpoints
Convergence achieved after 9 iterations
Backcast: 1980:2

Variable	Coefficient	Std. error	t-statistic	Prob.
C	0.006809	0.001464	4.651455	0.0000
AR(1)	0.742291	0.101186	7.335927	0.0000
MA(1)	−0.471431	0.161407	−2.920758	0.0047

R-squared	0.279356	Mean dependent var.	0.005942
Adjusted R-squared	0.258468	S.D. dependent var.	0.006687
S.E. of regression	0.005758	Akaike info criterion	−7.435603
Sum squared resid.	0.002288	Schwarz criterion	−7.340742
Log likelihood	270.6817	F-statistic	13.37388
Durbin–Watson stat.	1.876198	Prob(F-statistic)	0.000012

Inverted AR Roots	0.74	
Inverted MA Roots	0.47	

models have significant (for 90%) lags for the eighth and the 16th lag, suggesting that the residuals are serially correlated. So, again, here the ARMA(1,3) model seems to be the most appropriate. As an alternative specification, as an exercise for the reader, go back to step 4 (as step 6 suggests) and re-estimate a model with an AR(1) term and MA(1) and MA(3) terms, to see what happens to the diagnostics.

Table 13.5 Summary results of alternative ARMA(p, q) models

	ARMA(1,3)	*ARMA(1,2)*	*ARMA(1,1)*
Degrees of freedom	68	69	70
SSR	0.002093	0.002266	0.002288
ϕ(*t*-stat in parentheses)	0.71 (7.03)	0.72 (6.3)	0.74 (7.33)
θ_1(*t*-stat in parentheses)	−0.44 (−3.04)	−0.34 (−2.0)	−0.47 (−2.92)
θ_2(*t*-stat in parentheses)	−0.22 (−1.78)	−0.12 (0.9)	—
θ_3(*t*-stat in parentheses)	0.32 (2.85)	—	—
AIC/SBC	−7.4688/−7.3107	−7.4173/−7.2908	−7.4356/−7.3407
Adj R^2	0.301	0.254	0.258
Ljung–Box statistics	$Q(8) = 5.65(0.22)$	$Q(8) = 9.84(0.08)$	$Q(8) = 11.17(0.08)$
for residuals (sig	$Q(16) = 14.15(0.29)$	$Q(16) = 20.66(0.08)$	$Q(16) = 19.81(0.07)$
levels in parentheses)	$Q(24) = 19.48(0.49)$	$Q(24) = 24.87(0.25)$	$Q(24) = 28.58(0.15)$

The Box–Jenkins approach in Stata

The file ARIMA.dat contains quarterly data observations for the consumer price index (*cpi*) and gross domestic product (*gdp*) of the UK economy. In this example we shall give the commands for the identification of the best ARMA model for the *gdp* variable. The analysis is the same as in the EViews example presented earlier.

Step 1 To calculate the ACF and PACF, the command in Stata is:

```
corrgram gdp
```

The results obtained are shown in Figure 13.5. Additionally, Stata calculates the ACF and the PACF with graphs that show the 95% confidence limit. The commands for these are:

```
ac gdp
pac gdp
```

The graphs of these commands are shown in Figures 13.6 and 13.7, respectively.

Step 2 To take logs and first differences of the *gdp* series the following commands should be executed:

```
g lgdp = log(gdp)
g dlgdp = D.lgdp
```

Then again, for the correlograms, the commands are:

```
corrgram dlgdp
ac dlgdp
pac dlgdp
```

Step 3–5 We proceed with the estimation of the various possible ARMA models. The command for estimating ARIMA(p, d, q) models in Stata is the following:

```
arima depvarname , arima(#p,#d,#q)
```

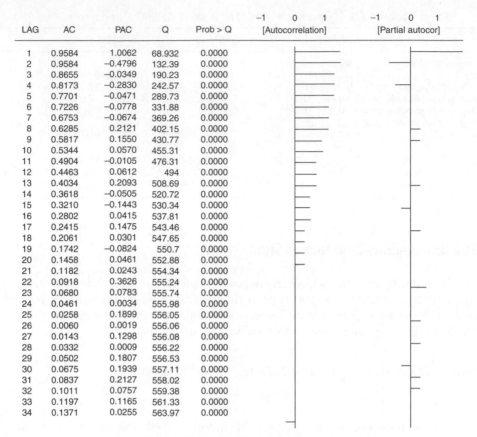

LAG	AC	PAC	Q	Prob > Q	[Autocorrelation]	[Partial autocor]
1	0.9584	1.0062	68.932	0.0000		
2	0.9584	−0.4796	132.39	0.0000		
3	0.8655	−0.0349	190.23	0.0000		
4	0.8173	−0.2830	242.57	0.0000		
5	0.7701	−0.0471	289.73	0.0000		
6	0.7226	−0.0778	331.88	0.0000		
7	0.6753	−0.0674	369.26	0.0000		
8	0.6285	0.2121	402.15	0.0000		
9	0.5817	0.1550	430.77	0.0000		
10	0.5344	0.0570	455.31	0.0000		
11	0.4904	−0.0105	476.31	0.0000		
12	0.4463	0.0612	494	0.0000		
13	0.4034	0.2093	508.69	0.0000		
14	0.3618	−0.0505	520.72	0.0000		
15	0.3210	−0.1443	530.34	0.0000		
16	0.2802	0.0415	537.81	0.0000		
17	0.2415	0.1475	543.46	0.0000		
18	0.2061	0.0301	547.65	0.0000		
19	0.1742	−0.0824	550.7	0.0000		
20	0.1458	0.0461	552.88	0.0000		
21	0.1182	0.0243	554.34	0.0000		
22	0.0918	0.3626	555.24	0.0000		
23	0.0680	0.0783	555.74	0.0000		
24	0.0461	0.0034	555.98	0.0000		
25	0.0258	0.1899	556.05	0.0000		
26	0.0060	0.0019	556.06	0.0000		
27	0.0143	0.1298	556.08	0.0000		
28	0.0332	0.0009	556.22	0.0000		
29	0.0502	0.1807	556.53	0.0000		
30	0.0675	0.1939	557.11	0.0000		
31	0.0837	0.2127	558.02	0.0000		
32	0.1011	0.0757	559.38	0.0000		
33	0.1197	0.1165	561.33	0.0000		
34	0.1371	0.0255	563.97	0.0000		

Figure 13.5 ACF and PACF for *gdp*

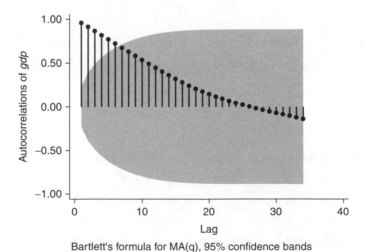

Bartlett's formula for MA(q), 95% confidence bands

Figure 13.6 ACF for *gdp* with 95% confidence bands

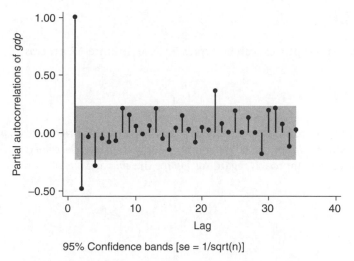

Figure 13.7   PACF for *gdp* with 95% confidence bands

where for #p we put the number of lagged AR terms (that is, if we want AR(4) we simply put 4) and so on. If we want to estimate an ARMA model, then the middle term is always defined as zero (that is for ARMA(2,3) we put arima(2,0,3)).

Therefore, the commands for the *gdp* variable are:

```
arima dlgdp , arima(1,0,3)
arima dlgdp , arima(1,0,2)
arima dlgdp , arima(1,0,1)
```

The results are similar to those presented in Tables 13.2, 13.3 and 13.4, respectively.

Questions and exercises

Questions

1 Explain the implication behind the AR and MA models by giving examples of each.

2 Define the concepts of stationarity and invertibility and state the conditions for stationarity in the AR models and invertibility for the MA models.

3 Define and explain the concepts of stationarity and invertibility. Why are they important in the analysis of time series data? Present examples of stationary and non-stationary, invertible and non-invertible processes.

4 Discuss analytically the three stages involved in the Box–Jenkins process for ARIMA model selection.

Exercise 13.1

Show that an MA(1) process can be expressed as an infinite AR process.

Exercise 13.2

The file ARIMA.wf1 contains quarterly data for the consumer price index (*cpi*) and gross domestic product (*gdp*) of the UK economy. Follow the steps described in the example for the Box–Jenkins approach regarding *gdp* for the *cpi* variable.

14 Modelling the Variance: ARCH–GARCH Models

CHAPTER CONTENTS

LEARNING OBJECTIVES

After studying this chapter you should be able to:

1. Understand the concept of conditional variance.
2. Detect 'calm' and 'wild' periods in a stationary time series.
3. Understand the autoregressive conditional heteroskedasticity (ARCH) model.
4. Perform a test for ARCH effects.
5. Estimate an ARCH model.
6. Understand the GARCH model and the difference between the GARCH and ARCH specifications.
7. Understand the distinctive features of the ARCH-M and GARCH-M models.
8. Understand the distinctive features of the TGARCH and EGARCH models.
9. Estimate all ARCH-type models using appropriate econometric software.

Introduction

Recent developments in financial econometrics have led to the use of models and techniques that can model the attitude of investors not only towards expected returns but also towards risk (or uncertainty). These require models that are capable of dealing with the volatility (variance) of the series. Typical are the autoregressive conditional heteroskedasticity (ARCH) family of models, which are presented and analysed in this chapter.

Conventional econometric analysis views the variance of the disturbance terms as being constant over time (the homoskedasticity assumption that was analysed in Chapter 7). However, often financial and economic time series exhibit periods of unusually high volatility followed by more tranquil periods of low volatility ('wild' and 'calm' periods, as some financial analysts like to call them).

Even from a quick look at financial data (see, for example, Figure 14.1, which plots the daily returns of the FTSE-100 index from 1 January 1990 to 31 December 1999) we can see that there are certain periods that have a higher volatility (and are therefore riskier) than others. This means that the expected value of the magnitude of the disturbance terms may be greater at certain periods compared with others. In addition, these riskier times seem to be concentrated and followed by periods of lower risk (lower volatility) that again are concentrated. In other words, we observe that large changes in stock returns seem to be followed by further large changes. This phenomenon is what financial analysts call volatility clustering. In terms of the graph in Figure 14.1, it is clear that there are subperiods of higher volatility; it is also clear that after 1997 the volatility of the series is much higher than it used to be.

Therefore, in such cases, it is clear that the assumption of homoskedasticity (or constant variance) is very limiting, and in such instances it is preferable to examine patterns that allow the variance to depend on its history. Or, to use more appropriate terminology, it is preferable to examine not the unconditional variance (which is the long-run forecast of the variance and can be still treated as constant) but the conditional variance, based on our best model of the variable under consideration.

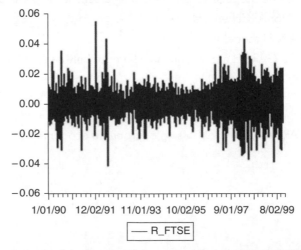

Figure 14.1   Plot of the returns of FTSE-100, 1 January 1990 to 31 December 1999

To understand this better, consider an investor who is planning to buy an asset at time t and sell it at time $t + 1$. For this investor, the forecast of the rate of return on this asset alone will not be enough; she/he would be interested in what the variance of the return over the holding period would be. Therefore, the unconditional variance is of no use either; the investor will want to examine the behaviour of the conditional variance of the series to estimate the riskiness of the asset at a certain period of time.

This chapter will focus on the modelling of the behaviour of conditional variance, or more appropriately, of conditional heteroskedasticity (from which comes the CH part of the ARCH models). The next section presents the first model that proposed the concept of ARCH, developed by Robert F. Engle in his seminal paper 'Autoregressive Conditional Heteroskedasticity with Estimates of the Variance of United Kingdom Inflation' published in *Econometrica* in 1982, and which began a whole new era in applied econometrics with many ARCH variations, extensions and applications. We shall then present the generalized ARCH (GARCH) model, followed by an alternative specification. Finally, illustrations of ARCH/GARCH models are presented using examples from financial and economic time series.

The ARCH model

Engle's model suggests that the variance of the residuals at time t depends on the squared error terms from past periods. Engle simply suggested that it is better to model simultaneously the mean and the variance of a series when it is suspected that the conditional variance is not constant.

Let's examine this in a more detailed way. Consider the simple model:

$$Y_t = a + \beta' \mathbf{X_t} + u_t \tag{14.1}$$

where $\mathbf{X_t}$ is a $k \times 1$ vector of explanatory variables and β is a $k \times 1$ vector of coefficients. Normally, we assume that u_t is independently distributed with a zero mean and a constant variance σ^2, or, in mathematical notation:

$$u_t \sim iid \ N(0, \sigma^2) \tag{14.2}$$

Engle's idea begins by allowing the variance of the residuals (σ^2) to depend on history, or to have heteroskedasticity because the variance will change over time. One way to allow for this is to have the variance depend on one lagged period of the squared error terms, as follows:

$$\sigma_t^2 = \gamma_0 + \gamma_1 u_{t-1}^2 \tag{14.3}$$

which is the basic ARCH(1) process.

The ARCH(1) model

Following on, the ARCH(1) model will simultaneously model the mean and the variance of the series with the following specification:

$$Y_t = a + \beta' \mathbf{X_t} + u_t \tag{14.4}$$

$$u_t | \Omega_t \sim iid\ N(0, h_t)$$

$$h_t = \gamma_0 + \gamma_1 u_{t-1}^2 \tag{14.5}$$

where Ω_t is the information set. Here Equation (14.4) is called the mean equation and Equation (14.5) the variance equation. Note that we have changed the notation of the variance from σ_t^2 to h_t. This is to keep the same notation from now on, throughout this chapter. (The reason it is better to use h_t rather than σ_t^2 will become clear through the more mathematical explanation provided later in the chapter.)

The ARCH(1) model says that when a big shock happens in period $t - 1$, it is more likely that the value of u_t (in absolute terms because of the squares) will also be bigger. That is, when u_{t-1}^2 is large/small, the variance of the next innovation u_t is also large/small. The estimated coefficient of γ_1 has to be positive for positive variance.

The ARCH(q) model

In fact, the conditional variance can depend not just on one lagged realization but on more than one, for each case producing a different ARCH process. For example, the ARCH(2) process will be:

$$h_t = \gamma_0 + \gamma_1 u_{t-1}^2 + \gamma_2 u_{t-2}^2 \tag{14.6}$$

the ARCH(3) will be given by:

$$h_t = \gamma_0 + \gamma_1 u_{t-1}^2 + \gamma_2 u_{t-2}^2 + \gamma_3 u_{t-3}^2 \tag{14.7}$$

and in general the ARCH(q) process will be given by:

$$h_t = \gamma_0 + \gamma_1 u_{t-1}^2 + \gamma_2 u_{t-2}^2 + \cdots + \gamma_q u_{t-q}^2$$

$$= \gamma_0 + \sum_{j=1}^{q} \gamma_j u_{t-j}^2 \tag{14.8}$$

Therefore, the ARCH(q) model will simultaneously examine the mean and the variance of a series according to the following specification:

$$Y_t = a + \beta' \mathbf{X_t} + u_t \tag{14.9}$$

$$u_t | \Omega_t \sim iid \ N(0, h_t)$$

$$h_t = \gamma_0 + \sum_{j=1}^{q} \gamma_j u_{t-j}^2 \tag{14.10}$$

Again, the estimated coefficients of the γs have to be positive for positive variance.

Testing for ARCH effects

Before estimating ARCH(q) models it is important to check for the possible presence of ARCH effects in order to know which models require the ARCH estimation method instead of OLS. Testing for ARCH effects was examined extensively in Chapter 7, but a short version of the test for qth order autoregressive heteroskedasticity is also provided here. The test can be done along the lines of the Breusch–Pagan test, which entails estimation of the mean equation:

$$Y_t = a + \beta' \mathbf{X_t} + u_t \tag{14.11}$$

by OLS as usual (note that the mean equation can also have, as explanatory variables in the $\mathbf{x}_t$ vector, autoregressive terms of the dependent variable), to obtain the residuals $\hat{u}_t$, and then run an auxiliary regression of the squared residuals ($\hat{u}_t^2$) on the lagged squared terms ($\hat{u}_{t-1}^2, \ldots, \hat{u}_{t-q}^2$) and a constant as in:

$$\hat{u}_t^2 = \gamma_0 + \gamma_1 \hat{u}_{t-1}^2 + \cdots + \gamma_q \hat{u}_{t-q}^2 + w_t \tag{14.12}$$

and then compute $R^2 \times T$. Under the null hypothesis of homoskedasticity ($0 = \gamma_1 = \cdots = \gamma_q$) the resulting test statistic follows a χ^2 distribution with q degrees of freedom. Rejection of the null suggests evidence of ARCH(q) effects.

Estimation of ARCH models by iteration

The presence of ARCH effects in a regression model does not invalidate completely the use of OLS estimation: the coefficients will still be consistent estimates, but they will not be fully efficient and the estimate of the covariance matrix of the parameters will be biased, leading to invalid t-statistics. A fully efficient estimator with a valid covariance matrix can, however, be calculated by setting up a model that explicitly recognizes the presence of ARCH effects. This model can no longer be estimated using a simple technique such as OLS, which has an analytical solution, but instead a non-linear maximization problem must be solved, which requires an iterative computer algorithm to search for the solution. The method used to estimate ARCH models is a special case of a general estimation strategy known as the maximum-likelihood approach. A formal exposition of this approach is beyond the scope of this book (see Cuthbertson *et al.*, 1992), but an intuitive account of how this is done is given here. Approaching the task, we assume we have the correct model and know the distribution of the error process; we select a set of values for the parameters to be estimated and can then in principle calculate the probability that the set of endogenous variables we have noted in our dataset would actually occur. We then select a set of parameters for our model that maximize this probability. These parameters are then called the maximum-likelihood parameters and they have the general property of being consistent and efficient (under the full set of CLRM assumptions, OLS is a maximum-likelihood estimator). Except in certain rare cases, finding the parameters which maximize this likelihood function requires the computer to search over the parameter space, and hence the computer will perform a number of steps (or iterations) as it searches for the best set of parameters. Packages such as EViews or Microfit include routines that do this very efficiently, though if the problem becomes too complex the program may sometimes fail to find a true maximum, and there are switches within the software to help convergence by adjusting a range of options. The next section explains step by step how to use EViews to estimate ARCH models, and provides a range of examples.

Estimating ARCH models in EViews

The file ARCH.wf1 contains daily data for the logarithmic returns FTSE-100 (named *r_ftse*) and three more stocks of the UK stock market (named *r_stock*1, *r_stock*2 and *r_stock*3, respectively). We first consider the behaviour of *r_ftse* alone, by checking whether the series is characterized by ARCH effects. From the time plot of the series in Figure 14.1, it can be seen clearly that there are periods of greater and lesser volatility in the sample, so the possibility of ARCH effects is quite high.

The first step in the analysis is to estimate an AR(1) model (having this as the mean equation for simplicity) for *r_ftse* using simple OLS. To do this, click **Quick/Estimate Equation**, to open the **Equation Specification** window. In this window we need to specify the equation to be estimated (by typing it in the white box of the **Equation Specification** window). The equation for an AR(1) model will be:

```
r_ftse c r_ftse(−1)
```

Next click **OK** to obtain the results shown in Table 14.1.

These results are of no interest in themselves. What we want to know is whether there are ARCH effects in the residuals of this model. To test for such effects we use the Breusch–Pagan ARCH test. In EViews, from the equation results window click on **View/Residuals Tests/ARCH-LM Test**. EViews asks for the number of lagged terms to include, which is simply the q term in the ARCH(q) process. To test for an ARCH(1) process, type 1, and for higher orders the value of q. Testing for ARCH(1) (by typing 1 and pressing **OK**), we get the results shown in Table 14.2.

The $T * R^2$ statistic (or Obs*R-squared, as EViews presents it) is 46.05 and has a probability value of 0.000. This clearly suggests that we reject the null hypothesis of

Table 14.1 A simple AR(1) model for the FTSE-100

Dependent variable: R_FTSE
Method: least squares
Date: 12/26/03 Time: 15:16
Sample: 1/01/1990 12/31/1999
Included observations: 2610

Variable	Coefficient	Std. error	t-statistic	Prob.
C	0.000363	0.000184	1.975016	0.0484
R_FTSE(−1)	0.070612	0.019538	3.614090	0.0003
R-squared	0.004983	Mean dependent var		0.000391
Adjusted R-squared	0.004602	S.D. dependent var		0.009398
S.E. of regression	0.009376	Akaike info criterion		−6.500477
Sum squared resid	0.229287	Schwarz criterion		−6.495981
Log likelihood	8485.123	F-statistic		13.06165
Durbin–Watson stat	1.993272	Prob(F-statistic)		0.000307

Table 14.2 Testing for ARCH(1) effects in the FTSE-100

ARCH test:

F-statistic	46.84671	Probability	0.000000
Obs*R-squared	46.05506	Probability	0.000000

Test equation:
Dependent variable: RESID^2
Method: least squares
Date: 12/26/03 Time: 15:27
Sample(adjusted): 1/02/1990 12/31/1999
Included observations: 2609 after adjusting endpoints

Variable	Coefficient	Std. error	t-statistic	Prob.
C	7.62E−05	3.76E−06	20.27023	0.0000
RESID^2(−1)	0.132858	0.019411	6.844466	0.0000
R-squared	0.017652	Mean dependent var		8.79E−05
Adjusted R-squared	0.017276	S.D. dependent var		0.000173
S.E. of regression	0.000171	Akaike info criterion		−14.50709
Sum squared resid	7.64E−05	Schwarz criterion		−14.50260
Log likelihood	18926.50	F-statistic		46.84671
Durbin–Watson stat	2.044481	Prob(F-statistic)		0.000000

homoskedasticity, and conclude that ARCH(1) effects are present. Testing for higher-order ARCH effects (for example order 6) the results appear as shown in Table 14.3.

This time the $T * R^2$ statistic is even higher (205.24), suggesting a massive rejection of the null hypothesis. Observe also that the lagged squared residuals are all highly statistically significant. It is therefore clear for this equation specification that an ARCH model will provide better results.

To estimate an ARCH model, click on **Estimate** in the equation results window to go back to the **Equation Specification** window (or in a new workfile, by clicking on **Quick/Estimate Equation** to open the **Equation Specification** window) and this time change the estimation method by clicking on the down arrow in the method setting

Table 14.3   Testing for ARCH(6) effects in the FTSE-100

ARCH test:

| F-statistic | 37.03529 | Probability | 0.000000 |
| Obs*R-squared | 205.2486 | Probability | 0.000000 |

Test equation:
Dependent variable: RESID^2
Method: least squares
Date: 12/26/03 Time: 15:31
Sample(adjusted): 1/09/1990 12/31/1999
Included observations: 2604 after adjusting endpoints

Variable	Coefficient	Std. error	t-statistic	Prob.
C	4.30E−05	4.46E−06	9.633006	0.0000
RESID^2(−1)	0.066499	0.019551	3.401305	0.0007
RESID^2(−2)	0.125443	0.019538	6.420328	0.0000
RESID^2(−3)	0.097259	0.019657	4.947847	0.0000
RESID^2(−4)	0.060954	0.019658	3.100789	0.0020
RESID^2(−5)	0.074990	0.019539	3.837926	0.0001
RESID^2(−6)	0.085838	0.019551	4.390579	0.0000

R-squared	0.078821	Mean dependent var	8.79E − 05
Adjusted R-squared	0.076692	S.D. dependent var	0.000173
S.E. of regression	0.000166	Akaike info criterion	−14.56581
Sum squared resid	7.16E−05	Schwarz criterion	−14.55004
Log likelihood	18971.68	F-statistic	37.03529
Durbin–Watson stat	2.012275	Prob(F-statistic)	0.000000

and choosing the **ARCH-Autoregressive Conditional Heteroskedasticity** option. In this new window, the upper part is devoted to the mean equation specification and the lower part to the ARCH specification, or the variance equation specification. In this window some things will appear that are unfamiliar, but they will become clear after the rest of this chapter has been worked through. To estimate a simple ARCH(1) model, assuming that the mean equation, as before, follows an AR(1) process, type in the mean equation specification:

```
r_ftse c rftse(−1)
```

making sure that the **ARCH-M** part selects **None**, which is the default EViews case. For the ARCH specification choose **GARCH/TARCH** from the drop-down **Model:** menu, which is again the default EViews case, and in the small boxes type 1 for the **Order ARCH** and 0 for the **GARCH**. The **Threshold Order** should remain at zero (which is the default setting). By clicking **OK** the results shown in Table 14.4 will appear.

Note that it took ten iterations to reach convergence in estimating this model. The model can be written as:

$$Y_t = 0.0004 + 0.0751 Y_{t-1} + u_t \qquad (14.13)$$
$$ (2.25) \qquad (3.91)$$

$$u_t | \Omega_t \sim iid\ N(0, h_t)$$

$$h_t = 0.000007 + 0.1613 u_{t-1}^2 \qquad (14.14)$$
$$ (35.97) \qquad (7.97)$$

Table 14.4   An ARCH(1) model for the FTSE-100

Dependent variable: R_FTSE
Method: ML–ARCH
Date: 12/26/03 Time: 15:34
Sample: 1/01/1990 12/31/1999
Included observations: 2610
Convergence achieved after 10 iterations

	Coefficient	Std. error	z-statistic	Prob.
C	0.000401	0.000178	2.257832	0.0240
R_FTSE(−1)	0.075192	0.019208	3.914538	0.0001

	Variance equation			
C	7.39E−05	2.11E−06	35.07178	0.0000
ARCH(1)	0.161312	0.020232	7.973288	0.0000

R-squared	0.004944	Mean dependent var	0.000391
Adjusted R-squared	0.003799	S.D. dependent var	0.009398
S.E. of regression	0.009380	Akaike info criterion	−6.524781
Sum squared resid	0.229296	Schwarz criterion	−6.515789
Log likelihood	8518.839	F-statistic	4.316204
Durbin–Watson stat	2.001990	Prob(F-statistic)	0.004815

with values of z-statistics in parentheses. Note that the estimate of γ_1 is highly significant and positive, which is consistent with the finding from the ARCH test above. The estimates of a and β from the simple OLS model have changed slightly and become more significant.

To estimate a higher-order ARCH model, such as the ARCH(6) examined above, again click on **Estimate** and this time change the **Order ARCH** to 6 (by typing 6 in the small box) leaving 0 for the **GARCH**. The results for this model are presented in Table 14.5.

Again, all the γs are statistically significant and positive, which is consistent with the findings above. After estimating ARCH models in EViews you can view the conditional standard deviation or the conditional variance series by clicking on the estimation window **View/Garch Graphs/Conditional SD Graph** or **View/Garch Graphs/Conditional Variance Graph**, respectively. The conditional standard deviation graph for the ARCH(6) model is shown in Figure 14.2.

You can also obtain the variance series from EViews by clicking on **Procs/Make GARCH Variance Series**. EViews automatically gives names such as GARCH01, GARCH02 and so on for each of the series. We renamed our obtained variance series as ARCH1 for the ARCH(1) series model and ARCH6 for the ARCH(6) model. A plot of these two series together is presented in Figure 14.3.

From this graph we can see that the ARCH(6) model provides a conditional variance series that is much smoother than that obtained from the ARCH(1) model. This will be discussed more fully later. To obtain the conditional standard deviation series plotted above, take the square root of the conditional variance series with the following command:

```
genr sd_arch1=arch1^(1/2)      [for the series of the ARCH(1) model]
genr sd_arch6=arch6^(1/2)      [for the series of the ARCH(6) model]
```

Table 14.5 An ARCH(6) model for the FTSE-100

Dependent variable: R_FTSE
Method: ML–ARCH
Date: 12/26/03 Time: 15:34
Sample: 1/01/1990 12/31/1999
Included observations: 2610
Convergence achieved after 12 iterations

	Coefficient	Std. error	z-statistic	Prob.
C	0.000399	0.000162	2.455417	0.0141
R_FTSE(−1)	0.069691	0.019756	3.527551	0.0004
Variance equation				
C	3.52E−05	2.58E−06	13.64890	0.0000
ARCH(1)	0.080571	0.014874	5.416946	0.0000
ARCH(2)	0.131245	0.024882	5.274708	0.0000
ARCH(3)	0.107555	0.022741	4.729525	0.0000
ARCH(4)	0.081088	0.022652	3.579805	0.0003
ARCH(5)	0.089852	0.022991	3.908142	0.0001
ARCH(6)	0.123537	0.023890	5.171034	0.0000

R-squared	0.004968	Mean dependent var	0.000391
Adjusted R-squared	0.001908	S.D. dependent var	0.009398
S.E. of regression	0.009389	Akaike info criterion	−6.610798
Sum squared resid	0.229290	Schwarz criterion	−6.590567
Log likelihood	8636.092	F-statistic	1.623292
Durbin–Watson stat	1.991483	Prob(F-statistic)	0.112922

A plot of the conditional standard deviation series for both models is presented in Figure 14.4.

A more mathematical approach

Consider the simple stationary model of the conditional mean of a series Y_t:

$$Y_t = a + \beta' \mathbf{X_t} + u_t \tag{14.15}$$

It is usual to treat the variance of the error term $Var(u_t) = \sigma^2$ as a constant, but the variance can be allowed to change over time. To explain this more fully, let us decompose the u_t term into a systematic component and a random component, as:

$$u_t = z_t \sqrt{h_t} \tag{14.16}$$

where z_t follows a standard normal distribution with zero mean and variance one, and h_t is a scaling factor.

In the basic ARCH(1) model we assume that:

$$h_t = \gamma_0 + \gamma_1 u_{t-1}^2 \tag{14.17}$$

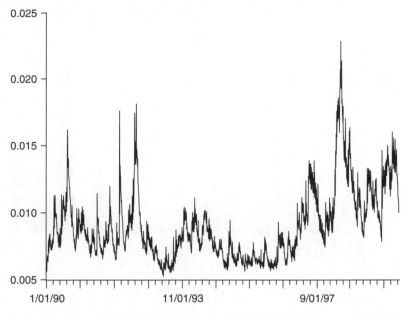

Figure 14.2 Conditional standard deviation graph for an ARCH(6) model of the FTSE-100

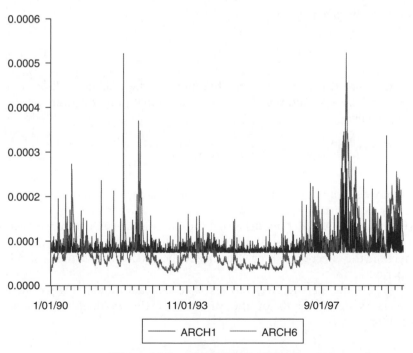

Figure 14.3 Plot of the conditional variance series

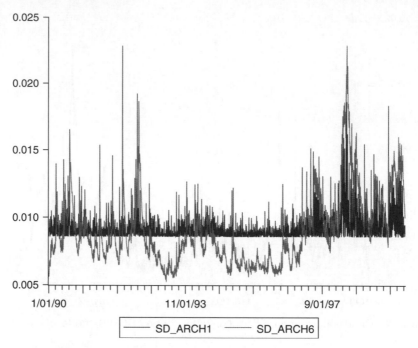

Figure 14.4   Plot of the conditional standard deviation series

The process for y_t is now given by:

$$y_t = a + \boldsymbol{\beta}'\mathbf{x_t} + z_t\sqrt{\gamma_0 + \gamma_1 u_{t-1}^2} \tag{14.18}$$

and from this expression it is easy to see that the mean of the residuals will be zero ($E(u_t) = 0$), because $E(z_t) = 0$. Additionally, the unconditional (long-run) variance of the residuals is given by:

$$Var(u_t) = E(z_t^2)E(h_t) = \frac{\gamma_0}{1 - \gamma_1} \tag{14.19}$$

which means that we simply need to impose the constraints $\gamma_0 > 0$ and $0 < \gamma_1 < 1$ to obtain stationarity.

The intuition behind the ARCH(1) model is that the conditional (short-run) variance (or volatility) of the series is a function of the immediate past values of the squared error term. Therefore the effect of each new shock z_t depends on the size of the shock in one lagged period.

An easy way to extend the ARCH(1) process is to add additional, higher-order lagged parameters as determinants of the variance of the residuals to change Equation (14.17) to:

$$h_t = \gamma_0 + \sum_{j=1}^{q} \gamma_j u_{t-j}^2 \tag{14.20}$$

which denotes an ARCH(q) process. ARCH(q) models are useful when the variability of the series is expected to change more slowly than in the ARCH(1) model. However, ARCH(q) models are quite often difficult to estimate, because they frequently yield negative estimates of the γ_js. To resolve this issue, Bollerslev (1986) developed the idea of the GARCH model, which will be examined in the next section.

The GARCH model

One of the drawbacks of the ARCH specification, according to Engle (1995), was that it looked more like a moving average specification than an autoregression. From this, a new idea was born, which was to include the lagged conditional variance terms as autoregressive terms. This idea was worked out by Tim Bollerslev, who in 1986 published a paper entitled 'Generalised Autoregressive Conditional Heteroskedasticity' in the *Journal of Econometrics*, introducing a new family of GARCH models.

The GARCH(p, q) model

The GARCH(p, q) model has the following form:

$$Y_t = a + \beta' \mathbf{X_t} + u_t \tag{14.21}$$

$$u_t | \Omega_t \sim iid\ N(0, h_t)$$

$$h_t = \gamma_0 + \sum_{i=1}^{p} \delta_i h_{t-i} + \sum_{j=1}^{q} \gamma_j u_{t-j}^2 \tag{14.22}$$

which says that the value of the variance scaling parameter h_t now depends both on past values of the shocks, which are captured by the lagged squared residual terms, and on past values of itself, which are captured by lagged h_t terms.

It should be clear by now that for $p = 0$ the model reduces to ARCH(q). The simplest form of the GARCH(p,q) model is the GARCH(1,1) model, for which the variance equation has the form:

$$h_t = \gamma_0 + \delta_1 h_{t-1} + \gamma_1 u_{t-1}^2 \tag{14.23}$$

This model specification usually performs very well and is easy to estimate because it has only three unknown parameters: γ_0, γ_1 and δ_1.

The GARCH(1,1) model as an infinite ARCH process

To show that the GARCH(1,1) model is a parsimonious alternative to an infinite ARCH(q) process, consider Equation (14.23). Successive substitution into the right-hand side of Equation (14.23) gives:

$$h_t = \gamma_0 + \delta h_{t-1} + \gamma_1 u_{t-1}^2$$

$$= \gamma_0 + \delta \left(\gamma_0 + \delta h_{t-2} + \gamma_1 u_{t-2}^2 \right) + \gamma_1 u_{t-1}^2$$

$$= \gamma_0 + \gamma_1 u_{t-1}^2 + \delta\gamma_0 + \delta^2 h_{t-2} + \delta\gamma_1 u_{t-2}^2$$

$$= \gamma_0 + \gamma_1 u_{t-1}^2 + \delta\gamma_0 + \delta^2 \left(\gamma_0 + \delta h_{t-3} + \gamma_1 u_{t-3}^2 \right) + \delta\gamma_1 u_{t-2}^2$$

$$\cdots$$

$$= \frac{\gamma_0}{1-\delta} + \gamma_1 \left(u_{t-1}^2 + \delta u_{t-2}^2 + \delta^2 \gamma_1 u_{t-3}^2 + \cdots \right)$$

$$= \frac{\gamma_0}{1-\delta} + \gamma_1 \sum_{j=1}^{\infty} \delta^{j-1} u_{t-j}^2 \qquad (14.24)$$

which shows that the GARCH(1,1) specification is equivalent to an infinite order ARCH model with coefficients that decline geometrically. For this reason, it is essential to estimate GARCH(1,1) models as alternatives to high-order ARCH models, because with the GARCH(1,1) there are fewer parameters to estimate and therefore fewer degrees of freedom are lost.

Estimating GARCH models in EViews

Consider again the *r-ftse* series from the ARCH.wf1 file. To estimate a GARCH model, click on **Quick/Estimate Equation**, to open the **Equation Specification** window, and again change the estimation method by clicking on the down arrow in the method setting and choosing the **ARCH-Autoregressive Conditional Heteroskedasticity** option. In this new **Equation Specification** window, the upper part is for the mean equation specification while the lower part is for the ARCH/GARCH specification or the variance equation. To estimate a simple GARCH(1,1) model, assuming that the mean equation as before follows an AR(1) process, in the mean equation specification window, we type:

```
r_ftse c rftse(-1)
```

making sure that within the **ARCH-M** part **None** is selected, which is the default in EViews. For the ARCH/GARCH specification choose **GARCH/TARCH** from the drop-down **Model:** menu, which is again the default EViews case, and in the small boxes type 1 for the **Order ARCH** and 1 for the **GARCH**. It is obvious that for higher orders, for example a GARCH(4,2) model, you would have to change the number in the small boxes by typing 2 for the **Order ARCH** and 4 for the **GARCH**. After specifying the number of ARCH and GARCH and clicking **OK** the required results appear. Table 14.6 presents the results for a GARCH(1,1) model.

Note that it took only five iterations to reach convergence in estimating this model. The model can be written as:

$$Y_t = 0.0004 + 0.0644 Y_{t-1} + \hat{u}_t \qquad (14.25)$$
$$\quad (2.57) \qquad (3.05)$$

$$u_t | \Omega_t \sim iid\ N(0, h_t)$$

$$h_t = 0.0000002 + 0.893 h_{t-1} + 0.084 \hat{u}_{t-1}^2 \qquad (14.26)$$
$$\quad (4.049) \qquad (59.43) \qquad (7.29)$$

Table 14.6   A GARCH(1,1) model for the FTSE-100

Dependent variable: R_FTSE
Method: ML–ARCH
Date: 12/26/03 Time: 18:52
Sample: 1/01/1990 12/31/1999
Included observations: 2610
Convergence achieved after 5 iterations

	Coefficient	Std. error	z-statistic	Prob.
C	0.000409	0.000158	2.578591	0.0099
R_FTSE(−1)	0.064483	0.021097	3.056426	0.0022
	Variance equation			
C	2.07E − 06	5.10E−07	4.049552	0.0001
ARCH(1)	0.084220	0.011546	7.294102	0.0000
GARCH(1)	0.893243	0.015028	59.43780	0.0000
R-squared	0.004924	Mean dependent var		0.000391
Adjusted R-squared	0.003396	S.D. dependent var		0.009398
S.E. of regression	0.009382	Akaike info criterion		−6.645358
Sum squared resid	0.229300	Schwarz criterion		−6.634118
Log likelihood	8677.192	F-statistic		3.222895
Durbin–Watson stat	1.981507	Prob(F-statistic)		0.011956

with values of z-statistics in parentheses. Note that the estimate of δ is highly significant and positive, as well as the coefficient of the γ_1 term. Taking the variance series for the GARCH(1,1) model (by clicking on **Procs/Make GARCH Variance Series**) it has been renamed as GARCH11 and this series has been plotted together with the ARCH6 series to obtain the results shown in Figure 14.5.

From this we observe that the two series are quite similar (if not identical), because the GARCH term captures a high order of ARCH terms as was proved earlier. Therefore, again, it is better to estimate a GARCH instead of a high order ARCH model because of its easier estimation and the least possible loss of degrees of freedom.

Changing the values in the boxes of the ARCH/GARCH specification to 6 in order to estimate a GARCH(6,6) model, the results shown in Table 14.7 are obtained, where the insignificance of all the parameters apart from the ARCH(1) term suggests that it is not an appropriate model.

Similarly, estimating a GARCH(1,6) model gives the results shown in Table 14.8, where now only the ARCH(1) and the GARCH(1) terms are significant; also some of the ARCH lagged terms have a negative sign. Comparing all the models from both the ARCH and the GARCH alternative specifications, we conclude that the GARCH(1,1) is preferred, for the reasons discussed above.

Alternative specifications

There are many alternative specifications that could be analysed to model conditional volatility, and some of the more important variants are presented briefly in this section. (Berra and Higgins (1993) and Bollerslev *et al.* (1994) provide very good reviews of these

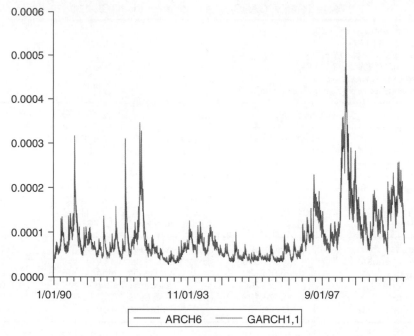

Figure 14.5   Plots of the conditional variance series for ARCH(6) and GARCH(1,1)

alternative specifications, while Engle (1995) collects some important papers in the ARCH/GARCH literature.)

The GARCH in mean or GARCH-M model

GARCH-M models allow the conditional mean to depend on its own conditional variance. Consider, for example, investors who are risk-averse and therefore require a premium as compensation for holding a risky asset. That premium is clearly a positive function of the risk (that is the higher the risk, the higher the premium should be). If the risk is captured by the volatility or by the conditional variance, then the conditional variance may enter the conditional mean function of Y_t.

Therefore, the GARCH-M(p,q) model has the following form:

$$Y_t = a + \beta' X_t + \theta h_t + u_t \tag{14.27}$$

$$u_t | \Omega_t \sim iid\ N(0, h_t)$$

$$h_t = \gamma_0 + \sum_{i=1}^{p} \delta_i h_{t-i} + \sum_{j=1}^{q} \gamma_j u_{t-j}^2 \tag{14.28}$$

Another variant of the GARCH-M type model is to capture risk not through the variance series but by using the standard deviation of the series having the following

Table 14.7 A GARCH(6,6) model for the FTSE-100

Dependent variable: R_FTSE
Method: ML–ARCH
Date: 12/26/03 Time: 19:05
Sample: 1/01/1990 12/31/1999
Included observations: 2610
Convergence achieved after 18 iterations

	Coefficient	Std. error	z-statistic	Prob.
C	0.000433	0.000160	2.705934	0.0068
R_FTSE(−1)	0.065458	0.020774	3.150930	0.0016
Variance equation				
C	1.70E−06	7.51E−06	0.227033	0.8204
ARCH(1)	0.038562	0.015717	2.453542	0.0141
ARCH(2)	0.070150	0.113938	0.615692	0.5381
ARCH(3)	0.022721	0.269736	0.084234	0.9329
ARCH(4)	−0.017544	0.181646	−0.096585	0.9231
ARCH(5)	0.011091	0.077074	0.143905	0.8856
ARCH(6)	−0.017064	0.063733	−0.267740	0.7889
GARCH(1)	0.367407	3.018202	0.121730	0.9031
GARCH(2)	0.116028	1.476857	0.078564	0.9374
GARCH(3)	0.036122	1.373348	0.026302	0.9790
GARCH(4)	0.228528	0.819494	0.278864	0.7803
GARCH(5)	0.217829	0.535338	0.406900	0.6841
GARCH(6)	−0.092748	0.979198	−0.094719	0.9245
R-squared	0.004904	Mean dependent var		0.000391
Adjusted R-squared	−0.000465	S.D. dependent var		0.009398
S.E. of regression	0.009400	Akaike info criterion		−6.643400
Sum squared resid	0.229305	Schwarz criterion		−6.609681
Log likelihood	8684.637	F-statistic		0.913394
Durbin–Watson stat	1.983309	Prob(F-statistic)		0.543473

specification for the mean and the variance equation:

$$Y_t = a + \beta' \mathbf{X_t} + \theta \sqrt{h_t} + u_t \tag{14.29}$$

$$u_t | \Omega_t \sim iid \ N(0, h_t)$$

$$h_t = \gamma_0 + \sum_{i=1}^{p} \delta_i h_{t-i} + \sum_{j=1}^{q} \gamma_j u_{t-j}^2 \tag{14.30}$$

GARCH-M models can be linked with asset–pricing models such as the capital asset–pricing models (CAPM) with many financial applications (for more, see Campbell *et al.* 1997; Hall *et al.* 1990).

Estimating GARCH-M models in EViews

To estimate a GARCH-M model in EViews, first click **Quick/Estimate Equation** to open the **Estimation Window**, then change the estimation method by clicking on the down arrow in the method setting and choosing the **ARCH-Autoregressive Conditional**

Table 14.8 A GARCH(1,6) model for the FTSE-100

Dependent variable: R_FTSE
Method: ML–ARCH
Date: 12/26/03 Time: 19:34
Sample: 1/01/1990 12/31/1999
Included observations: 2610
Convergence achieved after 19 iterations

	Coefficient	Std. error	z-statistic	Prob.
C	0.000439	0.000158	2.778912	0.0055
R_FTSE(−1)	0.064396	0.020724	3.107334	0.0019
Variance equation				
C	9.12E−07	2.79E−07	3.266092	0.0011
ARCH(1)	0.040539	0.013234	3.063199	0.0022
ARCH(2)	0.048341	0.025188	1.919235	0.0550
ARCH(3)	−0.027991	0.031262	−0.895354	0.3706
ARCH(4)	−0.037356	0.028923	−1.291542	0.1965
ARCH(5)	0.016418	0.028394	0.578219	0.5631
ARCH(6)	0.015381	0.023587	0.652097	0.5143
GARCH(1)	0.934786	0.011269	82.95460	0.0000

R-squared	0.004883	Mean dependent var	0.000391
Adjusted R-squared	0.001438	S.D. dependent var	0.009398
S.E. of regression	0.009391	Akaike info criterion	−6.646699
Sum squared resid	0.229310	Schwarz criterion	−6.624220
Log likelihood	8683.943	F-statistic	1.417557
Durbin–Watson stat	1.981261	Prob(F-statistic)	0.174540

Heteroskedasticity option. In this new **Equation Specification** window, the upper part is again for the mean equation specification while the lower part is for the ARCH/GARCH specification or the variance equation. To estimate a GARCH-M(1,1) model, assuming that the mean equation (as before) follows an AR(1) process, type in the mean equation specification:

```
r_ftse c rftse(−1)
```

and this time click on either **Std.Dev** or the **Var** selections from the **ARCH-M** part for versions of the mean Equations (14.29) and (14.27), respectively.

For the ARCH/GARCH specification choose **GARCH/TARCH** from the drop-down **Model:** menu, which is again the default EViews case, and in the small boxes specify by typing the number of the q lags $(1, 2, \ldots, q)$ for the **Order ARCH** and the number of p lags $(1, 2, \ldots, p)$ for the **GARCH**. Table 14.9 presents the results for a GARCH-M(1,1) model based on the specification that uses the variance series to capture risk in the mean equation, as given by Equation (14.27).

Note that the variance term (GARCH) in the mean equation is slightly significant but its inclusion substantially increases the significance of the GARCH term in the variance equation. Re-estimating the above model but this time clicking on the **Std.Dev** from the **ARCH-M** part to include the conditional standard deviation in the mean equation. The results are presented in Table 14.10, where this time the conditional

Table 14.9 A GARCH-M(1,1) model for the FTSE-100

Dependent variable: R_FTSE
Method: ML – ARCH
Date: 12/26/03 Time: 19:32
Sample: 1/01/1990 12/31/1999
Included observations: 2610
Convergence achieved after 13 iterations

	Coefficient	Std. error	z-statistic	Prob.
GARCH	6.943460	4.069814	1.706088	0.0880
C	−2.39E−05	0.000311	−0.076705	0.9389
R_FTSE(−1)	0.061006	0.020626	2.957754	0.0031
Variance equation				
C	7.16E-07	2.22E−07	3.220052	0.0013
ARCH(1)	0.049419	0.006334	7.801997	0.0000
GARCH(1)	0.942851	0.007444	126.6613	0.0000
R-squared	0.004749	Mean dependent var		0.000391
Adjusted R-squared	0.002838	S.D. dependent var		0.009398
S.E. of regression	0.009385	Akaike info criterion		−6.648319
Sum squared resid	0.229341	Schwarz criterion		−6.634831
Log likelihood	8682.056	F-statistic		2.485254
Durbin–Watson stat	1.974219	Prob(F-statistic)		0.029654

Table 14.10 A GARCH-M(1,1) for the FTSE-100 (using standard deviation)

Dependent variable: R_FTSE
Method: ML – ARCH
Date: 12/26/03 Time: 19:36
Sample: 1/01/1990 12/31/1999
Included observations: 2610
Convergence achieved after 13 iterations

	Coefficient	Std. error	z-statistic	Prob.
SQR(GARCH)	0.099871	0.080397	1.242226	0.2142
C	−0.000363	0.000656	−0.553837	0.5797
R_FTSE(−1)	0.063682	0.020771	3.065923	0.0022
Variance equation				
C	9.23E-07	2.72E−07	3.394830	0.0007
ARCH(1)	0.055739	0.007288	7.647675	0.0000
GARCH(1)	0.934191	0.008832	105.7719	0.0000
R-squared	0.005128	Mean dependent var		0.000391
Adjusted R-squared	0.003218	S.D. dependent var		0.009398
S.E. of regression	0.009383	Akaike info criterion		−6.648295
Sum squared resid	0.229253	Schwarz criterion		−6.634807
Log likelihood	8682.025	F-statistic		2.684559
Durbin–Watson stat	1.980133	Prob(F-statistic)		0.019937

standard deviation (or SQR(GARCH)) coefficient is not significant, suggesting that if there is an effect of the risk on the mean return, this is captured better by the variance.

The threshold GARCH (TGARCH) model

A major restriction of the ARCH and GARCH specifications above is that they are symmetric. By this we mean that what matters is only the absolute value of the innovation and not its sign (because the residual term is squared). Therefore, in ARCH/GARCH models a large positive shock will have exactly the same effect in the volatility of the series as a large negative shock of the same magnitude. However, for equities it has been observed that negative shocks (or 'bad news') in the market have a larger impact on volatility than do positive shocks (or 'good news') of the same magnitude.

The threshold GARCH model was introduced by the works of Zakoian (1990) and Glosten *et al.* (1993). The main target of this model is to capture asymmetries in terms of negative and positive shocks. To do this, simply add into the variance equation a multiplicative dummy variable to check whether there is a statistically significant difference when shocks are negative.

The specification of the conditional variance equation (for a TGARCH(1,1)) is given by:

$$h_t = \gamma_0 + \gamma u_{t-1}^2 + \theta u_{t-1}^2 d_{t-1} + \delta h_{t-1} \tag{14.31}$$

where d_t takes the value of 1 for $u_t < 0$, and 0 otherwise. So 'good news' and 'bad news' have different impacts. Good news has an impact of γ, while bad news has an impact of $\gamma + \theta$. If $\theta > 0$ we conclude that there is asymmetry, while if $\theta = 0$ the news impact is symmetric. TGARCH models can be extended to higher order specifications by including more lagged terms, as follows:

$$h_t = \gamma_0 + \sum_{i=1}^{q} (\gamma_i + \theta_i d_{t-i}) u_{t-i}^2 + \sum_{j=1}^{q} \delta_j h_{t-j} \tag{14.32}$$

Estimating TGARCH models in EViews

To estimate a TGARCH model in EViews, first click **Quick/Estimate Equation** to open the **Estimation Window**. Then change the estimation method by clicking on the down arrow in the method setting, to choose the **ARCH-Autoregressive Conditional Heteroskedasticity** option. In this new **Equation Specification** window we again have the upper part for the mean equation specification and the lower part for the ARCH/GARCH specification or the variance equation. To estimate a TGARCH(*p,q*) model, assuming that the mean equation follows an AR(1) process as before, type in the mean equation specification:

```
r_ftse c rftse(-1)
```

Table 14.11 A TGARCH(1,1) model for the FTSE-100

Dependent variable: R_FTSE
Method: ML–ARCH
Date: 12/27/03 Time: 15:04
Sample: 1/01/1990 12/31/1999
Included observations: 2610
Convergence achieved after 11 iterations

	Coefficient	Std. error	z-statistic	Prob.
C	0.000317	0.000159	1.999794	0.0455
R_FTSE(−1)	0.059909	0.020585	2.910336	0.0036
Variance equation				
C	7.06E − 07	1.90E − 07	3.724265	0.0002
ARCH(1)	0.015227	0.006862	2.218989	0.0265
(RESID<0)*ARCH(1)	0.053676	0.009651	5.561657	0.0000
GARCH(1)	0.950500	0.006841	138.9473	0.0000
R-squared	0.004841	Mean dependent var		0.000391
Adjusted *R*-squared	0.002930	S.D. dependent var		0.009398
S.E. of regression	0.009384	Akaike info criterion		−6.656436
Sum squared resid	0.229320	Schwarz criterion		−6.642949
Log likelihood	8692.649	*F*-statistic		2.533435
Durbin–Watson stat	1.972741	Prob(*F*-statistic)		0.026956

ensuring also that **None** was clicked on in the **ARCH-M** part of the mean equation specification.

For the ARCH/GARCH specification, choose **GARCH/TARCH** from the drop-down **Model:** menu, and specify the number of q lags $(1, 2, \ldots, q)$ for the **Order ARCH**, the number of p lags $(1, 2, \ldots, p)$ for the **Order GARCH** and the **Threshold Order** by changing the value in the box from 0 to 1 to have the TARCH model in action. Table 14.11 presents the results for a TGARCH(1,1) model.

Note that, because the coefficient of the (RESID < 0)*ARCH(1) term is positive and statistically significant, indeed for the FTSE-100 there are asymmetries in the news. Specifically, bad news has larger effects on the volatility of the series than good news.

The exponential GARCH (EGARCH) model

The exponential GARCH (EGARCH) model was first developed by Nelson (1991), and the variance equation for this model is given by:

$$\log(h_t) = \gamma + \sum_{j=1}^{q} \zeta_j \left| \frac{u_{t-j}}{\sqrt{h_{t-j}}} \right| + \sum_{j=1}^{q} \xi_j \frac{u_{t-j}}{\sqrt{h_{t-j}}} + \sum_{i=1}^{p} \delta_i \log(h_{t-i}) \tag{14.33}$$

where γ, the ζs, ξs and δs are parameters to be estimated. Note that the left-hand side is the log of the variance series. This makes the leverage effect exponential rather than quadratic, and therefore the estimates of the conditional variance are guaranteed to be non-negative. The EGARCH model allows for the testing of asymmetries as well as the TGARCH. To test for asymmetries, the parameters of importance are the ξs. If $\xi_1 = \xi_2 = \cdots = 0$, then the model is symmetric. When $\xi_j < 0$, then positive shocks (good news) generate less volatility than negative shocks (bad news).

Estimating EGARCH models in EViews

To estimate an EGARCH model in EViews, first click **Quick/Estimate Equation** to open the **Estimation Window**. Then change the estimation method by clicking the down arrow in the method setting to choose the **ARCH-Autoregressive Conditional Heteroskedasticity** option. In this new **Equation Specification** window we again have the upper part for the mean equation specification, while the lower part is for the ARCH/GARCH specification or the variance equation. To estimate an EGARCH(p,q) model, assuming that the mean equation follows an AR(1) process, as before type in the mean equation specification:

```
r_ftse c rftse(−1)
```

again making sure that **None** is clicked on in the **ARCH-M** part of the mean equation specification.

For the ARCH/GARCH specification now choose **EGARCH** from the drop-down **Model**: menu, and in the small boxes specify the number of the q lags $(1, 2, \ldots, q)$ for the **Order ARCH** and the number of p lags $(1, 2, \ldots, p)$ for the **GARCH**. Table 14.12 presents the results for an EGARCH(1,1) model.

Table 14.12   An EGARCH(1,1) model for the FTSE-100

Dependent variable: R_FTSE
Method: ML–ARCH
Date: 12/26/03 Time: 20:19
Sample: 1/01/1990 12/31/1999
Included observations: 2610
Convergence achieved after 17 iterations

	Coefficient	Std. error	z-statistic	Prob.
C	0.000306	0.000156	1.959191	0.0501
R_FTSE(−1)	0.055502	0.020192	2.748659	0.0060
Variance equation				
C	−0.154833	0.028461	−5.440077	0.0000
|RES|/SQR[GARCH](1)	0.086190	0.012964	6.648602	0.0000
RES/SQR[GARCH](1)	−0.044276	0.007395	−5.987227	0.0000
EGARCH(1)	0.990779	0.002395	413.7002	0.0000
R-squared	0.004711	Mean dependent var		0.000391
Adjusted R-squared	0.002800	S.D. dependent var		0.009398
S.E. of regression	0.009385	Akaike info criterion		−6.660033
Sum squared resid	0.229350	Schwarz criterion		−6.646545
Log likelihood	8697.343	F-statistic		2.465113
Durbin–Watson stat	1.964273	Prob(F-statistic)		0.030857

Note that, because the coefficient of the RES/SQR[GARCH](1) term is negative and statistically significant, indeed for the FTSE-100 bad news has larger effects on the volatility of the series than good news.

Adding explanatory variables in the mean equation

ARCH/GARCH models may be quite sensitive to the specification of the mean equation. Consider again for example, the FTSE-100 return series examined above. In all our analyses it was assumed (quite restrictively and without prior information) that a good specification for the mean equation would be a simple AR(1) model. It is obvious that, using daily data, AR models of a higher order would be more appropriate. Also, it might be more appropriate to use MA terms alongside the AR terms. Estimating an ARCH(1) and a GARCH(1,1) model for the FTSE-100 returns, assuming that it follows an ARMA(1,1) specification, in both cases gives results for the mean equation that are statistically insignificant. (We leave this as an exercise for the reader. To the mean equation specification, type in: r_ftse c AR(1) MA(1), and then arrange the number of ARCH(q) and GARCH(p) terms.) It should be clear that results, or even convergence of iterations, might be highly affected by wrong specifications of the mean equation, and if research using GARCH models is to be undertaken, the researcher has to be very careful first to identify the correct specification.

Adding explanatory variables in the variance equation

GARCH models also allow us to add explanatory variables in the specification of the conditional variance equation. We can have an augmented GARCH(q,p) specification such as the following:

$$h_t = \gamma_0 + \sum_{i=1}^{p} \delta_i h_{t-i} + \sum_{j=1}^{q} \gamma_j u_{t-j}^2 + \sum_{k=1}^{m} \mu_k X_k \tag{14.34}$$

where x_k is a set of explanatory variables that might help to explain the variance. As an example, consider the case of the FTSE-100 returns once again, and test the assumption that the Gulf War (which took place in 1994) affected the FTSE-100 returns, making them more volatile. This can be tested by constructing a dummy variable, named *Gulf*, which will take the value of 1 for observations during 1994 and 0 for the rest of the period. Then in the estimation of the GARCH model, apart from specifying as always the mean equation and the order of q and p in the variance equation, add the dummy variable in the box where EViews allows the entry of variance regressors, by typing the name of the variable there. Estimation of a GARCH(1,1) model with the dummy variable in the variance regression gave the results shown in Table 14.13, where it can be seen that the dummy variable is statistically insignificant, so the hypothesis that the Gulf War affected the volatility of the FTSE-100 returns can be rejected. Other examples with dummy and regular explanatory variables are given in

Table 14.13 A GARCH(1,1) model with an explanatory variable in the variance equation

Dependent variable: R_FTSE
Method: ML–ARCH
Date: 12/27/03 Time: 17:25
Sample: 1/01/1990 12/31/1999
Included observations: 2610
Convergence achieved after 10 iterations

	Coefficient	Std. error	z-statistic	Prob.
C	0.000400	0.000160	2.503562	0.0123
R_FTSE(−1)	0.068514	0.021208	3.230557	0.0012
Variance equation				
C	2.22E−06	6.02E−07	3.687964	0.0002
ARCH(1)	0.083656	0.013516	6.189428	0.0000
GARCH(1)	0.891518	0.016476	54.11098	0.0000
GULF	−4.94E−07	5.96E−07	−0.829246	0.4070
R-squared	0.004964	Mean dependent var		0.000391
Adjusted R-squared	0.003054	S.D. dependent var		0.009398
S.E. of regression	0.009384	Akaike info criterion		−6.644526
Sum squared resid	0.229291	Schwarz criterion		−6.631039
Log likelihood	8677.107	F-statistic		2.598278
Durbin–Watson stat	1.989232	Prob(F-statistic)		0.023694

the empirical illustration section below for the GARCH model of UK GDP and the effect of socio-political instability.

Estimating ARCH/GARCH-type models in Stata

All the analyses performed in the previous sections using Eviews can be performed with Stata, using the following commands. The data are given in the file named ARCH.dat. First, to obtain simple OLS results for the *r_ftse* daily time series regressed to a lag of the same series (r_ftse_{t-1}) the command is:

```
regress r_ftse L.rftse
```

where L. denotes the lag operator. The results are similar to those in Table 14.1.
   To test for ARCH effects, the command is:

```
estat archlm, lags(1)
```

The results are similar to those reported in Table 14.2 and suggest that there are ARCH effects in the series. To test for ARCH effects of a higher order (order 6 in the example reported in Table 14.3), the command is:

```
estat archlm, lags(6)
```

Then, to estimate the ARCH model, the command syntax is:

```
arch depvar indepvars , options
```

where `depvar` is replaced with the name of the dependent variable and `indepvars` with the names of the independent variables you want to include in the mean equation, and after the comma choose from the options which type of ARCH/GARCH model you wish to estimate (that is you specify the variance equation). Thus, for a simple ARCH(1) model of regressing *r_ftse* to *r_ftse*$_{t-1}$, in the mean equation the command is:

```
arch r_ftse L.r_ftse , arch(1)
```

Then, to obtain the h_t variance series of this ARCH(1) model, the command is:

```
predict htgarch1 , variance
```

(Here, `htgarch1` is a name that helps us remember that the series is a variance series for the ARCH(1) model; any other name the reader might want to give to the series will work just as well): while the command:

```
tsline htgarch1
```

provides a time plot of the variance series.

Continuing, the commands for an ARCH(6) model are:

```
arch r_ftse L.r_ftse , arch(6)
predict htgarch6 , variance
tsline htgarch6
```

For an ARCH-M(1) model:

```
arch r_ftse L.r_ftse , archm arch(1)
predict htgarchm1 , variance
tsline htgarchm1
```

For a GARCH(1,1) model:

```
arch r_ftse L.r_ftse , arch(1) garch(1)
predict htgarch11 , variance
tsline htgarch11
```

while for higher orders (that is for GARCH(3,4)) only the values in the parentheses should change:

```
arch r_ftse L.rftse , arch(1/3) garch(1/4)
```

The TGARCH(1,1,1) model is given by:

```
arch r_ftse L.r_ftse , arch(1) garch(1) tarch(1)
```

and, finally, the EGARCH(1,1,1) model is estimated by:

```
arch r_ftse L.r_ftse , arch(1) garch(1) earch(1)
```

All these commands are left as an exercise for the reader. The analysis and interpretation of the results are similar to those discussed previously in this chapter.

Estimating ARCH/GARCH models in Microfit

In Microfit, apart from the TGARCH model, all ARCH/GARCH-type models can be estimated automatically using Microfit's own menus. The data are given in the ARCH.fit file. The first step is to go to the volatility estimation menu by clicking on the **Volatility** Microfit button. This menu looks exactly like the single-equation menu, and here the mean equation to be estimated is defined. In this case, type:

```
r_ftse c r_ftse(-1)
```

then click on **Run**, which brings up the **GARCH estimation menu**. Here, a set of options is provided, and in each case you need to define which model you want to estimate from six possible choices:

```
GARCH
GARCH-M
AGARCH
AGARCH-M
EGARCH
EGARCH-M
```

Leaving aside cases 3 and 4 of absolute GARCH models, all the rest of the options are familiar to us from the theory in this chapter. So, to estimate a GARCH-M(1,1) model, choose option 2 from this list and click **OK**. Then Microfit requires you to specify the underlying distribution. This is left as the default case, which is the *z*-distribution. After clicking **OK** again a new window appears, where the orders of ARCH and GARCH terms in our model must be specified. First, type the number of the GARCH terms and then, separated by ";", the number of ARCH terms. Therefore, for GARCH-M(1,1) type:

```
1 ; 1
```

Then click **Run** again, which takes you to the window where you can specify the number of additional variables to be included in the Variance equation (we can leave this blank for this example). After clicking **Run** again the results appear, after a number of iterations that are shown on the screen while Microfit executes the calculations. The analysis and interpretation are similar to the cases that have been examined above. The rest of the ARCH/GARCH models have been left as exercises for the reader.

Empirical illustrations of ARCH/GARCH models

A GARCH model of UK GDP and the effect of socio-political instability

Asteriou and Price (2001) used GARCH models to capture the effects of socio-political instability in UK GDP. To approximate and quantify socio-political instability, they constructed indices that summarized various variables capturing phenomena of social unrest for the UK over the period 1960–97 using quarterly time series data. Specifically, their indices were constructed by applying the method of principal components to the following variables: *TERROR*, the number of terrorist activities that caused mass violence; *STRIKES*, the number of strikes that were caused by political reasons; *ELECT*, the number of elections; *REGIME*, a dummy variable that takes the value of one for government changes to different political parties, zero otherwise; *FALKL*, a dummy variable that takes the value of 1 for the period of the Falklands War (1982; q1–q4), zero otherwise; and finally *GULF*, a dummy variable which takes the value of 1 for the period of the first Gulf War (1991; q1–q4), zero otherwise. Their main results are presented below.

Results from GARCH models

Asteriou and Price (2001) estimated the following model:

$$\Delta \ln(Y_t) = a_0 + a_{1i} \sum_{i=0}^{4} \Delta \ln(Y_{t-i}) + a_{2i} \sum_{i=0}^{4} \Delta \ln(I_{t-i}) + \sum_{j=1}^{6} d_j X_{jt} + u_t \qquad (14.35)$$

$$u_t \sim N(0, h_t) \qquad (14.36)$$

$$h_t = b_1 e_{t-1}^2 + b_2 h_{t-1} \qquad (14.37)$$

That is, the growth rate of GDP (denoted by $\Delta \ln(Y_t)$) is modelled as an $AR(4)$ process, including the growth and four lags of investments (denoted by $\Delta \ln(I_t)$) plus the political instability proxies (X_{jt}), where the variance is conditioned on the lagged variance and lagged squared residuals.

Table 14.14, model 1 presents the results of a GARCH(1,1) model for GDP growth or reference without including political dummies. (In each case the model has first been estimated with four lagged terms of GDP per capita and four lagged terms of the rate of growth of investment, and subsequently reduced to a parsimonious model, including only the significant regressors.) Despite the low R^2, the variance part of the model fits well.

Continuing, Asteriou and Price re-estimated the above model, including in Equation (14.35) the political dummies. All the dummies entered the equation with the expected negative sign and three of them were statistically significant. The results of the parsimonious model are shown in Table 14.14, model 2, and from these we observe that *REGIME*, *TERROR* and *STRIKES* are highly significant and negative. The variance equation is improved and R^2, while it remains relatively low, is increased compared to the previous specification.

Table 14.14   GARCH estimates of GDP growth with political uncertainty proxies

	Dependent variable: $\Delta \ln(Y_t)$; *Sample: 1961q2–1997q4*			
Parameter	1	2	3	4
Constant	0.003 (3.49)	0.005 (3.78)	0.004 (3.80)	0.006 (5.66)
$\Delta \ln(Y_{t-3})$	0.135 (1.36)	0.194 (1.99)	0.186 (1.87)	0.270 (3.42)
$\Delta \ln(Y_{t-4})$	0.131 (1.23)	0.129 (1.22)	0.122 (1.48)	0.131 (1.29)
$\Delta \ln(I_{t-2})$	0.180 (2.25)	0.132 (1.48)	0.162 (1.92)	
REGIME		−0.012 (−4.91)		−0.012 (−5.63)
TERROR		−0.004 (−2.72)		−0.005 (−2.66)
STRIKES		−0.011 (−2.58)		−0.015 (−3.44)
PC1			−0.005 (−4.33)	
PC2			−0.003 (−2.02)	
		Variance equation		
Constant	0.00001 (1.83)	0.00001 (1.66)	0.000006 (1.16)	0.00006 (1.71)
ARCH(1)	0.387 (3.27)	0.314 (2.44)	0.491 (4.18)	0.491 (4.46)
GARCH(1)	0.485 (2.95)	0.543 (3.14)	0.566 (6.21)	0.566 (3.36)
R^2	0.006	0.099	0.030	0.104
S.E. of d.v.	0.010	0.010	0.010	0.010
S.E. of Reg.	0.010	0.010	0.010	0.010

The results from the alternative specification, with the inclusion of the *PCs* in place of the political instability variables (Table 14.14, model 3) are similar to the previous model. Negative and significant coefficients were obtained for the first and the third components.

Asteriou and Price (2001) also estimated all the above specifications without including the investment terms. The results for the case of the political uncertainty dummies are presented in the same table in model 4, and show clearly that the strong negative direct impact remains. Thus, the impact of political uncertainty on growth does not appear to operate through investment growth, leaving open the possibility of political uncertainty affecting the *level* of investment.

Results from GARCH-M models

Asteriou and Price (2001) argued that it is mainly political instability that affects uncertainty and thereby growth. So it was of considerable interest for them to allow uncertainty to affect growth directly. To do this they used the GARCH-M class of models, first to test whether uncertainty in GDP (conditioned by the 'in mean' term of the GARCH-M model) affects GDP growth, and second whether political instability (conditioned by the political dummies and by the *PCs* in the variance equation) affects GDP growth separately.

The GARCH-M model they estimated may be presented as follows:

$$\Delta \ln(Y_t) = a_0 + \sum_{i=0}^{4} a_{1i} \Delta \ln(Y_{t-i}) + \sum_{i=0}^{4} a_{2i} \Delta \ln(I_{t-i}) + \gamma h_t + u_t \tag{14.38}$$

$$u_t \sim N(0, h_t) \tag{14.39}$$

$$h_t = b_1 u_{t-1}^2 + b_2 h_{t-1} + \sum_{i=1}^{6} b_{3i} X_{it} \tag{14.40}$$

Table 14.15 GARCH-M(1,1) estimates with political uncertainty proxies

Parameter	1	2	3
Dependent variable: $\Delta \ln(Y_t)$; Sample: 1961q2–1997q4			
Constant	0.008 (2.67)	0.009 (4.22)	0.007 (4.33)
$\Delta \ln(Y_{t-3})$	0.154 (1.59)	0.175 (1.15)	0.161 (2.10)
$\Delta \ln(Y_{t-4})$	0.128 (1.24)	0.089 (0.81)	0.141 (1.84)
$\Delta \ln(Iv_{t-2})$	0.136 (1.69)	0.132 (1.33)	0.126 (1.84)
SQR(*GARCH*)	−0.498 (−1.40)	−0.674 (−3.07)	−0.444 (−2.42)
Variance equation			
Constant	0.00001 (1.68)	0.00005 (1.21)	0.000002 (0.80)
ARCH(1)	0.335 (3.07)	0.133 (1.33)	0.460 (4.05)
GARCH(1)	0.554 (3.53)	0.650 (4.00)	0.580 (6.64)
ELECT		0.007 (3.11)	
REGIME		0.006 (2.84)	
FAUKL		0.002 (5.11)	
STRIKES		0.066 (2.91)	
PC1			0.000047 (1.45)
PC2			0.000002 (0.09)
PC3			0.000031 (3.20)
R^2	0.054	0.053	0.064
S.E. of d.v.	0.010	0.0106	0.0106
S.E. of Reg.	0.010	0.0108	0.0107

That is, the growth rate of GDP is modelled as an *AR* process, including four lags of the growth rate of investments and the variance of the error term. Equation (14.39) defines h_t as the variance of the error term in Equation (14.38), and Equation (14.40) states that the variance of the error term is in turn a function of the lagged variance and lagged squared residuals as well as the political instability proxies X_{it}. To accept the first hypothesis it would be necessary for γ to be non-zero, while to accept the second hypothesis there should be evidence of positive statistically significant estimates for the coefficients of the political instability proxies (b_{3i}).

Table 14.15, model 1 reports the results of estimating a GARCH-M(1,1) model without political instability proxies. (Again, as in the previous section, the reported results are only from the parsimonious models.) The model is satisfactory given that the parameters (b_1, b_2) are strongly significant. The inclusion of the 'in mean' specification turns out to be redundant as γ is insignificant, suggesting that GDP uncertainty does not itself affect GDP growth. However, this turns out to be misleading and follows from the fact that political factors are ignored.

In estimating a GARCH-M(1,1) model including the political dummies in the variance equation (see Table 14.15, model 2), Asteriou and Price observed that all the political instability variables – with the exception of *REGIME* – entered the equation with the expected positive sign, indicating that political uncertainty increases the variance of GDP growth. All variables were statistically significant. The 'in mean' term is in this case highly significant and negative. The results from the alternative specification, with the inclusion of the *PCs* in the place of the political instability variables (Table 14.15, model 3) are similar to the previous one, with the exception that positive and significant coefficients were obtained only for the fifth component.

Continuing, Asteriou and Price estimated more general GARCH-M(1,1) models, first including the political dummies and the *PCs* in the growth equation, and then including political dummies and *PCs* in both the growth and the variance equation.

Table 14.16   GARCH-M(1,1) estimates with political proxies

Dependent variable: $\Delta \ln(Y_t)$; *Sample: 1961q2–1997q4*

Parameter	Estimate	Std. error	t-statistic
Constant	0.009	0.003	2.964
$\Delta \ln(Y_{t-3})$	0.206	0.093	2.203
$\Delta \ln(Y_{t-4})$	0.123	0.102	1.213
$\Delta \ln(I_{t-4})$	0.109	0.088	1.241
SQR(GARCH)	−0.447	0.365	−1.304
REGIME	−0.012	0.002	−5.084
TERROR	−0.005	0.001	−3.018
STRIKES	−0.012	0.004	−2.753
	Variance equation		
Constant	0.00001	0.000008	1.648
ARCH(1)	0.285	0.120	2.380
GARCH(1)	0.575	0.161	3.553
R^2	0.124		
S.E. of d.v.	0.0106		
S.E. of Reg.	0.0103		

Table 14.17   GARCH-M(1,1) estimates with political proxies

Dependent variable: $\Delta \ln(Y_t)$; *Sample: 1961q2–1997q4*

Parameter	Estimate	Std. error	t-statistic
Constant	0.005	0.001	3.611
$\Delta \ln(Y_{t-3})$	0.172	0.095	1.799
$\Delta \ln(Y_{t-4})$	0.123	0.090	1.353
$\Delta \ln(I_{t-4})$	0.181	0.089	2.023
SQR(GARCH)	−0.169	0.254	−0.667
REGIME	−0.013	0.006	−1.925
GULF	−0.007	0.003	−1.899
STRIKES	−0.020	0.006	−3.356
	Variance equation		
Constant	0.00002	0.00001	2.013
ARCH(1)	0.265	0.126	2.091
GARCH(1)	0.527	0.171	3.076
ELECT	0.00004	0.00001	2.608
REGIME	0.0001	0.0001	1.131
FALKL	0.00002	0.00002	1.326
R^2	0.141		
S.E. of d.v.	0.0106		
S.E. of Reg.	0.0103		

With the first version of the model they wanted to test whether the inclusion of the dummies in the growth equation would affect the significance of the 'in mean' term which captures the uncertainty of GDP. Their results, presented in Table 14.16, showed that GDP growth was significantly affected only by political uncertainty, captured either by the dummies or by the *PCs*, denoting the importance of political factors other than the GARCH process. (We report here only the results from the model with the political uncertainty dummies. The results with the *PCs* are similar but are not presented for economy of space. Tables and results are available from the authors on request.)

The final and most general specification was used to capture both effects stemming from political uncertainty, namely the effect of political uncertainty on GDP growth, and its effect on the variance of GDP. Asteriou and Price's results are presented in Table 14.17. After the inclusion of the political dummies in the variance equation, the model was improved (the political dummies significantly altered the variance of GDP), but the effect on GDP growth came only from the political uncertainty proxies that were included in the growth equation. The 'in mean' term was negative and insignificant.

The final conclusion of Asteriou and Price (2001) was that political instability has two identifiable effects. Some measures impact on the variance of GDP growth; others directly affect the growth itself. Instability has a direct impact on growth and does not operate indirectly via the conditional variance of growth.

Questions and exercises

Questions

1 Explain the meaning of ARCH and GARCH models, showing how each is a form of heteroskedasticity.

2 Explain how one can test for the presence of ARCH(q) effects in a simple OLS estimation framework.

3 Explain how one may estimate models with ARCH and GARCH effects.

4 What is meant by the comment that 'GARCH(1,1) is an alternative parsimonious process for an infinite ARCH(q) process'. Prove this mathematically.

5 Explain the meaning of asymmetries in news, and provide appropriate specifications for GARCH models that can capture these effects.

6 What should researchers be very careful of in estimating ARCH/GARCH models?

7 Provide a GARCH-M(q,p) model and explain the intuition behind this model.

8 Explain the effect of the dummy variable in the TGARCH model. Why does it enter the variance equation in a multiplicative form, and what is the rationale behind this?

Exercise 14.1

The file arch.wf1 contains daily data for the logarithmic returns FTSE-100 (named *r_ftse*) and three more stocks of the UK stock market (named *r_stock1*, *r_stock2* and *r_stock3*, respectively). For each of the stock series do the following:

(a) Estimate an AR(1) up to AR(15) model and test the individual and joint significance of the estimated coefficients.

(b) Compare AIC and SBC values of the above models and, along with the results for the significance of the coefficients, conclude which will be the most appropriate specification.

(c) Re-estimate this specification using OLS and test for the presence of ARCH(p) effects. Choose several alternative values for p.

(d) For the preferred specification of the mean equation, estimate an ARCH(p) model and compare your results with the previous OLS results.

(e) Obtain the conditional variance and conditional standard deviations series and rename them with names that will show from which model they were obtained (for example SD_ARCH6 for the conditional standard deviation of an ARCH(6) process).

(f) Estimate a GARCH(q,p) model, obtain the conditional variance and standard deviation series (rename them again appropriately) and plot them against the series you have already obtained. What do you observe?

(g) Estimate a TGARCH(q,p) model. Test the significance of the TGARCH coefficient. Is there any evidence of asymmetric effects?

(h) Estimate an EGARCH(q,p) model. How does this affect your results?

(i) Summarize all models in one table and comment on your results.

Exercise 14.2

You are working in a financial institution and your boss proposes to upgrade the financial risk-management methodology the company uses. In particular, to model the FTSE-100 index your boss suggests estimation using an ARCH(1) process. You disagree and wish to convince your boss that a GARCH(1,1) process is better.

(a) Explain, intuitively first, why a GARCH(1,1) process will fit the returns of FTSE-100 better than an ARCH(1) process. (Hint: You will need to refer to the stylized facts of the behaviour of stock indices.)

(b) Prove your point with the use of mathematics. (Hint: You will need to mention ARCH(q) processes here.)

(c) Estimate both models and try to analyse them in such a way that you can convince your boss about the preferability of the model you are proposing. Check the conditional standard deviation and conditional variance series as well. (Hint: Check the number of iterations and talk about computational efficiency.)

15 Vector Autoregressive (VAR) Models and Causality Tests

CHAPTER CONTENTS

LEARNING OBJECTIVES

After studying this chapter you should be able to:

1. Differentiate between univariate and multivariate time series models.
2. Understand Vector Autoregressive (VAR) models and discuss their advantages.
3. Understand the concept of causality and its importance in economic applications.
4. Use the Granger causality test procedure.
5. Use the Sims causality test procedure.
6. Estimate VAR models and test for Granger and Sims causality through the use of econometric software.

Vector autoregressive (VAR) models

It is quite common in economics to have models in which some variables are not only explanatory variables for a given dependent variable, but are also explained by the variables that they are used to determine. In these cases we have models of simultaneous equations, in which it is necessary to identify clearly which are the endogenous and which are the exogenous or predetermined variables.

The decision regarding such a differentiation among variables was heavily criticized by Sims (1980). According to Sims, if there is simultaneity among a number of variables, then all these variables should be treated in the same way. In other words, there should be no distinction between endogenous and exogenous variables. Therefore, once this distinction is abandoned, all variables are treated as endogenous. This means that in its general reduced form each equation has the same set of regressors, which leads to the development of VAR models.

The VAR model

When we are not confident that a variable really is exogenous, each variable has to be treated symmetrically. Take, for example, the time series y_t that is affected by current and past values of x_t and, simultaneously, the time series x_t to be a series that is affected by current and past values of the y_t series. In this case the simple bivariate model is given by:

$$y_t = \beta_{10} - \beta_{12}x_t + \gamma_{11}y_{t-1} + \gamma_{12}x_{t-1} + u_{yt} \tag{15.1}$$

$$x_t = \beta_{20} - \beta_{21}y_t + \gamma_{21}y_{t-1} + \gamma_{22}x_{t-1} + u_{xt} \tag{15.2}$$

where we assume that both y_t and x_t are stationary, and u_{yt} and u_{xt} are uncorrelated white-noise error terms. Equations (15.1) and (15.2) constitute a first-order VAR model, because the longest lag length is unity. These equations are not reduced-form equations, since y_t has a contemporaneous impact on x_t (given by $-\beta_{21}$), and x_t has a contemporaneous impact on y_t (given by $-\beta_{12}$). Rewriting the system using matrix algebra, we get:

$$\begin{bmatrix} 1 & \beta_{12} \\ \beta_{21} & 1 \end{bmatrix} \begin{bmatrix} y_t \\ x_t \end{bmatrix} = \begin{bmatrix} \beta_{10} \\ \beta_{20} \end{bmatrix} + \begin{bmatrix} \gamma_{11} & \gamma_{12} \\ \gamma_{21} & \gamma_{22} \end{bmatrix} \begin{bmatrix} y_{t-1} \\ x_{t-1} \end{bmatrix} + \begin{bmatrix} u_{yt} \\ u_{xt} \end{bmatrix} \tag{15.3}$$

or

$$\mathbf{B}z_t = \mathbf{\Gamma}_0 + \mathbf{\Gamma}_1 z_{t-1} + u_t \tag{15.4}$$

where

$$\mathbf{B} = \begin{bmatrix} 1 & \beta_{12} \\ \beta_{21} & 1 \end{bmatrix}, \quad z_t = \begin{bmatrix} y_t \\ x_t \end{bmatrix}, \quad \mathbf{\Gamma}_0 = \begin{bmatrix} \beta_{10} \\ \beta_{20} \end{bmatrix},$$

$$\mathbf{\Gamma}_1 = \begin{bmatrix} \gamma_{11} & \gamma_{12} \\ \gamma_{21} & \gamma_{22} \end{bmatrix} \quad \text{and} \quad u_t = \begin{bmatrix} u_{yt} \\ u_{xt} \end{bmatrix}.$$

Multiplying both sides by $\mathbf{B}^{-1}$ we obtain:

$$z_t = \mathbf{A}_0 + \mathbf{A}_1 z_{t-1} + \mathbf{e_t} \tag{15.5}$$

where $\mathbf{A}_0 = \mathbf{B}^{-1}\mathbf{\Gamma}_0$, $\mathbf{A}_1 = \mathbf{B}^{-1}\mathbf{\Gamma}_1$ and $\mathbf{e_t} = \mathbf{B}^{-1}u_t$.

For purposes of notational simplification we can denote as a_{i0} the ith element of the vector $\mathbf{A}_0$; a_{ij} the element in row i and column j of the matrix $\mathbf{A}_1$; and e_{it} as the ith element of the vector $\mathbf{e_t}$. Using this, we can rewrite the VAR model as:

$$y_t = a_{10} + a_{11}y_{t-1} + a_{12}x_{t-1} + e_{1t} \tag{15.6}$$

$$x_t = a_{20} + a_{21}y_{t-1} + a_{22}x_{t-1} + e_{2t} \tag{15.7}$$

To distinguish between the original VAR model and the system we have just obtained, we call the first a structural or primitive VAR system and the second a VAR in standard (or reduced) form. It is important to note that the new error terms, e_{1t} and e_{2t}, are composites of the two shocks u_{yt} and u_{xt}. Since $\mathbf{e_t} = \mathbf{B}^{-1}u_t$ we can obtain e_{1t} and e_{2t} as:

$$e_{1t} = (u_{yt} + \beta_{12}u_{xt})/(1 - \beta_{12}\beta_{21}) \tag{15.8}$$

$$e_{2t} = (u_{xt} + \beta_{21}u_{yt})/(1 - \beta_{12}\beta_{21}) \tag{15.9}$$

Since u_{yt} and u_{xt} are white-noise processes, it follows that both e_{1t} and e_{2t} are also white-noise processes.

Pros and cons of the VAR models

The VAR model approach has some very good characteristics. First, it is very simple. The econometrician does not have to worry about which variables are endogenous or exogenous. Second, estimation is also very simple, in the sense that each equation can be estimated separately with the usual OLS method. Third, forecasts obtained from VAR models are in most cases better than those obtained from the far more complex simultaneous equation models (see Mahmoud, 1984; McNees, 1986).

However, on the other hand, VAR models have faced severe criticism over various points. First, they are atheoretic, in that they are not based on any economic theory. Since initially there are no restrictions on any of the parameters under estimation, in effect 'everything causes everything'. However, statistical inference is often used in the estimated models so that some coefficients that appear to be insignificant can be dropped, in order to lead to models that might have an underlying consistent theory. Such inference is normally carried out using what are called causality tests. These are presented in the next section.

A second criticism concerns the loss of degrees of freedom. If we suppose that we have a three-variable VAR model and decide to include 12 lags for each variable in each equation, this will entail the estimation of 36 parameters in each equation plus the equation constant. If the sample size is not sufficiently large, estimating that great a number of parameters will consume many degrees of freedom, thus creating problems in estimation.

Finally, the obtained coefficients of the VAR models are difficult to interpret because of their lack of any theoretical background. To overcome this criticism, the advocates of VAR models estimate so-called impulse response functions. The impulse response function examines the response of the dependent variable in the VAR to shocks in the error terms. The difficult issue here, however, is defining the shocks. The general view is that we would like to shock the structural errors, that is, the errors in Equations (15.1) or (15.2), which we can interpret easily as a shock to a particular part of the structural model. However, we only observe the reduced-form errors in Equations (15.6) and (15.7) and these are made up of a combination of structural errors. So we have to disentangle the structural errors in some way, and this is known as the identification problem (this is quite different from the Box–Jenkins identification problem mentioned earlier). There are a variety of ways of doing this, though we are not going to explore these in this text. We would stress, however, that the different methods can give rise to quite different results and there is no objective statistical criteria for choosing between these different methods.

Causality tests

We said earlier that one of the good features of VAR models is that they allow us to test for the direction of causality. Causality in econometrics is somewhat different from the concept in everyday use; it refers more to the ability of one variable to predict (and therefore cause) the other. Suppose two variables, say y_t and x_t, affect each other with distributed lags. The relationship between these variables can be captured by a VAR model. In this case it is possible to state that (a) y_t causes x_t; (b) x_t causes y_t; (c) there is a bi-directional feedback (causality among the variables); and (d) the two variables are independent. The problem is to find an appropriate procedure that allows us to test and statistically detect the cause and effect relationship among the variables.

Granger (1969) developed a relatively simple test that defined causality as follows: a variable y_t is said to Granger cause x_t if x_t can be predicted with greater accuracy by using past values of the y_t variable rather than not using such past values, all other terms remaining unchanged.

The next section presents the Granger causality test, and this will be followed by an alternative causality test developed by Sims (1972).

The Granger causality test

The Granger causality test for the case of two stationary variables y_t and x_t involves as a first step the estimation of the following VAR model:

$$y_t = a_1 + \sum_{i=1}^{n} \beta_i x_{t-i} + \sum_{j=1}^{m} \gamma_j y_{t-j} + e_{1t} \qquad (15.10)$$

$$x_t = a_2 + \sum_{i=1}^{n} \theta_i x_{t-i} + \sum_{j=1}^{m} \delta_j y_{t-j} + e_{2t} \qquad (15.11)$$

where it is assumed that both ε_{yt} and ε_{xt} are uncorrelated white-noise error terms. In this model we can have the following different cases:

Case 1 The lagged x terms in Equation (15.10) may be statistically different from zero as a group, and the lagged y terms in Equation (15.11) not statistically different from zero. In this case we see x_t causes y_t.

Case 2 The lagged y terms in Equation (15.11) may be statistically different from zero as a group, and the lagged x terms in Equation (15.10) not statistically different from zero. In this case we see that y_t causes x_t.

Case 3 Both sets of x and y terms are statistically different from zero in Equations (15.10) and (15.11), so that there is bi-directional causality.

Case 4 Both sets of x and y terms are not statistically different from zero in Equations (15.10) and (15.11), so that x_t is independent of y_t.

The Granger causality test, then, involves the following procedure. First, estimate the VAR model given by Equations (15.10) and (15.11). Then check the significance of the coefficients and apply variable deletion tests, first in the lagged x terms for Equation (15.10), and then in the lagged y terms for Equation (15.11). According to the result of the variable deletion tests we may come to a conclusion about the direction of causality based on the four cases mentioned above.

More analytically, and for the case of one equation (we shall examine Equation (15.10), and it is intuitive to reverse the procedure to test for Equation (15.11)), we perform the following steps:

Step 1 Regress y_t on lagged y terms as in the following model:

$$y_t = a_1 + \sum_{j=1}^{m} \gamma_j y_{t-j} + e_{1t} \tag{15.12}$$

and obtain the RSS of this regression (the restricted one) and label it as RSS_R.

Step 2 Regress y_t on lagged y terms plus lagged x terms as in the following model:

$$y_t = a_1 + \sum_{i=1}^{n} \beta_i x_{t-i} + \sum_{j=1}^{m} \gamma_j y_{t-j} + e_{1t} \tag{15.13}$$

and obtain the RSS of this regression (the unrestricted one) and label it as RSS_U.

Step 3 Set the null and the alternative hypotheses as:

$$H_0: \quad \sum_{i=1}^{n} \beta_i = 0 \text{ or } x_t \text{ does not cause } y_t$$

$$H_1: \quad \sum_{i=1}^{n} \beta_i \neq 0 \text{ or } x_t \text{ does cause } y_t$$

Step 4   Calculate the F-statistic for the normal Wald test on coefficient restrictions given by:

$$F = \frac{(RSS_R - RSS_U)/m}{RSS_U/(n - k)}$$

which follows the $F_{m,n-k}$ distribution. Here $k = m + n + 1$.

Step 5   If the computed F-value exceeds the F-critical value, reject the null hypothesis and conclude that x_t causes y_t.

The Sims causality test

Sims (1980) proposed an alternative test for causality making use of the fact that in any general notion of causality it is not possible for the future to cause the present. Therefore, when we want to check whether a variable y_t causes x_t, Sims suggests estimating the following VAR model:

$$y_t = a_1 + \sum_{i=1}^{n} \beta_i x_{t-i} + \sum_{j=1}^{m} \gamma_j y_{t-j} + \sum_{\rho=1}^{k} \zeta_\rho x_{t+\rho} + e_{1t} \qquad (15.14)$$

$$x_t = a_2 + \sum_{i=1}^{n} \theta_i x_{t-i} + \sum_{j=1}^{m} \delta_j y_{t-j} + \sum_{\rho=1}^{k} \xi_\rho y_{t+\rho} + e_{2t} \qquad (15.15)$$

The new approach here is that, apart from lagged values of x and y, there are also leading values of x included in the first equation (and similarly, leading values of y in the second equation).

Examining only the first equation, if y_t causes x_t then we expect that there is some relationship between y and the leading values of x. Therefore, instead of testing for the lagged values of x_t we test for $\sum_{\rho=1}^{k} \zeta_\rho = 0$. Note that if we reject the restriction then the causality runs from y_t to x_t, and not vice versa, since the future cannot cause the present.

To carry out the test we simply estimate a model with no leading terms (the restricted version) and then the model as it appears in Equation (15.14) (the unrestricted model), and then obtain the F-statistic as in the Granger test above.

It is unclear which version of the two tests is preferable, and most researchers use both. The Sims test, however, using more regressors (because of the inclusion of the leading terms), leads to a greater loss of degrees of freedom.

Computer example: financial development and economic growth, what is the causal relationship?

The aim here is to investigate the effects of financial and stock market development on the process of economic growth in the UK. (This section is heavily based on Asteriou and

Price, 2000a.) The importance of the relationship between financial development and economic growth has been well recognized and emphasized in the field of economic development (see, for example, Gurley and Shaw, 1955; Goldsmith, 1969, among others). However, whether the financial system (with an emphasis on stock markets) is important for economic growth more generally is not clear. One line of research stresses the importance of the financial system in mobilizing savings, allocating capital, exerting corporate control and easing risk management, while, in contrast, a different line of research does not mention at all the role of the financial system in economic growth. We discuss the above points and test these questions empirically using the Granger causality test for the case of the UK.

Following standard practice in empirical studies (for example Roubini and Sala-i-Martin, 1992; King and Levine, 1993a, 1993b) our indicator for economic development is real GDP per capita.

The existing literature suggests as a proxy for financial development ratios of a broad measure of money, often M2, to the level of nominal GDP or GNP. This ratio measures directly the extent of monetization, rather than financial deepening. It is possible that this ratio may be increasing because of the monetization process rather than increased financial intermediation. An alternative is to deduct active currency in circulation from M2, or to use the ratio of domestic bank credit to nominal GDP. In our analysis, two alternative proxies of financial development are employed, based on two different definitions of money. The first is the currency ratio – the ratio of currency to the narrow definition of money (M0) (the sum of currency and demand deposits). The second is the monetization ratio given by a broader definition of money (M4) over nominal GDP, the inverse of velocity. The first variable is a proxy for the complexity of the financial market; a decrease in the currency ratio will accompany real growth in the economy, especially in its early stages, as there exists more diversification of financial assets and liabilities, and more transactions will be carried out in the form of non-currency. The monetization variable is designed to show the real size of the financial sector. We would expect to see the ratio increase (decrease) over time if the financial sector develops faster (slower) than the real sector.

A third measure of financial development is constructed in order to provide more direct information on the extent of financial intermediation. This is the ratio of bank claims on the private sector to nominal GDP (the 'claims ratio'). As it is the supply of credit to the private sector which, according to the McKinnon/Shaw inside model, is ultimately responsible for both the quantity and quality of investment and, in turn, for economic growth, this variable may be expected to exert a causal influence on real GDP per capita (Demetriades and Hussein, 1996).

To examine the connection between growth and the stock market, we have to construct individual indicators of stock market development. One important aspect of stock market development is liquidity (see Bencivenga *et al.*, 1996, and Holmstrom and Tirole, 1993), which can be measured in two ways. The first is to compute the ratio of the total value of trades of the capital market over nominal GDP. The second is to compute the 'turnover ratio', defined as the value of trades of the capital market over market capitalization, where market capitalization equals the total value of all listed shares in the capital market.

Finally, we need data for employment and for the stock of capital to construct the capital/labour ratio of an implicit Cobb–Douglas productivity function. The data for the stock of capital are available for the UK only on a yearly basis. Assuming that capital depreciates with a constant annual depreciation rate of δ, we applied the implicit annual rate to an initial value of the stock of capital for the first quarter of 1970 using the quarterly time series for gross fixed capital formation. This enabled us to simulate a quarterly time series for the stock of capital.

The data set used in estimation and testing consists of quarterly observations from the UK, and the sample period runs from 1970: q1–1997: q1, with the exception of the turnover ratio, which covers the period 1983: q1–1997: q1. The data were drawn from the UK's National Income and Expenditure Accounts, and from Datastream.

The conventional Granger causality test involves the testing of the null hypothesis 'x_t does not cause y_t', simply by running the following two regressions:

$$y_t = \sum_{i=1}^{m} a_i y_{t-i} + \sum_{j=1}^{n} b_j x_{t-j} + e_t \tag{15.16}$$

$$y = \sum_{i=1}^{m} a_i y_{t-i} + e_t \tag{15.17}$$

and testing $b_i = 0$ for every i.

The testing procedure for the identification of causal directions becomes more complex, however, when, as is common in macroeconomic time series, the variables have unit roots. In such a case – after testing for the existence of cointegration – it is useful to reparametrize the model in the equivalent ECM form (see Hendry *et al.*, 1984; Johansen, 1988) as follows:

$$\Delta y_t = \alpha_0 + \alpha_{1i} \sum_{i}^{m} \Delta x_{t-i} + \alpha_{2k} \sum_{k}^{n} \Delta z_{t-k} + \alpha_3 \upsilon_{t-1} + u_t \tag{15.18}$$

where $\upsilon_{t-1} = y_{t-1} - \alpha_1 x_{t-1} - \alpha_2 z_{t-1}$ is the residual of the cointegration equation. (This might seem difficult to follow at the moment, but it will become clearer after studying Chapters 16 and 17, which deal with the integration and cointegration of time series.)

The null hypothesis, now that x does not Granger cause y, given z, is $H_0(\alpha_1 = \alpha_3 = 0)$. This means that there are two sources of causation for y, either through the lagged terms Δx or through the lagged cointegrating vector. This latter source of causation is not detected by a standard Granger causality test. The null hypothesis can be rejected if one or more of these sources affects y (that is the parameters are different from zero). The hypothesis is tested again, using a standard F-test. Following Granger and Lin (1995), the conventional Granger causality test is not valid, because two integrated series cannot cause each other in the long run unless they are cointegrated. We therefore test for causality among the variables that are found to be cointegrated, using the VECM representations for the cointegrated variables. Results of these causality tests are presented in Table 15.1.

Causality in the long run exists only when the coefficient of the cointegrating vector is statistically significant and different from zero (Granger and Lin, 1995). In our analysis we apply variable deletion (F-type) tests for the coefficient of the cointegrating vector and for the lagged values of the financial proxies for the GDP per capital Vector Error Correction Model (VECM) and vice versa (testing for the validity of the supply-leading and demand-following, hypotheses, respectively). The results, reported in Table 15.1,

Table 15.1 Testing for long-run Granger causality

Model: $\Delta y_t = \alpha_0 + \alpha_{1i} \sum_i^m \Delta x_{t-i} + \alpha_{2k} \sum_k^n \Delta z_{t-k} + \alpha_3 \upsilon_{t-1} + u_t$
where $y = (GDP\ per\ capita);\ x = (turnover,\ monetization);\ z = (K/L\ ratio)$

x-variable	F-statistic		Lags	Causality relationship
turnover (ΔT)	$a_3 = 0$	$F(1,71) = 20.26^*$	1	$cv_{t-1} \rightarrow \Delta Y$
	$a_{2k} = 0$	$F(1,71) = 3.73^*$	1	$\Delta T \rightarrow \Delta Y$
monetization (ΔM)	$a_3 = 0$	$F(1,74) = 23.60^*$	6	$cv_{t-1} \rightarrow \Delta Y$
	$a_{2k} = 0$	$F(6,74) = 7.30^*$	6	$\Delta M \rightarrow \Delta Y$

Model: $\Delta y_t = \alpha_0 + \alpha_{1i} \sum_i^m \Delta x_{t-i} + \alpha_{2k} \sum_k^n \Delta z_{t-k} + \alpha_3 \upsilon_{t-1} + u_t$
where $y = (turnover,\ monetization);\ x = (GDP\ per\ capita);\ z = (K/L\ ratio)$

y-variable	F-statistic		Lags	Causality relationship
turnover (ΔT)	$a_3 = 0$	$F(1,71) = 5.88^*$	1	$cv_{t-1} \rightarrow \Delta Y$
	$a_{2k} = 0$	$F(1,71) = 1.07$	1	$\Delta T - / \rightarrow \Delta Y$
monetization (ΔM)	$a_3 = 0$	$F(1,74) = 12.81^*$	6	$cv_{t-1} \rightarrow \Delta Y$
	$a_{2k} = 0$	$F(6,74) = 0.836$	6	$\Delta M - / \rightarrow \Delta Y$

* Denotes the rejection of the null hypothesis of no causality.

show that there is strong evidence in favour of the supply-leading hypothesis. In both cases (turnover ratio and monetization ratio) the causality direction runs from the financial proxy variable to GDP per capita, while the opposite hypothesis – that GDP per capita causes financial development – is strongly rejected. We also observe in all cases that the coefficients of the cointegrating vectors are statistically significant and the F-type tests reject the hypothesis that those coefficients are equal to zero, suggesting that in all cases there is a long bi-directional causality relationship.

Estimating VAR models and causality tests in EViews, Stata and Microfit

Estimating VAR models in EViews

In EViews, to estimate a VAR model go to **Quick\Estimate VAR**. A new window opens that requires the model to be to specified. First, we have to specify whether it is an unrestricted VAR (default case) or a cointegrating VAR (we shall discuss this in Chapter 17). Leave this option as it is – that is, unrestricted VAR. Then the endogenous variables for our VAR model need to be defined by typing their names in the required box; the lag length (default is 1 2) by typing the start and end numbers of the lags we want to include; and the exogenous variable, if any (note that the constant is already included in the exogenous variables list).

As an example, we can use the data given in the file VAR.wf1. If we include as endogenous variables the series *r_ftse, r_stock1, r_stock2* and *r_stock3* and estimate the VAR model for 2 lags, we obtain the results reported in Table 15.2. EViews can calculate very quickly the Granger causality test for all the series in the VAR model estimated

Table 15.2 VAR model results

Vector autoregression estimates
Date: 04/21/10 Time: 13:54
Sample: 1/01/1990–12/31/1999
Included observations: 2610
Standard errors in ( ) & t-statistics in [ ]

	R_FTSE	R_STOCK1	R_STOCK2	R_STOCK3
R_FTSE(−1)	0.073909	0.026654	0.052065	0.061738
	(0.01959)	(0.03175)	(0.03366)	(0.03820)
	[3.77369]	[0.83939]	[1.54682]	[1.61634]
R_FTSE(−2)	−0.043335	−0.019181	−0.055069	−0.005584
	(0.01959)	(0.03176)	(0.03367)	(0.03821)
	[−2.21213]	[−0.60391]	[−1.63567]	[−0.14615]
R_STOCK1(−1)	0.002804	0.036453	0.000610	0.022188
	(0.01289)	(0.02091)	(0.02216)	(0.02515)
	[0.21748]	[1.74374]	[0.02751]	[0.88234]
R_STOCK1(−2)	−0.026765	−0.028422	0.056227	0.009408
	(0.01290)	(0.02091)	(0.02216)	(0.02515)
	[−2.07544]	[−1.35936]	[2.53691]	[0.37404]
R_STOCK2(−1)	0.003126	0.022653	0.001967	−0.030041
	(0.01225)	(0.01986)	(0.02106)	(0.02390)
	[0.25514]	[1.14034]	[0.09344]	[−1.25719]
R_STOCK2(−2)	0.008136	0.035131	−0.015181	−0.006935
	(0.01226)	(0.01988)	(0.02108)	(0.02392)
	[0.66344]	[1.76691]	[−0.72031]	[−0.28998]
R_STOCK3(−1)	0.004981	0.009964	0.031874	0.145937
	(0.01088)	(0.01763)	(0.01869)	(0.02121)
	[0.45799]	[0.56503]	[1.70519]	[6.87994]
R_STOCK3(−2)	0.012926	−0.021913	−0.073698	−0.071633
	(0.01087)	(0.01762)	(0.01868)	(0.02120)
	[1.18931]	[−1.24356]	[−3.94544]	[−3.37944]
C	0.000368	3.46E−05	0.000172	0.000504
	(0.00018)	(0.00030)	(0.00032)	(0.00036)
	[1.99918]	[0.11602]	[0.54520]	[1.40563]
R-squared	0.009126	0.005269	0.010114	0.024353
Adj. R-squared	0.006078	0.002209	0.007069	0.021352
Sum sq. resids	0.228332	0.600202	0.674418	0.868468
S.E. equation	0.009369	0.015191	0.016103	0.018273
F-statistic	2.994316	1.722159	3.321798	8.115318
Log likelihood	8490.567	7229.332	7077.190	6747.180
Akaike AIC	−6.499285	−5.532821	−5.416238	−5.163356
Schwarz SC	−6.479054	−5.512590	−5.396006	−5.143125
Mean dependent	0.000391	3.99E−05	0.000148	0.000565
S.D. dependent	0.009398	0.015208	0.016160	0.018471

Determinant resid covariance (dof adj.)	1.38E−15
Determinant resid covariance	1.36E−15
Log likelihood	29857.44
Akaike information criterion	−22.85168
Schwarz criterion	−22.77075

Table 15.3 Granger causality tests for VAR model

VAR Granger causality/block exogeneity wald tests
Date: 04/21/10 Time: 14:54
Sample: 1/01/1990–12/31/1999
Included observations: 2610

Dependent variable: R_FTSE

Excluded	Chi-sq	df	Prob.
R_STOCK1	4.330362	2	0.1147
R_STOCK2	0.506590	2	0.7762
R_STOCK3	1.792883	2	0.4080
All	5.798882	6	0.4461

Dependent variable: R_STOCK1

Excluded	Chi-sq	df	Prob.
R_FTSE	1.002366	2	0.6058
R_STOCK2	4.438242	2	0.1087
R_STOCK3	1.713987	2	0.4244
All	6.547766	6	0.3647

Dependent variable: R_STOCK2

Excluded	Chi-sq	df	Prob.
R_FTSE	4.732726	2	0.0938
R_STOCK1	6.447668	2	0.0398
R_STOCK3	17.03170	2	0.0002
All	24.44092	6	0.0004

Dependent variable: R_STOCK3

Excluded	Chi-sq	df	Prob.
R_FTSE	2.613544	2	0.2707
R_STOCK1	0.940452	2	0.6249
R_STOCK2	1.667499	2	0.4344
All	4.908218	6	0.5556

above. To do this, choose from the VAR window with the output **View/Lag Structure/Granger Causality–Block Exogeneity Tests**. The results of this Granger causality test are reported in Table 15.3 and show results for each equation of the VAR model, first for excluding the lagged regressors one by one and then all of them at once. EViews also quickly calculates Granger causality tests for different pairs of variables. This test is different from the one presented above because it assumes only the two variables that are being tested in the pair are endogenous in the VAR model. To do this very quick pairwise test, go to **Quick/Group Statistics/Granger Causality Test**, and in the window that appears define first the variables to be tested for causality (once again using *r_ftse, r_stock1, r_stock2* and *r_stock3*) and then the number of lags (default 2) that are needed for the test. By clicking **OK** we get the results reported in Table 15.3. The results report the null hypothesis, the *F*-statistic and the probability limit value for all possible pairs of variables. From the probability limit values, it is clear that, at a 95% significance level, the only case for which we can reject the null (prob < 0.05) is

Table 15.4 Pairwise Granger causality results from EViews

Pairwise Granger causality tests
Date: 04/21/10 Time: 13:56
Sample: 1/01/1990–12/31/1999
Lags: 2

Null hypothesis:	Obs	F-statistic	Prob.
R_STOCK1 does not Granger Cause R_FTSE	2610	1.39644	0.2477
R_FTSE does not Granger Cause R_STOCK1		0.44484	0.6410
R_STOCK2 does not Granger Cause R_FTSE	2610	0.28495	0.7521
R_FTSE does not Granger Cause R_STOCK2		2.03291	0.1312
R_STOCK3 does not Granger Cause R_FTSE	2610	0.65007	0.5221
R_FTSE does not Granger Cause R_STOCK3		1.35525	0.2581
R_STOCK2 does not Granger Cause R_STOCK1	2610	1.95921	0.1412
R_STOCK1 does not Granger Cause R_STOCK2		1.63311	0.1955
R_STOCK3 does not Granger Cause R_STOCK1	2610	0.55979	0.5714
R_STOCK1 does not Granger Cause R_STOCK3		0.28489	0.7521
R_STOCK3 does not Granger Cause R_STOCK2	2610	6.66531	0.0013
R_STOCK2 does not Granger Cause R_STOCK3		0.64888	0.5227

for '*r_stock3* does not cause *r_stock2*', concluding that *r_stock2* does indeed Granger cause *r_stock3*. The null hypothesis cannot be rejected in any other case.

Estimating VAR models in Stata

In Stata, the command for estimating a VAR model is:

```
varbasic endvariables , lags(#/#)
```

where `endvariables` is simply the names of the endogenous variables in the model, and after `lags` the number of lags is specified by stating the first and the last lag numbers in the parentheses. For example, using the data in the file VAR.dat, we can estimate a VAR model for *r_ftse*, *r_stock1*, *r_stock2* and *r_stock3* and for two lags with the use of the following command:

```
varbasic r_ftse, r_stock1, r_stock2 r_stock3 , lags(1/2)
```

The results are reported in Table 15.5. To obtain Granger causality results, after the estimation of the VAR model use the command:

```
vargranger
```

It is important to note here that this command should be executed immediately after obtaining the VAR model results, so that Stata knows which VAR model to use for the Granger causality test. The results obtained from this test are reported in Table 15.6 and are similar to those in Table 15.3. If you want to obtain pairwise test results, then the corresponding VAR model in each case should be performed first, followed by the

Table 15.5 VAR model results from Stata

Vector autoregression

Sample: 03janl990 − 22febl997		No. of obs	=	2608
Log likelihood = 29831.28		AIC	=	−22.84914
FPE = 1.40e-15		HQIC	=	−22.8198
Det(sigma_ml) = 1.36e-15		SBIC	=	−22.76816

Equation	parms	RMSE	R-sq	chi2	P>chi2
r_ftse	9	0.009373	0.0091	23.97894	0.0023
r_stockl	9	0.015196	0.0053	13.86606	0.0853
r_stock2	9	0.016105	0.0101	26.72685	0.0008
r_stock3	9	0.01828	0.0244	65.13587	0.0000

	Coef.	Std. err.	z	P>|z|	[95% conf. interval]	
r_ftse						
r_ftse						
Ll.	0.0738846	0.0195608	3.78	0.000	0.0355461	0.112223
L2.	−0.0432814	0.0195748	−2.21	0.027	−0.0816474	−0.0049154
r_stockl						
Ll.	0.0027893	0.0128777	0.22	0.829	−0.0224505	0.028029
L2.	−0.0267589	0.0128802	−2.08	0.038	−0.0520036	−0.0015143
r_stock2						
Ll.	0.0031296	0.0122359	0.26	0.798	−0.0208523	0.0271115
L2.	0.0081335	0.012247	0.66	0.507	−0.0158701	0.0321371
r_stock3						
Ll.	0.0049709	0.0108626	0.46	0.647	−0.0163194	0.0262611
L2.	0.012932	0.0108549	1.19	0.234	−0.0083432	0.0342071
_cons	0.0003672	0.0001837	2.00	0.046	7.19e−06	0.0007272
r_stockl						
r_ftse						
Ll.	0.0266341	0.031712	0.84	0.401	−0.0355204	0.0887885
L2.	−0.0194667	0.0317349	−0.61	0.540	−0.0816659	0.0427325
r_stockl						
Ll.	0.0364797	0.0208774	1.75	0.081	−0.0044392	0.0773985
L2.	−0.0285876	0.0208814	−1.37	0.171	−0.0695144	0.0123392
r_stock2						
Ll.	0.0226448	0.0198369	1.14	0.254	−0.0162348	0.0615244
L2.	0.0351782	0.0198549	1.77	0.076	−0.0037367	0.074093
r_stock3						
Ll.	0.0100071	0.0176105	0.57	0.570	−0.0245088	0.0445229
L2.	−0.0220191	0.017598	−1.25	0.211	−0.0565105	0.0124723
_cons	0.000032	0.0002978	0.11	0.914	−0.0005517	0.0006157
r_stock2						
r_ftse						
Ll.	0.0519944	0.0336099	1.55	0.122	−0.0138797	0.1178685
L2.	−0.0555804	0.033634	−1.65	0.098	−0.1215019	0.010341
r_stockl						
Ll.	0.0006448	0.0221268	0.03	0.977	−0.0427229	0.0440125
L2.	0.0558988	0.022131	2.53	0.012	0.0125228	0.0992749
r_stock2						
Ll.	0.0019564	0.021024	0.09	0.926	−0.0392499	0.0431628
L2.	−0.0150885	0.0210431	−0.72	0.473	−0.0563322	0.0261552
r_stock3						
Ll.	0.0319489	0.0186644	1.71	0.087	−0.0046325	0.0685304
L2.	−0.0739052	0.0186511	−3.96	0.000	−0.1104608	−0.0373497
_cons	0.0001665	0.0003156	0.53	0.598	−0.0004521	0.0007851

Continued

Table 15.5   Continued

r_stock3						
r_ftse						
Ll.	0.0618163	0.0381484	1.62	0.105	−0.0129532	0.1365858
L2.	−0.0058455	0.0381758	−0.15	0.878	−0.0806688	0.0689778
r_stockl						
Ll.	0.0222462	0.0251147	0.89	0.376	−0.0269777	0.0714701
L2.	0.0093423	0.0251195	0.37	0.710	−0.039891	0.0585757
r_stock2						
Ll.	−0.0300552	0.0238631	−1.26	0.208	−0.0768259	0.0167155
L2.	−0.0069142	0.0238847	−0.29	0.772	−0.0537273	0.0398989
r_stock3						
Ll.	0.1459849	0.0211847	6.89	0.000	0.1044636	0.1875062
L2.	−0.0716811	0.0211697	−3.39	0.001	−0.113173	−0.0301893
_cons	0.0005046	0.0003582	1.41	0.159	−0.0001975	0.0012068

Table 15.6   Granger causality results from stata

Equation	Excluded	chi2	df	Prob> chi2
r_ftse	r_stockl	4.3387	2	0.114
r_ftse	r_stock2	0.50782	2	0.776
r_ftse	r_stock3	1.7977	2	0.407
r_ftse	ALL	5.8109	6	0.445
r_stockl	r_ftse	1.0133	2	0.603
r_stockl	r_stock2	4.4583	2	0.108
r_stockl	r_stock3	1.7349	1	0.420
r_stockl	ALL	6.5914	6	0.360
r_stock2	r_ftse	4.7836	2	0.091
r_stock2	r_stock1	6.3918	2	0.041
r_stock2	r_stock3	17.177	2	0.000
r_stock2	ALL	24.578	6	0.000
r_stock3	r_ftse	2.6272	2	0.269
r_stock3	r_stock1	0.94498	2	0.623
r_stock3	r_stock2	1.673	2	0.433
r_stock3	ALL	4.93	2	0.553

Granger causality test. Therefore, to test for pairwise Granger causality between *r_stock1* and *r_stock2* use the following commands:

```
var r_stock1 r_stock2 , lags(1/2)
vargranger
```

We leave the rest of the cases as an exercise for the reader.

Estimating VAR models in Microfit

In Microfit, in order to estimate VAR models, first go to the **Multiple Equation Estimation Menu** by clicking on the **Multi** button. Then specify the number of lags by changing the default number in the small box to the one required for our case, and the variables for which you need to obtain VAR equations. If there are exogenous variables you want to include in the model, separate the endogenous and exogenous variables in the editor window with the '&' symbol. For this example we use the data given in the file VAR.fit. The endogenous variables you need to type in the window are:

```
r
_ftse r
_stock1 r
_stock2 r
_stock3
```

Then click **Run** and go to the **Unrestricted VAR Post Estimation Menu**. From this menu, to view the results, select option **1. Display Single Equation Estimation Results**. Microfit gives you the results equation by equation, so in the next window specify for which variable you want to see the results first and click **OK**. To see the results for the next equation, click **Close** on this result and go to option **0. Choose another equation to inspect**, and then again select option **1. Display Single Equation Estimation Results**, this time selecting the second variable, and so on.

For the Granger causality tests, Microfit does not provide the results automatically, but the results for each variable and each equation can be obtained by going first to option **2. Hypothesis Testing Menu** and then to option **5. Variable Deletion Test**. In each case, you must specify the variables you need to check for causality according to the theory developed in this chapter.

16 Non-Stationarity and Unit-Root Tests

CHAPTER CONTENTS

LEARNING OBJECTIVES

After studying this chapter you should be able to:

1. Understand the concept of stationarity.
2. Explain the differences between stationary and non-stationary time series processes.
3. Understand the importance of stationarity and the concept of spurious regressions.
4. Understand the concept of unit roots in time series.
5. Understand the meaning of the statement 'the series is integrated for order 1' or I(1).
6. Learn the Dickey–Fuller (DF) test procedure for testing for unit roots.
7. Differentiate among the three different DF models for unit-root testing.
8. Learn the Augmented Dickey–Fuller (ADF) test.
9. Learn the Philips-Perron (PP) test procedure.
10. Estimate the DF, ADF and PP tests using appropriate software.

Introduction

As we saw in Chapter 13, there are important differences between stationary and non-stationary time series. In stationary time series, shocks will be temporary, and over time their effects will be eliminated as the series revert to their long-run mean values. On the other hand, non-stationary time series will necessarily contain permanent components. Therefore, the mean and/or the variance of a non-stationary time series will depend on time, which leads to cases where a series (a) has no long-run mean to which the series returns; and (b) the variance will depend on time and will approach infinity as time goes to infinity.

We have also discussed ways of identifying non-stationary series. In general, we stated that a stationary series will follow a theoretical correlogram that will die out quickly as the lag length increases, while the theoretical correlogram of a non-stationary time series will not die out (diminish or tend to zero) for increasing lag length. However, this method is bound to be imprecise because a near unit-root process will have the same shape of autocorrelation function (ACF) as a real unit-root process. Thus, what might appear to be a unit root for one researcher may appear as a stationary process for another.

The point of this discussion is that formal tests for identifying non-stationarity (or, put differently, the presence of unit roots) are needed. The next section explains what a unit root is and discusses the problems regarding the existence of unit roots in regression models. Formal tests are then presented for the existence of unit roots, followed by a discussion of how results for the above tests can be obtained using EViews, Microfit and Stata. Finally, results are presented from applications on various macroeconomic variables.

Unit roots and spurious regressions

What is a unit root?

Consider the AR(1) model:

$$y_t = \phi y_{t-1} + e_t \tag{16.1}$$

where e_t is a white-noise process and the stationarity condition is $|\phi| < 1$.

In general, there are three possible cases:

Case 1 $|\phi| < 1$ and therefore the series is stationary. A graph of a stationary series for $\phi = 0.67$ is presented in Figure 16.1.

Case 2 $|\phi| > 1$ where the series explodes. A graph of a series for $\phi = 1.26$ is given in Figure 16.2.

Case 3 $\phi = 1$ where the series contains a unit root and is non-stationary. A graph of a series for $\phi = 1$ is given in Figure 16.3.

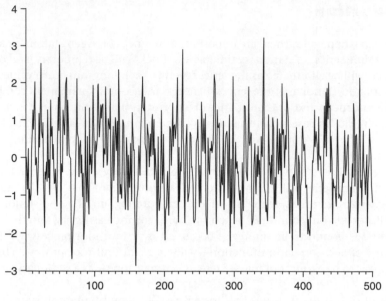

Figure 16.1   Plot of a stationary AR(1) model

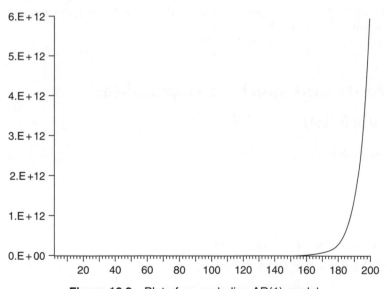

Figure 16.2   Plot of an exploding AR(1) model

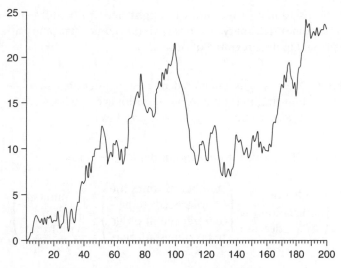

Figure 16.3 Plot of a non-stationary AR(1) model

To reproduce the graphs and the series that are stationary, exploding and non-stationary, type the following commands into EViews (or in a program file and run the program):

```
smpl @first @first+1
genr y=0
genr x=0
genr z=0
smpl @first+1 @last
genr z=0.67*z(-1)+nrnd
genr y=1.16*y(-1)+nrnd
genr x=x(-1)+nrnd
plot y
plot x
plot z
```

So if $\phi = 1$, then y_t contains a unit root. Having $\phi = 1$ and subtracting y_{t-1} from both sides of Equation (16.1) we get:

$$y_t - y_{t-1} = y_{t-1} - y_{t-1} + e_t$$
$$\Delta y_t = e_t \tag{16.2}$$

and because e_t is a white-noise process, so Δy_t is a stationary series. Therefore, after differencing y_t we obtain stationarity.

Definition 1 A series y_t is integrated of order one (denoted by $y_t \sim I(1)$) and contains a unit root if y_t is non-stationary but Δy_t is stationary.

In general, a non-stationary time series y_t might need to be differenced more than once before it becomes stationary. A series y_t that becomes stationary after d numbers of differences is said to be integrated of order d.

> **Definition 2** A series y_t is integrated of order d (denoted by $y_t \sim I(d)$) if y_t is non-stationary but $\Delta^d y_t$ is stationary; where $\Delta y_t = y_t - y_{t-1}$ and $\Delta^2 y_t = \Delta(\Delta y_t) = \Delta y_t - \Delta y_{t-1}$ and so on.

We can summarize the above information under a general rule:

$$\begin{pmatrix} \text{order of} \\ \text{integration} \\ \text{of a series} \end{pmatrix} \equiv \begin{pmatrix} \text{number of times the} \\ \text{series needs to be} \\ \text{differenced in order} \\ \text{to become stationary} \end{pmatrix} \equiv \begin{pmatrix} \text{number} \\ \text{of} \\ \text{unit roots} \end{pmatrix}$$

Spurious regressions

Most macroeconomic time series are trended and therefore in most cases are non-stationary (see, for example, time plots of the GDP, money supply and CPI for the UK economy). The problem with non-stationary or trended data is that the standard OLS regression procedures can easily lead to incorrect conclusions. It can be shown that in these cases the norm is to get very high values of R^2 (sometimes even higher than 0.95) and very high values of t-ratios (sometimes even greater than 4) while the variables used in the analysis have no interrelationships.

Many economic series typically have an underlying rate of growth, which may or may not be constant; for example, GDP, prices or the money supply all tend to grow at a regular annual rate. Such series are not stationary as the mean is continually rising; however, they are also not integrated, as no amount of differencing can make them stationary. This gives rise to one of the main reasons for taking the logarithm of data before subjecting it to formal econometric analysis. If we take the log of a series, which exhibits an average growth rate, we shall turn it into a series that follows a linear trend and is integrated. This can easily be seen formally. Suppose we have a series x, which increases by 10% every period, thus:

$$x_t = 1.1 x_{t-1}$$

Taking the log of this, we get:

$$\log(x_t) = \log(1.1) + \log(x_{t-1})$$

Now the lagged dependent variable has a unit coefficient and in each period it increases by an absolute amount equal to $\log(1.1)$, which is, of course, constant. This series would now be $I(1)$.

More formally, consider the model:

$$y_t = \beta_1 + \beta_2 x_t + u_t \tag{16.3}$$

where u_t is the error term. The assumptions of the CLRM require both y_t and x_t to have a zero and constant variance (that is, to be stationary). In the presence of non-stationarity, the results obtained from a regression of this kind are totally spurious (using the expression introduced by Granger and Newbold, 1974) therefore these regressions are called spurious regressions.

The intuition behind this is quite simple. Over time we expect any non-stationary series to wander around, as in Figure 16.3, so over any reasonably long sample the series will drift either up or down. If we then consider two completely unrelated series that are both non-stationary, we would expect that either both will go up or down together, or one will go up while the other goes down. If we then performed a regression of one series on the other we would find either a significant positive relationship if they are going in the same direction or a significant negative one if they are going in opposite directions, even though in fact both are unrelated. This is the essence of a spurious regression.

A spurious regression usually has a very high R^2 and t-statistics that appear to provide significant estimates, but the results may have no economic meaning at all. This is because the OLS estimates may not be consistent, and therefore the tests for statistical inference are not valid.

Granger and Newbold (1974) constructed a Monte Carlo analysis generating a large number of y_t and x_t series containing unit roots following the formulae:

$$y_t = y_{t-1} + e_{yt} \tag{16.4}$$

$$x_t = x_{t-1} + e_{xt} \tag{16.5}$$

where e_{yt} and e_{xt} are artificially generated normal random numbers.

Since y_t and x_t are independent of each other, any regression between them should give insignificant results. However, when Granger and Newbold regressed the various y_ts to the x_ts, as shown in Equation (16.3), they were surprised to find that they were unable to reject the null hypothesis of $\beta_2 = 0$ for approximately 75% of their cases. They also found that their regressions had very high R^2s and very low values of DW statistics.

To see the spurious regression problem, we can type the following commands into EViews (or into a program file and run the file several times) to see how many times the null of $\beta_2 = 0$ can be rejected. The commands are:

```
smpl @first @first+1
genr y=0
genr x=0
smpl @first+1 @last
genr y=y(-1)+nrnd
genr x=x(-1)+nrnd
scat(r) y x
smpl @first @last
ls y c x
```

An example of a scatter plot of y against x obtained in this way is shown in Figure 16.4. The estimated equation is:

$$y_t = -1.042 - 0.576x_t; \quad R^2 = 0.316; \quad DW = 0.118$$

$$(-1.743)(-9.572)$$

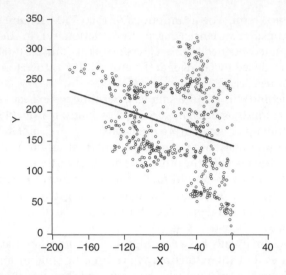

Figure 16.4   Scatter plot of a spurious regression example

Granger and Newbold (1974) proposed the following 'rule of thumb' for detecting spurious regressions: if $R^2 > DW$ statistic or if $R^2 \simeq 1$, then the regression 'must' be spurious.

To understand the problem of spurious regression better, it might be useful to use an example with real economic data. Consider a regression of the logarithm of real GDP (y) to the logarithm of real money supply (m) and a constant. The results obtained from such a regression are the following:

$$y_t = 0.042 + 0.453 m_t; \quad R^2 = 0.945; \quad DW = 0.221$$

$$\quad (4.743) \ (8.572)$$

Here we see very good t-ratios, with coefficients that have the right signs and more or less plausible magnitudes. The coefficient of determination is very high ($R^2 = 0.945$), but there is also a high degree of autocorrelation ($DW = 0.221$). This indicates the possible existence of spurious regression. In fact, this regression is totally meaningless because the money supply data are for the UK economy and the GDP figures are for the US economy. Therefore, while there should not be any significant relationship, the regression seems to fit the data very well, and this happens because the variables used in this example are, simply, trended (non-stationary).

So, the final point is that econometricians should be very careful when working with trended variables.

Explanation of the spurious regression problem

To put this in a slightly more formal way, the source of the spurious regression problem arises if two variables, x and y, are both stationary; then in general any linear combination of them will certainly also be stationary. One important linear combination of them is, of course, the equations error, and so if both variables are stationary the error in the equation will also be stationary and have a well-behaved distribution. However, when the variables become non-stationary then, of course, there is no guarantee that the errors will be stationary. In fact, as a general rule (although not always), the error itself becomes non-stationary, and when this happens the basic assumptions of OLS are violated. If the errors were non-stationary we would expect them to wander around and eventually become large. But OLS, because it selects the parameters to make the sum of the squared errors as small as possible, will select any parameter that gives the smallest error and so almost any parameter value can result.

The simplest way to examine the behaviour of u_t is to rewrite Equation (16.3) as

$$u_t = y_t - \beta_1 - \beta_2 x_t \tag{16.6}$$

or, excluding the constant β_1 (which only affects the u_t sequence, by shifting its mean):

$$u_t = y_t - \beta_2 x_t \tag{16.7}$$

If y_t and x_t are generated by Equations (16.4) and (16.5), with the initial conditions $y_0 = x_0 = 0$, we obtain:

$$u_t = \sum_{i=1}^{t} e_{yi} - \beta_2 \sum_{i=1}^{t} e_{xi} \tag{16.8}$$

Explanation of Equation (16.8)

This result comes from the solution by iteration of the difference equations given in Equations (16.4) and (16.5). Consider the solution only for y. Since:

$$y_1 = y_0 + e_{y1}$$

then for y_2 we shall have:

$$y_2 = y_1 + e_{y2} = y_0 + e_{y1} + e_{y2}$$

Continuing the process for y_3:

$$y_3 = y_2 + e_{y3} = y_0 + e_{y1} + e_{y2} + e_{y3}$$

and if the procedure is repeated t times we finally have that:

$$y_t = y_0 + \sum_{i=1}^{t} e_{yi}$$

The same holds for x_t.

From Equation (16.8) we see that the variance of the error term will tend to become infinitely large as t increases. Moreover, the error term has a permanent component in that $E_t e_{t+1} = e_t$ for all $i > 0$. Hence the assumptions of the CLRM are violated, and therefore any t-test, F-test or R^2 values are unreliable.

In terms of Equation (16.3) there are four different cases to discuss:

Case 1   Both y_t and x_t are stationary and the CLRM is appropriate, with OLS estimates being BLU.

Case 2 y_t and x_t are integrated of different orders. In this case the regression equations are meaningless. Consider, for example, the case where x_t now follows the stationary process $x_t = \phi x_{t-1} + e_{xt}$ with $|\phi| < 1$. Then Equation (16.8) is now $u_t = \sum e_{yi} - \beta_2 \sum \phi^i e_{xt-i}$. While the expression $\sum_{i=1}^{t} \phi^i e_{xt-i}$ is convergent, the e_t sequence still contains a trend component.

Case 3 y_t and x_t are integrated of the same order and the u_t sequence contains a stochastic trend. In this case we have spurious regressions and it is often recommended to re-estimate the regression equation in first differences or to respecify it.

Case 4 y_t and x_t are integrated of the same order and the u_t sequence is stationary. In this special case, y_t and x_t are said to be cointegrated. Cointegration will be examined in detail in the next chapter. For now it is sufficient to know that testing for non-stationarity is extremely important, because regressions in the form of Equation (16.3) are meaningless if cases 2 and 3 apply.

Testing for unit roots

Testing for the order of integration

A test for the order of integration is a test for the number of unit roots, and follows these steps:

Step 1   Test y_t to see if it is stationary. If yes, then $y_t \sim I(0)$; if no, then $y_t \sim I(n); n > 0$.

Step 2   Take first differences of y_t as $\Delta y_t = y_t - y_{t-1}$, and test Δy_t to see if it is stationary. If yes, then $y_t \sim I(1)$; if no, then $y_t \sim I(n); n > 0$.

Step 3   Take second differences of y_t as $\Delta^2 y_t = \Delta y_t - \Delta y_{t-1}$, and test $\Delta^2 y_t$ to see if it is stationary. If yes, then $y_t \sim I(2)$; if no, then $y_t \sim I(n); n > 0$ and so on until it is found to be stationary, and then stop. So, for example, if $\Delta^3 y_t \sim I(0)$, then $\Delta^2 y_t \sim I(1)$, and $\Delta y_t \sim I(2)$, and finally $y_t \sim I(3)$; which means that y_t needs to be differenced three times to become stationary.

The simple Dickey–Fuller (DF) test for unit roots

Dickey and Fuller (1979, 1981) devised a formal procedure to test for non-stationarity. The key insight of their test is that testing for non-stationarity is equivalent to testing for the existence of a unit root. Thus the obvious test is the following, which is based on the simple AR(1) model of the form:

$$y_t = \phi y_{t-1} + u_t \tag{16.9}$$

What we need to examine here is whether ϕ is equal to 1 (unity and hence 'unit root'). Obviously, the null hypothesis H_0: $\phi = 1$, and the alternative hypothesis H_1: $\phi < 1$.

A different (more convenient) version of the test can be obtained by subtracting y_{t-1} from both sides of Equation (16.9):

$$y_t - y_{t-1} = (\phi - 1)y_{t-1} + u_t$$
$$\Delta y_t = (\phi - 1)y_{t-1} + u_t$$
$$\Delta y_t = \gamma y_{t-1} + u_t \tag{16.10}$$

where of course $\gamma = (\phi - 1)$. Now the null hypothesis is H_0: $\gamma = 0$ and the alternative hypothesis H_a: $\gamma < 0$, where if $\gamma = 0$ then y_t follows a pure random-walk model.

Dickey and Fuller (1979) also proposed two alternative regression equations that can be used for testing for the presence of a unit root. The first contains a constant in the random-walk process, as in the following equation:

$$\Delta y_t = \alpha_0 + \gamma y_{t-1} + u_t \tag{16.11}$$

This is an extremely important case, because such processes exhibit a definite trend in the series when $\gamma = 0$ (as we illustrated in Chapter 13), which is often the case for macroeconomic variables.

The second case is also to allow a non-stochastic time trend in the model, to obtain:

$$\Delta y_t = \alpha_0 + a_2 t + \gamma y_{t-1} + u_t \tag{16.12}$$

The DF test for stationarity is then simply the normal t-test on the coefficient of the lagged dependent variable y_{t-1} from one of the three models (Equations (16.10), (16.11) or (16.12)). This test does not, however, have a conventional t-distribution and so we must use special critical values originally calculated by Dickey and Fuller.

MacKinnon (1991) tabulated appropriate critical values for each of the three models discussed above and these are presented in Table 16.1.

In all cases, the test focuses on whether $\gamma = 0$. The DF test statistic is the t-statistic for the lagged dependent variable. If the DF statistical value is smaller than the

Table 16.1 Critical values for the Dickey–Fuller test

Model	1%	5%	10%
$\Delta y_{t-1} = \gamma y_{t-1} + u_t$	−2.56	−1.94	−1.62
$\Delta y_{t-1} = \alpha_0 + \gamma y_{t-1} + u_t$	−3.43	−2.86	−2.57
$\Delta y_{t-1} = \alpha_0 + a_2 t + \gamma y_{t-1} + u_t$	−3.96	−3.41	−3.13
Standard critical values	−2.33	−1.65	−1.28

Note: Critical values are taken from MacKinnon (1991).

critical value then the null hypothesis of a unit root is rejected and we conclude that y_t is a stationary process.

The augmented Dickey–Fuller (ADF) test for unit roots

As the error term is unlikely to be white noise, Dickey and Fuller extended their test procedure by suggesting an augmented version of the test that includes extra lagged terms of the dependent variable in order to eliminate autocorrelation. The lag length on these extra terms is either determined by the Akaike information criterion (AIC) or the Schwartz Bayesian criterion (SBC), or more usefully by the lag length necessary to whiten the residuals (that is after each case we check whether the residuals of the ADF regression are autocorrelated or not through LM tests rather than the DW test).

The three possible forms of the ADF test are given by the following equations:

$$\Delta y_t = \gamma y_{t-1} + \sum_{i=1}^{p} \beta_i \Delta y_{t-i} + u_t \tag{16.13}$$

$$\Delta y_t = \alpha_0 + \gamma y_{t-1} + \sum_{i=1}^{p} \beta_i \Delta y_{t-i} + u_t \tag{16.14}$$

$$\Delta y_t = a_0 + \gamma y_{t-1} + a_2 t + \sum_{i=1}^{p} \beta_i \Delta y_{t-i} + u_t \tag{16.15}$$

The difference between the three regressions again concerns the presence of the deterministic elements a_0 and $a_2 t$. The critical values for the ADF tests are the same as those given in Table 16.1 for the DF test.

Unless the econometrician knows the actual data-generating process, there is a question concerning whether it is most appropriate to estimate Equations (16.13), (16.14) or (16.15). Doldado *et al.* (1990) suggest a procedure which starts from the estimation of the most general model given by Equation (16.15), answering a set of questions regarding the appropriateness of each model and then moving to the next model. This procedure is illustrated in Figure 16.5. It needs to be stressed here that, despite being useful, this procedure is not designed to be applied in a mechanical fashion. Plotting the data and observing the graph is sometimes very useful because it can indicate clearly the presence or not of deterministic regressors. However, this procedure is the most sensible way to test for unit roots when the form of the data-generating process is unknown.

The Phillips–Perron (PP) test

The distribution theory supporting the DF and ADF tests is based on the assumption that the error terms are statistically independent and have a constant variance. So, when using the ADF methodology, one has to make sure that the error terms are uncorrelated and that they really do have a constant variance. Phillips and Perron (1988) developed a generalization of the ADF test procedure that allows for fairly mild

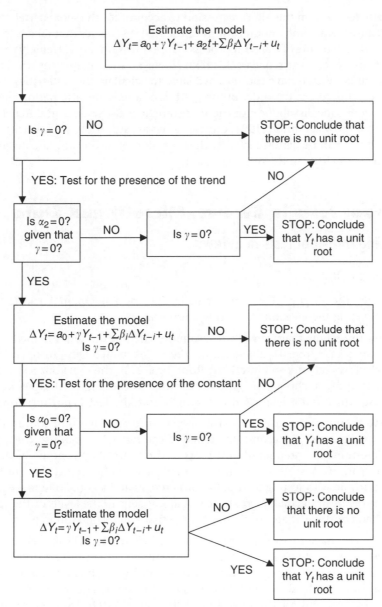

Figure 16.5 Procedure for testing for unit-root tests

Source: Enders (1995).

assumptions concerning the distribution of errors. The test regression for the PP test is the AR(1) process:

$$\Delta y_{t-1} = \alpha_0 + \gamma y_{t-1} + e_t \qquad (16.16)$$

While the ADF test corrects for higher-order serial correlation by adding lagged differenced terms on the right-hand side, the PP test makes a correction to the *t*-statistic of the coefficient γ from the AR(1) regression to account for the serial correlation in e_t. So the PP statistics are only modifications of the ADF t-statistics that take into account the less restrictive nature of the error process. The expressions are extremely complex to derive and are beyond the scope of this text. However, since many statistical packages (one of them is EViews) have routines available to calculate these statistics, it is good for the researcher to test the order of integration of a series by also performing the PP test. The asymptotic distribution of the PP t-statistic is the same as the ADF t-statistic and therefore the MacKinnon (1991) critical values are still applicable. As with the ADF test, the PP test can be performed with the inclusion of a constant, a constant and a linear trend, or neither in the test regression.

Unit-root tests in EViews, Microfit and Stata

Performing unit-root tests in EViews

The DF and ADF test

Step 1   Open the file gdp_uk.wf1 in EViews by clicking **File/Open/Workfile** and then choosing the file name from the appropriate path.

Step 2   Let us assume that we want to examine whether the series named GDP contains a unit root. Double-click on the series named 'gdp' to open the series window and choose **View/Unit-Root Test** ... In the unit-root test dialog box that appears, choose the type of test (that is the **Augmented Dickey–Fuller** test, which is the default) by choosing it from the **Test Type** drop-down menu.

Step 3   We then have to specify whether we want to test for a unit root in the level, first difference or second difference of the series. We can use this option to determine the number of unit roots in the series. As was noted in the theory section, we first start with the level and if we fail to reject the test there we continue with testing for the first differences and so on. So here we first click on **levels** in the dialog box to see what happens in the levels of the series and then continue, if appropriate, with the first and second differences.

Step 4   We also have to specify which model of the three ADF models we wish to use (that is whether to include a constant, a constant and a linear trend, or neither in the test regression). For the model given by Equation (16.13) click on **none** in the dialog box; for the model given by Equation (16.14) click on **intercept**; and for the model given by Equation (16.15) click on **intercept and trend**. The choice of the model is very important, since the distribution of the test statistic under the null hypothesis differs among these three cases.

Step 5   Finally, we have to specify the number of lagged dependent variables to be included in the model – or the number of augmented terms – to correct for the presence of serial correlation. EViews provides two choices: one is **User Specified**, which is used only in the event that we want to test for a predetermined specific lag length. If this is the case, we choose this option and enter the number of lags in the box next to it. The second choice is **Automatic Selection**, which is the default in EViews. If this option is chosen we need to specify from a drop-down menu the criterion we want EViews to use to find the optimal lag length. We have discussed the theory of the AIC and SBC criteria, which are referred to as the **Akaike Info Criterion** and the **Schwarz Info Criterion**, respectively, in EViews. We recommend choosing one of the two criteria before going on to the next step. EViews will present the results only for the optimal lag length determined from the criterion you have chosen.

Step 6 Having specified these options, click **OK** to carry out the test. EViews reports the test statistic together with the estimated test regression.

Step 7 We reject the null hypothesis of a unit root against the one-sided alternative if the ADF-statistic is less than (lies to the left of) the critical value, and conclude that the series is stationary.

Step 8 After running a unit-root test researchers should examine the estimated test regression reported by EViews, especially if unsure about the lag structure or deterministic trend in the series. You may want to rerun the test equation with a different selection of right-hand variables (add or delete the constant, trend or lagged differences) or lag order.

The PP test

Step 1 Open the file 'pp.wf1' in EViews by clicking **File/Open/Workfile** and then choosing the file name from the appropriate path.

Step 2 Let us assume that we want to examine whether the series GDP contains a unit root. Double-click on the series named *gdp* to open the series window and choose **View/Unit-Root Test** … In the unit-root test dialog box that appears, choose the type of test (that is the **Phillips–Perron** test) by selecting it from the **Test Type** drop-down menu.

Step 3 We then have to specify whether we want to test for a unit root in the level, first difference or second difference of the series. We can use this option to determine the number of unit roots in the series. As was stated in the theory section, first start with the level and if the test is not rejected in the level continue with testing for the first differences and so on. So here we first click on **levels** to see what happens in the levels of the series, and then continue, if appropriate, with the first and second differences.

Step 4 We also have to specify which model of the three to be used (that is whether to include a constant, a constant and a linear trend or neither in the test regression). For the random-walk model, click on **none** in the dialog box; for the random walk with drift model click on **intercept**; and for the random walk with drift and with deterministic trend model click on **intercept and trend**.

Step 5 Finally, for the PP test specify the lag truncation to compute the Newey–West heteroskedasticity and autocorrelation (HAC) consistent estimate of the spectrum at zero frequency.

Step 6 Having specified these options, click **OK** to carry out the test. EViews reports the test statistic together with the estimated test regression.

Step 7   We reject the null hypothesis of a unit root against the one-sided alternative if the ADF-statistic is less than (lies to the left of) the critical value.

Performing unit-root tests in Microfit

The DF and ADF test

Step 1   Open the file 'exdaily.fit' in Microfit by clicking **File/Open** and choosing the file name from the appropriate path.

Step 2   Let us assume that we want to examine whether the series named EUS (which is the US/UK exchange rate) contains a unit root. In the **process** editor, type:

```
ADF EUS(12)
```

where the number in parentheses specifies the maximum number of lagged dependent variables we want our model to include. Click **GO**.

Step 3   Microfit presents two alternative panels of results. The first is for a model that includes an intercept but not a trend, which is the model given by Equation (16.14). The second panel gives results for a model that includes both an intercept and a trend, which is the same as that given by Equation (16.15). Microfit does not give results for the first model that does not include either an intercept or a trend.

Step 4   The reported results include DF and ADF statistics for $0, 1, 2, \ldots, 12$ lags. These are statistical values for 13 different cases depending on the number of lags included in each case. Apart from the DF and ADF test statistics, we also have results for the AIC and SBC. We can use these two criteria to specify the appropriate number of lags to be included by minimizing both AIC and SBC. If they contradict, usually the SBC is preferable.

Step 5   Having specified which model is appropriate to examine according to the lag structure, we then reject the null hypothesis of a unit root against the one-sided alternative if the DF/ADF-statistic is less than (lies to the left of) the critical value, which is also reported by Microfit under each panel of results.

Note that while Microfit provides, very conveniently and quickly, results for 13 different cases of different numbers of lagged dependent variables (to do that in EViews we have to repeat the procedure 13 times, each time specifying a different number of lags), Microfit does not give us any details about the regression equation estimated in order to obtain those statistics. It is something like a black box in terms of information regarding the equation, and therefore in some cases where we may suspect a close unit root it might be preferable to obtain the test manually by running each regression model in the **single** editor.

In case we need to do that, we first have to define the new variable Δeus_t by typing in the **process** editor:

```
deus=eus-eus(-1)
```

and then going to the **single** editor and specifying the regression by typing:

```
deus c eus(-1) deus{1-4}
```

which will give us a *t*-statistic for *eus*(−1) that will be equivalent to the ADF(4) statistic for the previous test.

There is no standard procedure for performing the PP test in Microfit.

Performing unit-root tests in Stata

The DF and ADF test

In Stata, the command for the DF or ADF test for unit roots has the following syntax:

```
dfuller varname , options
```

where for `varname` in each case we type the name of the variable we want to test for order of integration. In the **options** we can specify the ADF type model to be estimated together with the number of lags for the augmentation (note that if we want to estimate the simple DF model we choose to set the lag equal to 0). It is easier to understand this through an example. The data are given in file gdp_uk.dat, which contains quarterly data for the log of the UK GDP (*lgdp*) series.

First, we estimate the model in Equation (16.3), which does not include constant and trend. The command is:

```
dfuller lgdp , regress noconstant lags(2)
```

The option `noconstant` defines the model as Equation (16.3), the option `regress` is to enable Stata to report the regression results together with the ADF-statistic, and the option `lags(2)` determines the number of lagged dependent variables to be included in the model. If we want to re-estimate the model for four lagged dependent variable terms, the command is:

```
dfuller lgdp , regress noconstant lags(4)
```

Continuing, assuming always that the lag length is 2, in order to estimate the ADF-statistic for the model in Equation (16.4) – with constant but no trend – the command is:

```
dfuller lgdp , regress lags(2)
```

Finally, for the model in Equation (16.5) – with constant and trend – the command is:

```
dfuller lgdp , regress trend lags(2)
```

If we conclude that the variable *lgdp* contains unit roots, then we need to reperform all tests for the variable in its first differences. This can easily be done in Stata with the difference operator (D). Therefore the commands for all three models, respectively, are:

```
dfuller D.lgdp , regress noconstant lags(2)
dfuller D.lgdp , regress lags(2)
dfuller D.lgdp , regress trend lags(2)
```

If we want to further difference the data to make them stationary, then second differences are required, and the commands change to:

```
dfuller D2.lgdp , regress noconstant lags(2)
dfuller D2.lgdp , regress lags(2)
dfuller D2.lgdp , regress trend lags(2)
```

and so on.

The PP test

The case of the PP test for unit roots is similar. The command is:

```
pperron varname , options
```

and, for the example we examined above:

```
pperron lgdp , regress noconstant lags(2)
```

which is the command for the model without constant and trend. Then:

```
pperron lgdp , regress lags(2)
```

is the command for the model that includes a constant but not a trend, and finally the command:

```
pperron lgdp , regress trend lags(2)
```

is for the model that includes both constant and trend. The difference operator can be used for conducting the test in first, second or even higher differences.

Computer example: unit-root tests on various macroeconomic variables

The data used in this example (see the file unionization.wf1) are drawn mainly from *International Historical Statistics* (Mitchell (1998)), where data on trade union membership, employment, unemployment rates, population, wages, prices, industrial production and GDP are available for most of the period between 1892 and 1997. We have also used some other sources (for example various issues of *Employment Gazette*, *Labour Market Trends* and OECD *Main Economic Indicators*) to amend and assure the quality of the data. (Data on capital stock were derived from the gross fixed capital formation series, assuming a rate of depreciation of 10% per year. The capital stock series is a little sensitive with respect to the initial value assumed, and for the period 1950–90 is highly correlated ($r = 0.9978$) with the UK capital stock series constructed by Nehru

Table 16.2 ADF test results

Model: $\Delta y_t = c_1 + by_{t-1} + c_2 t + \sum_{k=1}^{p} d_k \Delta y_{t-k} + v_t; H_0: b = 0; H_a: b > 0$

Unit-root tests at logarithmic levels

Variables	Constant	Constant and trend	None	k
GDP per capita (y/l)	−0.905	−2.799	−0.789	4
Unionization rate (TUD)	−1.967	−1.246	−0.148	4
Unemployment (Un)	−2.435	−2.426	−1.220	4
Wages (w)	−1.600	−1.114	−3.087*	4
Employment (l)	−1.436	−2.050	−1.854	4
Capital/labour (k/l)	−0.474	−2.508	2.161*	4

Unit-root tests at first differences

Variables	Constant	Constant and trend	None	k
GDP per capita (Δ)(y/l)	−6.163*	−6.167*	−6.088*	4
Unionization rate (ΔTUD)	−3.102*	−3.425*	−3.086*	4
Unemployment (ΔUn)	−4.283	−4.223	−4.305*	4
Wages (Δw)	−3.294*	−3.854*	—	4
Employment (Δl)	−4.572*	−4.598*	−4.115*	4
Capital/labour (Δ(k/l))	−3.814*	−3.787*	—	4

Notes: * Denotes significance at the 5% level and the rejection of the null hypothesis of non-stationarity. Critical values obtained from Fuller (1976) are −2.88, −3.45 and −1.94 for the first, second and third models, respectively. The optimal lag lengths k were chosen according to Akaike's FPE test.

and Dhareshwar, 1993.) Our aim is to apply tests that will determine the order of integration of the variables. We shall apply two asymptotically equivalent tests: the ADF test and the PP test.

We begin the ADF test procedure by examining the optimal lag length using Akaike's Final Prediction Error (FPE) criteria, before proceeding to identify the probable order of stationarity. The results of the tests for all the variables and for the three alternative models are presented in Table 16.2, first for their logarithmic levels (the unemployment and unionization rate variables are not logarithmed as they are expressed in percentages) and then (in cases where we found that the series contain a unit root) for their first differences and so on. The results indicate that each of the series is non-stationary when the variables are defined in levels. First differencing the series removes the non-stationary components in all cases and the null hypothesis of non-stationarity is clearly rejected at the 5% significance level, suggesting that all our variables are integrated of order one, as was expected. (There is an exception for the more restricted model and for the wages and capital/labour variables, where the tests indicate that they are I(0). However, the robustness of the two first models allows us to treat the variables as I(1) and proceed with cointegration analysis.)

The results of the PP tests are reported in Table 16.3, and are not fundamentally different from the respective ADF results. (The lag truncations for the Bartlett kernel were chosen according to Newey and West's (1987) suggestions.) Analytically, the results from the tests in the levels of the variables clearly point to the presence of a unit root in all cases. The results after first differencing the series robustly reject the null hypothesis of the presence of a unit root, suggesting therefore that the series are integrated of order one.

Table 16.3   PP test results

Model: $\Delta y_t = \mu + \rho y_{t-1} + \varepsilon_t$; H_0: $\rho = 0$; H_a: $\rho > 0$

Unit-root tests at logarithmic levels

Variables	Constant	Constant and trend	k
GDP per capita (y, l)	−2.410	−2.851	4
Unionization rate (TUD)	−1.770	−0.605	4
Unemployment (Un)	−2.537	−2.548	4
Wages (w)	2.310	−0.987	4
Employment (l)	−1.779	−2.257	4
Capital/labour (k/l)	−0.199	−2.451	4

Unit-root tests at first differences

Variables	Constant	Constant and trend	k
GDP per capita ($\Delta(y/l)$)	−11.107*	−11.050*	4
Unionization rate (ΔTUD)	−5.476*	−5.637*	4
Unemployment (ΔUn)	−8.863*	−8.824*	4
Wages (Δw)	−4.621*	−5.071*	4
Employment (Δl)	−7.958*	−7.996*	4
Capital/labour ($\Delta(k/l)$)	−10.887*	−10.849*	4

Notes: * Denotes significance at the 5% level and the rejection of the null hypothesis of non-stationarity. Critical values obtained from Fuller (1976) are −2.88, −3.45 and −1.94 for the first, second and third models, respectively. The optimal lag lengths *k* were chosen according to Akaike's FPE test.

Computer example: unit-root tests for the financial development and economic growth example

Consider again the data we described in the computer example of the previous chapter for the Granger causality tests. Here we report results of tests for unit roots and orders of integration of all the variables (see file finance.wf1).

We begin the ADF test procedure by examining the optimal lag length using Akaike's FPE criteria; we then proceed to identify the probable order of stationarity. The results of the tests for all the variables and for the three alternative models are presented in Table 16.4, first for their logarithmic levels and then (in cases where we found that the series contain a unit root) for their first differences and so on. The results indicate that each of the series is non-stationary when the variables are defined in levels. First differencing the series removes the non-stationary components in all cases and the null hypothesis of non-stationarity is clearly rejected at the 5% significance level, suggesting that all our variables are integrated of order one, as was expected.

The results of the PP tests are reported in Table 16.5, and are not fundamentally different from the respective ADF results. (The lag truncations for the Bartlett kernel were chosen according to Newey and West's (1987) suggestions.) Analytically, the results from the tests on the levels of the variables point clearly to the presence of a unit root in all cases apart from the claims ratio, which appears to be integrated of order zero. The results after first differencing the series robustly reject the null hypothesis of the presence of a unit root, suggesting therefore that the series are integrated of order one.

Table 16.4 ADF test results

Model: $\Delta y_t = c_1 + by_{t-1} + c_2 t + \sum_{k=1}^{p} d_k \Delta y_{t-k} + v_t$; H_0: $b = 0$; H_a: $b > 0$

Unit-root tests at logarithmic levels

Variables	Constant	Constant and trend	None	k
GDP per capita (Y)	−0.379	−2.435	−3.281*	1
Monetization ratio (M)	−0.063	−1.726	1.405	4
Currency ratio (CUR)	−1.992	1.237	1.412	9
Claims ratio (CL)	−2.829	−2.758	1.111	7
Turnover ratio (T)	−1.160	−2.049	−1.84	2
Capital/labour (K)	−0.705	−2.503	−2.539*	2

Unit-root tests at first differences

Variables	Constant	Constant and trend	None	k
GDP per capita (ΔY)	−6.493*	−6.462*	—	1
Monetization ratio (ΔM)	−3.025*	−4.100*	−2.671*	4
Currency ratio (ΔCUR)	−3.833*	−4.582*	2.585*	5
Claims ratio (ΔCL)	−6.549*	−6.591*	−6.596*	3
Turnover ratio (ΔT)	−6.196*	−6.148*	−5.452*	2
Capital/labour (ΔK)	−2.908*	−3.940*	—	2

Notes: * Denotes significance at the 5% level and the rejection of the null hypothesis of non-stationarity. Critical values obtained from Fuller (1976) are −2.88, −3.45 and −1.94 for the first, second and third models, respectively. The optimal lag lengths k were chosen according to Akaike's FPE test.

Table 16.5 PP test results

Model: $\Delta y_t = \mu + \rho y_{t-1} + \varepsilon_t$; H_0: $\rho = 0$; H_a: $\rho > 0$

Unit-root tests at logarithmic levels

Variables	Constant	Constant and trend	k
GDP per capita (Y)	−0.524	−2.535	4
Monetization ratio (M)	−0.345	−1.180	4
Currency ratio (CUR)	−2.511	0.690	4
Claims ratio (CL)	−4.808*	−4.968*	4
Turnover ratio (T)	−0.550	−3.265	3
Capital/labour (K)	−1.528	−2.130	4

Unit-root tests at first differences

Variables	Constant	Constant and trend	k
GDP per capita (ΔY)	−8.649*	−8.606*	4
Monetization ratio (ΔM)	−7.316*	−7.377*	4
Currency ratio (ΔCUR)	−11.269*	−11.886*	4
Claims ratio (ΔCL)	—	—	—
Turnover ratio (ΔT)	−11.941*	−11.875*	3
Capital/labour (ΔK)	−4.380*	−4.301*	4

Notes: * Denotes significance at the 5% level and the rejection of the null hypothesis of non-stationarity. Critical values obtained from Fuller (1976) are −2.88, −3.45 and −1.94 for the first, second and third models, respectively. The optimal lag lengths k were chosen according to Akaike's FPE test.

Questions and exercises

Questions

1 Explain why it is important to test for stationarity.

2 Describe how a researcher can test for stationarity.

3 Explain the term *spurious regression* and provide an example from economic time-series data.

Exercise 16.1

The file gdp_uk.wf1 contains data for the UK GDP in quarterly frequency from 1955 to 1998. Check for the possible order of integration of the *GDP* variable using both the ADF and the PP tests and following the steps described in Figure 16.5.

Exercise 16.2

The file Korea.wf1 contains data from various macroeconomic indicators of the Korean economy. Check for the order of integration of all the variables using both the ADF and PP tests. Summarize your results in a table and comment on them.

Exercise 16.3

The file Nelson_Ploser.wf1 contains data from various macroeconomic indicators of the US economy. Check for the order of integration of all the variables using both the ADF and PP tests. Summarize your results in a table and comment on them.

17 Cointegration and Error-Correction Models

CHAPTER CONTENTS

LEARNING OBJECTIVES

After studying this chapter you should be able to:

1. Understand the concept of cointegration in time series.
2. Appreciate the importance of cointegration and long-run solutions in econometric applications.
3. Understand the error-correction mechanism and its advantages.
4. Test for cointegration using the Engle–Granger approach.
5. Test for cointegration using the Johansen approach.
6. Obtain results of cointegration tests using appropriate econometric software.
7. Estimate error-correction models using appropriate econometric software.

Introduction: what is cointegration?

Cointegration: a general approach

The main message from Chapter 16 was that trended time series can potentially create major problems in empirical econometrics because of spurious regressions. We also made the point that most macroeconomic variables are trended and therefore the spurious regression problem is highly likely to be present in most macroeconometric models. One way of resolving this is to difference the series successively until stationarity is achieved and then use the stationary series for regression analysis. However, this solution is not ideal. There are two main problems with using first differences. If the model is correctly specified as a relationship between y and x (for example) and we difference both variables, then implicitly we are also differencing the error process in the regression. This would then produce a non-invertible moving average error process and would present serious estimation difficulties. The second problem is that if we difference the variables the model can no longer give a unique long-run solution. By this we mean that if we pick a particular value for x then regardless of the initial value for y the dynamic solution for y will eventually converge on a unique value. So, for example, if $y = 0.5x$ and we set $x = 10$, then $y = 5$. But if we have the model in differences, $y_t - y_{t-1} = 0.5(x_t - x_{t-1})$ then even if we know that $x = 10$ we cannot solve for y without knowing the past value of y and x, and so the solution for y is not unique, given x. The desire to have models that combine both short-run and long-run properties, and at the same time maintain stationarity in all of the variables, has led to a reconsideration of the problem of regression using variables that are measured in their levels.

The basic idea of this chapter follows from our explanation of spurious regression in Chapter 16, and in particular Equation (16.8), which showed that if the two variables are non-stationary we can represent the error as a combination of two cumulated error processes. These cumulated error processes are often called stochastic trends and normally we would expect them to combine to produce another non-stationary process. However, in the special case that X and Y are in fact related we would expect them to move together so the two stochastic trends would be very similar. When we put them together it should be possible to find a combination of them that eliminates the non-stationarity. In this special case we say that the variables are cointegrated. In theory, this should only happen when there is truly a relationship linking the two variables, so cointegration becomes a very powerful way of detecting the presence of economic structures.

Cointegration then becomes an overriding requirement for any economic model using non-stationary time series data. If the variables do not cointegrate we have problems of spurious regression and econometric work becomes almost meaningless. On the other hand, if the stochastic trends do cancel then we have cointegration and, as we shall see later, everything works even more effectively than we previously might have thought.

The key point here is that, if there really is a genuine long-run relationship between Y_t and X_t, then despite the variables rising over time (because they are trended), there will be a common trend that links them together. For an equilibrium or long-run relationship to exist, what we require, then, is a linear combination of Y_t and X_t that is a stationary variable (an $I(0)$ variable). A linear combination of Y_t and X_t can be taken directly from estimating the following regression:

$$Y_t = \beta_1 + \beta_2 X_t + u_t \tag{17.1}$$

and taking the residuals:

$$\hat{u}_t = Y_t - \hat{\beta}_1 - \hat{\beta}_2 X_t \tag{17.2}$$

If $\hat{u}_t \sim I(0)$ then the variables Y_t and X_t are said to be cointegrated.

Cointegration: a more mathematical approach

To put it differently, consider a set of two variables $\{Y, X\}$ that are integrated of order 1 (that is $\{Y, X\} \sim I(1)$) and suppose that there is a vector $\{\theta_1, \theta_2\}$ that gives a linear combination of $\{Y, X\}$ which is stationary, denoted by:

$$\theta_1 Y_t + \theta_2 X_t = u_t \sim I(0) \tag{17.3}$$

then the variable set $\{Y, X\}$ is called the cointegration set, and the coefficients vector $\{\theta_1, \theta_2\}$ is called the cointegration vector. What we are interested in is the long-run relationship, which for Y_t is:

$$Y_t^* = \beta X_t \tag{17.4}$$

To see how this comes from the cointegration method, we can normalize Equation (17.3) for Y_t to give:

$$Y_t = -\frac{\theta_2}{\theta_1} X_t + e_t \tag{17.5}$$

where now $Y^* = -(\theta_2/\theta_1)X_t$, which can be interpreted as the long-run or equilibrium value of Y_t (conditional on the values of X_t). We shall return to this point when discussing the error-correction mechanism later in the chapter.

For bivariate economic $I(1)$ time series processes, cointegration often manifests itself by more or less parallel plots of the series involved. As noted earlier, we are interested in detecting long-run or equilibrium relationships and this is mainly what the concept of cointegration allows.

The concept of cointegration was first introduced by Granger (1981) and elaborated further by Phillips (1986, 1987), Engle and Granger (1987), Engle and Yoo (1987), Johansen (1988, 1991, 1995a), Stock and Watson (1988), Phillips and Ouliaris (1990), among others. Working in the context of a bi-variate system with at most one cointegrating vector, Engle and Granger (1987) give the formal definition of cointegration between two variables as follows:

Definition 1 Time series Y_t and X_t are said to be cointegrated of order d, b where $d \geq b \geq 0$, written as $Y_t, X_t \sim CI(d, b)$, if (a) both series are integrated of order d, and (b) there exists a linear combination of these variables, say $\beta_1 Y_t + \beta_2 X_t$ which is integrated of order $d - b$. The vector $\{\beta_1, \beta_2\}$ is called the cointegrating vector.

A straightforward generalization of the above definition can be made for the case of n variables, as follows:

Definition 2   If Z_t denotes an $n \times 1$ vector of series $Z_{1t}, Z_{2t}, Z_{3t}, \ldots, Z_{nt}$ and (a) each Z_{it} is $I(d)$; and (b) there exists an $n \times 1$ vector β such that $Z_t'\beta \sim I(d - b)$, then $Z_t \sim CI(d, b)$.

For empirical econometrics, the most interesting case is where the series transformed with the use of the cointegrating vector become stationary; that is, when $d = b$, and the cointegrating coefficients can be identified as parameters in the long-run relationship between the variables. The next sections of this chapter will deal with these cases.

Cointegration and the error-correction mechanism (ECM): a general approach

The problem

As noted earlier, when there are non-stationary variables in a regression model we may get results that are spurious. So if Y_t and X_t are both $I(1)$, if we regress:

$$Y_t = \beta_1 + \beta_2 X_t + u_t \qquad (17.6)$$

we will not generally get satisfactory estimates of $\hat{\beta}_1$ and $\hat{\beta}_2$.

One way of resolving this is to difference the data to ensure stationarity of our variables. After doing this, $\Delta Y_t \sim I(0)$ and $\Delta X_t \sim I(0)$, and the regression model will be:

$$\Delta Y_t = a_1 + a_2 \Delta X_t + \Delta u_t \qquad (17.7)$$

In this case, the regression model may give us correct estimates of the $\hat{a}_1$ and $\hat{a}_2$ parameters and the spurious equation problem has been resolved. However, what we have from Equation (17.7) is only the short-run relationship between the two variables. Remember that, in the long-run relationship:

$$Y_t^* = \beta_1 + \beta_2 X_t \qquad (17.8)$$

so ΔY_t is bound to give us no information about the long-run behaviour of our model. Knowing that economists are interested mainly in long-run relationships, this constitutes a big problem, and the concept of cointegration and the ECM are very useful to resolve this.

Cointegration (again)

We noted earlier that Y_t and X_t are both $I(1)$. In the special case that there is a linear combination of Y_t and X_t (that is, $I(0)$), then Y_t and X_t are cointegrated. Thus, if this is the case, the regression of Equation (17.6) is no longer spurious, and it also provides us with the linear combination:

$$\hat{u}_t = Y_t - \hat{\beta}_1 - \hat{\beta}_2 X_t \tag{17.9}$$

which connects Y_t and X_t in the long run.

The error-correction model (ECM)

If, then, Y_t and X_t are cointegrated, by definition $\hat{u}_t \sim I(0)$. Thus we can express the relationship between Y_t and X_t with an ECM specification as:

$$\Delta Y_t = a_0 + b_1 \Delta X_t - \pi \hat{u}_{t-1} + e_t \tag{17.10}$$

which will now have the advantage of including both long-run and short-run information. In this model, b_1 is the impact multiplier (the short-run effect) that measures the immediate impact a change in X_t will have on a change in Y_t. On the other hand, π is the feedback effect, or the adjustment effect, and shows how much of the disequilibrium is being corrected – that is the extent to which any disequilibrium in the previous period affects any adjustment in Y_t. Of course $\hat{u}_{t-1} = Y_{t-1} - \hat{\beta}_1 - \hat{\beta}_2 X_{t-1}$, and therefore from this equation β_2 is also the long-run response (note that it is estimated by Equation (17.7)).

Equation (17.10) now emphasizes the basic approach of the cointegration and error-correction models. The spurious regression problem arises because we are using non-stationary data, but in Equation (17.10) everything is stationary, the change in X and Y is stationary because they are assumed to be $I(1)$ variables, and the residual from the levels regression (17.9) is also stationary, by the assumption of cointegration. So Equation (17.10) fully conforms to our set of assumptions about the classic linear regression model and OLS should perform well.

Advantages of the ECM

The ECM is important and popular for many reasons:

1 First, it is a convenient model measuring the correction from disequilibrium of the previous period, which has a very good economic implication.

2 Second, if we have cointegration, ECMs are formulated in terms of first differences, which typically eliminate trends from the variables involved, and they resolve the problem of spurious regressions.

3 A third, very important, advantage of ECMs is the ease with which they can fit into the general to specific approach to econometric modelling, which is in fact a search for the most parsimonious ECM model that best fits the given data sets.

4 Finally, the fourth and most important feature of the ECM comes from the fact that the disequilibrium error term is a stationary variable (by definition of cointegration). Because of this, the ECM has important implications: the fact that the two variables are cointegrated implies that there is some adjustment process preventing the errors in the long-run relationship from becoming larger and larger.

Cointegration and the error-correction mechanism: a more mathematical approach

A simple model for only one lagged term of X and Y

The concepts of cointegration and the error-correction mechanism (ECM) are very closely related. To understand the ECM it is better to think of it first as a convenient reparametrization of the general linear autoregressive distributed lag (ARDL) model.

Consider the very simple dynamic ARDL model describing the behaviour of Y in terms of X, as follows:

$$Y_t = a_0 + a_1 Y_{t-1} + \gamma_0 X_t + \gamma_1 X_{t-1} + u_t \qquad (17.11)$$

where the residual $u_t \sim iid(0, \sigma^2)$.

In this model the parameter γ_0 denotes the short-run reaction of Y_t after a change in X_t. The long-run effect is given when the model is in equilibrium, where:

$$Y_t^* = \beta_0 + \beta_1 X_t^* \qquad (17.12)$$

and for simplicity assume that

$$X_t^* = X_t = X_{t-1} = \cdots = X_{t-p} \qquad (17.13)$$

Thus, it is given by:

$$Y_t^* = a_0 + a_1 Y_t^* + \gamma_0 X_t^* + \gamma_1 X_t^* + u_t$$
$$Y_t^*(1 - a_1) = a_0 + (\gamma_0 + \gamma_1) X_t^* + u_t$$
$$Y_t^* = \frac{a_0}{1 - a_1} + \frac{\gamma_0 + \gamma_1}{1 - a_1} X_t^* + u_t$$
$$Y_t^* = \beta_0 + \beta_1 X_t^* + u_t \qquad (17.14)$$

So the long-run elasticity between Y and X is captured by $\beta_1 = (\gamma_0 + \gamma_1)/(1 - a_1)$. Here, we need to make the assumption that $a_1 < 1$ so that the short-run model in Equation (17.11) converges to a long-run solution.

We can then derive the ECM, which is a reparametrization of the original Equation (17.11) model:

$$\Delta Y_t = \gamma_0 \Delta X_t - (1 - a)[Y_{t-1} - \beta_0 - \beta_1 X_{t-1}] + u_t \tag{17.15}$$

$$\Delta Y_t = \gamma_0 \Delta X_t - \pi[Y_{t-1} - \beta_0 - \beta_1 X_{t-1}] + u_t \tag{17.16}$$

Proof that the ECM is a reparametrization of the ARDL

To show that this is the same as the original model, substitute the long-run solutions for $\beta_0 = a_0/(1 - a_1)$ and $\beta_1 = (\gamma_0 + \gamma_1)/(1 - a_1)$ to give:

$$\Delta Y_t = \gamma_0 \Delta X_t - (1 - a)\left[Y_{t-1} - \frac{a_0}{1 - a_1} - \frac{\gamma_0 + \gamma_1}{1 - a_1} X_{t-1}\right] + u_t \tag{17.17}$$

$$\Delta Y_t = \gamma_0 \Delta X_t - (1 - a)Y_{t-1} - a_0 + (\gamma_0 + \gamma_1)X_{t-1} + u_t \tag{17.18}$$

$$Y_t - Y_{t-1} = \gamma_0 X_t - \gamma_0 X_{t-1} - Y_{t-1} + aY_{t-1} - a_0 - \gamma_0 X_{t-1} - \gamma_1 X_{t-1} + u_t \tag{17.19}$$

and by rearranging and cancelling out terms that are added and subtracted at the same time we get:

$$Y_t = a_0 + a_1 Y_{t-1} + \gamma_0 X_t + \gamma_1 X_{t-1} + u_t \tag{17.20}$$

which is the same as for the original model.

What is of importance here is that when the two variables Y and X are cointegrated, the ECM incorporates not only short-run but also long-run effects. This is because the long-run equilibrium $Y_{t-1} - \beta_0 - \beta_1 X_{t-1}$ is included in the model together with the short-run dynamics captured by the differenced term. Another important advantage is that all the terms in the ECM model are stationary, and standard OLS is therefore valid. This is because if Y and X are $I(1)$, then ΔY and ΔX are $I(0)$, and by definition if Y and X are cointegrated then their linear combination $(Y_{t-1} - \beta_0 - \beta_1 X_{t-1}) \sim I(0)$.

A final, very important, point is that the coefficient $\pi = (1 - a_1)$ provides us with information about the speed of adjustment in cases of disequilibrium. To understand this better, consider the long-run condition. When equilibrium holds, then $(Y_{t-1} - \beta_0 - \beta_1 X_{t-1}) = 0$. However, during periods of disequilibrium, this term will no longer be zero and measures the distance the system is away from equilibrium. For example, suppose that because of a series of negative shocks in the economy (captured by the error term u_t) Y_t increases less rapidly than is consistent with Equation (17.14). This causes $(Y_{t-1} - \beta_0 - \beta_1 X_{t-1})$ to be negative, because Y_{t-1} has moved below its long-run steady-state growth path. However, since $\pi = (1 - a_1)$ is positive (and because of the minus sign in front of π) the overall effect is to boost ΔY_t back towards its long-run path as determined by X_t in Equation (17.14). The speed of this adjustment to equilibrium is dependent on the magnitude of $(1 - a_1)$. The magnitude of π will be discussed in the next section.

A more general model for large numbers of lagged terms

Consider the following two-variable Y_t and X_t ARDL:

$$Y_t = \mu + \sum_{i=1}^{n} a_i Y_{t-i} + \sum_{i=0}^{m} \gamma_i X_{t-i} + u_t \tag{17.21}$$

$$Y_t = \mu + a_1 Y_{t-1} + \cdots + a_n Y_{t-n} + \gamma_0 X_t + \gamma_1 X_{t-1} + \cdots + \gamma_m X_{t-m} + u_t \tag{17.22}$$

We want to obtain a long-run solution of the model, which would be defined as the point where Y_t and X_t settle down to constant steady-state levels Y^* and X^*, or more simply when:

$$Y^* = \beta_0 + \beta_1 X^* \tag{17.23}$$

and again assume X^* is constant

$$X^* = X_t = X_{t-1} = \cdots = X_{t-m}$$

So, putting this condition into Equation (17.21), we get the long-run solution, as:

$$Y^* = \frac{\mu}{1 - \sum a_i} + \frac{\sum \gamma_i}{1 - \sum a_i} X^*$$

$$Y^* = \frac{\mu}{1 - a_1 - a_2 - \cdots - a_n} + \frac{(\gamma_1 + \gamma_2 + \cdots + \gamma_m)}{1 - a_1 - a_2 - \cdots - a_n} X^* \tag{17.24}$$

or:

$$Y^* = B_0 + B_1 X^* \tag{17.25}$$

which means we can define Y^* conditional on a constant value of X at time t as:

$$Y^* = B_0 + B_1 X_t \tag{17.26}$$

Here there is an obvious link to the discussion of cointegration in the previous section. Defining e_t as the equilibrium error as in Equation (17.4), we get:

$$e_t \equiv Y_t - Y^* = Y_t - B_0 - B_1 X_t \tag{17.27}$$

Therefore, what we need is to be able to estimate the parameters B_0 and B_1. Clearly, B_0 and B_1 can be derived by estimating Equation (17.21) by OLS and then calculating $A = \mu/(1 - \sum a_i)$ and $B = \sum \gamma_i/(1 - \sum a_i)$. However, the results obtained by this method are not transparent, and calculating the standard errors will be very difficult. However, the ECM specification cuts through all these difficulties.

Take the following model, which (although it looks quite different) is a reparametrization of Equation (17.21):

$$\Delta Y_t = \mu + \sum_{i=1}^{n-1} a_i \Delta Y_{t-i} + \sum_{i=0}^{m-1} \gamma_i \Delta X_{t-i} + \theta_1 Y_{t-1} + \theta_2 X_{t-1} + u_t \tag{17.28}$$

Note: for $n = 1$ the second term on the left-hand side of Equation (17.28) disappears. From this equation we can see, with a bit of mathematics, that:

$$\theta_2 = \sum_{i=1}^{m} \gamma_i \qquad (17.29)$$

which is the numerator of the long-run parameter, B_1, and that:

$$\theta_1 = -\left(1 - \sum_{i=1}^{n} a_i\right) \qquad (17.30)$$

So the long-run parameter B_0 is given by $B_0 = 1/\theta_1$ and the long-run parameter $B_1 = -\theta_2/\theta_1$. Therefore the level terms of Y_t and X_t in the ECM tell us exclusively about the long-run parameters. Given this, the most informative way to write the ECM is as follows:

$$\Delta Y_t = \mu + \sum_{i=1}^{n-1} a_i \Delta Y_{t-i} + \sum_{i=0}^{m-1} \gamma_i \Delta X_{t-i} + \theta_1\left(Y_{t-1} - \frac{1}{\theta_1} - \frac{\theta_2}{\theta_1} X_{t-1}\right) + u_t \qquad (17.31)$$

$$\Delta Y_t = \mu + \sum_{i=1}^{n-1} a_i \Delta Y_{t-i} + \sum_{i=0}^{m-1} \gamma_i \Delta X_{t-i} - \theta_1(Y_{t-1} - \hat{\beta}_0 - \hat{\beta}_1 x_{t-1}) + u_t \qquad (17.32)$$

where $\theta_1 = 0$. Furthermore, knowing that $Y_{t-1} - \hat{\beta}_0 - \hat{\beta}_1 x_{t-1} = e_t$, our equilibrium error, we can rewrite Equation (17.31) as:

$$\Delta Y_t = \mu + \sum_{i=1}^{n-1} a_i \Delta Y_{t-i} + \sum_{i=0}^{m-1} \gamma_i \Delta X_{t-i} - \pi \hat{e}_{t-1} + \varepsilon_t \qquad (17.33)$$

What is of major importance here is the interpretation of π. π is the error-correction coefficient and is also called the adjustment coefficient. In fact, π tells us how much of the adjustment to equilibrium takes place in each period, or how much of the equilibrium error is corrected. Consider the following cases:

(a) If $\pi = 1$ then 100% of the adjustment takes place within a given period, or the adjustment is instantaneous and full.

(b) If $\pi = 0.5$ then 50% of the adjustment takes place in each period.

(c) If $\pi = 0$ then there is no adjustment, and to claim that Y_t^* is the long-run part of Y_t no longer makes sense.

We need to connect this with the concept of cointegration. Because of cointegration, $\hat{e}_t \sim I(0)$ and therefore also $\hat{e}_{t-1} \sim I(0)$. Thus, in Equation (17.33), which is the ECM representation, we have a regression that contains only $I(0)$ variables and allows us to use both long-run information and short-run disequilibrium dynamics, which is the most important feature of the ECM.

Testing for cointegration

Cointegration in single equations: the Engle–Granger approach

Granger (1981) introduced a remarkable link between non-stationary processes and the concept of long-run equilibrium; this link is the concept of cointegration defined above. Engle and Granger (1987) further formalized this concept by introducing a very simple test for the existence of cointegrating (that is long-run equilibrium) relationships.

To understand this approach (which is often called the EG approach) consider the following two series, X_t and Y_t, and the following cases:

(a) If $Y_t \sim I(0)$ and $X_t \sim I(1)$, then every linear combination of those two series

$$\theta_1 Y_t + \theta_2 X_t \qquad (17.34)$$

will result in a series that will always be $I(1)$ or non-stationary. This will happen because the behaviour of the non-stationary $I(1)$ series will dominate the behaviour of the $I(0)$ one.

(b) If we have that both X_t and Y_t are $I(1)$, then in general any linear combination of the two series, say

$$\theta_1 Y_t + \theta_2 X_t \qquad (17.35)$$

will also be $I(1)$. However, though this is the more likely case, there are exceptions to this rule, and we might find in rare cases that there is a unique combination of the series, as in Equation (17.35) above, that is $I(0)$. If this is the case, we say that X_t and Y_t are cointegrated of order (1, 1).

Now the problem is how to estimate the parameters of the long-run equilibrium relationship and check whether or not we have cointegration. Engle and Granger proposed a straightforward method involving four steps.

Step 1: test the variables for their order of integration

By definition, cointegration necessitates that the variables be integrated of the same order. Thus the first step is to test each variable to determine its order of integration. The DF and ADF tests can be applied in order to infer the number of unit roots (if any) in each of the variables. We can differentiate three cases which will either lead us to the next step or will suggest stopping:

(a) if both variables are stationary ($I(0)$), it is not necessary to proceed, since standard time series methods apply to stationary variables (in other words, we can apply classical regression analysis);

(b) if the variables are integrated of different order, it is possible to conclude that they are not cointegrated; and

(c) if both variables are integrated of the same order we proceed with step 2.

Step 2: estimate the long-run (possible cointegrating) relationship

If the results of step 1 indicate that both X_t and Y_t are integrated of the same order (usually in economics, $I(1)$), the next step is to estimate the long-run equilibrium relationship of the form:

$$Y_t = \beta_1 + \beta_2 X_t + e_t \qquad (17.36)$$

and obtain the residuals of this equation.

If there is no cointegration, the results obtained will be spurious. However, if the variables are cointegrated, then OLS regression yields 'super-consistent' estimators for the cointegrating parameter $\hat{\beta}_2$.

Step 3: check for (cointegration) the order of integration of the residuals

To determine if the variables are in fact cointegrated, denote the estimated residual sequence from this equation by $\hat{e}_t$. Thus, $\hat{e}_t$ is the series of the estimated residuals of the long-run relationship. If these deviations from long-run equilibrium are found to be stationary, then X_t and Y_t are cointegrated.

We perform a DF test on the residual series to determine their order of integration. The form of this DF test is:

$$\Delta\hat{e}_t = a_1\hat{e}_{t-1} + \sum_{i=1}^{n} \delta_i \Delta\hat{e}_{t-i} + v_t \qquad (17.37)$$

Note that because $\hat{e}_t$ is a residual we do not include a constant or a time trend. The critical values differ from the standard ADF values, being more negative (typically around -3.5). Critical values are provided in Table 17.1.

Obviously, if we find that $\hat{e}_t \sim I(0)$, we can reject the null that the variables X_t and Y_t are not cointegrated; similarly, if we have a single equation with more than just one explanatory variable.

Step 4: estimate the ECM

If the variables are cointegrated, the residuals from the equilibrium regression can be used to estimate the ECM and to analyse the long-run and short-run effects of the variables as well as to see the adjustment coefficient, which is the coefficient of the lagged residual terms of the long-run relationship identified in step 2. At the end, the adequacy of the model must always be checked by performing diagnostic tests.

Table 17.1 Critical values for the null of no cointegration

	1%	5%	10%
No lags	−4.07	−3.37	−3.3
Lags	−3.73	−3.17	−2.91

Important note. It is of major importance to note that the critical values for the cointegration test (the ADF test on the residuals) are not the same as the standard critical values of the ADF test used for testing stationarity. In fact, in order to have more robust conclusions regarding the evidence of cointegration, the critical values are more negative than the standard ADF ones. Engle and Granger (1987), in their seminal paper, performed their own Monte Carlo simulations to construct critical values for the cointegration tests. These values are shown in Table 17.1. There are two sets of critical values: the first is for no lagged dependent variable terms in the augmentation term (that is for the simple DF test); and the second is for including lagged dependent variables (that is for the ADF test). A more comprehensive set of critical values may be found in MacKinnon (1991), which is now the primary source.

Drawbacks of the EG approach

One of the best features of the EG approach is that it very easy both to understand and to implement. However, there are important shortcomings in the Engle–Granger methodology:

1 One very important issue is related to the order of the variables. When estimating the long-run relationship, one has to place one variable in the left-hand side and use the others as regressors. The test does not say anything about which of the variables can be used as a regressor and why. Consider, for example, the case of just two variables, X_t and Y_t. One can either regress Y_t on X_t (that is $Y_t = a + \beta X_t + u_{1t}$) or choose to reverse the order and regress X_t on Y_t (that is $X_t = a + \beta Y_t + u_{2t}$). It can be shown, with asymptotic theory, that as the sample goes to infinity, the test for cointegration on the residuals of those two regressions is equivalent (that is there is no difference in testing for unit roots in u_{1t} and u_{2t}). However, in practice in economics, there are rarely very big samples and it is therefore possible to find that one regression exhibits cointegration while the other does not. This is obviously a very undesirable feature of the EG approach, and the problem becomes far more complicated when there are more than two variables to test.

2 A second problem is that when there are more than two variables there may be more than one cointegrating relationship, and the Engle–Granger procedure using residuals from a single relationship cannot treat this possibility. So a most important point is that it does not give us the number of cointegrating vectors.

3 A third problem is that it relies on a two-step estimator. The first step is to generate the residual series and the second is to estimate a regression for this series to see whether the series is stationary or not. Hence, any error introduced in the first step is carried into the second.

All these problems are resolved with the use of the Johansen approach that will be examined later.

The EG approach in EViews, Microfit and Stata

The EG approach in EViews

The EG test is very easy to perform and does not require any more knowledge regarding the use of EViews. For the first step, ADF and PP tests on all variables are needed to determine the order of integration of the variables. If the variables (let's say X and Y) are found to be integrated of the same order, then the second step involves estimating the long-run relationship with simple OLS. So the command here is simply:

```
ls X c Y
```

or

```
ls Y c X
```

depending on the relationship of the variables (see the list of drawbacks of the EG approach in the section above). You need to obtain the residuals of this relationship, which are given by:

```
genr res_000=resid
```

where instead of 000 a different alphanumeric name can be entered to identify the residuals in question. The third step (the actual test for cointegration) is a unit-root test on the residuals, for which the command is:

```
adf res_000
```

for no lags; or:

```
adf(4) res_000
```

for 4 lags in the augmentation term, and so on. A crucial point here is that the critical values for this test are not those reported in EViews, but the ones given in Table 17.1 in this text.

The EG approach in Microfit

In Microfit, after testing for the order of integration of the variables, for the second step go to the **single** editor (by pressing the **single** button) and specify the equation you need to estimate and click **Start** to get the estimation results in the **results** window. Closing these results, go to the **Post Regression Menu** window and from this, after choosing **2. Move to Hypothesis Testing**, choose **3. Unit-Root Test on the Residuals**. Microfit asks you to determine the number of lags and then presents the ADF test results for this unit-root test. Again, you need to remember to compare the test statistics with the appropriate critical values shown in Table 17.1.

The EG approach in Stata

The commands for Stata are:

```
regress y x
predict res_000 , residuals
dfuller res_000 , noconstant
```

for no lags or the simple DF test; or:

```
dfuller res_000 , noconstant lags(4)
```

to include 4 lags in the augmentation term, and so on.

Cointegration in multiple equations and the Johansen approach

It was mentioned earlier that if there are more than two variables in the model, there is a possibility of having more than one cointegrating vector. This means that the variables in the model might form several equilibrium relationships governing the joint evolution of all the variables. In general, for n number of variables there can be only up to $n-1$ cointegrating vectors. Therefore, when $n=2$, which is the simplest case, if cointegration exists then the cointegrating vector is unique.

Having $n>2$ and assuming that only one cointegrating relationship exists where there are actually more than one is a serious problem that cannot be resolved by the EG single-equation approach. Therefore an alternative to the EG approach is needed, and this is the Johansen approach for multiple equations.

To present this approach, it is useful to extend the single-equation error-correction model to a multivariate one. Let us assume that we have three variables, Y_t, X_t and W_t which can all be endogenous; that is we have it that (using matrix notation for $Z_t = [Y_t, X_t, W_t]$)

$$Z_t = A_1 Z_{t-1} + A_2 Z_{t-2} + \cdots + A_k Z_{t-k} + u_t \tag{17.38}$$

which is comparable to the single-equation dynamic model for two variables Y_t and X_t given in Equation (17.21). Thus it can be reformulated in a vector error-correction model (VECM) as follows:

$$\Delta Z_t = \Gamma_1 \Delta Z_{t-1} + \Gamma_2 \Delta Z_{t-2} + \cdots + \Gamma_{k-1} \Delta Z_{t-k-1} + \Pi Z_{t-1} + u_t \tag{17.39}$$

where $\Gamma_i = (I - A_1 - A_2 - \cdots - A_k)$ $(i = 1, 2, \ldots, k-1)$ and $\Pi = -(I - A_1 - A_2 - \cdots - A_k)$. Here we need to examine carefully the 3×3 Π matrix. (The Π matrix is 3×3 because we assume three variables in $Z_t = [Y_t, X_t, W_t]$.) The Π matrix contains information regarding the long-run relationships. We can decompose $\Pi = \alpha\beta'$ where α will include the speed of adjustment to equilibrium coefficients while β' will be the long-run matrix of coefficients.

Therefore the $\beta' Z_{t-1}$ term is equivalent to the error-correction term $(Y_{t-1} - \beta_0 - \beta_1 X_{t-1})$ in the single-equation case, except that now $\beta' Z_{t-1}$ contains up to $(n-1)$ vectors in a multivariate framework.

For simplicity, we assume that $k = 2$, so that we have only two lagged terms, and the model is then the following:

$$
\begin{pmatrix} \Delta Y_t \\ \Delta X_t \\ \Delta W_t \end{pmatrix} = \Gamma_1 \begin{pmatrix} \Delta Y_{t-1} \\ \Delta X_{t-1} \\ \Delta W_{t-1} \end{pmatrix} + \Pi \begin{pmatrix} Y_{t-1} \\ X_{t-1} \\ W_{t-1} \end{pmatrix} + \mathbf{e_t} \tag{17.40}
$$

or

$$
\begin{pmatrix} \Delta Y_t \\ \Delta X_t \\ \Delta W_t \end{pmatrix} = \Gamma_1 \begin{pmatrix} \Delta Y_{t-1} \\ \Delta X_{t-1} \\ \Delta W_{t-1} \end{pmatrix} + \begin{pmatrix} a_{11} & a_{12} \\ a_{21} & a_{22} \\ a_{31} & a_{32} \end{pmatrix} \begin{pmatrix} \beta_{11} & \beta_{21} & \beta_{31} \\ \beta_{12} & \beta_{22} & \beta_{32} \end{pmatrix} \begin{pmatrix} Y_{t-1} \\ X_{t-1} \\ W_{t-1} \end{pmatrix} + \mathbf{e_t} \tag{17.41}
$$

Let us now analyse only the error-correction part of the first equation (that is for ΔY_t on the left-hand side), which gives:

$$
\Pi_1 Z_{t-1} = ([a_{11}\beta_{11} + a_{12}\beta_{12}] \quad [a_{11}\beta_{21} + a_{12}\beta_{22}]
$$

$$
[a_{11}\beta_{31} + a_{12}\beta_{32}]) \begin{pmatrix} Y_{t-1} \\ X_{t-1} \\ W_{t-1} \end{pmatrix} \tag{17.42}
$$

where Π_1 is the first row of the Π matrix.

Equation (17.42) can be rewritten as:

$$
\Pi_1 Z_{t-1} = a_{11}(\beta_{11}Y_{t-1} + \beta_{21}X_{t-1} + \beta_{31}W_{t-1})
$$
$$
+ a_{12}(\beta_{12}Y_{t-1} + \beta_{22}X_{t-1} + \beta_{32}W_{t-1}) \tag{17.43}
$$

which shows clearly the two cointegrating vectors with their respective speed of adjustment terms a_{11} and a_{12}.

Advantages of the multiple-equation approach

So, from the multiple-equation approach we can obtain estimates for both cointegrating vectors from Equation (17.43), while with the simple equation we have only a linear combination of the two long-run relationships.

Also, even if there is only one cointegrating relationship (for example the first only) rather than two, with the multiple-equation approach we can calculate all three differing speeds of adjustment coefficients $(a_{11} \quad a_{21} \quad a_{31})$.

Only when $a_{21} = a_{31} = 0$, and only one cointegrating relationship exists, can we then say that the multiple-equation method is the same (reduces to the same) as the single-equation approach, and therefore there is no loss from not modelling the determinants of ΔX_t and ΔW_t. Here, it is good to mention too that when $a_{21} = a_{31} = 0$, this is equivalent to X_t and W_t being weakly exogenous.

So, summarizing, only when all right-hand variables in a single equation are weakly exogenous does the single-equation approach provide the same result as a multivariate equation approach.

The Johansen approach (again)

Let us now go back and examine the behaviour of the Π matrix under different circumstances. Given that Z_t is a vector of non-stationary $I(1)$ variables, then ΔZ_{t-1} are $I(0)$ and ΠZ_{t-1} must also be $I(0)$ in order to have that $u_t \sim I(0)$ and therefore to have a well-behaved system.

In general, there are three cases for ΠZ_{t-1} to be $I(0)$:

Case 1   When all the variables in Z_t are stationary. Of course, this case is totally uninteresting since it implies that there is no problem of spurious regression and the simple VAR in levels model can be used to model this case.

Case 2   When there is no cointegration at all and therefore the Π matrix is an $n \times n$ matrix of zeros because there are no linear relationships among the variables in Z_t. In this case the appropriate strategy is to use a VAR model in first differences with no long-run elements as a result of the non-existence of long-run relationships.

Case 3   When there exist up to $(n-1)$ cointegrating relationships of the form $\beta' Z_{t-1} \sim I(0)$. In this particular case, $r \leq (n-1)$ cointegrating vectors exist in β. This simply means that r columns of β form r linearly independent combinations of the variables in Z_t, each of which is stationary. Of course, there will also be $(n-r)$ common stochastic trends underlying Z_t.

Recall that $\Pi = \alpha\beta'$ and so in case 3 above, while the Π matrix will always be dimensioned $n \times n$, the α and β matrices will be dimensioned $n \times r$. This therefore imposes a rank of r on the Π matrix, which also imposes only r linearly independent rows in this matrix. So underlying the full size Π matrix is a restricted set of only r cointegrating vectors given by $\beta' Z_{t-1}$. Reduced rank regression, of this type, has been available in the statistics literature for many years, but it was introduced into modern econometrics and linked with the analysis of non-stationary data by Johansen (1988).

Going back to the three different cases considered above regarding the rank of the matrix Π we have:

Case 1   When Π has a full rank (that is there are $r = n$ linearly independent columns) then the variables in Z_t are $I(0)$.

Case 2   When the rank of Π is zero (that is there are no linearly independent columns) then there are no cointegrating relationships.

Case 3   When Π has a reduced rank (that is there are $r \leq (n-1)$ linearly independent columns) and therefore there are $r \leq (n-1)$ cointegrating relationships.

Johansen (1988) developed a methodology that tests for the rank of Π and provides estimates of α and β through a procedure known as reduced rank regression, but the actual procedure is quite complicated and beyond the scopes of this text (see Cuthbertson, Hall and Taylor (1992) for more details).

The steps of the Johansen approach in practice

Step 1: testing the order of integration of the variables

As with the EG approach, the first step in the Johansen approach is to test for the order of integration of the variables under examination. It was noted earlier that most economic time series are non-stationary and therefore integrated. Indeed, the issue here is to have non-stationary variables in order to detect among them stationary cointegrating relationship(s) and avoid the problem of spurious regressions. It is clear that the most desirable case is when all the variables are integrated of the same order, and then to proceed with the cointegration test. However, it is important to stress that this is not always the case, and that even in cases where a mix of $I(0)$, $I(1)$ and $I(2)$ variables are present in the model, cointegrating relationships might well exist. The inclusion of these variables, though, will massively affect researchers' results and more consideration should be applied in such cases.

Consider, for example, the inclusion of an $I(0)$ variable. In a multivariate framework, for every $I(0)$ variable included in the model the number of cointegrating relationships will increase correspondingly. We stated earlier that the Johansen approach amounts to testing for the rank of Π (that is finding the number of linearly independent columns in Π), and since each $I(0)$ variable is stationary by itself, it forms a cointegrating relationship by itself and therefore forms a linearly independent vector in Π.

Matters become more complicated when we include $I(2)$ variables. Consider, for example, a model with the inclusion of two $I(1)$ and two $I(2)$ variables. There is a possibility that the two $I(2)$ variables cointegrate down to an $I(1)$ relationship, and then this relationship may further cointegrate with one of the two $I(1)$ variables to form another cointegrating vector. In general, situations with variables in differing orders of integration are quite complicated, though the positive thing is that it is quite common in macroeconomics to have $I(1)$ variables. Those who are interested in further details regarding the inclusion of $I(2)$ variables can refer to Johansen's (1995b) paper, which develops an approach to treat $I(2)$ models.

Step 2: setting the appropriate lag length of the model

The issue of finding the appropriate (optimal) lag length is very important because we want to have Gaussian error terms (that is standard normal error terms that do not suffer from non-normality, autocorrelation, heteroskedasticity and so on). Setting the value of the lag length is affected by the omission of variables that might affect only the short-run behaviour of the model. This is because omitted variables instantly become part of the error term. Therefore very careful inspection of the data and the functional relationship is necessary before proceeding with estimation, to decide whether to include additional variables. It is quite common to use dummy variables to take into account short-run 'shocks' to the system, such as political events that had important effects on macroeconomic conditions.

The most common procedure in choosing the optimal lag length is to estimate a VAR model including all our variables in levels (non-differenced data). This VAR model should be estimated for a large number of lags, then reducing down by re-estimating the model for one lag less until zero lags are reached (that is we estimate the model for 12 lags, then 11, 10 and so on until we reach 0 lags).

In each of these models we inspect the values of the AIC and the SBC criteria, as well as the diagnostics concerning autocorrelation, heteroskedasticity, possible ARCH effects and normality of the residuals. In general the model that minimizes AIC and SBC is selected as the one with the optimal lag length. This model should also pass all the diagnostic checks.

Step 3: choosing the appropriate model regarding the deterministic components in the multivariate system

Another important aspect in the formulation of the dynamic model is whether an intercept and/or a trend should enter either the short-run or the long-run model, or both models. The general case of the VECM, including all the various options that can possibly arise, is given by the following equation:

$$\Delta Z_t = \Gamma_1 \Delta Z_{t-1} + \cdots + \Gamma_{k-1} \Delta Z_{t-k-1} + \alpha(\beta Z_{t-1} \quad \mu_1 1 \quad \delta_1 t)$$
$$+ \mu_2 + \delta_2 t + \mathbf{u}_t \tag{17.44}$$

And for this equation we can see the possible cases. We can have a constant (with coefficient μ_1) and/or a trend (with coefficient δ_1) in the long-run model (the cointegrating equation (CE)), and a constant (with coefficient μ_2) and/or a trend (with coefficient δ_2) in the short-run model (the VAR model).

In general, five distinct models can be considered. While the first and the fifth models are not that realistic, all of them are presented for reasons of complementarity.

Model 1   No intercept or trend in CE or VAR ($\delta_1 = \delta_2 = \mu_1 = \mu_2 = 0$). In this case there are no deterministic components in the data or in the cointegrating relations. However, this is quite unlikely to occur in practice, especially as the intercept is generally needed to account for adjustments in the units of measurements of the variables in (Z_{t-1} 1 t).

Model 2   Intercept (no trend) in CE, no intercept or trend in VAR ($\delta_1 = \delta_2 = \mu_2 = 0$). This is the case where there are no linear trends in the data, and therefore the first differenced series have a zero mean. In this case, the intercept is restricted to the long-run model (that is the cointegrating equation) to account for the unit of measurement of the variables in (Z_{t-1} 1 t).

Model 3   Intercept in CE and VAR, no trends in CE and VAR ($\delta_1 = \delta_2 = 0$). In this case there are no linear trends in the levels of the data, but both specifications are allowed to drift around an intercept. In this case, it is assumed that the intercept in the CE is cancelled out by the intercept in the VAR, leaving just one intercept in the short-run model.

Model 4   Intercept in CE and VAR, linear trend in CE, no trend in VAR ($\delta_2 = 0$). In this model a trend is included in the CE as a trend-stationary variable, to take into account exogenous growth (that is technical progress). We also

Model 5 Intercept and quadratic trend in the CE intercept and linear trend in VAR. This model allows for linear trends in the short-run model and thus quadratic trends in the CE. Therefore, in this final model, everything is unrestricted. However, this model is very difficult to interpret from an economics point of view, especially since the variables are entered as logs, because a model like this would imply an implausible ever-increasing or ever-decreasing rate of change.

So the problem is, which of the five different models is appropriate in testing for co-integration. It was noted earlier that model 1 and model 5 are not that likely to happen, and that they are also implausible in terms of economic theory, therefore the problem reduces to a choice of one of the three remaining models (models 2, 3 and 4). Johansen (1992) suggests that the joint hypothesis of both the rank order and the deterministic components need to be tested, applying the so-called Pantula principle. The Pantula principle involves the estimation of all three models and the presentation of the results from the most restrictive hypothesis (that is r = number of cointegrating relations = 0 and model 2) to the least restrictive hypothesis (that is r = number of variables entering the VAR $- 1 = n - 1$ and model 4). The model-selection procedure then comprises moving from the most restrictive model, at each stage comparing the trace test statistic to its critical value, and stopping only when it is concluded for the first time that the null hypothesis of no cointegration is not rejected.

Step 4: determining the rank of Π or the number of cointegrating vectors

According to Johansen (1988) and Johansen and Juselius (1990), there are two methods (and corresponding test statistics) for determining the number of cointegrating relations, and both involve estimation of the matrix Π. This is a $k \times k$ matrix with rank r. The procedures are based on propositions about eigenvalues.

(a) One method tests the null hypothesis, that $Rank(\Pi) = r$ against the hypothesis that the rank is $r + 1$. So the null in this case is that there are cointegrating vectors and there are up to r cointegrating relationships, with the alternative suggesting that there are $(r + 1)$ vectors.

The test statistics are based on the characteristic roots (also called eigenvalues) obtained from the estimation procedure. The test consists of ordering the largest eigenvalues in descending order and considering whether they are significantly different from zero. To understand the test procedure, suppose we obtained n characteristic roots denoted by $\lambda_1 > \lambda_2 > \lambda_3 > \cdots > \lambda_n$. If the variables under examination are not cointegrated, the rank of Π is zero and all the characteristic roots will equal zero. Therefore $(1 - \hat{\lambda}_i)$ will be equal to 1 and, since $\ln(1) = 0$, each of the expressions will be equal to zero for no cointegration. On the other hand, if the rank of Π is equal to 1, then $0 < \lambda_1 < 1$ so that the first expression is $(1 - \hat{\lambda}_i) < 0$, while all the rest will be equal to zero. To test how many of the numbers of the characteristic roots are significantly different from zero this test uses the following statistic:

$$\lambda_{\max}(r, r+1) = -T \ln(1 - \hat{\lambda}_{r+1}) \tag{17.45}$$

As noted above, the test statistic is based on the *maximum eigenvalue* and is thus called the *maximal eigenvalue statistic* (denoted by $\lambda_{\max}$).

(b) The second method is based on a likelihood ratio test for the trace of the matrix (and because of that it is called the *trace statistic*). The trace statistic considers whether the trace is increased by adding more eigenvalues beyond the rth. The null hypothesis in this case is that the number of cointegrating vectors is less than or equal to r. From the previous analysis it should be clear that when all $\hat{\lambda}_i = 0$, then the trace statistic is also equal to zero. On the other hand, the closer the characteristic roots are to unity, the more negative is the $\ln(1 - \hat{\lambda}_i)$ term and therefore the larger the trace statistic. This statistic is calculated by:

$$\lambda_{trace}(r) = -T \sum_{i=r+1}^{n} \ln(1 - \hat{\lambda}_{r+1}) \tag{17.46}$$

The usual procedure is to work downwards and stop at the value of r, which is associated with a test statistic that exceeds the displayed critical value. Critical values for both statistics are provided by Johansen and Juselius (1990) (these critical values are directly provided from both EViews and Microfit after conducting a test for cointegration using the Johansen approach).

Step 5: testing for weak exogeneity

After determining the number of cointegrating vectors we proceed with tests of weak exogeneity. Remember that the Π matrix contains information about the long-run relationships, and that $\Pi = \alpha\beta'$, where α represents the speed of adjustment coefficients and β is the matrix of the long-run coefficients. From this it should be clear that when there are $r \leq n - 1$ cointegrating vectors in β, this automatically means that at least $(n - r)$ columns of α are equal to zero. Thus, once the number of cointegrating vectors has been determined, we should proceed with testing which of the variables are weakly exogenous.

A very useful feature of the Johansen approach for cointegration is that it allows us to test for restricted forms of the cointegrating vectors. Consider the case given by Equation (17.40), and from this the following equation:

$$\begin{pmatrix} \Delta Y_t \\ \Delta X_t \\ \Delta W_t \end{pmatrix} = \Gamma_1 \begin{pmatrix} \Delta Y_{t-1} \\ \Delta X_{t-1} \\ \Delta W_{t-1} \end{pmatrix} + \begin{pmatrix} a_{11} & a_{12} \\ a_{21} & a_{22} \\ a_{31} & a_{23} \end{pmatrix} \begin{pmatrix} \beta_{11} & \beta_{21} & \beta_{31} \\ \beta_{12} & \beta_{22} & \beta_{32} \end{pmatrix} \begin{pmatrix} Y_{t-1} \\ X_{t-1} \\ W_{t-1} \end{pmatrix} + \mathbf{e_t} \tag{17.47}$$

In this equation it can be seen that testing for weak exogeneity with respect to the long-run parameters is equivalent to testing which of the rows of α are equal to zero. A variable Z is weakly exogenous if it is only a function of lagged variables, and the parameters of the equation generating Z are independent of the parameters generating the other variables in the system. If we think of the variable Y in Equation (17.47), it is clearly a function of only lagged variables but in the general form above the parameters of the cointegrating vectors (β) are clearly common to all equations and so the parameters generating Y cannot be independent of those generating X and W as they are the same parameters. However, if the first row of the α matrix were all zeros then the βs would drop out of the Y equation and it would be weakly exogenous. So a joint test that a particular row of α is zero is a test of the weak exogeneity of the corresponding variable. If a variable is found to be weakly exogenous it can be dropped as an endogenous part of the system. This means that the whole equation for that variable can also be dropped, though it will continue to feature on the right-hand side of the other equations.

Step 6: testing for linear restrictions in the cointegrating vectors

An important feature of the Johansen approach is that it allows us to obtain estimates of the coefficients of the matrices α and β, and then test for possible linear restrictions regarding those matrices. Especially for matrix β, the matrix that contains the long-run parameters, this is very important because it allows us to test specific hypotheses regarding various theoretical predictions from an economic theory point of view. So, for example, if we examine a money–demand relationship, we might be interested in testing restrictions regarding the long-run proportionality between money and prices, or the relative size of income and interest-rate elasticities of demand for money and so on. For more details regarding testing linear restrictions in the Johansen framework, see Enders (1995) and Harris (1997).

The Johansen approach in EViews, Microfit and Stata

The Johansen approach in EViews

EViews has a specific command for testing for cointegration using the Johansen approach under group statistics. Consider the file money_ita.wf1, which has quarterly data from 1975q1 to 1997q4 for the Italian economy and for the following variables:

> $lm2\_p$ = the log of the real money supply measured by the M2 definition
>
> > deflated by the consumer price index (*cpi*);
>
> $lgdp\_p$ = the log of real income (again deflated by the CPI); and
>
> > r = the interest rate representing the opportunity cost of holding money.

The first step is to determine the order of integration of the variables. To do this, apply unit-root tests on all three variables that are to be tested for cointegration. Apply the Doldado *et al.* (1990) procedure to choose the appropriate model and determine the number of lags according to the SBC criterion. For example, for M2, the model with constant and trend showed that the inclusion of the trend was not appropriate (because its coefficient was statistically insignificant), and we therefore estimated the model that includes only a constant. This model was found to be appropriate and we concluded from that model that there is a unit root in the series (because the ADF-statistic was bigger than the 5% critical value). The results of all tests for levels and first differences are presented in Table 17.2.

Table 17.2   Unit-root test results

Variables	Model	ADF-stat.	No. of lags
	ADF tests in the levels		
lm3_p	Constant no trend	−2.43	2
lgdp_p	Constant and trend	−2.12	4
r	Constant and trend	−2.97	2
	ADF tests in first differences		
lm3_p	Constant no trend	−4.45	2
lgdp_p	Constant no trend	−4.37	4
R	Constant and trend	−4.91	2

The second step is to determine the optimal lag length. Unfortunately, EViews does not allow the automatic detection of the lag length (while Microfit does), so the model needs to be estimated for a large number of lags and then reduced down to check for the optimal value of AIC and SBC (as described in step 1 of the Johansen approach). By doing this we found that the optimal lag length was 4 lags (not surprising for quarterly data).

Then the Pantula principle needs to be applied to decide which of the three models to choose in testing for cointegration. Each of the three models for cointegration in Microfit are tested by opening **Quick/Group Statistics/Cointegration Test**. Then in the **series list** window enter the names of the series to check for cointegration, for example:

```
lgdp_p lm2_p r
```

then press **OK**. The five alternative models explained in the theory are given under the labels 1, 2, 3, 4 and 5. There is another option (option 6 in EViews) that compares all these models together. In our case we wish to estimate models 2, 3 and 4 (because, as noted earlier, models 1 and 5 occur only very rarely). To estimate model 2, select that model and specify the number of lags in the bottom-right corner box that has the (default by EViews) numbers '1 2' for the inclusion of two lags. Change '1 2' to '1 4' for four lags, and click **OK** to get the results. Note that there is another box that allows us to include (by typing their names) variables that will be treated as exogenous. Here we usually put variables that are either found to be $I(0)$, or dummy variables that possibly affect the behaviour of the model.

The results of this model are presented in Table 17.3 (we present only the results of the trace statistic needed for the Pantula principle; later we shall check all the results reported in the cointegration results window).

Doing the same for models 3 and 4 (in the **untitled group window** select **View/Cointegration Test** and simply change the model by clicking next to 3 or 4), we obtain the results reported in Tables 17.4 and 17.5.

The trace statistics for all three models are then collected together as in Table 17.6 to choose which model is the most appropriate. Start with the smaller number of cointegrating vectors $r = 0$, and check whether the trace statistic for model 2 rejects the null; if 'yes' proceed to the right, checking whether the third model rejects the null, and so on. In our case, model 3 suggests that the trace statistic is smaller than the 5% critical value, so this model does not show cointegration, and the analysis is stopped at this point.

Table 17.3 Cointegration test results (model 2)

Date: 04/07/04 Time: 17:14
Sample(adjusted): 1976:2 1997:4
Included observations: 87 after adjusting endpoints
Trend assumption: No deterministic trend (restricted constant)
Series: LGDP_P LM2_P R
Lags interval (in first differences): 1 to 4
Unrestricted Cointegration Rank Test

Hypothesized No. of CE(s)	Eigenvalue	Trace statistic	5% critical value	1% critical value
None**	0.286013	51.38016	34.91	41.07
At most 1*	0.139113	22.07070	19.96	24.60
At most 2	0.098679	9.038752	9.24	12.97

Note: *(**) denotes rejection of the hypothesis at the 5%(1%) level. Trace test indicates 2 cointegrating equations at the 5% level and 1 cointegrating equation at the 1% level.

Table 17.4 Cointegration test results (model 3)

Date: 04/07/04 Time: 17:27
Sample(adjusted): 1976:2 1997:4
Included observations: 87 after adjusting endpoints
Trend assumption: Linear deterministic trend
Series: LGDP_P LM2_P R
Lags interval (in first differences): 1 to 4
Unrestricted Cointegration Rank Test

Hypothesized No. of CE(s)	Eigenvalue	Trace statistic	5% critical value	1% critical value
None	0.166219	25.79093	29.68	35.65
At most 1	0.108092	9.975705	15.41	20.04
At most 2	0.000271	0.023559	3.76	6.65

Note: *(**) denotes rejection of the hypothesis at the 5%(1%) level. Trace test indicates no cointegration at both the 5% and 1% levels.

Table 17.5 Cointegration test results (model 4)

Date: 04/07/04 Time: 17:27
Sample(adjusted): 1976:2 1997:4
Included observations: 87 after adjusting endpoints
Trend assumption: Linear deterministic trend (restricted)
Series: LGDP_P LM2_P R
Lags interval (in first differences): 1 to 4
Unrestricted Cointegration Rank Test

Hypothesized No. of CE(s)	Eigenvalue	Trace statistic	5% critical value	1% critical value
None**	0.319369	52.02666	42.44	48.45
At most 1	0.137657	18.55470	25.32	30.45
At most 2	0.063092	5.669843	12.25	16.26

Note: *(**) denotes rejection of the hypothesis at the 5%(1%) level. Trace test indicates 1 cointegrating equation at both the 5% and 1% levels.

Table 17.6 The Pantula principle test results

r	$n - r$	Model 2	Model 3	Model 4
0	3	51.38016	25.79093*	52.02666
1	2	22.0707	9.975705	18.5547
2	1	9.038752	0.023559	5.669843

Note: * Indicates the first time that the null cannot be rejected.

For illustrative purposes for the use of EViews only, we consider the results from model 2 where only two cointegrating vectors were found to exist. From the full results (reported in Table 17.7) we see that both the trace and the maximal eigenvalue statistics suggest the existence of two cointegrating vectors. EViews then reports results regarding the coefficients of the α and β matrices, first unnormalized and then normalized. After establishing the number of cointegrating vectors, we proceed with the estimation of the ECM by clicking on **Procs/Make Vector Autoregression**. EViews here gives us two choices of VAR types; first, if there is no evidence of cointegration we can estimate the unrestricted VAR (by clicking on the corresponding button), or, if there is cointegration we can estimate the VECM. If we estimate the VECM we need to specify (by clicking on the **Cointegration** menu), which model we want and how many numbers of cointegrating vectors we wish to have (determined from the previous step), and to impose restrictions on the elements of the α and β matrices by clicking on the **VEC restrictions** menu. The restrictions are entered as $b(1, 1) = 0$ for the $\beta_{11} = 0$ restriction. More than one restriction can be entered and they should be separated by commas.

The Johansen approach in Microfit

To use the Johansen approach in Microfit, first go to the **multi** window by clicking the **multi** button. Then from the **Multivariate Menu** choose **Unrestricted VAR** and specify the required equation in the corresponding box. Here the names are entered of the variables to be checked for cointegration in order to determine the optimal lag length from the unrestricted VAR. After typing the names of the variables, click on **Start**, which takes you to the **Unrestricted VAR post estimation menu**. From this menu choose option **4. Hypothesis testing and lag order selection in the VAR**. Here, choose option **1. Testing and selection criteria for order (lag length) of the VAR**, and thus obtain the results reported in Table 17.8.

In Table 17.8 we see the AIC and SBC, together with some other statistics regarding estimations of simple VARs for 13 different lag structures (from lags 12 to 0). The aim is to choose the model that minimizes AIC and SBC. In this particular case both statistics suggest a lag length of 6 as being optimal (see the values in bold type in the table).

To test for cointegration among the variables, now go to the **Multivariate Menu** and choose **Cointegrating VAR Menu**. Five different options are offered, corresponding to the models of the structure of deterministic components examined in the theoretical explanation of the Johansen approach above. To apply the Pantula principle, again all three models (models 2, 3 and 4; we leave out models 1 and 5) should be estimated. By choosing the model and clicking on **Start** the results for the maximal and the trace eigenvalue statistics are obtained, together with their respective critical values. If the statistical values are bigger than the critical ones, the null of no cointegration is rejected in favour of the alternative. Then close the results and, following the **Cointegrating**

Table 17.7 Full results from the cointegration test (model 2)

Date: 04/07/04 Time: 17:41
Sample(adjusted): 1975:4 1997:4
Included observations: 89 after adjusting endpoints
Trend assumption: No deterministic trend (restricted constant)
Series: LGDP_P LM2_P R
Lags interval (in first differences): 1 to 2
Unrestricted Cointegration Rank Test

Hypothesized No. of CE(s)	Eigenvalue	Trace statistic	5% critical value	1% critical value
None**	0.219568	48.20003	34.91	41.07
At most 1**	0.193704	26.13626	19.96	24.60
At most 2	0.075370	6.974182	9.24	12.97

Note: *(**) denotes rejection of the hypothesis at the 5%(1%) level. Trace test indicates 2 cointegrating equation(s) at both the 5% and 1% levels.

Hypothesized No. of CE(s)	Eigenvalue	Max-Eigen statistic	5% critical value	1% critical value
None*	0.219568	22.06377	22.00	26.81
At most 1*	0.193704	19.16208	15.67	20.20
At most 2	0.075370	6.974182	9.24	12.97

Note: *(**) denotes rejection of the hypothesis at the 5%(1%) level. Max-eigenvalue test indicates 2 cointegrating equation(s) at the 5% level, and no cointegration at the 1% level.

Unrestricted Cointegrating Coefficients (normalized by b'*S11*b = I):

LGDP_P	LM2_P	R	C
−5.932728	4.322724	−0.226210	10.33096
4.415826	−0.328139	0.158258	−11.15663
0.991551	−17.05815	0.113204	27.97470

Unrestricted Adjustment Coefficients (alpha):

D(LGDP_P)	0.004203	0.001775	3.68E−05
D(LM2_P)	0.001834	−0.001155	0.003556
D(R)	0.228149	−0.399488	−0.139878

1 Cointegrating Equation(s):		Log likelihood	415.4267

Normalized cointegrating coefficients (std. err. in parentheses)

LGDP_P	LM2_P	R	C
1.000000	−0.728623	0.038129	−1.741351
	(0.61937)	(0.01093)	(1.17467)

Adjustment coefficients (std. err. in parentheses)

D(LGDP_P)	−0.024938
	(0.00583)
D(LM2_P)	−0.010881
	(0.00895)
D(R)	−1.353545
	(0.73789)

Continued

Table 17.7 Continued

2 Cointegrating Equation(s):		Log likelihood		425.0077

Normalized cointegrating coefficients (std. err. in parentheses)

LGDP_P	LM2_P	R	C
1.000000	0.000000	0.035579	−2.615680
		(0.01765)	(0.24340)
0.000000	1.000000	−0.003500	−1.199974
		(0.02933)	(0.40446)

Adjustment coefficients (std. err. in parentheses)

D(LGDP_P)	−0.017100	0.017588
	(0.00712)	(0.00417)
D(LM2_P)	−0.015981	0.008307
	(0.01112)	(0.00652)
D(R)	−3.117614	1.117312
	(0.86005)	(0.50413)

Table 17.8 Test statistics and choice criteria for selecting the order of the VAR model

Based on 258 observations from 1974M1 to 1995M6. Order of VAR = 12
List of variables included in the unrestricted VAR:
FF   ITL

Order	LL	AIC	SBC	LR test			Adjusted LR test	
12	−1326.9	−1354.9	−1460.2					
11	−1327.1	−1351.1	−1349.3	CHSQ (4) =	0.44302 [.979]		0.40181 [.982]	
10	−1328.1	−1348.1	−1339.2	CHSQ (8) =	2.4182 [.965]		2.1932 [.975]	
9	−1328.5	−1344.5	−1328.4	CHSQ (12) =	3.0913 [.995]		2.8037 [.997]	
8	−1332.1	−1354.1	−1320.9	CHSQ (16) =	10.2877 [.851]		9.3307 [.899]	
7	−1334.4	−1352.4	−1312.1	CHSQ (20) =	14.8836 [.783]		13.4991 [.855]	
6	−1335.7	**−1359.7**	**−1402.4**	CHSQ (24) =	17.6463 [.820]		16.0048 [.888]	
5	−1336.9	−1356.9	−1392.5	CHSQ (28) =	20.0586 [.862]		18.1927 [.921]	
4	−1337.2	−1353.2	−1381.6	CHSQ (32) =	20.5527 [.941]		18.6409 [.971]	
3	−1338.3	−1350.3	−1371.6	CHSQ (36) =	22.8243 [.957]		20.7011 [.981]	
2	−1341.0	−1349.0	−1363.2	CHSQ (40) =	28.1570 [.920]		25.5377 [.963]	
1	−1345.4	−1349.4	−1356.5	CHSQ (44) =	36.9251 [.766]		33.4902 [.875]	
0	−2836.3	−1336.3	−1336.3	CHSQ (48) =	3018.8 [.000]		2738.0 [.000]	

Note: AIC = Akaike information criterion; SBC = Schwarz Bayesian criterion.

VAR post estimation menu, specify the number of cointegrating relationships (which were determined earlier by the trace and max statistics) in choice 2, set the cointegrating vectors in choice 3 and so on, until choice 6 which leads to the **Long Run Structural Modelling Menu** from which restrictions can be imposed on the coefficients of the cointegrating vectors.

The Johansen approach in Stata

In Stata, the command for the Johansen cointegration test has the following syntax:

```
vecrank varnames , options
```

where in varnames type the names of the variables to be tested for cointegration. From the options given, specify the different models discussed in the theory. So, for each case (from models 1–5):

```
Model 1: trend(none)
Model 2: trend(rconstant)
Model 3: trend(constant)
Model 4: trend(rtrend)
Model 5: trend(trend)
```

Thus, if you want to test for cointegration between two variables (let's call them x and y) through the third model, the command is:

```
vecrank y x , max trend(constant) lags(2)
```

where the max is in the command for Stata to show both the max and trace statistics (if the max is omitted, Stata will report only the trace statistics). Also lags(#) determines the number of lags to be used in the test (in this case 2).

If it appears that there is cointegration, the command:

```
vec varnames , options
```

provides the VECM estimation results. The options are the same as above. So, the command:

```
vec y x , trend(trend) lags(3)
```

yields VECM results for the variables y and x and for three lagged short-run terms, when the cointegrating equation has been determined from the fifth model according to the theory.

Computer examples of cointegration

Here we again examine the test results from Asteriou and Price (2000a). The results for the order of integration of the variables included in their analysis were presented in the second computer example in Chapter 16. Once the stationarity order has been established, we can move on to cointegration tests.

Table 17.9 reports the results from using the Engle–Granger (EG) (1987) cointegration methodology. We first regressed GDP per capita to the capital/labour ratio and to every financial development proxy (one at each specification). The test statistics presented in Table 17.9 are the ADF tests relating to the hypothesis of a unit root in the cointegrating regression residuals of each specification. The results of the first method indicate that the hypothesis of the existence of a bivariate cointegrating relationship between the level of GDP per capita and each of the financial development proxies is clearly rejected in all cases (the critical value is -3.37; see Table 17.1).

However, as discussed earlier, the Engle–Granger procedure suffers from various shortcomings. One is that it relies on a two-step estimator; the first step is to generate the error series and the second is to estimate a regression for this series to see whether the series is stationary or not. Hence any error introduced by the researcher in the first step is carried into the second, in particular the misspecification in the short-run dynamics. The Johansen (1988) maximum-likelihood method circumvents the use of two-step

Table 17.9   Engle–Granger cointegration tests

Variables in cointegrating vector	ADF-statistic	k	n
Y, K, M	−2.6386	4	109
Y, K, CUR	−2.1290	6	109
Y, K, CL	−2.0463	4	104
Y, K, T	−3.3999	4	85

Note: k is the degree of augmentation of the ADF test, determined by the FPE test; n is the number of observations used in the first step of the Engle–Granger procedure.

estimators and, moreover, can estimate and test for the presence of multiple cointe-grating vectors. The Johansen (1988) test also allows us to test restricted versions of the cointegrating vectors and speed of adjustment parameters.

Thus we continue testing for cointegration with the Johansen method. First, we test for the presence of cointegrating vectors, introducing in each case only one financial development proxy variable, then we go on to include all four financial development proxies.

Monetization ratio

We want to test for the existence of cointegration relations among per capita GDP and the financial development variables. The first proxy variable for financial development is the monetization ratio. The Johansen method is known to be sensitive to the lag length (see Banerjee *et al.*, 1993), and we therefore estimate the VAR system compris-ing the monetization ratio, the capital/labour ratio and GDP per capita for various lag lengths, and calculate the respective Akaike information criterion (AIC) and the Schwarz Bayesian criterion (SBC) to determine the appropriate lag length for the coin-tegration test. Nine alternative VAR(p), $p = 1, 2, \ldots, 9$, models were estimated over the same sample period, namely 1972q1 – 1997q1, and as to be expected, the maximized values of the log likelihood (LL) increase with p. Both criteria indicated that the optimal lag length is two. The results in Table 17.10 show that the log likelihood ratio statistics suggest a VAR of order 7. By construct, both the AIC and the SBC suggest the use of two lags. Initially, we test for cointegration using only two lags in the VAR system.

We also need to determine the appropriate restrictions on the intercept and trends in the short- and long-run models. For this, we use the Pantula principle; that is, we estimate all three alternative models and move from the most restrictive to the least restrictive, comparing the trace or the maximal eigenvalue test statistic to its critical value, stopping (and therefore choosing the model) only when, for the first time, the null hypothesis is not rejected. The results from the three estimating models are presented in Table 17.11. The first time that the null hypothesis is not rejected is for the first model (restricted intercepts, no trends in the levels of the data) and we can see that both the trace and the maximal eigenvalue test statistics suggest the existence of one cointegrating relationship.

The results of the cointegration test are presented in Table 17.12. We observe one cointegration vector, given in the last row of the table, and the monetization ratio and the capital/labour ratios show the expected positive signs. However, the model selected suggests that there is no constant in the cointegrating vector. This may be interpreted as

Table 17.10 Test statistics and choice criteria for selecting the order of the VAR

Based on 101 obs. from 1972q1 to 1997q1
Variables included in the unrestricted VAR: Y, K, M

Order	LL	AIC	SBC	LR test	Adjusted LR test
8	1092.2	1014.2	912.1	—	—
7	1089.4	1020.4	930.1	$\chi^2(9) = 5.62\ [.777]$	4.17 [.900]
6	1068.0	1008.0	929.5	$\chi^2(18) = 48.33\ [.000]$	35.89 [.007]
5	1064.1	1013.1	946.3	$\chi^2(27) = 56.21\ [.001]$	41.74 [.035]
4	1060.7	1018.7	963.7	$\chi^2(36) = 62.97\ [.004]$	46.76 [.0108]
3	1051.1	1018.1	974.9	$\chi^2(45) = 82.15\ [.001]$	61.00 [.056]
2	1045.1	1021.1	989.7	$\chi^2(54) = 94.13\ [.001]$	69.90 [.072]
1	938.8	968.8	949.2	$\chi^2(63) = 216.58\ [.000]$	160.82 [.000]
0	284.5	275.5	270.7	$\chi^2(72) = 1615.1\ [.000]$	1199.4 [.000]

Note: AIC = Akaike information criterion; SBC = Schwarz Bayesian criterion.

Table 17.11 The Pantula principle for the monetization ratio proxy variable: $k = 2$

H_0	r	$n - r$	Model 1	Model 2	Model 3
λ max test					
	0	3	40.68	19.96	31.21
	1	2	13.13*	4.56	13.65
	2	1	3.69	0.07	4.17
λ trace test					
	0	3	57.50	29.60	42.03
	1	2	4.56*	4.46	17.82
	2	1	0.07	0.07	4.17

Note: * Denotes the first time when the null hypothesis is not rejected for the 90% significance level.

Table 17.12 Cointegration test based on Johansen's max. likelihood method: $k = 2$

Null hypothesis	Alternative hypothesis	Critical values	
		95%	90%
λ_{max} rank tests		λ_{max} rank value	
$H_0 : r = 0$	$H_a : r > 0$	40.68*	22.04	19.86
$H_0 : r \leq 1$	$H_a : r > 1$	13.13	15.87	13.81
$H_0 : r \leq 2$	$H_a : r > 2$	3.69	9.16	7.53
λ_{trace} rank tests		λ_{trace} rank value	
$H_0 : r = 0$	$H_a : r = 1$	57.50*	34.87	31.39
$H_0 : r = 1$	$H_a : r = 2$	16.82	20.18	17.78
$H_0 : r = 2$	$H_a : r = 3$	3.69	9.16	7.53
Normalized ecm: $Y = 0.408*K + 0.286*M + 8.392$				

Note: 107 observations from 1970q3 to 1997q1. * and ** denote rejection of the null hypothesis for the 5% and 10% significance levels respectively. Critical values from Ostervald–Lenum (1992).

Table 17.13 The Pantula principle for the monetization ratio proxy variable: $k = 7$

H_0	r	$n - r$	Model 1	Model 2	Model 3
λ *max test*					
	0	3	32.29	29.20	42.60
	1	2	27.27	8.76*	12.80
	2	1	8.58	0.19	8.61
λ *trace test*					
	0	3	69.32	38.17	64.02
	1	2	36.35	8.96*	21.41
	2	1	8.58	0.13	8.61

Note: * Denotes the first time when the null hypothesis is not rejected for the 90% significance level.

Table 17.14 Cointegration test based on Johansen's max. likelihood method: $k = 7$

Null hypothesis	Alternative hypothesis		Critical values	
			95%	90%
λ_{max} rank tests		λ_{max} rank value		
$H_0 : r = 0$	$H_a : r > 0$	29.20*	21.12	19.02
$H_0 : r \leq 1$	$H_a : r > 1$	8.76	14.88	12.98
$H_0 : r \leq 2$	$H_a : r > 2$	0.19	8.07	6.50
λ_{trace} rank tests		λ_{trace} rank value		
$H_0 : r = 0$	$H_a : r = 1$	38.17*	31.54	28.78
$H_0 : r = 1$	$H_a : r = 2$	8.96	17.86	15.75
$H_0 : r = 2$	$H_a : r = 3$	0.19	8.07	6.50
Normalized ecm: $Y = 0.376*K + 0.335*M$				

Notes: 102 observations from 1971q1 to 1997q1. * and ** denote rejection of the null hypothesis for the 5% and 10% significance levels respectively. Critical values from Ostervald–Lenum (1992).

evidence that the technological parameter in the production function is not significant, and that all the technological innovation is driven by the monetization ratio, but this is implausible. Also, the corresponding vector error-correction model (VECM) suffers from residual serial correlation and non-normality. This suggests that the lag length chosen may be too small and an alternative lag length might be used.

Thus, we re-estimated the model for a lag length of seven. (We also included intervention dummies for residual outliers to help accommodate non-normality.) The results in Table 17.13 indicate that the appropriate model this time has unrestricted intercepts and no trends, which is consistent with economic theory predictions; namely, that there is a stochastic trend in technical progress (see Greenslade *et al.*, 1999).

The results for the cointegration tests are presented in Table 17.14. Again we conclude that there exists one cointegrating relationship (as in the case with the two lags) which is reported in the last row of the table. We observe a strong positive relationship between the monetization ratio and the GDP per capita, which provides evidence in favour of the hypothesis that there is a link between financial development and economic growth.

Table 17.15 reports summary results from the VECMs and the basic diagnostics about the residuals of each error-correction equation. Namely, we present the coefficients and the corresponding *t*-statistics for the ecm_{t-1} component, which in this case have the expected signs and are statistically significant in the equations of Y and M. The insignificance of the ECM component for the capital/labour variable indicates that this ratio is

Table 17.15 Summary results from the VECMs and diagnostic tests

	ΔY	ΔK	ΔM
constant	0.904 (4.507)	−0.141 (−1.488)	−0.908 (−2.775)
ecm(−1)	−0.208 (−4.49)	0.004 (1.54)	0.280 (2.78)
R^2	0.79	0.75	0.79
S.E. of regression	0.006	0.002	0.01
$\chi^2_{S.C.}(4)$	0.639	2.748	8.195
$\chi^2_{Norm}(2)$	0.776	5.995	5.585
$\chi^2_{Het}(1)$	2.511	0.067	2.993
$\chi^2_{Arch}(4)$	1.445	4.781	3.239

Note: * Rejects null hypothesis at 5% significance level. *t*-statistics in parentheses.

Table 17.16 Test statistics and choice criteria for selecting the order of the VAR

Based on 77 obs. from 1978q1 to 1997q1
List of variables included in the unrestricted VAR: Y, K, T

Order	LL	AIC	SBC	LR test	Adjusted LR test
8	692.6	614.6	523.2	—	—
7	685.3	616.3	535.4	$\chi^2(9) = 14.54$ [.104]	9.63 [.381]
6	679.9	619.9	549.6	$\chi^2(18) = 25.24$ [.118]	16.72 [.542]
5	672.0	621.0	561.2	$\chi^2(27) = 41.17$ [.040]	27.26 [.449]
4	667.2	625.2	576.0	$\chi^2(36) = 50.80$ [.052]	33.64 [.581]
3	664.4	631.4	592.7	$\chi^2(45) = 56.42$ [.118]	37.37 [.783]
2	649.4	625.3	597.2	$\chi^2(54) = 86.55$ [.003]	57.32 [.353]
1	606.8	591.8	574.3	$\chi^2(63) = 171.48$ [.000]	113.58 [.000]
0	170.4	164.4	157.3	$\chi^2(72) = 1044.4$ [.000]	691.75 [.000]

Note: AIC = Akaike information criterion; SBC = Schwarz Bayesian criterion.

weakly exogenous to the model. The diagnostic tests involve χ^2 tests for the hypothesis that there is no serial correlation; that the residual follows the normal distribution; that there is no heteroskedasticity; and finally that there is no autoregressive conditional heteroskedasticity. In all equations the diagnostics suggest that the residuals are Gaussian, as the Johansen method presupposes.

Turnover ratio

Continuing, we turn to the next financial development proxy variable, which is the turnover ratio. The results of the tests for the lag length of this model (which includes GDP per capita, turnover ratio, capital/labour ratio, intercept and various structural dummy variables) are reported in Table 17.16 and indicate a lag length of order 2. For this choice, three alternative measures of the order of lag length agree. Here the selected model is the one with the unrestricted intercept but no trend in the levels of the data, consistent with our expectations (see Table 17.17). The results of the cointegration test are presented in Table 17.18. We observe one cointegration vector reported in the latter table with the expected signs, indicating that a positive long-run relationship exists between GDP per capita and the turnover ratio. Again, the diagnostics (reported in Table 17.19) show that the error terms are Gaussian. The ECM coefficients have the

Table 17.17   The Pantula principle for the turnover ratio proxy variable

H_0	r	$n - r$	Model 1	Model 2	Model 3
λ max test					
	0	3	49.86	24.11	27.76
	1	2	23.74	8.67*	17.96
	2	1	7.34	0.55	0.43
λ trace test					
	0	3	49.86	33.43	54.19
	1	2	23.74	9.23*	26.43
	2	1	7.34	0.55	8.46

Note: * Denotes the first time when the null hypothesis is not rejected for the 90% significance level.

Table 17.18   Cointegration test based on Johansen's max. likelihood method

Null hypothesis	Alternative hypothesis		Critical values	
			95%	90%
λ_{max} rank tests		λ_{max} rank value		
$H_0 : r = 0$	$H_a : r > 0$	24.11*	21.12	19.02
$H_0 : r \leq 1$	$H_a : r > 1$	8.67	14.88	12.98
$H_0 : r \leq 2$	$H_a : r > 2$	0.55	8.07	6.50
λ_{trace} rank tests		λ_{trace} rank value		
$H_0 : r = 0$	$H_a : r = 1$	33.43*	31.54	28.78
$H_0 : r = 1$	$H_a : r = 2$	9.23	17.86	15.75
$H_0 : r = 2$	$H_a : r = 3$	0.55	8.07	6.50
Normalized ecm: $Y = 0.376*K + 0.335*M$				

Note: 83 observations from 1976q3 to 1997q1. * and ** denote rejection of the null hypothesis for the 5% and 10% significance levels, respectively. Critical values from Ostervald-Lenum (1992).

Table 17.19   Summary results from the VECMs and diagnostic tests

	ΔY	ΔK	ΔT
ecm(−1)	−0.025 (−4.29)	0.006 (2.283)	0.44 (2.61)
R^2	0.59	0.77	0.42
S.E. of Regression	0.005	0.0027	0.171
$\chi^2_{S.C.}(4)$	6.48	5.56	3.03
$\chi^2_{Norm}(2)$	0.18	3.01	4.40
$\chi^2_{Het}(1)$	0.93	0.06	1.04
$\chi^2_{Arch}(4)$	3.89	11.45	1.88

Note: * Rejects null hypothesis at 5% significance level. *t*-statistics in parentheses.

expected signs and are statistically significant and different from zero. However, the low coefficient on capital is hard to interpret.

Claims and currency ratios

Extending our analysis to the other two financial development proxy variables (claims and currency ratios), we found in both cases that the most suitable model was the

Table 17.20 The Pantula principle for the claims ratio proxy variable

H_0	r	$n - r$	Model 1	Model 2	Model 3
λ max test					
	0	3	39.60	13.27*	31.73
	1	2	11.04	9.60	12.88
	2	1	7.60	0.24	9.34
λ trace test					
	0	3	58.25	23.12*	53.96
	1	2	18.65	9.58	22.22
	2	1	0.06	0.24	9.34

Note: * Denotes the first time that the null hypothesis is not rejected for the 90% significance level.

Table 17.21 The Pantula principle for the currency ratio proxy variable

H_0	r	$n - r$	Model 1	Model 2	Model 3
λ max test					
	0	3	39.11	11.20*	32.00
	1	2	7.70	7.51	10.87
	2	1	6.13	0.09	7.37
λ trace test					
	0	3	52.95	18.81*	50.25
	1	2	13.84	7.60	18.25
	2	1	6.13	0.09	7.37

Note: * Denotes the first time that the null hypothesis is not rejected for the 90% significance level.

second (unrestricted intercept, no trends), but there is no cointegration relationship between these variables and the GDP per capita (see Tables 17.20 and 17.21).

Thus with the Johansen procedure we found strong evidence of cointegration between two of the four financial development proxies (monetization and the turnover ratio) and GDP per capita.

A model with more than one financial development proxy variable

In this section we examine a specification that includes more than one financial development proxy. First, we estimated a model including all four proxy variables; the selected lag length was two (see Table 17.22) and the appropriate model includes unrestricted intercepts but no trends in the VECMs (see Table 17.23).

The results for the cointegration test are reported in Table 17.24. This time, there are two cointegrating vectors, which is consistent with the previous findings of cointegration among monetization and GDP per capita, and turnover and GDP per capita. The results from the VECM for all these variables are reported in Table 17.25, and indicate that the claims ratio and the currency ratio should be treated as weakly exogenous variables in the cointegrating model. Therefore we re-estimated, treating these two proxies as exogenous variables. However, while the results then clearly indicated the existence of one cointegrating vector with the correct – according to the theory – signs of the coefficients for the capital/labour ratio

Table 17.22   Test statistics and choice criteria for selecting the order of the VAR

Based on 77 obs. from 1978q1 to 1997q1
List of variables included in the unrestricted VAR: Y, K, T, M, CL, CUR

Order	LL	AIC	SBC	LR test	Adjusted LR test
8	1421.4	1121.4	769.8	—	—
7	1363.1	1099.1	789.7	$\chi^2(36) = 16.67$ [.000]	40.91 [.264]
6	1312.6	1084.6	817.4	$\chi^2(72) = 17.67$ [.000]	76.32 [.341]
5	1287.0	1095.0	869.9	$\chi^2(108) = 268.94$ [.000]	94.30 [.823]
4	1254.7	1098.7	915.8	$\chi^2(144) = 333.54$ [.000]	116.95 [.952]
3	1225.3	1105.3	964.6	$\chi^2(180) = 392.33$ [.000]	137.57 [992]
2	1190.3	1106.3	1007.9	$\chi^2(216) = 462.23$ [.000]	162.08 [.998]
1	1129.5	1081.5	1025.2	$\chi^2(252) = 583.96$ [.000]	204.76 [.987]
0	90.47	378.4	364.4	$\chi^2(288) = 2061.9$ [.000]	723.01 [.000]

Note: AIC = Akaike information criterion; SBC = Schwarz Bayesian criterion.

Table 17.23   The Pantula principle for all the financial development ratio proxy variables

H_0	r	n − r	Model 1	Model 2	Model 3
λ max test					
	0	6	51.37	51.12	56.60
	1	5	41.90	34.65	47.95
	2	4	29.81	18.37*	24.86
	3	3	17.37	10.80	17.20
	4	2	7.50	5.79	10.80
	5	1	5.70	0.86	5.76
λ trace test					
	0	6	153.68	121.99	163.23
	1	5	102.31	70.86	106.23
	2	4	60.40	36.20*	58.67
	3	3	30.58	17.46	33.80
	4	2	13.21	6.66	16.60
	5	1	5.70	0.86	5.79

Note: * Denotes the first time that the null hypothesis is not rejected for the 90% significance level.

and the financial proxies, we were in all cases unable to accept the exogeneity test conducted subsequently.

Thus we finally estimated a model including the financial development proxies, which we found are cointegrated with per capita GDP (namely the turnover and the monetization ratio). The results of the test for cointegration of this model are presented in Table 17.26. It is clear that we have one cointegrating vector, which is reported in the same table. From these results, we observe a positive relationship between GDP per capita and the capital/labour ratio with a higher coefficient than in the previous cases, as well as positive relationships between the dependent variable and the two financial development ratios. We do not wish to claim too much about the results of this final specification, but it seems to capture some of the implications of the underlying economic theory and is at least consistent with the previous findings of the tests for cointegration for each variable reflecting financial development separately.

Table 17.24 Cointegration test based on Johansen's maximum likelihood method

Null hypothesis	Alternative hypothesis		Critical values	
			95%	90%
λ_{max} rank tests		λ_{max} rank value		
$H_0 : r = 0$	$H_a : r > 0$	51.12*	39.83	36.84
$H_0 : r \leq 1$	$H_a : r > 1$	34.65*	33.64	31.02
$H_0 : r \leq 2$	$H_a : r > 2$	18.37	27.42	24.99
$H_0 : r \leq 3$	$H_a : r > 3$	10.80	21.12	19.02
$H_0 : r \leq 4$	$H_a : r > 4$	5.79	14.88	12.98
$H_0 : r \leq 5$	$H_a : r > 5$	0.86	8.07	6.50
λ_{trace} rank tests		λ_{trace} rank value		
$H_0 : r = 0$	$H_a : r = 1$	121.99*	95.87	91.40
$H_0 : r = 1$	$H_a : r = 2$	70.86*	70.49	66.23
$H_0 : r = 2$	$H_a : r = 3$	36.20	48.88	45.70
$H_0 : r = 3$	$H_a : r = 4$	17.46	31.54	28.78
$H_0 : r = 4$	$H_a : r = 5$	6.66	17.86	15.75
$H_0 : r = 5$	$H_a : r = 6$	0.86	8.07	6.50

Normalized ecm1: $Y = 0.138^*K + 0.130^*M + 0.252^*CUR + 0.098^*CL + 0.058^*T$
Normalized ecm2: $Y = 0.231^*K + 0.200^*M + 0.279^*CUR + 0.007^*CL + 0.089^*T$

Notes: 83 observations from 1976q3 to 1997q1. * and ** denote rejection of the null hypothesis for the 5% and 10% significance levels, respectively. Critical values from Ostervald-Lenum (1992).

Table 17.25 Summary results from the VECMs and diagnostic tests

	ΔY	ΔK	ΔM	ΔCUR	ΔCL	ΔT
constant	1.27(4.88)	−0.26(−1.93)	−0.01(−0.32)	−0.14(−0.35)	−0.01(−1.14)	−29.3(−2.57)
ecm1(−1)	0.007(1.2)	−0.007(−0.2)	0.01(1.79)	−0.01(−1.14)	−1.52(−5.91)	0.03(0.18)
ecm2(−1)	−0.03(−5.18)	0.007(2.27)	0.01(1.80)	−0.004(−0.44)	−0.33(−1.31)	0.35(1.78)
R^2	0.59	0.70	0.52	0.40	0.52	0.23
S.E. of Regression	0.005	0.003	0.1	0.009	0.25	0.19
$\chi^2_{S.C.}(4)$	3.95	8.69	13.95*	3.43	15.18*	22.29*
$\chi^2_{Norm}(2)$	0.52	3.32	15.53*	7.31*	69.74*	1.49
$\chi^2_{Het}(1)$	0.85	0.08	0.0001	0.62	0.004	0.64
$\chi^2_{Arch}(4)$	5.43	1.71	3.16	2.32	2.54	0.89

Note: * Rejects null hypothesis at 5% significance level. *t*-statistics in parentheses.

Table 17.26 Cointegration test based on Johansen's maximum likelihood method

Null hypothesis	Alternative hypothesis		Critical values	
			95%	90%
λ_{max} rank tests		λ_{max} rank value		
$H_0 : r = 0$	$H_a : r > 0$	30.24*	27.42	24.99
$H_0 : r \leq 1$	$H_a : r > 1$	14.29	21.12	19.02
$H_0 : r \leq 2$	$H_a : r > 2$	5.07	14.88	12.98
$H_0 : r \leq 3$	$H_a : r > 3$	0.02	8.07	6.50
λ_{trace} rank tests		λ_{trace} rank value		
$H_0 : r = 0$	$H_a : r = 1$	49.63*	48.88	45.70
$H_0 : r = 1$	$H_a : r = 2$	19.39	31.54	28.78
$H_0 : r = 2$	$H_a : r = 3$	5.09	17.86	15.75
$H_0 : r = 3$	$H_a : r = 4$	0.02	8.07	6.50

Normalized ecm: $Y = 0.122^*K + 0.110^*M + 0.073^*T$

Notes: 83 observations from 1976q3 to 1997q1. * and ** denote rejection of the null hypothesis for the 5% and 10% significance levels, respectively. Critical values from Ostervald-Lenum (1992).

Questions and exercises

Questions

1 Explain the meaning of cointegration. Why is it so important for economic analysis?

2 Why is it necessary to have series that are integrated of the same order to make cointegration possible? Give examples.

3 What is the error-correction model? Prove that the ECM is a reparametrization of the ARDL model.

4 What are the features of the ECM that make it so popular in modern econometric analysis?

5 Explain step by step how can one test for cointegration using the Engle–Granger (EG) approach.

6 State the drawbacks of the EG approach, and discuss these with reference to its alternative (that is the Johansen approach).

7 Is it possible to have two I(1) variables and two I(2) variables in a Johansen test for cointegration, and to find that the I(2) variables are cointegrated with the I(1)? Explain analytically.

Exercise 17.1

The file korea_phillips.wf1 contains data for wages and unemployment for the Korean economy. Test for cointegration between the two variables using the EG approach and comment on the validity of the Phillips curve theory for the Korean economy.

Exercise 17.2

The file cointegration.wf1 contains data on three variables (x, y and z). Test the variables for their order of integration and then apply the EG approach to the three different pairs of variables. In which of the pairs do you find cointegration?

Exercise 17.3

Use the file in Exercise 17.2 and verify your results by using the Johansen approach. Include all three variables in a multivariate Johansen cointegration test. What is your result? Can you identify the cointegrating vector(s)?

Exercise 17.4

The files Norway.wf1, Sweden.wf1 and Finland.wf1 contain data for GDP and various financial proxies as in the computer example for the UK case presented in this chapter. For each of these countries, test for cointegration among the pairs of variables by applying both the EG and the Johansen approach as in the computer example. After determining whether or not cointegration exists, estimate the respective ECMs.

18 Identification in Standard and Cointegrated Systems

CHAPTER CONTENTS

LEARNING OBJECTIVES

After studying this chapter you should be able to:

1. Understand the concept of identification and know how to use the rank and order conditions.
2. Appreciate the differences of identification between standard and cointegrating systems.
3. Know how to identify a cointegrating system of equations.

Introduction

In the previous chapter we discussed the case of estimating and testing cointegration when there are more than two cointegrating vectors. One important issue we did not address, however, is exactly how we interpret these vectors once there are more than one of them. Johansen in his original work was careful to describe his method as 'estimating the space spanned by the cointegrating vectors'. This may seem a confusing phrase, but it is in fact very important. The key to understanding this is to realize that if there are two cointegrating vectors an infinite number of other vectors can be constructed simply by combining them in different ways. For example, if the coefficients of each vector are added together that will produce a third vector which cointegrates, or subtracting the coefficients will produce another. So once there are two or more vectors we have really only defined a space that contains all the possible vectors we could calculate. The important issue, then, is how to locate a single set of vectors in this space that we can interpret from an economic viewpoint. This is the identification problem.*

This basic issue is not new to models that involve cointegration, and in fact it is a fundamental problem in all econometrics whenever researchers are dealing with more than one equation. In the 1950s an important group of econometricians called the Cowles Commission defined this problem for systems of simultaneous equations, and the extension to systems with cointegration is a relatively straightforward expansion of their ideas.

This chapter will define the problem of identification for standard models and then extend the idea to systems with cointegration. We shall then illustrate the procedure using an example based on US yield curve data.

Identification in the standard case

In this section we consider the standard issue of identification as it has been understood since the 1960s, without considering the issue of cointegration. Let us begin by considering a structural two-equation system as follows:

$$
\begin{aligned}
y_1 &= \alpha_1 y_2 + \beta_1 x_1 + \beta_2 x_2 + u_1 \\
y_2 &= \alpha_2 y_1 + \beta_3 x_1 + \beta_4 x_2 + u_2
\end{aligned}
\tag{18.1}
$$

where y_1 and y_2 are endogenous variables, x_1 and x_2 are exogenous variables and u_1 and u_2 are error terms. This is a simultaneous system because y_1 is a function of current y_2 and y_2 is a function of current y_1. We also interpret it as a pair of structural relationships, which simply means that we can give these equations a clear economic interpretation. This system can be written in matrix form as:

$$
AY = BX + U
\tag{18.2}
$$

---

*In econometrics, identification has a number of meanings. In time series it is sometimes related to choosing the correct form of the model, for example. But in this context it refers to being able to identify the economic structure that lies behind a set of data.

where

$$A = \begin{pmatrix} 1 & -\alpha_1 \\ -\alpha_2 & 1 \end{pmatrix} \quad B = \begin{pmatrix} \beta_1 & \beta_2 \\ \beta_3 & \beta_4 \end{pmatrix} \quad Y = \begin{pmatrix} y_1 \\ y_2 \end{pmatrix} \quad X = \begin{pmatrix} x_1 \\ x_2 \end{pmatrix} \quad \text{and } U = \begin{pmatrix} u_1 \\ u_2 \end{pmatrix}$$

The identification problem that exists in Equation (18.1) may be understood in a number of ways.

1 We may note that identical variables are in each of the two equations in Equation 18.1 so, apart from the fact that we have chosen to write y_1 on the left-hand side of the first one and y_2 on the left-hand side of the second, there is really no difference between them. If we were to try to estimate these two equations the data would make it impossible to discriminate between them.

2 Assuming that we know the parameters then, for any two values of the X-variables, we could solve these equations for the Y-variables. This would represent one point in a graph involving Y_1 and Y_2. But this point would not allow us to estimate the lines that pass through it, as any number of lines will pass through the same point. Even if we had many points this would not help, as every point could have an infinite number of lines passing through it.

3 The final way is in terms of the reduced form of the structural model. The reduced form is simply when we eliminate all the simultaneous effects by solving the model for the exogenous variables:

$$Y = A^{-1}BX + A^{-1}U = DX + E \tag{18.3}$$

In this form the D matrix has four elements. We can estimate these four parameters easily, but the issue is whether we can recover the structural form parameters A and B. A and B contain six unknown parameters, and so it is generally impossible to work out these from the four parameters we estimate in the reduced form in a unique way.

The identification problem then is understanding what we need to know about the system to allow us to estimate the structural form uniquely, either as a structural equation directly or by estimating the reduced form and then calculating the structural parameters. In essence, unless we know something about the system from theory, the system will always be unidentified. To identify the structure we must have some theoretical knowledge about the simultaneous structure we are trying to estimate. So, for example, if we interpret one equation as a demand equation and the other as a supply equation we might believe from theory that people's incomes affect demand but not supply; similarly, the supply curve might be affected by the firm's capital stock, which would not enter the demand equation. These types of theoretical expectations would then allow us to impose some restrictions on the simultaneous model, which might have the following form:

$$\begin{aligned} y_1 &= \alpha_1 y_2 + \beta_1 x_1 + u_1 \\ y_2 &= \alpha_2 y_1 + \beta_4 x_2 + u_2 \end{aligned} \tag{18.4}$$

Here, just as in the supply and demand example above, we assume that we know that x_2 does not enter the first equation and x_1 does not enter the second. Now the model is said to be exactly identified, and we can see this in terms of the three points made above:

1 The equations are now distinctly different from each other, and so it would be possible to estimate the two simultaneous equations in Equation (18.4.)

2 It is now possible to trace out either line in a unique way. Suppose we have two values for x_1 and x_2; this would give us two values for the y-variables. Now suppose only x_2 changed; this obviously does not move the first line at all, as x_2 is not in that equation; however, we would get a new solution for both y-variables. So the first line has not moved and we have two points on that line. If we join these two points we shall be drawing the first relationship. Similarly, if only x_1 changes we shall be able to join the solution points and draw out the second relationship. So, by excluding a variable from a relationship, we are able to identify that relationship.

3 Now the reduced form still has four parameters that can be estimated, but the structural form also has only four parameters. This means that in general we shall be able to move from the reduced form parameters to the simultaneous structural ones in a unique way.

In this simple case it is fairly obvious that excluding one variable from each equation will allow us to achieve identification of the model, but in more complex models this is not so easy to decide. However, there are two conditions that allow us to assess whether a particular equation is identified. These are called the order and the rank conditions. The order condition is relatively easy to calculate; it is a necessary condition, but not sufficient. This means that if an equation is identified then the order condition must hold, but even if it holds it does not guarantee that an equation is identified. The rank condition is more complex to calculate, but it is both necessary and sufficient. This means that if an equation is identified, the rank condition must hold, and if it holds, an equation is definitely identified.

The order condition

Let G be the total number of endogenous variables in a model, G_1 be the number of endogenous variables in a particular equation, K be the number of exogenous variables in a model, and K_1 the number of exogenous variables in a particular equation. Then the equation is identified if:

$$K - K_1 = G_1 - 1 \tag{18.5}$$

If $K - K_1 < G_1 - 1$ then the equation is not identified.
If $K - K_1 > G_1 - 1$ then the equation is over-identified; this case will be discussed below.

The rank condition

If a model contains G endogenous variables and G equations, then a particular equation is identified by the rank condition if and only if at least one non-zero determinant of order $(G-1) \times (G-1)$ can be constructed from the coefficients of the variables excluded from that equation.

The order condition is just checking that sufficient variables have been excluded from an equation for identification. The problem with this condition, however, is that it does not check the rest of the system. So we might believe that we have identified an equation by excluding a particular variable, but if that variable does not appear anywhere else in the system we would be mistaken in believing we had identified it. The rank condition checks not only that we have made sufficient exclusion restrictions but also that the variables excluded actually do something in the rest of the model that guarantees identification.

If a model is:

- **Under-identified:** this means that the structural form of the model cannot be uniquely determined and, in effect, that the theoretical specification of the model is inadequate.

- **Exactly identified:** this means that there is a unique mapping between the structural form parameters and the reduced form parameters. However, there may be a number of just identified models that give the same reduced form. It is then not possible to test between these different theoretical models. In this case we can take the reduced form model parameters and derive a number of different structural forms, all of which fit the data equally well, and so we cannot test between them.

- **Over-identified:** this means that we have more than the required just identifying restrictions, so when we go from the reduced form to the structural form we shall begin to reduce the explanatory power of the structural model. In this case, if we have a number of different structural models we can begin to construct a test of the best one. It is only in this case that we can begin to test one economic theory against another.

The above section has outlined the basic idea of identification in a standard economic model; we now turn to the extension of the case where we have cointegration in the system.

Identification in cointegrated systems

The basic idea behind identification in cointegrated systems parallels the above standard case in many ways, though it does have some crucial differences. Again, let us begin with a simultaneous structural system, but now in an ECM framework with cointegration. If we begin by writing out a matrix form of the structural version of Equation (17.41):

$$A_0 \Delta Y_t = \sum_{j=1}^{p} A_j \Delta Y_{t-j} + \alpha^s \beta^{s'} Y_{t-1} + u_t \qquad (18.6)$$

There are two ways in which this model is marked out as a structural one: first, we have the Γ_0 matrix, which means that the current terms are simultaneously interrelated; and second, the α and β matrices have an s superscript, which means that they are the structural and economically meaningful cointegrating vectors and loading weights that we would really like to know about. However, when we apply the Johansen method outlined in the last chapter, this is not the model we estimate; instead, what we actually estimate is the following reduced form model:

$$\Delta Y_t = \sum_{j=1}^{p} A_0^{-1} A_j \Delta Y_{t-j} + A_0^{-1} \alpha^s \beta^{s\prime} Y_{t-1} + A_0^{-1} u_t \tag{18.7}$$

or:

$$\Delta Y_t = \sum_{j=1}^{p} \Gamma_j \Delta Y_{t-j} + \alpha \beta' Y_{t-1} + \varepsilon_t \tag{18.8}$$

There are two issues to the identification problem: an issue around the dynamic terms (can we work out the elements of the A_0 matrix?); and an issue around the cointegrating vectors (can we get from the estimated α and β matrices back to the structural ones in which we are interested?). These two issues are completely separate; being able to solve one does not help in solving the other, so even if we knew A_0 this would not help us to solve for the structural α and β. We can see this clearly from the following statement:

$$A_0^{-1} \alpha^s \beta^{s\prime} = \alpha \beta' = \alpha P P^{-1} \beta' = \alpha^+ \beta^{+\prime}$$

where P is any positive semi-definite matrix; this shows that the reduced form loading weights and cointegrating vectors are not unique. This is just a formal statement of the cointegrating space.

However, this separation of the problem into two parts turns out to be a positive advantage, as normally we are only really interested in identifying the long run; that is, the structural α and β, and this means that we can concentrate only on that part of the problem.

The key insight as to how we identify the long-run cointegrating vectors was provided by Pesaran and Shin (2002). As in the standard case of identification, we need theoretical restrictions to allow us to identify the structure of a system. However, in this case we do not need restrictions on each equation but rather restrictions on each cointegrating vector. The first stage in identifying the cointegrating vectors is to know how many vectors there are; that is, to test for the cointegrating rank r. The previous chapter outlined the methodology for doing this. Once we know r, then we need k restrictions on the cointegrating vectors, where $k = r^2$. This is the order condition for identifying the long-run cointegrating vectors; it is a necessary condition but not sufficient. As before, we have three cases. If:

- $k < r^2$, then the model is under-identified and we cannot obtain unique estimates of the structural vectors from the reduced form.

- $k = r^2$, then the model is exactly identified, but it is statistically indistinguishable from any other exactly identified model.
- $k > r^2$, then the model is over-identified and we may test it against the data and against other over-identified models.

As an example, suppose we have two cointegrating vectors, $r = 2$, in a system of three variables. Then we would need $r^2 = 4$ restrictions to identify the system exactly. One possible set of restrictions would be:

$$0 = \alpha_1 x_1 + \alpha_2 x_2 + \alpha_3 x_3$$
$$0 = \beta_1 x_1 + \beta_2 x_2 + \beta_3 x_3 \tag{18.9}$$
$$\alpha_1 = -1, \alpha_2 = 0, \beta_2 = -1, \beta_3 = 0$$

This would amount to normalizing the first vector on x_1 and the second on x_2, and excluding x_2 from the first vector and x_3 from the second. These four restrictions would identify these two vectors exactly. However, the key difference here between identifying cointegrating vectors and the standard idea of identification is that here we place restrictions on individual vectors, not on each equation. As each equation in Equation (18.8) has all the cointegrating vectors, nothing is excluded from an actual equation.

A worked example

To see how this all works, and to help in understanding what is meant by moving around the cointegrating space, it is helpful to work through a simple example by hand. Consider the following simple system:

$$X_{1t} = 1 + X_{2t} + 0.8X_{1t-1} + u_{1t}$$
$$X_{2t} = 1 + X_{3t} + u_{2t}$$
$$\Delta X_{3t} = u_{3t} \tag{18.10}$$
$$u_{it} \sim NID(0, 1)$$

In this example we have three variables. X_3 is non-stationary as it is a random walk, X_2 is cointegrated with X_3 in the second equation with a vector which is $(0,-1,1)$, and in the first equation X_1 is cointegrated with X_2 with a vector $(-1,5,0)$.* The cointegrating vectors are identified, as X_3 is excluded from the first vector and X_1 is excluded from the second, and so with the two normalization restrictions we have $k = 4$ restrictions for $r = 2$ cointegrating vectors.

Now we have generated some artificial data from this system and used the data to estimate the three variable system and to test for cointegration. The following results were obtained for the maximum eigenvalue and trace test.

---

*We can see the long run by realizing that in the static solution $X_{1t} = X_{1t-1} = X_1$; hence $X_1 = 1 + X_2 + 0.8X_1$ and so $X_1 = 1 + 5X_2$.

Table 18.1 Tests of the cointegrating rank r

	Statistic	95% critical value
Max eigenvalue		
$r = 0$	114.3	22.0
$r = 1$	44.6	15.6
$r = 2$	1.26	9.2
Trace		
$r = 0$	160.2	34.9
$r = 1$	45.8	19.9
$r = 2$	1.26	9.2

Table 18.2 The estimated cointegrating vectors

	Vector 1	Vector 2
X_1	−0.014(−1)	0.013(−1)
X_2	0.085(5.9)	0.056(−4.3)
X_3	0.013(0.95)	−0.19(14.7)

The conclusion from Table 18.1 is clearly that there are two cointegrating vectors on both tests, which, of course, is the correct answer. However, the two estimated cointegrating vectors do not look very much like the theoretical ones we know lie behind the data. The estimated cointegrating vectors are given in Table 18.2.

The numbers in parentheses are simply the cointegrating vectors arbitrarily normalized on the first variable. These are quite unlike the underlying true cointegrating vectors that generated the data, which were (−1,5,0) and (0, −1,1), but it must be remembered that these are not the identified ones and we are simply looking at an arbitrary point in the cointegrating space. What we must do now is to move around this space to impose our identifying restriction. In the first vector we have −1 on the first variable and zero on the third. How can we achieve this? The idea is to make a series of linear combinations of the two vectors that are going to give this result. The coefficient on the third variable in the first vector is 0.013; if the coefficient on the second vector were to be −0.013 and we added the two vectors together this would give us a zero. So we need to construct a second vector with −0.013 in it. If we multiplied the whole second vector by 0.06842 this would give us the result we need. So, the following steps are to be carried out:

CV2	0.013	0.056	−0.19
CV2*0.06842=	0.00089	0.00383	−0.013
+CV1=	−0.013	0.088	0
Divide by 0.013 to normalize	−1	6.8	0

We have moved around the cointegrating space to construct a vector that obeys our two restrictions for the first cointegrating vector. Our estimate of the original true structural vector (−1,5,0) is, then, (−1,6.8,0); this is clearly not a bad estimate, but it was far from obvious that it was there in the original Johansen results. We can now turn to the identification of the second vector $(0,-1,1)$. Here we want to construct a vector with a zero in the first place and then normalize it. If we multiplied the first vector by 0.9285 we would get -0.13 in the first place and we could then just add the two vectors together to get a zero, as follows:

CV1	-0.014	0.085	0.013
CV1*0.9285	-0.013	0.079	0.012
+CV2	0	0.135	-0.178
Divide by -0.135 To normalize	0	-1	1.3

So our estimate of the true vector $(0,-1,1)$ is $(0,-1,1.3)$, again remarkably close considering that this was not at all obvious in the original results.

This chapter has explored the basic idea of identification in systems of equations, starting first with standard equations and then moving on to systems involving co-integration. While identification has always been important, it takes on a new and important role when we start to investigate systems of cointegrated equations. The reason for this is simply that the results which come out of the standard Johansen technique cannot be interpreted easily until the issue of identification has been fully resolved.

Computer example of identification

As an example of identification we are going to consider three points on the US Treasury bill yield curve. That is the rate of interest offered by US Treasury bills over 4 weeks, 3 months and 6 months over the period 31 July 2001 to 31 December 2009 on a daily basis: approximately 2,100 observations. This data is shown in Figure 18.1.

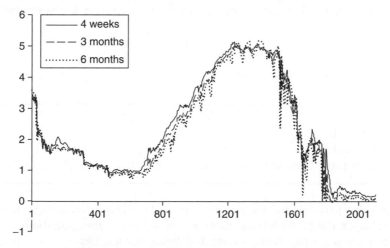

Figure 18.1 The US Treasury bill yield curve

The expectations theory of the yield curve suggests the 3-month rate should be equal to the average of the 4-week rate over the following 3 months, and similarly the 6-month rate should equal the average of the expected 4-week rate over the following 6 months. Figure 18.1 suggests that these three rates move closely together. We would expect that there are two cointegrating vectors linking the three rates, one linking the 3-month to the 4-week rate, and one linking the 6-month to the 4-week rate, hence $(1,-1,0)$ and $(1,0,-1)$. If we test for cointegration as outlined in the previous section we find two cointegrating vectors, but, as before, they do not look like the two vectors outlined above.

To identify these vectors in EViews we go to the VAR specification window and choose a vector error correction model for our three variables with lag length of 2. Under cointegration we choose 2 as the number of cointegrating vectors. Then, to identify the system, click on the tab **VEC RESTRICTIONS** and tick the box to impose restrictions. Then each restriction may be typed into the window below. To restrict the second coefficient in the first vector to be -1, type $B(1, 2) = -1$, and restrictions are separated by commas. So to enter the four restrictions we need to identify the system exactly. We type the following in the restriction box:

$$B(1, 2) = -1, \ B(1, 3) = 0, \ B(2, 3) = -1, \ B(2, 2) = 0$$

The resulting vectors will then look like this:

4-week	1.007	0.998	
3-month	-1	0	
6-month	0	-1	
SE of each equation	$EQ1 = 0.086$	$EQ2 = 0.0621$	$EQ3 = 0.0479$

This looks very close to the theoretical expectations. However, at this point we have only imposed an exactly identifying set of restrictions, so, while these results make sense, it would be equally possible to impose something absurd in the model and it would work equally well. Suppose we entered the following set of restrictions:

$$B(1, 2) = -1, \ B(1, 3) = 3, \ B(2, 3) = -1, \ B(2, 2) = 4$$

We would get the following results:

4-week	-1.99	-3.03	
3-month	-1	4	
6-month	3	-1	
SE of each equation	$EQ1 = 0.086$	$EQ2 = 0.0621$	$EQ3 = 0.0479$

The key thing to note is that the standard errors of each equation do not change, so we are not reducing the fit of each equation; we are simply rearranging them in different ways. So there is no way from a statistical point of view that we can discriminate between this nonsensical model and the one above.

However, if we now impose some overidentifying conditions we can begin to test between the two models. Our theory suggests more than four restrictions; in addition to the four we have imposed, we also believe that the coefficient on the 4-week rate in each vector should be 1. Hence the full set of restrictions would be:

$$B(1,1) = 1, \ B(1,2) = -1, B(1,3) = 0, \ B(2,1) = 1, \ B(2,3) = -1, \ B(2,2) = 0$$

If we impose these on the model we get the following results:

4-week	1	1	
3-month	-1	0	
6-month	0	-1	
SE of each equation	$EQ1 = 0.086$	$EQ2 = 0.0621$	$EQ3 = 0.0479$

The standard errors of each equation hardly change (not at all at this number of significant digits) which shows that imposing these extra two restrictions does not make the model fit very much worse, and at the beginning of the output EViews produces a likelihood ratio test of these restrictions that is 4.34 as a $\chi^2(2)$ test with a probability of 0.11. Hence we cannot reject these restrictions at either a 10% or a 5% critical value. So the sensible model is accepted by the data.

If we were to go back to our nonsensical model as follows:

$$B(1,1) = 1, B(1,2) = -1, B(1,3) = 3, B(2,1) = 1, B(2,3) = -1, B(2,2) = 4$$

We would get the following results:

4-week	1	1	
3-month	-1	4	
6-month	3	-1	
SE of each equation	$EQ1 = 0.088$	$EQ2 = 0.0622$	$EQ3 = 0.048$

The standard errors have now risen on each equation, which shows that the fit has deteriorated, but, more importantly, the likelihood ratio test of these restrictions is 125.2, with a probability value of zero to 6 decimal places, which means that we can immediately reject these restrictions as unacceptable to the data. So once we have some over-identifying restrictions we can begin to test one theory against another. But it is only in this case that we can do that.

Conclusion

In this chapter we have outlined the idea of identification in simultaneous systems which are either standard ones or built around cointegration. The identification stage is especially important when we are using the Johansen technique to estimate a number of cointegrating vectors, as the technique itself simply estimates the cointegrating space, and the identification of structural vectors is crucial.

19 Solving Models

CHAPTER CONTENTS

LEARNING OBJECTIVES

After studying this chapter you should be able to:

1. Understand the concept of model solution in econometrics.
2. Understand the concept of simultaneity in economic models.
3. Obtain and interpret impulse response functions of economic models.
4. Solve and evaluate economic models using EViews.

Introduction

Many economic models are non-linear; and even relatively simple models often consist of a mixture of log-linear equations and linear identities, so that in combination the model is non-linear. This means that, in general, such models cannot be solved analytically and hence we must resort to a set of numerical techniques to solve and analyse them. Eviews now has a powerful set of model solution and simulation procedures that allow it to be used for quite sophisticated forecasting and simulation exercises. This chapter will outline some of the principles of model solution, simulation and forecasting, and then show how these ideas are implemented in Eviews.

Solution procedures

Consider a general non-linear model comprising n endogenous variables Y_i, $i = 1 \ldots n$ and m exogenous variables X_j, $j = 1 \ldots m$:

$$Y_1 = f_1(Y, X)$$

$$\vdots \tag{19.1}$$

$$Y_n = f_n(Y, X)$$

In general, there is no way of solving these equations to reach an analytical solution; instead, one of a range of numerical techniques must be used to achieve a numerical solution. The most common technique used is the Gauss–Seidel solution algorithm, a simple technique that has proved itself to be both robust and efficient over the years. The idea of this algorithm is to assign an initial value to the endogenous variables, say Y^1, and then to run through the set of equations solving each in turn, successively updating the values of the endogenous variables, as follows:

$$Y_i^2 = f_i\left(Y_k^2, Y_l^1, X\right) \quad i = 1, \ldots n, \quad k = 1, \ldots i-1, \quad l = i+1, \ldots n \tag{19.2}$$

This is repeated until the value of the endogenous variables at the start of each iteration is sufficiently close to the value that comes out at the end of the iteration to allow the assumption that the whole process has converged; that is, $Y_i^2 - Y_i^1 < \varepsilon$ for all i. This process is not theoretically guaranteed to converge, even if the model does have a solution, but in practice over many years the technique has proved itself to be highly reliable. One of the earliest applications of the Gauss–Seidel technique in economic modelling was in Norman (1967), and more details may be found in Hall and Henry (1988).

The alternative to using Gauss–Seidel is to use one of the gradient-based methods of solution. These methods essentially make a linear approximation to the model and then solve the linearized model repeating the linearization until convergence results. EViews offers two of these algorithms: Newton's method and Broyden's method. Newton's method is the basic one; in this case we take Equation (19.1) and express it as:

$$0 = F(Y, X) \tag{19.3}$$

We perform a linearization around an arbitrary point Y^1:

$$F(Y, X) = F(Y^1, X) + \frac{\partial F(Y^1, X)}{\partial Y} \Delta Y \tag{19.4}$$

We can then update our initial guess Y^1 in the following way:

$$Y^2 = Y^1 + \left(\frac{\partial F(Y^1, X)}{\partial Y} \right)^{-1} F(Y^1, X) \tag{19.5}$$

This is guaranteed to converge, assuming a solution exists, but it can be much more expensive in computational time and computer memory than the Gauss–Seidel technique, as the matrix of derivatives will be an $n \times n$ matrix, which, as the size of the model grows, can become a very large matrix to calculate. Broyden's method is an extension of this technique, whereby instead of calculating the full matrix of derivatives this matrix is simply approximated and updated successively as the solution iterations continue.

The techniques outlined above do not need to be adapted in any significant way if the model is extended to include past values of either the Y- or X-variable. The only trivial extension that needs to be made is that some initial data values must be supplied for the period before the initial solution period, to allow for the lags in the model. However, if the model contains future values of the endogenous variables then the conventional solution methods need to be extended in an important way. So consider an extension of the model in Equation (19.3) to include lagged and future values of Y:

$$0 = F(Y_t, Y_{t-1}, Y_{t+1}, X) \quad t = 1 \ldots T \tag{19.6}$$

When the model is solved for period t, the values of Y at $t - 1$ are known, but not the values of Y at $t + 1$, and so the conventional sequential solution procedure breaks down. Models of the form given by Equation (19.6) are quite common where we have expectations effects, and a common procedure is to replace the expected value of future variables with their actual realization in the model. This is often referred to as a model consistent solution, and requires an extension to the solution techniques outlined above. While there have been a number of proposed solution techniques in the literature, one technique based on practical experience has come to dominate the others. This technique is called the stack algorithm and was first proposed by Hall (1985). The basic idea is quite straightforward; a conventional model such as Equation (19.3) consists of n equations solved over a number of time periods, say 1 to T, and typically the model is solved for each time period, one at a time. However, we can think of a model such as Equation (19.6) simply as a much larger set of equations:

$$0 = F(Y_1, Y_0, Y_2, X_1)$$
$$0 = F(Y_2, Y_1, Y_3, X_2)$$

$$\vdots \qquad\qquad\qquad (19.7)$$

$$0 = F(Y_T, Y_{T-1}, Y_{T+1}, X_T)$$

where we are stacking the n equations in each period over all T periods to give large set of nT equations. We can now use any of the standard techniques such as Gauss–Seidel to solve this large set of equations. The only remaining complication is that in the first equation in Equation (19.7) we have Y_0 and in the last equation, Y_{T+1}; these are both outside the solution period and must be supplied by extra information. Y_0 is usually trivial, as this is simply taken to be the historical data. Y_{T+1}, however, are more complex as these are generally unknown and must be supplied by a special set of equations called terminal conditions. These may be simple constant values or any other set of formulae the user may care to specify, such as a constant growth rate or constant level.

Model add factors

Add factors (or residuals) play a number of roles in manipulating models. As we shall see below, they allow us to interfere in the model's solution in a forecasting context, they allow us to shock the model, they allow us to investigate the implications of the stochastic nature of the model and they help in setting up simulations. In its most basic form an add factor is simply a value that is added to an equation in one form or another. In Eviews, two types of add factors can be generated. If we specify our model Equation (19.3) in a slightly different way:

$$f(Y_i) = f_i(Y, X) \quad i = 1, \ldots n \qquad\qquad (19.8)$$

where we have simply split the dependent variable from each equation and put it on the left-hand side with any possible non-linear transformation to which it has been subject, then there are two ways we may insert an add factor:

$$f(Y_i) = f_i(Y, X) + a_i^1 \quad i = 1, \ldots n \qquad\qquad (19.9)$$

or:

$$f(Y_i - a_i^2) = f_i(Y, X) \quad i = 1, \ldots n \qquad\qquad (19.10)$$

These two will, of course, differ depending on the non-linearity of the f function. In many contexts the two residuals can have quite different implications. Equation (19.10) is often referred to as an additive residual or add factor as it simply adds a fixed amount to the variable. Equation (19.9) will, of course, have different effects depending on the function f. For the most common case, where f is either a log function or the change in the log of Y_i, then Equation (19.9) may be thought of as a multiplicative residual, so that a value of 0.1 for a would increase Y by 10%. Using a residual such as Equation (19.9) in a log equation would also preserve the elasticities of the equation.

Simulation and impulse responses

One of the main uses of models is in policy analysis using either simulation exercises or impulse response analysis. The difference between the two is simply that a simulation is where the effect on the endogenous variables of changing an exogenous variable in a model is considered, while an impulse response considers the effect of applying a set of shocks to a model. The important difference between the two is that a simulation requires that the variable being changed is an exogenous one. Some models (for example a standard VAR model) may not have any exogenous variable and so a simulation does not make sense in that case. If we were to treat one of the endogenous variables as if it were exogenous and apply a fixed change to it, the simulation would have no clear meaning, as we would be cutting out an arbitrary part of the model's feedback structure. Of course, if we shocked an exogenous variable, then as there is no feedback from the model to the exogenous variable, the shock would have the same effect and interpretation as a simulation. Either a simulation or an impulse response is, then, simply a derivative of the endogenous variables with respect to the exogenous variable or the shock.

The basic process of a simulation, then, is to solve the model for a baseline solution. A change is then made, either to one of the add factors in the model, to represent a shock, or to one of the exogenous variables. The model is then solved again and the difference between the two model runs is the shock effect. It is also important to realize that, in the case of a non-linear model, it is generally true that its simulation properties will vary with the baseline from which the simulation was constructed just as a partial derivative of a non-linear function will generally change with the value of the variables in the function. Solving a model for a baseline is not always a simple procedure, and there are a number of options that might be adopted:

1 It may be possible to solve the model for its steady-state solution; that is, to set all the exogenous variables to a constant value and then solve the model for a long period of time. If it settles down to a constant solution then this steady state may be a good baseline from which to perform simulations.

2 If the model's simulation properties are base-dependent, we might argue that the historical data, or a relevant forecast, is the appropriate base to use. However, the model will typically not solve exactly for a historical set of data without some interference. This can be achieved, however, by defining a suitable set of add factors. Let $\bar{Y}$ be a vector of values of the endogenous variables to be used for the baseline of a simulation. We define:

$$f(Y_i^*) = f_i(\bar{Y}, X) \qquad (19.11)$$

that is, Y^* is the solution to each equation given when the desired base value of all the endogenous variables is put on the right-hand side of the equation. Then we may define either:

$$a_i^1 = f(\bar{Y}_i) - f(Y_i^*) \tag{19.12}$$

or:

$$a_i^2 = \bar{Y}_i - Y_i^* \tag{19.13}$$

And if we add these residuals to the model, the model will then replicate exactly the desired base. The difference between the two residuals is now quite important; the additive residuals in Equation (19.13) will preserve the properties of linear equations exactly, but will distort the elasticities of logarithmic equations. The non-linear residual in Equation (19.12) will generally preserve any elasticities exactly as specified in the original equation and hence will give a closer approximation to the simulation properties of a model with zero residuals.

3 Some researchers put considerable effort into constructing a reasonably smooth simulation base and then producing a set of residuals as outlined above to replicate this base. The argument here is that sudden movements in the baseline data can cause odd simulation properties in the model and this can be avoided by constructing a smooth baseline. This is certainly true if only additive add factors, as in Equation (19.13), are used, but the correct use of non-linear add factors should remove this effect.

Stochastic model analysis

Econometric models are by their very nature stochastic; they have uncertain parameters, the functional form may be wrong and they typically have residuals as they do not fit the data perfectly. The analysis of model solution and simulation given above makes no allowance for this, and so we would typically refer to these solution techniques as deterministic techniques, as they do not allow for the stochastic nature of the model. However, there is a broad set of techniques, called stochastic simulations, which allow us to explore the consequences of the stochastic nature of a model. Broadly speaking, once we recognize that a model is stochastic we must realize that the solution to the model is properly described by a complete joint density function of all the endogenous variables. In general, if the model is non-linear then even if all the sources of uncertainty in the model are normal, the density function of the endogenous variables will not be normal. This means that the deterministic model solution is not located easily on the joint density function; it is not the mode of the distribution and is not the same as the vector of marginal means.* Under certain, fairly weak, assumptions about the type of non-linearity, Hall (1988) demonstrated that the deterministic solution corresponds to the vector of marginal medians of the joint distribution of the endogenous variables. So, in a broad sense, the deterministic solution is at the centre of the joint distribution. There will, then, be a distribution around this central point that will measure the uncertainty attached to a forecast or simulation, and this will not generally be symmetric.

---

*The mean is essentially a univariate concept. If we are dealing with a joint distribution the mean of each variable can be defined by allowing all other variables to take all possible values; this is the marginal mean.

We can characterize the sources of model uncertainty by using the following decomposition, writing the model in the following general way:

$$Y = f(X, A, u)$$

where A are the estimated parameters of the model, X are the exogenous variables that may be measured with error, and u are a set of residuals which cause the model to replicate exactly the data Y. Now define:

$$Y^1 = f(X, A, 0) \tag{19.14}$$

$$Y^2 = \bar{f}(X, \bar{A}, 0) \tag{19.15}$$

$$Y^3 = \bar{f}(\bar{X}, \bar{A}, 0) \tag{19.16}$$

where Equation (19.14) is the solution to the model when the residuals are set to zero, Equation (19.15) is the solution when the correct functional form and parameters are used, and Equation (19.16) also uses the correct exogenous variables, then:

$$Y^1 - Y = (Y^1 - Y^2) + (Y^2 - Y^3) + (Y^3 - Y) \tag{19.17}$$

That is, the total error made by the model comprises a term that comes from the residuals of the model, a term that comes from the misspecified functional form, and a term that comes from the errors in the exogenous variables. So a complete understanding of the uncertainty surrounding a model should take into account all these factors.

Stochastic simulation is a computer technique that allows the investigation of these issues. Essentially, what goes on in a stochastic simulation is that a set of numbers are drawn for some combination of the residuals, the parameters and the exogenous variables, and the model is then solved. The solution is stored and the process is repeated with another set of numbers and that solution is also stored. The process is repeated many times and, given the law of large numbers, the set of solutions to the model will approximate the density function of the endogenous variables. The main issue is how these numbers are generated and precisely which parts of the model are subject to shocks.

The shocks may be generated as draws from a parametric distribution, or they may come from a historical set of observations. So, for example, we may follow the usual estimation assumptions and assume that the errors of each equation are normally distributed with a variance given by the equation estimation. The shocks to the model's residuals could then be generated as random numbers drawn from a normal distribution with this variance. Similarly, the shocks to an equation's parameters could be generated from a multivariate normal distribution with a variance–covariance matrix, which again comes from the equation's estimation. An alternative would be to try to get away from assuming a particular distribution for the residuals and simply to use a historical, observed set of residuals arising from the estimation. These residuals can then be used repeatedly, drawing them at random for each replication of the model. If the second option is used, the technique is generally referred to as a bootstrap procedure. More details on exactly how this may be done are given in Hall and Henry (1988).

Setting up a model in EViews

In this section we construct a small 'Dornbusch'-style macroeconomic model, which can be solved either with backward expectations or with model consistent expectations.

The first stage is to create a workfile in the usual way with all the necessary historical data. Then a special model object is created inside the workfile which will hold all the equations of the model in one place. This is done by clicking on the **object** tab in the workfile, then **new object**, then selecting **model** and naming the model to keep it permanently in the workfile. This will create an empty model object, and equations can now be added to this model. There are two main ways to add an equation to the model: either it may simply be typed into the model or an estimated equation may be linked to it. The heart of a Dornbusch-style model is the open arbitrage condition, which does not require estimation as such; hence we can simply type this equation into the model. To do this, go to the Model window, and anywhere in the main window right-click and click on **insert**. Then simply type the required equation into the box that appears:

$$\log(exr) = \log(exre) + sti/100 - stiw/100 \tag{19.18}$$

where *exr* is the nominal exchange rate, *exre* is the expected exchange rate next period, *sti* is the short term interest rate and *stiw* is the world short term interest rate. We now want to define the output gap, and so we define a simple trend output by regressing the following non-linear least squares model:

$$\log(yfr) = c(1) + c(2) * t \tag{19.19}$$

where *yfr* is real GDP and *t* is a time trend, we obtain $c(1) = 12.18$ and $c(2) = 0.029$. We then enter the equation for trend output into the model as:

$$\log(yfrt) = 12.18 + 0.029 * t \tag{19.20}$$

and define the output gap as:

$$ogap = \log(yfr) - \log(yfrt) \tag{19.21}$$

and the real exchange rate as:

$$rexr = exr * cxud/yfd \tag{19.22}$$

where *rexr* is the real exchange rate, *cxud* is US prices and *yfd* is the GDP deflator.

Now we can estimate a reduced-form IS relationship for GDP:

$$\log(yfr) = 12.11 + 0.07 * \log(rexr) - 0.2 * (sti - (\log(yfd)$$
$$- \log(yfd(-1))) * 100 + 0.03 * t + shock \tag{19.23}$$

where *shock* is an artificial variable, set to zero at the moment, which will be used later in the simulation stage. As this is an estimated equation it can be added it directly to the model from the equation object; simply right-click on the equation, and copy and paste it into the model workfile.

The next equation makes the prices a function of the output gap, so that when output goes up, prices also rise:

$$\log(yfd) = -0.003 + 0.85 * \log(yfd(-1)) + 0.135 * ogap \qquad (19.24)$$

And a Taylor rule type equation is used for interest rates:

$$sti = 8.7 + 1.5 * (\log(yfd) - \log(yfd(-1)) * 400 \qquad (19.25)$$

where the 400 turns quarterly inflation into annual inflation scaled in the same way as the short term interest rate. The model is now almost complete; all that is left is to specify a method for determining the expected exchange rate. Here we shall try two alternatives: first a backward-looking expectations mechanism:

$$exre = exr(-1) \qquad (19.26)$$

and then a model-consistent version where the expected exchange rate is set equal to the actual value in the next period of the solution:

$$exre = exr(+1) \qquad (19.27)$$

We shall begin by solving the backward version of the model, using Equation (19.26). Typically, a model of this type will not solve over a reasonable number of periods, given the poor fit of each individual equation. The first stage of solving the model, then, is to create a set of add factors for each equation that will cause it to solve exactly for the historical base period. To do this, go to the model workfile and in the **equation view** highlight each equation, one at a time. Then right-click on an individual equation and choose **properties**. This will bring up a window related to that individual equation; there are three tabs at the top, one of them for **Add factors**. Under **factor type** choose either the second or third option as described above. EViews will then create an add factor series in the main workfile. Finally, under **modify add factor**, choose the second option (so that this equation has no residuals at actuals), which will create a set of add factors that replicate exactly the historical baseline. Repeat this for all the equations in the model. We are then ready to solve the model; choose **Proc** in the main Model window and **solve model**. The default options should be fine, so just click on **OK**. In the main workfile now each endogenous variable in the model will have a second variable with the extension _0 added, so there will be *yfr* and *yfr_0*; the second variable now contains the model solution for *yfr*, and if the add factors have been correctly applied these two should be identical, so that the model has been solved endogenously to replicate exactly the historical base.

To undertake a simulation we need to set up a new scenario, change something in that scenario and finally resolve the model. We begin by creating a new scenario; in the Model window go to **view** and then **scenarios**, then click on **create new scenario**. This will have the default name of scenario 2. All that is left to do is to return to the main variable window and change one of the exogenous variables in the model. In this case we want to apply a 5% shock directly to *yfr*, which we might interpret as a temporary demand shock. In the *yfr* equation we had added a shock variable, which was initially zero, so to change this we simply click on shock_2 and go down to 1980, right-click and select **edit** and change the zero to 0.05. This has now produced a 5% shock to *yfr* in 1980 only.

The next step is simply to solve the model again. This will create a version of each variable in the model with a _2 after it, which holds the new solution values. We now have a number of options. We could simply look at the new solution variables and the base values, and the difference would be the simulation effect. It is usually more convenient to look at either the absolute change or the percentage change between the base values and the new solution, however. To do this, simply generate a new variable; for example, to look at how *exr* changes simply define:

$$exrd = (exr\_2 - exr)/exr \tag{19.28}$$

We can then look at either the values of *exrd* or a graph of it. The latter is shown in Figure 19.1 below. This figure shows that after a sudden one-off shock to demand there is a steady devaluation of the exchange rate, reaching around 1%.

We now turn to the model-consistent expectations version of the model based on Equation (19.27). The whole procedure follows exactly the same set of steps. We create add factors that exactly replicate the base; then we create a new scenario and adjust the shock_2 variable in exactly the same way. The only difference comes when solving

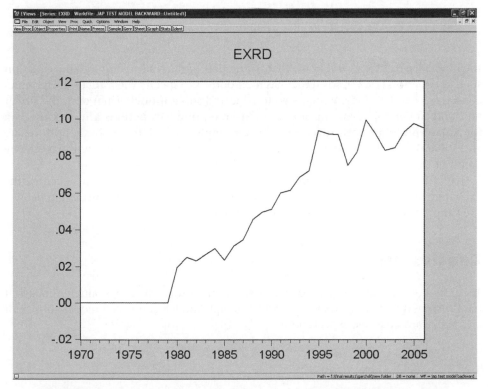

Figure 19.1 The change in the exchange rate under backward expectations

412 *Time Series Econometrics*

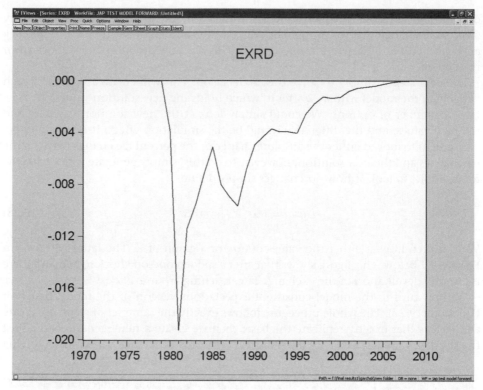

Figure 19.2 The change in the exchange rate under forward-looking expectations

the model itself. EViews will know that the model contains a forward-looking equation such as Equation (19.27), so all that has to be done is to specify the form of the terminal conditions. In the Model window go to **proc** and **solve model**. Then click the **solver** tab, and under **forward solution** select **user supplied in actuals** and tick the box for '**solve model in both directions**'. Then simply go back to the **basic options** tab and solve the model. Now we can again look at the effect of simulating the model by defining the variable *exrd*, and display it as shown in Figure 19.2.

Here the rise in demand causes an increase in interest rates, which causes the exchange rate to jump and then slowly return to its long-run value, just as happens in the simple textbook versions of the Dornbusch model.

Conclusion

This chapter has outlined the basic procedures used to solve and evaluate models. It has illustrated this in EViews for a relatively simple model using both model-consistent and backward-adaptive expectations.

Part

VI Panel Data Econometrics

20 Traditional Panel Data Models

CHAPTER CONTENTS

LEARNING OBJECTIVES

After studying this chapter you should be able to:

1. Understand how a panel differs from either a cross-section or a time series data set.
2. Understand the simple linear panel model with a common constant for all cross-sections.
3. Understand the fixed effects model, which allows for differences for each individual cross-section in a panel data set.
4. Understand the random effects model, which considers individual differences in the cross-sections to be random.
5. Compare and contrast the fixed effects model with the random effects model.
6. Use the Hausman test to assist in making a choice between fixed and random effects.
7. Estimate panel data models using appropriate econometric software.

Introduction: the advantages of panel data

Panel data estimation is often considered to be an efficient analytical method in handling econometric data. Panel data analysis has become popular among social scientists because it allows the inclusion of data for N cross-sections (for example countries, households, firms, individuals and so on) and T time periods (for example years, quarters, months and so on). The combined panel data matrix set consists of a time series for each cross-sectional member in the data set, and offers a variety of estimation methods. In this case, the number of observations available increases by including developments over time.

A data set consisting only of observations of N individuals at the same point in time is referred to as a cross-section data set. Some cross-section data sets also exist over time, so there may be a number of cross-section samples taken at different points in time. These data sets do not, however, constitute a panel data set, as it is generally not possible to follow the same individual member though time. Examples of such datasets would be household surveys that are repeated every year but where different households are surveyed in each case, so it would not be possible to follow the same household through time. A true panel data set would allow each individual in the panel to be followed over a number of periods.

If the panel has the same number of time observations for every variable and every individual, it is known as a balanced panel. Researchers often work with unbalanced panels where there are different numbers of time observations for some of the individuals. When a panel is unbalanced this does not cause major conceptual problems, but the data handling from a computer point of view may become a little more complex.

The basic idea behind panel data analysis arises from the notion that the individual relationships will all have the same parameters. This is sometimes known as the pooling assumption as, in effect, all the individuals are pooled together into one data set and a common set of parameters is imposed across them. If the pooling assumption is correct then panel data estimation can offer some considerable advantages: (a) the sample size can be increased considerably by using a panel, and hence much better estimates can be obtained; and (b) under certain circumstances the problem of omitted variables, which may cause biased estimates in a single individual regression, might not occur in a panel context. Of course, the disadvantage of panel estimation is that if the pooling assumption is not correct, there may be problems, though even in this case, which is often referred to as a heterogeneous panel (because the parameters are different across the individuals), normally the panel data estimator would be expected to give a representative average estimate of the individual parameters. However, we would warn that there are certain circumstances in which this might not happen and thus panel techniques can give quite biased results.

A common problem of time-series estimations is that, when estimating samples with very few observations, it is difficult for the analyst to obtain significant t-ratios or F-statistics from regressions. This problem is common with annual data estimations, since there are very few annual series that extend over more than 50 years. An efficient solution to the problem is to 'pool' the data into a 'panel' of time series from different cross-sectional units. This pooling of the data generates differences among the different cross-sectional or time-series observations that can be captured with the inclusion of dummy variables. This use of dummies to capture systematic differences among panel observations results in what is known as a fixed-effects model, the easiest way of dealing with pooled data. An alternative method is called the random-effects model.

The linear panel data model

A panel data set is formulated from a sample that contains N cross-sectional units (for example countries) that are observed at different T time periods. Consider, for example, a simple linear model with one explanatory variable, as given by:

$$Y_{it} = a + \beta X_{it} + u_{it} \tag{20.1}$$

where the variables Y and X have both i and t subscripts for $i = 1, 2, \ldots, N$ sections and $t = 1, 2, \ldots, T$ time periods. If the sample set consists of a constant T for all cross-sectional units, or in other words if a full set of data both across countries and across time has been obtained, then the data set is called *balanced*. Otherwise, when observations are missing for the time periods of some of the cross-sectional units then the panel is called *unbalanced*.

In this simple panel the coefficients a and β do not have any subscripts, suggesting that they will be the same for all units and for all years. We can introduce some degree of heterogeneity into this panel by relaxing the rule that the constant a should be identical for all cross-sections. To understand this better, consider a case where in the sample there are different subgroups of countries (for example high and low income, OECD and non-OECD, and so on), and that differences are expected in their behaviour. Thus our model becomes:

$$Y_{it} = a_i + \beta X_{it} + u_{it} \tag{20.2}$$

where a_i can now differ for each country in the sample. At this point there may be a question of whether the β coefficient should also vary across different countries, but this would require a separate analysis for each one of the N cross-sectional units and the pooling assumption is the basis of panel data estimation.

Different methods of estimation

In general, simple linear panel data models can be estimated using three different methods: (a) with a common constant as in equation (20.1); (b) allowing for fixed effects; and (c) allowing for random effects.

The common constant method

The common constant method (also called the pooled OLS method) of estimation presents results under the principal assumption that there are no differences among the data matrices of the cross-sectional dimension (N). In other words, the model estimates a common constant a for all cross-sections (common constant for countries). Practically, the common constant method implies that there are no differences between the estimated cross-sections and it is useful under the hypothesis that the data set is *a priori* homogeneous (for example we have a sample of only high-income countries, or EU-only countries and so on). However, this case is quite restrictive and cases of more interest involve the inclusion of fixed and random effects in the method of estimation.

The fixed effects method

In the fixed effects method the constant is treated as group (section)-specific. This means that the model allows for different constants for each group (section). So the model is similar to that in Equation (20.1). The fixed effects estimator is also known as the least squares dummy variable (LSDV) estimator because, to allow for different constants for each group, it includes a dummy variable for each group. To understand this better consider the following model:

$$Y_{it} = a_i + \beta_1 X_{1it} + \beta_2 X_{2it} + \cdots + \beta_k X_{kit} + u_{it} \tag{20.3}$$

which can be rewritten in a matrix notation as:

$$Y = D\alpha + X\beta' + u \tag{20.4}$$

where we have:

$$Y = \begin{pmatrix} Y_1 \\ Y_2 \\ \vdots \\ Y_N \end{pmatrix}_{NT \times 1}, \quad D = \begin{pmatrix} i_T & 0 & \cdots & 0 \\ 0 & i_T & & 0 \\ \vdots & \vdots & & \vdots \\ 0 & 0 & & i_T \end{pmatrix}_{NT \times N},$$

$$X = \begin{pmatrix} x_{11} & x_{12} & \cdots & x_{1k} \\ x_{21} & x_{22} & & x_{2k} \\ \vdots & \vdots & & \vdots \\ x_{N1} & x_{N2} & & x_{Nk} \end{pmatrix}_{NT \times k} \tag{20.5}$$

and:

$$\alpha = \begin{pmatrix} a_1 \\ a_2 \\ \vdots \\ a_N \end{pmatrix}_{N \times 1}, \quad \beta' = \begin{pmatrix} \beta_1 \\ \beta_2 \\ \vdots \\ \beta_k \end{pmatrix}_{k \times 1} \tag{20.6}$$

where the dummy variable is the one that allows us to take different group-specific estimates for each of the constants for each different section.

Before assessing the validity of the fixed effects method, we need to apply tests to check whether fixed effects (that is different constants for each group) should indeed be included in the model. To do this, the standard F test can be used to check fixed effects against the simple common constant OLS method. The null hypothesis is that all the constants are the same (homogeneity), and that therefore the common constant method is applicable:

$$H_0: \quad a_1 = a_2 = \cdots = a_N \tag{20.7}$$

The *F*-statistic is:

$$F = \frac{\left(R^2_{FE} - R^2_{CC}\right)/(N-1)}{\left(1 - R^2_{FE}\right)/(NT - N - k)} \sim F(N-1, NT - N - k) \qquad (20.8)$$

where R^2_{FE} is the coefficient of determination of the fixed effects model and R^2_{CC} is the coefficient of determination of the common constant model. If *F*-statistical is bigger than *F*-critical we reject the null.

The fixed effects model has the following properties:

1. It essentially captures all effects that are specific to a particular individual and do not vary over time. So, if we had a panel of countries, the fixed effects would take full account of things such as geographical factors, natural endowments and any other of the many basic factors that vary between countries but not over time. Of course, this means we can not add extra variables that also do not vary over time, such as country size, for example, as this variable will be perfectly co-linear with the fixed effect.

2. In some cases it may involve a very large number of dummy constants as some panels may have many thousands of individual members – for example, large survey panels. In this case the fixed effect model would use up *N* degrees of freedom. This is not in itself a problem as there will always be many more data points than *N*. However, computationally it may be impossible to calculate many thousands of different constants. In this case, many researchers would transform the model by differencing all the variables or by taking deviations from the mean for each variable, which has the effect of removing the dummy constants and avoids the problem of estimating so many parameters. However, differencing the model, in particular, might be undesirable as it may distort the parameter values and can certainly remove any long-run effects.

It is also possible to extend the fixed effect model by including a set of time dummies. This is known as the two-way fixed effect model and has the further advantage of capturing any effects that vary over time but are common across the whole panel. For example, if we were considering firms in the UK, they might all be affected by a common exchange rate and the time dummies would capture this.

The fixed effect model is a very useful basic model to start from; however, traditionally, panel data estimation has been applied mainly to data sets where *N* is very large. In this case a simplifying assumption is sometimes made that gives rise to the random effects model.

The random effects method

An alternative method of estimating a model is the random effects model. The difference between the fixed effects and the random effects method is that the latter handles the constants for each section not as fixed, but as random parameters. Hence the variability of the constant for each section comes from:

$$a_i = a + v_i \tag{20.9}$$

where v_i is a zero mean standard random variable. The random effects model therefore takes the following form:

$$Y_{it} = (a + v_i) + \beta_1 X_{1it} + \beta_2 X_{2it} + \cdots + \beta_k X_{kit} + u_{it} \tag{20.10}$$

$$Y_{it} = a + \beta_1 X_{1it} + \beta_2 X_{2it} + \cdots + \beta_k X_{kit} + (v_i + u_{it}) \tag{20.11}$$

One obvious disadvantage of the random effects approach is that we need to make specific assumptions about the distribution of the random component. Also, if the unobserved group-specific effects are correlated with the explanatory variables, then the estimates will be biased and inconsistent. However, the random effects model has the following advantages:

1 It has fewer parameters to estimate than the fixed effects method.
2 It allows for additional explanatory variables that have equal value for all observations within a group (that is it allows us to use dummies).

Again, to use random effects one needs to be very careful to check whether there are any implications when using them for our model compared with the fixed effects model. Comparing the two methods, one might expect that the use of the random effects estimator is superior to the fixed effects estimator, because the former is the GLS estimator and the latter is in fact a limited case of the random effects model (as it corresponds to cases where the variation in individual effects is relatively large). But, on the other hand, the random effects model is built under the assumption that the fixed effects are uncorrelated with the explanatory variables, an assumption that in practice creates strict limitations in panel data treatment.

In general, the difference between the two possible ways of testing panel data models is that the fixed effects model assumes that each country differs in its intercept term, whereas the random effects model assumes that each country differs in its error term. Generally, when the panel is balanced (that is, contains all existing cross-sectional data), one might expect that the fixed effects model will work better. In other cases, where the sample contains limited observations of the existing cross-sectional units, the random effects model might be more appropriate.

The Hausman test

The Hausman test is formulated to assist in making a choice between the fixed effects and random effects approaches. Hausman (1978) adapted a test based on the idea that under the hypothesis of no correlation, both OLS and GLS are consistent, but OLS is inefficient, while under the alternative OLS is consistent but GLS is not. More specifically, Hausman assumed that there are two estimators $\hat{\beta}_0$ and $\hat{\beta}_1$ of the parameter vector β and he added two hypothesis-testing procedures. Under H_0, both estimators are consistent but $\hat{\beta}_0$ is inefficient, and under H_1, $\hat{\beta}_0$ is consistent and efficient, but $\hat{\beta}_1$ is inconsistent.

For the panel data, the appropriate choice between the fixed effects and the random effects methods involves investigating whether the regressors are correlated with the individual (unobserved in most cases) effect. The advantage of the use of the fixed effects estimator is that it is consistent even when the estimators are correlated with the individual effect. In other words, given a panel data model where fixed effects would be appropriate, the Hausman test investigates whether random effects estimation could be almost as good. According to Ahn and Moon (2001), the Hausman statistic may be viewed as a distance measure between the fixed effects and the random effects estimators. Thus we actually test H_0, that random effects are consistent and efficient, versus H_1, that random effects are inconsistent (as the fixed effects will be always consistent). The Hausman test uses the following test statistic:

$$H = (\hat{\beta}^{FE} - \hat{\beta}^{RE})'[Var(\hat{\beta}^{FE}) - Var(\hat{\beta}^{RE})]^{-1}(\hat{\beta}^{FE} - \hat{\beta}^{RE}) \sim \chi^2(k) \tag{20.12}$$

If the value of the statistic is large, then the difference between the estimates is significant, so we reject the null hypothesis that the random effects model is consistent and use the fixed effects estimator. In contrast, a small value for the Hausman statistic implies that the random effects estimator is more appropriate.

Computer examples with panel data

Inserting panel data in EViews

One difficulty in working with panel data is that it is quite different from what we have seen so far when using EViews. To use panel data requires specific data manipulation in order to insert the data in EViews in a way that will allow us to get results from the different panel methods of estimation we have seen above.

Consider the following case: assume we have a data set formed of three variables (Y, X and E), and that we have panel data for those three variables for eight different sections (that is $i = 1, 2, \ldots, 8$) and for 40 different time periods (that is $t = 1, 2, \ldots, 40$) – for example, yearly data from 1960 to 1999. We want to enter these data into EViews to estimate a panel regression of the form:

$$Y_{it} = a_i + \beta_1 X_{it} + \beta_2 E_{it} + u_{it} \tag{20.13}$$

To do this we take the following steps:

Step 1 *Create a workfile.* We need to create a new EViews workfile by going to **File/New/Workfile** and setting values for the start and end periods of our data set (in this case, 1960 to 1999).

Step 2 *Create a pool object.* Next create a pool object. Go to **Object/New Object** and from the list of objects click on **Pool**, provide a name for the pool object in the top right-hand corner of the window **Name for the object** (let's say 'basic') and click **OK**. The pool object window will open with the first line reading:

```
Cross-Section Identifiers: (Enter identifiers below this line)
```

In this window enter names for our cross-section dimension. If, for example, we have different countries we can enter the names of the countries, specifying short names (up to three letters for each) to have an equal number of letters for the description of each. If we have different individuals, we could enter numbers instead of the names of the individuals and keep a log file in Excel to record numbers against names. Again, in setting numbers as identifiers, an equal number of digits should be used for each section.

Step 3 *Enter the identifiers*. In our example we have eight different sections so we can enter the identifiers with either names or numbers as we choose. Because we do not have (in this specific example) any information about the nature of the cross-sectional dimension, we may simply enter numbers for identifiers, as follows:

```
Cross-Section Identifiers: (Enter identifiers below this line)
01
02
03
04
05
06
07
08
```

Step 4 *Generate a variable*. We are now ready to generate variables that can be read in EViews as panel data variables. To do this, click on the button **PoolGenr** in the Pool Object window. This opens the Generate series by equation window, in which we specify our equation. Let's say that we want first to enter the Y variable; to do so we type:

```
y_?=0
```

and click **OK**. This will create eight different variables in the Workfile window, namely the variables y_01, y_02, y_03,...,y_08. To explain this a little more, it is the question mark symbol (?) that instructs EViews to substitute each of the cross-section identifiers at that point; and the underscore (_) symbol is used to make the names of the variables easy to see.

Step 5 *Copying and pasting data from Excel*. To do this we need first to explain how the data should look in Excel. If we open the eight variables (y_01, y_02, y_03,...,y_08) created from the previous step in a group (to do this select all eight variables and double-click on them to go to **group**) we will have a matrix of 40×8 dimensions of zeros; 40 because of the number of years in our file and 8 because of the number of cross-sections. This matrix is viewed as what we call 'years down – sections across', so it looks like this:

	section 1	section 2	section 3	····	section 8
1960					
1961					
1962					
···					
···					
1999					

Therefore, it is very important that we have our data in the same format in Excel. If, for example, the downloaded data were in the form 'sections down – years across', they would have to be transformed before being entered into EViews. (A simple way of doing this would be to select all the data, copy it (**Edit/Copy**) and finally paste it into a different sheet using the **Paste Special** function (**Edit/Paste Special**) after clicking on the choice **transpose**, to reformat the data as necessary.)

When the data is in Excel as desired (that is 'years down – sections across'), simply copy all the data (the values of the data only, not the years or the variables/sections names) and paste it into the EViews Group window with the zero values. To edit the Group window and paste the data needed to activate the window by pressing the **edit +/−** button, and then go onto **Edit/Paste**. Finally, press the **edit +/−** button once more to deactivate the window.

The same procedure should be followed for the rest of the variables (X and E). The file panel_test.xls contains the raw data in Excel and the file panel_test.wf1 the same data transferred in EViews.

As a second example, consider the file panel_eu.xls, which contains data for 15 EU countries (so $N = 15$) for the years 1960–99 unbalanced (so max $T = 40$) for three variables, GDP growth, gross fixed capital formation as percentage of GDP, and foreign direct investment (FDI) inflows as percentage of GDP. The reader should try as an exercise to transfer this data from Excel to EViews. (The result is in a file labelled panel_test.wf1.) We have used the following cross-section identifiers:

BEL	for Belgium
DEN	for Denmark
DEU	for Germany
ELL	for Greece
ESP	for Spain
FRA	for France
IRE	for Ireland
ITA	for Italy
LUX	for Luxembourg
NET	for Netherlands
OST	for Austria
POR	for Portugal
RFI	for Finland
SWE	for Sweden
UKA	for United Kingdom

Note that only the three letters should be written as names for the cross-section identifiers in the pool object. We have also used the following variable names: GDPGR95_?,
FDITOGDP_? and GFCFTOGDP_? (see file panel_eu.wf1).

Table 20.1   Common constant

Dependent variable: Y_?
Method: pooled least squares
Date: 04/03/04 Time: 22:22
Sample: 1960 1999
Included observations: 40
Number of cross-sections used: 8
Total panel (balanced) observations: 320

Variable	Coefficient	Std. error	t-statistic	Prob.
C	50.27199	2.040134	24.64151	0.0000
X_?	0.496646	0.018320	27.10964	0.0000
E_?	1.940393	0.153886	12.60930	0.0000

R-squared	0.739693	Mean dependent var.	105.2594
Adjusted R-squared	0.738051	S.D. dependent var.	5.254932
S.E. of regression	2.689525	Sum squared resid.	2293.034
Log likelihood	−769.1500	F-statistic	450.3965
Durbin–Watson stat.	1.061920	Prob(F-statistic)	0.000000

Table 20.2   Fixed effects

Dependent variable: Y_?
Method: pooled least squares
Date: 04/03/04 Time: 22:23
Sample: 1960 1999
Included observations: 40
Number of cross-sections used: 8
Total panel (balanced) observations: 320

Variable	Coefficient	Std. error	t-statistic	Prob.
X_?	0.473709	0.021889	21.64181	0.0000
E_?	1.845824	0.157163	11.74465	0.0000

Fixed effects

01–C	53.24391
02–C	53.35922
03–C	52.37416
04–C	52.89543
05–C	52.64917
06–C	53.34308
07–C	52.76667
08–C	51.85719

R-squared	0.746742	Mean dependent var.	105.2594
Adjusted R-squared	0.739389	S.D. dependent var.	5.254932
S.E. of regression	2.682644	Sum squared resid.	2230.940
Log likelihood	−764.7575	F-statistic	914.0485
Durbin–Watson stat.	1.030970	Prob(F-statistic)	0.000000

Estimating a panel data regression in EViews

After transferring the data into EViews, panel data estimation is carried out by using the **pool object**. Always double-click on **pool object** (labelled as **basic**) and work from there. Let us assume that we have the panel_test file open and that we want to estimate the following model:

$$Y_{it} = a_i + \beta_1 X_{it} + \beta_2 E_{it} + u_{it} \tag{20.14}$$

To do so from the **basic (pool object)**, first click on the **Estimate** button. The Pooled Estimation window opens which asks us to provide names for the dependent variable and the regressors. For the model above, insert as **dependent variable** Y_? (the ? indicates that the computer will include the data for all cross-sections from one to eight) and as regressors in the field **common coefficients** include the constant C followed by the X_? and E_? variables. We also have the option to change the sample (by typing different

Table 20.3   Random effects

Dependent variable: Y_?
Method: GLS (variance components)
Date: 04/03/04 Time: 22:24
Sample: 1960 1999
Included observations: 40
Number of cross-sections used: 8
Total panel (balanced) observations: 320

Variable	Coefficient	Std. error	t-statistic	Prob.
C	47.30772	1.340279	35.29692	0.0000
X_?	0.523554	0.012030	43.52132	0.0000
E_?	2.220745	0.149031	14.90118	0.0000

Random Effects

01–C	0.258081			
02–C	−2.415602			
03–C	0.848119			
04–C	−1.775884			
05–C	1.190163			
06–C	−1.573142			
07–C	0.472518			
08–C	2.995747			

GLS transformed regression

R-squared	0.716534	Mean dependent var.	105.2594
Adjusted R-squared	0.714746	S.D. dependent var.	5.254932
S.E. of regression	2.806617	Sum squared resid.	2497.041
Durbin–Watson stat.	1.140686		

Unweighted statistics including random effects

R-squared	0.594095	Mean dependent var.	105.2594
Adjusted R-squared	0.591534	S.D. dependent var.	5.254932
S.E. of regression	3.358497	Sum squared resid.	3575.601
Durbin–Watson stat.	0.796605		

Table 20.4 Common constant

Dependent variable: Y_?
Method: pooled least squares
Date: 04/30/10 Time: 12:11
Sample: 1960 1999
Included observations: 40
Cross-sections included: 8
Total pool (balanced) observations: 320

Variable	Coefficient	Std. error	t-statistic	Prob.
C	50.27199	2.040134	24.64151	0.0000
X_?	0.496646	0.018320	27.10964	0.0000
E_?	1.940393	0.153886	12.60930	0.0000
R-squared	0.739693	Mean dependent var.		105.2594
Adjusted R-squared	0.738051	S.D. dependent var.		5.254932
S.E. of regression	2.689525	Akaike info criterion		4.825937
Sum squared resid.	2293.034	Schwarz criterion		4.861265
Log likelihood	−769.1500	Hannan–Quinn criter.		4.840044
F-statistic	450.3965	Durbin–Watson stat.		1.061920
Prob(F-statistic)	0.000000			

starting and ending periods in the corresponding box), to include cross-section-specific coefficients for some of the explanatory variables (to induce heterogeneity – this will be examined later), or period-specific coefficients, by typing variable names into the corresponding boxes (for the present, these boxes are left blank) and to select a number of different estimation methods (fixed and random effects) by choosing different options from the drop-down menu. By leaving everything at the default setting **None** we get the common constant estimator results presented in Table 20.4. The interpretation of the results is as before.

To select the fixed effects estimator, click on **estimate** again, leave the equation specification as it is and choose **Fixed** in the cross-section drop-down menu of the **estimation method** choice frame. The results for fixed effects are given in Table 20.5. Similarly, we can obtain results for random effects by choosing **Random** from the cross-section drop-down menu (note that in all cases the period drop-down menu is left as **None**). The results for the random effects estimator are shown in Table 20.6.

We leave it as an exercise to the reader to estimate a model (using the data in the panel_eu.wf1 file) that examines the effects of gross fixed capital formation and FDI inflows to GDP growth for the 15 EU countries.

The Hausman test in EViews

After estimating the equation with random effects, the Hausman test can be conducted in EViews to identify the most appropriate method comparing the fixed and random effects estimator. To do the test, go to **View/Fixed-Random Effects Testing/Correlated Random Effects – Hausman Test**. The results of the test are reported in Table 20.7, and we can see that in this case the chi-square statistic is 7.868, which is larger than the critical. Hence we reject the null hypothesis of random effects in favour of the fixed effects estimator.

Table 20.5 Fixed effects

Dependent variable: Y_?
Method: pooled least squares
Date: 04/30/10 Time: 12:14
Sample: 1960 1999
Included observations: 40
Cross-sections included: 8
Total pool (balanced) observations: 320

Variable	Coefficient	Std. error	t-statistic	Prob.
C	52.81111	2.434349	21.69414	0.0000
X_?	0.473709	0.021889	21.64181	0.0000
E_?	1.845824	0.157163	11.74465	0.0000
Fixed effects (cross)				
01–C	0.432805			
02–C	0.548114			
03–C	−0.436944			
04–C	0.084326			
05–C	−0.161931			
06–C	0.531979			
07–C	−0.044436			
08–C	−0.953913			

Effects specification

Cross-section fixed (dummy variables)

R-squared	0.746742	Mean dependent var.	105.2594
Adjusted R-squared	0.739389	S.D. dependent var.	5.254932
S.E. of regression	2.682644	Akaike info criterion	4.842234
Sum squared resid.	2230.940	Schwarz criterion	4.959994
Log likelihood	−764.7575	Hannan–Quinn criter.	4.889258
F-statistic	101.5609	Durbin–Watson stat.	1.030970
Prob(F-statistic)	0.000000		

The Hausman test in Stata

To implement the Hausman test in Stata, first obtain the fixed and random effects estimates, save them and then compute the test statistic with the Hausman command. The full set of commands is as follows:

```
xtreg y x e , fe
estimates store fe
xtreg y x e , re
estimates store re
hausman fe re
```

The results and interpretation are similar to those provided in Table 20.7.

Inserting panel data into Stata

In Stata, the data should be imported in a different way from EViews. Stata needs to specify the data set as a panel through the command:

```
xtset panelvar timevar
```

Table 20.6   Random effects

Dependent variable: Y_?
Method: pooled EGLS (cross-section random effects)
Date: 04/30/10 Time: 12:21
Sample: 1960 1999
Included observations: 40
Cross-sections included: 8
Total pool (balanced) observations: 320
Swamy and Arora estimator of component variances

Variable	Coefficient	Std. error	t-statistic	Prob.
C	50.27199	2.034914	24.70472	0.0000
X_?	0.496646	0.018273	27.17917	0.0000
E_?	1.940393	0.153492	12.64165	0.0000
Random effects (cross)				
01–C	0.000000			
02–C	0.000000			
03–C	0.000000			
04–C	0.000000			
05–C	0.000000			
06–C	0.000000			
07–C	0.000000			
08–C	0.000000			

Effects specification				
			S.D.	Rho
Cross-section random			0.000000	0.0000
Idiosyncratic random			2.682644	1.0000

Weighted statistics				
R-squared	0.739693	Mean dependent var.		105.2594
Adjusted R-squared	0.738051	S.D. dependent var.		5.254932
S.E. of regression	2.689525	Sum squared resid.		2293.034
F-statistic	450.3965	Durbin–Watson stat.		1.061920
Prob(F-statistic)	0.000000			

Unweighted statistics				
R-squared	0.739693	Mean dependent var.		105.2594
Sum squared resid.	2293.034	Durbin–Watson stat.		1.061920

where `panelvar` is the name of the variable that contains the elements specifying the different sectors in the panel and `timevar` is the name of the variable containing elements specifying the time frame of the panel.

Therefore, we need to specify those two variables and obtain the data in the form of long series. Let us consider the following example of data (which is the same data set as the previous one for Eviews). Table 20.8 contains the data as they appear in Stata. We see that the first series (called id in this example) contains the number 1 for a range of values, followed by a large set of 2s, 3s and so on. These are the panel identifiers (1 for the first sector, 2 for the second and so on). The variable time, next to the id variable, takes the yearly values 1962, 1963,..., 1999 and then starts again from 1962, 1963,..., 1999, taking the same values for the second section (has the id value of 2) and the third

Table 20.7 The Hausman test

Correlated random effects – Hausman test
Pool: BASIC
Test cross-section random effects

Test summary	Chi-sq. statistic	Chi-sq. d.f.	Prob.
Cross-section random	7.868021	2	0.0196

** WARNING: estimated cross-section random effects variance is zero.

Cross-section random effects test comparisons:

Variable	Fixed	Random	Var(Diff.)	Prob.
X_?	0.473709	0.496646	0.000145	0.0570
E_?	1.845824	1.940393	0.001140	0.0051

Cross-section random effects test equation:
Dependent variable: Y_?
Method: panel least squares
Date: 04/30/10 Time: 12:25
Sample: 1960 1999
Included observations: 40
Cross-sections included: 8
Total pool (balanced) observations: 320

Variable	Coefficient	Std. error	t-statistic	Prob.
C	52.81111	2.434349	21.69414	0.0000
X_?	0.473709	0.021889	21.64181	0.0000
E_?	1.845824	0.157163	11.74465	0.0000

Effects specification

Cross-section fixed (dummy variables)

R-squared	0.746742	Mean dependent var.	105.2594
Adjusted R-squared	0.739389	S.D. dependent var.	5.254932
S.E. of regression	2.682644	Akaike info criterion	4.842234
Sum squared resid.	2230.940	Schwarz criterion	4.959994
Log likelihood	−764.7575	Hannan–Quinn criter.	4.889258
F-statistic	101.5609	Durbin–Watson stat.	1.030970
Prob(F-statistic)	0.000000		

section, and so on. These two variables provide the panel characteristics for Stata. The values for the Y, X and E variables, respectively, follow for each section and year.

Thus, to specify this data set as a panel in Stata the command is:

```
xtset id time
```

Stata responds with:

```
panel variable: id (strongly balanced)
time variable: time, 1960 to 1999
delta: 1 unit
```

This applies when the panel is balanced (that is, there are data available for all cross-sections and times). On getting this response from Stata (or a similar response that

Table 20.8 Data in Stata

id	time	Y	X	E
1	1960	100.0000	100	−0.8609
1	1961	102.5000	103.6334	1.251923
1	1962	104.7734	105.7995	1.705449
1	1963	107.2076	106.5128	0.583854
1	1964	107.888	107.6693	0.440685
⋮	⋮	⋮	⋮	⋮
1	1999	115.5558	125.8987	1.175648
2	1960	100.0000	100	1.368522
2	1961	102.4580	100.2264	−0.16229
2	1962	98.62976	96.24845	−0.74456
2	1963	96.27536	99.09063	−0.15279
2	1964	97.53818	99.18853	−0.02619
⋮	⋮	⋮	⋮	⋮
3	1960	100.0000	100	−0.57229
3	1961	101.5600	101.8093	1.954698
3	1962	98.93489	102.0647	−1.1432
3	1963	99.70796	100.4486	0.096794
3	1964	98.81096	99.48605	−0.37499
⋮	⋮	⋮	⋮	⋮

shows us that the data have been specified as a panel – that is, we don't get an error message) we can proceed with the Stata commands for panel methods of estimation.

Estimating a panel data regression in Stata

To estimate a panel regression in its simpler form (that is with the common constant method), the command is:

```
regress depvar indepvars , options
```

This means that we want to list the dependent variable followed by the independent variables, and in the options we specify the method of estimation. Since we want the common constant method, we leave the options blank and use the command:

```
xtreg y x e
```

The results of this estimation are similar to those obtained in Table 20.4. For the fixed effects estimator (select the option `fe`), the command is:

```
xtreg y x e , fe
```

while, similarly, for the random effects estimator (select the option `re`) the command is:

```
xtreg y x e , re
```

The results for these two methods are similar to those in Tables 20.5 and 20.6, respectively.

21

Dynamic Heterogeneous Panels

CHAPTER CONTENTS

LEARNING OBJECTIVES

After studying this chapter you should be able to:

1.   Understand the bias in dynamic panel models.
2.   Understand the solution to the bias problem.
3.   Know the mean group and pooled mean group estimators for dynamic heterogeneous panel models.

Introduction

A dynamic model is characterized by the presence of a lagged dependent variable among the regressors. The basic model is:

$$Y_{i,t} = a_i + \beta_i' X_{i,t} + \gamma Y_{i,t-1} + u_{i,t} \qquad (21.1)$$

where γ is a scalar, and β and $X_{i,t}$ are each $k \times 1$. Dynamic models are very important, especially in economics, because many economic relationships are dynamic in nature and should be modelled as such. The time dimension of panel data (unlike cross-sectional studies) enables us to capture the dynamics of adjustment.

In this simple dynamic model the only heterogeneity comes from the individual intercepts a_i, which are allowed to vary among different sections. However, sometimes in economics it is necessary to induce more heterogeneity in order to find specific coefficients for different groups for some cases. Later we shall consider the mean group and pooled mean group estimators that allow for greater heterogeneity in panel data models.

The problem with the dynamic panels is that the traditional OLS estimators are biased and therefore different methods of estimation need to be introduced. These issues are examined analytically in this chapter.

Bias in dynamic panels

Bias in the simple OLS estimator

The simple OLS estimator for simple static panels is consistent as n or $T \to \infty$ only when all explanatory variables are exogenous and are uncorrelated with individual specific effects. However, because the OLS estimator ignores the error-component structure of the model, it is not efficient. Also, things are quite different when the model includes a lagged dependent variable.

Consider the basic model presented in Equation (21.1) which can be rewritten (omitting the $X_{i,t}$ regressors for simplicity) as:

$$Y_{i,t} = a_i + \gamma Y_{i,t-1} + u_{i,t} \qquad (21.2)$$

It is easy to show that the OLS estimator for this model will be seriously biased because of the correlation of the lagged dependent variable with the individual specific effects (a_i), which are either random or fixed. Since $Y_{i,t}$ is a function of a_i, then $Y_{i,t-1}$ is also a function of a_i. Therefore $Y_{i,t-1}$, which is a regressor in the model, is correlated with the error term and this obviously causes OLS estimators to be biased and inconsistent even if the error terms are not serially correlated. The proof of this is quite difficult and requires much calculation using matrix algebra, and is thus beyond the scope of this text. Readers who would like a better insight into dynamic panels should read Baltagi (1995, ch. 8) or Hsiao (1986, ch. 6).

Bias in the fixed effects model

The bias and inconsistency of the OLS estimator stems from the correlation of the lagged dependent variable with the individual specific effects. It might therefore be thought that the within-transformation of the fixed effects model, given by:

$$Y_{i,t} - \bar{Y}_i = \gamma(Y_{i,t-1} - \bar{Y}_{i,t-1}) + (u_{i,t} - \bar{u}_i) \tag{21.3}$$

would eliminate the problem, because now the individual effects (a_i) are cancelled out. However, the problem is not solved that easily.

Consider again the model in Equation (21.1), which can be rewritten as:

$$Y_{i,t} = \mu_i + \gamma Y_{i,t-1} + u_{i,t} \tag{21.4}$$

where μ_i are now fixed effects. Let $\bar{Y}_i = 1/T \sum_{t=1}^{T} Y_{i,t}$; $\bar{Y}_{i,t-1} = 1/T \sum_{t=1}^{T-1} Y_{i,t-1}$ and $\bar{u}_i = 1/T \sum_{t=1}^{T} u_{i,t}$. It can be shown again that the fixed estimator will be biased for small 'fixed' T. The bias this time is caused by having to eliminate the unknown individual effects (constants) from each observation, which creates a bias $1/T$ between the explanatory variables in the within-transformed model and the residuals. Because $Y_{i,t}$ is correlated with $\bar{u}_i$ by construction (consider that $\bar{u}_i$ is an average containing $u_{i,t-1}$, which is obviously correlated with $Y_{i,t-1}$), $(Y_{i,t-1} - \bar{Y}_{i,t-1})$ will be correlated with $(u_{i,t} - \bar{u}_i)$ even if u_{it} are not serially correlated.

Bias in the random effects model

The problem with the generalized least squares (GLS) method of estimation of the random effects model is similar to that of the least squares dummy variable (LSDV) estimation of the fixed effects model. To apply GLS, it is necessary to quasi-demean the data. This demeaning unavoidably causes the quasi-demeaned dependent variable to be correlated with the quasi-demeaned residuals, and therefore the GLS estimator will also be biased and inconsistent.

Solutions to the bias problem (caused by the dynamic nature of the panel)

There are two proposed solutions to the bias problem presented above. One is to *introduce exogenous variables* into the model. If exogenous variables are added (to a first-order autoregressive process), the bias in the OLS estimator is reduced in magnitude but remains positive. The coefficients on the exogenous variables are biased towards zero. However, the LSDV estimator, for small T, remains biased even with added exogenous variables. A second way is to use the *instrumental variable methods* proposed by Anderson and Hsiao (1981, 1982) and Arellano and Bond (1991). The instrumental variable methods are quite complicated and beyond the scope of this text, but they are mentioned here since they are widely used in panels with small T dimensions. These instrumental variable estimators are sometime referred to as GMM estimators.

Bias of heterogeneous slope parameters

All panel data models make the basic assumption that at least some of the parameters are the same across the panel; this is sometimes referred to as the pooling assumption. Serious complications can arise if this assumption is not true and bias can again arise in both static and dynamic panels under certain circumstances. When the pooling assumption does not hold, a panel is referred to as a heterogeneous panel; this simply means that some of the parameters vary across the panel. If a constant parameter assumption is imposed incorrectly then serious problems may arise. Consider the following heterogeneous static model:

$$Y_{i,t} = \mu_i + \beta_i' \mathbf{X}_i + u_{i,t} \tag{21.5}$$

where heterogeneity is introduced, for example, because cross-sections are considered for a large number of countries in differing stages of economic development, or with different institutions, customs and so on. For simplicity, assume that there is only one explanatory variable, X_{it}, and suppose that the now heterogeneous β_i coefficients are:

$$\beta_i = \beta + v_i \tag{21.6}$$

In this case, Pesaran and Smith (1995) prove that both the fixed effects (FE) and the random effects (RE) estimators may be inconsistent.

Consider now the dynamic autoregressive distributed lag (ARDL) model:

$$Y_{i,t} = a_i + \gamma_i Y_{i,t-1} + \beta_i X_{i,t} + e_{i,t} \tag{21.7}$$

where all coefficients are allowed to vary across cross-sectional units. If we want to consider long-run solutions we have that:

$$\theta_i = \frac{\beta_i}{1 - \gamma_i} \tag{21.8}$$

is the long-run coefficient of X_{it} for the ith cross-sectional unit. Using this, Equation (21.7) can be rewritten as:

$$\Delta Y_{i,t} = a_i - (1 - \gamma_i)(Y_{i,t-1} - \theta_i X_{i,t}) + e_{i,t} \tag{21.9}$$

or substituting $(1 - \gamma_i)$ with ϕ_i:

$$\Delta Y_{i,t} = a_i - \phi_i(Y_{i,t-1} - \theta_i X_{i,t}) + e_{i,t} \tag{21.10}$$

Let us now consider a random coefficients model, which will mean that:

$$\phi_i = \phi + v_i \tag{21.11}$$

$$\theta_i = \theta + w_i \tag{21.12}$$

where v_i and w_i are two iid error terms. From this we have that the original coefficients in Equation (21.7) are:

$$\beta_i = \theta_i \phi_i = \theta \phi + \phi w_i + \theta v_i + w_i v_i \tag{21.13}$$

Having that $\gamma = 1 - \phi$, and that $\beta = \theta \phi$, and substituting these two in Equation (21.7) we obtain:

$$Y_{i,t} = a_i + \gamma_i Y_{i,t-1} + \beta_i X_{i,t} + v_{i,t} \tag{21.14}$$

$$v_{i,t} = e_{i,t} - v_i Y_{i,t-1} + (\phi w_i + \theta v_i + w_i v_i) X_{i,t} \tag{21.15}$$

From this analysis, it is clear that $v_{i,t}$ and $Y_{i,t-1}$ are correlated and therefore both the FE and the RE estimators are now inconsistent. This is an expected result, given that we know that the FE and RE estimators are inconsistent for small T and infinite N. The big problem here is that both estimators will be inconsistent even for $T \to \infty$ and $N \to \infty$.

Solutions to heterogeneity bias: alternative methods of estimation

Pesaran *et al.* (1999) (hereafter PSS) suggest two different estimators to resolve the bias caused by heterogeneous slopes in dynamic panels. These are the mean group (MG) estimator and the pooled mean group (PMG) estimator. Both methods are presented briefly below.

The mean group (MG) estimator

The MG estimator derives the long-run parameters for the panel from an average of the long-run parameters from ARDL models for individual countries. For example, if the ARDL is the following:

$$Y_{i,t} = a_i + \gamma_i Y_{i,t-1} + \beta_i X_{i,t} + e_{i,t} \tag{21.16}$$

for country i, where $i = 1, 2, \ldots, N$, then the long-run parameter θ_i for country i is:

$$\theta_i = \frac{\beta_i}{1 - \gamma_i} \tag{21.17}$$

and the MG estimators for the whole panel will be given by:

$$\hat{\theta} = \frac{1}{N} \sum_{i=1}^{N} \theta_i \tag{21.18}$$

$$\hat{a} = \frac{1}{N} \sum_{i=1}^{N} a_i \tag{21.19}$$

It can be shown that MG estimation with sufficiently high lag orders yields super-consistent estimators of the long-run parameters even when the regressors are $I(1)$ (see Pesaran *et al.*, 1999). The MG estimators are consistent and have sufficiently large asymptotic normal distributions for N and T. However, when T is small, the MG estimator of the dynamic panel data model is biased and can cause misleading results, and therefore should be used cautiously.

The pooled mean group (PMG) estimator

Pesaran and Smith (1995) show that, unlike the situation with static models, pooled dynamic heterogeneous models generate estimates that are inconsistent even in large samples. (The problem cannot be solved by extending the sample, as it flows from heterogeneity; and extending the dimension of the cross-section increases the problem.) Baltagi and Griffin (1997) argue that the efficiency gains of pooling the data outweigh the losses from the bias induced by heterogeneity. They support this argument in two ways. First, they informally assess the plausibility of the estimates they obtain for a model of gasoline demand using different methods. This is hard to evaluate as it relies on a judgement about what is 'plausible'. Monte Carlo simulations would make the comparison clearer. Second, they compare forecast performance. However, this is a weak test to apply to the averaging technique, which is designed only to estimate long-run parameters and not short-run dynamics. Baltagi and Griffin do not consider the method discussed next, the PMG. In the type of data set we are considering, T is large enough to allow individual country estimation. Nevertheless, we may still be able to exploit the cross-section dimension of the data to some extent. Pesaran and Smith (1995) observe that while it is implausible that the dynamic specification is common to all countries, it is at least conceivable that the long-run parameters of the model may be common. They propose estimation by either averaging the individual country estimates, or by pooling the long-run parameters, if the data allows, and estimating the model as a system. PSS refer to this as the pooled mean group estimator, or PMG. It possesses the efficiency of pooled estimation while avoiding the inconsistency problem flowing from pooling heterogeneous dynamic relationships.

The PMG method of estimation occupies an intermediate position between the MG method, in which both the slopes and the intercepts are allowed to differ across countries, and the classical fixed effects method in which the slopes are fixed and the intercepts are allowed to vary. In PMG estimation, only the long-run coefficients are constrained to be the same across countries, while the short-run coefficients are allowed to vary.

Setting this out more precisely, the unrestricted specification for the ARDL system of equations for $t = 1, 2, \ldots, T$ time periods and $i = 1, 2, \ldots, N$ countries for the dependent variable Y is:

$$Y_{it} = \sum_{j=1}^{p} \lambda_{ij} Y_{i,t-j} + \sum_{j=1}^{q} \delta'_{ij} X_{i,t-j} + \mu_i + \varepsilon_{it} \qquad (21.20)$$

where $X_{i,t-j}$ is the $(k \times 1)$ vector of explanatory variables for group i, and μ_i represents the fixed effects. In principle, the panel can be unbalanced and p and q may vary across countries. This model can be reparametrized as a VECM system:

$$\Delta Y_{it} = \theta_i(Y_{i,t-1} - \beta_i' X_{i,t-1}) + \sum_{j=1}^{p-1} \gamma_{ij} \Delta Y_{i,t-j}$$

$$+ \sum_{j=1}^{q-1} \gamma_{ij}' \Delta X_{i,t-j} + \mu_i + \varepsilon_{it} \tag{21.21}$$

where the β_i are the long-run parameters and θ_i are the equilibrium- (or error-) correction parameters. The pooled mean group restriction is that the elements of β are common across countries:

$$\Delta y_{it} = \theta_i(y_{i,t-1} - \beta' x_{i,t-1}) + \sum_{j=1}^{p-1} \gamma_{ij} \Delta y_{i,t-j}$$

$$+ \sum_{j=1}^{q-1} \gamma_{ij}' \Delta x_{i,t-j} + \mu_i + \varepsilon_{i,t} \tag{21.22}$$

Estimation could proceed by OLS, imposing and testing the cross-country restrictions on β. However, this would be inefficient as it ignores the contemporaneous residual covariance. A natural estimator is Zellner's SUR method, which is a form of feasible GLS. However, SUR estimation is only possible if N is smaller than T. Thus PSS suggest a maximum likelihood estimator. All the dynamics and the ECM terms are free to vary. Again it is proved by PSS that under some regularity assumptions the parameter estimates of this model are consistent and asymptotically normal for both stationary and non-stationary $I(1)$ regressors. Both MG and PMG estimations require the selection of the appropriate lag lengths for the individual country equations using the Schwarz Bayesian criterion.

There are also issues of inference. PSS argue that, in panels, omitted group-specific factors or measurement errors are likely to bias the country estimates severely. It is a commonplace in empirical panels to report a failure of the 'poolability' tests based on the group parameter restrictions. (For example, Baltagi and Griffin (1997, p. 308) state that despite the poolability test failing massively ($F(102,396) = 10.99$; critical value about 1.3), 'like most researchers we proceed to estimate pooled models'.) So PSS propose a Hausman test. This is based on the result that an estimate of the long-run parameters in the model can be derived from the average (mean group) of the country regressions. This is consistent even under heterogeneity. However, if the parameters are in fact homogeneous, the PMG estimates are more efficient. Thus we can construct the test statistic:

$$H = \hat{q}'[var(\hat{q})]^{-1}\hat{q} \sim \chi_k^2$$

where $\hat{q}$ is a $(k \times 1)$ vector of the difference between the mean group and PMG estimates and $var(\hat{q})$ is the corresponding covariance matrix. Under the null that the two estimators are consistent but only one is efficient, $var(\hat{q})$ is easily calculated as the difference between the covariance matrices for the two underlying parameter vectors. If the poolability assumption is invalid, then the PMG estimates are no longer consistent and the test fails.

Application: the effects of uncertainty in economic growth and investment

Asteriou and Price (2000) examine the interactions between uncertainty, investment and economic growth, using panel data for a sample of 59 industrial and developing countries between 1966 and 1992 to estimate the reduced-form equation:

$$\Delta \hat{y}_{i,t} = a_{0,i} + a_{1,i} h_{i,t} + \alpha_i \Delta \hat{k}_{i,t} + \epsilon_{i,t} \tag{21.23}$$

to explore the possible effects of uncertainty on economic growth and investment. The data used in their analysis are annual observations for GDP per capita (worker) (y_{it}) and capital per capita (k_{it}) taken from various issues of the Penn World Table. Before estimating the main model, they estimate GARCH(1,1) models for GDP per capita growth in order to obtain the variance series, used as uncertainty proxies ($h_{i,t}$) in the subsequent analysis.

Evidence from traditional panel data estimation

Asteriou and Price begin by estimating their main model using traditional panel data techniques; that is fixed effects and random effects. Acknowledging that these methods of estimation are inappropriate, they report them partly to illustrate how misleading they can be. The results are presented in Table 21.1, which reports estimates of Equation (21.23) for three alternative cases: first, assuming that the constant in the model is common and homogeneous for all countries, which is a rather restrictive assumption; second, assuming fixed effects; and third, assuming the existence of random effects (the country-specific constants have been omitted from Table 21.1). In all cases (see columns (a), (c) and (d) of Table 21.1), the reported coefficients are similar and significant. Where capital growth is included, the uncertainty proxy enters the equation negatively, so that higher levels of uncertainty are associated with lower levels of growth. Capital growth has the expected positive sign. However, when the term for the growth rate of capital per capita is excluded from the equation, the uncertainty proxy coefficients obtained are positive and highly significant (see columns (b), (d) and (f) of Table 21.1). This implies that investment increases with uncertainty. But regressions of the growth rate of capital on uncertainty (not reported) reveal that uncertainty has a significant negative impact. These results are therefore hard to interpret.

Mean group and pooled mean group estimates

Next, Asteriou and Price (2000) estimate and report results of the MG and PMG methodology. Table 21.2 shows the effects of uncertainty on GDP per capita growth in three cases: pooling only the effect of uncertainty; pooling only capital; and pooling

Table 21.1 Results from traditional panel data estimation

Variable	Common constant		Fixed effects		Random effects	
	(a)	(b)	(c)	(d)	(e)	(f)
Constant	0.01	0.01			0.01	0.02
	(12.6)	(5.13)			(8.5)	(9.7)
$h_{i,t}$	−0.10	0.63	−0.06	0.92	−0.08	0.48
	(−5.7)	(13.5)	(−2.6)	(13.5)	(−4.1)	(14.0)
$\Delta \hat{k}_{i,t}$	0.12		0.10		0.11	
	(7.2)		(6.4)		(6.7)	
R^2	0.05	0.08	0.14	0.11	0.13	0.05

Note: t-statistics in parentheses in this and subsequent tables.

Table 21.2 MG and PMG estimates: dep. var. output growth

Variable	PMG estimates		MG estimates		h-test
	Coef.	t-ratio	Coef.	t-ratio	
A. Common parameter on h					
Common long-run coefficients					
h	−0.061	−1.891	−26.618	−1.967	3.85[0.05]
Unrestricted long-run coefficients					
Δk	0.086	1.323	−0.214	−0.487	—
Error-correction coefficients					
ϕ	−0.952	−32.988	−0.926	−22.300	—
B. Common parameter on Δk					
Common long-run coefficients					
Δk	0.061	3.324	−0.214	−0.487	1.19[0.27]
Unrestricted long-run coefficients					
h	−10.325	−1.762	−26.618	−1.967	—
Error-correction coefficients					
ϕ	−0.929	−25.798	−0.926	−22.300	—
C. Common parameter on Δk **and** h					
Common long-run coefficients					
Δk	0.160	7.949	−0.214	−0.487	2.21[0.14]
h	−0.027	−1.019	−26.618	−1.967	3.86[0.05]
Joint Hausman test: 3.89[0.14]					
Error-correction coefficients					
ϕ	−0.945	−35.920	−0.926	−22.300	—

Table 21.3 MG and PMG estimates: dep. var. capital growth

Variable	PMG estimates		MG estimates		h-test
	Coef.	t-ratio	Coef.	t-ratio	
h	−5.956	−4.310	−316.0	−1.003	0.97[0.33]
Error-correction coefficients					
ϕ	−0.345	−5.972	−0.414	−7.409	—

both uncertainty and capital. The results show that the Hausman test rejects pooling of the long-run variance term, but accepts pooling of the capital stock effect. The joint test in column (c) accepts, but the individual test rejects. Thus the key results are those in column (b). (The inefficient MG results are given for comparison; the Δk term is incorrectly signed but insignificant.) The PMG coefficient on Δk is on the small side but correctly signed and significant. (As usual in growth studies, there is a potential difficulty in interpreting these results, as the equation is specified in first differences. These are marginal effects being observed.) The impact of uncertainty is apparently large, but the variance terms are small. The (average) error-correction coefficients reported show that adjustment is rapid, with 93% occurring within one year. Compared to the traditional estimates, the variance effect is larger by two orders of magnitude.

Table 21.2 shows the effect of uncertainty over and above that working through investment, while Table 21.3 reports the direct impact on investment. The PMG specification is easily accepted by the Hausman test. As discussed above, the impact of uncertainty is ambiguous, but we expect a negative coefficient, and this is in fact the case. Thus the conclusion from this application is that certainly MG and PMG estimators are appropriate for a dynamic heterogeneous panel of this nature, while the results from the estimation suggest that uncertainty (as proxied by the variance series of GARCH(1,1) models of the GDP per capita) has a negative effect on both growth rates and investment.

22 Non-Stationary Panels

CHAPTER CONTENTS

LEARNING OBJECTIVES

After studying this chapter you should be able to:

1. Appreciate the concept of stationarity in a panel data framework.
2. Understand the various panel unit-root testing procedures.
3. Perform panel unit-root tests using EViews.
4. Understand the concept of cointegration in a panel data framework.
5. Understand the various panel cointegration testing procedures.
6. Perform panel cointegration tests using EViews.

Introduction

Until very recently, panel data studies have ignored the crucial stationarity (ADF and PP) and cointegration (Engle–Granger and Johansen) tests. However, with the growing involvement of macroeconomic applications in the panel data tradition, where a large sample of countries constitutes the cross-sectional dimension providing data over lengthy time series, the issues of stationarity and cointegration have also emerged in panel data. This was mainly because macro panels had large N and T compared to micro panels with large N but small T. Consider, for example, the Penn-World Tables data (available from the NBER at http://www.nber.org) where data are available for a large set of countries, and at least some of the variables (GDP, for example) are expected to have unit roots. This has brought a whole new set of problems to panel data analysis that had previously been ignored.

While the relative literature on time-series studies answers stationarity issues successfully, the adoption and adjustment of similar tests on panel data is still in progress, mainly because of the complexity of considering relatively large T and N samples in the later studies. We can summarize the major differences between time series and panel unit-root tests below:

1 Panel data allows researchers to test the various approaches with different degrees of heterogeneity between individuals.

2 In panel data analysis to date one cannot be sure as to the validity of rejecting a unit root.

3 The power of panel unit-root tests increases with an increase in N. This power increase is much more robust than the size of the one observed in the standard low-power DF and ADF tests applied to small samples.

4 The additional cross-sectional components incorporated in panel data models provide better properties of panel unit-root tests, compared with the low-power standard ADF for time series samples.

Panel unit-root tests

Both DF and ADF unit-root tests are extended to panel data estimations, to consider cases that possibly exhibit the presence of unit roots. Most of the panel unit-root tests are based on an extension of the ADF test by incorporating it as a component in regression equations. However, when dealing with panel data, the estimation procedure is more complex than that used in time series. The crucial factor in panel data estimation appears to be the degree of heterogeneity. In particular, it is important to realize that all the individuals in a panel may not have the same property; that is, they may not all be stationary or non-stationary (or cointegrated/not cointegrated). So if a panel unit root test is carried out where some parts of the panel have a unit root and some do not the situation becomes quite complex.

A wide variety of procedures have been developed, with an emphasis on the attempt to combine information from the time-series dimension with that obtained from the cross-sectional dimension, hoping that in taking into account the cross-sectional dimension the inference about the existence of unit roots will be more precise and straightforward.

However, a variety of issues arise from this: one is that some of the tests proposed require balanced panels (not missing any data for either i or t), whereas others allow for unbalanced panel setting. A second issue is related to the formulation of the null hypothesis; one may form the null as a generalization of the standard DF test (that is, that all series in the panel are assumed to be non-stationary) and reject the null if some of the series in the panel appear to be stationary, while on the other hand one can formulate the null hypothesis in exactly the opposite way, presuming that all the series in the panel are stationary processes, and rejecting it when there is sufficient evidence of non-stationarity. In both cases, the consideration of a set of time series leads to a 'box-score' concept, wherein one makes an inference on the set of the series depending on the predominating evidence.

Another important theoretical consideration in the development of the panel unit-roots literature is related to the asymptotic behaviour of a panel's N and T dimensions. Various assumptions can be made regarding the rates at which these parameters tend to infinity. One may fix, for example, N and let T go to infinity and after that let N tend to infinity. Alternatively, one may allow the two indices to tend to infinity at a controlled rate, that is as $T = T(N)$; while a third possibility is to allow both N and T to tend to infinity simultaneously (see Phillips and Moon, 2000). All these are quite complicated issues and beyond the scope of this text. In the next section our aim is to present as simply as possible the major tests for unit roots and cointegration in panels and provide guidelines on how to use these tests in applied econometric work.

The Levin and Lin (LL) test

One of the first panel unit-root tests was that developed by Levin and Lin (1992). (The test was originally presented in a working paper by Levin and Lin in 1992 and their work was finally published in 2002 with Chu as co-author (see Levin *et al.*, 2002) but the test is still abbreviated as LL by the initials of the first two authors.) Levin and Lin adopted a test that can in fact be seen as an extension of the DF test. Their model takes the following form:

$$\Delta Y_{i,t} = a_i + \rho Y_{i,t-1} + \sum_{k=1}^{n} \phi_k \Delta Y_{i,t-k} + \delta_i t + \theta_t + u_{it} \tag{22.1}$$

This model allows for two-way fixed effects, one coming from a_i and the second from θ_t. So both unit-specific fixed effects and unit-specific time effects are included. The unit-specific fixed effects are a very important component because they allow for heterogeneity, since the coefficient of the lagged Y_i is restricted to being homogeneous across all units of the panel.

The null and the alternative hypotheses of this test are:

$$H_0: \quad \rho = 0$$

$$H_a: \quad \rho < 0$$

Like most of the unit-root tests in the literature, the LL test also assumes that the individual processes are cross-sectionally independent. Under this assumption, the test derives conditions for which the pooled OLS estimator of ρ will follow a standard normal distribution under the null hypothesis.

Thus the LL test may be viewed as a pooled DF or ADF test, potentially with different lag lengths across the different sections in the panel.

The Im, Pesaran and Shin (IPS) test

The major drawback of the LL test is that it restricts ρ to being homogeneous across all i. Im *et al.* (1997) extended the LL test, allowing heterogeneity on the coefficient of the $Y_{i,t-1}$ variable and proposing as a basic testing procedure one based on the average of the individual unit-root test statistics.

The IPS test provides separate estimations for each i section, allowing different specifications of the parametric values, the residual variance and the lag lengths. Their model is given by:

$$\Delta Y_{i,t} = a_i + \rho_i Y_{i,t-1} + \sum_{k=1}^{n} \phi_{ik} \Delta Y_{i,t-k} + \delta_i t + u_{it} \tag{22.2}$$

while now the null and alternative hypotheses are formulated as:

$$H_0: \quad \rho_i = 0 \text{ for all } i$$
$$H_a: \quad \rho < 0 \text{ for at least one } i$$

Thus the null of this test is that all series are non-stationary processes under the alternative that a fraction of the series in the panel are assumed to be stationary. This is in sharp contrast with the LL test, which presumes that all series are stationary under the alternative hypothesis.

Im *et al.* (1997) formulated their model under the restrictive assumption that T should be the same for all cross-sections, requiring a balanced panel to compute the $\bar{t}$-test statistic. Their $\bar{t}$-statistic is nothing other than the average of the individual ADF t-statistics for testing that $\rho_i = 0$ for all i (denoted by t_{ρ_i}):

$$\bar{t} = \frac{1}{N} \sum_{i=1}^{N} t_{\rho_i} \tag{22.3}$$

Im *et al.* (1997) also showed that, under specific assumptions, t_{ρ_i} converges to a statistic denoted as t_{iT} which they assume to be iid with finite mean and variance. They then computed values for the mean ($E[t_{iT}|\rho_i = 1]$) and for the variance ($Var[t_{iT}|\rho_i = 1]$) of the t_{iT} statistic for different values of N and lags included in the augmentation term of Equation (22.1). Based on these values, they constructed the IPS statistic for testing for unit roots in panels, given by:

$$t_{IPS} = \frac{\sqrt{N}\left(\bar{t} - 1/N \sum_{i=1}^{N} E[t_{iT}|\rho_i = 0]\right)}{\sqrt{Var[t_{iT}|\rho_i = 0]}} \tag{22.4}$$

which they have proved follows the standard normal distribution as $T \to \infty$ is followed by $N \to \infty$ sequentially. The values of $E[t_{iT}|\rho_i = 0]$ and $Var[t_{iT}|\rho_i = 0]$ are given in their paper. Finally, they also suggested a group mean Lagrange Multiplier test for testing for panel unit roots. Performing Monte Carlo simulations, they proved that both their LM and t-statistics have better finite sample properties than the LL test.

The Maddala and Wu (MW) test

Maddala and Wu (1999) attempted to improve to some degree the drawbacks of all previous tests by proposing a model that could also be estimated with unbalanced panels. Basically, Maddala and Wu are in line with the assumption that a heterogeneous alternative is preferable, but they disagree with the use of the average ADF-statistics by arguing that it is not the most effective way of evaluating stationarity. Assuming that there are N unit-root tests, the MW test takes the following form:

$$\Pi = -2 \sum_{i=1}^{N} \ln \pi_i \qquad (22.5)$$

where π_i is the probability limit values from regular DF (or ADF) unit-root tests for each cross-section i. Because $-2 \ln \pi_i$ has a χ^2 distribution with 2 degrees of freedom, the Π statistic will follow a χ^2 distribution with $2N$ degrees of freedom as $T_i \to \infty$ for finite N. To consider the dependence between cross-sections, Maddala and Wu propose obtaining the π_i-values using bootstrap procedures by arguing that correlations between groups can induce significant size distortions for the tests. (The bootstrapping method of estimation is quite complicated and therefore not presented in this text. For this reason, and only for illustrative purposes in the examples given in the next section for the MW test, we use π values that are given by the standard OLS method of the DF (or ADF) tests.)

Computer examples of panel unit-root tests

Consider the data in the panel_unit_root.wf1 file for 14 EU countries (Luxembourg is excluded because of limited data availability) and for the years 1970–99. There are two variables, namely GDP per capita (GDPPC) and FDI inflows. First, the $\bar{t}$-statistic from the Im *et al.* (1997) paper must be calculated. To do this we estimated 14 different regression equations of the standard ADF unit-root test using at first only a constant and then a constant and a trend in the deterministic components. From these tests we extracted the ADF test statistics for each section, which are reported in Table 22.1. The $\bar{t}$-statistic is simply the average from the individual ADF-statistics to enable us to put the data in Excel and calculate the average of the $N = 14$ different ADF-statistics. The $\bar{t}$-statistic is also reported in Table 22.1. Finally we calculated the t_{IPS} statistic given by Equation (22.4). The commands for these calculations in Excel are quite easy and are indicated for the first two cases in Table 22.1, where $E[t_{iT}|\rho_i = 0] = -1.968$ and $Var[t_{iT}|\rho_i = 0] = 0.913$ are taken by the IPS paper for $N = 25$ and number of lags

Table 22.1 IPS panel unit-root tests

	Intercept		Intercept and trend	
	FDIINFL	*GDPPC*	*FDIINFL*	*GDPPC*
Belgium	2.141	0.963	1.304	−1.797
Denmark	5.873	1.872	3.381	−1.981
Germany	2.852	0.603	2.561	−2.900
Greece	−2.008	2.466	−2.768	−0.156
Spain	−1.099	1.169	−2.958	−1.917
France	1.991	−0.189	0.558	−4.038
Ireland	2.718	2.726	2.465	1.357
Italy	−0.478	0.620	−2.392	−2.211
Netherlands	2.104	1.804	1.271	−0.990
Austria	−0.140	1.061	−0.577	−2.886
Portugal	−1.257	1.810	−2.250	−0.443
Finland	1.448	−0.008	0.809	−2.303
Sweden	3.921	−0.013	4.900	−2.361
United Kingdom	1.010	2.088	−0.996	−1.420
t-bar	1.362*	1.212	0.379	−1.718
IPS-stat	10.172**	9.612	9.191	0.980
ADF critical	−2.985	−2.959	−3.603	−3.561
IPS critical 5%	−1.960	−1.960	−1.960	−1.960

Notes: * = AVERAGE(B4:B17); ** = (SQRT(14)*(B19 − (−1.968)))/(SQRT(0.913)).

equal to 4. For simplicity, we have used the same number of lags (that is 4) for all ADF models. If the lag length is different in each case the formula is slightly more complicated because the mean of $E[t_{iT}|\rho_i = 0] = -1.968$ and $Var[t_{iT}|\rho_i = 0] = 0.913$ need to be used instead. (We leave this as an exercise for the reader.) From the results we see that, first, from the simple ADF test for each section we have unit roots in all cases, apart from the rare exception of France, for the GDPPC with trend and intercept which appears to be trend-stationary. However, from the t_{IPS} we conclude that the whole panel is stationary because the statistical values are clearly bigger than the critical value (distributed under the normal distribution).

For the MW test, the results are reported in Table 22.2. Here the first column reports statistics regarding the *p*-values (π) for each of the 14 cross-sections. Then in the next column the value $-2\ln\pi_i$ is calculated for each of the cross-sections and finally the sum of these values is calculated in order to construct the MW statistic given by Equation (22.5). The basic commands in Excel are reported below Table 22.2.

EViews has created algorithms to calculate very quickly the panel unit-root tests of the LL and IPS types. To obtain these results from the 'basic' pooled object choose **View/Unit Root test** and then specify the name of the variable you want to examine with the regular _? at the end (to include all cross-sections in the test). Then, the type of the test needs to be specified from the **Test type** drop-down menu (there are options other than the LL and IPS tests, which are not discussed in this textbook), and other options regarding the type of equation (none, intercept, intercept and trend) and the level of the data (level, first differences and second differences) that are similar to the standard unit-root tests and need to be specified. By clicking **OK** in each case the results are obtained very quickly and efficiently. The interpretation is as above.

Table 22.2 Maddala and unit-root tests

	Intercept				Intercept and Trend			
	FDIINFL		GDPPC		FDIINFL		GDPPC	
	pi	−2ln(pi)	pi	−2ln(pi)	pi	−2ln(pi)	pi	−2ln(pi)
Belgium	0.045	2.685*	0.345	0.925	0.209	1.361	0.085	2.142
Denmark	0.000	9.858	0.073	2.275	0.003	4.955	0.059	2.457
Germany	0.010	3.984	0.552	0.516	0.020	3.413	0.008	4.209
Greece	0.061	2.433	0.021	3.360	0.014	3.725	0.877	0.114
Spain	0.286	1.089	0.253	1.193	0.008	4.149	0.067	2.346
France	0.061	2.428	0.852	0.140	0.583	0.468	0.000	6.639
Ireland	0.014	3.731	0.012	3.876	0.024	3.241	0.187	1.455
Italy	0.638	0.390	0.541	0.533	0.028	3.110	0.037	2.869
Netherlands	0.049	2.621	0.083	2.159	0.220	1.315	0.332	0.958
Austria	0.890	0.101	0.299	1.049	0.571	0.487	0.008	4.180
Portugal	0.226	1.293	0.082	2.169	0.039	2.821	0.662	0.359
Finland	0.164	1.570	0.994	0.005	0.429	0.735	0.030	3.038
Sweden	0.001	6.074	0.990	0.009	0.000	7.875	0.027	3.148
United Kingdom	0.325	0.976	0.047	2.653	0.332	0.957	0.169	1.547
MW stat		39.233**		20.862		38.611		35.461
MW critical	41.330							

Notes: * = − 2*log(C5); ** = Sum(C5:C19).

Panel cointegration tests

Introduction

The motivation to test for cointegration is linked primarily with the need to investigate the problem of spurious regressions, which exists only in the presence of non-stationarity. The cointegration test between two variables is a formal way of investigating:

1 A simple spurious regression where both X_{it} and Y_{it} are integrated of the same order and the residuals of regressing Y_{it} to X_{it} (that is the u_{it} sequence of this panel data model) contains a stochastic trend; or

2 The special case in which, again, both X_{it} and Y_{it} are integrated of the same order, but this time the u_{it} sequence is stationary.

Normally, in the first case first differences are applied to re-estimate the regression equation, while in the second case we conclude that the variables X_{it} and Y_{it} are cointegrated. Thus, in order to test for cointegration, it is important to ensure that the regression variables are *a priori* integrated of the same order.

There are different possible tests for cointegration in panels, and the best-known are based on the Engle and Granger cointegration relationship. In the time series framework the remarkable outcome of the Engle–Granger (1987) procedure is that if a set of variables are cointegrated, there always exists an error-correcting formulation of the dynamic model, and vice versa. Their analysis consists of a standard ADF test on the residuals u_t under the null H_0 where the variables are not cointegrated, versus the alternative H_a, where they are cointegrated. If it is observed that the ADF-statistic is less than the appropriate critical value the null that there are no cointegrating relationships between the variables is rejected and the estimation of the ECM continues. The Engle–Granger procedure can also be used for the estimation of either heterogeneous or homogeneous panels, under the hypothesis of a single cointegrating vector, as will be shown below.

The Kao test

Kao (1999) presented DF- and ADF-type tests for cointegration in panel data. Consider the model:

$$Y_{it} = a_i + \beta X_{it} + \hat{u}_{it} \tag{22.6}$$

According to Kao, the residual-based cointegration test can be applied to the equation:

$$\hat{u}_{it} = e\hat{u}_{it-1} + v_{it} \tag{22.7}$$

where $\hat{u}_{it}$ is the estimated residuals from Equation (22.6). The OLS estimate of ρ is given by:

$$\hat{\rho} = \frac{\sum_{i=1}^{N} \sum_{t=2}^{T} \hat{u}_{it}\hat{u}_{it-1}}{\sum_{i=1}^{N} \sum_{t=2}^{T} \hat{u}_{it}^2} \tag{22.8}$$

and its corresponding t-statistic is given by:

$$t_\rho = \frac{(\hat{\rho} - 1)\sqrt{\sum_{i=1}^{N} \sum_{t=2}^{T} \hat{u}_{it}^2}}{1/(NT) \sum_{i=1}^{N} \sum_{t=2}^{T} (\hat{u}_{it} - \hat{\rho}\hat{u}_{it-1})^2} \tag{22.9}$$

Kao proposed four different DF-type tests. They are given below:

$$DF_\rho = \frac{\sqrt{N}T(\hat{\rho} - 1) + 3\sqrt{N}}{\sqrt{10.2}} \tag{22.10}$$

$$DF_t = \sqrt{1.25}t_\rho + \sqrt{1.875N} \tag{22.11}$$

$$DF_\rho^* = \frac{\sqrt{N}T(\hat{\rho} - 1) + 3\sqrt{N}\hat{\sigma}_v^2/\hat{\sigma}_{0v}^2}{\sqrt{3 + 36\hat{\sigma}_v^4/(5\hat{\sigma}_{0v}^4)}} \tag{22.12}$$

$$DF_t^* = \frac{t_\rho + \sqrt{6N}\hat{\sigma}_v/(2\hat{\sigma}_{0v})}{\sqrt{\hat{\sigma}_{0v}^2/(2\hat{\sigma}_v^2) + 3\hat{\sigma}_v^2/(10\hat{\sigma}_{0v}^2)}} \tag{22.13}$$

of which the first two (DF_ρ and DF_t) are for cases where the relationship between the regressors and the errors is strongly exogenous, and the last two (DF_ρ^* and DF_t^*) are for cases where the relationship between the regressors and the errors is endogenous.

Kao (1999) also proposed an ADF test, where the following regression can be run:

$$u_{i,t} = \rho u_{i,t-1} + \sum_{j=1}^{n} \phi_j \Delta u_{i,t-j} + v_{it} \tag{22.14}$$

The null hypothesis for this test as well as for the DF tests is that of no cointegration, and the ADF test statistic is calculated by:

$$ADF = \frac{t_{ADF} + \sqrt{6N}\hat{\sigma}_v/(2\hat{\sigma}_{0v})}{\sqrt{\hat{\sigma}_{0v}^2/(2\hat{\sigma}_v^2) + 3\hat{\sigma}_v^2/(10\hat{\sigma}_{0v}^2)}} \tag{22.15}$$

where t_{ADF} is the ADF-statistic of the regression in Equation (22.14). All five test statistics follow the standard normal distribution.

Kao's test imposes homogeneous cointegrating vectors and AR coefficients, but it does not allow for multiple exogenous variables in the cointegrating vector. Another drawback is that it does not address the issue of identifying the cointegrating vectors and the cases where more than one cointegrating vector exists.

The McCoskey and Kao test

McCoskey and Kao (1998) use a Lagrange multiplier test on the residuals. The major contribution of this approach is that it tests for the null of cointegration rather than the null of no cointegration. The model is:

$$Y_{it} = a_i + \beta_i X_{it} + u_{it} \tag{22.16}$$

where

$$u_{it} = \theta \sum_{j=1}^{t} e_{ij} + e_{it} \tag{22.17}$$

Thus the test is analogous to the locally best unbiased invariant for a moving average unit root and is also free of nuisance parameters. The null hypothesis is then H_0: $\theta = 0$, implying that there is cointegration in the panel, since for $\theta = 0$, $e_{it} = u_{it}$. The alternative, H_a: $\theta \neq 0$, is the lack of cointegration. The test statistic is obtained by using the following equation:

$$LM = \frac{1/N \sum_{i=1}^{N} 1/T^2 \sum_{t=2}^{T} S_{it}^2}{s^*} \tag{22.18}$$

where S_{it} is the partial sum process defined as $S_{it}^2 = \sum_{j=1}^{t} u_{ij}$ and s^* is defined as $s^* = 1/NT \sum_{i=1}^{N} \sum_{t=2}^{T} u_{it}^2$.

Estimation of the residuals can be applied by using OLS estimators and, more specifically, through the use of either FMOLS (fully modified OLS) or the DOLS (dynamic OLS) estimator.

The Pedroni tests

Pedroni (1997, 1999, 2000) proposed several tests for cointegration in panel data models that allow for considerable heterogeneity. Pedroni's approach differs from that of McCoskey and Kao presented above in assuming trends for the cross-sections and in considering as the null hypothesis that of no cointegration. The good features of Pedroni's tests are that they allow for multiple ($m = 1, 2, \ldots, M$) regressors, for the cointegration vector to vary across different sections of the panel, and for heterogeneity in the errors across cross-sectional units.

The panel regression model Pedroni proposes has the following form:

$$Y_{i,t} = a_i + \delta_t + \sum_{m=1}^{M} \beta_{mi} X_{mi,t} + u_{i,t} \tag{22.19}$$

Seven different cointegration statistics are proposed to capture the within and between effects in his panel, and his tests can be classified into two categories. The first category includes four tests based on pooling along the 'within' dimension (pooling the AR coefficients across different sections of the panel for the unit-root test on the residuals). These tests are quite similar to those discussed above, and involve calculating the average test statistics for cointegration in the time series framework across the different sections. The test statistics of these tests are given below:

1 The panel v-statistic

$$T^2 N^{3/2} Z_{\hat{v}NT} = \frac{T^2 N^{3/2}}{\left(\sum_{i=1}^{N} \sum_{t=1}^{T} \hat{L}_{11i}^{-2} \hat{u}_{it}^2\right)} \tag{22.20}$$

2 The panel ρ-statistic

$$T\sqrt{N} Z_{\hat{\rho}NT} = \frac{T\sqrt{N} \left(\sum_{i=1}^{N} \sum_{t=1}^{T} \hat{L}_{11i}^{-2} \left(\hat{u}_{it-1}^2 \Delta \hat{u}_{it}^2 - \hat{\lambda}_i\right)\right)}{\left(\sum_{i=1}^{N} \sum_{t=1}^{T} \hat{L}_{11i}^{-2} \hat{u}_{it}^2\right)} \tag{22.21}$$

3 The panel t-statistic (non-parametric)

$$Z_{tNT} = \sqrt{\tilde{\sigma}_{NT}^2 \sum_{i=1}^{N} \sum_{t=1}^{T} \hat{L}_{11i}^{-2} \hat{u}_{it-1}^2} \left(\sum_{i=1}^{N} \sum_{t=1}^{T} \hat{L}_{11i}^{-2} \left(\hat{u}_{it-1}^2 \Delta \hat{u}_{it}^2 - \hat{\lambda}_i\right)\right) \tag{22.22}$$

4 The panel t-statistic (parametric)

$$Z_{tNT} = \sqrt{\tilde{\sigma}_{NT}^{*2} \sum_{i=1}^{N} \sum_{t=1}^{T} \hat{L}_{11i}^{-2} \hat{u}_{it-1}^{*2}} \left(\sum_{i=1}^{N} \sum_{t=1}^{T} \hat{L}_{11i}^{-2} \left(\hat{u}_{it-1}^{*2} \Delta \hat{u}_{it}^{*2} - \hat{\lambda}_i\right)\right) \tag{22.23}$$

The second category includes three tests based on pooling the 'between' dimension (averaging the AR coefficients for each member of the panel for the unit-root test on the residuals). So for these tests the averaging is done in pieces and therefore the limiting distributions are based on piecewise numerator and denominator terms. These test statistics are given below:

5 The group ρ-statistic (parametric)

$$T\sqrt{N}\tilde{Z}_{\hat{\rho}NT} = T\sqrt{N}\frac{\sum_{t=1}^{T}\left(\hat{u}_{it-1}^2\Delta\hat{u}_{it}^2 - \hat{\lambda}_i\right)}{\sum_{i=1}^{N}\left(\sum_{t=1}^{T}\hat{u}_{it-1}^2\right)} \tag{22.24}$$

6 The group t-statistic (non-parametric)

$$\sqrt{N}\tilde{Z}_{tNT-1} = \sqrt{N}\sum_{i=1}^{N}\left(\sqrt{\tilde{\sigma}_i^2\sum_{t=1}^{T}\hat{u}_{it-1}^2}\right)\sum_{t=1}^{T}\left(\hat{u}_{it-1}^2\Delta\hat{u}_{it}^2 - \hat{\lambda}_i\right) \tag{22.25}$$

7 The group t-statistic (parametric)

$$\sqrt{N}\tilde{Z}_{tNT-1}^* = \sqrt{N}\sum_{i=1}^{N}\left(\sqrt{\tilde{s}_i^{*2}\sum_{t=1}^{T}\hat{u}_{it-1}^{*2}}\right)\sum_{t=1}^{T}\left(\hat{u}_{it-1}^{*2}\Delta\hat{u}_{it}^{*2}\right) \tag{22.26}$$

A major drawback of the above procedure is the restrictive *a priori* assumption of a unique cointegrating vector.

The Larsson *et al.* test

Larsson *et al.* (2001), in contrast to all the tests detailed above, based their test on Johansen's (1988) maximum likelihood estimator, avoiding the use of unit-root tests on the residuals and contemporaneously relaxing the assumption of a unique cointegrating vector (thus this model allows us to test for more multiply-cointegrating vectors). The model Larsson *et al.* proposed starts from the assumption that the data-generating process for each of the cross-sections can be represented by an ECM specification. So, we have the following model:

$$\Delta Y_{i,t} = \Pi_i Y_{i,t-1} + \sum_{k=1}^{n}\Gamma_{ik}\Delta Y_{i,t-k} + u_{i,t} \tag{22.27}$$

Larsson *et al.* propose the estimation of the above model separately for each cross-section using maximum likelihood methods for the calculation of the trace statistic for each cross-sectional unit LR_{iT}. Then the panel rank trace statistic, LR_{NT}, can be obtained as the average of the N cross-sectional trace statistics. The null and alternative hypotheses for this test are:

$$H_0: \quad rank(\Pi_i) = r_i \leq r \quad \text{for all } i = 1, \dots, N \tag{22.28}$$

$$H_a: \quad rank(\Pi_i) = p \quad \text{for all } i = 1, \dots, N \tag{22.29}$$

where p is the number of variables that were used to test for possible cointegration among them.

The standardized panel cointegration rank trace test-statistic (denoted by Y_{LR}) is then given by:

$$Y_{LR} = \frac{\sqrt{N}(LR_{NT} - E[Z_k])}{\sqrt{Var(Z_k)}} \qquad (22.30)$$

where LR_{NT} is the average of the trace statistic for each cross-sectional unit, and $E[Z_k]$ and $Var[Z_k]$ are the mean and variance of the asymptotic trace statistic reported in Larsson *et al.* (2001).

Computer examples of panel cointegration tests

EViews automatically performs the Kao and Pedroni tests for panel cointegration. To obtain these results, again we need to work from the 'basic' pool object. The option that needs to be selected is **View/Cointegration tests**. Then in the Panel Cointegration Test window type the names of the variables to be tested for possible cointegration (the variables are typed, as usual, as y_?, with the question mark denoting that all the cross-sections are to be included in the 'basic' object) and choose the method from a drop-down menu (as well as the Pedroni and Kao tests, there is also an option for the Fisher test, which is not discussed here). An example can illustrate this. We use the file panel_test.wf1, which contains yearly data for eight sectors $(01, 02, \ldots, 08)$ for three variables Y, X and E. Let us assume we want to test for panel cointegration between Y and X. First double-click on the 'basic' object to open it in a separate window. Then go to **View/Cointegration tests** and specify in the **Variables** frame:

```
Y_? X_?
```

First, we choose the Pedroni test, and specify from the **Deterministic trend speci-fication** frame that we want first to get results for the **Individual intercept** case. By clicking **OK** we obtain the results shown in Table 22.3. From these results we under-stand that for all possible test statistics (with the exception of the group **rho** statistic) we reject the null hypothesis and conclude in favour of cointegration. More specifi-cally, all test statistics are normally distributed (thus the critical value is ±1.64) with the panel v-statistic being based on a right-hand-side test (which means that the sta-tistical should be higher than the critical of +1.64 in order to reject the null) and all the rest being left-hand-side tests (that is the statistical values should be lower than the critical of −1.64 in order to reject the null).

Similarly, if we choose the Kao test from the **Test type** drop-down menu we get the results reported in Table 22.4. From these results, again, we conclude in favour of cointegration, because the ADF-statistic for the panel residuals obtained is sufficiently larger than the critical value.

We continue by applying the Larsson *et al.* (2001) test. To do this, we check for cointegration using the Johansen approach for the three variables in the file panel_eu.wf1 (FDITOGDP, GDPGR95 and GFCFTOGDP) for each of the 13 EU countries

Table 22.3 The Pedroni panel cointegration test results

Pedroni residual cointegration test
Series: Y_? X_?
Date: 04/30/10 Time: 17:34
Sample: 1960 1999
Included observations: 40
Cross-sections included: 8
Null Hypothesis: No cointegration
Trend assumption: No deterministic trend
User-specified lag length: 1
Newey-West automatic bandwidth selection and Bartlett kernel

Alternative hypothesis: common AR coefs. (within-dimension)

	Statistic	Prob.	Weighted statistic	Prob.
Panel v-statistic	3.470135	0.0003	2.658131	0.0039
Panel rho-statistic	−2.861077	0.0021	−2.989879	0.0014
Panel PP-statistic	−2.804523	0.0025	−2.878230	0.0020
Panel ADF-statistic	−7.003347	0.0000	−6.473866	0.0000

Alternative hypothesis: individual AR coefs. (between-dimension)

	Statistic	Prob.
Group rho-statistic	−1.561884	0.0592
Group PP-statistic	−3.478301	0.0003
Group ADF-statistic	−6.864051	0.0000

Cross-section specific results

Phillips–Perron results (non-parametric)

Cross ID	AR(1)	Variance	HAC	Bandwidth	Obs
01	0.778	3.339948	3.667992	4.00	39
02	0.691	3.889055	4.267406	3.00	39
03	0.501	3.874576	4.048139	2.00	39
04	0.340	7.545930	0.663966	38.00	39
05	0.655	4.785681	4.054810	6.00	39
06	0.774	6.910023	9.395697	3.00	39
07	0.591	7.255144	5.357614	6.00	39
08	0.600	9.926374	4.298425	6.00	39

Augmented Dickey–Fuller results (parametric)

Cross ID	AR(1)	Variance	Lag	Max lag	Obs
01	0.737	3.263971	1	−	38
02	0.592	3.480958	1	−	38
03	0.496	3.954906	1	−	38
04	0.047	6.318783	1	−	38
05	0.498	3.894017	1	−	38
06	0.544	4.650277	1	−	38
07	0.408	6.302087	1	−	38
08	0.388	7.295182	1	−	38

Table 22.4   The Kao panel cointegration test results

Kao residual cointegration test
Series: Y_? X_?
Date: 04/30/10 Time: 17:41
Sample: 1960 1999
Included observations: 40
Null Hypothesis: No cointegration
Trend assumption: No deterministic trend
User-specified lag length: 1
Newey-West automatic bandwidth selection and Bartlett kernel

	t-statistic	*Prob.*
ADF	−7.870900	0.0000
Residual variance	6.564957	
HAC variance	5.545143	

Augmented Dickey-Fuller test equation
Dependent variable: D(RESID?)
Method: panel least squares
Date: 04/30/10 Time: 17:41
Sample (adjusted): 1962 1999
Included observations: 38 after adjustments
Cross-sections included: 8
Total pool (balanced) observations: 304

Variable	Coefficient	Std. error	t-statistic	Prob.
RESID?(−1)	−0.491419	0.046898	−10.47841	0.0000
D(RESID?(−1))	0.367147	0.055535	6.611065	0.0000
R-squared	0.273775	Mean dependent var.		−0.076695
Adjusted *R*-squared	0.271371	S.D. dependent var.		2.734351
S.E. of regression	2.334036	Akaike info criterion		4.539632
Sum squared resid.	1645.213	Schwarz criterion		4.564087
Log likelihood	−688.0241	Hannan-Quinn criter.		4.549415
Durbin–Watson stat.	1.947289			

(Luxembourg and the Netherlands are excluded because of insufficient data). From this test we take the trace statistics and report them in Excel, as shown in Table 20.8.

The command for the cointegration test in EViews is:

```
coint gdpgr95_bel fditogdp_bel gfcftogdp_bel
```

for the case of Belgium (which is why we use the cross-section identifier **bel**), and changing the cross-section identifier for all other groups. The model chosen for this test is the one that includes a linear deterministic trend in the data and intercept in both CE and VAR. For simplicity, the lag length was chosen in all cases to be equal to 1. After obtaining the statistics it is easy to do the calculations (simply taking the average of all the trace statistics for each section) in order to compute LR_{NT}, and then using the $E[Z_k]$ and $Var[Z_k]$ obtained from Larsson *et al.* (2001) to calculate:

$$Y_{LR} = \frac{\sqrt{N}(LR_{NT} - E[Z_k])}{\sqrt{Var(Z_k)}} \qquad (22.31)$$

The commands for the calculations in Excel are given in Table 22.4. From the results for the individual cointegration tests we see that we can reject the null of no cointegration and accept that there is one cointegrating vector for all the cases apart from three (Denmark, France and UK suggest no cointegration among their variables), and reject the null of only one cointegrating vector in favour of two cointegrating vectors for three out of the 13 cases (Spain, Portugal and Sweden). However, the Y_{LR} statistic suggests that in the panel we have two cointegrating vectors because the statistical values are greater than the 1.96 critical value of the normal distribution.

Part

VII Using Econometric Software

23 Practicalities of Using EViews, Microfit and Stata

CHAPTER CONTENTS

459

About Microfit

Starting up with Microfit

After opening Microfit the first screen you see looks like this:

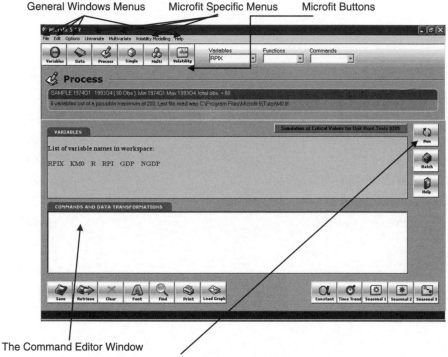

What can be seen immediately is that Microfit has the general Windows programs structure, with the menus **File**, **Edit**, **Options** and **Help** like any other Windows application, together with some menus unique to Microfit: the **Univariate**, **Multivariable** and **Volatility Clustering** menus. Below the menus, it has buttons labelled: **Variables**, **Data**, **Process**, **Single**, **Multi** and **Volatility**.

Description of Microfit buttons

The buttons across the top of the Command Editor are used to access other parts of the application. We shall discuss each button separately.

Variables: This button opens a new window showing your variables with brief descriptions (if any). It allows you to edit their names and/or descriptions.

Data: This button opens a new window that allows you to view your data in a spreadsheet (similar to Excel). This window allows you to enter data manually, edit the data and copy/paste data, either from Microfit to other software or the reverse (from other software to Microfit).

Process: This button gives you access to the Command Editor window. When the data has been inserted successfully, the Command Editor allows you to perform data transformations and preliminary analyses by using appropriate Microfit commands.

Single: This button gives you access to the Single Equation Estimation window, where you can estimate single equations using various estimation methods (ordinary least squares (OLS) is the default method; if you want to change method you can do so through the Univariate Menu).

Multi: This button gives you access to the System Estimation window, which allows you to estimate systems of multiple equations, or Vector Autoregressive (VAR) models. (Unrestricted VAR is the default method; if you want to change method this can be done using the Multivariate Menu.)

Volatility: This button gives you access to the Volatility Modelling Estimation window, which allows you to estimate ARCH/GARCH types of models (multivariate GARCH is the default method; if you want to change method this can be done using the Multivariate Menu).

Creating a file and importing data

Inputting directly from the keyboard is the most basic method of entering data. First make sure that you know:

- the frequency of the data (whether the data are undated, or are annual, half-yearly, quarterly or monthly);
- the number of variables in the data set; and
- the sample period of observations.

To input a new data set, click on the **File** menu and then choose **Input New Data from the Keyboard**. A window will open with different options for data frequency, start and end dates and number of variables. This window will look like this:

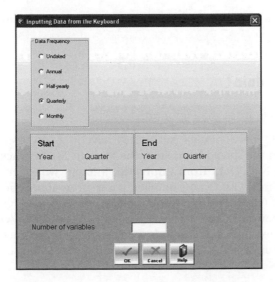

Under **Data Frequency** there are the following options:

Undated: This option is relevant for entering cross-sectional observations. Microfit assumes that the observations are unordered, and asks how many observations there are. If there is data containing variables such as employment, output and investment for a number of firms, then each firm represents an observation and the number of observations will be equal to the number of firms in your data set. If you have time series covering the period from 1990 to 2000 inclusive and wish to enter them as undated, the number of observations in the data will equal 11.

Annually, Half-yearly, Quarterly and Monthly: All these choices are for time series data. The program supplies the dates so you do not need to type them in. However, you will be asked to specify the dates for the start and end of your data by typing them in the corresponding cells. The next step is to type in and specify the number of variables you wish to have in your file.

Entering variable names

The Variables window contains the default variable names $X1$, $X2$, $X3$ and so on. You can enter your own choice of variables and/or add a description if you wish. When you are entering the desired names keep in mind the following:

- A valid variable can be at most nine characters long and must begin with a letter, not a symbol.

- MFit is not case sensitive. Lower and upper case letters are treated as equivalent.

- The underscore (_) character is allowed.

- Variable descriptions can be up to 80 characters long.

- You can return to the Variables window to edit your data by clicking the **Variables** button.

- When you have finished entering your observations, click **Close**.

Copying/pasting data

Opening a data file from the clipboard

To open a new data file from data you already have in a spreadsheet (such as Excel), copy the data from the spreadsheet. From the Microfit Menus click on the **File** menu and choose **Input New Data from Clipboard**. Microfit will open a window like the one below. This window asks you a number of questions about the format of the data on the spreadsheet (clipboard) you want to paste.

For example, if you have dates in the first column, in the **Dates/Observations** frame you should click next to **Dates/Obs** in first column. Similarly, choose the appropriate buttons for names of variables, descriptions, data frequency and so on. Once you have done that, click **OK** and you have your data in Microfit.

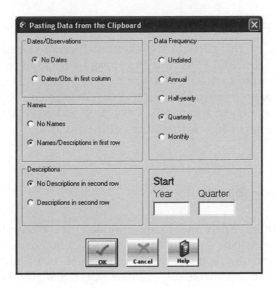

Pasting data into Microfit

To paste data from the clipboard into the **Data Editor**, choose **Paste Data** from the **Edit** menu. Then choose the frequency of your data by clicking the appropriate button. When you have finished entering your information, press **OK**. You will be asked to specify whether the variable names (up to nine characters) and/or variable descriptions (up to 80 characters) are included in the copied area of your data set. This relates to the format in which your copied data appear on the clipboard.

Copying data from MFit to the clipboard

Click the **Data** button to move to the **Data Editor** and select the data you want to copy. Now your data are ready to be pasted into any other software for use.

Saving data

To save your current data file, select **Save as...** from the **File** menu or click the **Save** button. Then select the type of file in which you want to save your data, from the drop-down list. If you are working with a file you have saved previously, save it again by choosing **Save** from the **File** menu. **Important:** Once you have inserted your data into Microfit it is good to save your file in the Microfit file format (filename.fit). This way you can access your .fit file in Microfit by simply choosing **File/Open File** from the Microfit menu without having to go through all the descriptive steps about your data. A good practice is to save your initial file with a sensible name (let's say Greek_Macro.fit) and then every time you make a change you save the file as Greek_Macro_01.fit, Greek_Macro_02.fit, Greek_Macro_03.fit and so on. This way you keep a log of the progress in your work, and if you lose or accidentally delete one of your files you do not waste all your work.

Creating a constant term, a time trend and seasonal dummies

To create a constant term, click on the **Constant** button (located in a set of buttons in the lower right-hand corner) in the process screen (go to the process screen by clicking the **Process** button) or choose from the **Edit** menu **Constant (intercept) Term**. **Constant** is a variable with all its all elements equal to unity, and Microfit asks you to supply a name (C, CON, INT and ALPHA are the most common choices). The procedure for creating a time trend and seasonal dummies is similar.

Basic commands in Microfit

The **Command Editor** is where one or more formula(e) or command(s) are entered. The different formulae need to be separated by semicolons (;). Standard arithmetic operators such as $+$, $-$, $/$, $*$ can also be used, as well as a wide range of built-in functions. For example, to create a new variable (for example $LOGX$) which is the logarithm of an existing variable (for example X) you need to type in the **Command Editor Process**:

$$LOG\,X = LOG(X) \tag{23.1}$$

and then click on **Run**. This operation places the natural logarithm of X in $LOG\,X$. Click on the **Variables** and **Data** buttons to view the new variable. In this context, you can also create the first differences (returns) of the series. To create a new variable (for example $D1X$), which is the first differences of the series of an existing variable (for example X), type:

$D1X = X - X(-1)$ if the variable is daily, yearly or undated

$D1X = X - X(-4)$ if the variable is quarterly

$D1X = X - X(-12)$ if the variable is monthly in the **Command Editor**

                                Process and then click on **GO**.

About EViews

Starting up with EViews

You need to familiarize yourself with the main areas in the EViews window shown in the figure that follows.

The title bar

The title bar, labelled EViews, is at the very top of the main window. When EViews is the active program in Windows, the title bar colour is enhanced; when another program is active, the title bar will be lighter in colour. EViews may be activated by clicking anywhere in the EViews window or by using Alt+Tab to cycle between applications until the EViews window is active.

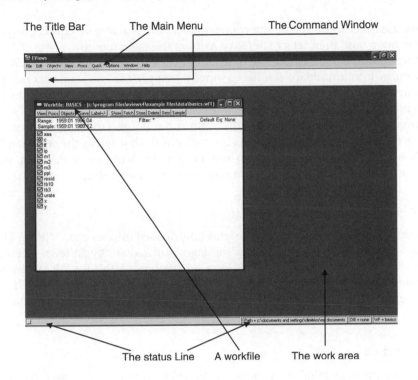

The Title Bar   The Main Menu   The Command Window

The status Line   A workfile   The work area

The main menu

Just below the title bar is the main menu. If you move the cursor to an entry in the main menu and left-click on it, a drop-down menu will appear. The main menu includes regular Windows software options, such as **File**, **Edit**, **Window** and **Help**, and some options specific to EViews, such as **Objects**, **View Procs**, **Quick**, **Options**. Clicking on an entry in the drop-down menu selects the highlighted item. Some of the items in the drop-down menu may be black, others grey; grey items are not available to be executed.

The Command window

Below the menu bar is an area called the Command window, in which EViews commands may be typed. The command is executed as soon as you click **ENTER**. The vertical bar in the command window is called the insertion point, which shows where the letters that are typed on the keyboard will be placed. As with standard word processors, if something is typed in the command area, the insertion point can be moved by pointing to and clicking on a new location. If the insertion point is not visible, it probably means that the command window is not active; simply click anywhere in the command window to activate it.

You can move the insertion point to previously executed commands, edit the existing command, and then click **ENTER** to execute the edited version of the command. The command window supports Windows cut-and-paste so you can easily move text between the command window, other EViews text windows, and other Windows programs. The contents of the command area may also be saved directly into a text file for later use (make certain that the command window is active by clicking anywhere in the window, and then select **File/Save As** from the main menu).

If more commands are entered than will fit in the command window, EViews turns this window into a standard scrollable window. Simply use the scroll bar or up and down arrows on the right-hand side of the window to see various parts of the list of previously executed commands.

You may find that the default size of the command window is too large or too small for your needs. It can be resized by placing the cursor at the bottom of the command window, holding down the mouse button and dragging the window up or down. Release the mouse button when the command window is the desired size.

The status line

At the very bottom of the window is a status line, divided into several sections. The left section will sometimes contain status messages sent to you by EViews. These messages can be cleared manually by clicking on the box at the far left of the status line. The next section shows the default directory that EViews uses to look for data and programs. The last two sections display the names of the default database and workfile.

The work area

The area in the middle of the window is the work area, where EViews displays the various object windows that it creates. Think of these windows as similar to the sheets of paper you might place on your desk as you work. The windows will overlap each other, with the topmost window being in focus or active. Only the active window has a darkened title bar. When a window is partly covered, you can bring it to the top by clicking on its title bar or on a visible portion of the window. You can also cycle through the displayed windows by pressing the **F6** or **CTRL+TAB** keys. Alternatively, you may select a window directly by clicking on the window menu item, and selecting the desired name. You can move a window by clicking on its title bar and dragging the window to a new location, or change the size of a window by clicking at the lower right corner and dragging the corner to a new location.

Creating a workfile and importing data

To create a workfile to hold your data, select **File/New/Workfile**, which opens a dialogue box to provide information about the data. Here you specify the desired frequency of the data set – for example, daily or 5 days a week – and the start and end dates – for example, 01:01:85 and 12:31:99 (note the order of month, then day, then year).

After filling in the dialogue box, click on **OK**. EViews will create an untitled workfile and display the workfile window. For now, notice that the workfile window displays two pairs of dates: one for the range of dates contained in the workfile and the second for the current workfile sample. Note also that the workfile contains the coefficient vector C and the series RESID. All EViews workfiles will contain these two objects.

Copying and pasting data

Copying data

The next step is to copy and paste the data. Note that, while the following discussion involves an example using an Excel spreadsheet, these basic principles apply to any other Windows application. The first step is to highlight the cells to be imported into EViews. Note that if we include column headings in our selection these will be used as EViews variable names, so don't leave empty cells after the variable name but start immediately with the data. Since EViews understands dated data, and we are going to create a daily workfile, we do not need to copy the date column. Instead, click on the column label 'B' and drag to the column label desired. The selected columns of the spreadsheet will be highlighted. Select **Edit/Copy** to copy the highlighted data to the clipboard.

Pasting into new series

Select **Quick/Empty Group (Edit Series)**. Note that the spreadsheet opens in edit mode, so there is no need to click the **Edit +/−** button. If you are pasting in the series names, click on the up-arrow in the scroll bar to make room for them. Place the cursor in the upper-left cell, just to the right of the second observation label. Then select **Edit/Paste** from the main menu (not **Edit +/−** in the toolbar). The group spreadsheet will now contain the data from the clipboard.

You may now close the group window and delete the untitled group without losing the two series. Note that, when importing data from the clipboard, EViews follows the Windows standard of tab-delimited free-format data with one observation per line. Since different applications use different whitespace and delimiter characters, attempting to cut-and-paste from non-standard applications may produce unanticipated results.

Pasting into existing series

You can import data from the clipboard into an existing EViews series or group spreadsheet by using **Edit/Paste** in the same fashion. There are only a few additional issues to consider:

1. To paste several series, first open a group window containing the existing series. The easiest way to do this is to click on **Show** and then type the series names in the order they appear on the clipboard. Alternatively, you can create an untitled group by selecting the first series, selecting each subsequent series (in order), and then double-clicking to open.

2. Next, make certain that the group window is in edit mode. If not, press the **Edit +/−** button to toggle between edit mode and protected mode. Place the cursor in the target cell and select **Edit/Paste**.

3. Finally, click on **Edit +/−** to return to protected mode.

Verifying and saving the data

First, verify that the data have been read correctly. Here, a group object is created that allows all your series to be examined. Click on the name of the first variable in the workfile window, and then press **CTRL** and click on all the rest of them (do not include RESID and C). All the new series should be highlighted. Now place the cursor anywhere in the highlighted area and double-click the left mouse button. EViews will open a pop-up menu providing several options. Choose **Open Group**. EViews will create an untitled group object containing all four of the series. The default window for the group shows a spreadsheet view of the series, which you can compare with the top of the Excel worksheet to ensure that the first part of the data has been read correctly. Use the scroll bars and scroll arrows on the right-hand side of the window to verify the remainder of the data.

Once you are satisfied that the data are correct, save the workfile by clicking **Save** in the workfile window. A **Save** dialog will open, prompting for a workfile name and location; enter a name and click **OK**. EViews will save the workfile in the specified directory with the specified name. A saved workfile can be opened later by selecting **File/Open/Workfile** from the main menu. A good practice is to save your initial file with a sensible name (let's say Greek_Macro.wf1) and then every time you make a change you save the file as Greek_Macro_01.wf1, Greek_Macro_02.wf2, Greek_Macro_03.wf3 and so on. This way you keep a log of the progress in your work, and if you lose or accidentally destroy one of your files you do not waste all your work.

Examining the data

You can use basic EViews tools to examine the data in a variety of ways. For example, if you select **View/Multiple Graphs/Line** from the group object toolbar, EViews displays line graphs of each of the series. You can select **View/Descriptive Stats/Individual Samples** to compute descriptive statistics for each of the series. Click on **View/Correlations**, for example, to display the correlation matrix of the selected (grouped) series.

You can also examine characteristics of the individual series. Since the regression analysis below will be expressed in either logarithms or growth rates (first differences in logarithms or returns), we can construct variables with the *genr* command (for generate).

Commands, operators and functions

The genr command

The *genr* command generates new series according to an equation specified by the user, in one of two ways. The first way is to click *genr* in the workfile area. A new window pops up, requesting you to enter the equation required. You need to define a new name and then enter the equation next to the name (followed by the = sign). For example, to take the logarithm of series $X01$, write:

$$LX01 = \text{LOG}(X01) \tag{23.2}$$

Table 23.1   Operators

Expression	Operator	Description
+	Add $x + y$	Adds the contents of x and y
−	Subtract $x - y$	Subtracts the contents of y from x
*	Multiply $x * y$	Multiplies the contents of x by y
/	Divide x/y	Divides the contents of x by y
∧	Raise to the power $x^\wedge y$	Raises x to the power of y

which will generate a new series named $LX01$, and this will be the logarithm of $X01$ (note that you can choose whatever name you like before the = sign).

Another way is to use the command line, where you simply write:

$$genr\ lx01 = \log(x01) \tag{23.3}$$

and get the same result as before. This way is sometimes very convenient; for example, you might have to take logs of many series. This can be easily done by generating a variable, x?? (? denotes numbers from 1 to 9). You can then return to the command line and change only the numbers in each case.

Obviously, taking logarithms is one of the many methods you can use to generate new series. The following tables show the basic operators, mathematical functions and time series functions that can be used with the *genr* command.

Operators

All the operators described in Table 23.1 may be used in expressions involving series and scalar values. When applied to a series expression, the operation is performed for each observation in the current sample. The precedence of evaluation is listed below. Note that you can enforce order-of-evaluation using appropriate parentheses.

Mathematical functions

The functions listed in Table 23.2 are designed to perform basic mathematical operations. When applied to a series, they return a value for every observation in the current sample. When applied to a matrix object, they return a value for every element of the matrix object. The functions will return NA (not applicable) values for observations where the input values are NAs, and for observations where the input values are not valid. For example, the square-root function, *@sqrt*, will return NA values for all observations that are less than zero. Note that the logarithmic functions are base-e (natural logarithms). To convert the natural logarithm into log10, use the relationship: $\log_{10}(x) = \log_e(x)/\log_e 10$.

Time series functions

The functions in Table 23.3 facilitate working with time series data. Note that NAs will be returned for observations for which lagged values are not available. For example, $d(x)$ returns a missing value for the first observation in the workfile, since the lagged value is not available.

Table 23.2   Mathematical functions

Function	Name	Examples/description
@abs(x);abs(x)	Absolute value	@abs(-3) = 3; abs(2) = 2
@ceiling(x)	Smallest integer	@ceiling(2.34) = 3; @ceiling(4) = 4
@exp(x); exp(x)	Exponential, e^x	@exp(1) = 2.71813
@fact(x)	Factorial, $x!$	@fact(3) = 6; @fact(0) = 1
@floor(x)	Largest integer	@floor(1.23) = 1; @floor(3) = 3
@inv(x)	Reciprocal, $1/x$	@inv(2) = 0.5
@log(x)	Natural logarithm ln(x)	@log(2) = 0.693; log(2.71813) = 1
@sqrt(x)	Square root	@sqrt(9) = 3; sqr(4) = 2

Table 23.3   Time series functions

Function	Name and description
d(x)	First difference; $(1 - L)X = X - X(-1)$
d(x, n)	nth order difference; $(1 - L)^n X$
d(x, n, s)	nth order difference with a seasonal difference at s; $(1 - L)^n(1 - L^s)X$
dlog(x)	First difference of the logarithm dlog(x, n) nth order difference of the logarithm
dlog(x, n, s)	nth order difference of the logarithm with a seasonal difference at s
@movav(x, n)	n-period backward moving average; @movav($x, 3$) = $(X + X(-1) + X(-2))/3$
@movsum(x, n)	n-period backward moving sum; @movsum($x, 3$) = $X + X(-1) + X(-2)$
@pch(x)	One-period percentage change (in decimal)
@pcha(x)	One-period percentage change annualized (in decimal)
@pchy(x)	One-year percentage change (in decimal)
@seas(n)	Seasonal dummy: returns 1 when the quarter or month equals n, and 0 otherwise

About Stata

Starting up with Stata

First, familiarize yourself with the Stata window. On opening Stata you see the screen shown in the figure that follows.

Review window: This window keeps a log of the commands you have entered during your session in Stata. It is helpful because if you want to reperform a task, instead of retyping the command in the Command window, you can click on the selected command and it will reappear in the Command window automatically.

Results window: This window displays all the results and any error messages arising from your commands. It shows the commands you have entered together with the results they have produced.

Variables window: This window shows all the variables in your data set (file) once you open/create a file in Stata. Because sometimes one might have to work with a very large number of variables, a very useful command that orders the variables in alphabetical order is the command *aorder*. So, by typing

```
aorder
```

in the Command window you will see all your variables listed in alphabetical order in the Variables window.

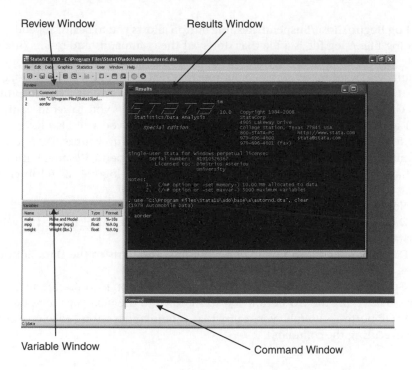

Review Window

Results Window

Variable Window

Command Window

Command window: In this window you type the commands you want to execute and by pressing the **ENTER** on your computer you obtain the results shown in the Results window. If you give a wrong command to Stata, the Results window will report an error message in red-coloured characters under the command you gave, and the command in the Review window will also be shown in red characters to indicate that it was a wrong command that did not produce any valuable results.

The Stata menu and buttons

The Stata menu contains options that are common to all Windows programs, such as **File**, **Edit**, **Window** and **Help**, together with unique Stata options such as **Data**, **Graphics**, **Statistics** and **User**. The most important is the **Statistics** option, which allows you to perform most of the estimations required through windows with instructions (very useful to someone who does not know the Stata commands). The **Help** menu provides very useful information for all Stata commands.

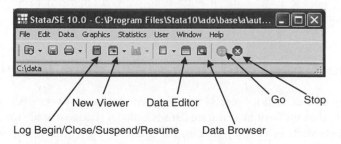

New Viewer   Data Editor   Go   Stop

Log Begin/Close/Suspend/Resume   Data Browser

The **Log Begin/Close/Suspend/Resume** button allows you to begin, append or overwrite a log file. A log file is a file that stores all the commands and results (including possible error messages) from your session in Stata. From there you can copy/paste the results you want for writing up your research report. To create a new log file, click on the **Log Begin/Close/Suspend/Resume** button. Stata will ask you to provide a name. Give a reasonable name (something that will help you to recall easily what it is all about). The file will have the suffix *.smcl and you will also have to specify the folder where you want to save your log file. During your work, or after you have finished, you can click on the **Log Begin/Close/Suspend/Resume** button again to (a) have a look at the log file, or (b) to suspend the log file, or (c) to close the log file.

The **New Viewer** button provides you with a search engine for help.

The **Data Editor** button allows you to view and, if necessary, change the values in your data set.

The **Data Browser** allows you to view your data (similarly to the **Data Editor**), but here you cannot make any changes.

The **GO** button is used in the event that the results obtained do not all fit in one window. By clicking the **GO** button you scroll down to the next page of results.

The **STOP** button is useful if you realize that a command is wrong and you want Stata to stop executing the command.

Creating a file when importing data

The simplest way to import data into Stata is manually, using the keyboard. Once you have opened Stata, click on the **Data Editor** button and a spreadsheet window will open. Here you can enter your data, variable by variable, using the keyboard. Each variable for which you enter data will be given the provisional name Var1, Var2 and so on by Stata. You can change these names, provide definitions/descriptions and so on by double-clicking on the Var1 cell (for the first variable) and providing the necessary information in the new window that appears. After you have finished entering the data manually, it is always advisable to save the data file in the Stata format (filename.dat) so that you can reopen the file in Stata without having to go repeatedly through the manual entry of the data.

Copying/pasting data

The simplest way to enter data in Stata is to copy them from Excel (or any other spreadsheet) and then paste them in the **Data Editor**.

Cross-sectional and time series data in Stata

Stata is set up as a default for receiving cross-sectional data. If you wish, you can even add a variable that will not be numeric (this is called a string variable for Stata), which can have labels such as country names, for example. However, if you want to work with time series data, Stata requires you to declare your data as time series. There are two possible ways: one is to copy/paste the data from Excel/EViews into Stata without including your time variable and then define the time variable in Stata according to your data set. A second way is to copy/paste the time variable together with the other variables and then try to define your data set as time series in Stata with the use of this variable. The first way (which is described in the next section) is easier, but sometimes (especially when there are missing dates in the data set) the second way is also required. The second, including a time variable, is described immediately after the following section and is recommended only when there are missing dates in the sample.

First way – time series data with no time variable

Sometimes it is possible to have time series data copied and pasted into Stata with the time variable in a format that Stata does not understand. The easiest way to make our data set into time series in Stata requires only the starting date and the frequency of our data set. The following commands are then executed in the Command window.

For daily data, with the starting date of 30 January 1973:

```
generate datevar = d(30Jan1970) + _n - 1
format datevar %td
tsset datevar
```

For weekly data, with starting date week 1 of 1985:

```
generate datevar = w(1985w1) + _n - 1
format datevar %tw
tsset datevar
```

For monthly data, with starting date July 1971:

```
generate datevar = m(1971m7) + _n - 1
format datevar %tm
tsset datevar
```

For quarterly data, with starting date the first quarter of 1966:

```
generate datevar = q(1966q1) + _n - 1
format datevar %tq
tsset datevar
```

For yearly data, starting from 1984:

```
generate datevar = y(1984) + _n - 1
format datevar %ty
tsset datevar
```

Second way – time series data with time variable

The difficulty is that first you have to create a series that will contain the dates in Stata in the format that Stata requires. Most of the time, when you copy/paste data from a source, the date column has a format similar to the following:

```
30 Jan 1973
30-Jan-1973
30/Jan/1973
```

and other possible variations of this kind. These variables in Stata are called string variables, or are described as having a string format. A string variable is basically a variable containing anything other than just numbers. What we want is to convert this variable into a date variable for Stata. To do this, we need to use a set of commands in Stata. To understand this better, below is an example for each frequency.

Time series – daily frequency

We start with daily frequency. We have copied/pasted a data set from Excel to Stata, with the variable labelled 'Time' as follows:

```
Time
30/01/1973
31/01/1973
01/02/1973
...
```

We need to convert this to daily time series. First, generate a new variable in Stata, which will be named 'datevar' using the *gen* command:

```
gen datevar=date(time, ''DMY'')
```

Note that after the *gen* command we give the name of the new variable, after the equals sign we set this variable to be a date, and in the parentheses we specify the name of the string variable we want to change (that is time), separated by a comma, and in "" we give the order in which the string variable time shows the date (that is first the day (D), followed by the month (M) and then the year (Y)).

The newly created variable (which we called 'datevar') from the above command will look like this:

```
    time        datevar
30/01/1973      4478
31/01/1973      4779
01/02/1973      4780
    ...          ...
```

These numbers (4478 denoting 30 January 1973) might look weird, but they are simply numeric values for dates for Stata, with a starting date of 1 January 1960 (that is this being set to 0). So 30 January 1973 is the 4478th day after 1 January 1960 (interesting, but let's leave this aside just now).

The next command we need, then, is to format the 'datevar' variable so that it can be set as a daily date variable for Stata. This command is:

```
format datevar %td
```

Here, after the percentage sign, *t* is for time and *d* is for daily. Finally, we need to sort the data with this variable and set the data as daily time series by the following two commands:

```
sort datevar
tsset datevar
```

and we are done.

Time series – monthly frequency

Let's do the whole exercise now for monthly frequency. We have copied/pasted a data set from Excel to Stata and we have the variable labelled 'Time' as follows:

```
Time
01/1973
02/1973
03/1973
...
```

We need to convert this to monthly time series. First, we generate a new variable in Stata, which we will name 'datevar', using the *gen* command:

```
gen datevar=monthly(time, ''MY'')
```

Note that again in "" we give the order in which the string variable time shows the date (that is first the month (M) and then the year (Y)).

The next command we need is to format the 'datevar' variable so that it can be set as a monthly date variable for Stata. This command is:

```
format datevar %tm
```

Here, after the percentage sign, *t* is for time and *m* is for monthly. Finally, we need to sort the data with this variable and set the data as daily time series by the following two commands:

```
sort monthly
tsset monthly
```

and we are done.

Table 23.4 Commands for transforming string variables into date variables in Stata

Frequency	Generate datevar command	Format command
Daily	*gen datevar=date(time, "DMY")*	*format datevar %td*
Weekly	*gen datevar=weekly(time, "WY")*	*format datevar %tw*
Monthly	*gen datevar=monthly(time, "MY")*	*format datevar %tm*
Quarterly	*gen datevar=quarterly(time, "QY")*	*format datevar %tq*
Half-yearly	*gen datevar=halfyearly(time, "HY")*	*format datevar %th*
Yearly	*gen datevar=yearly(time, "Y")*	*format datevar %ty*

All frequencies

It should probably by now be easy to understand the commands for all other frequencies. Details are given in Table 23.4.

Saving data

Once you have successfully performed all the transformations in Stata, save the data in Stata (*.dta) in the regular Windows way (that is following the File/Save As path) in order to be able to reopen the data without having to go through the same procedure again. Remember that it is always good to keep the original data set and record any progress you make in your work by saving your data with different file names. A good practice is to save your initial file with a sensible name (let's say Greek_Macro.dta) and then every time you make a change you save the file as Greek_Macro_01.dta, Greek_Macro_02.dta, Greek_Macro_03.dta and so on. In this way you keep a log of the progress in your work, and if you lose or accidentally destroy one of your files you do not waste all your work.

Basic commands in Stata

The summarize command

One basic descriptive command in Stata is:

```
summarize varname
```

where instead of *varname* type the name of the variable you want to summarize. This gives summary statistics for the specified variable (number of observations, mean, standard deviation, minimum and maximum). You can obtain the same information in a table in the Results window for more than one variable by typing the command

```
summarize var1 var2 var3 var4
```

where *var1* is the first variable, *var2* is the second variable and so on. A different way of getting summary statistics for one or more variables is by using the **Statistics** menu. Go to **Statistics/Summaries, Tables and Tests/Summary and Descriptive**

Table 23.5 Basic operators in Stata

Arithmetic	Logical	Relational (numeric and string)
+ addition	! not	> greater than
− subtraction	| or	< less than
* multiplication	& and	>= greater or equal
/ division		<= less or equal
ˆ power		== equal
		!= not equal

Statistics/Summary Statistics and then specify the variables you want to examine and the information you want to obtain.

The generate, *gen g*, command

The most basic command in Stata is the `generate` command (it can be abbreviated as *gen* or even as *g*). This command allows you to generate a new series by typing:

```
generate newvarname = expression
```

where *newvarname* is the name you will give to the new variable that you want to create, and *expression* is the expression that describes your new variable. If you have a variable (let's call it *xx*) and you want it squared, give the command:

```
generate xxsquared = xx*xx
```

or

```
generate xxsquared = xx^2
```

Operators

Stata uses a set of operators that can be used with the *generate* command to create new series. The most basic Stata operators are presented in Table 23.5. The operators are divided into arithmetic, logical and relational. Some additional time series operators are listed in Table 23.6. The logical and relational operators are very useful when used in conjunction with the `if` function. An example might be the case of a data set of 500 individuals, of whom 230 are male and 270 female. This is captured by the dummy variable `gender`, which takes the value of 1 for males and 0 for females. If the summarize command for basic descriptive statistics of the variable `income` is used, we can obtain the following:

```
summarize income
summarize income if gender == 1
summarize income if gender == 0
```

where, in the first case, summary statistics will be obtained for the whole sample, in the second only for the males in the sample, and in the third only for the females in the sample (note that the relational == sign was used here and not the simple = sign).

Table 23.6 Time series operators in Stata

Operator	Meaning
L.	Lag operator (lags the variable one time period) x_{t-1}
L2.	Lags the variable two periods x_{t-2}
...	... for higher lag orders x_{t-k}
F.	Forward/Lead operator x_{t+1}
F2.	Two period lead x_{t+2}
...	... for higher period leads x_{t+k}
D.	Difference operator $\Delta x = x_t - x_{t-1}$
D2.	Second difference (difference of difference) $\Delta^2 x = \Delta x_t - \Delta x_{t-1}$
...	Higher-order difference $\Delta^k x = \Delta^{k-1} x_t - \Delta^{k-1} x_{t-1}$
S.	'Seasonal' difference operator $x_t - x_{t-1}$
S2.	Lag two (seasonal) difference $x_t - x_{t-2}$
...	Higher lag (seasonal) difference $x_t - x_{t-k}$

Understanding command syntax in Stata

Stata is a command-based program with thousands of commands performing nearly every operation related to statistics and econometrics. The most important thing – for the user who wants to be competent in Stata, and use the Command window for fast and efficient calculations – is to learn the command syntax and usage. Command combined with the Stata help menu provides the user with unlimited capabilities. Let's look at an example of the command syntax. If we take the *arch* command (the syntax is similar to most commands), we have:

```
arch depvar [indepvars] [if] [in] [weight] [, options]
```

First, it is important to note that whatever is not in brackets has to be used/typed in the Command window, and anything in brackets is optional. Second, if something from the optional choices is used, type it in the command line without the brackets. So, to estimate an *arch* model with a dependent variable (described in Stata as *depvar*, so we substitute *depvar* with our variable name) a variable named *Y* and independent variables (described in Stata as *indepvars*) *X*1 and *X*2, the command is:

```
arch y x1 x2
```

If you want a GARCH(2,1) model, you need to use the options (for a set of possible options, see the Help menu):

```
arch y x1 x2 , arch(1/2) garch(1)
```

and so on.

It is similar in the case of every other command. What is important here is that Stata enables the less competent user to access nearly every application with no knowledge of commands, by using the Statistics menu.

We hope that readers will have found this chapter helpful to their understanding of applied econometrics in the other chapters of this book.

Appendix: Statistical Tables

Table A.1 *t*-table with right tail probabilities

df\p	0.4	0.25	0.1	0.05	0.025	0.01	0.005	0.0005
1	0.324920	1.000000	3.077684	6.313752	12.706200	31.820520	63.656740	636.619200
2	0.288675	0.816497	1.885618	2.919986	4.302650	6.964560	9.924840	31.599100
3	0.276671	0.764892	1.637744	2.353363	3.182450	4.540700	5.840910	12.924000
4	0.270722	0.740697	1.533206	2.131847	2.776450	3.746950	4.604090	8.610300
5	0.267181	0.726687	1.475884	2.015048	2.570580	3.364930	4.032140	6.868800
6	0.264835	0.717558	1.439756	1.943180	2.446910	3.142670	3.707430	5.958800
7	0.263167	0.711142	1.414924	1.894579	2.364620	2.997950	3.499480	5.407900
8	0.261921	0.706387	1.396815	1.859548	2.306000	2.896460	3.355390	5.041300
9	0.260955	0.702722	1.383029	1.833113	2.262160	2.821440	3.249840	4.780900
10	0.260185	0.699812	1.372184	1.812461	2.228140	2.763770	3.169270	4.586900
11	0.259556	0.697445	1.363430	1.795885	2.200990	2.718080	3.105810	4.437000
12	0.259033	0.695483	1.356217	1.782288	2.178810	2.681000	3.054540	4.317800
13	0.258591	0.693829	1.350171	1.770933	2.160370	2.650310	3.012280	4.220800
14	0.258213	0.692417	1.345030	1.761310	2.144790	2.624490	2.976840	4.140500
15	0.257885	0.691197	1.340606	1.753050	2.131450	2.602480	2.946710	4.072800
16	0.257599	0.690132	1.336757	1.745884	2.119910	2.583490	2.920780	4.015000
17	0.257347	0.689195	1.333379	1.739607	2.109820	2.566930	2.898230	3.965100
18	0.257123	0.688364	1.330391	1.734064	2.100920	2.552380	2.878440	3.921600
19	0.256923	0.687621	1.327728	1.729133	2.093020	2.539480	2.860930	3.883400
20	0.256743	0.686954	1.325341	1.724718	2.085960	2.527980	2.845340	3.849500
21	0.256580	0.686352	1.323188	1.720743	2.079610	2.517650	2.831360	3.819300
22	0.256432	0.685805	1.321237	1.717144	2.073870	2.508320	2.818760	3.792100
23	0.256297	0.685306	1.319460	1.713872	2.068660	2.499870	2.807340	3.767600
24	0.256173	0.684850	1.317836	1.710882	2.063900	2.492160	2.796940	3.745400
25	0.256060	0.684430	1.316345	1.708141	2.059540	2.485110	2.787440	3.725100
26	0.255955	0.684043	1.314972	1.705618	2.055530	2.478630	2.778710	3.706600
27	0.255858	0.683685	1.313703	1.703288	2.051830	2.472660	2.770680	3.689600
28	0.255768	0.683353	1.312527	1.701131	2.048410	2.467140	2.763260	3.673900
29	0.255684	0.683044	1.311434	1.699127	2.045230	2.462020	2.756390	3.659400
30	0.255605	0.682756	1.310415	1.697261	2.042270	2.457260	2.750000	3.646000
inf	0.253347	0.674490	1.281552	1.644854	1.959960	2.326350	2.575830	3.290500

Table A.2   Normal distribution tables

AREA BETWEEN ZERO AND Z

	0.00	0.01	0.02	0.03	0.04	0.05	0.06	0.07	0.08	0.09
0.0	0.0000	0.0040	0.0080	0.0120	0.0160	0.0199	0.0239	0.0279	0.0319	0.0359
0.1	0.0398	0.0438	0.0478	0.0517	0.0557	0.0596	0.0636	0.0675	0.0714	0.0753
0.2	0.0793	0.0832	0.0871	0.0910	0.0948	0.0987	0.1026	0.1064	0.1103	0.1141
0.3	0.1179	0.1217	0.1255	0.1293	0.1331	0.1368	0.1406	0.1443	0.1480	0.1517
0.4	0.1554	0.1591	0.1628	0.1664	0.1700	0.1736	0.1772	0.1808	0.1844	0.1879
0.5	0.1915	0.1950	0.1985	0.2019	0.2054	0.2088	0.2123	0.2157	0.2190	0.2224
0.6	0.2257	0.2291	0.2324	0.2357	0.2389	0.2422	0.2454	0.2486	0.2517	0.2549
0.7	0.2580	0.2611	0.2642	0.2673	0.2704	0.2734	0.2764	0.2794	0.2823	0.2852
0.8	0.2881	0.2910	0.2939	0.2967	0.2995	0.3023	0.3051	0.3078	0.3106	0.3133
0.9	0.3159	0.3186	0.3212	0.3238	0.3264	0.3289	0.3315	0.3340	0.3365	0.3389
1.0	0.3413	0.3438	0.3461	0.3485	0.3508	0.3531	0.3554	0.3577	0.3599	0.3621
1.1	0.3643	0.3665	0.3686	0.3708	0.3729	0.3749	0.3770	0.3790	0.3810	0.3830
1.2	0.3849	0.3869	0.3888	0.3907	0.3925	0.3944	0.3962	0.3980	0.3997	0.4015
1.3	0.4032	0.4049	0.4066	0.4082	0.4099	0.4115	0.4131	0.4147	0.4162	0.4177
1.4	0.4192	0.4207	0.4222	0.4236	0.4251	0.4265	0.4279	0.4292	0.4306	0.4319
1.5	0.4332	0.4345	0.4357	0.4370	0.4382	0.4394	0.4406	0.4418	0.4429	0.4441
1.6	0.4452	0.4463	0.4474	0.4484	0.4495	0.4505	0.4515	0.4525	0.4535	0.4545
1.7	0.4554	0.4564	0.4573	0.4582	0.4591	0.4599	0.4608	0.4616	0.4625	0.4633
1.8	0.4641	0.4649	0.4656	0.4664	0.4671	0.4678	0.4686	0.4693	0.4699	0.4706
1.9	0.4713	0.4719	0.4726	0.4732	0.4738	0.4744	0.4750	0.4756	0.4761	0.4767
2.0	0.4772	0.4778	0.4783	0.4788	0.4793	0.4798	0.4803	0.4808	0.4812	0.4817
2.1	0.4821	0.4826	0.4830	0.4834	0.4838	0.4842	0.4846	0.4850	0.4854	0.4857
2.2	0.4861	0.4864	0.4868	0.4871	0.4875	0.4878	0.4881	0.4884	0.4887	0.4890
2.3	0.4893	0.4896	0.4898	0.4901	0.4904	0.4906	0.4909	0.4911	0.4913	0.4916
2.4	0.4918	0.4920	0.4922	0.4925	0.4927	0.4929	0.4931	0.4932	0.4934	0.4936
2.5	0.4938	0.4940	0.4941	0.4943	0.4945	0.4946	0.4948	0.4949	0.4951	0.4952
2.6	0.4953	0.4955	0.4956	0.4957	0.4959	0.4960	0.4961	0.4962	0.4963	0.4964
2.7	0.4965	0.4966	0.4967	0.4968	0.4969	0.4970	0.4971	0.4972	0.4973	0.4974
2.8	0.4974	0.4975	0.4976	0.4977	0.4977	0.4978	0.4979	0.4979	0.4980	0.4981
2.9	0.4981	0.4982	0.4982	0.4983	0.4984	0.4984	0.4985	0.4985	0.4986	0.4986
3.0	0.4987	0.4987	0.4987	0.4988	0.4988	0.4989	0.4989	0.4989	0.4990	0.4990

Table A.3 F distribution for alpha 0.10

df2/df1	1	2	3	4	5	6	7	8	9	10	12	15	20	24	30	40	60	120	INF
1	39.86346	49.5	53.59324	55.83296	57.24008	58.20442	58.90595	59.43898	59.85759	60.19498	60.70521	61.22034	61.74029	62.00205	62.26497	62.52905	62.79428	63.06064	63.32812
2	8.52632	9	9.16179	9.24342	9.29263	9.32553	9.34908	9.36677	9.38054	9.39157	9.40313	9.42471	9.44131	9.44962	9.45793	9.46624	9.47456	9.48289	9.49122
3	5.53832	5.46238	5.39077	5.34264	5.30916	5.28473	5.26619	5.25167	5.24	5.23041	5.21562	5.20031	5.18448	5.17636	5.16811	5.15972	5.15119	5.14251	5.1337
4	4.54477	4.32456	4.19086	4.10725	4.05058	4.00975	3.97897	3.95494	3.93567	3.91988	3.89553	3.87036	3.84434	3.83099	3.81742	3.80361	3.78957	3.77527	3.76073
5	4.06042	3.77972	3.61948	3.5202	3.45298	3.40451	3.3679	3.33928	3.31628	3.2974	3.26824	3.23801	3.20665	3.19052	3.17408	3.15732	3.14023	3.12279	3.105
6	3.77595	3.4633	3.28876	3.18076	3.10751	3.05455	3.01446	2.98304	2.95774	2.93693	2.90472	2.87122	2.83634	2.81834	2.79996	2.78117	2.76195	2.74229	2.72216
7	3.58943	3.25744	3.07407	2.96053	2.88334	2.82739	2.78493	2.75158	2.72468	2.70251	2.66811	2.63223	2.59473	2.57533	2.55546	2.5351	2.51422	2.49279	2.47079
8	3.45792	3.11312	2.9238	2.80643	2.72645	2.66833	2.62413	2.58935	2.56124	2.53804	2.50196	2.46422	2.42464	2.4041	2.38302	2.36136	2.3391	2.31618	2.29257
9	3.3603	3.00645	2.81286	2.69268	2.61061	2.55086	2.50531	2.46941	2.44034	2.41632	2.37888	2.33962	2.29832	2.27683	2.25472	2.23196	2.20849	2.18427	2.15923
10	3.28502	2.92447	2.72767	2.60534	2.52164	2.46058	2.41397	2.37715	2.34731	2.3226	2.28405	2.24351	2.20074	2.17843	2.15543	2.13169	2.10716	2.08176	2.05542
11	3.2252	2.85951	2.66023	2.53619	2.45118	2.38907	2.34157	2.304	2.2735	2.24823	2.20873	2.16709	2.12305	2.10001	2.07621	2.05161	2.02612	1.99965	1.97211
12	3.17655	2.8068	2.60552	2.4801	2.39402	2.33102	2.28278	2.24457	2.21352	2.18776	2.14744	2.10485	2.05968	2.03599	2.01149	1.9861	1.95973	1.93228	1.90361
13	3.13621	2.76317	2.56027	2.43371	2.34672	2.28298	2.2341	2.19535	2.16382	2.13763	2.09659	2.05316	2.00698	1.98272	1.95757	1.93147	1.90429	1.87591	1.8462
14	3.10221	2.72647	2.52222	2.39469	2.30694	2.24256	2.19313	2.1539	2.12195	2.0954	2.05371	2.00953	1.96245	1.93766	1.91193	1.88516	1.85723	1.828	1.79728
15	3.07319	2.69517	2.48979	2.36143	2.27302	2.20808	2.15818	2.11853	2.08621	2.05932	2.01707	1.97222	1.92431	1.89904	1.87277	1.84539	1.81676	1.78672	1.75505
16	3.04811	2.66817	2.46181	2.33274	2.24376	2.17833	2.128	2.08798	2.05533	2.02815	1.98539	1.93992	1.89127	1.86556	1.83879	1.81084	1.78156	1.75075	1.71817
17	3.02623	2.64464	2.43743	2.30775	2.21825	2.15239	2.10169	2.06134	2.02839	2.00094	1.95772	1.91169	1.86236	1.83624	1.80901	1.78053	1.75063	1.71909	1.68564
18	3.00698	2.62395	2.41601	2.28577	2.19583	2.12958	2.07854	2.03789	2.00467	1.97698	1.93334	1.88681	1.83685	1.81035	1.78269	1.75371	1.72322	1.69099	1.65671
19	2.9899	2.60561	2.39702	2.2663	2.17596	2.10936	2.05802	2.0171	1.98364	1.95573	1.9117	1.86471	1.81416	1.78731	1.75924	1.72979	1.69876	1.66587	1.63077
20	2.97465	2.58925	2.38009	2.24893	2.15823	2.09132	2.0397	1.99853	1.96485	1.93674	1.89236	1.84494	1.79384	1.76667	1.73822	1.70833	1.67678	1.64326	1.60738
21	2.96096	2.57457	2.36489	2.23334	2.14231	2.07512	2.02325	1.98186	1.94797	1.91967	1.87497	1.82715	1.77555	1.74807	1.71927	1.68896	1.65691	1.62278	1.58615
22	2.94858	2.56131	2.35117	2.21927	2.12794	2.0605	2.0084	1.9668	1.93273	1.90425	1.85925	1.81106	1.75899	1.73122	1.70208	1.67138	1.63885	1.60415	1.56678
23	2.93736	2.54929	2.33873	2.20651	2.11491	2.04723	1.99492	1.95312	1.91888	1.89025	1.84497	1.79643	1.74392	1.71588	1.68643	1.65535	1.62237	1.58711	1.54903
24	2.92712	2.53833	2.32739	2.19488	2.10303	2.03513	1.98263	1.94066	1.90625	1.87748	1.83194	1.78308	1.73015	1.70185	1.6721	1.64067	1.60726	1.57146	1.5327
25	2.91774	2.52831	2.31702	2.18424	2.09216	2.02406	1.97138	1.92925	1.89469	1.86578	1.82	1.77083	1.71752	1.68898	1.65895	1.62718	1.59335	1.55703	1.5176
26	2.90913	2.5191	2.30749	2.17447	2.08218	2.01389	1.96104	1.91876	1.88407	1.85503	1.80902	1.75957	1.70589	1.67712	1.64682	1.61472	1.5805	1.54368	1.5036
27	2.90119	2.51061	2.29871	2.16546	2.07298	2.00452	1.95151	1.90909	1.87427	1.84511	1.79889	1.74917	1.69514	1.66616	1.6356	1.6032	1.56859	1.53129	1.49057
28	2.89385	2.50276	2.2906	2.15714	2.06447	1.99585	1.9427	1.90014	1.8652	1.83593	1.78951	1.73954	1.68519	1.656	1.62519	1.5925	1.55753	1.51976	1.47841
29	2.88703	2.49548	2.28307	2.14941	2.05658	1.98781	1.93452	1.89184	1.85679	1.82741	1.78081	1.7306	1.67593	1.64655	1.61551	1.58253	1.54721	1.50899	1.46704
30	2.88069	2.48872	2.27607	2.14223	2.04925	1.98033	1.92692	1.88412	1.84896	1.81949	1.7727	1.72227	1.66731	1.63774	1.60648	1.57323	1.53757	1.49891	1.45636
40	2.83535	2.44037	2.22609	2.09095	1.99682	1.92688	1.87252	1.82886	1.7929	1.76269	1.71456	1.66241	1.60515	1.57411	1.54108	1.50562	1.46716	1.42476	1.37691
60	2.79107	2.39325	2.17741	2.04099	1.94571	1.87472	1.81939	1.77483	1.73802	1.70701	1.65743	1.60331	1.54349	1.51072	1.47554	1.43734	1.3952	1.34757	1.29146
120	2.74781	2.34734	2.12999	1.9923	1.89587	1.82381	1.76748	1.72196	1.68425	1.65236	1.6012	1.545	1.48207	1.44723	1.40938	1.3676	1.32034	1.26457	1.19256
inf	2.70554	2.30259	2.0838	1.94486	1.84727	1.77411	1.71672	1.6702	1.63152	1.59872	1.54578	1.48714	1.4206	1.38318	1.34187	1.29513	1.23995	1.1686	1

Continued

Table A.3 F distribution for alpha 0.05

df2/df1	1	2	3	4	5	6	7	8	9	10	12	15	20	24	30	40	60	120	INF
1	161.4476	199.5	215.7073	224.5832	230.1619	233.986	236.7684	238.8827	240.5433	241.8817	243.906	245.9499	248.0131	249.0518	250.0951	251.1432	252.1957	253.2529	254.3144
2	18.5128	19	19.1643	19.2468	19.2964	19.3295	19.3532	19.371	19.3848	19.3959	19.4125	19.4291	19.4458	19.4541	19.4624	19.4707	19.4791	19.4874	19.4957
3	10.128	9.5521	9.2766	9.1172	9.0135	8.9406	8.8867	8.8452	8.8123	8.7855	8.7446	8.7029	8.6602	8.6385	8.6166	8.5944	8.572	8.5494	8.5264
4	7.7086	6.9443	6.5914	6.3882	6.2561	6.1631	6.0942	6.041	5.9988	5.9644	5.9117	5.8578	5.8025	5.7744	5.7459	5.717	5.6877	5.6581	5.6281
5	6.6079	5.7861	5.4095	5.1922	5.0503	4.9503	4.8759	4.8183	4.7725	4.7351	4.6777	4.6188	4.5581	4.5272	4.4957	4.4638	4.4314	4.3985	4.365
6	5.9874	5.1433	4.7571	4.5337	4.3874	4.2839	4.2067	4.1468	4.099	4.06	3.9999	3.9381	3.8742	3.8415	3.8082	3.7743	3.7398	3.7047	3.6689
7	5.5914	4.7374	4.3468	4.1203	3.9715	3.866	3.787	3.7257	3.6767	3.6365	3.5747	3.5107	3.4445	3.4105	3.3758	3.3404	3.3043	3.2674	3.3298
8	5.3177	4.459	4.0662	3.8379	3.6875	3.5806	3.5005	3.4381	3.3881	3.3472	3.2839	3.2184	3.1503	3.1152	3.0794	3.0428	3.0053	2.9669	2.9276
9	5.1174	4.2565	3.8625	3.6331	3.4817	3.3738	3.2927	3.2296	3.1789	3.1373	3.0729	3.0061	2.9365	2.9005	2.8637	2.8259	2.7872	2.7475	2.7067
10	4.9646	4.1028	3.7083	3.478	3.3258	3.2172	3.1355	3.0717	3.0204	2.9782	2.913	2.845	2.774	2.7372	2.6996	2.6609	2.6211	2.5801	2.5379
11	4.8443	3.9823	3.5874	3.3567	3.2039	3.0946	3.0123	2.948	2.8962	2.8536	2.7876	2.7186	2.6464	2.609	2.5705	2.5309	2.4901	2.448	2.4045
12	4.7472	3.8853	3.4903	3.2592	3.1059	2.9961	2.9134	2.8486	2.7964	2.7534	2.6866	2.6169	2.5436	2.5055	2.4663	2.4259	2.3842	2.341	2.2962
13	4.6672	3.8056	3.4105	3.1791	3.0254	2.9153	2.8321	2.7669	2.7144	2.671	2.6037	2.5331	2.4589	2.4202	2.3803	2.3392	2.2966	2.2524	2.2064
14	4.6001	3.7389	3.3439	3.1122	2.9582	2.8477	2.7642	2.6987	2.6458	2.6022	2.5342	2.463	2.3879	2.3487	2.3082	2.2664	2.2229	2.1778	2.1307
15	4.5431	3.6823	3.2874	3.0556	2.9013	2.7905	2.7066	2.6408	2.5876	2.5437	2.4753	2.4034	2.3275	2.2878	2.2468	2.2043	2.1601	2.1141	2.0658
16	4.494	3.6337	3.2389	3.0069	2.8524	2.7413	2.6572	2.5911	2.5377	2.4935	2.4247	2.3522	2.2756	2.2354	2.1938	2.1507	2.1058	2.0589	2.0096
17	4.4513	3.5915	3.1968	2.9647	2.81	2.6987	2.6143	2.548	2.4943	2.4499	2.3807	2.3077	2.2304	2.1898	2.1477	2.104	2.0584	2.0107	1.9604
18	4.4139	3.5546	3.1599	2.9277	2.7729	2.6613	2.5767	2.5102	2.4563	2.4117	2.3421	2.2686	2.1906	2.1497	2.1071	2.0629	2.0166	1.9681	1.9168
19	4.3807	3.5219	3.1274	2.8951	2.7401	2.6283	2.5435	2.4768	2.4227	2.3779	2.308	2.2341	2.1555	2.1141	2.0712	2.0264	1.9795	1.9302	1.878
20	4.3512	3.4928	3.0984	2.8661	2.7109	2.599	2.514	2.4471	2.3928	2.3479	2.2776	2.2033	2.1242	2.0825	2.0391	1.9938	1.9464	1.8963	1.8432
21	4.3248	3.4668	3.0725	2.8401	2.6848	2.5727	2.4876	2.4205	2.366	2.321	2.2504	2.1757	2.096	2.054	2.0102	1.9645	1.9165	1.8657	1.8117
22	4.3009	3.4434	3.0491	2.8167	2.6613	2.5491	2.4638	2.3965	2.3419	2.2967	2.2258	2.1508	2.0707	2.0283	1.9842	1.938	1.8894	1.838	1.7831
23	4.2793	3.4221	3.028	2.7955	2.64	2.5277	2.4422	2.3748	2.3201	2.2747	2.2036	2.1282	2.0476	2.005	1.9605	1.9139	1.8648	1.8128	1.757
24	4.2597	3.4028	3.0088	2.7763	2.6207	2.5082	2.4226	2.3551	2.3002	2.2547	2.1834	2.1077	2.0267	1.9838	1.939	1.892	1.8424	1.7896	1.733
25	4.2417	3.3852	2.9912	2.7587	2.603	2.4904	2.4047	2.3371	2.2821	2.2365	2.1649	2.0889	2.0075	1.9643	1.9192	1.8718	1.8217	1.7684	1.711
26	4.2252	3.369	2.9752	2.7426	2.5868	2.4741	2.3883	2.3205	2.2655	2.2197	2.1479	2.0716	1.9898	1.9464	1.901	1.8533	1.8027	1.7488	1.6906
27	4.21	3.3541	2.9604	2.7278	2.5719	2.4591	2.3732	2.3053	2.2501	2.2043	2.1323	2.0558	1.9736	1.9299	1.8842	1.8361	1.7851	1.7306	1.6717
28	4.196	3.3404	2.9467	2.7141	2.5581	2.4453	2.3593	2.2913	2.236	2.19	2.1179	2.0411	1.9586	1.9147	1.8687	1.8203	1.7689	1.7138	1.6541
29	4.183	3.3277	2.934	2.7014	2.5454	2.4324	2.3463	2.2783	2.2229	2.1768	2.1045	2.0275	1.9446	1.9005	1.8543	1.8055	1.7537	1.6981	1.6376
30	4.1709	3.3158	2.9223	2.6896	2.5336	2.4205	2.3343	2.2662	2.2107	2.1646	2.0921	2.0148	1.9317	1.8874	1.8409	1.7918	1.7396	1.6835	1.6223
40	4.0847	3.2317	2.8387	2.606	2.4495	2.3359	2.249	2.1802	2.124	2.0772	2.0035	1.9245	1.8389	1.7929	1.7444	1.6928	1.6373	1.5766	1.5089
60	4.0012	3.1504	2.7581	2.5252	2.3683	2.2541	2.1665	2.097	2.0401	1.9926	1.9174	1.8364	1.748	1.7001	1.6491	1.5943	1.5343	1.4673	1.3893
120	3.9201	3.0718	2.6802	2.4472	2.2899	2.175	2.0868	2.0164	1.9588	1.9105	1.8337	1.7505	1.6587	1.6084	1.5543	1.4952	1.429	1.3519	1.2539
inf	3.8415	2.9957	2.6049	2.3719	2.2141	2.0986	2.0096	1.9384	1.8799	1.8307	1.7522	1.6664	1.5705	1.5173	1.4591	1.394	1.318	1.2214	1

Continued

Table A.3 *F* distribution for alpha 0.025

df2/df1	1	2	3	4	5	6	7	8	9	10	12	15	20	24	30	40	60	120	INF
1	647.789	799.5000	864.1630	899.5833	921.8479	937.1111	948.2169	956.6562	963.2846	968.6274	976.7079	984.8668	993.1028	997.2492	1001.414	1005.598	1009.800	1014.020	1018.258
2	38.5063	39.0000	39.1655	39.2484	39.2982	39.3315	39.3552	39.3730	39.3869	39.3980	39.4146	39.4313	39.4479	39.4562	39.465	39.473	39.481	39.490	39.498
3	17.4434	16.0441	15.4392	15.1010	14.8848	14.7347	14.6244	14.5399	14.4731	14.4189	14.3366	14.2527	14.1674	14.1241	14.081	14.037	13.992	13.947	13.902
4	12.2179	10.6491	9.9792	9.6045	9.3645	9.1973	9.0741	8.9796	8.9047	8.8439	8.7512	8.6565	8.5599	8.5109	8.461	8.411	8.360	8.309	8.257
5	10.0070	8.4336	7.7636	7.3879	7.1464	6.9777	6.8531	6.7572	6.6811	6.6192	6.5245	6.4277	6.3286	6.2780	6.227	6.175	6.123	6.069	6.015
6	8.8131	7.2599	6.5988	6.2272	5.9876	5.8198	5.6955	5.5996	5.5234	5.4613	5.3662	5.2687	5.1684	5.1172	5.065	5.012	4.959	4.904	4.849
7	8.0727	6.5415	5.8898	5.5226	5.2852	5.1186	4.9949	4.8993	4.8232	4.7611	4.6658	4.5678	4.4667	4.4150	4.362	4.309	4.254	4.199	4.142
8	7.5709	6.0595	5.4160	5.0526	4.8173	4.6517	4.5286	4.4333	4.3572	4.2951	4.1997	4.1012	3.9995	3.9472	3.894	3.840	3.784	3.728	3.670
9	7.2093	5.7147	5.0781	4.7181	4.4844	4.3197	4.1970	4.1020	4.0260	3.9639	3.8682	3.7694	3.6669	3.6142	3.560	3.505	3.449	3.392	3.333
10	6.9367	5.4564	4.8256	4.4683	4.2361	4.0721	3.9498	3.8549	3.7790	3.7168	3.6209	3.5217	3.4185	3.3654	3.311	3.255	3.198	3.140	3.080
11	6.7241	5.2559	4.6300	4.2751	4.0440	3.8807	3.7586	3.6638	3.5879	3.5257	3.4296	3.3299	3.2261	3.1725	3.118	3.061	3.004	2.944	2.883
12	6.5538	5.0959	4.4742	4.1212	3.8911	3.7283	3.6065	3.5118	3.4358	3.3736	3.2773	3.1772	3.0728	3.0187	2.963	2.906	2.848	2.787	2.725
13	6.4143	4.9653	4.3472	3.9959	3.7667	3.6043	3.4827	3.3880	3.3120	3.2497	3.1532	3.0527	2.9477	2.8932	2.837	2.780	2.720	2.659	2.595
14	6.2979	4.8567	4.2417	3.8919	3.6634	3.5014	3.3799	3.2853	3.2093	3.1469	3.0502	2.9493	2.8437	2.7888	2.732	2.674	2.614	2.552	2.487
15	6.1995	4.7650	4.1528	3.8043	3.5764	3.4147	3.2934	3.1987	3.1227	3.0602	2.9633	2.8621	2.7559	2.7006	2.644	2.585	2.524	2.461	2.395
16	6.1151	4.6867	4.0768	3.7294	3.5021	3.3406	3.2194	3.1248	3.0488	2.9862	2.8890	2.7875	2.6808	2.6252	2.568	2.509	2.447	2.383	2.316
17	6.0420	4.6189	4.0112	3.6648	3.4379	3.2767	3.1556	3.0610	2.9849	2.9222	2.8249	2.7230	2.6158	2.5598	2.502	2.442	2.380	2.315	2.247
18	5.9781	4.5597	3.9539	3.6083	3.3820	3.2209	3.0999	3.0053	2.9291	2.8664	2.7689	2.6667	2.5590	2.5027	2.445	2.384	2.321	2.256	2.187
19	5.9216	4.5075	3.9034	3.5587	3.3327	3.1718	3.0509	2.9563	2.8801	2.8172	2.7196	2.6171	2.5089	2.4523	2.394	2.333	2.270	2.203	2.133
20	5.8715	4.4613	3.8587	3.5147	3.2891	3.1283	3.0074	2.9128	2.8365	2.7737	2.6758	2.5731	2.4645	2.4076	2.349	2.287	2.223	2.156	2.085
21	5.8266	4.4199	3.8188	3.4754	3.2501	3.0895	2.9686	2.8740	2.7977	2.7343	2.6368	2.5338	2.4247	2.3675	2.308	2.246	2.182	2.114	2.042
22	5.7863	4.3828	3.7829	3.4401	3.2151	3.0546	2.9338	2.8392	2.7628	2.6998	2.6017	2.4984	2.3890	2.3315	2.272	2.210	2.145	2.076	2.003
23	5.7498	4.3492	3.7505	3.4083	3.1835	3.0232	2.9023	2.8077	2.7313	2.6682	2.5699	2.4665	2.3567	2.2989	2.239	2.176	2.111	2.041	1.968
24	5.7166	4.3187	3.7211	3.3794	3.1548	2.9946	2.8738	2.7791	2.7027	2.6396	2.5411	2.4374	2.3273	2.2693	2.209	2.146	2.080	2.010	1.935
25	5.6864	4.2909	3.6943	3.3530	3.1287	2.9685	2.8478	2.7531	2.6766	2.6135	2.5149	2.4110	2.3005	2.2422	2.182	2.118	2.052	1.981	1.906
26	5.6586	4.2655	3.6697	3.3289	3.1048	2.9447	2.8240	2.7293	2.6528	2.5896	2.4908	2.3867	2.2759	2.2174	2.157	2.093	2.026	1.954	1.878
27	5.6331	4.2421	3.6472	3.3067	3.0828	2.9228	2.8021	2.7074	2.6309	2.5676	2.4688	2.3644	2.2533	2.1946	2.133	2.069	2.002	1.930	1.853
28	5.6096	4.2205	3.6264	3.2863	3.0626	2.9027	2.7820	2.6872	2.6106	2.5473	2.4484	2.3438	2.2324	2.1735	2.112	2.048	1.980	1.907	1.829
29	5.5878	4.2006	3.6072	3.2674	3.0438	2.8840	2.7633	2.6686	2.5919	2.5286	2.4295	2.3248	2.2131	2.1540	2.092	2.028	1.959	1.886	1.807
30	5.5675	4.1821	3.5894	3.2499	3.0265	2.8667	2.7460	2.6513	2.5746	2.5112	2.4120	2.3072	2.1952	2.1359	2.074	2.009	1.940	1.866	1.787
40	5.4239	4.0510	3.4633	3.1261	2.9037	2.7444	2.6238	2.5289	2.4519	2.3882	2.2882	2.1819	2.0677	2.0069	1.943	1.875	1.803	1.724	1.637
60	5.2856	3.9253	3.3425	3.0077	2.7863	2.6274	2.5068	2.4117	2.3344	2.2702	2.1692	2.0613	1.9445	1.8817	1.815	1.744	1.667	1.581	1.482
120	5.1523	3.8046	3.2269	2.8943	2.6740	2.5154	2.3948	2.2994	2.2217	2.1570	2.0548	1.9450	1.8249	1.7597	1.690	1.614	1.530	1.433	1.310
inf	5.0239	3.6889	3.1161	2.7858	2.5665	2.4082	2.2875	2.1918	2.1136	2.0483	1.9447	1.8326	1.7085	1.6402	1.566	1.484	1.388	1.268	1.000

Table A.4 Chi-square distribution

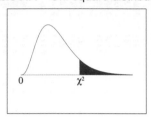

The shaded area is equal to α for $\chi^2 = \chi_\alpha^2$.

df	$\chi_{.995}^2$	$\chi_{.990}^2$	$\chi_{.975}^2$	$\chi_{.950}^2$	$\chi_{.900}^2$	$\chi_{.100}^2$	$\chi_{.050}^2$	$\chi_{.025}^2$	$\chi_{.010}^2$	$\chi_{.005}^2$
1	0.000	0.000	0.001	0.004	0.016	2.706	3.841	5.024	6.635	7.879
2	0.010	0.020	0.051	0.103	0.211	4.605	5.991	7.378	9.210	10.597
3	0.072	0.115	0.216	0.352	0.584	6.251	7.815	9.348	11.345	12.838
4	0.207	0.297	0.484	0.711	1.064	7.779	9.488	11.143	13.277	14.860
5	0.412	0.554	0.831	1.145	1.610	9.236	11.070	12.833	15.086	16.750
6	0.676	0.872	1.237	1.635	2.204	10.645	12.592	14.449	16.812	18.548
7	0.989	1.239	1.690	2.167	2.833	12.017	14.067	16.013	18.475	20.278
8	1.344	1.646	2.180	2.733	3.490	13.362	15.507	17.535	20.090	21.955
9	1.735	2.088	2.700	3.325	4.168	14.684	16.919	19.023	21.666	23.589
10	2.156	2.558	3.247	3.940	4.865	15.987	18.307	20.483	23.209	25.188
11	2.603	3.053	3.816	4.575	5.578	17.275	19.675	21.920	24.725	26.757
12	3.074	3.571	4.404	5.226	6.304	18.549	21.026	23.337	26.217	28.300
13	3.565	4.107	5.009	5.892	7.042	19.812	22.362	24.736	27.688	29.819
14	4.075	4.660	5.629	6.571	7.790	21.064	23.685	26.119	29.141	31.319
15	4.601	5.229	6.262	7.261	8.547	22.307	24.996	27.488	30.578	32.801
16	5.142	5.812	6.908	7.962	9.312	23.542	26.296	28.845	32.000	34.267
17	5.697	6.408	7.564	8.672	10.085	24.769	27.587	30.191	33.409	35.718
18	6.265	7.015	8.231	9.390	10.865	25.989	28.869	31.526	34.805	37.156
19	6.844	7.633	8.907	10.117	11.651	27.204	30.144	32.852	36.191	38.582
20	7.434	8.260	9.591	10.851	12.443	28.412	31.410	34.170	37.566	39.997
21	8.034	8.897	10.283	11.591	13.240	29.615	32.671	35.479	38.932	41.401
22	8.643	9.542	10.982	12.338	14.041	30.813	33.924	36.781	40.289	42.796
23	9.260	10.196	11.689	13.091	14.848	32.007	35.172	38.076	41.638	44.181
24	9.886	10.856	12.401	13.848	15.659	33.196	36.415	39.364	42.980	45.559
25	10.520	11.524	13.120	14.611	16.473	34.382	37.652	40.646	44.314	46.928
26	11.160	12.198	13.844	15.379	17.292	35.563	38.885	41.923	45.642	48.290
27	11.808	12.879	14.573	16.151	18.114	36.741	40.113	43.195	46.963	49.645
28	12.461	13.565	15.308	16.928	18.939	37.916	41.337	44.461	48.278	50.993
29	13.121	14.256	16.047	17.708	19.768	39.087	42.557	45.722	49.588	52.336
30	13.787	14.953	16.791	18.493	20.599	40.256	43.773	46.979	50.892	53.672
40	20.707	22.164	24.433	26.509	29.051	51.805	55.758	59.342	63.691	66.766
50	27.991	29.707	32.357	34.764	37.689	63.167	67.505	71.420	76.154	79.490
60	35.534	37.485	40.482	43.188	46.459	74.397	79.082	83.298	88.379	91.952
70	43.275	45.442	48.758	51.739	55.329	85.527	90.531	95.023	100.425	104.215
80	51.172	53.540	57.153	60.391	64.278	96.578	101.879	106.629	112.329	116.321
90	59.196	61.754	65.647	69.126	73.291	107.565	113.145	118.136	124.116	128.299
100	67.328	70.065	74.222	77.929	82.358	118.498	124.342	129.561	135.807	140.169

Table A.5 Durbin–watson significance

Table A-1
Models with an intercept (from Savin and White)

Durbin–Watson Statistic: 1% significance points of dL and dU

n	k'*=1 dL	dU	k'=2 dL	dU	k'=3 dL	dU	k'=4 dL	dU	k'=5 dL	dU	k'=6 dL	dU	k'=7 dL	dU	k'=8 dL	dU	k'=9 dL	dU	k'=10 dL	dU
6	0.390	1.142	-----	-----	-----	-----	-----	-----	-----	-----	-----	-----	-----	-----	-----	-----	-----	-----	-----	-----
7	0.435	1.036	0.294	1.676	-----	-----	-----	-----	-----	-----	-----	-----	-----	-----	-----	-----	-----	-----	-----	-----
8	0.497	1.003	0.345	1.489	0.229	2.102	-----	-----	-----	-----	-----	-----	-----	-----	-----	-----	-----	-----	-----	-----
9	0.554	0.998	0.408	1.389	0.279	1.875	0.183	2.433	-----	-----	-----	-----	-----	-----	-----	-----	-----	-----	-----	-----
10	0.604	1.001	0.466	1.333	0.340	1.733	0.230	2.193	0.150	2.690	-----	-----	-----	-----	-----	-----	-----	-----	-----	-----
11	0.653	1.010	0.519	1.297	0.396	1.640	0.286	2.030	0.193	2.453	0.124	2.892	-----	-----	-----	-----	-----	-----	-----	-----
12	0.697	1.023	0.569	1.274	0.449	1.575	0.339	1.913	0.244	2.280	0.164	2.665	0.105	3.053	-----	-----	-----	-----	-----	-----
13	0.738	1.038	0.616	1.261	0.499	1.526	0.391	1.826	0.294	2.150	0.211	2.490	0.140	2.838	0.090	3.182	-----	-----	-----	-----
14	0.776	1.054	0.660	1.254	0.547	1.490	0.441	1.757	0.343	2.049	0.257	2.354	0.183	2.667	0.122	2.981	0.078	3.287	-----	-----
15	0.811	1.070	0.700	1.252	0.591	1.465	0.487	1.705	0.390	1.967	0.303	2.244	0.226	2.530	0.161	2.817	0.107	3.101	0.068	3.374
16	0.844	1.086	0.738	1.253	0.633	1.447	0.532	1.664	0.437	1.901	0.349	2.153	0.269	2.416	0.200	2.681	0.142	2.944	0.094	3.201
17	0.873	1.102	0.773	1.255	0.672	1.432	0.574	1.631	0.481	1.847	0.393	2.078	0.313	2.319	0.241	2.566	0.179	2.811	0.127	3.053
18	0.902	1.118	0.805	1.259	0.708	1.422	0.614	1.604	0.522	1.803	0.435	2.015	0.355	2.238	0.282	2.467	0.216	2.697	0.160	2.925
19	0.928	1.133	0.835	1.264	0.742	1.416	0.650	1.583	0.561	1.767	0.476	1.963	0.396	2.169	0.322	2.381	0.255	2.597	0.196	2.813
20	0.952	1.147	0.862	1.270	0.774	1.410	0.684	1.567	0.598	1.736	0.515	1.918	0.436	2.110	0.362	2.308	0.294	2.510	0.232	2.174
21	0.975	1.161	0.889	1.276	0.803	1.408	0.718	1.554	0.634	1.712	0.552	1.881	0.474	2.059	0.400	2.244	0.331	2.434	0.268	2.625
22	0.997	1.174	0.915	1.284	0.832	1.407	0.748	1.543	0.666	1.691	0.587	1.849	0.510	2.015	0.437	2.188	0.368	2.367	0.304	2.548
23	1.017	1.186	0.938	1.290	0.858	1.407	0.777	1.535	0.699	1.674	0.620	1.821	0.545	1.977	0.473	2.140	0.404	2.308	0.340	2.479
24	1.037	1.199	0.959	1.298	0.881	1.407	0.805	1.527	0.728	1.659	0.652	1.797	0.578	1.944	0.507	2.097	0.439	2.255	0.375	2.417
25	1.055	1.210	0.981	1.305	0.906	1.408	0.832	1.521	0.756	1.645	0.682	1.776	0.610	1.915	0.540	2.059	0.473	2.209	0.409	2.362
26	1.072	1.222	1.000	1.311	0.928	1.410	0.855	1.517	0.782	1.635	0.711	1.759	0.640	1.889	0.572	2.026	0.505	2.168	0.441	2.313
27	1.088	1.232	1.019	1.318	0.948	1.413	0.878	1.514	0.808	1.625	0.738	1.743	0.669	1.867	0.602	1.997	0.536	2.131	0.473	2.269
28	1.104	1.244	1.036	1.325	0.969	1.414	0.901	1.512	0.832	1.618	0.764	1.729	0.696	1.847	0.630	1.970	0.566	2.098	0.504	2.229
29	1.119	1.254	1.053	1.332	0.988	1.418	0.921	1.511	0.855	1.611	0.788	1.718	0.723	1.830	0.658	1.947	0.595	2.068	0.533	2.193
30	1.134	1.264	1.070	1.339	1.006	1.421	0.941	1.510	0.877	1.606	0.812	1.707	0.748	1.814	0.684	1.925	0.622	2.041	0.562	2.160
31	1.147	1.274	1.085	1.345	1.022	1.425	0.960	1.509	0.897	1.601	0.834	1.698	0.772	1.800	0.710	1.906	0.649	2.017	0.589	2.131
32	1.160	1.283	1.100	1.351	1.039	1.428	0.978	1.509	0.917	1.597	0.856	1.690	0.794	1.788	0.734	1.889	0.674	1.995	0.615	2.104
33	1.171	1.291	1.114	1.358	1.055	1.432	0.995	1.510	0.935	1.594	0.876	1.683	0.816	1.776	0.757	1.874	0.698	1.975	0.641	2.080
34	1.184	1.298	1.128	1.364	1.070	1.436	1.012	1.511	0.954	1.591	0.896	1.677	0.837	1.766	0.779	1.860	0.722	1.957	0.665	2.057
35	1.195	1.307	1.141	1.370	1.085	1.439	1.028	1.512	0.971	1.589	0.914	1.671	0.857	1.757	0.800	1.847	0.744	1.940	0.689	2.037
36	1.205	1.315	1.153	1.376	1.098	1.442	1.043	1.513	0.987	1.587	0.932	1.666	0.877	1.749	0.821	1.836	0.766	1.925	0.711	2.018
37	1.217	1.322	1.164	1.383	1.112	1.446	1.058	1.514	1.004	1.585	0.950	1.662	0.895	1.742	0.841	1.825	0.787	1.911	0.733	2.001
38	1.227	1.330	1.176	1.388	1.124	1.449	1.072	1.515	1.019	1.584	0.966	1.658	0.913	1.735	0.860	1.816	0.807	1.899	0.754	1.985
39	1.237	1.337	1.187	1.392	1.137	1.452	1.085	1.517	1.033	1.583	0.982	1.655	0.930	1.729	0.878	1.807	0.826	1.887	0.774	1.970
40	1.246	1.344	1.197	1.398	1.149	1.456	1.098	1.518	1.047	1.583	0.997	1.652	0.946	1.724	0.895	1.799	0.844	1.876	0.749	1.956
45	1.288	1.376	1.245	1.424	1.201	1.474	1.156	1.528	1.111	1.583	1.065	1.643	1.019	1.704	0.974	1.768	0.927	1.834	0.881	1.902
50	1.324	1.403	1.285	1.445	1.245	1.491	1.206	1.537	1.164	1.587	1.123	1.639	1.081	1.692	1.039	1.748	0.997	1.805	0.955	1.864
55	1.356	1.428	1.320	1.466	1.284	1.505	1.246	1.548	1.209	1.592	1.172	1.638	1.134	1.685	1.095	1.734	1.057	1.785	1.018	1.837
60	1.382	1.449	1.351	1.484	1.317	1.520	1.283	1.559	1.248	1.598	1.214	1.639	1.179	1.682	1.144	1.726	1.108	1.771	1.072	1.817
65	1.407	1.467	1.377	1.500	1.346	1.534	1.314	1.568	1.283	1.604	1.251	1.642	1.218	1.680	1.186	1.720	1.153	1.761	1.120	1.802
70	1.429	1.485	1.400	1.514	1.372	1.546	1.343	1.577	1.313	1.611	1.283	1.645	1.253	1.680	1.223	1.716	1.192	1.754	1.162	1.792
75	1.448	1.501	1.422	1.529	1.395	1.557	1.368	1.586	1.340	1.617	1.313	1.649	1.284	1.682	1.256	1.714	1.227	1.748	1.199	1.783
80	1.465	1.514	1.440	1.541	1.416	1.568	1.390	1.595	1.364	1.624	1.338	1.653	1.312	1.683	1.285	1.714	1.259	1.745	1.232	1.777
85	1.481	1.529	1.458	1.553	1.434	1.577	1.411	1.603	1.386	1.630	1.362	1.657	1.337	1.685	1.312	1.714	1.287	1.743	1.262	1.773
90	1.496	1.541	1.474	1.563	1.452	1.587	1.429	1.611	1.406	1.636	1.383	1.661	1.360	1.687	1.336	1.714	1.312	1.741	1.288	1.769
95	1.510	1.552	1.489	1.573	1.468	1.596	1.446	1.618	1.425	1.641	1.403	1.666	1.381	1.690	1.358	1.715	1.336	1.741	1.313	1.767
100	1.522	1.562	1.502	1.582	1.482	1.604	1.461	1.625	1.441	1.647	1.421	1.670	1.400	1.693	1.378	1.717	1.357	1.741	1.335	1.765
150	1.611	1.637	1.598	1.651	1.584	1.665	1.571	1.679	1.557	1.693	1.543	1.708	1.530	1.722	1.515	1.737	1.501	1.752	1.486	1.767
200	1.664	1.684	1.653	1.693	1.643	1.704	1.633	1.715	1.623	1.725	1.613	1.735	1.603	1.746	1.592	1.757	1.582	1.768	1.571	1.779

*k' is the number of regressors excluding the intercept

n	k'*=11 dL	dU	k'=12 dL	dU	k'=13 dL	dU	k'=14 dL	dU	k'=15 dL	dU	k'=16 dL	dU	k'=17 dL	dU	k'=18 dL	dU	k'=19 dL	dU	k'=20 dL	dU
16	0.060	3.446	-----	-----	-----	-----	-----	-----	-----	-----	-----	-----	-----	-----	-----	-----	-----	-----	-----	-----
17	0.084	3.286	0.053	3.506	-----	-----	-----	-----	-----	-----	-----	-----	-----	-----	-----	-----	-----	-----	-----	-----
18	0.113	3.146	0.075	3.358	0.047	3.557	-----	-----	-----	-----	-----	-----	-----	-----	-----	-----	-----	-----	-----	-----
19	0.145	3.023	0.102	3.227	0.067	3.420	0.043	3.601	-----	-----	-----	-----	-----	-----	-----	-----	-----	-----	-----	-----
20	0.178	2.914	0.131	3.109	0.092	3.297	0.061	3.474	0.038	3.639	-----	-----	-----	-----	-----	-----	-----	-----	-----	-----
21	0.212	2.817	0.162	3.004	0.119	3.185	0.084	3.358	0.055	3.521	0.035	3.671	-----	-----	-----	-----	-----	-----	-----	-----
22	0.246	2.729	0.194	2.909	0.148	3.084	0.109	3.252	0.077	3.412	0.050	3.562	0.032	3.700	-----	-----	-----	-----	-----	-----
23	0.281	2.651	0.227	2.822	0.178	2.991	0.136	3.155	0.100	3.311	0.070	3.459	0.046	3.597	0.029	3.725	-----	-----	-----	-----
24	0.315	2.580	0.260	2.744	0.209	2.906	0.165	3.065	0.125	3.218	0.092	3.363	0.065	3.629	0.043	3.629	0.027	3.747	-----	-----
25	0.348	2.517	0.292	2.674	0.240	2.829	0.194	2.982	0.152	3.131	0.116	3.274	0.085	3.410	0.060	3.538	0.039	3.657	0.025	3.766
26	0.381	2.460	0.324	2.610	0.272	2.758	0.224	2.906	0.180	3.050	0.141	3.191	0.107	3.325	0.079	3.452	0.055	3.572	0.036	3.682
27	0.413	2.409	0.356	2.552	0.303	2.694	0.253	2.836	0.208	2.976	0.167	3.113	0.131	3.245	0.100	3.371	0.073	3.490	0.051	3.602
28	0.444	2.363	0.387	2.499	0.333	2.635	0.283	2.772	0.237	2.907	0.194	3.040	0.156	3.169	0.122	3.294	0.093	3.412	0.068	3.524
29	0.474	2.321	0.417	2.451	0.363	2.582	0.313	2.713	0.266	2.843	0.222	2.972	0.182	3.098	0.146	3.220	0.114	3.338	0.087	3.450
30	0.503	2.283	0.447	2.407	0.393	2.533	0.342	2.659	0.294	2.785	0.249	2.909	0.208	3.032	0.171	3.152	0.137	3.267	0.107	3.379
31	0.531	2.248	0.475	2.367	0.422	2.487	0.371	2.609	0.322	2.730	0.277	2.851	0.234	2.970	0.193	3.087	0.160	3.201	0.128	3.311
32	0.558	2.216	0.503	2.330	0.450	2.446	0.399	2.563	0.350	2.680	0.304	2.797	0.261	2.912	0.221	3.026	0.184	3.137	0.151	3.246
33	0.585	2.187	0.530	2.296	0.477	2.408	0.426	2.520	0.377	2.633	0.331	2.746	0.287	2.858	0.246	2.969	0.209	3.078	0.174	3.184
34	0.610	2.160	0.556	2.266	0.503	2.373	0.452	2.481	0.404	2.590	0.357	2.699	0.313	2.808	0.272	2.915	0.233	3.022	0.197	3.126
35	0.634	2.136	0.581	2.237	0.529	2.340	0.478	2.444	0.430	2.550	0.383	2.655	0.339	2.761	0.297	2.865	0.257	2.969	0.221	3.071
36	0.658	2.113	0.605	2.210	0.554	2.310	0.504	2.410	0.455	2.512	0.409	2.614	0.364	2.717	0.322	2.818	0.282	2.919	0.244	3.019
37	0.680	2.092	0.628	2.186	0.578	2.282	0.528	2.379	0.480	2.477	0.434	2.576	0.389	2.675	0.347	2.774	0.306	2.872	0.268	2.969
38	0.702	2.073	0.651	2.164	0.601	2.256	0.552	2.350	0.504	2.445	0.458	2.540	0.414	2.637	0.371	2.733	0.330	2.828	0.291	2.923
39	0.723	2.055	0.673	2.143	0.623	2.232	0.575	2.323	0.528	2.414	0.482	2.507	0.438	2.600	0.395	2.694	0.354	2.787	0.315	2.879
40	0.744	2.039	0.694	2.123	0.645	2.210	0.597	2.297	0.551	2.386	0.505	2.476	0.461	2.566	0.418	2.657	0.377	2.748	0.338	2.838
45	0.835	1.972	0.790	2.044	0.744	2.118	0.700	2.193	0.655	2.269	0.612	2.346	0.570	2.424	0.528	2.503	0.488	2.582	0.448	2.661
50	0.913	1.925	0.871	1.987	0.829	2.051	0.787	2.116	0.746	2.182	0.705	2.250	0.665	2.318	0.625	2.387	0.586	2.456	0.548	2.526
55	0.979	1.891	0.940	1.945	0.902	2.002	0.863	2.059	0.825	2.117	0.786	2.176	0.748	2.237	0.711	2.298	0.674	2.359	0.637	2.421
60	1.037	1.865	1.001	1.914	0.965	1.964	0.929	2.015	0.893	2.067	0.857	2.120	0.822	2.173	0.786	2.227	0.751	2.283	0.716	2.338
65	1.087	1.845	1.053	1.889	1.020	1.934	0.986	1.980	0.953	2.027	0.919	2.075	0.886	2.123	0.852	2.172	0.819	2.221	0.789	2.272
70	1.131	1.831	1.099	1.870	1.068	1.911	1.037	1.953	1.005	1.995	0.974	2.038	0.943	2.082	0.911	2.127	0.880	2.172	0.849	2.217
75	1.170	1.819	1.141	1.856	1.111	1.893	1.082	1.931	1.052	1.970	1.023	2.009	0.993	2.049	0.964	2.090	0.934	2.131	0.905	2.172
80	1.205	1.810	1.177	1.844	1.150	1.878	1.122	1.913	1.094	1.949	1.066	1.984	1.039	2.022	1.011	2.059	0.983	2.097	0.955	2.135
85	1.236	1.803	1.210	1.834	1.184	1.866	1.158	1.898	1.132	1.931	1.106	1.965	1.080	1.999	1.053	2.033	1.027	2.068	1.000	2.104
90	1.264	1.798	1.240	1.827	1.215	1.856	1.191	1.886	1.166	1.917	1.141	1.948	1.116	1.979	1.091	2.012	1.066	2.044	1.041	2.077
95	1.290	1.793	1.267	1.821	1.244	1.848	1.221	1.876	1.197	1.905	1.174	1.943	1.150	1.963	1.126	1.993	1.102	2.023	1.079	2.054
100	1.314	1.790	1.292	1.816	1.270	1.841	1.248	1.868	1.225	1.895	1.203	1.922	1.181	1.949	1.158	1.977	1.136	2.006	1.113	2.034
150	1.473	1.783	1.458	1.799	1.444	1.814	1.429	1.830	1.414	1.847	1.400	1.863	1.385	1.880	1.370	1.897	1.355	1.913	1.340	1.931
200	1.561	1.791	1.550	1.801	1.539	1.813	1.528	1.824	1.518	1.836	1.507	1.847	1.495	1.860	1.484	1.871	1.474	1.883	1.462	1.896

*k' is the number of regressors excluding the intercept

Table A-2
Models with an intercept (from Savin and White)

Durbin–Watson Statistic: 5% significance points of dL and dU

n	k'=1 dL	dU	k'=2 dL	dU	k'=3 dL	dU	k'=4 dL	dU	k'=5 dL	dU	k'=6 dL	dU	k'=7 dL	dU	k'=8 dL	dU	k'=9 dL	dU	k'=10 dL	dU
6	0.610	1.400	-----	-----	-----	-----	-----	-----	-----	-----	-----	-----	-----	-----	-----	-----	-----	-----	-----	-----
7	0.700	1.356	0.467	1.896	-----	-----	-----	-----	-----	-----	-----	-----	-----	-----	-----	-----	-----	-----	-----	-----
8	0.763	1.332	0.559	1.777	0.367	2.287	-----	-----	-----	-----	-----	-----	-----	-----	-----	-----	-----	-----	-----	-----
9	0.824	1.320	0.629	1.699	0.455	2.128	0.296	2.588	-----	-----	-----	-----	-----	-----	-----	-----	-----	-----	-----	-----
10	0.879	1.320	0.697	1.641	0.525	2.016	0.376	2.414	0.243	2.822	-----	-----	-----	-----	-----	-----	-----	-----	-----	-----
11	0.927	1.324	0.758	1.604	0.595	1.928	0.444	2.283	0.315	2.645	0.203	3.004	-----	-----	-----	-----	-----	-----	-----	-----
12	0.971	1.331	0.812	1.579	0.658	1.864	0.512	2.177	0.380	2.506	0.268	2.832	0.171	3.149	-----	-----	-----	-----	-----	-----
13	1.010	1.340	0.861	1.562	0.715	1.816	0.574	2.094	0.444	2.390	0.328	2.692	0.230	2.985	0.147	3.266	-----	-----	-----	-----
14	1.045	1.350	0.905	1.551	0.767	1.779	0.632	2.030	0.505	2.296	0.389	2.572	0.286	2.848	0.200	3.111	0.127	3.360	-----	-----
15	1.077	1.361	0.946	1.543	0.814	1.750	0.685	1.977	0.562	2.220	0.447	2.471	0.343	2.727	0.251	2.979	0.175	3.216	0.111	3.438
16	1.106	1.371	0.982	1.539	0.857	1.728	0.734	1.935	0.615	2.157	0.502	2.388	0.398	2.624	0.304	2.860	0.222	3.090	0.155	3.304
17	1.133	1.381	1.015	1.536	0.897	1.710	0.779	1.900	0.664	2.104	0.554	2.318	0.451	2.537	0.356	2.757	0.272	2.975	0.198	3.184
18	1.158	1.391	1.046	1.535	0.933	1.696	0.820	1.872	0.710	2.060	0.603	2.258	0.502	2.461	0.407	2.668	0.321	2.873	0.244	3.073
19	1.180	1.401	1.074	1.536	0.967	1.685	0.859	1.848	0.752	2.023	0.649	2.206	0.549	2.396	0.456	2.589	0.369	2.783	0.290	2.974
20	1.201	1.411	1.100	1.537	0.998	1.676	0.894	1.828	0.792	1.991	0.691	2.162	0.595	2.339	0.502	2.521	0.416	2.704	0.336	2.885
21	1.221	1.420	1.125	1.538	1.026	1.669	0.927	1.812	0.829	1.964	0.731	2.124	0.637	2.290	0.546	2.461	0.461	2.633	0.380	2.806
22	1.239	1.429	1.147	1.541	1.053	1.664	0.958	1.797	0.863	1.940	0.769	2.090	0.677	2.246	0.588	2.407	0.504	2.571	0.424	2.735
23	1.257	1.437	1.168	1.543	1.078	1.660	0.986	1.785	0.895	1.920	0.804	2.061	0.715	2.208	0.628	2.360	0.545	2.514	0.465	2.670
24	1.273	1.446	1.188	1.546	1.101	1.656	1.013	1.775	0.925	1.902	0.837	2.035	0.750	2.174	0.666	2.318	0.584	2.464	0.506	2.613
25	1.288	1.454	1.206	1.550	1.123	1.654	1.038	1.767	0.953	1.886	0.868	2.013	0.784	2.144	0.702	2.280	0.621	2.419	0.544	2.560
26	1.302	1.461	1.224	1.553	1.143	1.652	1.062	1.759	0.979	1.873	0.897	1.992	0.816	2.117	0.735	2.246	0.657	2.379	0.581	2.513
27	1.316	1.469	1.240	1.556	1.162	1.651	1.084	1.753	1.004	1.861	0.925	1.974	0.845	2.093	0.767	2.216	0.691	2.342	0.616	2.470
28	1.328	1.476	1.255	1.560	1.181	1.650	1.104	1.747	1.028	1.850	0.951	1.959	0.874	2.071	0.798	2.188	0.723	2.309	0.649	2.431
29	1.341	1.483	1.270	1.563	1.198	1.650	1.124	1.743	1.050	1.841	0.975	1.944	0.900	2.052	0.826	2.164	0.753	2.278	0.681	2.396
30	1.352	1.489	1.284	1.567	1.214	1.650	1.143	1.739	1.071	1.833	0.998	1.931	0.926	2.034	0.854	2.141	0.782	2.251	0.712	2.363
31	1.363	1.496	1.297	1.570	1.229	1.650	1.160	1.735	1.090	1.825	1.020	1.920	0.950	2.018	0.879	2.120	0.810	2.226	0.741	2.333
32	1.373	1.502	1.309	1.574	1.244	1.650	1.177	1.732	1.109	1.819	1.041	1.909	0.972	2.004	0.904	2.102	0.836	2.203	0.769	2.306
33	1.383	1.508	1.321	1.577	1.258	1.651	1.193	1.730	1.127	1.813	1.061	1.900	0.994	1.991	0.927	2.085	0.861	2.181	0.796	2.281
34	1.393	1.514	1.333	1.580	1.271	1.652	1.208	1.728	1.144	1.808	1.079	1.891	1.015	1.978	0.950	2.069	0.885	2.162	0.821	2.257
35	1.402	1.519	1.343	1.584	1.283	1.653	1.222	1.726	1.160	1.803	1.097	1.884	1.034	1.967	0.971	2.054	0.908	2.144	0.845	2.236
36	1.411	1.525	1.354	1.587	1.295	1.654	1.236	1.724	1.175	1.799	1.114	1.876	1.053	1.957	0.991	2.041	0.930	2.127	0.868	2.216
37	1.419	1.530	1.364	1.590	1.307	1.655	1.249	1.723	1.190	1.795	1.131	1.870	1.071	1.948	1.011	2.029	0.951	2.112	0.891	2.197
38	1.427	1.535	1.373	1.594	1.318	1.656	1.261	1.722	1.204	1.792	1.146	1.864	1.088	1.939	1.029	2.017	0.970	2.098	0.912	2.180
39	1.435	1.540	1.382	1.597	1.328	1.658	1.273	1.722	1.218	1.789	1.161	1.859	1.104	1.932	1.047	2.007	0.990	2.085	0.932	2.164
40	1.442	1.544	1.391	1.600	1.338	1.659	1.285	1.721	1.230	1.786	1.175	1.854	1.120	1.924	1.064	1.997	1.008	2.072	0.952	2.149
45	1.475	1.566	1.430	1.615	1.383	1.666	1.336	1.720	1.287	1.776	1.238	1.835	1.189	1.895	1.139	1.958	1.089	2.022	1.038	2.088
50	1.503	1.585	1.462	1.628	1.421	1.674	1.378	1.721	1.335	1.771	1.291	1.822	1.246	1.875	1.201	1.930	1.156	1.986	1.110	2.044
55	1.528	1.601	1.490	1.641	1.452	1.681	1.414	1.724	1.374	1.768	1.334	1.814	1.294	1.861	1.253	1.909	1.212	1.959	1.170	2.010
60	1.549	1.616	1.514	1.652	1.480	1.689	1.444	1.727	1.408	1.767	1.372	1.808	1.335	1.850	1.298	1.894	1.260	1.939	1.222	1.984
65	1.567	1.629	1.536	1.662	1.503	1.696	1.471	1.731	1.438	1.767	1.404	1.805	1.370	1.843	1.336	1.882	1.301	1.923	1.266	1.964
70	1.583	1.641	1.554	1.672	1.525	1.703	1.494	1.735	1.464	1.768	1.433	1.802	1.401	1.838	1.369	1.874	1.337	1.910	1.305	1.948
75	1.598	1.652	1.571	1.680	1.543	1.709	1.515	1.739	1.487	1.770	1.458	1.801	1.428	1.834	1.399	1.867	1.369	1.901	1.339	1.935
80	1.611	1.662	1.586	1.688	1.560	1.715	1.534	1.743	1.507	1.772	1.480	1.801	1.453	1.831	1.425	1.861	1.397	1.893	1.369	1.925
85	1.624	1.671	1.600	1.696	1.575	1.721	1.550	1.747	1.525	1.774	1.500	1.801	1.474	1.829	1.448	1.857	1.422	1.886	1.396	1.916
90	1.635	1.679	1.612	1.703	1.589	1.726	1.566	1.751	1.542	1.776	1.518	1.801	1.494	1.827	1.469	1.854	1.445	1.881	1.420	1.909
95	1.645	1.687	1.623	1.709	1.602	1.732	1.579	1.755	1.557	1.778	1.535	1.802	1.512	1.827	1.489	1.852	1.465	1.877	1.442	1.903
100	1.654	1.694	1.634	1.715	1.613	1.736	1.592	1.758	1.571	1.780	1.550	1.803	1.528	1.826	1.506	1.850	1.484	1.874	1.462	1.898
150	1.720	1.747	1.706	1.760	1.693	1.774	1.679	1.788	1.665	1.802	1.651	1.817	1.637	1.832	1.622	1.846	1.608	1.862	1.593	1.877
200	1.758	1.779	1.748	1.789	1.738	1.799	1.728	1.809	1.718	1.820	1.707	1.831	1.697	1.841	1.686	1.852	1.675	1.863	1.665	1.874

*k' is the number of regressors excluding the intercept

	k'*=11		k'=12		k'=13		k'=14		k'=15		k'=16		k'=17		k'=18		k'=19		k'=20	
n	dL	dU	dL	dU	dL	dU	dL	dU	dL	dU	dL	dU	dL	dU	dL	dU	dL	dU	dL	dU
16	0.098	3.503	-----	-----	-----	-----	-----	-----	-----	-----	-----	-----	-----	-----	-----	-----	-----	-----	-----	-----
17	0.138	3.378	0.087	3.557	-----	-----	-----	-----	-----	-----	-----	-----	-----	-----	-----	-----	-----	-----	-----	-----
18	0.177	3.265	0.123	3.441	0.078	3.603	-----	-----	-----	-----	-----	-----	-----	-----	-----	-----	-----	-----	-----	-----
19	0.220	3.159	0.160	3.335	0.111	3.496	0.070	3.642	-----	-----	-----	-----	-----	-----	-----	-----	-----	-----	-----	-----
20	0.263	3.063	0.200	3.234	0.145	3.395	0.100	3.542	0.063	3.676	-----	-----	-----	-----	-----	-----	-----	-----	-----	-----
21	0.307	2.976	0.240	3.141	0.182	3.300	0.132	3.448	0.091	3.583	0.058	3.705	-----	-----	-----	-----	-----	-----	-----	-----
22	0.349	2.897	0.281	3.057	0.220	3.211	0.166	3.358	0.120	3.495	0.083	3.619	0.052	3.731	-----	-----	-----	-----	-----	-----
23	0.391	2.826	0.322	2.979	0.259	3.128	0.202	3.272	0.153	3.409	0.110	3.535	0.076	3.650	0.048	3.753	-----	-----	-----	-----
24	0.431	2.761	0.362	2.908	0.297	3.053	0.239	3.193	0.186	3.327	0.141	3.454	0.101	3.572	0.070	3.678	0.044	3.773	-----	-----
25	0.470	2.702	0.400	2.844	0.335	2.983	0.275	3.119	0.221	3.251	0.172	3.376	0.130	3.494	0.094	3.604	0.065	3.702	0.041	3.790
26	0.508	2.649	0.438	2.784	0.373	2.919	0.312	3.051	0.256	3.179	0.205	3.303	0.160	3.420	0.120	3.531	0.087	3.632	0.060	3.724
27	0.544	2.600	0.475	2.730	0.409	2.859	0.348	2.987	0.291	3.112	0.238	3.233	0.191	3.349	0.149	3.460	0.112	3.563	0.081	3.658
28	0.578	2.555	0.510	2.680	0.445	2.805	0.383	2.928	0.325	3.050	0.271	3.168	0.222	3.283	0.178	3.392	0.138	3.495	0.104	3.592
29	0.612	2.515	0.544	2.634	0.479	2.755	0.418	2.874	0.359	2.992	0.305	3.107	0.254	3.219	0.208	3.327	0.166	3.431	0.129	3.528
30	0.643	2.477	0.577	2.592	0.512	2.708	0.451	2.823	0.392	2.937	0.337	3.050	0.286	3.160	0.238	3.266	0.195	3.368	0.156	3.465
31	0.674	2.443	0.608	2.553	0.545	2.665	0.484	2.776	0.425	2.887	0.370	2.996	0.317	3.103	0.269	3.208	0.224	3.309	0.183	3.406
32	0.703	2.411	0.638	2.517	0.576	2.625	0.515	2.733	0.457	2.840	0.401	2.946	0.349	3.050	0.299	3.153	0.253	3.252	0.211	3.348
33	0.731	2.382	0.668	2.484	0.606	2.588	0.546	2.692	0.488	2.796	0.432	2.899	0.379	3.000	0.329	3.100	0.283	3.198	0.239	3.293
34	0.758	2.355	0.695	2.454	0.634	2.554	0.575	2.654	0.518	2.754	0.462	2.854	0.409	2.954	0.359	3.051	0.312	3.147	0.267	3.240
35	0.783	2.330	0.722	2.425	0.662	2.521	0.604	2.619	0.547	2.716	0.492	2.813	0.439	2.910	0.388	3.005	0.340	3.099	0.295	3.190
36	0.808	2.306	0.748	2.398	0.689	2.492	0.631	2.586	0.575	2.680	0.520	2.774	0.467	2.868	0.417	2.961	0.369	3.053	0.323	3.142
37	0.831	2.285	0.772	2.374	0.714	2.464	0.657	2.555	0.602	2.646	0.548	2.738	0.495	2.829	0.445	2.920	0.397	3.009	0.351	3.097
38	0.854	2.265	0.796	2.351	0.739	2.438	0.683	2.526	0.628	2.614	0.575	2.703	0.522	2.792	0.472	2.880	0.424	2.968	0.378	3.054
39	0.875	2.246	0.819	2.329	0.763	2.413	0.707	2.499	0.653	2.585	0.600	2.671	0.549	2.757	0.499	2.843	0.451	2.929	0.404	3.013
40	0.896	2.228	0.840	2.309	0.785	2.391	0.731	2.473	0.678	2.557	0.626	2.641	0.575	2.724	0.525	2.808	0.477	2.829	0.430	2.974
45	0.988	2.156	0.938	2.225	0.887	2.296	0.838	2.367	0.788	2.439	0.740	2.512	0.692	2.586	0.644	2.659	0.598	2.733	0.553	2.807
50	1.064	2.103	1.019	2.163	0.973	2.225	0.927	2.287	0.882	2.350	0.836	2.414	0.792	2.479	0.747	2.544	0.703	2.610	0.660	2.675
55	1.129	2.062	1.087	2.116	1.045	2.170	1.003	2.225	0.961	2.281	0.919	2.338	0.877	2.396	0.836	2.454	0.795	2.512	0.754	2.571
60	1.184	2.031	1.145	2.079	1.106	2.127	1.068	2.177	1.029	2.227	0.990	2.278	0.951	2.330	0.913	2.382	0.874	2.434	0.836	2.487
65	1.231	2.006	1.195	2.049	1.160	2.093	1.124	2.138	1.088	2.183	1.052	2.229	1.016	2.276	0.980	2.323	0.944	2.371	0.908	2.419
70	1.272	1.987	1.239	2.026	1.206	2.066	1.172	2.106	1.139	2.148	1.105	2.189	1.072	2.232	1.038	2.275	1.005	2.318	0.971	2.362
75	1.308	1.970	1.277	2.006	1.247	2.043	1.215	2.080	1.184	2.118	1.153	2.156	1.121	2.195	1.090	2.235	1.058	2.275	1.027	2.315
80	1.340	1.957	1.311	1.991	1.283	2.024	1.253	2.059	1.224	2.093	1.195	2.129	1.165	2.165	1.136	2.201	1.106	2.238	1.076	2.275
85	1.369	1.946	1.342	1.977	1.315	2.009	1.287	2.040	1.260	2.073	1.232	2.105	1.205	2.139	1.177	2.172	1.149	2.206	1.121	2.241
90	1.395	1.937	1.369	1.966	1.344	1.995	1.318	2.025	1.292	2.055	1.266	2.085	1.240	2.116	1.213	2.148	1.187	2.179	1.160	2.211
95	1.418	1.930	1.394	1.956	1.370	1.984	1.345	2.012	1.321	2.040	1.296	2.068	1.271	2.097	1.247	2.126	1.222	2.156	1.197	2.186
100	1.439	1.923	1.416	1.948	1.393	1.974	1.371	2.000	1.347	2.026	1.324	2.053	1.301	2.080	1.277	2.108	1.253	2.135	1.229	2.164
150	1.579	1.892	1.564	1.908	1.550	1.924	1.535	1.940	1.519	1.956	1.504	1.972	1.489	1.989	1.474	2.006	1.458	2.023	1.443	2.040
200	1.654	1.885	1.643	1.896	1.632	1.908	1.621	1.919	1.610	1.931	1.599	1.943	1.588	1.955	1.576	1.967	1.565	1.979	1.554	1.991

*K' is the number of regressors excluding the intercept

Bibliography

Ahn, S.C. and H.R. Moon (2001) 'Large-N and Large-T Properties of Panel Data Estimators and the Hausman Test, August 2001', USC CLEO Research Paper no. C01–20.

Akaike, H. (1970) 'Statistical Predictor Identification', *Annals of the Institute of Statistical Mathematics*, 22, pp. 203–17.

Akaike, H. (1974) 'A New Look at Statistical Model Identification', *IEEE Transactions on Automatic Control*, 19, pp. 716–23.

Almon, S. (1965) 'The Distributed Lag Between Capital Appropriations and Expenditures', *Econometrica*, 30, pp. 178–96.

Anderson, T.W. and C. Hsiao (1981) 'Estimation of Dynamic Models with Error Components', *Journal of the American Statistical Association*, 76, pp. 598–606.

Anderson, T.W. and C. Hsiao (1982) 'Formulation and Estimation of Dynamic Models Using Panel Data', *Journal of Econometrics*, 18, pp. 47–82.

Arellano, M. and S. Bond (1991) 'Some Tests of Specification for Panel Data: Monte Carlo Evidence and an Application to Employment Equations', *Review of Economic Studies*, 58, pp. 277–320.

Asteriou, D. and G. Kavetsos (2003) 'Testing for the Existence of the January Effect in Transition Economies', City University Working Paper No. 107.

Asteriou, D. and S. Price (2000a) 'Financial Development and Economic Growth: Time Series Evidence for the Case of UK', *Ekonomia*, 4(2), pp. 122–41.

Asteriou, D. and S. Price (2000b) 'Uncertainty, Investment and Economic Growth: Evidence from a Dynamic Panel', City University Working Paper No. 88.

Asteriou, D. and S. Price (2001) 'Political Uncertainty and Economic Growth: UK Time Series Evidence', *Scottish Journal of Political Economy*, 48(4), pp. 383–89.

Baltagi, B.H. (1995) *Econometric Analysis of Panel Data*. New York: John Wiley.

Baltagi, B.H. and J.M. Griffin (1997) 'Pooled Estimators vs their Heterogeneous Counterparts in the Context of Dynamic Demand for Gasoline', *Journal of Econometrics*, 77, pp. 303–27.

Banerjee, A., J.J. Dolado, J.W. Galbraith and D.F. Hendry (1993) *Cointegration, Error-Correction and the Econometric Analysis of Non-Stationary Data*. Oxford: Oxford University Press.

Bencivenga, V., B. Smith and R. Starr (1996) 'Equity Markets, Transactions Costs, and Capital Accumulation: An Illustration', *The World Bank Economic Review*, 10(2), pp. 241–65.

Berra, A.K. and M.L. Higgins (1993) 'ARCH Models: Properties, Estimation, and Testing', *Journal of Economic Surveys*, 7, pp. 305–62.

Bollerslev, T. (1986) 'Generalised Autoregressive Conditional Heteroskedasticity', *Journal of Econometrics*, 31, pp. 307–27.

Bollerslev, T., R.F. Engle and D.B. Nelson (1994) 'ARCH Models', in R.F. Engle and D. McFadden (eds), *Handbook of Econometrics*, Volume IV. Amsterdam: North-Holland, pp. 2959–3038.

Box, G.E.P. and D.R. Cox (1964) 'An Analysis of Transformations', *Journal of the Royal Statistical Society*, Series B.

Box, G.E.P. and G.M. Jenkins (1976) *Time Series Analysis: Forecasting and Control*, revd edn. San Francisco: Holden-Day.

Breusch, T. (1978) 'Testing for Autocorrelation in Dynamic Linear Models', *Australian Economic Papers*, 17, pp. 334–55.

Breusch, T. and A. Pagan (1979) 'A Simple Test for Heteroskedasticity and Random Coefficient Variation', *Econometrica*, 47, pp. 1278–94.

Cagan, P. (1956) 'The Monetary Dynamics of Hyper Inflations', in M. Friedman (ed), *Studies in the Quantity Theory of Money*. Chicago, IL: University of Chicago Press.

Campbell, H.Y., A.W. Lo and A.C. MacKinley (1997) *The Econometrics of Financial Markets*. Princeton, NJ: Princeton University Press.

Chow, G. (1960) 'Tests of Equality between Sets of Coefficients in Two Linear Regressions', *Econometrica*, 28, pp. 591–605.

Cochrane, D. and G. Orcutt (1949) 'Application of Least Squares Regression to Relationships Containing Autocorrelated Error Terms', *Journal of the American Statistical Association*, 44, pp. 32–61.

Craven, P. and G. Wahba (1979) 'Smoothing Noisy Data with Spline Functions', *Numerische Mathematik*, 31, pp. 377–403.

Cuthbertson, K., S.G. Hall and M.P. Taylor (1992) *Applied Econometric Techniques*. New York: Simon and Schuster.

Davidson, R. and J.G. MacKinnon (1993) *Estimation and Inference in Econometrics*. Oxford: Oxford University Press.

Demetriades, P.O. and K.A. Hussein (1996) 'Does Financial Development Cause Economic Growth? Time-Series Evidence from 16 Countries', *Journal of Development Economics*, 51, pp. 387–411.

Dickey, D.A. and W.A. Fuller (1979) 'Distribution of the Estimators for Autoregressive Time Series with a Unit Root', *Journal of the American Statistical Association*, 74, pp. 427–31.

Dickey, D.A. and W.A. Fuller (1981) 'Likelihood Ratio Statistics for Autoregressive Time Series with a Unit Root', *Econometrica*, 49, pp. 1057–72.

Doldado, J., T. Jenkinson and S. Sosvilla-Rivero (1990) 'Cointegration and Unit Roots', *Journal of Economic Surveys*, 4, pp. 249–73.

Durbin, J. (1970) 'Testing for Serial Correlation in Least Squares Regression – When Some of the Variables are Lagged Dependent Variables', *Econometrica*, 38, pp. 410–21.

Durbin, J. and G. Watson (1950) 'Testing for Serial Correlation in Least Squares Regression I', *Biometrica*, 37, pp. 409–28.

Enders, W. (1995) *Applied Econometric Time Series*. New York: John Wiley.

Engle, R.F. (1982) 'Autoregressive Conditional Heteroskedasticity with Estimates of the Variance of U.K. Inflation', *Econometrica*, 50, pp. 987–1008.

Engle, R.F. (1995) *ARCH Selected Readings (Advanced Texts in Econometrics)*. Oxford: Oxford University Press.

Engle, R.F. and C.W.J. Granger (1987) 'Co-integration and Error Correction: Representation, Estimation, and Testing', *Econometrica*, 55, pp. 251–76.

Engle, R.F., D.M. Lilien and R.P. Robins (1987) 'Estimating Time Varying Risk Premia in the Term Structure: The ARCH-M Model', *Econometrica*, 55, pp. 391–407.

Engle, R.F. and B. Yoo (1987) 'Forecasting and Testing in Cointegrated Systems', *Journal of Econometrics*, 35, pp. 143–59.

Fuller, W.A. (1976) *Introduction to Statistical Time Series*. New York: John Wiley.

Gilbert, C.L. (1986) 'Professor Hendry's Econometric Methodology', *Oxford Bulletin of Economics and Statistics*, 84, pp. 283–307.

Glesjer, H. (1961) 'A New Test for Multiplicative Heteroskedasticity', *Journal of the American Statistical Association*, 60, pp. 539–47.

Glosten, L., R. Jogannathan and D. Ruknle (1993) 'Relations between the Expected Nominal Stock Excess Return, the Volatility of the Nominal Excess Return and the Interest Rate', *Journal of Finance*, December, 48(5), pp. 1779–801.

Godfrey, L.G. (1978) 'Testing for Higher Order Serial Correlation in Regression Equations when the Regressions Contain Lagged Dependent Variables', *Econometrica*, 46, pp. 1303–10.

Goldfeld, S. and R. Quandt (1965) 'Some Tests for Homoscedasticity', *Journal of the American Statistical Association*, 60, pp. 539–47.

Goldsmith, R. (1969) *Financial Structure and Development*. New Haven, CT: Yale University Press.

Granger, C.W.J. (1969) 'Investigating Causal Relations by Econometric Models and Cross Spectral Methods', *Econometrica*, 35, pp. 424–38.

Granger, C.W.J. (1981) 'Some Properties of Time Series Data and their Use in Econometric Model Specification', *Journal of Econometrics*, 16, pp. 121–30.

Granger, C.W.J. (1988) 'Some Recent Developments in the Concept of Causality', *Journal of Econometrics*, 39, pp. 199–211.

Granger, C.W.J. and J. Lin (1995) 'Causality in the Long-run', *Econometric Theory*, 11, pp. 530–6.

Granger, C.W.J. and P. Newbold (1974) 'Economic Forecasting: The Atheist's Viewpoint', in G.A. Renton (ed.), *Modelling the Economy*. London: Heinemann.

Granger, C.W.J. and P. Newbold (1996) *Forecasting Economic Time Series*. New York: Academic Press.

Greenslade, J.V., S.G. Hall and S.G.B. Henry (1999) 'On the Identification of Cointegrated Systems in Small Samples: Practical Procedures with an Application to UK Wages and Prices', *Computing in Economics and Finance*, Society for Computational Economics, p. 643.

Gujarati, D. (1978) *Basic Econometrics*. New York: McGraw-Hill.

Gultekin, M.N. and N.B. Gultekin (1983) 'Stock Market Seasonality: International Evidence', *Journal of Financial Economics*, 12, pp. 469–81.

Gurley, J.G. and E.S. Shaw (1955) 'Financial Aspects of Economic Development', *American Economic Review*, 45, pp. 515–38.

Hall, S.G. (1985) 'On the Solution of Large Economic Models with Coherency in Expectations', *Bulletin of Economic Research*, 37(2), pp. 157–61.

Hall, S.G. (1988) 'Rationality and Siegels' Paradox, The Importance of Coherency in Expectations', *Applied Economics*, 20(11), pp. 1533–41.

Hall, S.G. and S.G.B. Henry (1988) 'Macroeconomic Modelling', Contributions to Economic Analysis, series. Amsterdam: North Holland.

Hall, S.G., D.K. Miles and M.P. Taylor (1990) 'A Multivariate GARCH in Mean Estimation of the Capital Asset Pricing Model', in K.D. Patterson and S.G.B. Henry (eds), *Issues in Economic and Financial Modelling*. London: Chapman & Hall.

Hannan, E.J. and B. Quin (1979) 'The Determination of the Order of an Autoregression', *Journal of the Royal Statistical Society*, Series B14, pp. 190–5.

Harris, R. (1995) *Using Cointegration Analysis in Econometric Modelling*. London: Prentice Hall.

Harvey, A. (1976) 'Estimating Regression Models with Multiplicative Heteroscedasticity', *Econometrica*, 44, pp. 461–5.

Hausman, J. (1978) 'Specification Tests in Econometrics', *Econometrica*, 46, pp. 1251–71.

Hendry, D.F., A.R. Pagan and J.D. Sargan (1984) 'Dynamic Specification', in Z. Griliches and M.D. Intriligator (eds), *Handbook of Econometrics*. Amsterdam: North-Holland.

Hendry, D.F. and J.F. Richard (1983) 'The Econometric Analysis of Economic Time Series', *International Statistics Review*, 51, pp. 3–33.

Hildreth, C. and J. Lu (1960) 'Demand Relations with Autocorrelated Disturbances', Technical Bulletin No. 276, Michigan State University Agricultural Experiment Station.

Holmstrom, B. and J. Tirole (1993) 'Market Liquidity and Performance Monitoring', *Journal of Political Economy,* 101(4), pp. 678–709.

Hsiao, C. (1986) *Analysis of Panel Data*, Econometric Society monographs no. 11. New York: Cambridge University Press.

Im, K.S., M.H. Pesaran and Y. Shin (1997) 'Testing for Unit Roots in Heterogeneous Panels', MS, Department of Applied Economics, University of Cambridge.

Jaffe, J.F. and R. Westerfield (1989) 'Is There a Monthly Effect in Stock Market Returns?', *Journal of Banking and Finance,* 13, pp. 237–44.

Jarque, C.M. and A.K. Berra (1990) 'Efficient Tests for Normality, Homoskedasticity and Serial Independence of Regression Residuals', *Economic Letters*, 6, pp. 255–9.

Johansen, S. (1988) 'Statistical Analysis of Cointegration Vectors', *Journal of Economics Dynamics and Control*, 12, pp. 231–54.

Johansen, S. (1991) 'Estimation and Hypothesis Testing of Cointegration Vectors in Gaussian Vector Autoregressive Models', *Econometrica*, 59, pp. 1551–80.

Johansen, S. (1992) 'Determination of Cointegration Rank in the Presence of a Linear Trend', *Oxford Bulletin of Economics and Statistics*, 54, pp. 383–97.

Johansen, S. (1995a) *Likelihood-based Inference in Cointegrated Vector Autoregressive Models*. Oxford: Oxford University Press.

Johansen, S. (1995b) 'A Statistical Analysis of I(2) Variables', *Econometric Theory*, 11, pp. 25–59.

Johansen, S. and K. Juselius (1990) 'The Maximum Likelihood Estimation and Inference on Cointegration – with Application to Demand for Money', *Oxford Bulletin of Economics and Statistics*, 52, pp. 169–210.

Kao, C. (1999) 'Spurious Regression and Residual-Based Tests for Cointegration in Panel Data', *Journal of Econometrics*, 90, pp. 1–44.

King, R. and R. Levine (1993a) 'Finance and Growth: Schumpeter Might Be Right', *Quarterly Journal of Economics*, 108(3), pp. 717–38.

King, R. and R. Levine (1993b) 'Finance, Enterpreneurship and Growth Theory and Evidence', *Journal of Monetary Economics*, 32(3), pp. 513–42.

Klein, L.R. and J.N. Morgan (1951) 'Results of Alternative Statistical Treatment of Sample Survey Data', *Journal of American Statistical Association*, 47, pp. 399–407.

Kmenta, J. (1986) *Elements of Econometrics*. New York: Macmillan.

Koyck, L.M. (1954) *Distributed Lags and Investment Analysis*. Amsterdam: North-Holland.

Larsson, R., J. Lyhagen and M. Lothgren (2001) 'Likelihood Based Cointegration Tests in Heterogeneous Panels', *Econometrics Journal*, 4, pp. 109–42.

Levin, A. and C.F. Lin (1992) 'Unit Root Tests in Panel Data: Asymptotic and Finite Sample Properties', University College of San Diego Working Paper No. 92–3.

Levin, A., C.F. Lin and C.S. Chu (2002) 'Unit Root Tests in Panel Data: Asymptotic and Finite Sample Properties', *Journal of Econometrics*, 108, pp. 1–24.

Ljung, G. and G. Box (1979) 'On a Measure of Lack of Fit in Time Series Models', *Biometrika*, 66, pp. 265–70.

MacKinnon, J.G. (1991) 'Critical Values for Cointegration Tests', in R.F. Engle and C.W.J. Granger (eds), *Long-run Economic Relationships: Readings in Cointegtion*. Oxford: Oxford University Press.

Maddala, G.S. (2001) *Introduction to Econometrics*, 3rd edn. London: John Wiley.

Maddala, G.S and S. Wu (1999) 'A Comparative Study of Unit Root Tests with Panel Data and a New Simple Test', *Oxford Bulletin of Economics and Statistics*, special issue, 61, pp. 631–52.

Mahmoud, E. (1984) 'Accuracy in Forecasting: A Survey', *Journal of Forecasting*, 3, pp. 139–59.

McCoskey, S. and C. Kao (1998) 'A Residual-Based Test for the Null of Cointegration in Panel Data', *Econometric Reviews*, 17, pp. 57–84.

McCulloch, J. Huston (1985) 'On Heteroskedasticity', *Econometrica*, p. 483.

McFadden, D. (1973) 'Conditional Logit Analysis of Qualitative Choice Behavior', in P. Zarembka (ed.), *Frontiers in Econometrics*. New York: Academic Press.

McNees, S. (1986) 'Forecasting Accuracy of Alternative Techniques: A Comparison of US Macroeconomic Forecasts', *Journal of Business and Economic Statistics*, 4, pp. 5–15.

Mitchell, B. (1998) *International Historical Statistics: Europe, 1750–1993*, 4th edn. London: Macmillan.

Mizon, G. and J. Richard (1986) 'The Encompassing Principle and Its Application to Testing Nonnested Models', *Econometrica*, 54, pp. 657–78.

Nehru, V. and A. Dhareshwar (1993) 'A New Database on Physical Capital Stock: Sources, Methodology and Results', *Rivista de Analisis Economico*, 8(1), pp. 37–59.

Nelson, D.B. (1991) 'Conditional Heteroskedasticity in Asset Returns: A New Approach', *Econometrica*, 59, pp. 347–70.

Newey, W. and K. West (1987) 'A Simple Positive Semi-Definite, Heteroskedasticity and Autocorrelation Consistent Covariance Matrix', *Econometrica*, p. 51.

Norman, M. (1967) 'Solving a Non-linear Econometric Model by the Gauss-Siedel Iterative Method', Paper presented at the Econometric Society Meeting, December.

Okun, A. (1962) 'Potential GNP: Its Measurement and Significance', *Proceedings of the Business and Economics Statistics Section of the American Statistical Association*, pp. 98–104.

Osterwald-Lenum, M. (1992) 'A Note with Fractiles of the Asymptotic Distribution of the Likelihood Rank Statistics: Four Cases', *Oxford Bulletin of Economics and Statistics*, 54, pp. 461–72.

Park, R. (1966) 'Estimating with Heteroscedastic Error Terms', *Econometrica*, 34, p. 888.

Pedroni, P. (1997) 'Panel Cointegration: Asymptotic and Finite Sample Properties of Pooled Time Series with an Application to the PPP Hypothesis: New Results', Working Paper, Indiana University.

Pedroni, P. (1999) 'Critical Values for Cointegration Tests in Heterogeneous Panels with Multiple Regressors', *Oxford Bulletin of Economics and Statistics*, special issue, 62, November, pp. 653–70.

Pedroni, P. (2000) 'Fully Modified OLS for Heterogeneous Cointegrated Panel', *Advances in Econometrics*, 15, pp. 93–130.

Pesaran, M.H. and Y. Shin (2002) 'Long-Run Structural Modelling', *Econometric Reviews*, 21, pp. 49–8.

Pesaran, M.H., Y. Shin and R. Smith (1999) 'Pooled Mean Group Estimation of Dynamic Heterogeneous Panels', *Journal of the American Statistical Association*, 94, pp. 621–34.

Pesaran, M.H. and R. Smith (1995) 'Estimation of Long-Run Relationships from Dynamic Heterogeneous Panels', *Journal of Econometrics*, 68, pp. 79–113.

Phillips, P.C.B. (1986) 'Understanding Spurious Regression', *Journal of Econometrics*, 33, pp. 311–40.

Phillips, P.C.B. (1987) 'Time Series Regressions with a Unit Root', *Econometrica*, 55, pp. 165–93.

Phillips, P.C.B. and H.R. Moon (2000) 'Linear Regression Theory for Non-Stationary Panel Data', *Econometrica*, 67, pp. 1057–111.

Phillips, P.C.B. and P. Perron (1988) 'Testing for a Unit Root in Time Series Regression', *Biometrika*, 75, pp. 335–46.

Phillips, P.C.B. and S. Ouliaris (1990) 'Asymptotic Properties of Residual Based Tests for Cointegration', *Econometrica*, 58, pp. 165–93.

Ramsey, J.B. (1969) 'Tests for Specification Error in Classical Least Squares Regression Analysis', *Journal of the Royal Statistical Society*, B31, pp. 250–71.

Rice, J. (1984) 'Bandwith Choice for Nonparametric Kernel Regression', *Annals of Statistics*, 12, pp. 1215–30.

Roubini, N. and X. Sala-i-Martin (1992) 'Financial Repression and Economic Growth', *Journal of Development Economics*, 39, pp. 5–30.

Runkle, D.E. (1987) 'Vector Autoregression and Reality', *Journal of Business and Economic Statistics*, 5, pp. 437–54.

Schwarz, G. (1978) 'Estimating the Dimension of a Model', *Annals of Statistics*, 6.

Shibata, R. (1981) 'An Optimal Selection of Regression Variables', *Biometrica*, 68, pp. 45–54.

Sims, C.A. (1972) 'Money, Income and Causality', *American Economic Review*, 62, pp. 540–52.

Sims, C.A. (1980) 'Macroeconomics and Reality', *Econometrica*, 48, pp. 1–48.

Stock, J. and M. Watson (1988) 'Testing for Common Trends', *Journal of the American Statistical Association*, 83, pp. 1097–107.

Studenmund, A.H. (2001) *Using Econometrics: A Practical Guide*. Reading, MA: Addison-Wesley Longman.

White, H. (1980) 'A Heteroscedasticity-Consistent Covariance Matrix Estimator and a Direct Test for Heteroscedasticity', *Econometrica*, 48, pp. 817–38.

Zakoian, J.-M. (1994) 'Threshold Heteroskedastic Models', *Journal of Economic Dynamics and Control*, 18, pp. 931–55.

Index